By Donald Honig

Fiction

Sidewalk Caesar
Walk Like a Man
The Americans
Divide the Night
No Song to Sing
Judgment Night
The Love Thief
The Severith Style
Illusions
I Should Have Sold Petunias
The Last Great Season
Marching Home

Nonfiction

The Image of Their Greatness (*with Lawrence Ritter*)
The 100 Greatest Baseball Players of All Time (*with Lawrence Ritter*)
The Brooklyn Dodgers: An Illustrated Tribute
The New York Yankees: An Illustrated History
Baseball's 10 Greatest Teams
The Los Angeles Dodgers: The First Quarter Century
The Boston Red Sox: An Illustrated Tribute
The National League: An Illustrated History
The American League: An Illustrated History
Baseball America
The World Series: An Illustrated History
The New York Mets: The First Quarter Century
The All-Star Game: A Pictorial History
Mays, Mantle, Snider
Baseball in the '50s
Baseball's Greatest Pitchers
Baseball's Greatest First Basemen

For Young Readers

Frontiers of Fortune
Jed McLane and Storm Cloud
Jed McLane and the Stranger
In the Days of the Cowboy
Up From the Minor Leagues
Dynamite
Johnny Lee
The Journal of One Davey Wyatt
An End of Innocence
Way to Go Teddy

Playing for Keeps
Breaking In
The Professional
Coming Back
Fury on Skates
Hurry Home
Running Harder
Going the Distance
Winter Always Comes

Editor

Blue and Gray: Great Writings of the Civil War
The Short Stories of Stephen Crane

A DONALD HONIG READER

BASEBALL WHEN THE GRASS WAS REAL

BASEBALL BETWEEN THE LINES

EXCERPTS FROM:

THE OCTOBER HEROES

THE MAN IN THE DUGOUT

DONALD HONIG
FOREWORD BY LAWRENCE RITTER

A FIRESIDE BOOK   PUBLISHED BY SIMON & SCHUSTER INC.

New York London Toronto Sydney Tokyo

First Fireside Edition, 1988

Published by the Simon & Schuster Trade Division
by arrangement with the author.
Simon & Schuster Building
Rockefeller Center
1230 Avenue of the Americas
New York, New York 10020

FIRESIDE and colophon are registered trademarks
of Simon & Schuster Inc.

Designed by Bonni Leon
Manufactured in the United States of America

10 9 8 7 6 5 4 3 2 1 Pbk.

Library of Congress Cataloging in Publication Data

Honig, Donald.
    [Selections. 1988]
    A Donald Honig reader / Donald Honig; foreword by Lawrence Ritter.
—1st Fireside ed.
        p.   cm.—(Fireside sports classic)
    A Fireside Book.
    Contents: Baseball when the grass was real—Baseball between the
lines—Excerpts from The October heroes. The man in the dugout.
    1. Baseball—United States—History.   I. Title.
    GV863.H64 1988
    796.357′0973—dc19   88-6749
                                                                             CIP
ISBN 0–671–66339–9 Pbk.
Excerpts from the chapter on Pete Reiser have appeared in *Sports Illus-
trated*. Excerpts from the chapter on Wes Ferrell have appeared in *Atlantic
Monthly*.

CONTENTS

FOREWORD

The best thing about baseball today is its yesterdays.

That's nothing new. For generations, reminiscing about the game has been at least as popular as watching or playing it. In the old days, for example, when *The Sporting News* was truly the bible of baseball because that's all it contained, the "hot stove league" flourished every winter. The name "hot stove league" stemmed from the image of half a dozen cronies sitting around an old-fashioned potbellied stove arguing about whether they'd rather have Babe Ruth or Ty Cobb on their team, about whether teenager Bobby Feller threw as hard as the immortal Walter Johnson, about what would have happened if Joe DiMaggio played his home games in Fenway Park while Ted Williams played his in Yankee Stadium.

Players talked baseball as much as the fans in those days. Lefty O'Doul, who had a distinguished career in the big leagues in the twenties and thirties, complained in the sixties that times had changed and not for the better. "Ballplayers don't want to talk baseball anymore," he said. "They'd rather talk about stocks, bonds, real estate, their commercials. They don't care to discuss baseball. Of course, when I was playing there wasn't much else to do. We'd sit around on long train rides and in hotel lobbies in the evening and talk about girls and baseball. Mostly baseball, believe it or not. In St. Louis there was a fountain at the old Buckingham Hotel, and on hot nights we'd sit around that fountain and talk about how to beat the guys the next day. We talked baseball day and night, never got tired of it."

The year was 1964, O'Doul was holding forth in the back room of his San Francisco restaurant after closing, and I was the entire audience. At the time, I was flying around the country lugging a 25-pound reel-to-reel Tandberg tape recorder, searching for old-time ballplayers. The end result eventually became *The Glory of Their Times,* a book of tape-recorded first-person oral histories about the early days of baseball that was published in 1966.

(Today *Glory* is frequently mentioned as a pioneer in the field of oral history, but in fact it had distinguished precursors. With primitive recording equipment, John and Alan Lomax, father and son, spent years traveling the length and breadth of the land unearthing bits and pieces of America's folk-song heritage; John Lomax told the story in *Adventures of a Ballad Hunter,* 1947. And anthropologist Oscar Lewis further opened my eyes to the potentialities of the tape recorder with his taped inquiries into the daily lives of the urban poor in *Five Families: Case Studies in the Culture of Poverty,* 1959, and *The Children of Sanchez,* 1961.)

The spark that ignited my own travels was the death of Ty Cobb in 1961. The early stars of the game were rapidly disappearing—Babe Ruth was already gone, as well as Honus Wagner, John McGraw, Christy Mathewson, Walter Johnson, Tris Speaker, and too many others—and with them, of course, went priceless memories about the people and events that shaped the game in the extraordinary first two decades of the twentieth century. The thought occurred to me: if the Lomaxes could track down obscure folksingers and Oscar Lewis could tape the nuances of an entire subculture, why not try to do something along similar lines with a pathbreaking generation of ballplayers?

That my own father died at about the same time only added a sense of personal urgency to the whole idea. After all, it had been my father, observing a traditional American ritual, who in 1932 had taken me, hand in hand, to my first major-league game.

Happily, it soon became obvious that there is a comfortable fit between ballplayers and tape recorders. The game lends itself to memories, because although baseball is a team game, and it is teams that win or lose, it is *individuals* who clearly and unmistakably bear responsibility for victories or defeats. Unlike most football players, baseball players do their thing singly and alone; they are praised or blamed, become heroes or goats, depending on their individual performances in the full glare of the spotlight.

One evening, in the midst of a long conversation with Paul

Waner, the great Pittsburgh hitting star suddenly said, "You know why old ballplayers love to reminisce? It's because each of us has so many memories stored away in the old noggin, memories that are just begging to pour out. Think about it. We used to play 154 games a season, each one with at least eighteen players on the field. I bet that after each game every one of those eighteen could have told a story or two about the game, something that struck him as especially interesting. It might have been something technical about the way the game was played, or something mainly of human interest, or maybe something funny, or whatever. You can figure it out: 18 times 154, and that's just for a single season."

The Glory of Their Times barely nudged the tip of the iceberg. It contained the life stories of only 22 men (including Lefty O'Doul and Paul Waner, both of whom unfortunately died before the end of the sixties). The pressure of other responsibilities, however, made it impossible for me to continue running all over the country dragging my tape recorder behind me. As a result, the publication of *Glory* in 1966 was followed by a hiatus of almost a decade during which no further baseball oral-history collections appeared.

But then—to fans' gratitude—the drought ended when Donald Honig—novelist, short-story writer, onetime pitcher in the Red Sox farm system, and longtime good friend—bought a tape recorder and turned his considerable talents to interviewing ex–major leaguers.

Interviewing is not a simple matter. To be a good oral historian requires a combination of skills. Naturally, one must be a good and patient listener; be profoundly knowledgeable about the topic under discussion; be congenial, warm, empathic, and perceptive as a human being; and after the interview itself has ended, be able to organize vast amounts of material and write it up in a logical and interesting manner.

Donald Honig possesses all these qualities in abundance, which is why his four oral-history books have passed with flying colors the most difficult test of all, the test of time. When the books first appeared in the late seventies, readers responded with great delight. *Baseball When the Grass Was Real* (1975) was followed by *Baseball Between the Lines* (1976), *The Man in the Dugout* (1977), and *The October Heroes* (1979).

The present volume reprints all of the first two books and large portions of the third and fourth.

In addition to the traits mentioned above, Honig has another quality: he knows whom to talk to. The great superstars are here, of course—like Lefty Grove, Charlie Gehringer, and Bob Feller—but also the ordinary players, the foot soldiers, the ones whom many fans remember with particular affection—like Elbie Fletcher, Doc Cramer, Frank McCormick, Bobby Shantz, and Billy Goodman. Indeed, they frequently tell the best stories and are the most spontaneous, simply because they haven't been asked about their lives and careers as often as their more celebrated contemporaries.

In addition to pure nostalgia, there is much gripping, first-rate baseball history in these pages. For example, Honig sought out Les Bell, who was playing third base for the St. Louis Cardinals in the 1926 World Series, to hear just what happened when Grover Cleveland Alexander came in from the Cardinals' bullpen in the seventh game of the Series to strike out Yankee second baseman Tony Lazzeri.

Similarly, we are privy to Babe Ruth's famous "called shot" home run in the 1932 World Series, when he is said to have pointed to the center-field bleachers at Wrigley Field and then hit the next pitch to that very spot. We hear recollections of that moment from a variety of perspectives—from New York Yankee Joe Sewell (who swears to Honig that Ruth did it) to Chicago Cubs Burleigh Grimes and Billy Herman (who swear he didn't).

Speaking of Ruth brings to mind Elbie Fletcher's poignant memories of the greatest player of all time in spring training in 1935. Fletcher was an eighteen-year-old rookie and the Babe was on his last legs. "He was forty years old," Fletcher told Honig. "He couldn't run, he could hardly bend down for a ball, and of course he couldn't hit the way he used to. It was sad watching those great skills fading away. One of the saddest things of all is when an athlete begins to lose it. And to see it happening to Babe Ruth, to see Babe Ruth struggling on a ball field, well then you realize we're all mortal and nothing lasts forever."

There is a wide range of emotion in these pages, from regret to exhilaration, from sadness to elation; there is wonderment and awe, satisfaction for what was and wistfulness for what almost was. It is as if once played and completed, a baseball game, a season, or a World Series retains a certain organic quality, a pulsebeat lying quiet in time, waiting for an interlocutor as skilled as Mr. Honig to seek it out and gently raise its decibel count.

If anyone doubts the sanctified place that baseball occupies in the national consciousness, one need only think of the millions upon millions of statistics—they cover a player, a game, a season, a team, a league—that bind together the history of our national sport. Everything that occurs is duly recorded in a kind of double-entry accounting that proves out at the end of every game. This staggering compendium of numbers tells us without embellishment the measures of success and failure, of individual heroics and disappointments.

But it is the stories that accompany these statistics which put them in vivid perspective and humanize them. Memories of the participants permeate and set into focus the games and seasons of the past. Replayed and retold for each succeeding generation, the stories never lose their freshness, their drama, their capacity to give pleasure. They have become as much a part of American folklore as George Washington's cherry tree, Paul Bunyan, and Johnny Appleseed.

The Donald Honig Reader gives us box seats at many of baseball's most memorable events. No—even better, we are in the dugout, on the field, and later in the clubhouse, seeing and hearing and sharing the emotions of the moment. We have always known *what* happened. Now we know how the participants *felt* at the time, as history that is uniquely American passes before us in the pages that follow.

Lawrence S. Ritter

BASEBALL

WHEN THE

GRASS

WAS REAL

WES FERRELL

Wesley Cheek Ferrell
Born: February 2, 1908, Greensboro, North Carolina; Died:
  December 9, 1976
Major-league career: 1927–41, Cleveland Indians, Boston Red
  Sox, Washington Senators, New York Yankees, Brooklyn
  Dodgers, Boston Braves
Lifetime record: 193 wins, 128 losses

On the mound, Wes Ferrell was tough, competitive, and a winner. Pitching for teams that were seldom in contention, he nevertheless won more than 20 games six times, including two seasons of 25 victories. A hard-hitting pitcher, Ferrell left behind a lifetime .280 batting average and a total of 38 home runs, a record for pitchers.

Ferrell teamed with his brother Rick at Boston and Washington for several years to form one of the great brother batteries of all time.

There were seven of us boys in the family, and we learned farming before we learned anything else. My father owned 150 of the prettiest acres in North Carolina, or anywhere else for that matter. Driving in here, you probably saw those old bulldozers snortin' away. Well, that's our old farm they're bulldozing. They're fixin' to put up apartments, right smack over that beautiful land.

We raised hay, wheat, corn, and tobacco, too, of course, and we raised that old sorghum molasses, that we cook down here in this part of the country. And we had livestock, too, about sixty or seventy cows.

But more than anything else we raised ballplayers on that

17

farm. We'd go out into the fields after harvest time and hit for hours. Just hit an old beat-up nickel ball far as it'd go and chase it down and throw it around. Saturday and Sunday were our big days, of course. That's when we played team ball, around the countryside here.

You know, back in those days baseball was the only sport you could make a living at. My folks didn't quite understand how I could make any money out of playing baseball. They thought I was sort of spending my time doing nothing. But me and Rick, we worked darn hard at it; we never let up. Brother Rick had a great career: caught more games than any catcher in American League history.

Rick was my catcher when we were growing up. We were always real close. Slept together, ate together, went rabbit hunting together. We always said we were going to make baseball players of ourselves. That was what we was wanting to do. It was just a dream back then, of course, but it turned out to come true. And it happened so doggone fast, too. It seemed that one day I was thinking about my boyhood hero Babe Ruth, and then almost overnight I was standing on the mound in Cleveland trying to strike him out. Overnight isn't far from the fact either. Spring of '27 I was still living on the farm, and in the fall I pitched a few innings for Cleveland. Eighteen years old.

After high school I went to a military school in Oak Ridge, not far from home. I was playing ball, too, of course, and looking pretty good. What happened was, some college boy down here saw me pitch and told me I ought to go up to East Douglas, Massachusetts, and pitch for that club in the Blackstone Valley League. Semipro ball. So I did that. I was getting $300 a month, plus free lodging and free food. That was in the summer of '27.

I did okay up there, because I got a letter from a Cleveland scout named Bill Rapp. He asked me if I would sign with Cleveland and how much I wanted. I wrote back telling him $800 a month and $3,000 to sign a contract. What the heck . . . why not lay it on real fancy. Pretty tall figures for those days, particularly for a kid who'd only pitched a few months of semipro ball. But he wrote back and told me to go to Cleveland and see Mr. E. S. Barnard, who was president of the club at that time, that he thought I could get the money.

So here I go, still a little old country boy with a drawl thick as molasses, getting on the train and heading out to Cleveland. When I got off the train I asked somebody how to get out to League Park. They put me on a streetcar, and I told the conductor where I wanted to get off. It was quite a long ride, and finally he looked around at me and said, "This is it."

I get off the streetcar, and I'm looking for a ball park. Now the only ball parks I'd ever seen were back home and in East Douglas, and what those were were playing fields with little wooden fences around them. So I'm looking around, and I don't see a ball park. Some kids were playing in the street, and I asked them where League Park was. They pointed and said, "That's it." Well, I turned around and looked up, and there's this great stone structure. Biggest thing I ever saw in my life. They called this a ball park? I couldn't believe it. Then I heard a little noise in the back of my mind: *major leagues.* The sound of those two words was like instant education.

So I took a tighter hold on my suitcase and walked through the gates of that thing, staring up and around at everything like I was walking through a palace. I went past all those great stone pillars and got up onto a concrete runway and looked way down and there at the end was a beautiful green ball field and guys playing ball on it. There was a game going on. And all of a sudden the notion of baseball got as big as all get-out in my mind. Seeing it being played down there in that setting was just beautiful. It was inspiring.

Then I remembered why I was there, and asked directions to Mr. Barnard's office. When I walked in, I saw this sharp-eyed, half-bald guy. I introduced myself and we shook hands.

"I understand you want eight hundred a month and three thousand to sign a contract," he said.

"Yes, sir," I said. I was trying to keep my eyes off of all those pictures he had on the wall: Tris Speaker, Walter Johnson, Christy Mathewson, Ty Cobb, as if I felt funny asking for all that money in front of *those* guys.

E.S. Barnard was smiling at me.

"Son," he said, "look down there." He had a window, and looking through it, you could see the ball field. "See that center fielder?" he said. "He's a regular on this ball club, and *he's* not making eight hundred dollars a month. Now I don't know if you're good enough to make this club or that we even want you. I don't know. But I'll tell you what I'll do. I'll give you three thousand to sign a contract and five hundred a month, for two years. And if after that time we retain you, we'll give you an additional three-thousand-dollar bonus."

I mulled it over, took another glance at those pictures, and said, "I'll take it."

The next spring I went to spring training with Cleveland down in New Orleans. I pitched good ball. Hell, I was as good as anybody they had on that club. Then the season opens, and I can't get in there. They've got me throwing batting practice for two weeks. Finally I got sick of it. So the next day I went into the outfield and stood there. Next thing I know they're calling me.

"Get in there and throw some batting practice."

"The hell with you," I said. "I didn't come up here for that."

That startled them. Here's the kid telling them what he's not going to do.

So they sent me to Terre Haute, which was fine with me. I won myself 20 ball games. I came back to Cleveland the next year, 1929, and I stuck. First club I got in against was the Tigers. They had a great ball club. Harry Heilmann, Bob Fothergill, Dale Alexander, Charlie Gehringer. Hitters. I was sitting in the bullpen. Just a kid, still scared at seeing so many people in the stands, still feeling more like a fan than a player.

It was a cold April day, and I've got the horse blanket covering me. I figured I'd be the last guy in the world to be in that ball game. But then our pitcher started getting in trouble, and Roger Peckinpaugh, the manager, starts waving down to the pen. Glenn Myatt, the bullpen catcher, got up.

"Hey, Wes," he says. "Come on."

"What do you mean?"

"You're first relief pitcher."

"Me?" I said. "What are you talkin' about?"

I was scared. I didn't want to get out there in front of that big crowd. But I loosened up fast, cold or no cold. They finally got our pitcher out of there, and here I go, walking in across that green grass—I don't think I even touched it. I get out to the mound and look around, and there's all those people staring at me. "Hell, boy," I told myself, "here you are. Do the job or go home."

First guy I faced was Harry Heilmann, standing up there

with that big bat like a tin soldier, feet close together. Four times American League batting champ. I threw that ball by him so fast he never did see it. Got him out, got them all out. Two innings of shutout ball. Throwing the ball harder than I ever dreamed I could. I guess I was so excited or something, or maybe I just grew into it all of a sudden.

They made me a starter after that. Had a good year, right along. But I'm still making only $500 a month, playing out the second year of that contract. That's around $3,000 a year. We had this pitcher with us, Johnny Miljus, used to be with the Pirates. He liked me. He told me, "If you don't get ten grand next year, I'm gonna beat your brains out."

They called me up into the office in the middle of August. I'd won about 16 by that time. Billy Evans was the general manager.

"Wes," he said, "I want to sign you up for next year. We want to give you a two-thousand-dollar bonus and five hundred a month."

"Mr. Evans," I said, "I don't care anything about a bonus. I'll tell you what you do. You give me eighty-five hundred for the year and I'll take it."

"You'll never get it," he said.

Then we went on a long road trip, and every day Miljus is saying to me, "You get that ten grand next year." Then it was near the end of the season, and I'm a 20-game winner. My rookie year this is.

I was shagging flies in the outfield before a game when Mr. Evans waved me in.

"Wes," he said, "we're gonna give it to you."

"Mr. Evans," I said, "I want more money now."

Doggone if I don't get my ten grand. Plus they had to give me an additional three thousand for retaining me for two years. So I had some money. And I'll tell you where I was real lucky. Wall Street had just gone busted, so I didn't have the opportunity to make bad investments, like so many of the fellows did. If I'd made that money the year before, it would've flown right out of my pocket.

The next year I won 25, and they gave me a two-year contract calling for $15,000 and $18,000. I won 91 games my first four years; four 20-game seasons—21, 25, 22, 23. Nobody's ever done that, before or since.

What would I be making today with that record? You name it. But I'll tell you something, $18,000 was a lot of money in those days. That was during the Depression. Those were bad days. Why, I think I had more money than Mr. Bradley did—and he was the president of that ball club then. I was sure as hell driving a finer automobile that he was. I'll say things were bad. After my fourth straight 20-game season I got *cut* $7,000. The ball club couldn't help themselves; they were barely surviving.

Being a big league star was exciting. I was going to the best hotels in the biggest cities and meeting the most famous people. You were always a star in somebody's eye; you were popular; you were known. You never waited on line; you never wanted for service, wherever you went. You never looked for that sort of thing; it just naturally came your way. People *want* to do it. Makes them feel good, I guess.

It builds your pride; at least it did mine. I wanted to look better, to dress better, to be a better guy. You stop to think that here are people who have driven maybe 300 miles to see you pitch a ball game, and then they hang around and want your autograph. It's very flattering. And if you're lucky and take it in the right spirit, it makes you a better person.

You know, off the field I was shy. I'd just come up from the farm and wasn't used to seeing lots of people and surely wasn't used to having crowds cheering me and looking for my autograph. It was a struggle for me because I didn't want to seem conceited.

Now on the field I was different. I had to be. I gave the impression that I was mean. After all, this was my job, my livelihood. So I put an act on. I'd look wild warming up. I'd stomp and storm around out there like a bear cat, fight my way through a ball game, fight like the devil, do anything to win. And I got that reputation for being temperamental and mean, and it stuck, even with people who should have known better. I'll tell you something that struck me as so damned funny. In 1933 we had the first All-Star game, in Chicago. Connie Mack was managing the American League team, and he always liked me. Well, we were having our meeting at the hotel before going out to the ball park. Connie is telling us all what to do.

"Lefty Gomez," he says, "you're starting. Ruth, you're playing right field. Gehringer, you're playing second base. Gehrig, you're on first. Simmons, you're in center field." And so on, right down the lineup. All these great stars. Then he says, "Wes Ferrell."

"Yes, Mr. Mack?" I said.

"I want you to be in the bullpen for the first six innings. *Will that be all right with you?*"

Well, that was the funniest thing I ever heard. Here he is, telling all these great stars what to do and then asking me if that was all right with me. I guess Connie thought I was the meanest man in the world.

Of course the game was tougher then, in my opinion. When I first came up, just a kid, they'd tell me to throw at a hitter.

"What do you mean, 'throw at him'?" I asked.

"Throw at his head," they said.

"I'll kill him," I said.

"That's an order, Ferrell. You throw at him."

I'm in Philadelphia one time, and a fellow named Hale is playing third base for Connie Mack's club. Peckinpaugh tells me I've got to throw at Hale. So I powdered one at him, and his feet went up and his head went down. Damn near took the button off his cap. When he got up, he was white as a sheet. They took him out of the ball game—which is what Peckinpaugh wanted.

That's when they had the art of hitting, in those days. There were so many good hitters you just had to go out there and take command. A team had a string of guys in the lineup hitting .320, .330, .340. Like facing machine-gun fire. When a guy hit a home run in those days, the next two hitters went down. They knew it was coming. Once, in a game in Detroit, somebody hit a home run off of me, and up comes Fothergill. A real hitter. I lowered the boom on him, putting it right over his head. He gets up, dusts himself off, and I get him out. Next fellow comes up—I forget his name—and lies down flat on his back in the batter's box.

"Hey, Wes," he yells, "I'm already down. You don't have to throw at me."

I got to laughing so hard I just laid one right in there, and damn if he doesn't knock it back through my legs for a base hit.

I never threw at Ruth, though. You just didn't want to do

that. He was baseball. What was it like pitching to him? Like looking into a lion's jaw, that's what. Hell, man, you're pitching to a *legend!* And you knew, too, that if he hits a home run, he's gonna get the cheers, and if he strikes out, he's still gonna get the cheers. You were *nothing* out there when Ruth came up.

You look around, and your infielders are way back and your outfielders have just about left town, they're so far back. And here you are, 60 feet away from him. You got great encouragement from your infielders, too. The first baseman says pitch him outside; the third baseman says pitch him inside. They're worried about having their legs cut off. "Take it easy, boys," I told them. "I'm closer to him than you are, and I'm not worryin'." The hell I wasn't. Ruth could swivel your head with a line drive.

But I always had pretty good luck with Babe. He was a guess hitter, you know. I'd watch that right leg; it told me what he was looking for. Sometimes he'd have his back almost to the pitcher, with that right leg pulled around toward the catcher. That's when he was looking for curves or slow stuff. When he was looking for a fastball, he'd place that right leg differently. So I'd pitch accordingly to him. Ruth hit only three home runs off me in the seven years I pitched to him. And he never beat me a ball game.

After the Babe died, I went to an old-timers' game in New York. After the game we all went to Toots Shor's restaurant for the shindig. Mrs. Ruth was there. I'd never met her, so I went up and introduced myself.

"You're Wes Ferrell?" she said.

"That's right," I said.

"Babe said a lot of things about you."

"What do you mean?" I asked.

"He'd come home and say how tough it was to get a base hit off of you. It upset him quite a bit."

Well, that flattered me more than anything in the world.

I had my troubles with Roger Peckinpaugh, you know. But I always worked hard for him, same as any manager I ever pitched for. Starting, relieving, pinch-hitting; I was always on call, happy to do anything to help out the ball club. Hurts my arm today just to think about it.

There was this game against the Athletics, in 1931. It was

supposed to be a home game for the Athletics, but there was no Sunday ball in Philadelphia at that time, so we caught the sleeper out of Philly on Saturday and went back to Cleveland. Connie Mack figured there was no sense bringing the whole team for just the one game, and he left some of his ballplayers home. So he was short of pitchers.

I forget who started for the A's, but we got him out of there in the first inning. Eddie Rommel came in and pitched the rest of the game—seventeen innings. We got about 30 hits off him. Johnny Burnett, our shortstop, set a record that game: he got 9 hits. Alva Bradley, the Cleveland owner, said later it was the most exciting ball game he ever saw. Well, I didn't think it was so damned exciting.

I relieved Willis Hudlin in the seventh and pitched right on into the eighteenth inning before they beat me with a bad-hop base hit. Jimmie Foxx got a single, and then Eric McNair hit a line drive to left that took a crazy hop over Joe Vosmik's head. Jimmie came tearing around, and I'm beat. I should've won it in the ninth, you know, but Eddie Morgan made an error at first on the easiest ground ball you ever saw and that tied it.

Now, that was just a little relief stint, those eleven innings. A few days later I'm taking my *regular* turn, against the Yankees in New York. I go out there, and I just don't have anything on the ball. They beat me. I'm sitting in the clubhouse after the game, and Peckinpaugh comes over and says, "Hey, why didn't you bear down out there?"

"What the hell are you talking about?" I said. I was steamin'. "I've been winning twenty games a year for you and pitching out of turn whenever you needed me, and you ask me why I wasn't bearing down? I *always* bear down. I just didn't have anything to bear down *with* today."

Well, that didn't sit too good with him. Then we go up to Boston, and I start another ball game. They get one or two runs off me in the second inning, and he wants to take me out.

"Hell," I said. "I ain't coming out. I just got in here."

Finally I had to leave, and the next thing I know I'm suspended. They called it insubordination or something like that. I went back to Cleveland and sat around doing nothing for fourteen days, in the middle of one of my finest years. What a waste of time.

Couldn't get along with Peckinpaugh, no matter what. The guy hardly ever spoke to me. He got fired in 1933, and Walter Johnson came over to manage. Here was a fine guy, nice as could be. Religious type of person, a real gentleman. He had some drawbacks as a manager, though. Had trouble expressing himself. He'd hold a meeting, and you'd hear him say, "Now, dadgummit, confound it, I want you boys, doggonnit, to get out there and get 'em." That's how he'd tell you. Never profane, though. A very kind person. Never had any trouble with his ballplayers. Not even with Fiery Wes Ferrell. Fiery Wes Ferrell. Boy, I've got to laugh at that. I guess I've still got the reputation, but reputations aren't always justified. Here, listen to this. I was with the Red Sox and pitching a game in Yankee Stadium against Monte Pearson. I had them beat going into about the fifth or sixth inning. The Yankees had two men on and DiMaggio is up. I walked over to Eric McNair, who's playing shortstop. Cronin, who was the manager and the regular shortstop, wasn't playing that day. I forget why.

I tell McNair, "Now, I'm gonna throw him a slider and try to make him hit it to you."

I go back to the mound and make my pitch, get it right where I want, and doggone if Joe doesn't hit it right straight to McNair. But the ball was hit right off the end of the bat and had such spin on it that when it hit the ground, it got away from McNair. Two runs scored. I figured I should have been out of the inning, and I got mad. Then a couple base hits followed on top of that.

I look over at Cronin. He's standing up in the dugout with his hands in the air. I thought he wanted to take me out. I look around, and my infielders are standing around with their hands on their hips, looking at the ground. I figured I'm gone, and I walked off the mound. In those days you had to go through the Yankee dugout to get to the clubhouse. I went right past brother Rick—he was with the Red Sox too then— and he didn't say anything to me. I was told later that Cronin started to yell at me not to leave, but I didn't hear anything. I thought I was out.

Next thing I know I'm sitting in my hotel room, and somebody calls me on the telephone to tell me I'm suspended, fined $1,000, and a lot of stuff like that. Boy, I nearly hit the ceiling! I couldn't believe what I was hearing. I would *never* walk out of a ball game. Ask Peckinpaugh—he needed a lasso to get me out of the game that other time.

They had a big meeting that night, and I told Cronin that it was all a misunderstanding, that he knew my record, how hard I worked, how willingly, and that I was the last one in the world to run out on a ball club.

Well, nobody said much. They send me back to Boston and I find the newspapers filled with the story: "Wes Ferrell Suspended. Walks Out of Ball Game." A lot of crap like that. Two days later I was out pitching again, in my regular turn. Wasn't fined, wasn't suspended. It was all a misunderstanding and was soon forgotten by all concerned. But that's how you get a reputation as being this or that sort of fellow.

Like I say, Rick was there with me on the Red Sox. When I got traded over to Boston in 1934, he was already there. We got along real fine. Usually thought alike. Brother or no brother, he was a great catcher and ought to be in the Hall of Fame. He was a real class receiver. You never saw him lunge for the ball; he never took a strike away from you. He'd get more strikes for a pitcher than anybody I ever saw, because he made catching look easy.

Well . . . I say we got along real fine, and we did . . . but I'll always remember a game I was pitching against the Detroit Tigers. Brother Rick is giving me the signs, the little old one-two-three for fastball, curve, straight change-up. I kept shaking him off; I wanted to throw my change-up curve. Finally he got tired of squatting there and being shaken off, and he got up and walked around in front of the batter.

"Throw any damn thing you please," he said. "You can't fool me no way. I know you well enough."

Boy, that made me mad! That's all I wanted to know. I wanted to powder that ball by him so fast he wouldn't see it. "A great star like me?" I says to myself. Me winning all those games, and he thinks he's going to catch me without signs? I kicked the mound around a little bit, pulled my cap down tight on my head. Then I fired him a curveball—one of the best I'd ever thrown, I swear—and he just reached down across his body and caught it backhanded with that mitt of his. Showboating. I'd throw him my best fastballs and he'd catch them soft—you know, wouldn't let it pop.

Well, we went through the whole ball game that way. Just

a-stormin', and a-throwin', and a-powderin' that ball. And here's Cronin, standing out at shortstop, wondering what in the world's going on up there—he's not seeing any signs!

I pitched a two-hitter. Beat the Tigers 3–0. One of my finest games. I was so happy I was tickled to death. After it's over, I go into the clubhouse and I'm sitting there. Everybody's coming over to shake my hand on the game. And there's brother Rick, sitting two stools away. He won't look at me. I keep glancing over, but he won't look. We're pulling our socks and uniforms off. Finally I glance around again, and now he's looking at me.

"Well," he says, "you pitched a pretty good ball game. But damn you, if you'd listened to me, you'd of pitched a *no*-hitter!"

I'd already had a no-hitter, you know, in 1931, against the St. Louis Browns. And guess who almost beat me out of it? That's right. Brother Rick. He came up in the late innings and hit one to Bill Hunnefield at short. Hunnefield came up with it and threw a little high, and they called it an error. And I'll tell you, I never saw anybody run harder than Rick did going down that line—and that's the way it's supposed to be.

I held out the year I was traded to Boston. Missed most of spring training. I was just sitting tight, right down here on the farm. Rick told me to keep quiet, not make any noise, that he'd heard the Red Sox were trying to get me. I was keeping myself in shape as best I could, running, throwing.

Now, the Lucky Strike tobacco people over here in Reidsville had a ball club, and they wanted me to come out and pitch for them against some amateur club from Virginia. They said they'd give me $100. Well, I thought this was great. I'd get the chance to pitch a game, give myself a workout against a bunch of humpty-dumpties and make $100 in the bargain.

So I went over to Reidsville. A real country ball park. I had to dress in the boiler room of a factory, leaving my clothes in this filthy place that was dusty and smelly and full of cobwebs, and then go on out to the ball park. It was no Yankee Stadium, I can tell you. The fence was half broken down; the little bleacher section they had was rickety. But a lot of people showed. They came from miles around, some of them in horse and buggies. Come to see the great Wes Ferrell pitch. The man who had pitched to Ruth and Gehrig and Foxx and Simmons; come to see him dazzle a collection of country boys.

They came crowding around me while I'm warming up, talking to me the whole time. "Hi ya, Wes." "How's it look, Wes?" And I'm smiling and nodding and saluting them off of the peak of my cap and telling them that it looks just fine.

Then the game starts. The first guy comes up. Left-handed hitter. Wearing overalls and tennis shoes and a faded little cap. And smoking a cigarette! I get two strikes on him. He steps out and flips away the cigarette. Oh, I'm thinking, what a smooth way to earn $100. I wind up and give him my high hard one . . . and he hits it over the center-field fence. Well, that was the pattern. The great Wes Ferrell never pitched harder in his life, and those guys killed me. Line drives all over the place. I finished out the game in the outfield. Never been so embarrassed in my life.

After the game they paid me off in nickels and dimes and quarters and dollar bills. I wanted to turn my back when I took it, I was so embarrassed. I went back to the boiler room and dressed, and soon after that I came up with the biggest case of crabs you ever heard of, from leaving my clothes in that damn filthy boiler room. By God, what a day!

Of course, people always ask me who was the greatest hitter I ever faced. They expect I would say Gehrig or Ruth or Simmons or Foxx. But I don't. I say Gehringer. Charlie Gehringer was the toughest hitter I ever faced. The reason I say this is because he'd never offer to hit the first pitch. You could just lob it in there, throw it right down the middle of the plate, and he'd just stand there and follow it into the catcher's mitt. Sometimes he'd spot you *two* strikes. And you say to yourself, "Well, as good a pitcher as I am, I'm gonna get him out." But you couldn't do it. He'd hit that ball. And he'd beat you ball games. Yes, he would.

You threw it down the middle to Ruth, he'd knock you off the mound. Gehrig too, and Foxx and Simmons and Greenberg and DiMaggio. They'd kill you, those fellows. You had to start pitching hard to them, first pitch. Why did Gehringer do that? I don't know. I never asked him.

I didn't have too much trouble with Simmons. He was a great hitter, though. Believe that. Foxx was another great one. I'd strike him out three times, and then he'd hit a home run so far out of Shibe Park that you just had to stand there and admire it. A man hit a ball that far? No way you could get mad at him. You had to admire it. Foxx was a wonderful guy, too. Always smiling, always looking to have a good time. Loved his golf, like so many ballplayers. In fact, he ran his own golf course down in St. Petersburg for a while.

Hey, all this talk about pitching, don't forget I was a pretty fair hitter, too. I hit nine home runs in 1931, and that's still a record for pitchers. In 1933, when Vosmik broke his wrist, and my arm was a little sore, they put me in the outfield, and I hit close to .300.

One time I was pitching against Hod Lisenbee of the Athletics. He had me beat 1–0 going into the eighth inning and I hit a home run to tie it. Then in the thirteenth inning I hit another home run to beat him, 2–1.

Another time, when I was with the Red Sox, Grove was pitching and he was getting beat by one run going into the last of the ninth. Now, you know Lefty; he was a great competitor and a hard loser. A *very* hard loser. He's sure he's lost his ball game and is madder'n hell over it. He goes into the clubhouse. We get a man on base, and Cronin sends me up to hit. Tommy Bridges is the pitcher. Well, I hit the first pitch I see and knock it over the left field fence, and we win the ball game.

So we all rush into the clubhouse, laughing and hollering, the way you do after a game like that. And here's Lefty, sitting there, still thinking he's lost his game. When he saw all the carrying-on, I tell you, the smoke started coming out of his ears.

"I don't see what's so funny," he says. "A man loses a ball game, and you're all carrying on."

Then somebody says, "Hell, Lefty, we won it. Wes hit a home run for you."

Well, I was sitting across the clubhouse from him, pulling my uniform off, and I notice he's staring at me, with just a trace of smile at the corners of his mouth. Just staring at me. He doesn't say anything. I give him a big grin and pull my sweat shirt up over my head. Then I hear him say, "Hey, Wes." I look over and he's rolling a bottle of wine across to me—he'd keep a bottle of one thing or another stashed up in his locker. So here it comes, rolling and bumping along the clubhouse floor. I picked it up and thanked him and put it in my locker. At the end of the season I brought it back to

Carolina with me and let it sit up on the mantel. It sat up there for years and years. Every time I looked at it I thought of Old Left. He rolled it over to me.

He was my idol. Lefty Grove. Fastest pitcher I ever saw. The greatest. Why, I wasn't good enough to carry his glove across the field. Dizzy Dean was great, and so was Koufax. And Bob Feller was fast, of course. Bob had spectacular stuff. Didn't have to fool around on the corners; just get it over the plate. But Grove was faster. He'd throw that ball in there, and you'd wonder where it went to. It would just *zing!* and disappear. You can believe he was that fast because that's all he threw. He'd just keep fogging them in there. He didn't start throwing breaking stuff until late in his career.

I got to know Lefty when we were both with the Red Sox, from '34 to '37. He was just about the finest friend I ever had.

I'll give you another good pitcher—Bobo Newsom. And what a character he was! One time I started walking toward him during a game and everybody thought we were going to fight, but it wasn't that at all. You see, what happened was, when I was warming up before the game Bobo came walking by. He'd finished his warm-ups.

"Hey, Wes," he says, "the one that gives up the first hit to the other has got to come over and shake his hand." I don't know how he thought these things up.

"That's okay with me," I said. I figured I was a better hitter than he was, so there was no problem.

We went along until about the sixth inning, and neither of us has got a hit off of the other. Then Newsom comes up and the SOB bites into one and hits it up against the left-field stands for a double. The fans are all yelling and cheering, and I'm standing out on the mound, knowing what I've got to do. I didn't know whether to cuss or laugh. Finally I turn around and here I go, walking toward second base. The umpires thought I was going to fight, and they started coming over. I walked up to Bobo, and he's grinning a mile across his face and I start laughing too, couldn't help myself.

"What are you doing, Ferrell?" the umpire asks.

"I've got to shake this SOB's hand," I said. "We made a deal."

I shook hands with old Bobo and turned around and walked

back to the mound. The fans went crazy over it; they didn't know what it was all about, but they loved it.

Who was the toughest team to pitch against? Well, I'll tell you how to figure that. You've got to look at their pitching staff. If I'm pitching against the Yankees, it's not Ruth or Gehrig or DiMaggio I'm worrying about, because I know I can get those boys out often enough to win. It's Gomez, say, or Ruffing I've got to worry about—because they can shut my club out. Same with the A's. It's not Foxx or Simmons, great as they were—it's Grove or Earnshaw that's going to beat me. That's the way you look at it.

I'm with Washington in 1938, winning 13 and losing 8, and Clark Griffith turns me loose. I was getting a big salary, and I guess he figured he'd save some money. Joe McCarthy called me the next day and asked me to join the Yankees, which naturally I was happy to do. They had a great ball club, with the pennant just about sewed up. McCarthy always liked me. Some years before, when I was still with Cleveland, I'd made some favorable comments on his ability to handle his pitching staff, and Joe never forgot that.

I thought McCarthy was a great manager. Still do. He was all business running his ball club, very professional. You didn't see guys running around all night and then kicking your game away the next day, which experience I'd had.

When I got up to the stadium, he called me into his office.

"We've got one rule around here," he said. "We don't second-guess the manager."

And he meant it. He was very professional. You got up there, you saw why the Yankees were winning all those pennants. They were all business, all baseball.

You know what burned up old Griffith? When he let me go he had to give me ten days' pay. And then I sign up with the Yankees right away. So I'm getting paid double. Well, we went down to Washington a few days later, and McCarthy starts me. I beat them in eleven innings—and Griffith is still paying me out. Oh, that did him to a turn, paying money to the guy who's beating him.

You know, something happened in that game. I thought it was curious at the time, though now I can understand it. We should've won the game in nine innings, but Gehrig made a bad play on a ground ball and let the tying run in. Instead of going to the plate and throwing the man out, he went the easy way, to first base. It was the kind of play you'd never expect him to make. Nobody knew at the time, of course, that Gehrig was dying. All we knew was that he wasn't swinging the bat the way he could nor running the way he could.

The next year, in spring training, it got worse. I was in the clubhouse with him one day down in St. Petersburg. The rest of the team was out on the field. Lou got up on the bench to look out the window to see what was going on on the field. It was some little effort for him to do that, and he wasn't too steady. All of a sudden he fell over, right down to the floor. Just like that. He fell hard, too, and lay there for a second, frowning, like he couldn't understand what was happening.

"You hurt yourself, Lou?" the trainer asked.

"No, I'm okay," he said. He got up and didn't say anything more about it. I suppose he didn't know what was wrong, any more than the rest of us. He'd hit a ball into right-center, a sure double, and run and run as hard as he could—he *always* hustled—and get thrown out by a mile. In workouts you'd see him straining and huffing and puffing, running as hard as he could, and not getting anywhere. The fellows would laugh and kid him. "Hey, Lou, you're getting old." That sort of thing. Nobody knew the truth.

I remember one time out on the golf course, it was during the St. Petersburg Open. A lot of us went out to watch the pros. I was following the crowd, and I noticed Lou, walking all by himself along the edge of the woods. I watched him for a while and noticed something peculiar. Instead of wearing cleats, which normally he would have worn for walking across the grass, he was wearing tennis sneakers and was *sliding* his feet as he went along, instead of picking them up and putting them down. Looking back now, I realize why. His muscles were so deteriorated that just the effort of lifting his feet a few inches to walk had already become too much. God, it was sad to see—Lou Gehrig having to slide his feet along the grass to move himself.

Yep, there's a lot of things that stay with you as the years pile up. It's all been so long ago now that I find it hard to believe I ever did it, that I was ever there. For a while after you leave the game, you dream about it a lot. You dream you're going to pitch and that you can't get your uniform on.

You dream you can't get to the park, that you've lost your way. Crazy dreams, huh? But maybe not so crazy after all.

All of a sudden you're out of the big time, out of reach of all the glory you had. You had everything, all the time. I met so many fine people, all the celebrities. Musicians, singers, actors, politicians. Was even made a Kentucky colonel. It's great when somebody comes along and tells you they saw you pitch, how good they thought you were, how much they enjoyed it. But little by little it dwindles down, until you're back where you started.

Like I said, we sold off the old farm a couple of years ago to some developers, and they're bustin' and churnin' that earth now. Putting up apartments on the fields and pastures where me and Rick and all the rest of us used to play ball.

But still I've got those memories. I played against a lot of great stars. You name 'em. Ruth, Gehrig, Greenberg, Gehringer, Simmons, Foxx, Grove, DiMaggio, Cochrane, Feller. I saw them all. And they saw me. You bet they did.

CHARLIE GEHRINGER

CHARLES LEONARD GEHRINGER
Born: May 11, 1903, Fowlerville, Michigan
Major-league career: 1924–1942, Detroit Tigers
Lifetime average: .320

Charlie Gehringer was known as "The Mechanical Man" for the smooth, seemingly effortless style of his play. He batted over .300 thirteen times, including a league-leading .371 in 1937, the year he was selected the American League's Most Valuable Player. One of the greatest second basemen of all time, Gehringer amassed a lifetime total of 2,839 hits.

Gehringer was elected to the Hall of Fame in 1949.

This was back in 1923. Bobby Veach, who was in the Tiger outfield with Cobb and Heilmann in those days, used to come out to Fowlerville to hunt. Fowlerville was where I lived, not all that far from Detroit. One of Veach's hunting companions was a local man, a fellow who was a great baseball fan. He'd seen me play quite a bit. He suggested that Bobby take me down to Detroit for a tryout because he felt that I had a future in baseball. Veach had never seen me play, but he took this man's word for it, and it was through Veach that it was arranged.

So I went to the Tigers' ball park for a tryout. Was I nervous? What do you think? Walking out onto that ball field was something I'd never even dared to dream of. I thought I might get there someday by working my way up through the minors, but *suddenly* to be there was just unbelievable. And of course Ty Cobb was the manager, and to be on the same field with him was just overwhelming for a kid. A frightening experience.

They were all out there, Cobb, Heilmann, the whole bunch.
I hit with the scrubs. Cobb was watching me, but I couldn't
believe he was paying attention. After I hit, I went into the
outfield. I just stood around, still nervous, maybe a little embarrassed about being there.

Then Cobb was calling me in. I figured he wanted me to get
out of the way. But when I came in, he said, "Get in there and
hit again."

By this time the regulars were taking batting practice, and
they didn't like the idea of me getting in with them. They
didn't like that one bit. But it was by Cobb's orders. I stepped
in and started hitting again. This time Cobb wouldn't take his
eyes off me; I could *feel* him staring at me. Then they were all
watching me—Heilmann, Manush, Veach, the whole gang. I
guess they liked what they saw because they stopped grumbling about me being in there. It was eerie. The only sound in
that big, empty ball park was me standing there hitting line
drives, with the whole Tiger ball club watching me.

Then Cobb sent me out to second base, and I started picking
up grounders. I guess I was always pretty good with the glove.
It came to me quite naturally. I never thought much about
what I was doing. I just went and picked them up.

What happened next really amazed me. Cobb left the field
and in full uniform, spikes and all, went up to Mr. Navin's
office—he owned the ball club—and told Mr. Navin to come
down to the field and watch me.

I worked out that whole week, and then they signed me. No,
no bonus. But I did get a lot of tips on the stock market from
Cobb, which didn't do me any good; I didn't have the money to
invest.

Sure I wanted to play for the Tigers. They were my team. I
used to cut all the pictures of Detroit players out of the paper
and keep a scrapbook, and then sit and stare at them. I guess
I couldn't help but to be a Tiger fan; I was born so close to
Detroit.

I was born on a farm in Michigan, near Lansing. The near-
est town was Fowlerville, where I went to school. It was general farming. We had a lot of dairy cattle, raised practically
all the crops. I had an older brother who ran all the equipment, and I had to do the hard work, like shocking the wheat
and picking up the corn and hoeing the weeds and working in

the garden, and things like that. I think that's what gave me the idea of turning to something that might be easier, where at least the hours might be shorter.

I guess I started playing ball as soon as I was able to handle a bat, probably when I was about seven years old. When I was a kid, baseball was about the only sport you had in the country. And there was no television in those days, fewer ways to amuse yourself. So you played baseball.

I wasn't always an infielder. I pitched all through high school. I had a big roundhouse curve and good control, and it got me through the high school competition. But then I pitched a couple of semipro ball games, and that roundhouse wasn't fooling too many guys, and I decided I'd better try something else. So I switched to second base, though I played third when I attended the University of Michigan for two semesters.

Cobb took me under his wing right away. He kept telling me I was going to be tremendous. He really took care of me the first year or two. Went out of his way to teach me, and he taught me an awful lot. He more or less told me how to hit, where to stand in the batter's box against certain pitchers, how to spray hit—which I got to be able to do pretty well.

He always said that after Eddie Collins I was the best second baseman he ever saw. That was nice to hear, coming from a man who knew the game as well as Cobb did and who was kind of sparing with his compliments. So I guess he was satisfied with the way I took his instructions.

But he was tough to play for. Very demanding. He was so great himself that he couldn't understand why if he told players how to do certain things, they couldn't do it as well as he did. He just didn't seem to realize that it wasn't possible, and he got very frustrated with a lot of guys. But if you had the talent, then he could really help you. I think he made a fine hitter out of Manush, who pretty much followed Cobb's advice and, of course, had the talent to take advantage of it.

One of the things he always told me was, "Now, if you go to bat four times in a game and don't get a hit, work harder on that fifth time. Try not to get out of a game without a hit." That's one of the things he tried to impress upon me: Never give up. No matter what the score is, no matter what the situation. Always try harder and harder to get that base hit. That's what he preached, and that's what he practiced. Every time at bat for him was a crusade, and that's why he's off in a circle by himself.

He taught himself to hate those pitchers. It was a real vendetta between him and them. Of course, while he's got all those records today, I think it took a lot out of him as far as being a human being was concerned. You can't turn that kind of competitive drive on and off. He was the same off the field as he was on; he was always fighting with somebody. He was a holy terror.

I became a regular with the Tigers in 1926. That was when I really got to know Cobb. He got tough. Oh, he got tough with me. I was supposed to start the season in '26, but somehow in spring training I said something, or didn't say something, that provoked him and he took me out of the lineup about a week before we came home, and I never got to start. He never explained it to me, and nobody else ever did. He wouldn't even talk to me. The only way I managed to get into the lineup was because our second baseman, Frank O'Rourke, got the measles. So Cobb had no other choice but to put me in. But even then he wouldn't tell me to bunt or to hit or to do this or do that. He'd tell the coaches to tell me what to do.

To this day I don't know why he got sore at me. The only thing I can think of is something that happened in spring training. You know, those games get so dull, and Cobb was always after you to shake it up out there, make a little noise. He said that to me one time when I was coming in off the field, and I said to him, "Well, I'm making most of the noise out there. I'm making more noise than anybody else." That might have done it. I can't remember anything else I ever said or did that might have turned him sour. He was awfully touchy. I don't think anybody really got along with him. Of course, he'd never pick on Heilmann, say; Heilmann was too big a star. He'd pick on guys he knew couldn't battle back with him.

I remember one time, in St. Louis, he kept me after school, like a teacher would. Just kept me sitting in the clubhouse for an hour after everybody had left the ball park. This was because I'd let Ken Williams, who Cobb disliked very much, beat out a bunt. Now Ken Williams was a very powerful hitter. How are you going to play him up on the grass so he can't beat out a bunt? He'll knock your teeth out. I thought that was ridiculous. But he kept me sitting there for an hour.

He sure was a peculiar man.

Cobb left during the '26 season, and George Moriarty took over. He was a former ballplayer and had been an umpire too. His main forte was stealing bases, and home plate in particular. He wrote a book once called *Don't Die on Third*. He had everybody stealing home, whether you could run or not. He'd even get you in a hotel lobby and demonstrate how it should be done. He would show you how to get a lead. Then he'd start jockeying around between the potted palms and the furniture, and people would look at him like he'd gone balmy. I'll bet we set a record that year for having guys thrown out trying to steal home.

We generally had a heavy-hitting ball club over the years I was with the Tigers. We had guys like Heilmann, Manush, Greenberg, Rudy York, Pete Fox, Gerald Walker, Goose Goslin, Bob Fothergill. Fothergill was a likable character. He was a fun-loving fellow, always had a weight problem. Navin was always raking him over the coals about it. There was a story that I heard about Fothergill coming into Navin's office one winter's day to talk contract. Fothergill as usual was way overweight, and to conceal it, he came to the office wearing this big, heavy overcoat. Navin spotted him in the outer office and sensed what Bob was up to. So Navin went into his office, turned the heat way up, and then told Fothergill to come in.

Bob was anxious to get in and out of there as quickly as he could. But Navin sat back and began talking about one thing and another, and the sweat began pouring off of poor Fothergill.

"Why don't you take that coat off, Bob?" Navin asked. "Make yourself comfortable."

"No, it's okay," Fothergill said. "I'm comfortable."

Well, Navin just kept him there, talking, and Fothergill must have felt like he was in a steam bath. But he wouldn't take that coat off. Finally Bob said, "Let's get this over with." I don't know what he signed for that time, but I'm sure it wasn't for the figure he had in mind, he was so anxious to get out of there.

Walter Johnson was near the end of his career when I came into the league, but he could still throw hard. Del Baker, our coach, had seen Johnson in his prime, and said he threw the ball so hard you could hear it. Of course, in those days they didn't toss a ball out of the game as quickly as they do today, so if it had a little rough spot on it I imagine it did whir.

I think Grove was the fastest I ever saw, but guys who had hit against them both said Johnson was still faster. It's hard to believe that anyone could throw harder than Lefty Grove, though. Most of the time the right-handed batters couldn't pull him. I could always pull Feller—of course, he was right-handed—but I could never pull Grove until the tail end of his career. I'd go up there telling myself I was going to swing the minute he let it go. I'd do that and still hit a ground ball to the third baseman. And as good a pull hitter as Heilmann was, he'd always hit Grove to right field.

Grove's fastball wasn't all that alive. It carried a little but never did anything tricky. But it was so fast that by the time you'd made up your mind whether it was going to be a strike or a ball, it just wasn't there anymore. A lot of times he'd come in to relieve when it was near dark, and then it was hopeless.

Does Grove say I used to give him trouble? Well, that's hard for me to believe. Though once I did hit two home runs in succession off him. Just guessed right, I suppose. No, he didn't knock me down the next time. But I'll tell you, he once hit me as hard as I've ever been hit. This was when I'd first come in the league, one of the first few times I faced him. Everybody told me, "One thing you don't have to worry about—he's never wild inside." Well, he let this one get away and got me on the elbow. I thought the ball stuck there, that's how hard it came in. I had to leave the game, and that was the only time I ever saw Mr. Navin come into the clubhouse. He thought for sure that my arm was broken.

Wes Ferrell was another topflight pitcher in those days, and a good hitter, too. He won a lot of his own games with his bat. I think both of those Ferrell boys deserve some recognition. Rick was a fine catcher, and he probably hit better than some guys you've got in the Hall of Fame. You could do worse than put both those boys in the Hall of Fame.

Wes was one of your great competitors. He just hated to lose. I remember one time we were in Washington, playing the Senators. Ferrell had us beat by about 6–0 in the fourth inning, and he's going great guns. Then it started to rain. The skies turned black, and I tell you it just poured. Naturally the game was held up. I was sitting in the dugout, looking across at Wes, and I could almost *see* what he was thinking: God, am I going to lose this easy victory? After about fifteen minutes the rain stopped and the sun came out, and even before they could get the canvas off the field, there's Wes out there loosening up. He's determined to get that one more inning in to make it an official game.

I happened to be the first man he faced after the delay, and I hit a home run. That started it off. We began hitting and didn't stop until we'd tied the score. Bucky Harris was managing Washington then, and for some reason he left Wes in. Well, the next inning we get two more runs. That finished Wes. He went over to the bench, sat down, threw his glove disgustedly to the dugout floor, clamped down on it with his spikes and gritted his teeth and reached over and just started pulling that glove all to pieces, tearing up the fingers, the webbing, the stuffing, the whole thing.

And you know, there was an aftermath to that game. Mr. Briggs, who was then owner of the team, was listening to the game on the radio, and he was so happy with the way we won that game, coming from behind and all, that he bought everybody a tailor-made suit of clothes—which was quite a thing to do for twenty-five men.

One day I read in the paper about this kid the Indians had, named Bob Feller. He'd pitched three innings in an exhibition game against the Cardinals and struck out eight men. On our next trip to Cleveland Earl Averill said to me, "Boy, wait till you see this kid we've got. He'll remind you you're in the big leagues."

"I read about him," I said. "He must be pretty good, huh?"

"No," Averill said. "He's better than that. In fact, he's even better than *that.*"

Well, he was. Feller had terrific speed, and what made him even harder to hit was that tremendous curve ball. And he'd throw it to you anytime. This made him tough. There were a lot of guys in those days who could throw awfully hard, but the fact that Feller could snap off that curve made him all the tougher to hit. And he was just wild enough so you had to be foot-free up there.

We had a fine pitcher with us in Detroit in those days. Schoolboy Rowe. In fact, when he first came up, he was a great pitcher. He had one of the finest fastballs I ever stood behind.

Of course, he was so tall, and looking at that ball from second base, I swear it looked like it was going to hit the ground; but they were strikes. That ball would carry in there, and it had plenty of smoke on it. For about four years he was really throwing hard; then he hurt his arm.

I remember when Rowe was going for the record for consecutive wins, in 1934. He had 15, one under the record held by Joe Wood, Walter Johnson, and Grove. We were playing Washington and losing by one run, late in the game. We were really breaking our backs for him; we wanted to see him make it. Greenberg came up with two men on and drove them in with a double. That gave Rowe what he needed, and he beat them, I think it was 3–2. But the next time out, when he was trying to set a new record, he got bombed by the Athletics.

We had Tommy Bridges on our staff, too. One of the finest curve ball pitchers I ever saw. I always said I was glad I didn't have to bat against him.

With a little luck, we might have had Carl Hubbell pitching for us too. What a front three that would have been—Rowe, Bridges, Hubbell. Hubbell was with the Tigers for a while when I was a rookie. Cobb gave up on him finally, and the Tigers let him go. Then the Giants scouted him pitching somewhere down South and bought him. This was after he had developed that screwball—which he didn't have when he was with the Tigers. He was in the Detroit system for four or five years and just wasn't getting them out with what he had. He never had a great fastball or curve. It was the screwball that made him. Later on, of course, when he became a great pitcher, everybody wanted to know why we'd let him go. Well, it was nobody's fault; he was a completely different pitcher when we had him.

When we had him, he sure wasn't the pitcher he was in the '34 All-Star game, was he? I guess what he did in that game still ranks as one of the greatest pitching performances of all time. You know, I led off that game against him. Got a single to center. Then he walked Manush. So there we were, on first and second, with Ruth, Gehrig, and Foxx coming up. I figured we were good for at least a couple of runs, that there was no way he could get by our three best hitters.

But he struck out Ruth, and on the strikeout we pulled a double steal. So now I was on third, Manush was on second, there was still only one out, and Gehrig and Foxx were coming to bat. Still a pretty good situation for us. But he struck out Gehrig. And then he struck out Foxx. To start off the next inning he struck out Simmons. And then he struck out Cronin. Bill Dickey finally broke the string by getting a single. I'm glad he did. It was starting to get embarrassing.

A lot of us went on a trip to Japan that year, after the Series. It was quite a good ball club we took over there. We had Foxx, Ruth, Gehrig, Frank Hayes, Eric McNair, Bing Miller, Earl Averill, Lefty O'Doul. O'Doul arranged it. He'd been to Japan a few times and had been impressed with the Japanese love of baseball. He was instrumental in introducing professional baseball to Japan.

We went over by boat, and when we arrived, you never saw so many people as greeted us at the dock and then later on the streets when we drove to our hotel. It seemed like all of Tokyo was out, waving and yelling. We could hardly get our cars through, the streets were so jammed. What was interesting was that they knew who we all were. You'd think being so many miles away and being such a different culture, the whole thing would have been strange to them. But apparently they'd been following big-league baseball for years and gee, they knew us all. Especially Ruth, of course. They made a terrific fuss over him, and he loved it.

Those Japanese fans had never seen anything like those big guys—Ruth, Foxx, Gehrig. They just couldn't believe anybody could hit a ball so far. Of course, the Japanese were so much smaller than our guys. I remember a few games Ruth played first base—Gehrig was in the outfield—and whenever one of the Japanese got to first, Ruth would stand on the bag to make them look smaller. The fans loved it. They loved everything he did. His magic was unbelievable.

The stadium in Tokyo held about 60,000 people, and you know, it was the darnedest thing—even before we got on the field to work out, the place was jam-packed. It was that way every day; we'd go out to loosen up and there they were, every seat filled—to watch the pregame workout!

We did a lot of crazy things. Sometimes we'd take infield practice without a ball. We'd go through the motions, whipping our arms through the air and yelling and throwing nothing. And then wouldn't you know it? After about a week the

Japanese started taking infield practice without a ball. Probably thought that was the way to do it.

I got to know Ruth fairly well. He was a big lovable kid. Always a laugh, always a joke. You know, with all his great power, he never hit a ball hard on the ground. Ruth had that uppercut swing, and if he hit the ball on the ground, he more or less topped it, and it would be a big bouncer. Now Gehrig, he could really lash ground balls at you; he'd knock your shins off. But if Ruth hit a ball hard, it was gone; either that or one of those nose-dive line drives.

I'll tell you who hit probably the most wicked ground ball to second base—Al Simmons. He had that long bat, and he stood quite a ways back from the plate, and they tried to pitch him outside to keep him from knocking it upstairs, so then he'd hit it to the right side. And he'd slice them. You'd think you were in front of it, but you kept moving to your left and finally wound up catching it one-handed. He could blister it. He hit a miserable ground ball.

Remember the G-men? That's what they called FBI men back in the thirties. It was short for government men. Well, that's what they called us in the Tiger lineup, the G-men: Greenberg, Goslin, Gehringer. Goslin came over in '34 and helped us win two pennants. And of course, Greenberg was a great one. Hank was a self-made ballplayer. He made himself a great hitter through hard work and determination. When he first came up, he couldn't hit that curve ball, but he learned to hang in there. When they took him off of first base and put him in the outfield, everybody thought he'd get killed out there, but he worked hard at it, and he became pretty good in the field.

Hank loved to drive those runs in. If there was a man on first, he'd always say to me, "Get him over to third, just get him over to third." He drove them in, too. Had over 180 one year.

In 1937 we had four men with over 200 hits—Greenberg, Gerald Walker, Pete Fox, and myself. That must be a record. And a few years earlier we had four men on the infield who together drove in 460 runs—Hank, Billy Rogell, Marv Owen, and myself. That's nice hitting to have in your infield.

Rudy York was with us, too, in those years. Another powerful slugger. I roomed with Rudy for a while. He used to lead the league in burned-up mattresses. He would always go to bed smoking a cigarette. And he would fall asleep. If the cigarette burned his fingers, he'd wake up and put it out. But if it didn't, then he was in trouble. And so was his roommate. He burned up quite a few mattresses that way. He had to pay for them, too. I roomed with him for a year or two until I decided that my chances were better in some other part of the hotel.

I had kind of a long wait for my first World Series. It didn't come until 1934. The year before, we finished fourth. But then Cochrane took over as player-manager, and we got Goose Goslin from Washington, and apparently that was all we needed.

There's nothing like a World Series, no matter how many of them you might get into. It's a situation where you're not just up for every game, you're up for every pitch.

We played the Cardinals in '34, and they beat us, even though we had them down, three games to two. We felt we should have won the sixth game, but we got a bad umpiring decision at third base from Brick Owens. We had a bunt play on, with men on first and second. Cochrane was going to third, and Owens called him out. The pictures showed later that he was safe. That was a turning point in the game. We did get one or two runs that inning, but we should have had the bases full and nobody out, and maybe we would have got Paul Dean out of the ball game, and who could tell what would have happened? We got beat, 4–3. That tied the Series at three games apiece, and Dizzy beat us the next day. But we always felt that call at third probably cost us the Series, that there should never have been a seventh game.

Dizzy shut us out that seventh game, and we got clobbered, 11–0. That was the game where we had the riot. I guess you've heard of that. In the sixth inning Joe Medwick hit one for extra bases. He went tearing around like all those Cardinals did—that was the Gas House Gang, and they were all do-or-die guys. Marv Owen was straddling the bag waiting for the relay, and Medwick came flying in there and took Owen with him. The fans didn't like it—this was in Detroit. The ball game was lost by that time—the score was something like 9–0—and our fans were pretty disheartened. So when Medwick took his position in left field at the bottom of the inning, they seemed to focus on that play and let all their frustrations out on Medwick. They started throwing things at him, mostly fruit and vegetables. I don't know where they got all that produce from—it was fairly late in the game and you'd have thought they would have eaten most of it by then—but it seemed like the supply was endless. You almost thought that trucks were pulling up to the gates making deliveries.

Judge Landis finally took Medwick out of the game, and everything calmed down after that.

We won it again in '35, and this time we played the Cubs. They had a good ball club, with some very strong pitching. Lon Warneke and Bill Lee pitched fine ball games against us, but we got some good pitching ourselves from Tommy Bridges and Alvin Crowder. We went into the sixth game leading them, three games to two. Same situation as the year before. We'd come close in '34, losing in seven, and when you've come that close, well, you know what it is to *almost* win; that's a very itchy feeling.

We won it in the last of the ninth. The game was tied, 3–3. Larry French was pitching for them. Cochrane opened with a single, and I was the next batter. Well, I tied into one and thought for sure I'd got myself a two-base hit down the right field line. But Phil Cavarretta had never moved away from the bag. I've talked to him a dozen times since, and he always says, "I don't know why I didn't get off. I just stayed there." He should have gotten off the minute the ball was pitched, since I'm more apt to hit one to his right than to his left. But for some reason he stayed right there, and I hit it like a shot right at him, so hard that it handcuffed him and trickled away. If he had caught it, he would have had an easy double play, since Cochrane was off and running. So I was out, but Cochrane got to second.

Goose Goslin was the next hitter. He hit a looper into center field that was just out of everybody's reach, and Cochrane scored. That was the thrill of a lifetime. You don't realize what the world championship means until you've won it. It was the first championship ever for Detroit, and the town really went wild. So did we.

Cochrane was great, a great inspirational leader. Boy, he was a hard loser, the hardest loser I think I ever saw. He was a good manager, strict but fair. He wouldn't stand for any tomfoolery. He wanted everybody to put out as hard as they could, and he set the example himself. Always hustling, always battling. Cochrane was in charge out there, that's what you could say about him—he was in charge.

How would I compare him with Dickey? Well, it's hard. Dickey could throw a little better, I think. Cochrane was probably a better all-around guy; he could run faster, he could do more with the bat, he could do more things to beat you. He didn't have quite the power that Dickey did, though. It's a hard choice to make. You might be more inclined to pick Cochrane over Dickey because of Mickey's aggressiveness. But Dickey certainly made catching look easy.

You know, I was on deck when Cochrane got beaned. That was at Yankee Stadium in 1937. Bump Hadley was the pitcher, and he could throw hard. He let a high inside pitch get away, and Mickey never saw it. He didn't even flinch. The ball hit him so hard it bounced straight back to Hadley. Cochrane went down like he'd been hit with an ax. He had a terrible fracture, way back through his head. Some doctors said that if the ball had hit him an inch lower, he probably never would have awakened. I've never seen anybody hit harder than that. It about finished Cochrane's career, and it was a blow to the team. He was our quarterback.

He told me later that he'd lost track of the ball the moment Hadley let go of it. That happens a lot of times, and you just have to hope it's not coming at you. Yankee Stadium had a very bad background for hitting. The ball would get lost in all those white shirts out in the center field bleachers, and you just couldn't see it.

You get these nicknames in baseball, they're hard to shake off, they stay with you forever. The one they pinned on me was The Mechanical Man. I think it was Gomez who started that one. He was supposed to have said, "You wind him up in the spring, turn him loose, he hits .330 or 340, and you shut him off at the end of the season."

Well, as a matter of fact, I always did look at the fielding part of it as being very mechanical. You just get that part done so you can go back and hit. I think hitting is the thing people remember most vividly, the home run or the base hit that wins the ball game. You can make the greatest fielding play in the world, and they probably won't remember it the next day. Particularly in the infield. Of course we remember some great catches made by Willie Mays or Joe DiMaggio, because an outfielder has the opportunity to run a long distance or leap against a wall. But a great infield play just happens too quickly for the imagination to seize upon it. You ask somebody what's the greatest infield play they ever saw, and they probably couldn't tell you.

Take the double play, for instance. I don't think people appreciate how difficult that really is, especially when you have two guys running in different directions. The timing has to be perfect. You're throwing the ball to the base, not to the man, and he's not only got to be there at the same time the ball is, but he's got to be able to handle the throw and at the same time get out of the base runner's way. It may look easy and automatic, but if your timing is off just a fraction, you've messed it up.

I can tell you a good one on the old "Mechanical Man." Once we were playing the St. Louis Browns. I hit a ground ball to somebody, and they threw me out. That made two out, but I thought it was three, so I kept running, on around first and out to my position. In those days you used to leave your glove out on the field between innings, and I ran over and picked it up and took my position. I didn't realize it, but I was standing right next to the Browns' second baseman, Oscar Melillo.

"Charlie," he says, "thanks all the same, but I don't need any help."

Talk about a long walk back to the dugout.

I had a reputation for taking the first pitch, and I guess I did do that a lot. Why? I thought I was a better hitter with a strike or two on me. Too many times you go up there with the attitude of "Well, this is the first pitch, I'll take a swing at it." You're apt to be a bit careless, try to go for distance, and the next thing you know you've popped up. But with one strike or even two strikes, you're not going to be careless. You really knuckle down. You're going to get a good pitch, and you're going to hit it.

Yes, I had a good, long career. No regrets about any of it. I guess I had my share of the fun and the base hits. Getting into the Hall of Fame in 1949 was another great thrill. You know, these days I'm on the Old Timers Committee that votes on candidates for the Hall of Fame. If you've been out of baseball twenty years or more, you come under our jurisdiction. Who are my top choices? Well, I think Earl Averill should be in, and I think Billy Herman should be in, definitely. One of the greatest second basemen that ever lived. And there are some other guys who I think are deserving, like Freddy Fitzsimmons and Arky Vaughn and Joe Sewell and Ernie Lombardi. Chuck Klein is another one I always vote for.

I went into the service after the 1942 season. I'd about had it as a player. It was getting to be work, getting harder and harder to prime myself for the games.

I was stationed in California for two years. Then they sent me to the naval air station in Jacksonville. Ted Williams was stationed there at the time. They had a league of service teams down there.

Upon arriving in Jacksonville, I went to see the CO. He was a great sports fan, and he told me how happy he was to see me.

"We're going to have a fine team here," he said.

"I hope so," I said. "But as for myself, I think I'll just coach and not play."

"No," he said. "You're going to play."

"I'd rather just coach," I said.

"You're going to play," he said.

"But—"

"Because if you don't play," he said, "I'll send you so far they won't know where to find you."

"Okay," I said. "I'll play. I'll be happy to."

Later I was talking to Williams. Ted was so hepped up about flying those night fighters he couldn't think about anything else. I asked him if he was going to come out for the team.

"Gee," he said, "I've got such a heavy schedule that I just can't."

"Have you spoken to the CO yet?" I asked.

"No," he said.

"Ted," I said, "I think you're going to play."

"No, Charlie."

"Ted," I said. "Yes."

He did. He sure did. Those commanding officers took the whole baseball thing pretty seriously. Once we had a game scheduled at Montgomery Air Base, in Alabama, and they came and picked us up and flew us to Montgomery for the game and then flew us back again. Talk about wasting the taxpayers' money.

You know, when I came out of the service, I was in great shape. I think I probably could have played another year or so. I should have, too, to have gone after 3,000 hits. I fell short by about 160 or so. It didn't seem important when I was playing, but looking back now, it would be nice to have.

ELBIE FLETCHER

ELBURT PRESTON FLETCHER
Born: March 18, 1916, Milton, Massachusetts
Major-league career: 1934–35, 1937–49, Boston Braves, Pittsburg Pirates
Lifetime average: .271

A popular and highly respected ballplayer, Elbie Fletcher was a slick-fielding, sharp-hitting first baseman who starred for many years for the Braves and the Pirates. Appearing in a big league lineup for the first time in 1934 as an eighteen-year-old fresh from high school glory, Fletcher stayed in the big leagues until 1949 (with time out for two years in the Navy). An indication of the respect opposing pitchers had for him is the fact that four times Fletcher received more than 100 bases on balls in a season, twice leading the league.

Did you know that I'm in the Hall of Fame? I sure am.

Whenever I tell that to anybody they look at me like I'm crazy. "We know your record, Fletcher," they say. "You were a pretty good first baseman, but not good enough for that." And I tell them, "Look, when you get to Cooperstown I want you to go over to where they have the records on Johnny Vander Meer. Look at the box scores of his two consecutive no-hitters. In one of those games—the one against the Braves—you'll see my name: Elbie Fletcher: 0 for 2."

Sure, I still kid around a lot. I was always that way. Life is too short not to have your laughs. Did I kid around when I was playing ball? Well, not in the sense that I didn't take the game seriously. I took it very seriously, but I also enjoyed it. Heck, it was still the same game I loved on the sandlots. And when you can play it in the big leagues—well, you're on top of the world.

I grew up in a little town outside Boston, not too far from both Fenway Park and Braves Field. It was great having two big league teams nearby; it meant that there was always a ball game. When I was a kid, I worked in a vegetable market in town. I got twenty-five cents a day. And I would take that quarter and buy myself a seat at either Fenway Park or Braves Field; it didn't make any difference. I'd sit close as I could get to first base, and I'd rivet my eyes on the first baseman, watching every move he made. You know George Sisler finished up with the Braves in '29 and '30, and he was still something to see around that bag.

I don't know when it got fixed in my mind that I was going to be a big league first baseman; as a matter of fact, I can't remember a time when I *didn't* want to be a big league first baseman.

I got my opportunity to go into professional baseball by winning a newspaper contest. A newspaper in the Boston area asked the fans to write in and recommend a high school player and say why they thought he might possibly have the qualifications to eventually become a big leaguer. Well, I organized a campaign on behalf of Elbie Fletcher. I had all my uncles and aunts and cousins and friends and everybody else write in recommending me. And as fate would have it, I won the contest. The prize was a free trip to Florida and spring training with the Braves. Talk about a dream coming true! This was in 1934.

So I got on a train and headed south. First time ever away from home. I was so excited I couldn't sleep. I just sat there and kept my nose pressed against the train window all the way to Bradenton.

Bill McKechnie was the manager then. He was a very kindly man. One of the coaches, Hank Gowdy, sort of kept an eye on me and on some of the other younger players. I don't know if he had been asked to do it or whether he was doing it on his own. Hank was an old-timer—he was the catcher for the 1914 Miracle Braves—and he was kind of strict and stern with us, though he was also very generous and good-hearted.

Well, when I got down there, they said to me, "Now, when

you go into the restaurant to eat, you order right off the menu and just sign the check."

I couldn't believe it. This was just great. Eat all you want and whatever you want, and just sign your name! So the first morning I went into the restaurant with another boy, and we picked up the menus. I saw "breakfast steak" printed there. Well, back home I'd be lucky to see steak once a month. And here it was, right on the menu—and just sign your name!

So the waitress came over and waited for us to order. To tell you the truth, I was a little scared about ordering steak for breakfast, even though it was on the menu.

"What'll it be, boys?" the waitress asked.

I kept staring at "breakfast steak," biting my lip. I could just hear McKechnie or Gowdy saying: "Steak for breakfast? Listen, kid, who do you think you are, Babe Ruth or somebody?" But finally I got my courage up and said, "What about the steak?"

"What about it?" she said.

"Maybe I'll have the steak," I said.

Nothing happened. By that I mean she just wrote it down and walked away.

So that started it. I had steak every morning, for five or six mornings in a row. The waitress even got to know me. I'd come in and sit down and she'd say, "Steak, kid?" Then I started feeling sick. I was all bound up inside and was getting sicker by the minute. I didn't say anything to anybody at first; I was afraid they'd send me home. Then I told one guy, and word started getting around. Finally it got around to McKechnie, and he heard what was happening every morning at the breakfast table. He came up to me on the field and said, "I want you in the clubhouse tomorrow morning at nine thirty."

"I'll be there," I said.

Now that was pretty early, before the ballplayers came in. So I showed up at nine thirty, and there he was. Just the two of us.

"I understand you're having a problem," he said.

"Sort of," I said.

"Not feeling too well."

"No, sir."

"Wait here," he said.

He went away, and when he came back, he was holding this

big bag filled with liquid, with sort of a nozzle on it. I looked at it and wondered what he was up to. He handed me the bag. I didn't know what in the world this thing was. He saw the puzzlement on my face and explained how I was to work the thing.

It was the first time in my life I'd ever had an enema.

When I was ready to leave the clubhouse, he said to me, "Fletcher. One more thing. From now on you're having breakfast with Hank Gowdy."

So every morning after that I sat down with old Hank and he'd pick up the menu, study it very sternly, and then bark up to the waitress, "Prunes and All-Bran."

God, it was awful.

You know, I was still in high school when I went away with the Braves that spring. When I got down to Bradenton, the Braves sent me to school for a couple of hours a day—I guess they had to do that. That enabled me to keep up with my studies, and when I got back to Milton High School, I was able to graduate with my class.

The day after I graduated I was in Harrisburg, Pennsylvania, making $250 a month, which was darn good money in those days. That was during the Depression, remember, and a lot of men with families weren't making anywhere near as much as I was.

I'll tell you how I happened to be getting that much money. Judge Fuchs was the owner of the Braves, and his son Bobby came around to my house and left a contract for me to sign. It called for $150 a month. Because I was underage, my dad had to sign for me. But he was a salesman, and he was on the road at the time. So there I was, sitting with that contract and unable to sign it. I was going out of my mind—I figured the Braves would forget about me if I didn't get that contract right back to them.

After a few days went by, I got a letter from the Braves telling me to disregard that contract, that they were enclosing one that called for $250 a month. Now $150 a month was more money than I'd ever seen in my life, so you can imagine how I felt about $250. The crazy thing was—I found this out later— the Braves thought I was holding out! My father was still on the road. I was having fits; nobody could control me. I must've asked my mother every fifteen minutes for days when he was coming home. "I told you when he's coming home," she'd say. "Now be still." Be still? How could I be still?

When finally my father came home, I didn't even give him a chance to say hello; I dragged him over to the table and made him sign that contract.

I think my father was tickled to death to get rid of me. I was in my senior year in high school at the time, and he was wondering where he was going to get the dough to send me to college. I had a brother who was a couple of years older, and he wanted to become a doctor. So we had to skimp and save for that, and I guess we were living pretty close to the mark. I was wishing I could do something to make it easier. So when the Braves came along with their offer, it was an answer to a lot of problems.

I liked it in the minors. Sure, living conditions weren't the best, but you just didn't take notice of that. We were allowed $1.50 a day for meals. We rode the buses and stayed in the worst hotels in town. We'd sleep eight in a room, just put the mattresses down on the floor and go to sleep. In fact, we'd only take two rooms and that would take care of the whole ball club. But it was fun. We'd have water fights and pillow fights. Hell, we were all seventeen and eighteen years old. It was a great experience, being away from home, having people make a fuss over you because you were a ballplayer. You'd be on the field and make a good play or get a base hit and everybody would cheer, and you'd be asked for your autograph and then later go up to your room and hit somebody over the head with a pillow. That was the minor leagues.

I came up to stay in 1937. Casey Stengel was managing the Braves then. Unfortunately, we had a bad ball club. But life was made tolerable by the pranksters we had, guys like Al Lopez, Tony Cuccinello, Danny MacFayden. Now Danny had been wearing the same pair of old white shoes for weeks, and they looked terrible. He always used to put those shoes very neatly right in front of his chair, and later he'd slip his feet into them and get up and walk away. One day Cuccinello and Lopez nailed the shoes to the floor. Then they took a razor blade and cut along the soles, right around the whole shoe. After the game MacFayden showered and dressed and then slipped his feet into the shoes and got up and took a few steps and stopped. He looked down and found himself wearing the tops of his shoes. The laughter went all around the clubhouse till Stengel finally came over to see what it was all about. There was MacFayden still standing there dumbstruck, wearing the tops of his shoes and looking back over his shoulder at the soles nailed to the floor. Stengel just shook his head.

Are there more laughs on a second division club? I don't see why there should be. Unfortunately, I was never on a pennant winner. I was always on teams that were out of contention. But I'll tell you something—it doesn't affect the way you play. You still play hard; you want that base hit, that run batted in; you want to dig out that low throw, make that good play. You're a professional, a big leaguer, and you take pride in that. Getting the base hit that wins the ball game is one of the greatest thrills you can have, whether you're in first place or last.

I guess the tightest pennant race I ever saw was in 1938. That was the year when Gabby Hartnett hit his famous "home run in the dark" that just about knocked Pittsburg out of the pennant and won it for the Cubs. That's very vivid in my mind because I was traded over to Pittsburgh the next year to replace Gus Suhr.

And you know, it was sad, because that's all they talked about on that Pirate club that year: Hartnett's home run. I knew we weren't going to win it. That home run was still on everybody's mind, haunting them like a ghost. Management knew it, and that's why they were trying to shake up the club. But it didn't help. They talked about Hartnett's shot all year and finished sixth.

Pie Traynor was the manager when I was sold to Pittsburgh. He was a very fine man, extremely soft-spoken. You never saw him kicking lockers or throwing things after a tough game. He kept it inside.

Now Frankie Frisch was as different from Traynor in that respect as you could possibly get. Frisch took over in 1940. He was aggressive and fiery and, God, teed off all the time. He'd fine you as quick as look at you. He fined me $250 once. That was during spring training one year, in San Bernardino. I was watching the floor show at a nightclub and sort of let the night slip by.

I don't know what time it was when I got back to the hotel, but when I looked into the lobby, there was Frisch, Honus

Wagner—he was one of our coaches—and Mr. Benswanger, the owner of the club. I walked around the block a couple of times, but each time I came back they were still there. Hell, I thought, they must be waiting for me. So I figured why make bad enough worse, and walked in. I marched right by them, said, "Good evening, gentlemen," and went upstairs. When I got up to my room, Debs Garms, my roomie, said, "They've been looking for you." "I know," I said. "I found them."

The next morning I went down to get my mail, and here's the letter in my box, addressed to Mr. Elburt P. Fletcher, with the Pittsburgh Pirate insignia on the envelope. It said: "Dear Mr. Fletcher: Due to the fact that you broke training rules you are hereby fined the sum of—" and it started with $50, but that was crossed out, and so was $100, $150, $200. They were all crossed out. It ended with $250.

Then I got to thinking I'd better call my wife because I knew some of the players would be writing home that Fletcher was fined $250, and I knew it wouldn't be long before she heard about it. So I put in a long-distance call and told her the story.

"All right," she said. "I'll go to the bank and take out two hundred and fifty dollars, and we won't say anything more about it."

Later I got a bill for $28 for the phone call. So that episode cost me $278. To see a floor show. I went into the service not long after that, for two years. When I got out and returned to the ball club, there was Frisch, welcoming me back with a big smile on his face.

"Elbie," he said, "do you know what we're going to do for you? We're going to give you back the two fifty we fined you a couple of years ago."

That was Frisch. Always unpredictable.

He always said he was never taught how to lose, and when he was with those great Gashouse Gang teams in St. Louis, he didn't lose very often. Then all of a sudden he gets with a ball club that's giving him an education in losing.

It was a pity we didn't do better in those years because we had some good ballplayers. We had Arky Vaughan, Johnny Rizzo, Bob Elliott, and of course the Waners. Paul was kind of along in years when I joined the club, but he could still hit. He was a master. You know how some players have their favorite bat, how they rub it and hone it and baby it along? Well, Paul maintained that the bat had nothing to do with it. One day, just to prove his point, he told us to pick out any bat we wanted and he'd use it in the game. Each time he went up to the plate we'd toss him a different bat. Well, he went four for five.

"It's not the bat that counts," he said after the game. "It's the guy who's wheeling it."

That Joe Medwick was something to watch in his great years, too. A great bad ball hitter. In fact, when we used to discuss how to pitch to him, the word was, "Don't get cute. Throw him strikes." Now that sounds crazy, but the truth was that the ball Joe could hit best was the one that was outside or practically over his head. He'd pound the stuffings out of them.

Medwick came up through that St. Louis organization, and all of those guys were bearcats. They were mean players, and hungry. Remember Pepper Martin? I used to hate to see that guy come to bat. He'd hit the ball and you could hear him leave home plate, stompin' and chuggin', coming down the line like his life depended on him beating that ball. I used to try to get the ball and lift my foot off the base as quick as I could. I remember one time he cut the heel right out of my shoe. And that was a brand-new expensive pair of spikes. He wouldn't cut you on purpose; he was just an aggressive player. When we'd get him in a rundown, it was like being in a cage with a tiger. He'd never give up, and you knew that when it finally came to the tag, he'd be diving or kicking, doing anything he could to get that ball out of your hand.

I'll tell you about another guy—Pete Reiser. There was a sweet ballplayer. Aggressive too, like Martin. He led the league his first full year up, in 1941. What a future he had, but he crashed into those fences too often trying to catch flyballs. He would do anything to get a ball. You know, a lot of times a fellow would get a base hit, and we'd stand on first and shoot the breeze a little. I was a friendly sort of guy. But Reiser wouldn't talk. Never would say a word. He'd get on base, and he'd be all concentration. And you just *knew* what he was thinking about: How am I going to get to second? How am I going to get to third? How am I going to score? Oh, but he had speed. He was *fast*. The slightest mistake, and he was gone.

Jackie Robinson was the same way. I remember when he came into the league. He was on first one time, and there was a pickoff play, and the ball got away and rolled not more than six feet from me. He saw where that ball was a split second before I did, and that's all he needed. By the time I picked it up I didn't even have a play at second on him. That's how quick he was. Unbelievable reflexes. And alert, always alert.

Sure, there was some grumbling when Jackie came into the league. I guess some of the Southern ballplayers didn't like the idea. But I tell you, every day that Robinson played he made them eat every word they were saying. He took a lot, but he stuck. I heard him called some awful things, by a lot of guys who didn't have the guts to back up what they were saying. Lucky for him, Jackie was playing in the right place. Those Brooklyn fans loved him and appreciated him.

I'll never forget those Brooklyn fans. Most rabid in the league. Ebbets Field was the most fantastic place to play in; I think everybody in the league always enjoyed going to Brooklyn. Never a dull moment. You'd be standing around during batting practice, and you'd hear some guy with lungs like a cannon yell out, "Fletcher, ya bum ya!" Not with any hard feelings or anything like that; just to let you know he was there. But I'll say one thing: If you made a good play, they were the first to acknowledge it. And of course that right field wall at Ebbets Field was always nice for a left-handed hitter to shoot at.

Now that old Braves Field up in Boston was another story. There was always this terrific wind blowing in from right field. You'd hit a scorcher out there, a shot that would go out of any other park—and you'd see the right fielder come trotting in for it. Al Lopez caught up there for a few years, and I asked him one time in spring training what he did over the winter. "Well," he said, "now and then I'd turn on the electric fan and sit in front of it and think of Braves Field."

One thing I'll never forget as long as I live. In 1938 we were playing a game there against Chicago. The wind was whipping up stronger than usual, and the sky was getting dark. But we kept playing. Then a big billboard behind the left field fence blew over. The infield dirt was whirling around like crazy, and now and then a guy's hat flew off. But we still kept playing. Finally somebody hit a high pop fly. I called for it behind the mound. Then the shortstop was calling for it. Then the left fielder was calling for it. And then the wind took it and blew it right out of the ball park. At that point the umpires said, "Okay, boys. That's all for today."

You know what that was? That was the day of the big hurricane of 1938, probably the worst ever to hit New England. I could barely drive home, it was so awful, with trees lying all over the street. But that's how bad the wind was in Braves Field—we were playing in a hurricane and didn't know the difference!

In 1935 I went back to spring training with the Braves. Still just a kid, eighteen years old. That was the spring Babe Ruth joined the team, right at the very end of his career. We were all awed by his presence. He still had that marvelous swing, and what a follow-through, just beautiful, like a great golfer.

But he was forty years old. He couldn't run, he could hardly bend down for a ball, and of course he couldn't hit the way he used to. It was sad watching those great skills fading away. One of the saddest things of all is when an athlete begins to lose it. A ball goes past you that you know you would have been on top of a few years before. And then, being a left-handed hitter, you begin to realize that most of your good shots are going to center and left-center, and you know you've lost just that fraction of a second and can't always pull the ball the way you used to. And to see it happening to Babe Ruth, to see Babe Ruth struggling on a ball field, well, then you realize we're all mortal and nothing lasts forever.

In those days none of us were going to make enough money to give us real security when we retired. When you were through playing, you went out to look for a job. But that didn't depress me. I'd had many years of doing the thing I'd always wanted to do, that I loved most, and not many men can say that. A lot of people said that I was too easygoing, that I loved to play too much to have been as serious about it as I should have been. But I got everything out of it that I wanted to, and I have no regrets.

I still live in the town where I grew up, and the old diamonds are still there. Once in a while I go out with my sons and have a catch on the fields where I played as a kid. I look out at right field where I used to hit them so many years ago and think to myself, Gee, that wasn't such a long clout after all.

LEFTY GROVE

ROBERT MOSES GROVE

Born: March 6, 1900, Lonaconing, Maryland. Died: May 23, 1975

Major-league career: 1925–41, Philadelphia Athletics, Boston Red Sox

Lifetime Record: 300 wins, 141 losses

Lefty Grove was dour and cantankerous, shy and likable, and above all, one of the greatest left-handed pitchers ever to take the mound—perhaps the greatest. Winner of an even 300 games, he led the American League in strikeouts his first seven years, and still holds the record for most times leading in earned run average (nine). In his heyday, he was considered the fastest pitcher in baseball.

Grove was elected to the Hall of Fame in 1947.

Remember that time I was going for my seventeenth straight win, in 1931? I remember that all right. Boy, do I remember that! Would have set a new American League record if I'd have made it. Fellow named Dick Coffman with the St. Louis Browns beat me, 1–0. After I lost that game, I came back and won six or seven in a row. Would have had about 24 straight wins except for that 1–0 loss. After that game I went in and tore the clubhouse up. Wrecked the place. Tore those steel lockers off the wall and everything else. Ripped my uniform up. Threw everything I could get my hands on—bats, balls, shoes, gloves, benches, water buckets; whatever was handy. Giving Al Simmons hell all the while. Why Simmons? Because he was home in Milwaukee, that's why. Still gets me mad when I think about it.

See, Simmons should've been in left field, but he wasn't. He went home to Milwaukee, for some reason that I can't remember, and we had a fellow by name of Jim Moore playing in his place. Misjudged a fly ball. He ran in on the darn thing and it dropped over his head and that scored the run that beat me, with two men out in the seventh inning. I didn't say anything to Jim Moore, 'cause he was just a young guy just come to the team and he never played in St. Louis before. It was Simmons' fault. He's the one I blame for it.

So now I'm tied with Joe Wood and Walter Johnson and Schoolboy Rowe at 16 straight for the American League record. But I would have had 24 if Simmons had been out there where he belonged.

I never graduated from high school, you know. There were too many kids in the family—four boys and three girls—and I had to go to work. My dad was a coal miner. Didn't get much in those days for digging coal; about half a buck a ton. All my brothers were coal miners. Me too. For two weeks. That was in 1916. My brother had sprained his ankle, and I took his place for a couple of weeks. I helped load around fifteen ton of coal a day, and at half a dollar a ton you can figure out what I made. Not a heck of a lot. The last day, when I knew my brother was going to come back the next week, I said to my father, "Dad, I didn't put that coal in here, and I hope I don't have to take no more of her out."

I never went back. That was it.

Then I was working in the B&O railroad shops in Cumberland, Maryland. Mechanic's flunky. An apprentice. Working in the roundhouse, on the big steam engines. Tearing them down, fixing them, taking the heads off the big cylinders, cleaning them, putting them together again. That was in 1918 and '19.

I played ball that year, in 1919, with Midland. We had no team in Lonaconing, where I lived. Midland was three miles up the road. I pitched amateur ball there one season. Sort of amateur ball. We got $20 apiece at the end of the season. We put all the money together, see, what we'd made during the season passing the hat or at the places where we had closed parks. At Midland the park was fenced in, and we charged a quarter. Then at the end of the season we split the money among ourselves.

There was this fellow, Bill Lowden. He was the manager of the Martinsburg team. Blue Ridge League. Class C. He lived only eight miles from me, had a garage down there. He came around and asked me to sign up to pitch for Martinsburg.

So I went to my master mechanic in Cumberland and said, "I want a furlough for a month and a pass to Martinsburg."

"What are you going to do up there?" he asked.

"I'm going to play ball. Or try to, anyway."

So he gave me my thirty-day furlough from the job and a pass for the B&O train. That was the winter of 1919.

Neither of my parents had any objections. My father thought it was great, me becoming a ballplayer. As long as I was getting paid. And I was getting a lot more playing ball than they paid in the mines. My dad was a baseball fan, though he hardly ever got to see any baseball. Didn't have much time. Hardly ever saw daylight. In those days the miners went to work when it was dark and came back when it was dark. They worked ten, eleven hours a day in the mines. Not much chance to see ball games, except on Sundays.

I went to Martinsburg, and we started training in April, I think it was. I won three and lost three there, and then Jack Dunn of the Baltimore Orioles in the International League came up and saw me pitch and bought me, for $3,500 and a pitcher. The reason Martinsburg sold me was because their ball park was just a little one and they built a new grandstand and a fence all the way around the park and they needed some money to pay for it. So Martinsburg got a new grandstand and fence, and Baltimore got me. Five years later Dunn sold me to Connie Mack for $100,600, so you might say he made himself a pretty good deal.

I went to Baltimore around the end of June and was 12 and 2 for the rest of that season. That was 1920. Won all those games with fastballs. Didn't have a curve then. Didn't know what a curve was.

They tell you I was tough to get along with in those days? Well, maybe. I was doing my work—that's where I was tough. Out there on that field, that's where. You've got to remember that a lot of guys against me were tough, so why shouldn't I be too?

Heck, when I broke in, those old guys were tough on us youngsters who were trying to get a toehold. In Baltimore, I mean. We had Irvin Jenkins, Fritz Maisel, Otis Lary, Jack Bentley, Old Ben Egan, guys like that. They were tough to get along with. Criminy, they wouldn't even speak to you. They figured you were coming there to take away somebody's job. I was there about two weeks before they let on they knew I was around—and I'd already won three or four games by then. Oh, boy.

At Baltimore I won two or three in a row before I lost one. Just fastballs. Didn't start throwing the curve until a couple of years later. About 1923 I started working on it. I tried to throw a curveball as fast as the fastball, and it would only break a little ways. Maybe six inches. Just a wrinkle. Maybe they'd call it a slider today. I don't know. We didn't have sliders. We had spitballs, we had emery balls, we had mud balls, shine balls, fork balls, knuckleballs, but no sliders. Now they've got sliders and palm balls and I don't know what else.

George Earnshaw was with me in Baltimore. So was Al Thomas, who later pitched for the White Sox. Joe Boley was my shortstop, Max Bishop my second baseman, at Baltimore and then later on at Philadelphia. Our pitching staff was Harry Frank, Rube Parnham, Earnshaw, Johnny Ogden, Thomas, and myself. That was a pretty good pitching staff. They all came up to the big leagues except Harry Frank. Parnham was up and back. Parnham, he was a funny guy. He'd pitch today and then get on a train and go back home, and it was hard to tell just when he was going to come back. So when he did come back he'd pitch a doubleheader to make up for lost time. I saw him pitch a doubleheader a couple of times.

See, we had an easygoing club. Real loose. No rules. No clubhouse meetings. It was a good life. Dunnie was hardly ever in the clubhouse. After his son died, he wouldn't put a uniform on. Young Dunnie died in the winter of 1921. Before that the old man used to wear a uniform and manage and coach at third base. But after his son died, he didn't even come on the bench. Fritz Maisel and some of the others managed the club. It took a couple of years before he finally came back. But every once in a while, even then, he'd think about his son, and things wouldn't be right, and he wouldn't be there.

We had a ball club at Baltimore, boy, it was a ball club. I've seen that ball club sit up in the hotel playing cards all night

... no night games then, see ... and we'd have a Pierce-Arrow limousine hired waiting for us at the hotel at a certain time, and around one or two in the afternoon we'd go downstairs and pile into that son of a gun car and get to the ball park just in time to start the game. No practice or nothing. Fifteen minutes after we got there the game would start. And that team won seven straight International League pennants.

We caught the Little World Series that first year I was there, which was the first year they had the Little World Series. International League against the American Association. Old man Dunn came into the clubhouse in Toronto and told us about it. The Toronto Maple Leafs were right behind us, and we were playing them four games.

"Boys," he said, "if we win the pennant we're going to have a Little World Series, and the money will be split sixty-forty."

We thought about that for a minute, and then somebody said, "Well, what are we gonna do this winter—eat snowballs or steaks?"

And everyone yelled, "We're gonna eat steaks!"

We went out and beat Toronto four games, and they couldn't catch us after that.

After we started the Little World Series, against St. Paul, Mr. Dunn came into the clubhouse in Baltimore and said, "Now, boys, if you win this gosh-hank Series, I'll give you my share of the money."

Oh, boy, that was something *more*. So boy, we just went out and beat St. Paul, and coming back on the train from St. Paul, we got both checks—the players' cut and the owner's too. I forget what the amount was. Around $1,800 apiece, in total. That was a lot of dough in those days, 1920.

I was in the Little World Series in 1920, '21, '22, '23 and '24. We won the International League pennant every year I was there. Altogether, Baltimore won seven straight pennants: 1919 through 1925.

Let me tell you, those were some teams. We had a lot of guys good enough for the big leagues. See, there was no big-league draft from the International League. They can draft them from anywhere now. But not then. Anyway, we were satisfied to stay there. We were getting bigger salaries down there in Baltimore in the International League than lots of clubs were paying in the big leagues. So why leave? We couldn't get $750 to $1,000 a month in the big leagues in those days. Not on lots of clubs. But that's what we were getting in Baltimore. And Dunnie was good to us. We'd play exhibition games with the big league teams, and all the money was pooled and we got a cut. Plus we got the Little World Series money every year. I started off there at $250 a month, and by the time I got sold to Connie I was up over $750. We did fine.

Did I ever have any doubts about making that Baltimore team? No, sir. I always thought I could make any team I went with. I just had my mind made up I'd make it. Never bothered me who was up there with the bat. I'd hit 'em in the middle of the back or hit 'em in the foot, it didn't make any difference to me. But I'd never throw at a man's head. In all my years I've thrown at guys, but never at their heads. Never believed in it.

I used to pitch batting practice. You know, take my turn at it in Philadelphia. Those guys, Doc Cramer and them, used to hit one back through the box, and they knew damn well when they did, they'd better get out of there, 'cause I'd be throwing at their pockets. They'd try to hit one through the box their last swing, those guys, just to rile me up. Yessir, boy, I was just as mean against them as I was against the others. You can count on two fingers the guys who wouldn't throw at anybody in those days. Walter Johnson was one, and Herb Pennock was the other.

The Giants offered $75,000 for me, you know. But Dunn wouldn't sell me for less than $100,000, and I'm glad for that. I wouldn't have wanted to play for Mugsy McGraw. We wouldn't have got along. That was the winter of '23. I went to Connie Mack and the Philadelphia Athletics in the winter of '24.

Connie always called me Robert. When I got there in 1925, he was sixty-three years old. He sat on the bench in civilian clothes and a derby hat, waving his scorecard when he wanted to position somebody. I got along fine with him. He was just like a father to everyone. He knew how to treat each man.

I didn't do too well that first year with the A's. I think that was the only year I ever was under .500. I was just wild that year, that's all. Didn't pitch enough, I guess. I opened the American League season in 1925, in Philadelphia. Pitched against Walter Johnson. He beat me, 4–2. Ol' Walter. I don't know why Connie picked on me, a rookie. Guess he figured

Walter'd win anyway, so why waste a good pitcher? But I can tell you that I opened a few more seasons after that, and I didn't lose 'em.

Walter Johnson. I used to go from home to watch that bugger pitch. We'd take a train from Lonaconing down to Washington—three- or four-hour trip in those days—on Sundays to see him pitch. We idolized that guy. Just sat there and watched him pitch. Down around the knees—whoosh! One after the other. He had something all right. I pitched against a lot of guys and saw a lot of guys throw, and I haven't seen one yet come close to as fast as he was.

Bob Feller? I ought to know about him—I pitched against him. Feller wasn't as fast as Walter. *Heck,* no. I'd say Earnshaw we had pitching for us in Philadelphia was as fast as Feller. Big George Earnshaw.

The league was chock-full of hitters in those days. You had guys like Goose Goslin, George Sisler, Baby Doll Jacobson, Cobb, Speaker, Heilmann, Joe Sewell, Ruth, Gehrig. Gee whiz. Those days if you didn't hit .300, they didn't think much of you.

With us, Al Simmons, Jimmie Foxx, and those guys. Simmons, he was great. Bucketfoot Al. Always pulled that left foot down the third base line when he swung at the ball. Like to spike the third baseman. Big long bat, long as the law'd allow. Could he ever hit that ball! Whew! One year he held out till the season started—finally signed for $100,000 for three years—and came into opening day, no spring training or nothing, and got three hits. And hey, he was a great outfielder. They didn't give him much credit for it. They always watched his hitting. Good fielder. Never threw to the wrong base. Like Ruth. He'd know the runner. Mule Haas, Doc Cramer, Bing Miller. Great outfielders—don't think they weren't.

And I'll tell you something—their gloves were just a piece of leather. Little pancakes. I bring my old glove along now when I go to Old Timers' Days, and these kids, these modern players, look at it in the clubhouse and can't believe it.

"Christ," they say, "you didn't use that glove, did you?"

"I sure did," I tell them. "Kind of glove you got there," I say, "I used to use on the Eastern Shore to get minnies and crabs. We called them crab nets."

Best catcher ever caught me was Mickey. Best I ever saw.

Then Dickey's next. Greatest catcher of them all, Cochrane was. Great ballplayer, all around. Good hitter, good runner, good arm, smart. Hardly ever shook him off. If Mickey was living today, he'd tell you I only shook him off about five or six times all the years he caught me. Funny, before I'd even look at him, I had in my mind what I was going to pitch, and I'd look up and there'd be Mickey's signal, just what I was thinking. Like he was reading my mind. That's the kind of catcher he was.

Jimmie Foxx? Oh, boy, what a ballplayer. He could hit that ball! You ever been in the White Sox ball park? You know how far it is from home plate to the left-center-field fence? There was a tennis court back of the ball park there, and Foxx hit two into that tennis court. Over the double-deck stand and everything. Two in one day. At Yankee Stadium he hit one into the third deck off of Gomez. It was like a damn rocket. Gomez said, "Christ, if I was on that son of a bitch, I'd be back in California now." That was no bunt there, that wasn't.

Foxx would hit all those home runs and *still* hit .330. Nowadays home run hitters are considered great if they hit .270. When I was pitching, I used to love to see those guys come up to the plate who swung from the heels. I'd laugh to myself because I knew I had them. When they swing that hard, they're bound to take their eye off the ball. Tickled me pink to see those guys come up there. It's the guys who came up with their bats choked, like Joe Sewell and Charlie Gehringer, who would give you trouble.

Foxx didn't choke up; Simmons didn't. But they didn't cut like they do today. Neither did Ruth. The Babe. We called him the Big Monkey, the Big Baboon. Babe didn't care a hell of a lot for me, you know. The Yankees used to come through Baltimore to play exhibition games, and he knew I was wild and I didn't give a damn whether I hit him or not; didn't make any difference to me. He quit the game one day. I was wild, and I tore a couple buttons off his shirt. He didn't even go to first base. He just said, "I don't want any of that," and went in and dressed. Babe never had much to say to me after that.

Well, after pitching for more than fifteen years, I went and got myself a sore arm in '34. Got it in spring training first year I was with the Red Sox. Don't know how I got it. First one I ever had, and it stayed sore all that year. The muscles in my arm were torn, but I was okay the next season.

Then in '38 I lost the pulse in my left arm. Can you believe that? Pitched against Detroit one day, and Charlie Gehringer hit a swinging bunt down along the third base line, and I picked it up and threw. I must have thrown my arm along with the ball.

They took me in the clubhouse, and the doctor felt my pulse and said, "Hey, Mose, by God you're dead. You haven't got a pulse."

They took me to St. Elizabeth's Hospital, and boy, talk about a guy being a guinea pig. They had seven doctors there. They couldn't figure out what happened to my pulse! They finally put my arm in a glass boot. A glass container, and these rubber attachments moved it up and down. They'd put my arm in there in the morning for three hours, from nine to twelve, and again from six to nine at night. Six hours a day. Soon as my arm would come out of the "boot," they'd slap it on a machine to check the pulse. That went on for fifteen days. Then the needle started to move. Came back and won 15 games next year.

Remember that '29 Series against the Cubs? Lots of surprises in that one. Biggest surprise was Howard Ehmke starting the first game. That sure was something. Nobody ever guessed it. It was supposed to be me or Earnshaw to start that Series. Up until the meeting that morning in Chicago—and that's when we found out. Connie said I was going to be a bullpen pitcher for the Series; all the lefties were. He thought the Cubs would be murder on lefties—they had all those right-handed hitters—Rogers Hornsby, Kiki Cuyler, Riggs Stephenson, Hack Wilson.

I relieved in two of the games. I relieved Earnshaw in the second game in Chicago—we struck out 13 between us that day—and then I relieved in that ten-run seventh inning game. Went into the last of the seventh trailing 8–0, but that didn't mean anything. We never thought we were out of it. We had a team, it was hard to tell what we'd do. Once against Cleveland we were losing 15–4, and we scored thirteen runs and beat 'em 17–15.

So I was down in the bullpen when that seventh inning merry-go-round started. Simmons started it off with a home run, and before it was over, fifteen men had batted and we'd scored 10 runs. 'Course three or four were due to misjudged fly balls. Poor Hack Wilson was blinded by the sun a few times. It was tough out there, what with the sun coming just over the edge of the stands.

I came in and pitched the last two innings. Saw six men and struck out four of them.

We closed it out the next day. Went into the bottom of the ninth trailing 2–0 and scored three runs. Boy, some ball club, huh? Haas hit one out with a man on to tie it. Then Simmons doubled and Foxx walked, and then Bing Miller got the hit that won the son of a gun. I tell you, the place went wild when Simmons crossed the plate.

My three hundredth win? Durn right I'd made up my mind to get it. I *wanted* that. When I got to 275, I said, "By gosh, I'm gonna win three hundred or bust." And when I got number 300 in Boston in 1941—I beat Cleveland 10–5 that day—then that was all. Never won another game.

I knew it was time to go. You know how your ol' body feels. I just couldn't do it anymore. I wouldn't even go to a ball game for a couple years after that. I didn't coach anywhere—had plenty of offers—just had nothing to do with baseball. Not a thing. I just stayed up in the mountains and went down to the river and fished. Stayed home in Lonaconing. That's an Indian name. Means "meeting of the waters." Streams come out of the mountains there and meet and make one body.

I enjoyed every damn year I was in baseball except the first year with the A's, when I was a rookie learning the ropes, and the first year in Boston, when I had a sore arm. Except for those two years, I enjoyed it all. I loved baseball.

If I had to do it all over, I'd do the same thing. If they said, "Come on, here's a steak dinner," and I had a chance to go out and play a game of ball, I'd go out and play the game and let the steak sit there. I would.

BUCKY WALTERS

WILLIAM HENRY WALTERS
Born: April 19, 1909, Philadelphia, Pennsylvania
Major-league career: 1934–48, 1950, Boston Red Sox, Philadelphia Phillies, Cincinnati Reds, Boston Braves
Lifetime record: 198 wins, 160 losses

Coming to the major leagues originally as a third baseman, Bucky Walters made the transition from infielder to pitcher with astonishing ease and instant success (he led the league in shutouts his second year). In 1939 Walters was voted the National League's Most Valuable Player, after recording the league's lowest earned run average and winning 27 games. (Since 1918, only three National League pitchers have won more games in a season than Walters—Dazzy Vance, Dizzy Dean, and Robin Roberts.)

In 1934 I was twenty-five years old and figured I had just about won myself a job in the big leagues as an infielder. Finally. I'd bounced around with the Braves and the Red Sox for a few years, trying to convince somebody I could play the infield in the big leagues if only they'd give me the chance. I thought for sure I was going to stick with the Red Sox in the spring of '34, but around cut-down time they sold me to the Philadelphia Phillies. I finished out that year at third base for the Phillies and did all right, I thought.

Near the end of the season Jimmie Wilson, the manager, said to me, "Hey, the season's practically over, how about pitching a game or two?"

"Listen," I said, "I'm a third baseman."

"Who said you weren't? Anyway, what has one thing got to do with the other?"

So I pitched three innings in Brooklyn against the Dodgers and did pretty well—shut them out. Then I started another game, against Boston, in old Baker Bowl, the Phillies' park. Did pretty well again. Then the season was over, and I went home and spent the winter thinking about how to improve my play at third base and how I might do something to pick up that .260 batting average of mine.

You see, I'd never thought much about pitching during those early years, even though it was suggested to me many times by different players. They'd see that good arm and tell me I should be a pitcher. But I'd tell them that wasn't for me. I liked to play every day. I liked to be in there.

When I got to spring training in '35, the Phillies had made a deal. They'd traded Dick Bartell to the Giants for, among others, Johnny Vergez, the third baseman. So that left me in a battle for third base with Vergez, and I thought I could beat him out. But then one day at Orlando I had a pretty bad game at third. I made a couple of errors and went hitless.

That night Wilson and a couple of the coaches, Hans Lobert and Dick Spalding, got me aside and began telling me what a great future I'd have as a pitcher if I'd make the switch.

"Bucky," they said, "you can learn all there is to learn about pitching. But what you've already got is something that nobody can ever teach you—that great arm and that great fastball."

So I tried it. I found that I didn't mind pitching. Maybe it was because in the back of my mind I still felt I'd be going back to third base. I wanted to play every day. That was the thing of it. But I must admit I felt right at home on the mound. And I think I even had a certain edge, having been in the league for a little while, because I had always paid attention to what the hitters liked, what their strengths and weaknesses were, so that it was mainly a matter of me getting the ball there.

I was mostly a fastball pitcher when I started. I learned the curveball later on, but in the beginning it was that fastball. It had a tendency to sink, which was a great advantage for me, because most hitters tend to uppercut a little. So with that bat coming up and that ball sinking, you've got an advantage—*if* you can keep the ball down.

You won't be surprised if I tell you I was never keen about pitching in Baker Bowl. The place was a pitcher's nightmare. It was about 270 feet to the right field wall, and it ran straight across that way. It was high, with a big fence. What a target! No matter how well you went, it seemed you always had three on base and some big lefty was standing at the plate looking at that right field wall. Visiting pitchers used to get sore arms the minute the train pulled into Philly, and all the crippled hitters got better and ran over each other to get into the lineup.

But with the good fastball and the hitters not being too sure of my control, I did all right. I was 9 and 9 around the first of August, then got a sore arm and went on the shelf.

The arm came around in spring training the next year and I was able to pitch. I won 11 and lost 21 that year. Now that may sound like a pretty poor year, but I tell people that was one of my best years, because I pitched a lot of good ball that season. Jimmie Wilson said to me, "Look, don't be feeling bad about that record. If you weren't a darned good pitcher, you wouldn't have got the chance to lose twenty-one ball games."

If you look back over the years, I guess you'll find that some pretty fair pitchers lost 20 games in a season. Red Ruffing is one; Paul Derringer's another. Derringer lost 27 one year, believe it or not. A couple of years later, when we were both with Cincinnati, we won 52 games between us. Neither one of us were doing anything we hadn't done before; it just shows you what a different ball club and a different ball park can do.

Did I always want to be a ballplayer? Well, I guess I did. I can't remember when I didn't play baseball. I mean, you don't just start playing when you're nineteen or twenty. I always had a ball, and I always had a glove, from the time I can remember.

In those days—the late twenties—it wasn't so easy to get into professional baseball. A lot of the clubs didn't have more than one or two scouts, and the farm systems hadn't really started up yet, most of the minor league clubs being independently owned. So very often it was word of mouth. If somebody was good, word got around.

In my case, I was playing on the sandlots around Philadelphia. One day a fellow who had a contact with a club in Montgomery, Alabama, saw me playing shortstop, and after the game he asked me if I'd like to play pro ball. I guess he heard the quickest "Yes, sir" anybody ever heard.

My family wasn't too crazy about the idea. I'd never been away from home before, never been on a train, and they thought Montgomery was a long way to go just for a tryout, with no return ticket—I'd have had to hitchhike back if I didn't make it. But you never think about not making it, do you? I would've gone to China if I'd had to. Didn't make any difference to me. As long as it was pro ball.

I was the oldest of seven, and there wasn't much money in the family; but my grandmother dug up $10 somewhere and bought me a suitcase. First suitcase I ever owned; in fact, I think it was the first suitcase *any* of us ever owned.

Well, I didn't make it in Montgomery, but I must've made some kind of an impression, because they sent me up to High Point, North Carolina, in the Piedmont League. That began my travels through the minor leagues. Played everywhere from Portland, Maine, to San Francisco. I was property of the Braves for a while, and in '32 they sold me outright to San Francisco in the Coast League. I went out there and was having a great year, hitting around .380. Eddie Collins, who was general manager for the Red Sox at that time, saw me and bought me, and back across the country I went. In '34 they sold me to the Phillies. Still an infielder then.

I guess I was pretty lucky. Things were tough back in those days. Not many people today remember how tough. There weren't so many of those old greenbacks around. People were hurtin'. There weren't jobs. There wasn't anything. You saw guys selling apples on street corners. People were hocking their possessions, selling their houses, doing whatever they could to keep some food on the table. The bleacher people and the box-seat people both. Everybody.

Minor leagues were disbanding all over. I was playing in Portland in 1930, and in the middle of the season the league folded. Just weren't drawing. But I was lucky. I caught on with another club, another league. I was able to hang on. You had no guarantees in those days; you couldn't be sure of anything. As far as baseball was concerned, you just had to be fortunate enough to hang on until you got a break.

It was rough going in the big leagues, too. I can remember going on Western trips with the Phillies when sometimes you wouldn't see 500 people in the stands. The Phillies would make a western trip just praying they wouldn't get rained out in Chicago on Saturday or Sunday, so they'd have enough money to get home. Why, very often they used to have to sell a player or two just to be able to take the club to spring training.

Life is a little different today for a ballplayer. They get so many opportunities thrown at them away from the field there's a lot more money to be made. These fellows have got things going for them now that we never used to think of. Some guys would take a job in the wintertime, but in most cases when the baseball season was over, they just went home and took their shoes off or went hunting or played golf or goofed around. Is that what I used to do? Yes, sir. I made a job out of bummin'. A good one. Maybe it wasn't the smartest thing to do, but it was pretty much the style back then.

In my first year as a pitcher with the Phillies, 1935, I had the pleasure of pitching to Babe Ruth. I used to see him in spring training when I was with the Braves, because we both trained in St. Petersburg. I played third base in some of those games against the Yankees. And just for the hell of it I used to move in on the grass when he'd come up, to try to get him to hit one at me—and don't think he couldn't whistle them down that line if he wanted to. Why did I do that? I don't know. Maybe just to get him to look at me, take notice of me.

Well, when I faced him as a pitcher, he was past his peak, but he was still Babe Ruth, this great guy that I'd admired all my life. All I had then was the fastball, and I said to myself, "Well, if he's gonna hit it, he's gonna get the best one I've got." I wasn't trying to walk him, but I was trying to nick that outside corner. Well, I kept missing and ended up walking him. That's the only time I ever faced him. And I'll tell you the truth—I wouldn't have minded being one of his victims. Not at all.

Now, in 1938, around the middle of June, I'd won 4 and lost 8, and it looked like another one of those years where you were going to end up losing twice as many as you won, no matter how well you pitched. Then Jimmie Wilson called me one day and said, "We just made a deal for you. You're going to Cincinnati."

You might say that was a big break for me, going from a tail ender to a team that was shaping up to take two pennants, but actually I didn't want to go. I'd have rather stayed in the East, with my family. But that's the way things work in baseball.

I joined the Cincinnati club at an interesting moment—right in between Vander Meer's two no-hitters. He'd already pitched his first one, in Cincinnati against Boston. I joined the club in Brooklyn. It was the first night game ever in Ebbets Field, and Vander Meer was starting.

Well, he starts off that game, and you can see he had real good stuff. He had a powerful fastball and an exceptionally sharp curve. But he was wild that night, and it seemed he had men on base nearly every inning. But no hits. Then the crowd started getting tense—you know how they get when they start to smell a no-hitter. And this wasn't going to be any old no-hitter, of course. But he was wild, and working hard, going to three and two on almost every hitter.

In about the sixth or seventh inning, Bill McKechnie looked at me and said, "Sneak down to the bullpen." That was one of his favorite expressions, "Sneak down."

So I "sneaked down." Meanwhile, Vander Meer's still got the no-hitter going. And we had about four or five runs. But I thought to myself, "By God, if I'm going to get into this game, I'm going to be ready." So I started to warm up. I began to hear some booing. I looked around, couldn't see anything going on, and continued to loosen up. And they continued to boo. The harder I threw, the louder they booed, until I realized why they were doing it: It was *me* they were booing, the fact that I was warming up. There was no way they wanted to see Vander Meer come out of there as long as he had that no-hitter going.

John stayed wild; in fact, he walked the bases loaded in the ninth. But he got Durocher on an easy fly ball to Harry Craft in center, and that was it. The only double no-hitter in baseball history.

Like I said, Cincinnati was shaping up to take those two pennants in '39 and '40. I could tell from pitching against them that they were coming along. Their farm system had produced some good ballplayers, and on top of that they made the right trades.

We had pretty good hitting, plenty of speed, and a great

defense. We played a lot of tight, low-scoring ball games, and in the good years we won those games. We had Frank McCormick at first base, a very strong hitter; and Lonny Frey, Billy Myers, and Bill Werber at second, short, and third—all good, fast, smart ball players. In the outfield we had Wally Berger, Harry Craft—what a center fielder he was—and a good all-around ballplayer in right, Ival Goodman.

And big Ernie Lombardi catching. Everybody loved that guy. A sweet, quiet man. One of the most powerful hitters in baseball. He might have been slow afoot, but I'll tell you something you might think sounds strange—he was a good base runner. By that I mean when Lombardi went for a base, he always just made it, he was never just thrown out. I've seen plenty of these speedsters who can run like the wind get thrown out on close plays. But not Lombardi—he was always just in there. And how he could hit! He used to have infielders playing 20 and 30 feet back on the outfield grass for him.

Cincinnati hadn't won a pennant in twenty years when we brought it in for them in 1939. Going into the Series, the Yankees were the favorites, naturally. They'd won the championship three years running, and they had those great teams, with DiMaggio, Keller, Dickey, Gordon, and fellows like that.

Derringer pitched the first game, at Yankee Stadium, and it was a shame the way he lost it. It was 1–1 going into the bottom of the ninth. Keller hit a long fly that Goodman just couldn't hold onto, and it went for a triple. We walked DiMaggio, but Dickey looped one over short, and that was the ball game. A real heartbreaker.

I lost the next game, 4–0. Monte Pearson pitched a two-hitter against us. In fact, he had a no-hitter going into the eighth, when Lombardi got a single. We moved to Cincinnati for the third game, and they clobbered us. I remember Keller hit a couple out. He had a great Series.

Derringer started the fourth game. I came in in the eighth to hold a 4–2 lead. I didn't relieve very much, but in the spot we were in, down three games to none, there was no tomorrow. You've got all winter to either count your money or count your mistakes, depending on how it goes. Well, we messed up a double-play ball in the ninth, and the Yankees tied it.

It all came apart in the tenth. You wouldn't believe it, but we made three errors in that inning. We just never played that kind of ball. DiMaggio got the key hit, a single to right with two men on. Goodman bobbled the ball and the base runners were flying. Then that play occurred that they still talk about—"Lombardi's swoon." Swoon, my neck. The throw came home, and Lombardi took it just as Charlie Keller was coming across. Well, Keller ran into him hard and knocked him down, and the ball kicked away. Lombardi was stunned, he was hurt. If you want to criticize somebody, you can start with yours truly—I should have been there backing up, because that ball was just lying there. DiMaggio saw the situation, and he came home too.

They made that the big story of the Series. But it was a big story about nothing, because that run didn't mean anything. They beat us 7–4.

We got another crack at it in 1940. This time it was the Detroit Tigers. They came in with a good strong ball club—Hank Greenberg, Charlie Gehringer, Rudy York, Pinky Higgins, Barney McCosky, fellows of that caliber. And good pitching—Bobo Newsom, Tommy Bridges, Schoolboy Rowe. This wasn't going to be any picnic either.

We went into that Series without Lombardi. He'd hurt his foot and couldn't do much more than pinch-hit. My old Philadelphia manager, Jimmie Wilson, who had become one of our coaches, had to be pressed into service and he caught most of the Series for us. He was forty years old and hadn't caught in a couple of years, but he did a great job.

Derringer started the first game, and they got to him early. The final score was 7–2, Tigers. It looked like here we go again. The National League hadn't won a Series game since 1937—ten straight losses.

I started the second game, and the first eight pitches I threw were balls. Walked two men right off the bat. Boy, it looked like that rut we'd fallen into was getting deeper and deeper. Wilson walked out to me, very slowly; I swear it seemed like it took him five minutes.

"Now look," he said, "just calm down. You're throwing too hard. Just be yourself. Let them hit the ball."

He was right, I *was* throwing the ball too hard; I was trying to strike everybody out.

Let them hit it. Well, Gehringer obliged me very nicely. He rapped it into right field, and that brought in one run and left men on first and third. And up steps Greenberg. Well, here's where I got one of the biggest breaks of my life. He went for a bad ball, a curve, and grounded into a double play. The run came in, but we were able to get out of the inning not hurting too badly. So we got the break we needed. You've got to get a few breaks in the game, or you can't win. Right?

Then we started coming back. Jimmy Ripple hit a home run for us, we got some other hits, and went on to win, 5–3.

Tommy Bridges beat us the next game, but then Derringer came back to tie it at two games. Newsom shut us out on three hits in the fifth game, and we were in trouble.

We came back to Cincinnati for the sixth game (and, we hoped, the seventh). I pitched that game, and I was up for it. I shut them out, 4–0. I even hit a home run—hey, don't forget that now; make sure you get that in the book. Hit it off Freddy Hutchinson. He made a mistake, and it went out. That's what usually do go out of the park—the mistakes.

Somebody said to me later, "Hey, why didn't you trot around?"

"I was," I said.

"No, you weren't. You tore around those bases like you were trying to catch a train."

The truth is I was floating. What a nice feeling.

Derringer came back in the seventh game against Newsom. It was the third game for both of them, but boy, they were sharp. It was a real duel. Newsom had us 1–0 going into the bottom of the seventh, but then we got two runs. Jimmy Ripple got a key hit in there, a double. Derringer held them off and we won it, 2–1. Won the world championship. And we felt pretty good about it, believe me. We'd beaten a good team, and it was about time the National League had won one of those things.

You know, I used to read the box scores all the time and watch the lineups. In 1942 I began seeing this guy Musial in the Cardinal lineup. A new face, you know. We hadn't played St. Louis for a while, so I'd never seen him. Next time we went into Chicago I went over to Jimmie Wilson. He was managing the Cubs then—he got around, didn't he?

"Who's this guy Musial down there at St. Louis?" I asked him. "He hit you guys pretty good."

"Yeah," he said. "He sure did. But you know, Bucky, I think you can get him inside. Good and tight."

Well, the next time I pitched against the Cardinals I waited for Musial to come up. Then he stepped into the batter's box, with that funny little stance he had—remember it? I said to myself, "Well, here I go. Might as well find out something right now." I put one inside. I thought I'd got it in there pretty good and tight. Boy, he hit a screaming line drive down the right-field line, I'll bet he put blisters on that ball. Well, I thought, there goes that theory. You could see that this fellow was going to make a lot of money in the big leagues, and that it wasn't going to be for stealing bases.

The most money I ever made? Well, after winning 27 games in 1939 and being voted the National League's Most Valuable Player—about $22,000. But that was my own fault. I should've made more. I thought I'd be around forever, and money really didn't mean that much. But I'm not complaining. There's more to baseball than a payday. Baseball got me a lot of nice things. I'd go back and do it again for the same price. As a matter of fact, I'd do it for half as much.

JOHNNY MIZE

John Robert Mize
Born: January 7, 1913, Demorest, Georgia
Major-league career: 1936–1953, St. Louis Cardinals, New
  York Giants, New York Yankees
Lifetime average: .312

A big quiet man, with a strong, graceful swing, Johnny Mize is one of the great sluggers in National League history. He hit .300 or better his first nine years in the majors, leading the league with .349 in 1939. Four times he led the league in home runs (twice tying with Ralph Kiner) and in 1947 became one of the very few ever to hit 50 or more home runs in a season, when he hit 51. Six times Mize hit three home runs in a game, still a major league record.

In mid-season 1949, Mize was traded to the Yankees, where he remained as a part-time player and devastating pinch-hitter for five years, five pennants, and five world championships.

I grew up in Demorest, Georgia, in the northeastern part of the state. Was it a small town? Well, I played more basketball than anything else in those days because it was easier to get up a basketball team than a baseball team. In fact, I played more tennis as a kid than either baseball or basketball because it took even fewer people.

I never thought too much about being a ball player back then. You know how it is when you're a kid; you just go from day to day, growing up, not giving much thought to tomorrow. Tell you the truth, when I was attending Piedmont College in Demorest, the coach had to beg me to get me to go out for baseball.

After college, I started playing with different town teams every Saturday. I hooked on for a while with a lumber company team from Helen, Georgia. I got $5 or $10 a game. They might be playing some team out of Atlanta or from Gainesville or Chicopee, which were cotton mill towns. The manager of the lumber company team would call me up and say, "We've got a rough game Saturday and want you to come down and play with us." I played first base some and the outfield some; when you're playing semipro ball with town teams, you're liable to play any position.

I guess I was busting the ball pretty good, and Frank Rickey, Branch's brother, heard about me and came down for a look. The Morris Lumber Company out of Rochester, New York, had this mill in Helen, where I was playing. They way I heard the story, somebody kept telling Warren Giles, who was connected with the Rochester club then, about me. He sent Frank Rickey down to take a look. He had his look and offered me a contract.

I guess I was pleased with the idea of going into pro ball. Things were pretty rough around home then—this was 1930—and playing ball meant you'd have a little money to spend. The Depression hit hard down in Demorest, though I suppose no harder than anywhere else. Some people worked; some didn't. You had your own gardens and raised what you could. And you had relatives around, and they all had some type of farm, so there was always food, nobody was going to starve. Whenever somebody came to visit, they'd bring vegetables and lay them on the table. We got by.

Let me tell you about that contract I signed. It wasn't legal. The Cardinals never knew that. I was only seventeen then—underage—so Frank Rickey went to Atlanta and got my mother to sign the contract. You see, my father and mother separated when I was very young and I lived most of the time with my grandmother. It was my grandmother who actually was my legal guardian. So I was never legally signed.

I always had that in back of my mind, but I never did anything about it. I've often thought that when I was twenty years old, I should have got my release from the Cardinals and signed with somebody else for a good bonus. By then I was playing for Rochester in the International League, one step below the majors, and hitting around .350. But I didn't, and

I've regretted it ever since, the way things turned out. I've found out that in baseball they don't care a darn thing about you. Once you've stopped producing, you're gone. I went through this with the Cardinals. "You go along with us," they told me. "You'll always be with us, and we'll take care of you." The next year I was sold. So you take them at their word, you go along, and you find out where you end up.

In 1934 I was running out a double and tore the large muscle loose from the pelvic bone. That slowed me up a bit, I guess. So in the spring of '35 Branch Rickey offered me to Cincinnati, on a trial basis. I went to spring training with the Reds, but they didn't keep me. The way I heard it, Larry MacPhail, who was running the Reds at that time, wanted to buy me on condition my leg was all right, but if it wasn't, they'd return me to St. Louis and get their money back. But Rickey said no. "You either buy him or you don't. No conditions." Well, the Reds had just spent a lot of money buying ballplayers from the Cardinals. They'd bought Ival Goodman, Lew Riggs, and Billy Myers, and MacPhail felt he couldn't afford to gamble on me. So they turned me back, and the Cardinals sent me to Rochester.

Then I hurt my other leg, in a game at Montreal. I was running down the line after a foul ball, looking up in the air, and stepped in a hole. Same injury. That finished me for the season, and I went home. The injury was so bad that the club doctor recommended I retire from baseball. That didn't sound so good to me, so I got another opinion. I ended up having both legs operated on and came back okay after that.

I joined the Cardinals in '36. Rip Collins was the first baseman. I started out just as a pinch hitter, but when the year was over, I'd played in about 125 ball games. After the season they traded Collins to the Cubs.

The newspapers had pinned a name on that Cardinal team: "The Gas House Gang." That came from Pepper Martin sliding headfirst, and the dirty uniforms, and a general style of play. It was a good name to give them. Martin was the main one, I guess, when you come right down to it. He was the chief wild man and joker.

One time we were rained out in Philadelphia, and Pepper didn't have anything to do, and when Pepper was idle, you just knew that a situation was going to load up. So Pepper and

Dizzy Dean and somebody else got hold of some overalls and workmen's caps and all kinds of tools and went downstairs to remodel the hotel. They went into the barbershop and told the barber they had to take his sink out. He chased them out, and they went into the dining room. They started crawling under the tables where people were eating and began hammering and moving things around. This went on until the complaints started reaching the front desk. The hotel manager came around to see what was going on, but by that time the boys had gone. They would do things like that. Anytime, anyplace.

Dean enjoyed the clowning and cutting up as much as anybody. But when he wanted to pitch, he could pitch. If he said he was going to shut them out today, why, he'd come pretty close to doing it. He was one guy who could pop off and back it up. Was he the best pitcher I ever saw? Well, when you've faced guys like Feller and Hubbell, too, it's hard to tell which one is the best. I faced Feller a lot in spring training when I was with the Giants. He was fast all right, but probably not as fast as Rex Barney. What made Feller tough was he had a real fast curve. A lot of pitchers do you a favor when they throw you a curve ball, but his was wicked. You couldn't lay back for it.

In 1939 I led the league in hitting with .349. Naturally after a year like that you look forward to talking contract. But when I sat down with Rickey, he said, "Well, your home run production stayed pretty much the same." No mention of my batting average. So the next year I hit 43 home runs, which is still the Cardinal club record, and led the league in runs batted in. But my batting average went down. When I went in to talk contract this time, he said, "Well, your batting average wasn't so good. Would you be willing to take a cut?" I led the league in hitting, then I led the league in home runs and runs batted in, and he wanted to know if I'd take a cut!

We always had good ball clubs in St. Louis, but most of the time we needed just a little bit more help. They had plenty of good ballplayers in the minor leagues in those years, but they kept selling them off. Guys like Bob Klinger, Bill Lee, Fritz Ostermueller, Cy Blanton. Those guys were good pitchers, Bill Lee especially. He was a great one for the Cubs. If the Cardinals had brought them up, we might have won a few pennants during those years. I heard later that Rickey got 25 percent of whatever he sold a player for. That's why every year he was selling these players. He sold Johnny Rizzo, too, and those other fellows I mentioned, Riggs, Goodman, Myers.

In '41 Slaughter collided with Terry Moore, and Slaughter broke his shoulder. Here we're fighting the Dodgers for a pennant. Rickey said we didn't have anybody in the minor leagues to help us. Then in September he brings up Musial. Why didn't he bring Musial up earlier? That's what all the players wanted to know. We might have gone ahead and won the pennant.

I'll tell you what the talk used to be about Rickey: Stay in the pennant race until the last week of the season, and then get beat. I heard some talk to the effect that that was what he preferred. That way he drew the crowds all year, and then later on the players couldn't come in for the big raise for winning the pennant and maybe the World Series. I don't know if it's true or not, but that was the talk.

I got married to a St. Louis girl. Her father was a good friend of Sam Breadon, who owned the ball club. Breadon gave me $500 as a wedding gift. The next year when I was talking contract to Rickey, he said, "Well, you made seventy-five hundred last year." "No," I said, "I only made seven thousand." He said, "Really? Where's that five hundred that Breadon gave you?" That was Rickey.

You know, back when I broke in, throwing at hitters was part of the game. It was expected. If you couldn't take it, you were better off going home, because once they found out you couldn't take it then they would really let you have it. It never worried me. I always figured any guy that threw at me knew I could hit him, because the only reason you throw at a guy is to try and scare him. You let a pitcher scare you, and you might as well go up there without a bat in your hands. I always bore down harder against any man that threw at me.

Sure, I got hit in the head a few times. Those things will happen. Harry Gumbert hit me once; Brecheen hit me once. Were they throwing at me? I don't know. But one of them was a sinkerball pitcher; the other one was a control pitcher. And on each occasion I'd hit a home run the time before. Take it from there.

I was with the Giants when Brecheen hit me. We had a left-hander pitching for us that game named Monte Kennedy.

He was wilder than a March hare. Fast and wild. Well, after I was hit, Mel Ott, who was managing, told Kennedy, "When Brecheen comes to bat, throw at him. Not at his head; hit him in the knee." He's telling this to a fellow who generally had a hard time just keeping his pitches in the ball park. But, son of a gun, when Brecheen came up, first pitch Kennedy hit him right in the knee. Brecheen was out for ten days. That's probably one of the mysteries of baseball, that Kennedy, wild as he was, could hit a guy on the knee with his first pitch.

Before I was traded to the Giants, I thought I was going to Brooklyn. Durocher called me in the winter of '41 and asked me what I thought about playing in Brooklyn. In fact, the day he got in touch with me was Pearl Harbor Day, December 7. I was down in the Ozarks, bird hunting. A guy told me I was wanted on the telephone. As I was walking to the phone, he said to me, "By the way, the Japanese have bombed Pearl Harbor." I thought he was nuts. Didn't pay him any attention. I got on the phone and my father-in-law told me there was a message to get in touch with Durocher. I called Leo, and he asked me if I wanted to play with the Dodgers. He said they were trying to make a deal for me. I told him it didn't mean a damn to me where I played. Then I got into the car and turned on the radio and found out that fellow was right about Pearl Harbor. That was a hell of a piece of news, and I didn't know what to think about it. When something like that happens, you don't know what's coming next until it comes.

Four days later I was traded to the Giants. I wasn't too crazy about playing in the Polo Grounds, because I wasn't that much of a pull hitter. Maybe if I'd have got there earlier in my career, I might have become a pull hitter, to take advantage of that short right field, but after hitting straightaway for so many years, I didn't want to start changing around.

In the middle of 1949 we were playing the Yankees an exhibition game. Before the game Stengel said to me, "How do you feel?"

"All right," I said. "But I'm not playing much."

"If you were over here, you'd play," he said.

"Well," I said, "make the deal."

I was only kidding, but then late in August they did just that. They were up against the Red Sox for the pennant that year, and it seems the Red Sox were after me, too; in fact, the

Red Sox had one of their scouts following me around. Well, the Yankees got wind of that, and they made the deal first.

It was a good trade for me, going from the Giants to the Yankees. I got into a string of World Series. Five straight, starting in '49. I hurt my shoulder before the '49 Series and couldn't throw, but I pinch-hit twice and got two hits. One of them helped beat the Dodgers in the third game, at Ebbets Field. I got a single off of Ralph Branca in the ninth inning with the bases loaded, and that helped win that game.

After all those years in the National League I finally get into a World Series and find myself getting the base hit that helps win for the American League. So you don't want to get too sentimental about things, do you?

TED LYONS

Theodore Amar Lyons
Born: December 28, 1900, Lake Charles, Louisiana; Died: July
    25, 1987
Major-league career: 1923–46, Chicago White Sox
Lifetime record: 260 wins, 230 losses

*In a curious way, Ted Lyons embodies baseball history in
this century. He pitched to Ty Cobb, who came to the big
leagues in 1905, and he pitched to Ted Williams, who left the
big leagues in 1960. Lyons himself came to the Chicago White
Sox straight from the campus of Baylor University and remained in the American League for twenty-one years, not
counting three years out for service in the Marine Corps, in
which he enlisted in 1942 at the age of forty-two.*

Lyons was elected to the Hall of Fame in 1955.

It's true that I spent a long career with a team that was in the
second division most of the time. But I didn't find it frustrating. I would have liked to have won more, but I'll say this: My
ball club always hustled for me. I never could find fault with
a ball club that put out. As long as I lived, I never complained
about an error. We had a young shortstop who became one of
the greatest, Luke Appling. He had a great arm, and once in
a while he'd uncork one, and it would go up in the third row
of seats. I'd say to him, "That's the way to throw it, Luke.
Don't let up on the ball. Put something on it." You've got to
encourage a guy after he's made an error. If you get on him for
booting one, he's going to boot two more before it's over.

But I never resented the fact that we usually finished down
in the standings. Sure, you'd have liked to finish higher; it

would have been more pleasant once in a while. And if we could have won a pennant, just one, to see what it was like, it would have been nice. But I never regretted being with Chicago all those years. It's a wonderful town, with wonderful fans, and I can't say enough for them.

Each day you start anew. Every day you start you think you can win. And something different happens every day. You never see two games alike. At least I never have, and I've been paying attention for a long time.

I started playing ball when I was eight years old. With a sock ball. Do you know what that is? That's an old sock that you fold up tight as you can and then get your mother to sew up. We used a broomstick for a bat. That was down in southeastern Louisiana, a long time ago.

I occupied myself as a boy by playing baseball. All summer long, and then every other chance I could, between school time. I was a 90-pound second baseman in high school. I used a big Joe Jackson bat—I don't know whether you remember Shoeless Joe Jackson's name; he was one of the greatest hitters that ever lived—and I had to choke it up maybe two-thirds of the way and kind of push at the ball. A few years later I got up to 135 pounds, and I started pitching. I was sixteen years old then.

I always had my mind set on being a ballplayer. But I wanted to be a lawyer, too. I studied one term of law and then came to realize I had a little better fast ball and curve than I did a vocabulary. So I went to baseball. My family was wonderful about it. They said, "Well, you've played baseball all your life, from the time you were eight years old, through high school, through college." They told me to make my own choice. Their feeling was that if they talked me out of it and I went into something else and wasn't happy with it, they would feel responsible. I think they showed some wisdom there, and I think I made the right decision.

The scouting systems weren't so extensive then. But there had been several people down in that neighborhood. As a matter of fact, Connie Mack's Athletics trained in Lake Charles, about 20 miles from where I lived. Connie offered to pay my way through college if I signed with him. (For all he knew he might have been paying for an eight-year course—he didn't know if I was dumb or smart.) But I turned him down.

Connie was a wonderful old fellow with a great memory, because in '29, when he won the pennant, he said to me, "You see, young fellow, if you would have taken my offer, you'd be pitching on a pennant winner." I said, "That's right. Or maybe I'd be at Oscaloosa trying to make it to the big leagues." You never can tell, can you?

I signed with the White Sox in 1923. I was in my senior year at Baylor University, in Waco, Texas. The White Sox were training nearby, and they decided to come over to Baylor and breeze around and watch the college workout. One of the newspapermen said to the coach, "Say, how about letting Ray Schalk catch one of your pitchers?" He was trying to work up some kind of an angle for a story, see.

The coach said that would be all right, and he called out my name—my middle name, which is Amar, a very unusual name, and I never did like it much. Ray Schalk got a kick out of it, and he called me Amar from then on.

Anyway, the coach said, "Amar, come over here and throw a few for Ray Schalk." So I went over and threw to Schalk for about two or three minutes. I had a pretty good fast ball back then, and I let him know it.

After the workout Schalk and some of the other fellows came over and said there was a possibility they might contact me. That pleased me because the White Sox were one of my favorite teams when I was a kid. At the end of the school year in June, after I'd graduated, I signed up. I got a $1,000 bonus. I took it and bought myself a Ford car. A brand-new 1923 Model T. That was my first car. Cost me $428. What would you say a new Ford would cost today?

I joined the ball club in St. Louis. Actually, I got there a day ahead of them; they were in Cleveland. Detroit was in town, and I stayed at the same hotel they did, the Buckingham. After I had my dinner that night, I went outside. There was a little place out front where the ballplayers used to sit and talk. I saw all the stars there—Ty Cobb, Harry Heilmann, Bob Fothergill, Hookie Dauss. I sat around for an hour and a half, listening to them talk baseball. I got a big kick out of it. I thought that was a pretty good start for a fellow his first night in town.

The next day the White Sox came in from Cleveland, and I was assigned to room with Hollis Thurston, who they called

Sloppy, even though he was very neat. I never could figure that nickname. He walked into the room—we were perfect strangers—and he said, "Oh, so you're the college kid, eh?" He was one year older than I was.

So I joined the White Sox that day at the hotel, went out to the ball park with them, and pitched an inning in the first major-league game I ever saw. I was sitting on the bench enjoying the ball game, even though we were behind by five or six runs. Eddie Collins was filling in as manager—Kid Gleason had to go back to Chicago, for some reason—and Eddie looked back at me. In those days, in the old Browns ball park, you had two benches, one in front of the other. Naturally I was sitting on the back bench. Collins looked at me and said, "Hey, go down and warm up. I'll let you pitch an inning." I turned around to see who he was talking to, but there was nobody behind me. I kind of swallowed a little bit. "Do you mean me?" I asked. He said, "Yeah."

So I went down and warmed up. This was my debut, and I was beginning to wonder how I was going to do. When I walked out on the mound, I felt enclosed. You see, I'd been used to playing on pastures, where when somebody hit a ball you had to stop it from rolling. Well, this field had fences around it. And of course in those days the Browns had big crowds, because they were usually contenders, so there was a lot of noise.

I can remember the guys I faced: Urban Shocker, a spitball pitcher; Johnny Tobin, the leadoff hitter; and Baby Doll Jacobson. I got them out in order. I don't remember exactly how they went out, but I'd got off on the right foot and was tickled to death.

I received wonderful treatment from everybody when I was breaking in. They couldn't have been nicer. Great fellows. The White Sox at that time had Harry Hooper, Eddie Collins, Ray Schalk, Red Faber. All four of those fellows are Hall of Famers today. And they had Bibb Falk in the outfield, and Johnny Mostil, who was a great center fielder, one of the greatest. He could go get 'em. It was like turning a rabbit loose when the ball was hit out to center field. And they had Willie Kamm at third base. That was Willie's first year in the major leagues, and what a fine career he had ahead of him.

I guess I'm one of the few who have had long big league

careers without ever having played in the minors. Frankie Frisch never played in the minors; neither did Eppa Rixey or Mel Ott. Bob Feller is another one; he came right out of high school. You can name some others, but not too many.

I think if you've played four years of college ball and you had good coaching, you've learned a lot of fundamentals. Of course, on top of that you have to have a little intelligence, to help yourself. And on top of that, you've got to have a pretty good arm. That's the biggest thing. I'll tell you a little story that happened around 1927. Walter Johnson was near the end of his career, and he came up with a sore arm. Well, so did I. One day I was walking down the clubhouse steps, working my shoulder with my hand. And here comes Walter, walking up the clubhouse steps, doing the same thing to his shoulder. We both stopped and looked at each other and grinned sort of self-consciously.

"How's your arm, Walter?" I asked.

"It's terrible," he said. "How's yours?"

"The same thing," I said.

"That old stuff about pitching with your head doesn't go, does it?" he said.

That's what I mean, you see. You've got to have your arm in good shape. And in the big leagues it's got to be in good shape all the time. You couldn't go out there with a bad arm.

Well, I mentioned Walter Johnson. You have to mention Walter, don't you? He was just terrific. He was another one who never played in the minor leagues. He came up to the big leagues around 1907, just a green kid out of the West, and stepped right in, and nobody had ever seen anything like him. The thing that I think was so much in his favor was his delivery. He had long arms, and he came from down under, and his ball sank in onto a right-hand hitter. It was tough to hit. A left-hand hitter had the ball going away from him. I can't say Walter was the speediest I ever saw because he was past his prime when I came into the league. When I saw him, he wasn't quite as fast as Grove or as Feller. But Walter's ball did so much. And some of the other fellows who had batted against him six or eight years before told me that he just threw the ball by you, right over the plate.

I pitched against Grove quite a bit. I was in the league just a few years ahead of him, and I saw him come up. Of course I knew who he was even before he came into the league. He was with Baltimore of the International League, and we played them an exhibition game one time. He struck out fifteen of our batters. Here's this minor-league pitcher throwing nothing but fastballs and blowing them right past everybody. They knew what they were going to get, but it didn't make any difference. Somebody said, "Well, he'll never make it in the big leagues. All he can do is throw a fastball." And somebody else said, "Yeah, and all Galli-Curci can do is sing."

Oh, he was fast. He was terrific. I remember one time we sent Butch Henline up to pinch-hit against Lefty. Butch had just come over from the National League and had never hit against Lefty. It was in the ninth inning, and we had men on second and third. I don't know how they got there, unless we cheated. So Butch steps up, and Lefty pours in two strikes, throwing so hard you wondered the cover didn't fly off the ball. Then he threw the third one, and he had more on that than he did on the other two. Back comes Butch. He's absolutely demoralized. When he sat down on the bench, I said, "Butch, do you know that's the first time I ever saw him let up on oh and two? I'm surprised you didn't whale it." Well, he looked at me and his eyes got as big as silver dollars. "Let up?" he said. "Whale it? What are you talking about? I couldn't even *see* that thing!"

Bob Feller was another swifty. We'd all heard about him, about how fast he was and everything. But it wasn't until you hit against him that you knew how fast he really was, until you saw with your own eyes that ball jumping at you. You've heard about a fast ball being alive. Well, with Feller that wasn't just a figure of speech—his ball really moved. Do you remember Eric McNair? He'd be right on top of the plate, all the time. Well, one day in Cleveland Feller threw one right under McNair's chin. Almost got him. Then Feller struck him out, and when he came back to the bench, McNair said, "Fellas, you know I never give anybody an inch up at that plate. But I'm giving old Rapid Robert about a foot and a half from now on, because I don't mind being killed outright, but I don't want to be maimed the rest of my life."

I saw quite a bit of Cobb. I'd say he was probably the greatest all-around batter. He could hit the ball anywhere he wanted to, and he'd hit it wherever you pitched it. And he had so many gimmicks. In the spring he'd wear a long-sleeve shirt down to his wrists, and if you pitched a ball inside to him, he'd contrive to have it hit that baggy sleeve and he'd get on first base. In a close ball game I tried to keep it away from him, not give him a chance to do that to me, because he was a streak on those bases. He could upset a whole ball club.

Eddie Collins was a guy like Ty with the bat—he could do anything with it. He very seldom struck out. Eddie was just plain great, all-around. He could do everything. And he was a very intelligent guy. It was a pleasure to listen to him talk baseball. He'd never ramble, always came right to the point, and he was seldom wrong. If he told you how to pitch to a batter, well, you'd better do it. I'm pitching against Washington one time. Do you remember Goose Goslin? He could hit the ball a mile. Especially fastballs. Well, I kept trying to throw a fastball by him. I said I was going to throw a fastball by that Goslin if I had to try a hundred times. I really got stubborn about it. And Collins kept warning me about it. "Don't give that fella any fastballs," he said.

It comes down to the eighth or ninth inning, and the infield is in. Collins is our manager and is calling the signals for the catcher from second base. Goslin comes up, and Collins keeps calling curveball signs. I threw Goose two or three curves, and he fouled them off. I decided I was going to throw him a fastball. Buck Crouse was catching, and he gave me a curveball sign. I shook him off. He kept doing that, and I kept saying no. Finally he gave me a fastball. I threw it in, and Goslin hit it like a bullet. It hit Collins right on the shin and bounced out into left center field. Collins didn't go after the ball; he came after me. "I told you not to throw him a fastball!" he yelled.

After the game he rolled up his trouser leg to show me a big black and blue mark on his leg.

"Look what you did," he said.

"It's all right, Eddie," I said. "We won the game, didn't we?"

Then he started to laugh. "I guess we did," he said. Then he said, "But listen to me, Ted, you'd better let me call the signs after this, or you're liable to get somebody crippled out there."

You know, it's like I was telling someone not long ago. There are great stars in every era. You can go back to 1900, there were stars. And there are great stars today. But I would have to say that in the twenties we probably saw more great hitters than in any other era. Just think of some of those fellows: Cobb, Speaker, Gehrig, Sisler, Ruth, Simmons, Goslin, Heilmann, Foxx, and plenty of others. The only way you could pitch to them was by changing speeds. I always tried to keep the ball outside to them, but of course, when you do that, you're taking a chance on getting hit with a line drive because some of those big hitters would send that ball through the middle and pick you right off the hill. The only way you could get a fastball by was when you caught one of them guessing. If you'd been feeding him a lot of slow stuff, you might take a little chance . . . on untying the ball game.

I mean, it could be unnerving pitching to fellows like Ruth and Gehrig and Foxx. Foxx was something to look at up at the plate. He had great powerful arms, and he used to wear his sleeves cut off way up, and when he dug in and raised that bat, those muscles would bulge and ripple. One day I was pitching to him, and he swung and topped the ball around home plate. I came running in for it, but the ball kicked foul. I stood there looking at him.

"How much air you carrying in those arms, Jimmie?" I asked.

"Thirty-five pounds," he said.

"Looks it," I said. And it did. His biceps looked like tires carrying thirty-five pounds. He could hit a ball as far as anybody. You say you've heard stories about Jimmie's long-distance hitting? Well, I don't know which stories in particular you've heard, but I'd say you wouldn't go far wrong if you believed them all.

Harry Heilmann was one of the most marvelous men I ever met in baseball and one of the greatest right-hand hitters. He was a different type of hitter than, say, Hornsby; Hornsby had a smooth stroke with a beautiful follow-through; Harry had a choppy stroke, but powerful. He was a tough man to pitch to. That whole Tiger ball club was tough to pitch to in those years. I remember one year, until about June, they had three .400 hitters in the lineup. Heilmann, Manush, and Fothergill. Cobb couldn't even get into the lineup. I'd call that hitting, wouldn't you? Keeping Cobb on the bench! Fothergill came over to the White Sox a few years later, and he'd love to tell about that. "Remember the time Cobb couldn't get in the lineup?" he'd say, and he'd laugh and laugh.

Ted Williams was a Ty Cobb, as far as being an intelligent batter. He wouldn't hit at a bad ball. I got to know Ted fairly well; I pitched against him a lot, and I was in the service with him, out in Hawaii. We rode together in a jeep every day, in and out of Honolulu. All he'd want to talk about was hitting. One day we were riding back from Honolulu, and all of a sudden from out of the blue he says to me, "Ted, do you think I'm as good a hitter as Babe Ruth?"

I said, "Well, wait till you get dry behind the ears. You've only been in the league a few years." I was just kidding him.

You know, he wouldn't talk to me all the way home. He just sat there brooding. I had to laugh; I knew what was eating him.

When we got back to the base, I said, "Now, let's get back to the subject. Listen, Ted, you're a little different from Ruth. Babe would hit at balls up around his cap—and those are the ones he'd hit nine miles. You wouldn't swing at one above your letters. Babe didn't mind going after a bad ball. You won't go a half inch out of the strike zone. You're two completely different hitters." And then I told him, "Of course you're as good a hitter as he was."

Then he was all right again.

I pitched a no-hitter, back in 1926, against the Red Sox. Do I remember much about it? Listen, I remember everything about it. You ever want to clear up a pitcher's memory, just ask him about his no-hitter. I'll tell you what I remember about it more than anything else. I'd been under the weather for a couple of days before that. I started the ball game by walking the first batter on four pitches. The next batter comes up, and the first two pitches to him are way off. So it looked like a bad day for old Mudville. The next pitch the batter hit, a line drive out to center field. It looked like a base hit, but our jackrabbit out there, Johnny Mostil, charged in and made a shoestring catch and doubled the runner off first base. From then on there wasn't but one base on balls. And no hits, of course. A fellow said to me later, "It's a good thing Bill Barrett was in right field." And I said, "Well, yeah, I'd never been able to pitch it without a right fielder." But I knew what he meant. Bill Barrett did make some nice catches. The wind was blowing in that day, and he played extra short, and he caught a few balls that might have been hits.

The last play of the game I remember very well. The batter was an old Texas A&M boy named Topper Rigney. I got two fast strikes on him with curve balls. Then I didn't know what to throw him. I wasn't sure whether I wanted to waste one or not. Johnny Grabowski, my catcher, called for another curve ball. I decided to throw as good a curve as I could, but break it outside for a ball. Well, I got it outside, but it hit the corner of the plate, and he smacked it. It went to the right of Earl Sheely, our first baseman. He made a good backhand stop, and I ran over to cover first. When I took the throw, I just kept on running because the kids were already pouring out of the stands, coming to try and get that ball away from me.

I guess I had my little superstitions. Most ballplayers do. When I was going good on the mound, I liked to keep using the same ball. I didn't want the infielders throwing it around for fear it would get away and some fan pick it up. But talking about superstitions, I'll tell you a story about Wes Ferrell. There was a real fine pitcher. He'd battle you all the way. He kept you busy all right. Well, one time Wes and I had each won 10 straight games. He came into Chicago, and we were going to pitch against one another. Now, Wes was superstitious about having his picture taken on the day he was going to pitch, and I knew that. I knew, too, that if there was one way to upset a ballplayer, it was to monkey around with his superstitions.

We had this photographer who used to sit on our bench, named Brown.

"Hey, Brownie," I said, "how about getting a picture of Ferrell and me when he comes out, shaking hands and wishing each other bad luck?"

"He won't let me," he said. "You know how he feels about that."

"I know," I said. "But you just insist. Tell him we've both won ten games in a row, and this is a picture you really want. You seldom get two pitchers starting against each other who've won ten games in a row." And I gave him some more baloney.

"Okay," he said. "I'll try."

So Ferrell comes out. Temperamental, but a wonderful guy. Brown walks up to him.

"Wes," he says, "how about stepping over here and having a picture taken with Ted?"

"I don't like to have a picture taken before I pitch," Wes says.

So at about that time I walked over.

"Here's Ted right now," Brown says. "How about letting me get a little shot? It's a real occasion, with both of you having won ten straight. It'll be a great picture."

Wes shrugged. "Oh, all right," he says.

So Brown took a picture of us shaking hands, and while we were doing that, I said to Wes, "He's taking a picture of us shaking hands and wishing each other bad luck."

He laughed, but he gave me a funny look. I'm sure that was on his mind the whole game. I beat him, 2–1. Well, there was a big potbellied stove in the clubhouse, and he went in and pretty near tore that thing up. He stomped around in there for about an hour, steaming and snorting.

I saw Wes in Florida a few years ago, and I reminded him of that game. Did he remember it? Need you ask?

"I knew you guys were up to something the minute you started," he said.

"That's the only way we could have beat you," I said. "With that picture."

I played a number of years for Jimmy Dykes. He was a great manager. And he was a witty man, with a wonderful sense of humor. That came in handy during those years.

One time I was pitching a game against Feller, in Cleveland. Feller was really rough to beat. If you beat him, it was 1–0 or 2–1. This particular game was close, 1–1, in the ninth inning. They get a man on second base, and Ray Mack was the hitter. There was one out, and Feller was up next.

Dykes calls time and comes walking out to the mound.

"Let's walk this guy and get to Feller," he says.

"No, Jim," I said. "Let's not walk him. I'll make him hit something." In baseball parlance that means you're not going to give him anything too good to swing at, hope he'll go for a bad pitch.

Jimmy wasn't too sure.

"If we get Mack," I said, "it'll be two out, and they might put in a hitter for Feller." If they did that, we'd be rid of Bobby.

"All right," Jimmy said. "Okay."

I don't think he'd got back to the dugout when he heard something go *whack!* This fellow Mack hit a line drive into left center for a double, and there went the ball game.

So I walk off the mound, and Jimmy is waiting for me in the dugout. You know, most managers would have been a little sore about that. But Jimmy said, "Well, I'll say one thing. You did what you said you were going to do—you made him hit something."

You know, Jocko Conlon has just now gone into the Hall of Fame as one of the great umpires of all time. Well, there's a little story behind how Jocko became an umpire. He was with the White Sox for a while in the thirties, as a utility out-fielder. Jocko was always a good-natured guy, and playful. We were in the shower one day, and we started boxing. That was dumb because there was soap all over the floor and it was slick in there. I put up my elbow; he hit me there and broke his thumb. He called me Elbows McFadden after that.

The next day Jocko comes to the ball park with his thumb in a cast. He gives Dykes some cock-and-bull story how it happened, and that's that.

A few days later we were playing in St. Louis. It was the middle of the summer, and the heat was murderous. Umpires were always passing out in St. Louis. I happened to be looking at Red Ormsby, and all of a sudden he just keeled over, knocked out by the heat. In those days you only had two umpires. So what they did was get a player from our club and a player from the Browns to umpire the bases. Jocko had that broken thumb, so Dykes told him to get out there. Well, he umpired at third base, and he called some of the best plays you ever saw. I told him later, "Jocko, you might have found your career." You see, he was just hanging on in the big leagues at that time. So he went into umpiring and became one of the best, and today he's in the Hall of Fame. Thanks to old "Elbows McFadden."

Toward the end of my career I became known as the Sunday pitcher. They figured I could only pitch once a week. I could have pitched more often than that, I think, but they put me on that schedule. Every Sunday I went out and pitched my ball game. And you want to know the funny thing about that? When I was a kid, my mother wouldn't let me play ball on

Sunday. Then for three or four years that's the *only* day I played.

I try to keep up with baseball today as much as I can. I watch it on television, and I read *The Sporting News*. Sure I still read *The Sporting News*. I want to tell you how I first got to reading that paper. When we were kids down in Vinton, Louisiana, my best friend and I, we read everything about baseball we could get our hands on. Now my friend's brother worked at the Southern Pacific depot in town. Well, one day a train was going through town, and a fellow threw a newspaper out of the window. My friend's brother picked it up and gave it to us that afternoon.

"Here's something for you fellows," he said.

We looked at it and couldn't believe it. Page one was all baseball. We looked at the second page: all baseball. We looked at the third page: all baseball. Why, the whole paper was baseball! You never saw kids so elated. We subscribed right away. This was about 1914 or so. And I haven't missed an issue of *The Sporting News* since.

GEORGE PIPGRAS

GEORGE WILLIAM PIPGRAS
Born: December 20, 1899, Ida Grove, Iowa; Died: October 19, 1986
Major-league career: 1923–24, 1927–35, New York Yankees, Boston Red Sox
Lifetime record: 102 wins, 73 losses

A member of the 1927 Yankees, George Pipgras was an ace pitcher on the great teams of the late twenties and early thirties. Pipgras' best year was 1928, when he won 24 games. After his playing days were prematurely ended by a freak accident, Pipgras returned to the minor leagues as an umpire and worked his way back to the American League in that capacity.

When I came out of the Army in 1918, I went up to Fulda, Minnesota, a little old country town, to pitch semipro ball. There was a train that ran right behind center field, and every so often when I was pitching, I'd notice the train would stop and just stand still out there in deep center field. I didn't know it at the time, but I was being scouted by the train conductor. He was a fellow that was interested in baseball, and he recommended me to the White Sox.

Can you imagine that fellow stopping the train to watch a ball game? I hope his passengers were baseball fans.

The White Sox signed me and sent me to Saginaw, Michigan. But I couldn't get the ball over the plate, and they released me. I had a good fast ball, but I was wild, and I stayed wild, right through my big league career. Always walked a lot of men.

In 1922 I was pitching for Charleston, South Carolina, had

a good year, and the Yankees brought me up. I went to spring training with them in 1923, had one look at that pitching staff, and wondered how in the world I was going to win myself a job. They had Herb Pennock, Bob Shawkey, Waite Hoyt, Sam Jones, Bullet Joe Bush. As a matter of fact, I didn't start pitching regularly until 1927. Dutch Ruether was with us then, and he was supposed to pitch one day. But he wasn't feeling well. So Miller Huggins told me I was going to start.

Well, I won the ball game, and after that I took Ruether's place. Shows you how chancy baseball is—if Ruether hadn't turned up sick that day, who knows when I might have got my opportunity and what would have happened?

Those '27 Yankees had everything. I don't think any ball club in history could beat them. They were tops. Any team that has Ruth and Gehrig has a head start, doesn't it? They gave a pitcher confidence. You knew that if you were behind a run or two late in the game, it didn't matter; Ruth would hit one, or Gehrig would, or they both would. Then we had Earle Combs, Tony Lazzeri, Joe Dugan, Bob Meusel. Every one a great ballplayer.

Bob Meusel had the best arm I ever saw. You know, even Cobb wouldn't run on him. I remember once, Cobb was on third with one out and somebody lifted a fly ball to Meusel. Ordinarily on a ball like that Ty would have come in. Wally Schang was the catcher, and when that ball went out to Meusel, Wally took off his mask and stood at the plate and yelled down to Cobb, "Come on in, Ty. Come on in." Taunting him. Cobb just stood there. Meusel caught the ball and held onto it. Schang waved to Cobb: Come on in. But Ty just stood there with his hands on his hips, scowling at Schang. Cobb was aggressive, but not foolish. He knew Meusel's arm, and he wasn't about to challenge it.

We won 110 games that year, 1927, plus four straight in the Series against Pittsburgh. I wasn't supposed to start in that Series. At least not as far as I knew. Urban Shocker was supposed to start the second game. Well, in about the seventh or eighth inning of the first game, right out of the blue, Miller Huggins looks over at me.

"George," he says, "can you pitch tomorrow?"

"Well, sure I can."

"Okay," he says. "Get a good night's rest."

A good night's rest! I'll tell you what I did. I went back to the hotel and began studying that Pirate lineup until my eyes started to hurt. How was I going to pitch to them? They had some good hitters——the Waner brothers, Pie Traynor, Joe Harris, Glenn Wright.

I guess I was a bit nervous when I got to the ball park the next day. Heck, I was pitching for a team that had won 110 games. I was *expected* to win. I got some great encouragement from Urban Shocker in the clubhouse—he was going to be first out of the bullpen if I got into trouble.

"Listen," he said, "when you leave the game, leave the ball rough." He was a spitball artist, you see.

"Sure," I said. "I'll do that."

But I had no intention of getting out of there. I started off kind of shaky. Lloyd Waner led off and hit me for a triple, and he scored. But we came back with three in the third and three more in the eighth and beat them, 6–2. I was fast that day. Didn't throw but three curves. They kept coming up there looking for the curve but never got it.

We took the next two games for a clean sweep. As a matter of fact, I played in three World Series, and we swept each one in four games, in '27 against the Pirates, '28 against the Cardinals, and '32 against the Cubs.

I had a nice year in '28—24 wins. Huggins started me in the second game of the Series, against St. Louis. I drew an interesting opponent, Grover Cleveland Alexander. He was past his prime, of course, but that fellow still knew how to pitch. One thing I'll never forget. Alex had this reputation as being a pretty good man with the bottle. You've heard that. Anyway, you know how they always ask the starting pitchers to pose for pictures before a World Series game? Well, when I got together with Alex, I put out my hand for him to shake and he reached for it and I swear missed it by a foot, he was so drunk; either that or he had a wicked hangover. He just waved his hand around in the air until we made contact.

You knew that Alex wasn't right. He could throw the ball through the eye of a needle, but in that particular game he walked four or five men and gave up a lot of hits, and by the third inning we had him out of there. Lou Gehrig hit a tremendous home run off him. It was a ball that the center fielder broke in on, but it just kept rising and rising and finally hit the scoreboard. If you know where that scoreboard was in Yankee Stadium, you know what a clout that was. We won that game, 9–3.

Ruth and Gehrig hit home runs all over the place in that Series. What a Series those fellows had! Between them they hit seven home runs and averaged something like .600. There never was a one-two punch in any lineup like those two. At least I can't think of any. Can you?

In 1933 I was traded over to the Red Sox. I didn't like the idea, of course, but there's nothing you can do about it. Here I was leaving a winning ball club and going to a losing one.

We had Bucky Walters playing third base in Boston. What an arm! When he fired that ball across from third, it really moved. In fact, the first baseman sometimes had trouble handling it. They weren't thinking about making him into a pitcher then. Seems to me I heard some talk about his ball being too alive, but that would be nonsense since I can't believe a pitcher can have a ball that's too alive. Well, you know what happened. A few years later they did make him into a pitcher, in the National League, and he became one of the great ones.

You know, I broke my arm throwing a ball. Sounds incredible, doesn't it? It happened soon after I'd joined the Red Sox. I was pitching against Detroit. The batter was a fellow named Doljack. I had him oh and two and figured I'd waste a pitch. The moment I let go of the ball I felt my arm pop.

They sent me to a bone specialist in Chicago. He said that because of the amount of pitching I'd done through the years, the muscles in that arm had become stronger than the bone, and when I'd snapped off that pitch, well, the bone just wouldn't take it anymore. It's not a common thing; as far as I know, it's only happened a few times.

That finished me as a pitcher. I was only thirty-three years old and hadn't given much thought to the future, and frankly I didn't know what to do. So I talked to Tom Yawkey about it. Now there's a good man. He's a man who cares about his players and cares about baseball. He's a millionaire many times over and just as regular a guy as you'd want to find. I remember I was hunting with him at his plantation in South Carolina. This was right after I'd finished as a pitcher.

"I don't know what I'm going to do," I said to him. "Baseball has been my whole life. I just don't know anything else."

"Look," he said, "you know the game, you know the rules. Why don't you think about umpiring? If you want, I'll sponsor you."

Well, I went home and talked to my wife about it, thought it over for a month or so, and decided to take a shot at it. I called Yawkey and told him I'd do it. He got the American League to give me a job, in the Eastern League.

Well, I liked it fine, and I got along pretty well. I came into the American League in 1939. I was in baseball for seventeen years and was never put out of a game. I always remembered something Herb Pennock told me when I was just breaking in: "You're going to make a lot more mistakes than the umpire." So when the players used to get on me, I'd run them. I just wouldn't take it.

One time in Chicago, in a game between the White Sox and the Browns, I ran seventeen men out of there. They kept jumping on me, and I kept bouncing them out, off of both benches. That night Will Harridge called me—he was the league president.

"George," he said, "have you gone crazy?"

"No, I haven't gone crazy," I said. "They're going to let me alone out there, or I'm not going to be there."

"Don't you think you were a little bit rough on them?" he asked.

"Not at all."

"But *seventeen* men, George."

"All that yelling from the bench isn't necessary," I said. "I never read anything that said you had to yell at the umpire in order to play ball."

So the players knew I wasn't going to take it. And I worked a number of years with another fellow who wasn't going to take it—Bill Summers. When we walked out on that field, we were in charge, and everybody knew it.

Sure, we made mistakes. And when we did, we'd admit it. And once we'd admitted it, most of the players and managers would understand. Bill Dickey was a great one for that. He'd say, "What was wrong with that pitch?" And I'd say, "Nothing. I missed it." And he wouldn't say another word. Jimmy Dykes was another one like that. You've heard about Jimmy being rough on umpires, but I never found that so. He'd come storming out and I'd say, "Jimmy, I kicked it. Now let's get on with the game."

You know, most of the time when you see the manager out there, it's to protect his players. After all, the manager is sitting in the dugout, and say there's a close play at second base. There's no way he can see it. But he sees his player on the edge of getting the thumb, and he comes out there to break it up, to keep his player in the game. He's also got to let his players know he'll back them up in an argument. He's got to do that.

I was umpiring when Ted Williams broke in. There was a hitter. I never saw him swing at a bad ball. He had the greatest pair of eyes I ever saw. He'd take a ball an inch or two off the plate and never flinch. I'll tell you, he kept you on your toes, the way he took pitches. And when he took a pitch and you called it a strike, you couldn't help but to think you'd missed it. But Ted was great. He'd never look around at you. All the great ballplayers were that way—they'd never try to show you up.

People always ask me who was the fastest pitcher I ever saw. Well, I saw Grove and Feller in their prime, and you can't believe anybody could be quicker than those two fellows. But I'll tell you something. When I broke into the league, I batted against Walter Johnson. He'd been around a long time at that point, seventeen years or so. Well, I stepped into the batter's box, took two called strikes, and stepped out of the batter's box. I turned around and looked at Muddy Ruel, who was catching. I could see he had a little smile on his face, behind his mask. He knew what I was going to say.

"Muddy," I said, "I never saw those pitches."

"Don't let it worry you," he said. "He's thrown a few that Cobb and Speaker are still looking for."

And Johnson was past his prime then, remember. They told me that he'd slowed down a bit by then. So if that was Walter Johnson past his prime . . . well, who was the fastest pitcher of all time? I don't know . . . but I have a sneaking suspicion.

I like to play golf these days, you know. Well, the other day I was getting ready to putt the ball and some people were making noise. My partner asked me if that didn't bother me. "Look," I said, "if you've ever had the experience of standing out on a pitching mound, with seventy thousand people yelling their lungs out, with the bases loaded, the count three and two, and Jimmie Foxx at bat, why, you're not going to be bothered by a couple of people talking on a golf course."

BILLY HERMAN

WILLIAM JENNINGS BRYAN HERMAN
Born: July 7, 1909, New Albany, Indiana
Major-league career: 1931–47, Chicago Cubs, Brooklyn Dodgers, Boston Braves, Pittsburgh Pirates
Lifetime average: .304

Billy Herman had the reputation for being one of the most intelligent, as well as ablest, players of his day. In 1935 his 227 base hits led the league, and in 1935–36 he put together back-to-back seasons of 57 doubles. Herman was a winning player, superlative in the field, an incomparable hit-and-run man, a driving force on four pennant winners.

In February, 1975, Herman was voted into the Hall of Fame.

I came up to the Cubs from Louisville of the American Association in August, 1931. It was a bad ball club to be breaking in with because of that pitching staff. Biggest bunch of head-hunters you ever saw. Charlie Root. Off the field, a very quiet man. Out on that mound, he was mean. So was Pat Malone. And so was Lon Warneke. Guy Bush, too. That was a mean staff. Every time they'd throw at a hitter naturally somebody on our club would get it right back. I think I must've had my tail in the batter's box as often as my feet. But I was young and agile then, and it didn't bother me. Not much.

But of course, you had a lot of that back in those days. It was bad. The rules they have today are better in that respect. The umpires will stop that sort of thing. But back then, say you had a little trouble with a ball club on opening day. Well, now you're playing them twenty-one more games. That trouble would pop up every one of those games. Maybe even carry over into the next year. You had some really bad throwing contests. And I mean bad ones. It's a wonder a lot more players didn't get hurt.

I remember a game we were playing in Chicago against the Giants, when Bill Terry was managing them. We went into the bottom of the tenth, the game tied. There's two out and a man on first. Hal Schumacher is pitching for them, and Chuck Klein is the batter. Klein ties into one, hits it for a double, and we win the game.

The next day Charlie Root is pitching for us against Hubbell. Charlie puts them down in order in the first inning, getting Terry for the third out. Klein is our third hitter, and when he comes up, Hubbell throws two pitches right behind his head. Getting even for the day before, see. Well, we knew Hubbell's control. He could throw strikes at midnight. He's not going to miss that far unless he's told to. So we're pretty mad. We're yelling and cursing on the bench. Everybody but Root. Charlie just sits there like a mummy, not saying a thing. He goes out and pitches the next inning and doesn't come close to anybody. We wondered about that, but nobody said anything.

Then in the third inning up comes Mr. Terry again. He steps in and cocks that bat; Root winds up and with his first pitch hits him right in the neck. Terry staggered around but didn't go down. Then he starts for the mound, and Root, being a gentleman, doesn't want to make Terry walk that far. He comes right out to meet him.

"What the hell did you do that for?" Terry yells.

"Why'd you make Hubbell throw at Klein?" Charlie yells back.

Well, we broke it up before they got together. But that's the way it was then.

You know, when I was a kid, baseball was about the only sport around. There wasn't much basketball or football to speak of. So I started to play ball. That was back in Indiana, in a little town called New Albany. I played on the high school team and then in an amateur league in Louisville, which wasn't too far away. I wasn't thinking of pro ball in those days, but when I got a chance, I jumped at it. Once I signed that first contract, well, then I had visions of going to the big leagues. That became my ambition.

Baseball was a good job in those years, after the Depression began. I was damn lucky to be playing ball. In 1932 I made $7,000, which was a ton of money then. I came from a big family, and some of my brothers were struggling just to earn eating money.

Rogers Hornsby was the manager when I joined the Chicago club in 1931. He was all business. You couldn't smoke or even drink a soda in the clubhouse or read a paper or anything like that. Sort of an odd guy, too. If you were a rookie, he wouldn't talk to you. Never say hello. You might get a grunt out of him, but that was about all. The only time you'd hear his voice with your name in it was when you did something wrong, and then you heard it loud and clear. If he ignored you, then you knew you were doing all right.

Hornsby wasn't popular with the players, which didn't bother him a damn. We had some good ballplayers, too. Gabby Hartnett was on that club, and Charlie Grimm, Kiki Cuyler, Woody English, Riggs Stephenson, Hack Wilson, plus all those hard-nosed pitchers.

Breaking in was kind of rough back in those days. Much rougher than it is now. A kid comes to a major-league club today, everybody talks to him and tries to help him along. But back then they more or less resented a young kid coming to the team; they knew he was going to take some older guy's job, and that older guy was their friend. So you were pretty much on your own.

I was a serious-minded player, and I didn't go out of my way to try and make friends with the older players. I figured that if I could show them I could play and that I meant to stay, they'd warm up. And that's just what happened. I played in twenty-five games that September and hit .327. Then I went to spring training in 1932 and won the job.

That was quite a year for a first-year man. We were rolling along just great, fighting Pittsburgh for the pennant. And then all of a sudden, in August, Hornsby gets fired. He'd been having some trouble with the general manager, Mr. Veeck— that's Bill Veeck's father. Veeck was questioning Hornsby's handling of the pitchers, and one thing or another. Hornsby, of course, wasn't the type who took criticism gracefully, and it finally got to the point where he had to go.

Most of the players were pretty happy about the change,

especially since it was Charlie Grimm who took over. Grimm was as popular with the players as Hornsby was unpopular. Sometimes that kind of shake-up can demoralize a team, but it seemed to perk us up, and we went on to win the pennant. Root, Warneke, Bush, and Malone did most of the pitching for us coming down the stretch, and they were just great. But we should have gone home after winning the pennant; the World Series was a disaster.

We played the Yankees that year, and they clobbered us in four straight. You know, you hate to say it, but we were overmatched, strictly overmatched, and we were a damn *good* ball club. But they just had too much, in every department. We matched them in speed and defense and pitching, but they had that extra good power.

They had kind of a fat guy, with little skinny ankles, playing right field named Babe Ruth, and Lou Gehrig, Tony Lazzeri, Earle Combs, Bill Dickey, Frankie Crosetti, Ben Chapman. To give you an example of what we were facing, the Cubs as a team that year hit around 70 home runs; Ruth and Gehrig between *themselves* hit 75.

We had a lot of fire and spirit on the Cubs, but when we went out that first day and watched the Yankees take batting practice, our hearts just sank. They were knocking those balls out of sight. We were awestruck.

That was the Series in which Ruth supposedly called his shot. I say "supposedly." He didn't really do it, you know. I hate to explode one of baseball's great legends, but I was there and saw what happened. Sure, he made a gesture, he pointed—but it wasn't to call his shot. Listen, he was a great hitter and a great character, but do you think he would have put himself on the spot like that? I can tell you what happened and why it happened.

We were a young team and a fresh team. We had some guys on the bench that got on Ruth as soon as the Series started. And I mean they were rough. Once all that yelling starts back and forth it's hard to stop it, and of course, the longer it goes on, the nastier it gets. What were jokes in the first game became personal insults by the third game. By the middle of that third game things were really hot.

I think it was around the fifth inning when Ruth came up. Of course, it was always an occasion when that guy stepped up to the plate, but this time it seemed even more so. He'd already hit a home run, in the first inning with two on, and the Chicago fans were letting him have it, and so was our bench. I was standing out at second base, and I could hear it pouring out of the bench. Charlie Root was pitching. He threw the first one over, and Ruth took it for a strike. The noise got louder. Then Root threw another one across, and Ruth took that, for strike two. The bench came even more alive with that. What Ruth did then was hold up his hand, telling them that was only two strikes, that he still had another one coming and that he wasn't out yet. When he held up his hand, that's where the pointing came in. But he was pointing out toward Charlie Root when he did that, not toward the center-field bleachers. And then, of course, he hit the next pitch out of the ball park. Then the legend started that he had called his shot, and Babe went along with it. Why not?

But he didn't point. Don't kid yourself. I can tell you just what would have happened if Ruth had tried that—he would never have got a pitch to hit. Root would have had him with his feet up in the air. I told you, Charlie Root was a mean man out on that mound.

But, like I say, it's still a great story, and those who want to believe it will go on believing it, regardless of what anybody says.

You know, we had a great showman over in the National League, too. Dizzy Dean. What a sweet pitcher he was. He had all the equipment—good fastball, a great curve, and a good slow curve. But I wouldn't say he was the fastest pitcher in the league when I was there. I think Van Lingle Mungo was possibly the fastest pitcher I ever saw.

Dean was hardheaded out on the mound. He wanted to throw the ball past everybody. If he'd thrown more curves and changes, he wouldn't have had to work so hard. He could be smart and cagey out there when he wanted to—he proved that later, when he was pitching for us in Chicago after he'd lost his great fastball. But when he had it, he loved to show it off.

But I always had very good luck with him, better luck than I had with his brother Paul, even though Dizzy was a lot better pitcher. I always used to kid Diz about how well I hit him. I'll tell you a story about that. In 1960 Billy Jurges was managing the Red Sox, and I signed on as one of his coaches.

We were training out in Arizona, and Diz was living nearby in Phoenix.

Dean invited us out to his house one night. He showed us around and then took us into the den. The walls were decorated with pictures and trophies and all the mementos of his career. He also had a lot of box scores framed and hung up there. We got to kidding him about the year he won 30 games. He was proud as hell of that, and with good reason. But he always had a hard time beating the Cubs, and we let him know about that. So Diz pointed to one of the box scores.

"There," he said. "There's one I beat you."

Well, for some reason I went over and looked at the box score.

"No wonder," I said.

"What do you mean?" he asked.

"There's a reason why you won that game, Diz," I said.

"What are you talking about?" he asked.

"I didn't play that day," I said.

Diz gave me an indignant look and squinted at the box score. Sure enough, I wasn't in the lineup that game. It was the first time I ever saw Dean where he couldn't say a word.

I guess the only match in the league for Dean in those years was Carl Hubbell. What a great pitcher and fine competitor he was. I'll tell you something about Hubbell. When he was pitching, you hardly ever saw the opposing team sitting back in the dugout; they were all up on the top step, watching him operate. He was a marvel to watch, with that screwball, fastball, curve, screwball again, changes of speed, control. He didn't have really overpowering stuff, but he was an absolute master of what he did have, and he got every last ounce out of his abilities. I never saw another pitcher who could so fascinate the opposition the way Hubbell did.

But I had great luck with Hubbell. I was the type of hitter that he didn't like to pitch to. He liked those guys who swung hard and soon; he'd throw that little screwball, and they'd be out in front of it, hitting it off the end of the bat. But I was a right field hitter anyway, and a late swinger, so when that screwball was turning off, I'd go right along with it. But that Hal Schumacher—I couldn't hit him at all. He had a sinker, and I couldn't hit those guys. Bucky Walters, too. Same kind of pitcher. Sinking fast balls. Gave me fits.

I saw quite a bit of Pie Traynor, though he'd been around for a while by the time I came into the league. Son of a gun, he was a great player. Most marvelous pair of hands you'd ever want to see. The only problem he had was throwing. He was wild. They told me he was always wild. But the thing that helped Traynor was his quick release. You'd hit a shot at him, a play that he could take his time on, and he'd catch it and throw it right quick, so that if his peg was wild, the first baseman had time to get off the bag, take the throw and get back on again. It was the only way Traynor could throw; if he took his time, he was *really* wild.

But the best third baseman I ever saw, for a couple of years, was Billy Cox. He made the most outstanding plays I've ever seen. Brooks Robinson is great, and so was Clete Boyer; but Cox was amazing. He just made your eyes pop. Ballplayers have their own special lingo, you know, and what they said about Cox was that he had plenty of "cat." You couldn't believe how quick he was, going in any direction. And an arm like a rifle.

I'll tell you about another guy who awed me: Ernie Lombardi. For raw ability with a bat, I don't think anybody could top him. But he was so slow afoot that those infielders could play him so deep that he just didn't have any place to hit the ball. He had to hit it over the fence or against the fence or just too hard for anybody to be able to make a play on. If he was playing today, on this artificial surface, I don't know where the infielders would play him. The ball comes off there like a rocket, and the way Lombardi hit it he might kill an infielder today. He could hit a ball as hard as anybody I ever saw, and that includes Ruth and Foxx.

Nineteen thirty-five was a hell of a year. All season we were in third place watching the Cardinals and Giants battle it out. And then in September we suddenly got hot. I don't mean just hot—we sizzled. We took off and won twenty-one straight games. We played an eighteen-game home stand and won every one. Talk about the virtues of home cooking, huh? Then we went into St. Louis for a five-game series, needing only two to clinch. In the opener Lon Warneke beat Paul Dean, 1–0, and the next day Bill Lee beat Dizzy for the clincher. Lee was almost unbeatable that year. What an overhand curve that guy had!

How do you explain a ball club getting that hot? I don't know. Maybe it's the power of positive thinking. All of a sudden we got the notion that we couldn't lose; there was no way we could lose. Winning can become an infection, just like losing can. We rode that streak right into the World Series.

We played Detroit that fall. It was a fine World Series, and an exciting one, even though, dammit, we lost. Three of the games were decided by one run. We were down three games to two and got beat a real tough ball game in Detroit. That Series should've gone seven games. We got some great pitching from Warneke and Lee, and a timely hit or two here and there would have made all the difference. But you've heard that story before, haven't you?

Detroit had a solid club. Some real hitters. Mickey Cochrane, Pete Fox, and those G-men: Gehringer, Greenberg, and Goslin. Tommy Bridges beat us two games.

Bridges started the last game, in Detroit, and that's a ball game I don't think I'll ever forget. Detroit up to that time had never won a World Series, and the fans were screaming from the first pitch. We went into the top of the ninth tied, 3–3. I got lucky against Bridges that day and had knocked in all our runs; even got myself a World Series home run. Larry French was pitching for us.

Stan Hack led off the top of the ninth with a triple. So there he was, the tie-breaking run, standing on third base and nobody out. How many ways to get him in? Count 'em: base hit, fly ball, ground ball, balk, wild pitch, passed ball, error. Jurges came up. Bridges struck him out. Then came something they're still second-guessing Charlie Grimm for. He let Larry French hit for himself. Why did he do that? Well, Larry wasn't a bad hitter, for one thing, and for another, he was pitching pretty well and Grimm wanted to keep him in there. I didn't give it much thought at the time. When you're sitting on the bench, in the middle of all the action, you tend to go along with the manager's moves. The second-guessing comes later. That's what second-guessing is all about, isn't it?

Anyway, French tapped back to the mound. So now there were two out, and Hack is still standing on third, and he's looking lonelier and lonelier out there. Augie Galan was the batter. He got hold of one and hit a long fly ball, but it was caught. That fly ball had come too late.

When I think back to the 1935 World Series, all I can see is Hack standing on third base, waiting for somebody to drive him in. Seems to me now he stood there for hours and hours.

In the bottom of the ninth Cochrane got a hit. Then Gehringer hit a line shot that Cavarretta knocked down and got one out on. But Cochrane got to second. Goslin came up. And he got the hit that beat us. It was one of those hits that begins dying the moment it leaves the bat. I ran out for it, Billy Jurges ran out for it. Frank Demaree came in from center for it, but nobody could quite catch up to it and it just dropped onto the grass in center field, and Cochrane scored. Damn, that was so frustrating, running after the ball that's got the World Series riding on it, knowing that you're not going to catch it and knowing that you're not going to miss it by much. It just drops onto the grass and breaks your heart.

That 1935 team, damn it all, we had everything. It was one of the two best I ever played on—the '41 Dodgers was the other. The '35 Cubs were chock-full of good ballplayers. Some people said Chicago had the best infield that year that they ever had—even better than the Tinker-Evers-Chance infield. Well, it's not for me to say which was better, but besides myself we had Phil Cavarretta, Billy Jurges, and Stan Hack. Then we had Hartnett catching, and Chuck Klein, Frank Demaree, and Augie Galan in the outfield.

We'd gotten Klein from the Phillies. He'd had a half dozen really sensational years over there. He got off to a great start with us and then pulled a hamstring muscle. He tried to play with it and it got worse. He was a hell of a competitor, but he was just tearing up that leg. The blood started to clot in it, and I swear, that leg turned black, from his thigh all the way down to his ankle. I think it just about ruined his career. He couldn't run anymore; he couldn't swing the bat so well anymore. I think it all stemmed from that injured leg.

Chuck was a real nice guy, and strong, very, very strong. They said he could rip a telephone directory in half with his bare hands, and I can believe it. But he was extremely good-natured, and serious, all business. Now we had Augie Galan. Augie was one of my best friends on the ball club. He loved to laugh and fool around, and he had a great imagination for practical jokes. His favorite victim was Klein. Say, why is it that the little guys—Augie wasn't too big—always like to pull pranks on the big strong guys? Is it because they know the big guy won't belt them? Well, whatever the reason, Augie had Klein figured pretty well, because even though Chuck would sometimes get furious at Augie, he never stayed mad—he wasn't that kind of a guy. But one time in New York, Augie almost got it. Boy, I'll tell you, he never came closer to having his head handed to him than that day.

Chuck invited Augie and me up to his room for a beer after the game. This was at the Commodore Hotel, right near Grand Central Station. Chuck was in a real happy mood—his fianceé was coming in on the train from Philadelphia, and he was looking forward to taking her out for a night on the town. So we went up to his room, and Chuck called room service, and they came around with a tray of beer and a couple of bowls of peanuts.

We were sitting and drinking beer and eating the peanuts for a while, and then there's a knock on the door, and the valet comes in. He's got Chuck's suit on a hanger, all cleaned and pressed. Chuck's face lit up when he saw how nice the suit looked. You know how a fellow wants to look good when he's taking his best girl out. He tipped the valet and hung the suit up in the closet. Then he looked at his watch—it was getting near time for that train from Philly to come in.

"Listen," he said, "you guys sit around and finish your beer. I've got to go and meet the train. I'll be back in a little while."

So Augie and me are sitting there. He's pretty quiet for a while, staring at the bowl of peanuts on the table next to him. And then he gets a brilliant idea. He goes over to the window and opens it about eight or ten inches or so and then pulls the blind down to that level. He sprinkles some peanuts onto the windowsill, then steps around and hides behind the blind. Well, there were always a lot of pigeons around that area, and sure enough they start coming to peck at the peanuts. As soon as one of them lands, Augie shoots his hand out and captures it. He takes the pigeon over to the closet, opens the door, throws the pigeon in, and closes the door. He does this about three or four times and then sits down and has another beer.

About a half hour later Chuck comes back. He's checked his fianceé into the hotel, and now he's going to change and get ready for his big night out. He opens the closet to get his suit and the pigeons come roaring out, right in his face. Chuck was so startled he stumbled back and sat down on the edge of the bed, and just sat there watching the pigeons circle around and around the room until they found the open window and got the hell out.

Chuck looked at Galan—he knew who'd done it—and just shook his head. That was okay. But when he took his suit out and looked at it I thought he'd explode: the pigeons had shit all over it. I'll never forget him standing there holding that suit up on the hanger, his eyes getting bigger and bigger. Oh, he was mad. I thought he was going to throw Augie out of the window. I really thought he was going to do it, he was so goddamned mad. Augie was lucky to get out of that room alive.

You know, the other night I heard a sportscaster commenting on how tough the schedule is today for the ballplayer. Well, I had to laugh. The players today don't know how easy they have it. Say you're leaving Chicago to go play a series in St. Louis and a series in Cincinnati. You know how they make that trip today? Buses to and from the ball park. Short plane rides. And everything air-conditioned, of course: buses, planes, hotels, clubhouses.

Now, back when I played, here's how you went from Chicago to St. Louis to Cincinnati—and I'm talking about July and August, when it's always 90 or more degrees in those towns. You got on a train at midnight, and maybe that train has been sitting in the yards all day long, under a broiling sun. It feels like 150 degrees in that steel car. Sometimes they'd have these blowers on either end of the car to circulate the air, and sometimes they wouldn't. You get into St. Louis at six thirty in the morning, grab your own bag, fight to get a cab, and go to the hotel. By the time you get to the hotel it's seven thirty, and you have an afternoon ball game to play. So you hurry into the dining room—and it's hot in there, no air conditioning—and you eat and run upstairs to try and get a few hours' rest. Then you go to the ball park, where it's about 110 degrees. You finish the ball game around five or five thirty and go into the clubhouse. It's around 120 degrees in there. You take your shower, but there's no way you can dry off; the sweat just keeps running off of you. You go out to the street and try to find a cab back to the hotel. You get back to the hotel and go up to your room, and you lose your breath, it's so hot in there. But the dining room isn't much better, so you order room service and stay right there and eat. Then you go to bed and try to sleep, but you can't, you're sweating so much. So you get up and pull the sheet off the bed and soak it with cold water and go back and roll up in a wet sheet; but it dries out after an hour or two, and you have to get up and soak it again. This goes on for four days in St. Louis, and you go on to Cincinnati and it's the same thing. For eight days you haven't had a decent night's sleep. And they talk about tough conditions today!

But hell, if you wanted to play ball, you played ball, no matter what conditions were like. And I guess you can tolerate almost anything as long as you don't know how much better it can be.

That 1938 pennant race was a pip. We were battling it out with the Pirates. It was brutally close, the kind of race where you knew somebody was going to go home after the season and think all winter about that one bad break or that one good break, depending on which side you were on. And, boy, that's just what happened.

There were just a few games left to play, and the Pirates came into Chicago for a three-game series, leading us by a game and a half. This was do or die, no question about it.

Gabby Hartnett was our manager, and he took a gamble in the first game. He started Dean. Dizzy's arm was gone; all he could throw were curves and changes. But he had guts. And he pitched one hell of a ball game for us. He had them shut out until the ninth, 2–0. Then they got a man on, and Lee Handley doubled with two out, putting the tying runs on. Al Todd was the batter. Hartnett had a tough decision to make right then and there: Leave Diz in or take him out? Well, he took him out and brought in Bill Lee. Bill had been just marvelous for us coming down the stretch. But Lee's first pitch was wild, and a run came in. You could almost hear the second-guessers cranking up. But Lee bore down and struck Todd out. One of the most beautiful strikeouts I've ever seen. That left us just a half game out, and set the stage for the next day. They're still talking about what happened that next day. Whenever you're talking about baseball's great moments, you've got to include what happened in that game.

We came into the bottom of the ninth tied, 3–3. Mace Brown

was on the mound for the Pirates. He was their ace relief pitcher, and a real good one. It had been a drawn-out game, and by the time we came into the last of the ninth it was pretty dark, and it was obvious this was going to be the last inning. The Pirates were, in effect, playing for a tie at that point.

Brown got the first two men out, and then Hartnett was the batter. It was getting darker by the minute, and it looked for sure like we were going to have to play a doubleheader the next day, which would have put us in a bind because we were short on pitchers.

Brown got two strikes on Hartnett, and we were getting ready to go to the clubhouse. Then Brown threw the next pitch, and he came right in with it. I don't know why he didn't waste one; maybe he figured it was so dark Hartnett couldn't see it anyway. But Gabby swung and rode it right out of there. You never saw such excitement in a ball park! The fans came pouring out onto the field, and it seemed to take Hartnett forever to get around the bases. He had to fight his way through to touch third and then fight his way through to touch home plate.

Well, that broke Pittsburgh's back. We went out the next day, and we could've beaten nine Babe Ruths. We beat them by something like 10–1. They were totally demoralized, even though technically they were still in the race. If they'd won that last game, they would have left town a half game ahead. But their backs were broken. That sort of thing can happen to a team, any team, big league or not. What it does, most of the time, is upset you badly for two or three days, and when it happens late in the season, you just don't have the time to recover.

You know, the Cubs had this odd pattern of winning pennants every three years. They won it in 1929—I wasn't there then—1932, 1935, and 1938. Well, they didn't win it in 1941, but I got into the World Series just the same. I was traded over to the Dodgers soon after the season opened in 1941.

I was surprised by the deal, but maybe I shouldn't have been. I wasn't a kid anymore, and at that particular time the Cubs had a young second baseman they'd brought up from the Coast League, named Lou Stringer. He had a great spring training, and they thought he was going to be a fine ballplayer. So they figured I was expendable.

We were in New York at the time, at the Commodore Hotel. I remember Larry MacPhail called me at two thirty in the morning.

"I've just made a deal for you," he said.

"At two thirty in the morning?" I asked.

"What's the difference?" he said.

The Cubs were playing the Giants, and the Pirates were playing the Dodgers. So I got my gear out of the Polo Grounds and went over to Ebbets Field. I got four for four my first game.

I walked right into a real hot pennant race with the Dodgers. We fought the Cardinals all summer. I remember we went into St. Louis late in the year—every damned game that year seemed crucial—and we just had to beat them. Another one of those head-on collisions, when it's all on the table. The opening game of that series was just unforgettable. One of the greatest ball games I ever played in. Whitlow Wyatt was pitching for us against Mort Cooper. There was no score going into the eighth inning, and on top of it Cooper was pitching a no-hitter. Then, with two out, Dixie Walker hit a double, and I came up. Boy, you really want a base hit in a spot like that! We needed that game, and I hated to see Wyatt lose after the way he'd pitched. Well, Cooper gave me a pitch to hit, and I busted it for a double to score Dixie. That was the only run of the game. I'll remember that game as long as I live.

But I guess I didn't have much luck in World Series. Three with the Cubs, and three losers; and then another loser with the Dodgers, in '41. I'll tell you what happened to me in that Series. It was a very odd thing, something I'd never had happen to me before. We were taking batting practice before the third game, in Brooklyn. I was practicing hitting the ball to right field, and on my last cut I swung kind of awkwardly and pulled a rib cage muscle. The pain just rushed into me; I could hardly breathe. I went into the clubhouse, and they taped me up, but I was in a lot of pain. Still, I was determined to play. The last thing in the world you want to do is sit out a World Series. I came up to bat in the bottom of the first inning and hit the ball well, but I almost collapsed from the pain. I had to leave the game, and I was pretty much finished for the Series.

That was the game where Fred Fitzsimmons had the Yankees shut out into the seventh. Then Marius Russo hit one back off Fred's knee and made him leave the game. Hugh Casey came in, got nicked for a couple, and we lost, 2–1. The fourth game was the one where Mickey Owen let the third strike get away from him.

You've probably heard all kinds of stories about what happened there. Was it a spitter? Did Casey cross Mickey up? Well, Casey swore it was a curveball. I think Owen might have "nonchalanted" the ball, putting his glove out for it instead of shifting his whole body to make the catch. Owen had a habit of doing that, and maybe that's what happened there. And the ball got away. But let's give the Yankees some credit, too. They jumped right in and took advantage of the break. They had the type of club in those days that wouldn't let you up once you were down. And we stayed down, too. We were licked before we went out on the field the next day. We couldn't have beaten a girls' team.

Say, listen, can we skip 1942? People ask me what went wrong in 1942, and I say to them: "What went wrong? We won a hundred and four games, didn't we? That's pretty damned good, isn't it?" You bet your life that was pretty damned good. The only problem was, the Cardinals won 106.

That was some season, beginning with spring training. We took spring training in Havana that year. We had a lot of hell raisers on that club. It was a wild time. Why, MacPhail had detectives trailing some of the guys.

You know, Ernest Hemingway lived in Havana at that time, and I spent a night with him I'll never forget. Hemingway liked to hang around with ballplayers, and one day he invited a few of us out to this gun club where he and his wife were members. Hemingway took a lot of pride in all this manly stuff, guns and boozing and fighting, things like that. He was a big, brawny man, and when he'd had a few drinks, he got mean, real mean.

So he invited Hugh Casey, Larry French, Augie Galan, and myself out to the gun club. Believe me, this was no Coney Island shooting gallery. It was a real fancy place. You had a guy with a portable bar following you around. You'd get up, take your shots, and there'd be a drink ready for you. This went on from three o'clock in the afternoon until dark. At that point Hemingway said, "Ah, the hell with this. Come on up to the house, and let's have a few drinks."

So we all went up to his house. He had a big beautiful home. He took us into a huge dining room-living room combination, with all terrazzo floors, and told us to make ourselves comfortable while he went and got the drinks.

He came back with an enormous silver tray, with all the bottles, the mixers, the glasses, the ice—the whole works. He set it up on this little bookstand in the middle of the floor. And we started drinking. Hemingway was a real great host. He couldn't do enough for you. He gave us each an autographed copy of *For Whom the Bell Tolls,* his book about the Spanish Civil War.

We talked a lot about the war. The war had just started, in December, and this was in March. Hemingway started talking about the Japanese and how far they were going to go. And you know, events proved him right. He said they were going to go down the Malay Peninsula, that they were going to take Burma, and this island and that island. He'd been a foreign correspondent in different parts of the world and knew a hell of a lot about a lot of things, and it was fascinating.

We had quite a bit to drink; then he laid out some food. After we ate, we had a few more drinks. It was getting pretty late now, and Mrs. Hemingway excused herself and went to bed. Hemingway was good and loaded by this time.

Now Hugh Casey was a very quiet man, and he wasn't saying much. Hugh never said much. But he was a drinker. I'd say that of everybody in the room, Hugh and Hemingway were feeling the best. But everything was still serious, with talk about the war and one thing and another. Then out of a clear blue sky Hemingway looked over at Casey, sort of sizing him up. Hemingway had this funny little grin; I assumed it was friendly, but then it might not have been.

"You know, Hugh," he said, "you and I are about the same size. We'd make a good match."

Casey just grinned.

"Come on," Hemingway said. "I've got some boxing gloves. Let's just spar. Fool around a little bit."

Casey grinned and shrugged his shoulders. Hemingway went and got the boxing gloves. He came back and slipped on a pair of gloves and handed Casey the other pair. As Hugh was pulling his gloves on, Hemingway suddenly hauled off and belted him. He hit him hard, too. He knocked Casey into that bookstand and there goes the tray with all the booze and glasses smashing over the terrazzo floor. It must have echoed all through the house because Hemingway's wife came running out.

"What happened?" she asked.

"Oh, it's all right, honey," he said. "Hughie and I are just having a little fun. You go on back to bed."

She looked at him, looked at Casey, looked at the mess on the floor, and then went back to bed.

Casey didn't say anything about the sneak punch. He just got up and finished putting his gloves on. Then they started sparring. Hemingway didn't bother to pick up the tray or anything, and they were moving back and forth across the broken glass and you could hear it cracking and crunching on the terrazzo floor whenever they stepped on it.

Boom, Casey starts hitting him. And hitting him. Then Casey started knocking him down. Hemingway didn't like that at all. Then Casey belted him across some furniture, and there was another crash as Hemingway took a lamp and table down with him. The wife came running out again, and Hemingway told her it was all right, to go back to bed, that it was all in fun. She went away, but this time she was looking a little bit doubtful about the whole thing.

Hemingway was getting sore. He'd no sooner get up than Hugh would put him down again. Finally he got up this one time, and made a feint with his left hand, and kicked Casey in the balls.

That's when we figured it had gone far enough. We made them take the gloves off. Then everything was all right.

"Let's have another drink," Hemingway said.

But it was getting very late now; we had to be back at the hotel at twelve o'clock. We told him that.

"Well," he said, "I'm too drunk to drive you back to Havana. I'll have my chauffeur drive you."

As we were going to the door, he grabbed Casey by the arm.

"Look," Hemingway said, "you stay here. The chauffeur'll take them. You stay here. Spend the night. Tonight we're both drunk. But tomorrow morning we'll wake up, we'll both be sober. Then you and me will have a duel. We'll use swords, pistols, whatever you want. You pick it." And he's dead serious about it. He wanted to kill Casey. Hughie'd got the better of him, and Hemingway wanted to kill him.

"Unh-unh," Casey said, shaking his head. He didn't want any part of it. So we left.

The next day Hemingway's wife brought him down to the ball park. You never saw a man so embarrassed, so ashamed. He apologized to everybody. "Don't know what got into me," he said. Well, I can tell you what got into him. About a quart.

Yeah, that was one hell of a spring we had in Havana in '42. When we got back to Daytona Beach to finish training, Mac-Phail called us together in the clubhouse for a meeting. He's got a sheaf of papers in his hand.

"Gentlemen," he said in an icy tone of voice, "I'd like to read you something."

What he had there were the reports from the detectives. You never saw so many faces turn red. Oh, that was quite a crew. Johnny Allen was with us then. There was a wild man. And mean. Hemingway was lucky he didn't ask Allen to stay for a duel. Johnny would have hung around for it.

Later that year, MacPhail called another meeting, around the middle of August. We had about an eight- or ten-game lead over the Cardinals, and I guess we were feeling pretty good about ourselves. But MacPhail called this meeting in the Dodger clubhouse one night.

"You guys are not going to win this," he said.

We could hardly believe what he was saying. I think it was Dixie Walker who spoke up.

"What the hell are you talking about, Larry?" he said. "We've got an eight-game lead."

"I know," MacPhail said. "But you're not going to win it. You're just going to have to play outstanding ball, or else the Cardinals are going to catch you and beat you."

Well, we didn't know whether MacPhail had had a few drinks or was just trying to needle us or what. But by God, he was right. Of course, we won 104 games, but the Cardinals won 106. You couldn't stop them. They just kept on coming. There was one point, late in the season, when we won six or seven in a row and *lost* ground. The Cardinals took eight or nine in a row over the same stretch.

It was a wild year all around. We had some wicked throwing contests. I remember one particular time. See, when I was traded from Chicago to Brooklyn, Jimmie Wilson, who was managing the Cubs at the time, made some remarks about me. He said that I was all through and that I wouldn't help the Dodgers. But I had a good year, and I guess he felt that made him look bad.

We were in Chicago one day, and Wilson had a fellow named Bithorn pitching and a fellow named Hernandez catching. Two Latins. That was the battery. I came up to the plate, and Wilson starts hollering from the dugout for them to knock me down. But they wouldn't do it. Bithorn throws one pitch to me, which is outside, and Wilson stops the game. He walks to the mound and takes Bithorn out and brings in this big Paul Erickson, who threw bullets. And then he puts in Clyde Mc-Cullough to catch. I mean, he's really determined to get me knocked down.

The game starts up again, and I step in.

"Well, Willie boy," McCullough says to me, "you know what they made this change for, don't you?"

"Sure, I know," I said.

So that goddamned Erickson, the first pitch he throws is right at my head. I don't know which way to go. Finally I go out across the plate and the ball whistles behind me. The next pitch is the same identical thing, and out over the plate I go again. So now it's three and nothing. I look down at Dressen, who's coaching third base, and they're going to let me hit three and nothing. Now, that seldom happened to me—I wasn't a power hitter. I guess they knew how goddamned mad I was.

So now he's got to throw a strike, and he does—and I hit it right out of the ball park. Three and nothing, and I hit a home run after they threw at me twice. That was one of the sweetest hits I ever got.

Talk about sweet hits, though, I was directly involved in one that somebody else got. Ted Williams has said a number of times that one of the greatest thrills he ever had in baseball was hitting the home run that won the 1941 All-Star game. Well, I can remember that home run as vividly as Ted, but for a different reason.

That game was played in Detroit, in Briggs Stadium, and we were leading, 5–3, going into the last of the ninth. I was playing second base for the National League. The first batter went out. Then Ken Keltner got a hit, and Joe Gordon got a hit. Cecil Travis drew a walk, filling the bases. The next two batters were Joe DiMaggio and Ted Williams. Interesting situation, huh? Claude Passeau was pitching and he was a good one, and a tough competitor. Well, he got DiMaggio to hit it on the ground to Eddie Miller at short. It should have been a double play, ending the game. Miller played the ball cleanly over to me, but I made a poor throw, pulling the first baseman off the bag. Now a lot of people said that Travis slid in there hard and made me hurry my throw. But that's not true. I simply made a bad throw. So instead of the double play and the game being over, Williams got the chance to hit. And he hit that home run. You know, if you talk about the most famous home runs in baseball history, I was there for three of them: the one Ruth supposedly called in the '32 Series, Hartnett's home run in the twilight, and Williams'. I guess the only one I missed was Bobby Thomson's.

What's the funniest thing I ever saw on a baseball field? Well, I've been in baseball for forty-five years, so that's a tough one. Funny things aren't supposed to happen on a ball field, are they? But they do, of course. I can tell you what happened in St. Louis one day. I was with Brooklyn then. It was in either '41 or '42. We were playing the Cardinals and getting the hell beat out of us, by something like 14–2. We're looking terrible. Durocher is so goddamned mad he can't see. He's sitting in the corner of the dugout, right up against the stone wall. That wall jutted out a few feet and behind it were the box seats. I happened to be sitting next to him.

Well, a photographer comes over and wants to take Leo's picture. Leo's hardly in the mood and waves him off. But the guy stays there.

"Get away," Leo says. "Get the hell away."

But the guy doesn't move. He wants to get his picture. So Leo mutters something and reaches up into the bat rack and pulls out one of those Louisville Sluggers, and the minute he does that, the photographer ducks behind that stone wall, out of sight.

Well, why Durocher didn't put the bat back I don't know. But he held onto it. He's sitting there, gripping the bat handle in his hands. The next thing I know, out of the corner of my eye I see the lens of this camera coming around the wall. The guy is going to try and sneak a picture. Leo see it too. He looked at me, and he was just speechless he was so mad. The guy kept edging the camera out further and further. Suddenly Leo jumps up and swings the bat right into the camera, breaking the damn thing into pieces. The guy took off running, and Leo throws the bat after him, cursing and yelling.

Leo was a character. He was all business on that field, though. He was a good baseball man, a fine baseball man. But, like I say, a character, a real individualist. You just *knew* he wasn't going to get along with Bobo Newsom. Bobo was with us for a while in '42 and '43. He was a colorful guy in his own right.

Around midseason in '43 we were playing a ball game and Bobby Bragan was catching. Now Bobby had just recently made the switch from infielder and wasn't too adept behind the plate. There was a real tough situation, and Bobo throws a good pitch, a strike, and it gets by Bragan and we lose the ball game. Now, here's the thing about Newsom. Durocher had a real sharp tongue. Well, so did Newsom. He was quick and witty, and he always had an answer. (I guess it wasn't always the right answer—he was traded about fifteen times in his career.) After the game Durocher said something to him— I don't know exactly what it was—and Bobo answered him back. They got into a big argument, and Durocher fined and suspended him.

The next morning I was having breakfast together with Galan and Arky Vaughan at the New Yorker Hotel, where we were staying. Vaughan, you know, was a guy who always had everybody's respect, as a ballplayer and as a man. He never said too much, but everybody admired and respected him.

Arky's reading the paper. Durocher had given an interview saying that Newsom had crossed Bragan up, giving him a spitball, and that was why Bobo was suspended. But it had been building up, you see. Newsom had been getting to Durocher for weeks, throwing cutting little remarks at him. Bobo didn't mean any harm, but Leo was getting madder and madder. So finally he had a chance to stick it to Bobo, and he did.

So Vaughan's reading this, and he's very quiet, not saying anything to anybody. But something's bothering him, we could tell. So we go to the ball park. Durocher isn't there yet. We put on our uniforms and went out and loosened up. After batting practice we all went back to the clubhouse. By this time Durocher is in his office.

Well, Arky had been waiting all this time to ask Durocher if he'd been quoted correctly. He goes into the office, with a newspaper in his hand.

"Leo," he said, "did you tell this to the writers?"

"Yeah," Durocher said, "I told them that."

Arky didn't say another word. He went back to his locker and took off his uniform—pants, blouse, socks, cap—made a big bundle out of it and went back to the office.

"Take this uniform," he said, "and shove it right up your ass." And he threw it in Durocher's face. "If you would lie about Bobo," he said, "then you would lie about me and everybody else. I'm not playing for you."

Well, then everybody decides not to play. All of a sudden we're on strike. Finally, about ten minutes before game time Durocher is running around telling everybody it's going to be straightened out and asking them if they would play. A few of the guys started to relent, and he finally got nine men. But no Vaughan. Arky wouldn't play.

Around the seventh inning Branch Rickey—he was running the club then—came down to the clubhouse. Vaughan was still sitting there. Rickey started to work on him. He told Arky that he understood the situation, that he could sympathize, and one thing and another. Rickey could be very persuasive when he wanted to. But Vaughan wouldn't budge. Then Rickey said, "All I want you to do is put on your uniform, go out and sit on the bench for a few minutes and then come back. If you don't at least make an appearance, we'll have to discipline you. We'll have no alternative." Finally Vaughan agreed. He put on his uniform, walked into the dugout, and then turned around and walked right back out again.

Well, they straightened it out as best they could. I think they rescinded the action against Bobo. But it seemed to me like they got rid of Newsom pretty quick after that.

Leo was always fiery. A great baseball man, and he kept you on your toes. But sometimes he could really irritate you. One day we were playing the Giants in Brooklyn. This was in 1943. Some of our better players had gone into the service, and I had become our fourth place hitter, which I'd never been. We got down to about the sixth inning, and we loaded the bases with one out, trailing by a run or two. I come up. The cleanup hitter now. The count goes to two and nothing. I look down to Charley Dressen, and he's giving me the take sign. Well, you don't take in a situation like that. But the sign was out, and I had to take. It was a strike. The next pitch is outside, and now it's three and one. I look down at Dressen again, and again it's the take sign. Boy, by this time I'm boiling. Hell, I was hitting around .330, and he's got me batting fourth. So I take again, and it's a strike. Full count now. The next pitch comes in, and I whale it—a line shot right at the third baseman, and boom, it's a double play. The inning's over, and now I'm really mad. I'm steaming.

I went out to my position, and Camilli is rolling the ball around the infield to us. He throws it to me, and I pick it up, and as I do, I see Durocher sitting on the bench with his chin in his hand, looking down. Well, I don't know what possessed me, but instead of throwing to Camilli, I fired it toward the dugout as hard as I could. It skipped off the grass in front of the dugout and hit Durocher square in the forehead. Down he goes, headfirst, right out on the floor of the dugout.

Albie Glossop, who was playing shortstop, yells over to me, "Goddamn, you hit Durocher. Right between the eyes."

"That's exactly where I was aiming," I said.

Well, I figured I'm in for a good healthy fine. Leo gets up and goes to the ice bucket, takes out a big piece of ice, wraps it in a towel, and for the rest of that inning he's sitting there holding that ice up against his head. When the inning's over, I come in and sit down, not next to him, but not too far away either. I figured I'm going to get it now. But he didn't say anything. Not a word. He never said a word about it. So I got to thinking he believed it was an accident, that he didn't even know who had thrown it.

I went into the service after that season and didn't come back until spring training of 1946. Three years later. We were all in the clubhouse one morning, suiting up, getting ready to go out on the field. Durocher and Herman Franks, who were good friends, were clowning around down at the other end of the clubhouse, and all of a sudden Franks says, "Hey, Leo, do you remember the time you got hit between the eyes sitting on the bench in Brooklyn?" I was buttoning up my shirt, and I had to pause and smile; I hadn't thought of that in years. And then I hear Leo say, "Yeah. That goddamned Herman."

That was the first time I realized that Leo had known where that ball came from. But, goddamn, he'd never said a word about it. How do you figure a guy like that?

JAMES "COOL PAPA" BELL

JAMES BELL
Born: 1903, Starkville, Mississippi

James "Cool Papa" Bell was for more than two decades a star of the Negro Leagues. Considered by many one of the game's all-time ranking center fielders, a peer of Speaker, Mays, and DiMaggio, Bell's speed and baserunning feats were legendary. It was commonplace for him to score from second base on fly balls and groundouts. Kept from his true place as a major league star because of the color barrier, Bell played baseball all over the United States, as well as in Mexico, Cuba, the Dominican Republic, and Puerto Rico, for nearly thirty years.

In 1974 Bell's extraordinary talents were given belated recognition by organized baseball when he was inducted into the Hall of Fame at Cooperstown.

Of course, most of the time nobody kept any records, so I don't know what my lifetime batting average is. Nobody knows. If I had to guess, I'd say around .340 or .350. I batted .437 one year in the Mexican League. I batted .407 in 1944, .411 in 1946. I played twenty-nine years of baseball, and the lowest I ever batted was .306, in 1945. Other than that it was .340 on up to .400. That's twenty-nine seasons, 1922 through 1950. Plus twenty-one winter seasons. That makes a total of fifty seasons. That's the way you have to count it, by seasons.

I was born in Starkville, Mississippi, in 1903; at least that's what I always figured, because that's what I was told. See, in Jackson, Mississippi, they've got two different ages for me. They didn't keep good age records back then. I went by what my mother told me, and she said it was 1903.

I started playing ball as soon as I could, just like the average kid. Everybody played baseball; there were neighborhood teams, but no uniforms or anything like that.

My mother always said that when we got old enough to work, she would send us away from Starkville because she didn't want us to come up the way she came up. She wanted us to try to get the best education we could. We didn't have a high school in Starkville, which meant I wasn't going to get much education there. So she sent me to St. Louis, in 1920.

I had brothers already living in St. Louis, you see, which is why she sent me there. I told my mother I'd go to school, but once I got to the big city, there was so much going on I didn't have time for school. So I hired on at the packinghouse, at fifty-three cents an hour. It was my first job in St. Louis.

I had five brothers, all good athletes. When I got to St. Louis, four of them were playing with a semipro team, the Compton Hill Cubs. I joined up with them, as a left-hand pitcher. I didn't have any trouble making the team; I'd been playing ball with grown men since I was thirteen. I never had trouble making any team, as a matter of fact.

I was a pretty good pitcher, but I wanted to play every day. I was with the Cubs about a year and a half, playing Sundays and holidays and during the week working in the packinghouse.

Then one day I pitched a good game against the St. Louis Stars, a professional team with a lot of first-rate ballplayers. A few nights later my brother, who owned a restaurant, said to me, "The manager of the St. Louis Stars was over here. Wants you to play ball."

Well, that sounded pretty good to me. But my mother and my sister didn't want me to play professional baseball. My sister wrote home to my mother and said I was going to play ball and leave St. Louis and they wouldn't see me anymore. But my brother said, "Now look, you go ahead on and play. It doesn't matter if you make a whole lot of money or not. You can live here when you're in St. Louis and don't worry about the rent, and you can eat here, too. Just so you can say you played pro ball."

So I went with the Stars and pitched for them for two years, making $90 a month. Then they switched me to the outfield. See, every time I pitched I'd get two or three hits. Some of the older fellows on the team told me I should be playing every day, and then the manager got the same idea. That was in 1924.

We played five days a week. We were in what they called the Western League, and we played against Chicago, Indianapolis, Detroit, Kansas City, Cleveland, Dayton, and Toledo. Then there was an Eastern League, with teams in the East. It was on the same basis as the white major leagues, only it was a lower scale. But the fields were pretty good, and in 1928 or '29 we installed lights, years before the major leagues did. We drew crowds of 3,000 to 5,000, and more than that once we got the lights.

When I started, they thought I was going to be afraid playing in front of big crowds, because I was a country boy. When I joined the team, Gatewood, the manager, said to me, "We're going on the road for a month. Now you just watch everything. You got a lot to learn."

Our first stop was Indianapolis. They beat us three games. So Gatewood said, "What the heck, I'd just as soon put you in there. But don't be afraid. Don't pay any attention to the crowd."

We got a big lead in the fourth game, and he put me in to pitch the last two innings. I struck a couple of them out, and some of the fellows said, "Hey, that kid's mighty cool. He takes everything cool."

So they started calling me Cool. When I'd go in, they'd yell, "C'mon, Cool," like that. But that didn't sound right. That's not enough of a name, they said, got to put something else on it. They added Papa to it and started calling me Cool Papa. That's where it came from. In 1922.

I was with the Stars from 1922 through 1931. Then the league broke up and I went with the Homestead Grays in Pittsburgh. I played with them in part of 1932, but then they stopped paying us. That was the worst of the Depression then, 1932. So I moved from there to the Kansas City Monarchs and finished the season with them. No salary there either. We were on percentage, barnstorming around. We wound up playing in Mexico City that winter, but still hardly making any money.

In the Negro Leagues the audience was mixed but mostly colored. Even down South there were some white people at the games. When we played the Birmingham Black Barons in their park, there were always lots of whites in the crowd, but they were separated by a rope. You could be sitting right next to a white man, but that rope was always there. That was the system they had in those days. That's what they called states' rights. States' rights doesn't mean much to the Negro. You don't get justice with states' rights. Which is a bad thing to happen.

In 1933 I joined the Pittsburgh Crawfords and stayed with them four years. Left there in 1937 to go to the Dominican Republic. Remember Trujillo, the dictator? He was killed a few years ago, you know. Well, they were fixin' to do that back in 1937. But they like baseball down there and they were having championship games, and they said if he would win, they would keep him in office.

So Trujillo got a lot of boys from the States, as well as from Cuba and Panama and Puerto Rico. Mostly he wanted Satchel Paige. We were down in New Orleans in spring training in 1937 and Trujillo's men came there to get Satchel. But he didn't want to go. He kept ducking them for three or four days, but finally one day they trailed him to the hotel and came in looking for him—leaving their chauffeur out in the car. Paige slipped out the side door and jumped in his car to try to get away, but they crossed their car over the street and blocked it.

They told him they wanted him to go down there, and he said he didn't want to go. See, he'd just jumped his team in North Dakota the year before, and everybody was still mad at him, and he didn't want to jump again. That's why he was ducking them. But they showed him a lot of money, offered him a big salary, and he jumped again and went to the Dominican Republic.

But even with Satchel they needed some more ballplayers, because they were losing. So they asked him to send back and get some players from the Negro Leagues. He called Pittsburgh, when I was with the Crawfords. Now, I never did jump nowhere unless something was going bad, and that year it was going bad. The owner of the Crawfords was losing money, and he was giving us ballplayers a tough time, not paying us. Matter of fact, the whole league was going bad at that time. So I was *looking* for somewhere to go when Satchel called.

"We're in trouble down here," he said. "We're supposed to

win this championship. I want you and some of the boys to come down. They'll give you eight hundred dollars, your transportation, and all your expenses for six weeks. Will you do it?"

"No," I said. "But make it a thousand and I'll say yes."

Satchel put the head man on the phone, and he said okay, he'd give us each $1,000. Then I said how about us getting some of the money before we get there.

"No," he said, "we can't do that."

"I have to have *something* before I leave," I said.

He said he would talk to his people about it and call us back. When he called back, he said, "Okay, we'll give you half of it in Miami, before you get here. We'll have the consul in Miami meet your plane on your way down, and he'll give each of you five hundred dollars."

They sent us the tickets, and we went to Miami. This man met us at the airport, and he took us to a restaurant. He never mentioned money, and he sure didn't look like he had any on him. But after we ate, he finally gave each of us the $500.

When we got to the Dominican Republic, we went to San Pedro de Macoris—about 40 miles from Santo Domingo— which is the little town they kept the ball club in. And there was Satchel. Boy, was he happy to see us.

They kept us under guard at a private club. Had a head man there with us all the time, with a .45 pistol. We were allowed out on only two days of the week. They said they were going to kill Trujillo if we didn't win.

The best team there was Santiago, and we beat them, finally, and we won the championship. We won it the last day of the season. I guess we saved Trujillo's life, but the people finally got rid of him later.

Then from 1938 through 1941 I played in Mexico, first with Tampico, then with Torreón. In 1942 I came back to the United States and played with the Chicago American Giants.

In 1943 the Giants wouldn't give me the money they'd promised me the year before, and at the same time the Memphis team wanted me. The owner of the Memphis team told me to come there; he promised to pay my way down. But when I got there, he said, "No, I never pay transportation for no ballplayers." And then he said, "Also, I have to fix your teeth. All my ballplayers have got to have their teeth fixed."

"There's nothing wrong with my teeth," I said.

"Yes, there is," he said.

See, besides owning the ball club, he was a dentist. All his players had to have their teeth fixed by him. Then he'd take his pay out of their salary.

"Look," I said, "it don't seem like we're gonna get along here. If this is the way you run your team, then I'm going home."

The Homestead Grays had been trying to get me, and I got in touch with them. So they started fighting over my contract. But that didn't mean anything. We always had contracts, but they didn't mean much. They wouldn't pay you your money, and that was that. You'd just go somewhere else.

In those days, the thirties, after the big-league season was over, the major leaguers would go barnstorming. We played against all of them. In 1931 Max Carey brought a team to St. Louis to play us. Bill Walker—he'd had a great year with the Giants—was scheduled to pitch the first game. We knocked him out in the very first inning. We beat 'em about 18–3. They had a good team, too: O'Neill catching, Bill Terry at first, Durocher at short, Wally Berger and the two Waner boys in the outfield, and some others I can't remember.

We played a team of big leaguers in 1929, with Charlie Gehringer on it. He was one of the best ballplayers I ever saw. That was a good team we played against. They had O'Neill and Wally Schang catching, Art Shires playing first base, Gehringer at second, Red Kress at short, Manush, Simmons, and Bing Miller in the outfield, Willis Hudlin, Bob Quinn, Earl Whitehill, and George Uhle pitching. We won six out of eight. Gehringer was the only one who looked good. He was some ballplayer.

Here's the thing. In a short series we could beat those guys. In a whole summer, with the team we had, we couldn't. We only had fourteen or fifteen men to a team. We'd play about 130 league games, and *another* 130 exhibition games. Anywhere from 250 to 300 games a season.

Later on there were those famous games where Satchel pitched against Dizzy Dean. I was in center field most all of those games. Dean was a good pitcher, no mistake about that. The feature for those games was always Paige and Dean. Nobody else got any publicity.

Dean beat us a game in New York broke our heart. We had beaten them four in a row, and we went to New York, and everybody said we couldn't do it again. Dean shut us out, 3–0, at Yankee Stadium.

There was a play that day I still remember. I was on second, and Josh Gibson was up. He hit one on a line way back in deep center field. Jimmy Ripple caught it, and I tagged up and rounded third and came all the way home. The ball came in to the catcher—Mike Ryba—the same time I did, but high, and I slid in under it before he came down with the tag. And the umpire said, "Out!" I said I was safe, but the umpire laughed, and said, "I'm not gonna let you do that on major leaguers. Maybe you can do that in *your* league, but not against major leaguers."

Heck, I often scored from second on a long outfield fly.

We went from there to York, Pennsylvania. Dizzy was supposed to pitch. They had guaranteed him $350, but the people were kind of slow coming in, so the man in charge decided to hold the game up a while till the crowd got bigger. Dizzy said he wouldn't pitch a ball until he got his $350. I was told he was afraid the receipts wouldn't cover his guarantee.

Finally the crowd got a little bigger, though not by much. The promoter came to us and said, "Look, you boys play here several times a year. All we've taken in is a little more than I've already promised Dean. Would you play anyway?"

So we said, "Okay, we're here, so we might as well."

Then Dizzy came into the clubhouse and said, "Listen, don't you all hit me. I just pitched Sunday, and my arm is still tired. So don't hit me, y'hear." He wanted to look good, you know.

Sure, Diz, we told him. Then we went out and got four runs the first inning. First three men got on, and Gibson hit a home run, and the score was 4–0 before Dean knew what happened. Then four more in the second inning. People were booing and everything. Dizzy wouldn't pitch anymore, and he went to play second base, which he couldn't do very well.

We wound up winning by a big score, and all we got was about $7 apiece, while Dean got his $350.

It was rough barnstorming. We traveled by bus, you see. You'd be surprised at the conditions we played under. We would frequently play two and three games a day. We'd play a twilight game, ride 40 miles, and play another game, under the lights. This was in the 1940's. On Sundays you'd play three games—a doubleheader in one town and a single night game in another. Or three single games in three different towns. One game would start about one o'clock, a second about four, and a third at about eight. Three different towns, mind you. Same uniform all day, too. We'd change socks and sweat shirts, but that's about all. When you got to the town, they'd be waiting for you, and all you'd have time to do would be to warm your pitcher up. Many a time I put on my uniform at eight o'clock in the morning and wouldn't take it off till three or four the next morning.

Every night they'd have to find us places to stay if we weren't in a big city up North. Some of the towns had hotels where they'd take us. Colored hotels. Never a mixed hotel. In New York we'd stay at the Theresa, in Harlem, or the Woodside. In the larger cities in the South we'd stay at colored hotels. In smaller towns we'd stay at rooming houses or with private families, some of us in each house.

You could stay better in small towns in the South than you could in the North, because in a small town in the North you most of the time don't find many colored people living there. And those that are there have no extra rooms. But in a small town in the South there are enough colored people living there so you can find room in their homes.

Once we were going from Monroe, Louisiana, to New Orleans. We had to cross the bridge over the river at Vicksburg, Mississippi. We were planning to eat lunch at a little town called Picayune. We stopped at a colored restaurant and asked if they had any food.

"Oh, not for all those men," they said. "It'll take us too long to fix food for all those men." It was spring training, and we had about twenty-five men.

When the restaurant people went outside and looked at our bus standing there, they said, "Say, whose bus is this? Any white boys in it?"

"No," we said.

"Who owns it?"

"We have an owner."

"Is he white or colored?"

"Colored."

"And all these boys on the bus are colored?"

"Yeah," we said.

"Well," they said, "you all better get out of the state of Mississippi quick as you can."

"Why?"

" 'Cause if you don't, they gonna take this bus and all you guys in it and put you all working on that farm out there. They need farm workers real bad. There's a lot of people now out there on the farm they caught passing through. They jail 'em for speeding and put 'em to serving their sentence out on that farm."

So we got back on the bus and drove straight through till we were out of the state of Mississippi.

When I was manager of the Kansas City Monarchs' farm team, we played a lot against the House of David. That was in 1948, '49, '50. They had a lot of ex-minor- and -major-league players on their teams. They had to wear a beard. We barnstormed with them through California, Colorado, Nebraska, Iowa, North and South Dakota, and Canada.

We met a lot of good people, but also a lot that weren't so good. Some of them wanted to be good. All the people that you see that say, "I don't want you to do this or that"—they aren't bad people, they're worried people a lot of time, worried about the public. When we traveled with the House of David, they had no trouble finding accommodations, so they had all their reservations made out before the season started. But we had to go to places where we never did know whether we could sleep. Most of the time we'd stay in these cabins on the edge of town. They call them motels today, but in those days they called them cabins.

We went into a lot of small towns where they'd never seen a colored person. In some of those places we couldn't find anyplace to sleep, so we slept on the bus. If we had to, we could convert the seats into beds. We'd just pull over to the side of the road, in a cornfield or someplace, and sleep until the break of day, and then we'd go on into the next town, hoping we'd find a restaurant that would be willing to serve colored people.

All those things we experienced, today people wouldn't believe it. The conditions and the salaries, and what we had to go through. Lots of time for months and months I played on percentage—all of us did—and we'd be lucky to make $5 a game.

But I had a lot of fun in baseball. Saw a lot of great ballplayers. Guys you probably never heard of. Pitcher named Theodore Trent. He'd beat Paige an awful lot of the time. And he never lost a game to a big-league team barnstorming.

When we played Max Carey's all-stars, Trent struck those guys out again and again, with that great curveball he had. One game he struck Bill Terry out four times.

Trent was a great pitcher, but he got TB and died young.

Satchel was the fastest, though. I never saw a pitcher throw harder; you could hardly time him. I've seen Walter Johnson, I've seen Dizzy Dean, Bob Feller, Lefty Grove, all of them. Also Dick Redding and Smokey Joe Williams among our boys. *None* of them threw as hard as Paige at the time I saw them. All he threw for years was that fastball; it'd be by you so fast you could hardly turn. And he had control. He could throw that ball right by your knees all day.

Josh Gibson was a good catcher, but not outstanding. He didn't have good hands, and he wasn't the best receiver, though he had a strong arm. But he was a hitter, one of the greatest you ever saw. The most powerful. Never swung hard at the ball either. Just a short swing. Never swung all the way around. Pretty big man. About 190, 195 pounds. About 6'1". He died when he was only thirty-six.

Ruth used to hit them *high*. Not Gibson. He hit them *straight*. Line drives, but they kept going. His power was to center field, right over the pitcher's head. I played against Foxx, but Gibson hit harder and further more often than Foxx or any other player I ever saw.

But they rate Oscar Charleston the greatest Negro ballplayer of them all. He played outfield and first base. Then there was Buck Leonard, a very powerful hitter, and Judy Johnson, a wonderful third baseman, one of the best ever. So many of them, so many great players.

After I was through playing, I tried to get a coaching or scouting job in organized baseball, but nobody would hire me. The one man who might have given me a job was Bill Veeck, but I never could get to see him. Every time I went to see Mr. Veeck when he had the St. Louis Browns' franchise the people in the front office wouldn't let me in to see him. I'd been in baseball all my life and wanted to stay in it, but nobody wanted me.

But I'm not looking back at the past; I'm looking ahead to the future. I'm not angry at Mississippi or anyplace else. That's the way it was in those days. I pray that we can all live in peace together.

CLYDE SUKEFORTH

CLYDE LEROY SUKEFORTH
Born: November 30, 1901, Washington, Maine
Major-league career: 1926–34, 1945, Cincinnati Reds,
  Brooklyn Dodgers
Lifetime average: .264

Clyde Sukeforth came to the big leagues with the Cincinnati Reds in 1926, and his affiliation with baseball remains intact to this day; he is currently the Atlanta Braves' chief scout for the New England area. Sukeforth's finest season was 1929, when he hit .354.

Well, I've been in baseball for about fifty years now, and it's never been dull. Disappointing sometimes, yes; frustrating sometimes, certainly; and sometimes it's been downright infuriating. But never dull. I've been a player, coach, manager, scout. So I've seen the game from every possible angle.

Cincinnati brought me up from the Manchester club in the New England League at the end of the 1926 season. Cincinnati was pretty much a second-division club in those years. It wasn't the fault of the pitchers, though; we had some good ones. There was Carl Mays, Dolf Luque, Jakie May, Pete Donohue, Eppa Rixey.

Rixey was a great pitcher and a great characater. He's in the Hall of Fame today, of course. One of the fine left-handers. He was a fierce competitor and a hard loser. When he pitched, you didn't have to ask who won the game, all you had to do was look at the clubhouse later. If he'd lost, the place would look like a tornado had gone through it. Chairs would be broken up, tables knocked over, equipment thrown around.

The ball club didn't like that, needless to say, but what were they going to say to Rixey? That fellow was an institution in Cincinnati.

He was an old Southern boy, you know, and I guess he took his history as seriously as he did his baseball. Word got around that you could get his goat by whistling "Marching Through Georgia"—that was one of the songs the Union soldiers sang while they were ripping up the South during the Civil War. One time he was throwing batting practice and some fellow on the other bench started whistling that song at him. Rixey got the ball and fired it right into the dugout at him. Boy, did they scatter in there! Later we were sitting on the bench. Rixey was slouched down, his thumbs in his belt, scowling at the dugout floor.

"Eppa," I said, "why does that song make you so mad?"

He thought about it for a few moments.

"That song doesn't make me mad," he said. "The thing that makes me mad is that they *think* they're making me mad."

Hornsby was in his heyday when I broke in. The greatest hitter of all time, I'd say, or if not, then damn close to it. How did you pitch to him? You pitched and you prayed, was how. There was no way you could fool him. Just look at those averages. When Hornsby stepped into the cage to take batting practice before a game, everything on the field stopped. Everybody turned to watch him swing. And that included the old-timers, the tough old pros. Now that's an impressive tribute, I'd say. And he wasn't what you'd call a popular ballplayer either. Hornsby was a brutally frank man who always spoke his mind. But when he had a bat in his hand, he had nothing but admirers.

In the spring of 1932 I was traded over to the Dodgers. We didn't exactly burn up the league there either. But we had some live ones, like Van Mungo, Lefty O'Doul, Hack Wilson. Hack, you know, holds the National League record for home runs in a season—56, in 1930. Everybody knows that, right? Well, I'll tell you something that everybody doesn't know—he hit 57 that year, except that the record book doesn't show it. He hit one in Cincinnati one day, way up in the seats, hit it so hard that it bounced right back onto the field. The umpire had a bad angle on it and ruled that it had hit the screen and bounced back. I was sitting in the Cincinnati bullpen, and of course, *we* weren't going to say anything. But Hack really hit 57 that year.

Hack didn't look much like a ballplayer. He was stocky and muscular. Looked like a fire plug. Very strong. In fact, he was nicknamed after Hackenschmidt, the wrestler. Nice guy. Wonderful disposition. Easygoing. And I guess something of a playboy. He liked his beer, and occasionally he kept his own hours. He was involved in what I think is one of the best baseball stories ever. It happened in 1934, when Stengel was managing the Dodgers.

We had a pitcher, Boom-Boom Beck. Walter Beck. He was a pretty good pitcher. But he started to have his troubles. He got tattooed a few times, and it got to the point where his job was in jeopardy, and he realized it. Well, he gets what he thinks is probably his final start, in Philadelphia. And they start hitting him. They just kept knocking one after the other off of that right field fence in old Baker Bowl. It looked like a carousel, the way they were going around those bases.

Now, it was a real hot day. A scorcher. Hack was in right field, and maybe he didn't get all the sleep the night before that he should have had. And he's running down those balls one after the other. He'd no more than get into his position before somebody else would tattoo that fence and Hack would have to run it down and fire it into the infield.

Finally Stengel goes out to get Beck. Walter, I guess, feels that he's blown his last chance, and naturally he isn't feeling too happy about it. So when he sees Stengel coming, he takes the ball and in disgust turns and just throws it out against the right field fence. And there's Hack, grateful for a moment's rest, bent over out there with his hands on his knees, staring at the grass, huffing and puffing. All of a sudden he hears that ball hit the fence and takes off after it. Picks it up and fires it into second base.

Perfect peg, too.

I stayed with the Brooklyn organization after my playing days were over. I did some scouting, minor-league managing, coaching, even managed the Dodgers for a couple of games at the beginning of the 1947 season, after Durocher was suspended and before Burt Shotton came in. That was a job I was glad to get *out* of. That wasn't for me. You've got to have the right temperament to manage a big league ball club.

Branch Rickey took over as general manager during the war, and we got along fine. When he moved on to Pittsburgh in 1950, I went with him, to scout for the Pittsburgh organization.

Things were pretty rough in Pittsburgh in the early fifties. We were starving. Didn't have a dime. Couldn't win a ball game. One day during the 1954 season Mr. Rickey called me into his office.

"The Dodgers have just sent Joe Black to Montreal," he said. "Montreal is opening a five-game series with Richmond, in Richmond. I want you to go there and stay until Black pitches. Look him over. We might be able to make a deal for him."

So I went to Richmond. I got out to the ball park early the next evening, wanting to see everything I could. Montreal came out for fielding practice, and here's this baby-faced kid in right field with a real great arm. I mean, a rifle. Outstanding. Naturally you've got to notice that. Well, the game starts, and he isn't playing.

Around the seventh inning Montreal was behind, and who should go up to pinch-hit but this kid? He hits a routine ground ball to shortstop and turns it into a bang-bang play at first base. God, he could run. He could fly. Well, I said to myself, there's a boy who can do two things as well as any man who ever lived. Nobody could throw any better than that, and nobody could run any better than that.

They'd announced his name when he came up to pinch hit, and I made a note of it: Clemente.

The next night I'm out there bright and early, watching batting practice. Up comes Clemente. He's kind of an unorthodox hitter, but he's got the good wrists and the quick bat. Well, the same thing: He doesn't play, except to pinch-hit.

I stay around for five days, and Joe Black hasn't pitched yet. Max Macon was managing the Montreal club. Now I knew Max; he'd played for me when I was managing Montreal. I asked him about Black, and he told me Joe wasn't ready, that he had a little arm trouble, and it was uncertain when he would pitch. I was disappointed, naturally, but by that time I had something else on my mind. You see, Pittsburgh was going to be finishing last, and the National League had the first draft pick that year.

I said to Macon, "Max, I want to ask you a favor."

"What's that?" he asked.

"I want you to take care of our boy Clemente. He's just a young boy, away from home for the first time. Don't let him get into any trouble. Just look after him the same as you would your own boy. Protect him for us, Max," I said, "because he's just as good as on our own club."

Max laughed. "You mean you want *him?*"

I didn't know if he was trying to move me off the trail or not, but I just said, "Do me that favor, Max."

You see, I had found out in the meantime that the Dodgers had signed Clemente for a $10,000 bonus, and at that time there was a thing called the $4,000 bonus rule. Any boy that had signed for more than $4,000 had to go through the draft before he could be taken up to the big leagues—*if* he had been signed to a minor-league contract. The Dodgers had made a critical mistake here. They'd given Clemente the $10,000 and signed him to a Montreal contract instead of protecting him by signing him to a Brooklyn contract and optioning him down. I guess somewhere along the line they realized their mistake and were trying to cover it up by playing Clemente as little as possible.

So I sat down and wrote Mr. Rickey a letter. "You and I will never live long enough," I wrote, "to draft a boy with this kind of ability for $4,000 again. This is something that happens once in a lifetime. Now, if you don't take my word for it, see him for yourself. *But don't lose him.*"

Later in the season we held our draft meeting out at Mr. Rickey's farm just outside Pittsburgh. All the scouts from around the country were there.

"Well, boys," Mr. Rickey said, "we're finishing last, so we've got the first draft choice. Who is it going to be?"

Somebody suggested a pitcher out on the coast. Somebody else said an infielder out of the Southern League. Then he looked at me.

"Clyde, do you have a candidate?"

"Yes, sir," I said as emphatically as I could. "Clemente, with Montreal."

"Any of you other boys seen Clemente?" he asked, looking around.

One fellow spoke up.

"I have," he said. "I didn't like him."

"What didn't you like about him?" Mr. Rickey said.

"I didn't like his arm," the fellow said.

"Clyde," the old man said, "did you see this fellow Clemente throw?"

"I sure did," I said.

"What did you think of his arm?"

"Well," I said, "there's a question in my mind as to whether or not it's better than Furillo's." (Furillo had the best arm in the league at that time.) "It's right in the same class as Furillo's, and it may even be a little bit better."

"I see," Mr. Rickey said. "There seems to be some difference of opinion here. One man doesn't like the arm, while another says it's as good as the best. We'll have to sort this out."

So he sent George Sisler and another scout up to Montreal to see Clemente. I guess they decided he could throw, as well as do a few other things, because they recommended we draft him. That's how the Pirates got Clemente, for $4,000.

I never did get to see Joe Black pitch.

Mr. Rickey sent me out on another assignment which I guess you might describe as memorable. This was in August, 1945. We were still with Brooklyn. He called me into his office one day and told me to have a seat.

"The Kansas City Monarchs are playing the Lincoln Giants in Chicago on Friday night," he said. "I want you to see that game. I want you to see that fellow Robinson on Kansas City. Talk to him before the game. Tell him who sent you. Tell him I want to know if he's got a shortstop's arm, if he can throw from the hole. Ask Robinson to have his coach hit him some balls in the hole."

Mr. Rickey had been talking about establishing a Negro club in New York called the Brooklyn Brown Bombers, and we had been scouting the Negro Leagues for more than a year. But you know, there was always something strange about it. He told us he didn't want this idea of his getting around, that nobody was supposed to know what we were doing. So instead of showing our credentials and walking into a ball park, as we normally would have done, we always bought a ticket and made ourselves as inconspicuous as possible.

"Now, Clyde," the old man went on, "if you like this fellow's arm, bring him in. And if his schedule won't permit it, if he can't come in, then make an appointment for me and I'll go out there."

Mr. Rickey go out there? To see if some guy named Robinson was good enough to play shortstop for the Brooklyn Brown Bombers? Well, I'm not the smartest guy in the world, but I said to myself, *This could be the real thing.*

So I went to Chicago and started calling every hotel I thought a Negro club might be staying at. But I couldn't contact him. Later I found out why—they'd come in from somewhere out in Iowa the night before by bus, saving themselves a hotel bill.

I went out to Comiskey Park the next day and bought myself a ticket. I sat down front and began studying my scorecard. This was in August, and those scorecards are so often inaccurate that late in the year; but I seemed to remember that this fellow Robinson's number was eight. A few fellows came out, and one of them had number eight on him. I stood up and said, "Hey, Robinson." He walked over. I introduced myself and told him just what I was supposed to tell him.

He listened carefully and when I was through, he spoke right up—Jackie was never shy, you know.

"Why is Mr. Rickey interested in my arm?" he asked. "Why is he interested in me?"

And I said, "That is a good question. And I wish I had the answer for you. But I don't have it."

"Well," he said, "I'd be happy to show you what arm I have, but I'm not playing. I've got a bad shoulder, and I can't throw the ball across the infield."

I talked to the guy for a while, and I thought to myself: Mr. Rickey has had this fellow scouted. The only thing he's concerned about is his arm. Is it a shortstop's arm? Well, I had heard reports that he was outstanding in every way. A great athlete. So I thought: Supposing he doesn't have a shortstop's arm? There's always second base, third base, outfield. I liked this fellow.

"Look," I said, "you're not in the lineup. If you could get away for two or three days, it won't arouse anybody's suspicions. Tell your manager that you'll be back in a few days. We'll go into New York; I think the old man would like to talk to you."

Now this is Friday night, and Sunday I have to see a second baseman in Toledo. So I asked Robinson to meet me down at the Stevens Hotel after the game, and we would talk some more. He said all right.

Later it occurred to me that they might not let him in. This was 1945, remember. So when I got to the hotel, I saw the bellman out front, and I gave him a couple of bucks and I said, "There's going to be a colored fellow coming along here, and I want you to show him to the elevator." He said he would do that.

Evidently Jackie had no trouble getting in, because he came up to the room later on. And he starts right off.

"Why is Mr. Rickey interested in my arm? Why does he want to see me?"

"Jack," I said, "I can't answer that. I don't know."

"You can't blame me for being curious, can you?"

"I can't blame you," I said, "because I'm just as curious as you are."

You could feel it boiling inside of him: *Why is Mr. Rickey interested in my arm?*

"Look, Jack," I said, "you know that the old man has originated a lot of things, he's revolutionized a lot of things, and I'm hopeful it's something along those lines . . . but I just don't know."

But he wouldn't let up. He kept pressing me.

"Tell me what he said."

"I told you," I said.

"Tell me again."

"He told me to come out and see if you've got a shortstop's arm. He *also* said that if you couldn't come to Brooklyn to see him, he would come to see you."

The significance of that last part wasn't lost on him. I could see that. He was no fool, this fellow. Don't ever sell Robinson cheap. No, sir!

The more we talked, the better I liked him. There was something about that man that just gripped you. He was tough, he was intelligent, and he was *proud.*

"Mr. Sukeforth," he said, "what do *you* think?"

I was honest. I'd learned in a short time that that was the way you had to deal with Robinson.

"Jack," I said, "this could be the real thing."

It evidently sat well with him. It pleased him. Was he afraid of the idea? He was never afraid of anything, that fellow.

Then I told him I had to be in Toledo on Sunday. I asked him if he would meet with me in the Toledo ball park, and in the meantime I would make transportation arrangements to New York.

"I'll meet you in Toledo," he said.

"You got money?" I asked.

"I've got money," he said.

So I'm in Toledo on Sunday. I look up between games of the doubleheader, and there's Robinson, sitting back up in the stands, watching me. I don't know how long he'd been sitting there, his eyes on me. I waved to him to come down and join me.

"I'm glad you made it," I said when he sat down.

He didn't say much; he was pretty quiet. Evidently this thing had been going around in his mind.

We boarded the sleeper for New York that night. I got up the next morning, somewhere in New York State, and he's already up.

"Jack," I said, "let's go get some breakfast."

"No," he said, "I'll eat with the boys." He meant the porters.

I didn't make an issue of it. I went and got breakfast and came back, and we sat and talked on the way in. When we got to New York, I took him straight out to the Brooklyn Dodgers' office, at 215 Montague Street.

I brought him into Mr. Rickey's office and made the introductions. Then I said, "Mr. Rickey, I haven't seen this fellow's arm. I just brought him in for you to interview."

But the old man was so engrossed in Robinson by that time he didn't hear a damn word I said. When he met somebody he was interested in, he studied them in the most profound way. He just stared and stared. And that's what he did with Robinson—stared at him as if he were trying to get inside the man. And Jack stared right back at him. Oh, they were a pair, those two! I tell you, the air in that office was electric.

Listen, Mr. Rickey was under a lot of pressure too for signing Robinson. He was criticized by a lot of people, including some of the big wheels in the Brooklyn organization. They thought it was a bad move. But he was always that much ahead of everybody else. He knew this thing was coming. He knew that with the war over, things were going to change, that they were going to *have* to change. When you look back on it, it's almost unbelievable, isn't it? I mean here you've had fellows going overseas to fight for their country, putting their lives on the line, and when they come back home again, there are places they're not allowed to go, things they're not allowed to do. It was going to change all right, but not by itself, not by itself. Somewhere along the line you needed a coming together.

Do you know for how long the idea was in Mr. Rickey's head? More than forty years. For more than forty years he was waiting for the right moment, the right man. And that's what he told Robinson.

"For a great many years," he said, "I have been looking for a great colored ballplayer. I have reason to believe that you're that man. But what I'm looking for is *more* than a great player. I'm looking for a man that will take insults, take abuse—and have the guts *not to fight back!* If some guy slides into second base and calls you a black son of a bitch, you're coming up swinging. And I wouldn't blame you. You're justified. But," Mr. Rickey said, "that would set the cause back twenty years."

He went on along those lines, talking about turning the other cheek and things like that. He told Jack that we wanted to sign him for the Brooklyn organization, to play at Montreal. He described some of the things Robinson would have to face—the abuse, the insults, from fans, newspapermen, from other players, including some of his own teammates.

When the old man was through, Robinson just sat there, pondering it, thinking about it. I'd say he sat there for the better part of five minutes. He didn't give a quick answer. This impressed Mr. Rickey.

Finally Jackie said, "Mr. Rickey, I think I can play ball in Montreal, I think I can play ball in Brooklyn. But you're a better judge of that than I am. If you want to take this gamble, I will promise you there will be no incident."

Well, I thought the old man was going to kiss him.

Yes, that's about thirty years ago now, since those two came together. I guess you could say that history was made that day.

What was I doing while it was going on? Listen, I was pretty uneasy—remember, I hadn't seen the guy's arm!

DOC CRAMER

Roger Maxwell Cramer
Born: July 22, 1905, Beach Haven, New Jersey
Major-league career: 1929–48, Philadelphia Athletics, Boston
  Red Sox, Washington Senators, Detroit Tigers
Lifetime average: .296

If consistency is indeed the hobgoblin of little minds, as Emerson contends, it nevertheless is the hallmark of substantial ballplayers. Few were ever more consistent, and efficiently so, than Roger "Doc" Cramer. Posting a .296 batting average for 29 big-league seasons, Cramer also set a major-league record by seven times leading the league in at bats. In his 20 years Cramer accumulated a modest 345 strikeouts, a figure approached by some of today's finest hitters every two years.

I think I'm one of the few guys in the whole history of baseball who's ever gone six for six twice. Did it once against Chicago— got a few of those hits off of Ted Lyons, I believe—and once against Detroit. Actually, the first time I did it I didn't even know it. I knew I had a lot of hits, but I didn't realize I was going for number six. Second time I knew every hit.

I don't know if it was the first time or the second time, but one more hitter and I'd have been up again, for a seventh try. Maxie Bishop hit a line drive, and somebody made a good play on it; otherwise I'd been up for the seventh time. We scored 19 runs that day, I think. Why, I had five hits in five innings. That's a record.

I played twenty years in the big leagues. Two decades. I worked winters as a carpenter all the time I was playing ball.

152

Built my house with my own hands. Two years before I went with the A's, Brooklyn wanted me to go with them. But I turned them down. You see, I had two years' in carpentry and I wanted to finish my apprenticeship. Once I did that I was ready for anything.

I was playing semipro ball in Beach Haven, here in New Jersey, around 1928. Cy Perkins and Jimmy Dykes came over from Philadelphia one Sunday (Philadelphia didn't play Sunday ball at that time). I fancied myself a pitcher in those days, and I always could hit pretty good. Anyway, I must have done something to impress them because they came up to me after the game.

"What about coming to Philadelphia for a tryout?" they asked.

"When?" I asked.

"Wednesday."

"Can't make it," I said. "Got to work."

I never will forget that. I couldn't believe what I was hearing myself saying. Anyway, I went, and never came back to stay until twenty years later.

My dad didn't think much of my playing ball. See, I was a carpenter and had steady work. He'd say, "Look, you've got a good job and baseball don't amount to nothing"—that's the way he put it. But he got over it. They didn't want me to go away, that was the thing; they just didn't want me to leave because I'd never been anywhere.

Did I want to play ball? Well, the A's gave me a contract for I think about $3,500, and I'd have paid *them* that much to let me play. I stayed the rest of that year with the A's, working out—I wasn't into any games.

In '29 they sent me to Martinsburg, West Virginia. Blue Ridge League. They considered me a pitcher at first. But I hit so well every time I pitched that Mr. Mack heard about it and sent word for them to change me to an outfielder. So they sent me to center field, and that's where I stayed; never played any other place.

I liked it in Martinsburg. But you know, if you're having a good year, it doesn't much matter where you're playing. Did I have a good year? I guess I did. I hit .404. I won the batting championship, but not until the last day. I was being chased by Joe Vosmik—remember Joe? Good hitter. He was with

Frederick. Well, we played Frederick the last game of the season, so it came down to Joe and me swinging against each other for the batting championship. Just before the game the manager came up to me and said, "Well, Doc, you pitched on opening day, so you might as well pitch on closing day."

I'll tell you what happened that day. I got four or five hits, and at the same time I walked Vosmik four times. So he didn't get a chance to swing, and I beat him out. Oh, was he steaming! Years later, when we were on the Red Sox together and were good friends, he'd still bring it up. He'd really tell me about it. "Remember that day in Frederick?" he'd say. Did I walk him on purpose? Well, maybe only three times.

In 1928, the year I sat on the bench with the A's, they had a pretty good outfield. They had Al Simmons, Mule Haas, and Bing Miller, plus a couple of other guys who were just finishing up—Ty Cobb and Tris Speaker.

A lot of people didn't like Cobb, but that never seemed to bother him. Anyway, he was very nice to me. I liked him.

I don't think Cobb ever wanted to quit. He hit over .320 his last year, but he was forty-two years old and couldn't move in the outfield anymore. He had slowed up so much he'd lose a game for you. Ty Cobb. Yes, sir. In fact, he lost a series in New York late in 1928 that cost the A's a pennant. Mr. Mack had those other guys to put in there, but he played Cobb and Speaker for drawing cards. It cost them. Mr. Mack admitted it later, said it was a big mistake.

Speaker was a great guy, both on and off the field. I learned a lot just from watching him. He was a good teacher. He'd take you out there and show you how to do it. Cobb wouldn't do that. He'd talk to you, tell you all about it, but he wouldn't take you out there.

But Eddie Collins was my man. To me he was the real baseball man. He just about ran the Philadelphia Athletics at that time. Mr. Mack didn't do too much without talking to Collins first. Eddie Collins was the greatest second baseman I ever saw and one of the best ballplayers. He could hit, he could run, throw, field, and he had it upstairs, too. Smartest baseball man I ever met. Eddie could stand at third coaching, and I don't care who was pitching, in two innings he'd have their signs; he'd know what that pitcher was going to throw and call them.

How was I treated as a rookie with the A's? Well ... it

could've been a lot better. It wasn't like it is today. You couldn't even go up and have batting practice. The regulars would crowd you out; you couldn't mix in with them until you'd shown them you could play. That's the way it was in those days.

One day up in Boston Mr. Mack called me in and said, "You're my center fielder from now on, until you show me that you're not my center fielder."

That's the way he told me. He said I was going to hit second, in Haas' place. So I went out to hit with the regulars, and the next thing I knew they were jumping all over me, wanting to know what I was doing out there. One in particular got pretty hot about it.

"What are you doing out here?" he wanted to know. "You're supposed to hit in the morning." That's when the subs took batting practice, in the morning.

"Mr. Mack told me to hit here," I said. "I'm playing today."

"You are, huh? Well, nobody told me anything about it."

"Why should they?" I said. "You're just another ballplayer around here."

"Is that so?" he said.

"As far as I'm concerned."

Just another ballplayer! I've got to laugh now when I look back on it. I was talking to Al Simmons.

I really don't know how to tell you about Connie Mack. He was as good a man as ever lived, any way you take him. And he knew baseball. I'd say he was the best outfielder that ever lived. We played by his scorecard; that's all we played by. He'd move us into position by waving that scorecard of his, you see. Of course after you'd played a year or so for him you knew where to position yourself.

We were playing in St. Louis one time, right after I'd broken in. We had a one run lead in the ninth inning, two out, and Goose Goslin was the hitter. Eddie Rommel was pitching for us. Now, Eddie was a good pitcher, but they could pull him. So I played Goslin back about where I thought we always did play him. But Mr. Mack kept waving me in with his scorecard, until I swear I wasn't more than fifty feet in back of second base—for *Goslin*.

Well, Rommel threw the ball, Goslin swung, and I just stood right there and caught the ball. Never moved an inch. Right where he put me.

I asked Mr. Mack about it later, and he said, "That was just a hunch, boy, that was all. Just a hunch."

First time I met him, tell you the truth I was scared to death. Plumb afraid, that's all. I'd never been out of Manahawkin or Beach Haven; going to Philadelphia was like going to Europe, for me. I went up on the train in the morning, at six o'clock. Went to Camden, crossed over on the ferry, and then took the trolley car out to the ball park. That's the way you got there in those days.

I'll tell you, after I'd talked with him for five minutes, why, he was just like a father to me. He was a good man. He'd never bawl you out for a mistake till the next day. Then you'd go up to that little office up there, and he'd be waiting for you. Boy, he could tell it to you when he had to. That's if you'd made some sort of mistake that he thought you shouldn't have. I don't mean errors. He'd never get on a man for making an error. "You're supposed to make them," he'd say. "I know you're trying when you make an error."

In my first year, in '29, he put me up to pinch-hit. It was in Washington, against Fred Marberry. I had the count three and one. I looked down to Collins, who was coaching at third, and I thought I got the sign to hit. Well, it was "take." I swung and popped up. Collins jumped me about it, said I'd missed it. I didn't think anymore about it after that.

Then we got on the train that night, going back to Philadelphia. I was walking through the car and there he was, Mr. Mack. He crooked his finger toward me, and I went over and sat with him.

"Young man," he said, "you're going to Portland, Oregon, tomorrow morning."

I said, "How come?"

He said, "You're going out there to learn the signs. And you might as well learn how to field too while you're out there."

"By God," I said, "I'm not goin'."

"Yes, you are," he said.

I thought about it for a while. Then I said, "Portland, *Oregon?*"

"That's right," he said.

I told him, "Well, you kept me in the United States, didn't you?"

"Just about," he said.

Then, after he'd won the three pennants in '29, '30, '31, Mr. Mack went broke. Lost all his money in the stock market, like a lot of other people at that time. So he had to start selling everybody. Attendance had started to fall off, too. See, the fans knew we were going to win, so they stopped coming out. Nobody could beat us in those days. God, we had Grove, Earnshaw, Walberg, Quinn, Rommel pitching. We'd pitch Grove, Earnshaw, and Walberg the first three games, and we didn't care who they pitched—we had 'em wore out.

Grove was quick. I'll say he was. Whew! You haven't got anything today as quick. Koufax? No, sir. I've seen him pitch. Nobody was any quicker than Grove, that I ever saw. Well, just one instance. We were in New York one time, and Jack Quinn was pitching. We had them beat by a run. They got the bases full in the ninth with nobody out. Mr. Mack brought Lefty in to relieve. Ten pitches and we were in the clubhouse. He struck out Ruth, Gehrig, and Lazzeri on ten pitches— Lazzeri fouled a ball. And Grove threw only fast balls. Didn't have much of a curve until he was near finished. That's what I mean by him being so fast. Everybody in the league knew what he was going to throw, and they still couldn't hit it.

Lefty Grove. Mr. Mack always called him Robert.

But he was a tough loser, Grove was. Nicest guy you'd ever want to meet, but a tough loser. He hated to get beat—and they didn't beat him often. Why, when he was just pitching batting practice—you hit one through the box, and you'd go down on the next pitch. In *batting practice*. On the last swing we'd try to hit one back through him, just to rile him up. Once I hit a home run off of him in a game in Fort Myers, Florida. It was just a scrimmage between the team. I was on the scrubs. Next time I come up Cochrane says to me, "Hey, kid, be ready—he's gonna throw at you."

Well, I was young, I didn't hardly know what it meant. But I found out in a hurry! Boy, he hit me in the ribs, I thought it was going to come out the other side. Knocked me right down. But he wouldn't ever throw at anybody's head. He'd hit 'em in the pockets—that was the way he said it.

I was always on Grove's team. I never hit at him, except for one year, because I went to Boston a year after he did. Ted Lyons was one of the toughest I ever hit at. Great stuff, great control. I hit at Bob Feller a lot, but I had awful good luck with him. In fact, he walked me one time to pitch to Cecil Travis; I never did forget it. I could hit Bob pretty good. But he had great stuff, a really good curve. Johnny Allen was a good pitcher, and Wes Ferrell, when he was with Cleveland. Wes was like Grove—he wanted to win. I saw him stomp a brand-new wristwatch one day in the clubhouse after he'd got beat. He was putting the watch on, it slipped and fell, and he stomped it right there.

"Well, I won't drop you anymore!" he said.

I mentioned Cochrane before. You've got to talk about him. God, he was a great catcher, that fellow. He could do it all. I used to have a lot of assists, you know. I could throw pretty good. But you didn't have to make a perfect throw to Cochrane. If it was out a little ways, he'd go and get it and come back and get that guy. I'll tell you, there were few things as exciting as watching somebody trying to get in there on a close play with Cochrane. Home plate was *his,* you see. You had to take it away from him. Tough? Just the same as a piece of flint.

He was a tough loser, too. That whole gang were tough losers. You have Grove pitching and Cochrane catching, and you lose 1–0, you're a little timid about going into that clubhouse. I've seen it happen.

There was the time when Grove had won 16 straight games—which tied him for the league record with Walter Johnson and Smoky Joe Wood—and was going after number seventeen. Well, Dick Coffman of the St. Louis Browns beat him, 1–0, on a misjudged fly ball no less. Well, it's hard to believe what happened in the clubhouse after that game unless you were there to see it.

I was in center field in that game, and Jim Moore was in left field—he was the boy who misjudged the ball. Simmons should have been out there, but he'd told Mr. Mack he was going to Milwaukee for a couple of days for one reason or another, and he did. Back then they'd let you take off some time once in a while if you needed it. Well, to this day, if you talk to Grove about that game, he doesn't blame Jim Moore for losing it, he blames Simmons, because Simmons went to Milwaukee. That's the one he blames. He'll tell you that if Al had been in left field that day where he belonged, it never would have happened.

It was Oscar Mellilo who hit the ball. Moore ran under it, and it got away. There was a man on base when it happened. I retrieved the ball and threw it in, but the run scored. Coffman had good stuff and he beat us. Before you start blaming anybody for anything, you've got to remember that the man shut us out.

So we went into the clubhouse. The sparks were flying off Grove. Oh, I mean to tell you. I knew it. I knew it was going to happen. Well, he was about three lockers down from me. I saw him stand up and take hold of the top of his shirt with both hands—we had buttons on our shirts in those days—stand like that for a second, and then *rrrip!* He tore that shirt apart so fast and so hard that I saw the buttons go flying past me, three lockers away. Then everything went flying—bats, balls, gloves, shoes, benches. He broke up a couple of chairs. He kicked in a couple of lockers. Nobody said a word. There was no point. You had to wait till the steam went out of him. Next day he was all right. But I never will forget those buttons flying past me.

Grove was a tough customer all right. Wasn't afraid of anybody—Babe Ruth included. I'll tell you something about Ruth. You might have fellows today hitting more home runs than Babe Ruth, but you still don't have Babe Ruth. To me it was remarkable what a drawing card that man was. The fans—grown-ups as well as kids—would ache just to touch him.

One time we lost six or seven straight, coming off a Western trip. We didn't expect much of a crowd. We were playing the Yankees. Twelve o'clock they put up a sign, Standing Room Only. That was Ruth, that's all it was. He could fill any ball park, no matter where he went.

He was a great outfielder, too. You couldn't just go from first to third on him; you wanted to be sure because he could throw you out. That's all there was to it. He could fire that ball, and most of the time not on a hop either—it would come whistling in there on a line.

He was a great guy personally, too. I've been out to dinner with him, gone over to his house. I knew his wife and daughter. You just had to admire him, any way you take him. If you have a kid sick, he'd come visit and leave the kid a $100 bill and think nothing of it.

I went barnstorming out West with him one year. We played a game in Billings, Montana. The fences were way back. They told Ruth that nobody had ever hit one out of there. He laughed, and said, "The Baby'll hit one out"—he called himself the Baby.

First time up, right on out of the ball park it went. Tommy Thomas was the pitcher, from the White Sox. Ball parks didn't make any difference to Ruth; when he got a-hold of the ball, it was gone. I don't care what park—and some cornfields, it would go out of them, too.

He could hit a ball so hard it was tough to handle in the outfield. Sometimes it would come out to you and then sink, like a spitball or a knuckler. I never saw anybody else hit a ball like that.

Foxx was the same kind of hitter as Ruth, only right-handed. Once I saw him hit a ball in Chicago, a line drive against the center field fence, he had to slide to get into second base. The ball was hit so hard that when Appling went out to get the relay, it bounced right back into his glove; he turned and threw, and Foxx just made it—and Jimmie could run. That's how hard Foxx could hit them. He was strong.

Now Gehrig, he had plenty of ability, too. We respected Lou pretty much as we did Ruth up at the plate, I'll tell you that. You could fool Gehrig a little more than you could Ruth, but you weren't fooling him much.

Gehrig put on the biggest one-man show I ever saw in a ball game—four home runs, in Shibe Park. That was in 1932. He hit the first three off of Earnshaw, who was one of the best, and the fourth one off of Lee Roy Mahaffey. And I'll tell you— he pretty near hit five, because Simmons made a spectacular play on him in center field. One of the greatest plays you ever saw. Lou would've had five home runs that game. Still, four ain't a bad day's work, is it? They beat us, 20–13. Lost by a touchdown.

Grove never threw much at Gehrig. Didn't want to wake him up, he said. Lou was a quiet, good-natured sort of guy, and you didn't want to get him mad. "Let him sleep," Grove always said. Ruth, too; though once in a while he'd put one under Babe's chin, just for luck. Ruth just laughed. You expected that sort of thing in those days. If you hit a home run, you'd expect to be knocked down the next time up. That's the way it was. Or if you beat a guy a ball game, you wanted to be ready next time that fellow pitched against you. He'd let you have it.

Johnny Allen was the worst I ever saw for that. I said to him one day, "I believe you'd throw at your own mother."

"Oh, no," he said. "I wouldn't throw at her. But I might brush her back a little."

I was with the Red Sox when Williams broke in. First time I saw Teddy it was just like DiMaggio—you knew this fellow was going to be a ballplayer. And he wasn't shy, that boy. First day he walked into the clubhouse he called Cronin Skip. Ted was a great boy. I liked him.

That first spring he was with the team, we were coming up from the South, heading for Boston. We stopped off in Atlanta to play a game with the Atlanta Crackers. Ted was playing right field. Somebody hit the ball out to him, and it went between his legs, all the way to the wall. He chased it down, mad as the dickens at himself for missing it, and when he got to it, he picked it up and just threw that ball over the right field fence—right through Sears, Roebuck's plate glass window, we learned later on.

I was there alongside him when he threw it. I had to hold my hand over my mouth to keep from laughing. Then I looked around and sure enough, he was coming—Cronin. Walking out from shortstop, ver-r-r-y slow.

So I said, "Ted, here comes Cronin. Now keep your mouth shut. Don't say anything. 'Yes' him. That's all there is to it."

Cronin didn't say much. Wasn't much he could say. He just took Ted right out of there and sat him on the bench. It didn't bother Ted too much, except he wanted to stay in and hit. That boy loved to hit. With good reason.

Cronin said to me a few days later, "I want you to take Ted out and teach him how to field."

I said all right. So I had him out there with somebody hitting them to him. He'd miss one, catch one, then miss a couple more. Finally he said, "Ah, Doc, the hell with this. They don't pay off on me catching these balls. They're gonna pay me to hit. That's what they're gonna do."

And I said, "Well, I can see that, Ted. They're gonna pay you to hit."

There was no trouble seeing that. He had that swing.

Now, you know during the war the caliber of play went down somewhat, but hell, it was still baseball, and in 1945 we won the pennant. I was with Detroit then. Hank Greenberg had come out of the service in midseason. Hank won it for us with a grand slammer on the last day of the season, in the ninth inning. That was doing it with style—which was generally the way Hank Greenberg did things.

I always kid Greenberg about that. I was hitting third and he was hitting fourth that game. Nelson Potter was the pitcher We had men on second and third, and they walked me to get to Greenberg, loading the bases. They were looking for the double play. But I swear, before I got to first base, Greenberg hit one into the bleachers and we won the pennant.

So anytime I go anywhere and Hank is there, I always say, "You know, once they walked me to get to Greenberg"—and never tell 'em what happened, and then Hank always jumps in and says, "Hey, tell 'em what happened."

But I never do; I just let it go at that.

We played the Cubs in the Series and beat them in seven games. Claude Passeau beat us one game with a one-hitter, and Hank Borowy beat us twice. Then he came back for the seventh game, and we clobbered him. Five runs in the first inning. Newhouser went all the way for us and we beat them.

In twenty years in the big leagues, that was my only world's championship. It's a great feeling. You know you've done it all then. We drank champagne on the train all the way back to Detroit.

MAX LANIER

HUBERT MAX LANIER
Born: August 18, 1915, Denton, North Carolina
Major-league career: 1938–46, 1949–53, St. Louis Cardinals,
New York Giants, St. Louis Browns
Lifetime record: 108 wins, 82 losses

Although many fans today associate Max Lanier's name primarily with his "jump" to the Mexican League in 1946, Lanier was at the time of his departure one of the best left-handers in the National League. From 1941 through 1944 his highest earned run average was 2.98, his lowest 1.90 in 1943. With Army service, his time in Mexico, and his subsequent suspension, Lanier lost the greater part of five prime big league seasons.

Looking back on it all, I can tell you that it happened too quick. It doesn't seem like it could be that long ago. Time really flies. I know when I signed that first contract, it looked as big as this room.

I was pitching a high school game, down home in North Carolina. I won it, 2–0. When I came out of the ball park later, this guy was standing there waiting for me.

"Hi, Max," he said.

"Hi yourself," I said. I didn't know who he was.

"Can I give you a ride back to the school?" he asked.

"Well, I don't know you," I said.

He pulled out his identification and showed it to me. Frank Rickey, Branch's brother. Representing the St. Louis Cardinals.

"You interested in playing pro ball?" he asked.

"Yes indeed," I said. That was one of my dreams. I was already playing semipro ball while I was still in high school. We had a pretty good semipro club there in Denton, North Carolina. This was around 1934.

Frank Rickey signed me to a contract when I was sixteen years old. My family wasn't too enthused about the idea. You see, I'd been offered a scholarship by Duke University, and my parents wanted me to accept it, but I turned it down to play pro ball.

I signed right out of high school, with a class B club. I stayed there a week and then they wanted to send me to a D club, Huntington, West Virginia, for $70 a month. I didn't go for that, and I quit and came home. That was my first money dispute with the Cardinals. It didn't take long, did it? One week.

I started playing semipro ball again, in Ashbury, North Carolina. In 1936 I won 16 straight games. That's against no losses. One day I walk out of the ball park, and there's Frank Rickey standing there.

"Back again, are you?" I asked.

"How would you like to go to Columbus in the American Association?" he asked.

"Why should I?" I asked.

"It would be a great opportunity for you," he said. "That's Triple-A ball."

"I might consider it," I said. "Under one condition—that you guarantee I'll be on the ball club the whole year."

I guess you talk that way when you've got a 16-0 record, no matter who you've won them against.

"How do you know you can pitch in Triple-A?" he asked.

"I think I can," I said, "because we've got a lot of ballplayers right here who are that good, and I'm doing all right against them."

He went along with it. I was talking tough, but to tell you the truth, you couldn't afford to bargain too much with the Cardinals back then, because they had so many ballplayers. They were way ahead of everybody else in that respect. At one time they had about thirty farm clubs. And they kept us hungry. That was Branch Rickey's philosophy: a hungry ballplayer was a better ballplayer. I'll tell you one thing about him: he could tell you how much he paid you for each pitch, not how many games you won or lost.

The competition was murder. When I was coming up, they had, just in left-hand pitchers, fellows like Howie Pollet, Al Brazle, Harry Brecheen, Ernie White, Preacher Roe. That was pretty stiff competition. Why, Preacher Roe couldn't even make the club!

I got lucky at Columbus and won 10 and lost 4. The next year I went up to the Cardinals. Frisch was managing then. He was tough on young ballplayers. I didn't appreciate it then, but I did later. He'd find faults no matter what you did, but if you paid attention to him, you'd find yourself learning something. He was a good baseball man and a full-fledged character at the same time. I remember one time Paul Waner was wearing us out with line drives. Finally Frisch stood up in disgust and yelled, "Who on this ball club can get that Waner out?" Max Macon was sitting on the bench—this was before he went to the Dodgers. Well, Max liked to pop off a little anyway, and he said, "I can get him out." Frisch was delighted to hear that. He clapped his hands and said, "Atta boy. Get down there and warm up." Waner comes up again. Frisch brings in Macon. The first pitch Waner hits a line drive and breaks Macon's little finger. Frisch couldn't help but lie down on the bench and laugh himself silly.

Pepper Martin was on that ball club. I'd say he was the most colorful ballplayer I ever saw. He was a real fun lover. He'd come into the clubhouse and tie your uniform into knots or nail your shoes to the floor. Sometimes during a game you'd be out there pitching, and he'd walk over from third base to talk to you and slap a wad of chewing gum onto your wrist.

One day, I think it was in Chicago, he pulled a beauty. He was great at throwing paper sacks full of water out the window. Well, there was a mezzanine in the lobby of this hotel, with a staircase leading up to it from the ground floor. Pepper got himself a paper sack full of water and hung around by the mezzanine window, with a newspaper in his hand. He was waiting for Frisch. When Frisch came along, Pepper dropped his water bomb right on Frank's head, then tore back down the stairs, threw himself into a big chair, crossed his legs and opened the newspaper and looked as though he'd been sitting there all day.

Frisch came storming in, wringing wet. He ran up to Pepper

and said, "Damn you, if I wasn't seeing you sitting there, I'd swear it was you that did it!"

Pepper brought his paper down, looked at him as innocent as a baby, and said, "Did what, Frank?"

Another time, we lost a doubleheader in the Polo Grounds. That's pretty rough going, when you lose two. You don't hear a voice in the clubhouse, much less see anybody smile. So we trudged into the clubhouse, and it's like a tomb. Buzzy Wares, our first-base coach, goes to light up a cigar. Well, Pepper had switched matches on him, and the matches were loaded. Buzzy strikes a match, and it explodes. Buzzy exploded right along with it.

"Damn you guys!" he yells. "Lose a doubleheader and you're still pulling pranks."

He went and got another book of matches. But Pepper had loaded the cigar, too. Everybody's sitting there watching Buzzy light it. When twenty-five guys are sitting stone still watching you light your cigar, you ought to suspect something. But I guess Buzzy was too mad to take notice. Boy, he took notice a second later. The damn thing blew up in his face, and he had tobacco in his eyes, his ears, his nose. Twenty-five guys turned around and looked into their lockers, their shoulders shaking. You wouldn't want to be caught laughing then, would you?

Pepper kept you loose all right.

Joe Medwick was in his heyday when I joined the ball club. So was Johnny Mize, one of the greater left-hand hitters. He and Medwick were as good a pair of hitters as I've seen. Of course, after Joe took that beaning, he seemed to lose some of his edge. That was in 1940, at Ebbets Field, soon after he'd been traded over to the Dodgers. I've heard stories that there was some bad blood, that we were throwing at him, but I never believed it.

I was rooming with the fellow that hit him, Bob Bowman, and I didn't know of any reason for Bob to be throwing at him. Here's what I think happened. Charley Dressen was coaching third for Brooklyn, and he always tried to call the pitches. He was skilled at that, but sometimes he called them wrong. Bowman was wrapping his curveball, and then he wrapped a fastball the same way, and it faked Dressen. Medwick stepped right into it, thinking it was going to be the curve. I think that's what happened. And Joe got hit hard.

Bowman was upset about it, I know. He never showed up in the room that night. He was supposed to be in at twelve, and he didn't come in. I thought, gosh, maybe something's happened to him. I didn't want to call the manager, because there was the chance Bob might be out having a couple of drinks, and I didn't want to get him in dutch. So I called Pepper, and he told me that they'd sent Bowman on to Boston. They wanted to get him out of town because they were afraid some of those very rabid Dodger fans might try something the next day. But I wished somebody had told me about it.

We had some pretty good throwing contests with the Dodgers in '41 and '42. Guys like Whitlow Wyatt and Mort Cooper would come close to you when they wanted. Of course, we never threw to hit anybody, but we'd brush them back. We had some great battles with the Dodgers.

Somebody would start throwing close, or there would be some jockeying from the dugout, and that would start it off. Durocher was a great one for that. You could hear him in the dugout: "Stick it in his ear. Knock him down." Stuff like that. You never knew when he meant it. You take that kind of thing, some mean pitchers, a great rivalry, and put it in the middle of a tense pennant race, and you're going to have some fun out there.

I remember this one time Marty Marion was taking a throw at second and Medwick slid into him pretty high. I guess Marty didn't like spikes up in his face, so he just flipped Joe. The next thing you knew the whole gang was out there. I was pitching that day. Dixie Walker ran right by me and made a diving tackle into Kurowski, and then Jimmy Brown and me went after Walker. Oh, it was a great one. Players rolling and scrambling and wrestling all over the grass. Nobody got hurt. Nobody ever gets hurt in those things. Safest place to be in a baseball fight is right in the middle of it.

Another time, in St. Louis, in 1942, I saw Stan Musial get mad. It was the only time I ever saw Musial really get mad. Les Webber was pitching for the Dodgers, and he threw four pitches behind Musial's head. That's the worst place to throw, because a guy's instinct is to jerk back from a close pitch.

Musial was steaming. The whole ball club was steaming.

You just knew something was going to happen. Walker Cooper was the next hitter. He hit a ground ball, and when he went across first, he jarred Augie Galan. Augie was playing first that game. Mickey Owen was backing up the play, and he didn't like what Cooper had done. What does Mickey do but jump right up on Cooper's back. Mickey was a scrapper, but he wasn't too big, and Cooper was like an ox. I remember looking at that sight and thinking, What in the world is he doing up on Cooper's back, how's he going to get off, and what's going to happen when he does get off?

Well, Cooper, he was so strong, he just threw Mickey right over on the ground and held him there. Next thing you knew, we were all out there again.

I had particularly good luck against the Dodgers. One of the reasons, I think, was Durocher. He'd sit in that dugout and holler at me and get me mad. He thought he was going to upset me, but the madder I got, the better I could pitch.

I believe there was more pressure in '42 than in '41. We were 10½ games behind the Dodgers in August. Then we went on the road and won something like twenty-three out of twenty-six ball games. Finally we got within two games of the Dodgers and went into Ebbets Field. Mort Cooper pitched the opener, and he beat Whitlow Wyatt a close game. That put us just one back.

I was scheduled for the next day, but I'd been having a little trouble with my elbow. Billy Southworth came up to me in the clubhouse.

"Max," he said, "I believe I'll pitch Beazley today and let you rest that elbow."

"No, sir" I said. "I've beaten them four times already, and I think I can beat them once more."

He thought about it for a moment, then handed me the ball.

I beat Max Macon 2–1 that day. Kurowski hit a home run in the second inning with one on, and then they got one run in the second inning. And that was it.

I can tell you who was the last hitter I faced. Billy Herman. One of the best. I threw him a fastball and he took it. Well, I knew Billy—when he takes a pitch, he's looking for something else. So I wasted my curve and threw him another fastball for a strike. He was a guess hitter, and I figured he was guessing on the curve. So I threw him another fastball, right down the middle, and he took it for strike three. And we were tied with the Dodgers for first place.

We went on from there to Boston. Naturally you're not supposed to look at the scoreboard, and naturally you do. We were behind late in the game, and when we saw the Dodgers had lost, we went and came up with a big inning and won the game. We took over first place, and from then on they never caught us.

We played the Yankees in the Series that year. The Yankees had been in a lot of World Series and they were a little bit cocky, though any ball club that had won as many pennants as they had had a right to be. I think we were kind of nervous in the first game. They beat us, 7–4, but something happened in that game that took away our nervousness and gave us confidence. We were behind 7–0 going into the last of the ninth. We scored four runs and had the tying run at the plate. Musial was the hitter, and he flied out to deep right.

Well, that rally made us feel better, even though we lost the game. It showed we could throw a scare into the Yankees. And then we did more than scare them. We beat them four straight. I think that was one of the biggest World Series upsets ever.

I'll tell you, beating the Yankees in '42 will always be the highlight for me, more so than winning in '44 against the Browns, even though I beat them in the sixth game for the championship.

I went into the service in 1945 and missed most of that year. I came back in '46. I reported to the club in St. Pete. I was rarin' to go, but I hadn't signed my contract yet, so they wouldn't let me work out. The reason I hadn't signed was the old bugaboo, money. I'd won 17 in 1944, plus the big game in the Series. I was making $10,000 and was holding out for more.

Eddie Dyer was the manager then, and he was anxious for me to start working out. I was hanging around the clubhouse, waiting to get the thing settled. Eddie saw me there.

"Come into my office," he said.

I followed him into the office, and he closed the door.

"I'm going to call Mr. Breadon in St. Louis," he said.

"Think it'll do any good?" I asked.

"I don't know," he said. "We can try. You get on the other phone."

So I listed to the conversation.

"Mr. Breadon," Eddie said, "this boy is worth more money than what you've offered him."

"Do you think so?" Breadon asked.

"Yes, I do think so," Eddie said.

"Well," Breadon said, "I'll give him five hundred more. He can take it or go home."

So I had to take it. I wasn't satisfied; but I took it. I felt I'd been dealt with unfairly, but there wasn't much I could do about it.

When the season started, it seemed I couldn't do anything wrong. In the first month I had six starts, six complete games, six wins. I was pitching great ball, but I still wasn't entirely happy, because of the way I'd been treated by Breadon.

One night I was leaving the ball park in Philadelphia, and a couple of guys approached me. One of them was Bernardo Pasquel. He was the brother of Jorge Pasquel, a multimillionaire Mexican who owned a league in Mexico. They were offering a lot of money to big leaguers who were willing to jump. Some guys, like Mickey Owen and Sal Maglie, had already gone.

That first conversation didn't amount to much, but he said he would contact me in New York, which was our next stop. I didn't say much to him one way or the other at the time.

When we got into New York, I found out that Lou Klein, our second baseman, and Fred Martin, a pitcher, had already agreed to go to Mexico. They started talking to me about going with them. Then Pasquel contacted me, and we all met at the Roosevelt Hotel. I was a little hesitant; after all, it was quite a big move to be contemplating. But I'll tell you something. I'd had some trouble with my elbow the last few games. Nobody knew about it but me. I wasn't letting on to anybody, but I was getting concerned. I knew if that elbow went, I'd be in trouble. I'd be nowhere then. You know what a pitcher with a bad elbow is worth.

So I began to get receptive. Pasquel's first offer wasn't good enough, but finally he made me the right offer. I got a bonus of $25,000 to sign and $20,000 a year for five years. I couldn't turn it down. I said, shucks, I'll pitch the rest of my life for the Cardinals and come out with nothing. I think the highest-paid guy on the ball club at that time was $14,000, and I'm talking about a ball club that had won three out of the last four pennants and had a lot of top stars on it.

After the meeting I went back with Klein and Martin to the Hotel New Yorker, where the Cardinals were staying. After thinking it over, I let Pasquel know the next day. We didn't tell anybody, not the Cardinals, not anybody. We went to St. Louis and from there drove to Mexico City.

I thought I was making the right move at the time. Remember, I'd just received this shabby treatment from Breadon. In the long run, though, I think that whole business probably didn't help us as much as it did some of the rest of the players because I do know the Cardinals started paying more money.

When I got down there, Jorge Pasquel told me just to run and work out for a couple of days to get used to the high altitude. But my third day there I got into a ball game. It was the damnedest thing. I was sitting on the bench, watching the game. In the ninth inning the other team got the bases loaded with nobody out. All of a sudden the game stops. I look around to see what's happening, and Jorge Pasquel is coming out of his box. He walks across the field and comes to our dugout and says to Mickey Owen, who was managing the team, "I want Max to go in." Mickey didn't say anything; he just looked over at me and shrugged, as if to say, "It's his money."

So they stopped the game long enough for me to warm up. And I went out there and threw nine pitches and struck the side out. Pasquel came into the clubhouse after the game and patted me on the back and said, "Max, I won this game, didn't I?"

Pasquel owned the whole league, you see. They said he was worth something like $70,000,000. He used to sit up in his box during the game and eat off silver trays.

Conditions down there weren't too good. Half the time you couldn't play, you were so sick. You know, problems with the water. Mexico City was the only place where you didn't have to boil the drinking water; they had artesian wells there. And I got to where I was eating out of cans most of the time; I was afraid to eat the food.

I couldn't believe there was that much difference between two countries that were so close together. The conditions in the smaller cities were terrible. Tampico. San Luis Potosí.

Puebla. Gosh, that Tampico was hot. I'd be so tired after pitching a game there that I couldn't talk above a whisper. There was no air conditioning, for one thing. Didn't even have screens in the windows. They had these overhead fans with the big black blades that used to go around and around very slowly and not do a damn thing.

Sometimes we traveled by plane, sometimes by bus. Those bus rides through the mountains were hell. They'd drive on either side of the road, didn't make any difference. The one that had the loudest horn had the right-of-way, I'll tell you.

The whole thing didn't last very long. I stayed in Mexico about a year and a half. We found out later why the Pasquel brothers were after the big leaguers to come down there. At that time Alemán was running for President, and I think there was some family relationship between him and Jorge Pasquel. Now the people in Mexico loved baseball. It was worked out so Alemán got the credit for us coming down there. They figured he'd get some votes out of it. And he did get elected. So I think the whole thing was strictly a political deal. After the election Pasquel started cutting everybody. He cut me from $20,000 a year to $10,000. That's when we started jumping back to the States.

Of course, everybody who went to Mexico was suspended from the big leagues for five years. I thought that was a little stiff. Heck, we didn't go down there to hurt anybody. We just didn't think we were making enough money.

After I got back, this was in '48, I formed an all-star team, and we went on the road and played about eighty ball games against college and semi-pro teams. We played all over, Kansas, Iowa, Nebraska, Wisconsin, Indiana, Louisiana. But do you know, we got to where we couldn't get a ball game. I'm not especially against Happy Chandler—I suppose he had his job to do—but he tried to stop us from playing. We knew we couldn't play in professional ball parks against professional ballplayers, but he shouldn't have tried to stop us from playing against colleges and semipro clubs. But he did.

We were supposed to be suspended for five years, but in '48 we started a lawsuit against baseball, and that's how we got back. We had them by the tail then because the suspension was illegal.

I went up to Drummondville, Canada, in '49 and was play-ing ball there. Around the end of June I got a phone call from Fred Saigh, who now owned the Cardinals.

"You've been reinstated," he said. "You ready to come back?"

"Sure," I said. "If the price is right."

"Look," he said, "you did the club an injustice when you went to Mexico, and we can't give you any more money."

"You don't have any reason to say that," I told him, "be-cause you didn't even own the ball club then. You can forget about it if you think I'm going to come back for the same amount of money I was getting before I left. I'm making more money here in Drummondville than you're offering me."

Eddie Dyer got on the phone then.

"Max," he said, "we sure would like to have you back. We think we can win the pennant, and the fellows would like to have you back."

"Eddie," I said, "if you were managing in the minor leagues making more money than the major leagues offered, what would you do?"

"I'd probably stay where I was," he said.

"Well," I said, "those are exactly my circumstances right now."

Saigh called me back the next day.

"We'll double your salary," he said. "And we'll give you expense money if you can get to St. Louis by the Fourth of July."

Well, that sounded just great to me. As a matter of fact, I was there on the second of July.

I pitched for the Cardinals for a few more years and then in '52 was traded to the Giants. The next year I went back to St. Louis, but this time it was with the Browns. Bill Veeck owned the ball club, and what a great guy he was. Veeck was a generous and good-natured man and a real hell raiser when he wanted to be. Of course, we didn't have a very good ball club, but that didn't seem to dampen his spirits any. One time we'd lost eight straight, and he decided to give a party, to loosen us up.

This was in Cleveland, at the Aviation Room in the Carter Hotel. It was a pretty fancy place, decorated with a lot of airplane stuff, and had a big, glass-framed picture of Eddie Rickenbacker on the wall. Veeck told the whole ball club to be there, every man. He hired a piano player, and he had plenty of food and drink laid out. It was a great time; we were singing songs and laughing and telling stories. You'd have thought we had just won the World Series instead of riding an eight-game losing streak.

Around one o'clock in the morning a few of us started getting ready to leave. But Veeck got by the door and said, "Nobody can leave until I say they can leave." Then he started opening champagne and squirting it at everybody. Vic Wertz and myself, we caught him and poured a bottle of it right down his back. He was laughing so hard we could hardly hold him. Then there was one bottle of scotch left and Veeck grabbed it and threw it at Eddie Rickenbacker's picture and smashed the glass frame into a thousand pieces.

It was a great party. Cost him $1,850, Veeck said. We went out the next day, nice and loose, and lost our ninth straight.

SPUD CHANDLER

Spurgeon Ferdinand Chandler
Born: September 12, 1907, Commerce, Georgia
Major-league career: 1937–47, New York Yankees
Lifetime record: 109 wins, 43 loses

Spud Chandler stands as the hardest-to-defeat pitcher in baseball history, with a lifetime won-lost percentage of .717. His earned run average of 1.64 in 1943 is the third lowest recorded in the era of the lively ball—since 1919. In 1947, at the age of 40, Chandler led the American League in earned run average for a second time.

When Joe McCarthy was asked who were the greatest pitchers he ever managed, he named Lefty Gomez, Red Ruffing— and Spud Chandler.

I used to have this reputation for keying myself up before a game to the point where I was so angry people couldn't talk to me. They said I used to sit in the clubhouse and scowl and glower, and that not until I was full of rancor was I ready to go out and pitch.

Well, that just wasn't true. I was just so determined to win that it might have looked that way. But I never got what you would call mad, or disgruntled, or overbearing. But that's the idea people got. Milton Gross, who used to cover the Yankees, wrote a story one time, "The Yankees' Angry Ace," and it was on the cover of the *Saturday Evening Post*. My father-in-law read it and began wondering what kind of monster his daughter was married to!

Angry? No. No reason to be. Determined, that's all I was.

Jeeminney, without determination how are you going to be a winner?

Well, maybe I should qualify it a little. I was kind of sore once before a game. It was my first start in the big leagues, in the spring of 1937, against the White Sox. I had the butterflies about as bad as you can get them. Joe McCarthy noticed that, and he called me into his office. He had a very stern look on his face.

"Chandler," he said, "what are you playing baseball for?"

"I'm playing baseball because I love it," I said, "and because it's my livelihood." I didn't know what in the world he was driving at.

"Do you think you're any good?" he asked.

"Yes, sir," I said. "I think I'm pretty good."

"You do, huh?"

"Yes, sir." I was getting irritated now.

"Do you think you're going to win today?"

"There's only one way to tell," I said. "Get your uniform on and come on out and we'll see."

Well, I pitched a four-hitter and got beat, 1–0. Zeke Bonura hit a home run.

McCarthy had seen how nervous I was, you see, and what he was trying to do was get my mind off that by getting me irritated. A little of the old psychology. He had a way of sticking the ice pick in you when it was real cold. But he had a reason for it. He always had a reason for everything he did.

I never heard McCarthy second-guess a pitcher the whole time I was with the Yankees. He was a terrific manager. You couldn't help but respect him, and he demanded respect, and he received it from every player on the club.

I was going along fine in 1937 until I hurt my arm. I had seven wins and two losses, and then I was pitching in Cleveland and hurt my arm. It became very doubtful whether I would pitch anymore that season. The Yankees wanted to strengthen their pitching staff a little bit, so they got Ivy Andrews from Cleveland and sent me to Newark for the rest of the season.

The Newark Bears in 1937 were unbelievable. You know, that was a big league ball club. They were tremendous. If my memory serves me correctly, just about every man on that club went to the major leagues except one, and he was an older pitcher that had pitched in the major leagues and came back down there as a relief guy. His name was Phil Page. But every one of the pitchers, the two catchers, the entire infield and outfield went to the major leagues. That had to be the greatest assemblage of minor-league players in the history of baseball.

The catchers were Willard Hershberger and Buddy Rosar. We had George McQuinn at first base, Joe Gordon at second, Nolan Richardson at shortstop, and Babe Dahlgren at third. The regular outfield was Charlie Keller, Bob Seeds, and Jimmy Gleason. The pitching staff was Atley Donald, Steve Sundra, Vito Tamulis, Joe Beggs, Phil Page, Marius Russo, and myself. Frank Kelleher was a utility man. There were others, too, but I can't remember them all now.

We won the pennant by 25½ games. Funny thing about the way the Little World Series turned out. We played Columbus, the Cardinals' Triple-A farm club. They came into Newark and beat us three straight. So a lot of people thought it was a long train ride from Newark, New Jersey, to Columbus, Ohio, just to play one game. But we went out and beat them four times and won the Little World Series. That was the 1937 Newark Bears. There's never been anything quite like them in baseball before or since. Who else but the Yankees of that era were good enough to have a major-league farm club in the minors?

In those years every kid wanted to play for the Yankees. That was the magic name. You didn't have to offer a kid a bonus to sign; that Yankee contract was bonus enough. But things have changed drastically since then. It changed when the other clubs began pouring out those big bonuses.

When I was finished as a player, I became a scout for the Yankees. I tried to sign Herb Score, and I begged and cried and pleaded for the money to get him with. Score wanted to go to the Yankees, too. Mr. Weiss used to tell me, "Now, don't just get a major-league prospect, get a Yankee type." What was a Yankee type? Well, I guess what he meant by that was a guy who really wanted to go with the Yankees and was willing to take whatever he was offered. Score had the greatest arm I ever saw on a young pitcher. Cleveland got him. I missed Frank Lary by $2,000. I missed Lary, I missed Score, and when you miss those kind, you're about ready to quit. That's what I did.

I guess it was that Yankee magic that got me. They were always the number one club in my mind. I'll tell you something, and a lot of people might think this is farfetched. But I made a statement one time in Yankee Stadium in a football uniform. I was with the University of Georgia football team, and we were in New York for a game with New York University. This was in 1929 or '30. It was on a Friday afternoon, the day before the game. During the preliminary workouts I was standing on the pitching mound, with a football in my hand, and I made the statement to two or three of the guys: "Right here is where I'm going to be."

I graduated from high school in 1928, in a little town in northeast Georgia by the name of Carnesville. It's the county seat of Franklin County. Then I went to the University of Georgia and played baseball there for four years, along with football and track. But baseball was always my first love. In the summers I worked all week on a construction job, from Monday morning till Saturday noon, then jumped in a Model T Ford and rode 20 miles and pitched one game and played outfield in the other.

The Cardinals tried to sign me in the summer of 1929 and the Cubs in the spring of 1932, but I continued in school and then signed with the Yankees after I graduated. You know, I received a much greater offer to go with the Cubs than I did with the Yankees—but there you are, that Yankee magic.

I ran into some trouble along the way in the minor leagues and was four and a half years getting to the majors. Even after I was with the Yankees for a few years, it still took a while before I became what I considered firmly established. That was in 1941. I came up with an extra pitch, a slider, and that turned everything around for me. I lost very few games after that. For the rest of my career my winning percentage was something like .750 or thereabouts.

I started the second game of the World Series that year, against Brooklyn. I thought I had real good stuff, but Whitlow Wyatt beat me, 3–2. People said at the time that I got tired running the bases and lost some of my effectiveness after that.

You see, we had instructions to take the extra base on Pete Reiser. We were told that he had a sore arm and couldn't throw too well. Well, we were ahead 2–0 in the fourth inning, and Joe Gordon opened with a single. I forced him at second.

Then Johnny Sturm dropped a single into short center, and I elected to try for third. I shouldn't have gone over, but I did. I could run pretty good and thought I had a chance. But I was thrown out on a close play.

After that I ran into trouble, and they blamed it on the running I had done, but I don't think it was that. I wasn't hit all that hard. Joe Gordon made a bad throw in the sixth to let a man on, and then Billy Herman got a single, and I was out of there. We lost the game, 3–2.

That was the Series where Mickey Owen let that third strike get away and turned the ball game around. It was all the opening we needed. All hell broke loose after that. Base hits like thunder. One of those freak games. Like the one Bevens pitched in Ebbets Field in the '47 Series. It always happens in Brooklyn, doesn't it? Sure seems that way. Everything is going along fine, and then boom! it explodes in your face and it's over. The no-hitter is gone, the game is gone, everything is gone, and you're in the clubhouse scratching yourself and wondering where it all went.

Bevens had good stuff in that game but he was wild. Walking men all over the place. What did I think when I saw Lavagetto's shot heading out toward right field? I was wishing the park was just a little bit bigger, so Henrich could catch it. But it wasn't, and he didn't, and that's the way those things happen. Nothing you can do about them. You have to take the bitter with the sweet, don't you? Like the day Deacon Jones, the umpire, cleaned off the Athletics' bench. Wally Moses was sitting down there in the corner, and Wally, you know, never said an unkind word to anybody in his life. So when Deacon Jones started to run them all, Wally just sat there.

"Wally," Deacon says, "you've got to go, too."

Wally jumped up and said, "You know I didn't say anything."

"Well, that's true," Deacon says. "But you know, when the law raids a house of prostitution, the innocent have got to go with the guilty. So get going!"

You know, you always hear about the Yankee power. We had it, of course. But we had to pitch just as hard as anybody to win because everybody was always out to beat us. The other clubs always had their best pitchers stacked up for us; often they would take them out of rotation to have them ready for us. You go to Detroit, and you know you're going to get Bridges, Rowe, Newsom. Same thing with the White Sox— you're going to get Thornton Lee, Ted Lyons. Cleveland always had Bob Feller and Mel Harder waiting. Those fellows didn't give up many runs, and you had to work hard to beat them. And we did beat them. Don't underestimate that Yankee pitching staff. It was *strong*.

Of course we had Joe DiMaggio, and that was a ball club in itself. For all-around ability and everyday play, DiMaggio was the greatest player I ever saw. Williams might have been a little better hitter, but he could only beat you one way, where DiMaggio could beat you about four. The most complete ballplayer I ever saw. And he was a great team man, very loyal to the ball club; he gave his best, he never caused any trouble, he never got into any arguments.

I want to tell you a story that happened to me. I'm in Maryville, Tennessee, three or four years after I retired as an active player. I'm sitting in the ball park with a scout from the Milwaukee Braves. We're looking at Tennessee State Teachers and Kentucky State Teachers playing a baseball game. Three college kids come in and sit down right beside us. A few minutes later somebody hits a long clout to center field. It was over the center fielder's head, and he turned and ran and made a leaping catch with his back to the playing field. It was a terrific play as far as I'm concerned, as good as you'll ever see.

One of the collegians jumped up and started giving the center fielder a cheer but one of the other boys said, "What's all the excitement?"

"Well, that's the greatest play I ever saw."

And the other one said, "That was nothing. You should have seen the one I saw one time."

Of course I can't help but to be overhearing all this.

"I hate to interfere with your conversation," I said. "But you mean you've seen a better play than that?"

"You bet I have," he says.

And I say, "Well, if you have, I bet you I can tell you where it was, who hit it, who caught it, who pitched it, and what the pitch was."

The fellow looks at me as if I'm a real wise guy.

"Was it in Yankee Stadium?" I ask him.

"Yes, sir," he says.

"Did DiMaggio catch it?"

"Yes."

"Well, Greenberg hit it, didn't he?"

"Yes," he says.

"Well," I said, "I'm the guy that threw it, and it was a fastball."

Talk about things coming back to you. Here I am, in the hills of Tennessee, and a kid is talking about the greatest play he ever saw.

It was probably the greatest play a lot of people ever saw. It's hard to believe that a fellow could hit a ball as high and as far as Greenberg did and have it caught. When the ball was caught, Greenberg was at second base—that's how far he'd run before it came down. It was hit all the way to what we used to call the graveyard out there in center field by those monuments. About 460 feet. DiMaggio—who played a comparatively short center field—took off at the crack of the bat, on a dead run, going at kind of an angle toward the fence. I don't think he ever looked back; he just seemed to have it in his head where that ball was going to come down. Right at the fence, at the 460 mark, he just flicked out his glove and caught the ball.

That occurred late in the season in 1939. We were way behind in the game at the time, and nothing was at stake. But that's the way Joe played ball—everything was at stake for him, all the time.

Another fellow I have nothing but praise for is Bill Dickey. He was a great guy to work with. He was real patient with a young pitcher, he'd always encourage you, and he seemed to know what to call for. I never questioned Bill but one time in a ball game. We were playing in New York, and I was pitching against Washington. Through the first seven innings I hadn't thrown anything but fast balls. As we went into the dugout at the bottom of the seventh, I said, "Bill, when are you gonna call for a curve ball?"

He sat down on the bench and began to undo his chest protector. Without looking at me, he said, "When they start hitting your fastball."

"Well," I said, "I don't think they're gonna start hitting it this late in the ball game, but I'm getting tired of throwing it. My arm is getting bored."

He called for one curve in the eighth and one in the ninth.

Then Detroit came in, and he called for but three curveballs in that game. I guess he saw that my fastball was running and sinking so good he'd stick with it. But I threw only five curveballs in two games and won them both easily. You didn't argue with Bill Dickey.

Ted Williams? He got me in his book the first game I pitched against him. Didn't take him long. He hit a ball way back in right field in the Stadium. I saw right then that there was no way I could pitch him with fastballs without him hitting those home runs. So I didn't throw him any fastballs; not for strikes anyway. He was the only hitter that I was ever a defensive pitcher against. I usually went after every hitter from the first pitch right on down. But with Williams it had to be different. I'd always set him up for the fastball and never give it to him. I'd make him hit the curves, the sliders, the changes, and I had great luck with him doing that. You always had to maneuver the ball around with Ted, no matter what the count was. He was such a great hitter. You just couldn't throw him a fast ball. He'd hit it. Feller's, anybody's. A tremendous hitter.

He said to me once, "You son of a gun, I always thought you'd eventually try to slip that fastball by me, and I was always ready for it. I was going to hit it out of the park. But I never got it."

He made a statement once that the three toughest pitchers he ever hit against were Bob Lemon, Hal Newhouser, and myself.

The Yankees always had this reputation for being all business, and on the field I guess we were. But off the field, well, we had our moments, just like anybody else. I'll tell you one that Atley Donald and I pulled on George Stirnweiss and Bud Metheny, when they were rookies on the club.

We were in Detroit, and we had a rainy day. Donald and me are sitting in our room watching the raindrops strike the windows.

"Hey," Donald says, "what do you say we get old Metheny and Stirnweiss on the phone and sell them some Huskies?"

"What are you talking about?" I ask him.

"We'll tell them we're coming up with a new breakfast product, and its name is gonna be Huskies, and we want their endorsements."

So he gets on the phone, with his hand sort of over the mouthpiece to disguise his voice, and he gives them a real sales pitch. Stirnweiss, you know, had set a record in the International League the year before stealing bases. So we were going to give him $500. Then he gets Metheny on the line.

"Well, Mr. Metheny," he says, "it's true you led your league in runs batted in, but somebody does that every year; you didn't set any records. So we can't give you but three hundred."

You should have heard Metheny. He really put up a battle, telling how important runs batted in were. But Atley finally got him to agree to $300.

"We'll pick you up in the lobby at four o'clock," he says.

At four o'clock we go down to the lobby. We get off the elevator, and there's Stirnweiss and Metheny, looking at everybody, waiting for the Huskies people. We pretended we had some business at the desk, sat around awhile, then went outside. We came back about thirty minutes later, and they're still sitting there.

That night we're going over to Cleveland, by boat. We get down to the dock and I say to Atley, "We ought to send them a night letter, explaining why we didn't make it."

"That's a great idea," he says.

So we sent them a night letter, and the address we gave was a bar that was right down the street from the Cleveland ball park. We were staying at the Cleveland Hotel, and from the end of one of the hallways there you could see down the street to the ball park. You also could see that bar. We told them in the night letter we were going to meet them there at ten o'clock in the morning.

We got into Cleveland at about eight o'clock in the morning and went straight to the hotel. At ten o'clock Donald and I go out into the hallway to that window. We're watching for a few minutes and then here they come, walking across the street. They walk down a block to the bar. And the bar is closed. Doesn't open till one o'clock. So they stand there and start shaking the doorknob and beating on the door. Then they backed up and started talking. I think they were beginning to get the idea that somebody was pulling their leg.

They came to the clubhouse that day, and they were looking

at everybody with a big grin, wondering who had been selling them the Huskies. We never did 'fess up, though.

That little escapade took place in 1943, which also happens to be the year I like best to remember. That was my peak. I was 20-4 and with any luck could've been 24-0. The most they scored off of me in any one ball game was four runs. I had 19 wins and 2 losses, and I lost an extra-inning ball game to Cleveland, and then after that I lost 3–2 in extra innings to Washington. My last start was in the stadium against Detroit, and it went fourteen innings before I won it, 2–1. After that game some photographer wanted a picture of Dickey and me, and while we were getting ready for that, Bill said, "This game got you the Most Valuable Player Award. You just won it, I guarantee you that." Well, I hadn't been thinking about that, but it turned out he was right.

I won the opening game of the World Series against the Cardinals in New York. And then I shut them out in the fifth game to win the Series. I wasn't what you'd call brilliant that game, even though I shut them out. I gave up ten base hits and a couple of walks. They left eleven men on base.

To my mind, the turning point in the ball game came in the fourth inning. There was still no score. Whitey Kurowski got on with a hit, and I walked Ray Sanders on four pitches. The next batter was Johnny Hopp. My first three pitches to him were wide of the mark. I'm in pretty deep trouble right here.

Dickey came out at that point to talk to me.

"What's the matter?" he asked.

"Nothing," I said.

"Then get the ball over the plate," he said, and went back.

Well, I got the next two over, and he took them for strikes. So now it's three and two. And I'll tell you what was in the back of my mind as much as anything else. Mort Cooper was looking great for the Cardinals. He'd struck out the first five men he faced and was throwing hard. The only way we were going to beat him was to hold the Cardinals down and wait for something to happen.

I made that three-and-two pitch to Hopp and I never will forget it as long as I live. It was a fastball, and it had to be at least eight to ten inches outside—and he swung at it and missed. I got the next two men on ground balls and was out of the inning. When I went back to the bench, I was so elated I said, "Fellows, there's no way I can lose today."

Cooper continued to be tough. But then in the sixth inning we broke through. With two out Keller got a single and Dickey hit one over the right-field roof. And that was it. That wound up 1943. That beautiful year.

FRANK McCORMICK

Frank Andrew McCormick
Born: June 9, 1911, New York, New York; Died: November
  21, 1982
Major-league career: 1934, 1937–48, Cincinnati Reds, Phila-
  delphia Phillies, Boston Braves
Lifetime average: .299

*Frank McCormick entered the National League as a spectac-
ular rookie and remained to become one of its most warmly
regarded veterans. In his first full year, 1938, he hit .327 and
led the league in hits; in his second year he hit .332 and led the
league in hits and runs batted in; in his third year he hit .309
and led the league in hits and doubles. In 1941 McCormick
struck out just 13 times in 603 at bats, a remarkable statistic
for a power hitter.*

I can remember, when I was about seventeen years old, I was
talking with my father, and he said to me, "What are you
planning to do with your life, Frank?"

Well, out of a clear blue sky, I said, "I'm going to be a
baseball player."

Believe me, a few seconds after I said that, I was scared to
death, wondering why I had ever said such a thing. My father
didn't say anything; I think he was as surprised as I was. But
he understood my love for the game and sympathized with my
determination to make good at it, and he went along with me.
Later, as things began to materialize for me, he was delighted.
But I don't think he ever quite got over that first shock of
hearing about it.

It wasn't that I didn't have baseball on my mind; I'd been

thinking about it an awful lot and, of course, playing. At that time I was playing ball on Sundays for a man named George Halpern, who had a team that traveled out of the Bronx.

When I first joined that team, they had only so many uniforms. I came out there week after week and had to sit on the bench, because they couldn't suit me up. Halpern kept giving the uniform he promised me to a guy named Harry. Finally one day we were playing up in Mosholu Field in the Bronx— it's called Frankie Frisch Field now—near the New York Central Railroad tracks, and my family and my friends all came out to see the game. So I went to Halpern.

"George," I said, "I've got to play today."

"Gee, Frank," he said, "I'm sorry, but Harry's going to have the uniform."

"Listen," I said, "I've been with you four or five weeks now, sitting on the bench, and I've never complained. But now my family's here, my friends are here, and I want to play."

He thought about it for a couple of moments.

"Okay, Frank," he said. "You can get in there today."

So I put the uniform on and played that day. I got two home runs and a double. After that, the uniform was waiting for me every Sunday. That's how I got started in high-caliber sandlot ball.

It was around that time that the Athletics brought me up to Yankee Stadium for a tryout. I met Connie Mack in the dugout, and we shook hands.

"Fine pair of hands, young man," he said to me. "Now get out there and let's see if you can hit."

So I went out on the field and stepped into the batting cage. Ed Rommel, the old pitcher, was on the mound. Now, I don't know what kind of mood he was in, playful, mischievous, nasty, or what, but he started throwing knuckleballs. And I mean big-league knuckleballs. I could hardly believe what I was seeing, much less hit them. So I went flat on my face in that tryout. I got to know Rommel well later on, and we used to chuckle over that. He'd just been having his fun, that's all. And who knows—if Rommel had thrown me fast balls that day, I might have wound up with the A's.

You know, I worked out with the Giants, too, for a whole week once. That was about in 1932; Bill Terry had just taken over. I'd been working in the shipping room of an art gallery in New York. One day I was holding some Early American glass, a cream pitcher and a sugar bowl. They were worth about $450. Well, somebody attracted my attention, and I sort of bumped them together and broke them. Some pair of hands! So I got fired. It was soon after that that I went up to the Polo Grounds to try out.

I thought I did all right, but they said to me, "Son, if you have a good job, keep it."

And that was right after I'd lost the job. This was during the Depression, remember, and jobs weren't easy to come by. So I was feeling pretty low when I took the subway home that day.

At that time some friends suggested to me that I take the test for the police department. I was sure I could pass, and it was for that very reason that I *didn't* take the test, because I knew if I passed, I probably would have taken the bird in hand and never known whether I could make the big leagues or not. And I'd made up my mind that I was going to be a baseball player. At least, I was going to give it my best shot, give myself every chance, and not ever have to be one of these frustrated athletes who goes through life wondering what might have been.

Six years later I was a unanimous choice as the National League's all-star first baseman, and Bill Terry—who'd turned me down at the Polo Grounds—was one of the men who picked me. I guess it would have been nice to play for the Giants, being a New York boy, but to tell the truth, I just wanted to get to the big leagues, and it didn't much matter who it was with.

Anyway, Larry MacPhail was running the Cincinnati Reds in those days, and George Halpern eventually inveigled Mac-Phail to send me a bus ticket to a tryout camp in Beckley, West Virginia. This was in 1934. I was an outfielder then, and just before I left, Halpern came up with a suggestion.

"Look, Frank," he said, "there's going to be about a hundred and fifty kids down there at that camp, and a lot of them are going to be outfielders. Why don't you buy yourself a first baseman's mitt? You'll have a better shot if you do."

I took his advice, and it turned out to have been a pretty good idea.

So my uncle loaned me fifty bucks—which didn't last very long—and I took a bus down to Beckley. It was up in the mountains of West Virginia, and it was cold. Sure enough, the field was flooded with kids trying out. But I'd made up my mind that I was going to make it. Anytime somebody hit a long ball, I'd tell myself that I was going to hit one further, and I did. One thing I could do was hit, and I was determined to show them that. I guess after a few days I was feeling good about myself, because Bobby Wallace, an old-time shortstop who was one of the scouts running the camp, came up to me and said, "You've got a good bat, kid, but how are you with that glove?"

"Try me," I said.

"I'm going to hit one through your legs," he said.

"No, you're not," I told him. Now that was pretty fresh, wasn't it? Bobby Wallace had played in the big leagues for *twenty-five* years!

So he took me out there, and for about a half hour he slashed them down to me. He marked up my shins, my knees, my arm, my chest, but he didn't get one through my legs. When it was over, I said to him, "Let's try it again tomorrow."

He laughed. "No, thanks. You've worn me out."

When I saw that I was going to make the team, I really began to feel my oats. I had a letter that said I'd get $100 a month if I made the team. But the contract they offered me called for only $90. I wouldn't sign.

"The letter says a hundred," I told them, and thought to myself, *Holy mackerel, McCormick, you're a holdout.*

"We can't change the contract," they said.

"So what are you going to do about it?" I asked.

They thought it over, then said, "Okay. We'll give you ten bucks under the table every month."

And that's what they did.

Life in the minors can be rough, there's no question about that. But I'll tell you, you can like it an awful lot if you know you have a chance to make the big leagues. I felt I had a good chance, so I enjoyed it. And you know, when some of us get together today, the reminiscing we do more often than not is not about the major leagues and the good times, the good money, the good food; it's about the days when we traveled by car and by bus. You talk about the days when you had to eat hot dogs by the roadside and slept all night on the bus, and the times when the bus broke down and you had to get out in the middle of the night and push the darn thing along a country road until you found a garage. You remember the clubhouses that didn't have showers and the ball parks without dugouts, where you had to sit out in the broiling sun throughout a Sunday doubleheader. Those days seem like the great days, when things were tough, when you were young, when you had all that drive and desire and ambition going for you, when you had that lovely goal at the end of the rainbow—the big leagues.

I had a good year at Beckley. Hit around .350. Our season closed in Charleston, West Virginia, and I was told then that the Reds were bringing me up for the last weeks of the major-league season.

I got on the train and rode all night in the coach car. Didn't sleep a wink. I just sat there stiff as a board, staring out the window. Couldn't sleep, couldn't eat, couldn't even think. The Reds were in Brooklyn then, and that's where I was heading.

My first time at bat in the major leagues was at Brooklyn, in old Ebbets Field. Charley Dressen, who was managing Cincinnati then, sent me up to pinch-hit. Dutch Leonard was the pitcher. I was so nervous that if you had put a brick between my knees, I'd have ground it into dust—that's how bad I was shaking.

I guess you never forget that first big league at bat. I hit a scorcher that handcuffed the second baseman, but they scored it an error. Later on, when I got to know Dutch Leonard, he said to me, "You know, Frank, they should have scored that a hit."

But you know the old story—if the guy gets his glove on it, it's an error.

Then we went into the Polo Grounds. I was sitting in the dugout when Carl Hubbell went out to warm up for the Giants. You should have heard the moaning on our bench: "Oh, it's that guy again." "Here's where I get the collar." Talk like that. Gee whiz, I thought, these guys are whipped even before they walk out on the field. I made up my mind that wasn't going to happen to me.

In the middle of the game I was sent up to pinch-hit against Hubbell. I walked up there thinking: Hubbell or no Hubbell, the guy has to throw the ball over the plate, and it's up to me to swing or not to swing. Well, I hit one right past him into center field. Dressen let me stay in the game, and the next time up I got myself another single to center. Two hits off of Carl Hubbell. Boy, my chest was all swelled up. I was half expecting a ticker-tape parade.

You know, a funny thing, I always had pretty good luck against Carl Hubbell—until he lost his stuff. That's right. Seems I just couldn't get it into my head that he didn't have that real great stuff anymore, and I'd go up there looking for it and keep getting fooled.

Later on, in St. Louis, I pinch-hit against Dizzy Dean. I hit a ball to deep short to Durocher. If there hadn't been a runner on first, who got forced out, I would have had a hit to deep short. The things you remember, huh? Well, why not? It's only forty years ago.

I guess I'd have to say that Dean and Feller were the fastest I ever saw. Flip a coin between them. They threw aspirin tablets up there. Now, I know you've heard that expression a thousand times—but it's still the best description.

I was farmed out the next few years and came back for good in 1938. Bill McKechnie was the Reds' manager then. He was the real fatherly type. You liked to play for him. He was very understanding, sympathetic. And yet I'll tell you one thing— when he put his hand across his chest and looked at you over his bifocals, he was mad. And as fine a gentleman as he was, he could be rough as a corncob when he thought you hadn't done the right thing.

We knew in 1938 that we had a good team in Cincinnati. We could feel it happening. We went to spring training the next year, in 1939, in a confident mood. After about the first six weeks of the season we became conscious of the fact that we could win the pennant. And we did win it. Bucky Walters and Paul Derringer won 52 games between them that year. Those guys were just remarkable.

Then of course there was the World Series that year. I should say, "What Series?" The Yankees took us four straight. I'll tell you though, it was the way that we lost the first game in Yankee Stadium that I think took the heart out of us. A fly ball in the ninth inning that might have been caught was the crucial play. Paul Derringer pitched brilliantly, but we lost, 2–1. If we had won that game we would have made, at least, a more presentable Series out of it.

We won the pennant again in 1940 and this time went against the Detroit Tigers in the Series. That 1940 World Series was an exciting one; it went the full seven games. They had us three games to two, but we still had Walters and Derringer. Bucky shut them out in the sixth game to even it up, and Derringer started the seventh game against Bobo Newsom.

Bobo was a tough character in that game. In fact, he was tough every game we saw him. He'd already beaten us twice and had us down 1–0 going into the bottom of the seventh of the last game. I came up and led off with a double. Then Jimmy Ripple hit one out to right field that Bruce Campbell just missed catching, and I scored the tying run. Jimmie Wilson sacrificed Ripple to third, and then Billy Myers hit a long fly ball to score Ripple. They couldn't score off Derringer the last two innings, and we won it, 2–1.

I'll tell you, winning that championship is quite something. It isn't just the money; it's the honor and the prestige, the pride you take in being called champion. You can't imagine what this means and how it feels until you've done it.

There was some icing on the cake for me that winter. I was voted the National League's Most Valuable Player. Well, coming on top of the World Series victory, that was quite a dividend. That's the ultimate, of course. There are a lot of honors in baseball, like being in the opening-day lineup, playing in the All-Star game, the World Series. But getting that MVP award is a special thing. That's in a class by itself.

I look back on 1940 as being a great season for the team and for me personally, but unfortunately it was marred by a very sad and tragic incident. In August, one of our catchers, Willard Hershberger, took his own life. There seemed to be no apparent reason for it; I suppose it was just one of those things that builds up inside a man until it reaches a point where he can't fight it off anymore.

It happened while we were in Boston. Most of the time Willard was a nice, easygoing fellow, but he could be moody; sometimes his spirits would be way up, other times way down. The night before it happened, he was way down. We were all in the lobby, and we saw him come out of the elevator with McKechnie. Willard obviously was in some emotional distress; his eyes were all welled up with tears. We saw that and turned away. Nobody said anything. He and McKechnie went into the dining room and had dinner, just the two of them.

The following day, no Hershberger at the ball park. Then somebody came hollering for McKechnie, and we knew something had happened. We learned later that Willard had taken a razor and cut his throat behind a locked door in his hotel room.

Why things like that happen is not for me to say. I couldn't tell you. The only one who could have shed some light on it was McKechnie. "I know what the story is," he said later. "I know what happened, but I'm going to my grave with it." And he did. Whatever it was that Willard confided in him, McKechnie would never tell it. That's the kind of man he was.

RIP SEWELL

Truett Banks Sewell
Born: May 11, 1907, Decatur, Alabama
Major-league career: 1932, 1938–49, Detroit Tigers, Pittsburgh Pirates
Lifetime record: 143 wins, 97 losses

Inventor and sole owner and proprietor of the famous blooper pitch, Rip Sewell has won himself a place in baseball folklore for his mastery of this baffling and effective delivery. Lest the blooper overshadow his other achievements, however, it should be remembered that Sewell was an ace pitcher for the Pirates for a decade, twice winning 21 games in a season and in 1943 leading all National League pitchers in complete games.

In 1931 I was attending Vanderbilt University, in Nashville, Tennessee. I was there on a football scholarship, even though baseball was still my favorite sport. I always had my eye on a career in professional baseball; ever since I was a kid growing up in Decatur, Alabama.

I was studying mechanical engineering at Vanderbilt, but I soon came to realize I wasn't going to make it as a mechanical engineer. Tell you the truth, a degree didn't seem so attractive in those days. This was during the Depression. You saw quite a few fellows with degrees under each arm trying to get a job, any job.

So I left school and went to work for Dupont, in Old Hickory, Tennessee, right across the river from Nashville. Got a job in the plant. I also started playing semipro ball in Old Hickory. Still had that baseball bug. The baseball virus.

The sports editor of the Nashville *Banner,* Freddie Russell, was a fraternity brother of mine. I went to him and said, "Freddie, I know I can play ball. I just want an opportunity to prove it to somebody."

He took me down to see the owner of the Nashville Vols. I worked out there, and they signed me to a contract for $400 a month. That was the most money I'd ever seen in my life. When I signed the contract, they told me, "If we sell you before the year is over, you'll get ten percent of the selling price." It was a verbal agreement, nothing in writing. Sure enough, Detroit bought me. They paid $10,000 and three ballplayers for me, Detroit did. But I still haven't seen any part of that $10,000 or of the three ballplayers either for that matter.

I was up with the Tigers for a while in 1932. They used me in relief, though I didn't see too much action. I can tell you about the game that knocked me out of the big leagues at that time. It was one pitch that did it. I went in to relieve against the Athletics. There were a couple of men on base, and Jimmie Foxx was up. To this day I can see him standing there, his big-muscled arms looking like piano legs hanging out of a churn. I threw him one of my best pitches—I thought—and he hit it over the left field wall. The next day I was on my way to Toronto.

The Tigers recalled me in 1934, and I went to spring training with them in Lakeland, Florida. I had high hopes of sticking this time, but something happened down there that put a damper on my chances. About a week before camp broke, I had a fight with Hank Greenberg, who at that time was one of their up-and-coming young players. It was just one of those things that happens for no good reason and that you're real sorry about later. Hank and I had played together at Beaumont, and we'd been good friends, so this thing just came out of nowhere.

It started on a bus ride, coming back from Bradenton, after a game with the Cardinals. Tex Carleton had shut us out, 3–0. He'd struck Greenberg out two or three times. Sidearm fastballs, you know, and Hank didn't like it one bit. He was brooding on it.

After the ball game we got on the bus to go back to Lakeland. Greenberg gets on and sits down next to an open window, somewhere around the middle of the bus. Denny Carroll, the trainer, and Gerald Walker got on and went to the back of the bus together. When Gerald went by Hank—Gerald was a character anyway—he rubbed his hand over Hank's face and said, "Why don't you get that sour look off your puss?" Something like that. That didn't help Hank's disposition, I'm sure.

I was sitting two seats behind Greenberg, and in front of me was a kid pitcher. You know, the kind you call bush. Once the bus got going, the wind started blowing and it was getting cool. Denny Carroll called out to Greenberg, "Henry"—he called him Henry—"pull that window down. You'll give everybody back here a cold."

Greenberg didn't do anything. Just sat there.

The bus kept going, and the wind kept blowing in, and it was getting real chilly.

"Henry," Denny Carroll called out again, "pull that window down. Everybody back here's getting a chill."

Greenberg didn't say nuts. He just sat there.

So the kid pitcher is sitting behind him, and I'm sitting behind the kid pitcher. The kid could have reached forward and pulled the window down. I tapped him on the shoulder and said, "Hey, bush, pull the window down."

Well, Greenberg evidently thought I was talking to him. So he turned around and said to me, "Who you calling a bush, you Southern son of a bitch?"

Well, you know that's fightin' words in my part of the country. Son of a bitch is bad enough, but *Southern* son of a bitch, that was the kicker. So I said, "You, you big Jew son of a bitch, if it fits you." So I got right back. I didn't back off from anybody.

He said, "I'm gonna take your ass on when we get to Lakeland."

I said, "You can stop the damn bus right now if you want to do that."

There wasn't another word said until we got to Lakeland. We pulled up right in front of the hotel. Mickey Cochrane, who was the manager, and Frank Navin, who owned the club, were sitting there—they'd taken a car back. They were sitting in wicker chairs in the big front window, their feet up on the windowsill.

We started getting off the bus. Greenberg was ahead of me. When I stepped off, he hit me right upside the damn head. He must've had a ring on or something, because he just took the skin right off.

Well, we fought; hell, it must've been a half hour. And Cochrane and Navin sat there in that big window and watched. We just fought and fought and fought. Off the curb and into the street, out of the street and across the grass and through the hedges. He was a big guy, and so was I. Nobody tried to stop it. Finally a plainclothes cop came walking across the street and pulled out a blackjack. "Y'all stop this damn fight," he said, "or I'm gonna bop both of you." So he was the one who finally stopped it, this plainclothes cop. Then Cochrane told us to get up to our rooms and he'd see us in the morning. Why didn't Cochrane break it up? Well, I guess he figured he didn't start it. Only thing I can think of. Mickey was from the old school.

But after that I knew I was gone. I knew it. The next day Cochrane called me in and said, "Rip, don't think I feel any the less about you for it; in fact, I think more of you. But we've got thirty pitchers and only one first baseman. What do you think I'm going to do?"

"Well," I said, "I know what you're going to do."

I spent that summer in Toledo.

You know, just to jump ahead, in 1947 Greenberg joined the Pirates when I was still there, and we became good friends. He didn't stay with the Pirates but one year, but we were real close friends then, I'm happy to say.

The Pirates bought me from Buffalo at the end of the 1937 season. I went to spring training with them in '38 and made the club. Pie Traynor was managing then, but I didn't really get a chance to pitch until Frankie Frisch took over a year or so later. Frisch gave me my chance, and I owe everything to him.

Arky Vaughan was in his heyday at shortstop for the Pirates when I got there. I'd say that he was as good a man at short as I ever saw. He could do it all. And he was a good hitter. He could hit for power, and he could hit for average. And could he ever fly around those bases! I never saw anybody who could go from first to third or from second to home faster than Vaughan. Like we used to say, when he went around second his hip pocket was dipping sand. That's how sharp he cut those corners.

Paul and Lloyd Waner were still in the outfield for the

Pirates. You liked to see those fellows out there when you were pitching. And they could still wheel those bats. You know, they came from back on the farm in Oklahoma. They used to raise corn there, and they always used to have a great big stack of corncobs after shelling the corn and getting rid of it for the grain feed. Lloyd told me that's where he and Paul learned how to be good batters. They'd throw wet corncobs all day and try to hit them. You take a wet corncob and break it in half and throw it, and it'll go like a rocket. He said that was their pastime out there when they were kids growing up. For a bat they'd use an old pick handle or anything else they could come by.

You say you want to know the story of the blooper pitch? Well, that started with a shotgun blast in the Ocala National Forest on December 7, 1941. So that's a date I'll remember for more than one reason. I was out deer hunting that day. I was walking through the woods when another hunter spotted something moving. What he spotted was me, but he didn't realize that until he had turned suddenly and discharged two loads of buckshot out of a twelve-gauge shotgun at about thirty feet. Caught me in both legs. That shot tore holes in me as big as marbles. One of them smashed up the big toe which I pitched off of.

I had to learn to walk all over again, keeping that big toe up when I moved. Naturally my whole pitching motion had to be changed. I had to pitch just like I walked, like I was taking a step forward, all the while keeping that big toe up.

That's how the blooper ball came about, from having to learn to pitch with that motion, like I was walking toward you. I was the only pitcher to pitch off of the tip of his toes, and that's the only way you can throw the blooper. It's got to be thrown straight overhand. I was able to get a terrific backspin on the ball by holding onto the seam and flipping it off of three fingers. The backspin held it on its line of flight to the plate. So that ball was going slow but spinning fast. Fun to watch, easy to catch, but tough to hit. It helped me win 21 games in '43 and again in '44.

I was fooling around with Al Lopez in the bullpen one time and started looping the ball and dropping it into his glove. All of a sudden Lopez said, "Why don't you throw that in a game?"

I laughed. "Man, no," I said. "Frisch would get after me, and so would everybody else if I threw it in a game."

Then we were in Muncie, Indiana, playing an exhibition game against the Detroit Tigers. Dick Wakefield was at bat, with two out. Out of a clear blue sky I decided I was going to throw him that blooper ball. So I wound up and let it go. The thing went way up in the air, and coming down, it looked like it was going to be a perfect strike. He started to swing, he stopped, he started again, he stopped, and then he swung and missed it by a mile. I thought everybody was going to fall off the bench, they were laughing so hard.

Later I was sitting in the clubhouse, and all the newspaper boys came around to ask me what in the hell that was. Maurice Van Robays was sitting next to me. Maurice says, "That's an eephus ball."

Somebody said, "What's an eephus ball?"

Maurice says, "Eephus ain't nothin', and that's what that ball is."

So then they started calling it the eephus pitch. That's the way it got started. I got more funny reactions from that than you can imagine. The fans loved it. And a lot of times some of the players on the opposing team would whistle out to me, when one of their own players was at bat, and make their fingers dive up and down through the air, telling me to throw it. You see, most guys usually swung at it no matter where it was. It was like waving a red flag in front of a bull. Made them mad as hell. It looked like anybody could knock it out, and they always tried.

I had as good control of it as I did of my fastball and curve. I'd spot it around here and there, when they were least expecting it. It reached an arc of about 25 feet.

When I first started throwing that thing, I had more trouble from the umpires with it than I did from the batters. Some of the umpires said they wouldn't call it a strike, no way. I heard about that and told Frisch. He became concerned because that damned pitch was becoming a drawing card. We had people coming in from West Virginia and Ohio and everywhere else just to see it.

The Pirate management got hold of Bill Klem. He was the supervisor of National League umpires at that time. And of course you know Klem's reputation—the greatest umpire of them all. So he came to Pittsburgh and came into the clubhouse to see me. He told me to get a catcher and a batter and to go out to the mound. We did that, and he got behind the plate to see if it was true the blooper was a strike. I began demonstrating it. He watched me throw it in for a while, and then he said, "Okay. It's a strike, and I'll see that they call it." From then on they called it.

I guess the most famous blooper pitch was the one I threw to Ted Williams in the '46 All-Star game in Fenway Park. Before the game, Ted said to me, "Hey, Rip, you wouldn't throw that damned crazy pitch in a game like this, would you?"

"Sure," I said. "I'm gonna throw it to you."

"Man," he said, "don't throw that ball in a game like this."

"I'm gonna throw it to you, Ted," I said. "So look out."

Well, if you remember that game, they had us beat 8–0 going into the last of the eighth. It was a lousy game, and the fans were bored. I was pitching that inning, and Ted came to bat. You know how Ted used to be up there at the plate, all business. I smiled at him. He must've recalled our conversation because he shook his head from side to side in quick little movements, telling me not to throw it. I nodded to him: You're gonna get it, buddy. He shook his head again. And I nodded to him again. He was gonna get it. So I wound up like I was going to throw a fastball, and here comes the blooper. He swung from Port Arthur and just fouled it on the tip of his bat.

He stepped back in, staring out at me, and I nodded to him again: You're gonna get another one. I threw him another one, but it was outside and he let it go. Now he was looking for it. Well, I threw him a fastball, and he didn't like that. Surprised him. Now I had him one ball, two strikes. I wound up and threw him another blooper. It was a good one. Dropping right down the chute for a strike. He took a couple of steps up on it—which was the right way to attack that pitch, incidentally—and he hit it right out of there. And I mean he *hit* it.

Well, the fans stood up, and they went crazy. I walked around the base lines with Ted, talking to him. "Yeah," I told him, "the only reason you hit it is because I told you it was coming." He was laughing all the way around. I got a standing ovation when I walked off the mound after that inning. We'd turned a dead turkey of a ball game into a real crowd pleaser.

And he was the only man ever to hit a home run off the blooper. Ted Williams, in the '46 All-Star game.

BOB FELLER

ROBERT WILLIAM ANDREW FELLER
Born: November 3, 1918, Van Meter, Iowa
Major-league career: 1936–56, Cleveland Indians
Lifetime record: 266 wins, 162 losses

In a sport not noted for its prodigies, Bob Feller stands supreme. Achieving star status at seventeen with a suddenness that was as dramatic as it was remarkable, Feller became baseball's most electrifying performer since Babe Ruth. In all of sport, there are few names that match the magic and glamor of Bob Feller's. Among the most eye-catching of his many achievements, in addition to his three no-hitters and record-breaking strikeout performances, were the 12 one-hitters he pitched.

Feller was elected to the Hall of Fame in 1962.

How fast? Well, it so happens I can give you a precise answer, because they tested it once. This was in Washington, D.C., in 1946. When we got into town, I read in the paper that Clark Griffith was going to set up a speed meter at home plate and that I was going to throw the ball through it to measure my velocity.

Griffith's attendance was down at the time. He had a terrible ball club that year—they'd cinched last place by about Mother's Day. So, to help draw a crowd, he got this photoelectric-cell device from the ordnance plant in Aberdeen, Maryland. Aberdeen was a proving ground where the government tested the speed of projectiles, of ammunition, and so forth. He had it set up over home plate and loud and clear announced that I was going to throw through it. Without asking me.

Nobody had ever asked me about it. Griffith hadn't told me or the Cleveland ball club a thing about it.

Well, all I had going for me at the time was I was tied with Hal Newhouser in wins, I was trying to break the strikeout record for a season, and I was leading the league in earned run average. So I was in no way going to go out there and throw through that Mickey Mouse–Rube Goldberg device without being *asked*. And I never was asked, until Griffith came into the clubhouse before the game.

"Bob," he said, "the fans are waiting out there now. We've got the device set up over the plate. So why don't you get out there and take your warm-up pitches and throw through the meter before you start the ball game?"

"How many times do I have to throw through it?" I asked.

"Oh, about thirty or so," he said.

"And then go out and pitch my ball game. Well, I'll tell you, Mr. Griffith, I have a contract based upon my number of wins, so I have a lot going for me every time I pitch. You're asking me to throw a lot of pitches that could jeopardize my game. So it'll take a thousand bucks for me to go out there and throw through that bunch of wires."

When I said that, his head and his feet changed places.

"Bob," he said, "this kind of promotion is good for baseball. The fans really appreciate this sort of thing."

"That's all well and good," I said. "But you've got thousands and thousands of people out there who've come to watch it. You're not losing anything on it, are you?"

"That's not the point," he said.

I don't know if we ever decided what the point was, but he finally talked me down to $700 to go out there and do it.

I lost the ball game that night. I don't know if I wore myself out on that damned machine, but I lost the game something like 2–1 in ten or eleven innings. Griffith probably made over $20,000 on the deal, if you want to count the concessions. And I got my $700. But all he had to do was ask me first, and I probably would have done it for nothing.

What did the ball clock in at? 98.6 miles an hour as it crossed the plate. I threw thirty or forty times. I guess I was as fast as I ever was that night. I was as fast in '46 and the early part of '47 as I ever was.

At that rate of speed it took about a third of a second for the ball to leave my fingers and get up to the plate. Which means the hitter had that much time to make up his mind whether it was a curve or a fastball or a slider, a ball or a strike, whether to take it or to swing at it, and where he wanted to hit. I think it takes more ability to be a complete ballplayer than it does to play any major sport that I know of. Good reflexes, good eye, good coordination. You'd better have them.

Where did it all start? Van Meter, Iowa. I grew up there on a farm, about three miles outside town. It was a corn and hog farm. I did the usual chores that any kid does on a farm—milk the cows, feed the pigs, clean out the barn on Saturdays, put up fences.

In the early thirties the dust storms, the grasshoppers, the lack of rain played havoc with us. The cattle were starving and dying of thirst. Perhaps it wasn't so bad in that part of Iowa as it was further out in Nebraska and Kansas and the Dakotas. But we had to carry water out of the river, when the river had water in it, and put it in the wagon and dump it into a tank and haul it for the livestock. The streams were very low. Nothing would grow. The dust would pile up along the fence lines like snow.

Things were pretty tough, but we always managed to have a garden, and we had enough water to water it, so we had fruit and vegetables. And we did have the livestock, and we did have corn and grain in storage, which we fed them. Farmers, at least in that part of the country, usually had enough to eat, one way or the other. It may not have been enough, but it was something.

But whatever we didn't have, we always had baseball. I guess I could always throw hard, even when I was eight or nine years old. I used to play catch with my father in the house. I'd throw from the kitchen into the living room and he'd sit there on the davenport and catch me with a pillow. It wasn't long after that that he got a mitt for himself and a glove for me, and bats and balls.

Then he made a home plate in the yard, and I'd throw to him over it. He even built me a pitching rubber. When I was twelve, we built a ball field on our farm. We fenced off the pasture, put up the chicken wire and the benches and even a little grandstand behind first base. We formed our own team and played other teams from around the community on week-

ends. We had tournaments. The field was up on a little hill
and we called it Oak View because you looked right down over
the Raccoon River and saw a lot of oaks in the forest there.
The crops and the trees and the river made a very pretty view.
Artistically speaking, it was rather an interesting ball park.

Obviously my father loved baseball, and he cultivated my
talent for the game. I don't think he ever had any doubt in his
mind that I would play professional baseball someday. There
was no question about it being his ambition for me.

We practiced together constantly. In the wintertime we'd
throw in the barn. In 1924 we got a Delco plant to electrify the
property—this was about fifteen years before the power lines
came in. We had a windcharger, and on a windy day that
would charge the batteries, and we would use the lights in the
barn to play night baseball—if you want to call it that—two
or three nights a week to keep my arm in condition.

Dad would have me pitching under game conditions. We
would simulate an entire game. I'd pitch with men on base,
and we had a standard which he moved from side to side in the
batters box so I'd have to pitch to both right- and left-hand
hitters.

One summer's night we were in the barn, and I was pitching
a "game." My father crouched down to give me the sign. He
put out two fingers to call for a curveball and got set for it.
Well, it was kind of late in the evening, around nine or nine
thirty, and getting dark in there, and I thought he'd called for
a fastball. So instead of the ball breaking down and away, as
he expected, it came in straight, with a hop, and hit him in the
side and broke a couple of ribs. They had to tape him up from
his waist to under his armpits, and for a farmer to have to
work under those conditions was miserable.

I played four years of American Legion ball, beginning
when I was twelve. In 1934 some of the umpires in Legion ball
started telling Cy Slapnicka of the Cleveland Indians about
me. At first he didn't pay much attention to them—scouts are
always getting these rave reports on kids from one source or
another. But they kept after him. You know how people can
be—the less attention you pay them, the more enthusiastic
they're apt to become. So they kept bombarding Slapnicka
about me. "Greatest thing since sliced bread," etc. etc.

He didn't get out to see me until 1935, and even then I think it was just to humor those umpires and get them off his back. He came out there, figuring he'd have a look at the farmboy and then go on and attend to some serious business—he was planning to scout Claude Passeau, who was pitching for Des Moines, in the Western League.

Well, he never did see Passeau. He didn't buy Passeau. He bought me. Gave me a big bonus, too—an autographed ball and $1—to sign a contract for $75 a month. I was glad to get it, and my relationship with the Cleveland ball club, and Cy Slapnicka in particular, and the fans in Cleveland in general, and the writers, was a very happy one. I'm glad I didn't get a bonus. I think you're supposed to get paid after you do your job. I was well paid in Cleveland and have no complaints whatsoever.

This was in June, 1935. I was sixteen years old then. I was supposed to go to Fargo, North Dakota, when high school was out. But then I pitched five games in eight days in the state high school tournament, and I strained my arm. I couldn't throw. I informed the Cleveland ball club, and they brought me to Cleveland for the trainer to fix my arm up. All I needed really was some rest. I worked out with the club, played pepper, did some running. I had no broken bones or torn cartilages, so for what was bothering me, rest was the great healer.

In 1936 I stayed with the Cleveland ball club. Slapnicka was general manager then. What he did, in order to make me eligible to pitch for Cleveland, was put through a series of phony transfers of my contract through different minor league clubs until it was switched to Cleveland. This was clearly in violation of the rules, and Judge Landis caught up to him later on it.

I spent the spring of '36 with Cleveland trying to learn my business. And I had a lot to learn. Pitching in the big leagues is more than just throwing a fastball. Then, on July 6, during the All-Star game break, the St. Louis Cardinals came to town for an exhibition game. Slapnicka suggested I pitch a few innings, kind of as a lark, to save the pitching staff. Of course, he knew me better than anyone else did and figured, kid or no kid, I probably wouldn't embarrass myself.

The Cardinals had a pretty good lineup—Joe Medwick, Frankie Frisch, Pepper Martin, Rip Collins, Leo Durocher.

No, I wasn't nervous. I never had any concern about the hitters as long as I could get that ball over the plate. My own concern that day was the crowd. I'd never seen so many people before in my life.

If anybody was nervous that day, it was the Cardinals. I was very wild and had them scared half to death. The first big league batter I ever pitched to was Leo Durocher. The first pitch was over his head and into the screen. The next one was behind him. And of course those pitches were pretty fast. The next two pitches were strikes. Then Steve O'Neill, who was catching, said, "You'd better be careful, Leo. He's liable to stick this next one right in your ear." So Leo, who'd been pretty loose up there, dropped the bat and ran back to the dugout and hid behind the water cooler, pretending he was scared. Cal Hubbard, who was umpiring, told him to come back up to the plate, that he had another strike coming. Leo leaned out from behind the water cooler and cupped his hands around his mouth and yelled, "The hell with you, Hubbard. You take it for me." Dizzy Dean was sitting there laughing his head off. Leo was the first big-league hitter I ever struck out.

I pitched three innings and fanned eight out of nine. There's a story that went around at the time, that after the game some photographer asked Dean if he would pose for a picture with me, and Dean is supposed to have said, "You'd better ask *him* if he'll pose with *me*."

Right after that I joined the Cleveland pitching staff, getting into games that were lost, mopping up, that sort of thing. Then they started me, against the St. Louis Browns. This was in August. I had very good stuff and felt confident. I went out there and struck out 15. That hit the newspapers pretty hard. It wasn't that 15 strikeouts was so great, it was because I was so young. I was only seventeen. But also you have to remember that generally there were fewer strikeouts in those days. You had more choke hitters, they weren't swinging so hard.

I threw the fastball primarily in that game, but I had a curve then, too. I always had a good curve, even when I was a kid back in Iowa. I think if you talk to the guys who hit against me, they'll tell you, "Fastball hell, look at the curve he had." I struck out as many with the curve as I did with the fastball.

Three weeks later I struck out 17 Philadelphia Athletics,

and that broke the American League record. I was pretty excited over that. I knew I was approaching the record. I was counting those whiffs. There's no way you can duck it. And the closer I got to that record, the more I wanted to break it. I just kept pouring them in, trying to keep the ball over, hoping the guys wouldn't start choking up on the bat and start pushing the ball around.

That hit the newspapers like thunder and lightning, and I guess that's when people began to realize I was for real.

Was I the most famous kid in America in 1936? Come on now. You're forgetting about Shirley Temple, aren't you? And what about those kids in the *Our Gang* comedies? Anyway, I was seventeen years old. You want to call that a kid? Okay, maybe by baseball standards.

I tried not to let it all bother me too much. I went back to the farm, went hunting with my friends, went to basketball games. Sure, people would gawk at me and point me out like I was some sort of circus freak, and it took awhile to get accustomed to. I didn't pay that much attention to it. My father had a lot of common sense, and he saw to it that I didn't get swell-headed about it. He told me that people would be nitpicking and asking silly questions and trying to use me, that people always wanted to bask in reflected notoriety, good, bad, or indifferent. Sometimes your best friends are your worse enemies, wanting to keep you out late at night so they can be seen with you. These things happen in all walks of life, not only baseball.

So my life didn't change as much as it might have, given all the circumstances. I knew where the stakes were set, due to the fact my parents told me where they were set. They gave me a pretty good idea of values. My mother was a schoolteacher, and it was important to her that I get that high school diploma, and it was important to me too. I didn't exactly crack the books until three o'clock in the morning, but I did graduate.

In the winter of '36 Slapnicka's manipulating of my contract came to the attention of Judge Landis. You see, in those days major-league clubs couldn't sign free agents. Minor-league clubs would sign all the players and then sell them to the major-league clubs to make ends meet financially. This was by agreement. Well, the major-league clubs were all cheating.

They were signing players off the sandlots, and Judge Landis knew it. I was one of them. So it became within his authority to make me a free agent. If he had done that, I could've picked up $100,000 or more in bonus money. There were scouts sitting in the Chamberlain Hotel in Des Moines with blank checks in their hands, just waiting.

But I was loyal to the Cleveland club, and so were my parents. The ball club had done a great deal for us and had been very friendly. When my arm was bad, they took care of it, brought me along with compassion and understanding, instead of shooting me up to Fargo, where I might have injured it permanently and wound up milking cows the rest of my life—nothing wrong with that, but it wasn't my life's ambition to be a dairy farmer. I wanted to be a baseball player.

Well, my father and I met several times with Judge Landis. The judge said he was going to declare me a free agent. My father didn't like that one bit.

"The Cleveland ball club has treated us fair," he told the judge. "It's our intention for him to play for Cleveland, if they want him, and they want him. And if you won't permit that, then we're going to sue you in civil court, because we have a civil law contract and we want to test it to see if baseball law supersedes civil law."

Well, the judge wanted no part of that. He didn't want to hear anything about it, and this is why I was able to stay with Cleveland.

How did I feel about it? Well, sure I could have gotten $100,000. But I didn't care about that. I wanted to stay where I was. I was happy. I was pitching major-league baseball and was quite successful. I figured if I was worth that kind of money, I'd make it later, after I'd proved I was worth it. And if I wasn't worth it, then I had no business having it.

It took me about three years to learn how to pitch in the big leagues. Like I said, it's more than just a fastball. You have to learn how to hold runners on, how to field your position, how to *think* out on the mound. By the end of 1938 I'd absorbed a lot of that. That was my first really big year, 1938. Coming down to the last day of the season, I was running close with Bobo Newsom for the lead in strikeouts. I was anxious to lead the league, and so was Bobo. Well, I pitched my game and went into the clubhouse. I no sooner get in there than I get a phone call. It's from Bobo. Long distance. I forget where he was, St. Louis or someplace.

"Hey, Bob," he says,"how are you?"

"Pretty good, Bobo," I said. "How are you?"

"Okay," he says. "Listen, it's been a hell of a race for strike-outs, hasn't it?"

"Sure has."

"I think I beat you out," he says. "I struck out twelve today. What kind of a game did you have?"

"Well, I lost four to one, Bobo."

"That's too bad."

"But I struck out eighteen."

There was a long silence, which was unusual with Bobo, and then he said, "Congratulations."

Yeah, that was the day I broke the record. October 2, 1938. That's a day I'll always remember. It was the last day of the season, and we were playing the Tigers a doubleheader in Municipal Stadium in Cleveland. There must've been about 30,000 people in the stands. But they weren't there to see me; they were there to see Hank Greenberg try and break Ruth's record. Hank had 58 home runs, and this was going to be his last whack at that record.

In anticipation of Hank's breaking that record, there were newsreel cameras in from New York and elsewhere to document it. Well, instead of getting Hank breaking a home run record, they got me breaking the major-league strikeout record for one game, which was nice for me, because it's all recorded on film.

I was fast that day and had a very good curve. If I remember correctly, I struck out the side in the second, third, and fourth. I know that by the end of five innings I had 12 strikeouts. At the end of seven I had 15. I got one more in the eighth and went into the ninth inning needing one to tie the record—which I held jointly with Dizzy Dean—and two to set a new record.

I tied the record by fanning the leadoff man, Pete Fox. Then Greenberg came up. I'd already fanned Hank twice, and this time he hit a long fly ball to center. The next batter was Chet Laabs. I'd been feasting on him all afternoon—striking him out four times. So he was as determined as he could be not to strike out again. I ran the count to one and two. Then I threw him a fastball around the knees, close to the corner. He made a move as if he was going to swing, but he didn't swing. He took it. It could have been called either way. Cal Hubbard called it a strike. Number 18.

It was a nice way to end the season, and I basked in that one all winter long, even though I lost the game.

The 1940 season started off on a high note for me. We opened in Chicago against the White Sox. It was a cool day, I remember, the temperature in the 40's. My parents were there, and my sister, and some friends and relatives from Iowa.

We got a run in the fourth inning. Jeff Heath singled, and Rollie Hemsley tripled. That was the only run of the game. I don't think I had particularly good stuff that day, but when it came down to two out in the ninth, I had a no-hitter going. Taft Wright was the hitter. He was always tough for me. Sure enough, he hit a hard shot between first and second that Ray Mack, the second baseman, made a tremendous play on. He speared the ball about five feet back on the grass, did a complete 360-degree turn, and threw Taft Wright out by a step at first base. It was a tough play; the ball was well hit.

I got a big kick out of that. It was my first no-hitter and still the only one ever pitched on opening day.

We were running well in 1940; in fact, we were about 5½ games ahead in August. But we were having a problem with our manager, Oscar Vitt. It went back to when he first came to the team in 1938. Some of the players didn't like him for one reason or another. They thought his strategy was bad, his selection of pitchers was bad, his batting order was bad. Oscar Vitt is dead now, so I won't go into the details completely. But a lot of the players felt that tactically he just was not an able manager and that we wouldn't win the pennant unless he changed his approach.

So some of us went to the club president, Alva Bradley, and told him what we thought. We told him we felt we should have a change in field management. Mr. Bradley always said that Oscar Vitt talked too much, and he happened to be right. In fact, he told Oscar that when he hired him. If you talk too much, inevitably you're going to say the wrong thing. That goes for anybody, myself included.

But Vitt stayed till the end of the year, and we blew the pennant. I don't think our rebellion—if you want to call it that—had anything to do with it because that happened in June and we blew the pennant in September. Naturally the situation with Vitt wasn't conducive to a happy summer. It got into the papers, and the fans picked it up. One of the players had squealed to a friend in the press about the meeting with Bradley. I know who it was, but never mind. It shouldn't have been in the paper—it was a family squabble, you might say—but this guy wanted to get himself in good with one of the writers and told him about the meeting, and the thing ignited. So we got the name "crybabies," but that was a lot of nonsense. We felt we were justified in what we were doing.

At the very end of the season the Tigers came in for a three-game series needing only one win to clinch it. We really had our backs to the wall. I started the first game on a Friday afternoon. I'd been pitching real fine ball against the Tigers and was hoping to get us started off on the right foot.

The Tigers had a great pitching staff. They had Bobo Newsom, Tommy Bridges, Schoolboy Rowe. Each man was a fine pitcher, and experienced. Whichever one went out that day would give us a battle. But the damnedest thing happened. Detroit didn't start any of them. They started a fellow named Floyd Giebell, who they'd brought in from Buffalo a few weeks earlier. I don't think anybody had ever heard of him before. I blinked when I saw him come out to warm up. I had no idea who he was.

You see what they were doing. They didn't want to start any of their big pitchers against me; they were going to save them for the last two games. So they threw Giebell in as a give-up. Some give-up! All he did was shut us out. We got some hits off of him, a few walks, but we left a lot of men on base. Floyd Giebell pitched the game of his life and shut us out.

I gave up just three hits, but one of them came after a walk to Charlie Gehringer. Rudy York hit one that was in on his fists and lifted it down the left field line, and it went just far enough to carry over the barrier for a home run. That was the ball game, right there. And the pennant.

Floyd Giebell never won another game in the big leagues,

but I guess he made a place for himself in baseball history that day.

Joe DiMaggio? Sure, Joe gave me a lot of trouble—listen, he gave everybody a lot of trouble. He was a very fine hitter, with great power. He could do everything. He was a tremendous base runner; he could go from first to third, break up the double play. Wonderful arm; always threw to the right base. And he could cover the territory. He was an inspirational ballplayer, a real pro.

I started getting him out later on, after I'd learned how to pitch to him, but that was about the time he hung up his spikes. I started throwing him fastballs in tight, around his fists and his belt, crowding him, pushing him back. If I'd have done that earlier, I would have been all right. But I didn't do that. I was afraid I'd hit him, and I didn't want to hit him, any more than I wanted to hit anybody else, but particularly Joe and Ted Williams, because they were such great hitters and great competitors and drew a lot of people into the ball park. I didn't want to be boring in on them any more than they wanted to hit line drives through the box.

Did I ever throw intentionally at anybody? No, heavens no. It's only a game, you know. Now, when I say that, I don't mean anything derogatory about conditioning yourself, about preparing yourself to win and trying to win and doing all you can to win. But none of that gives you a license to go out there and maim somebody.

Williams hit me well at times and not so well at other times. Nobody had his number. I never could get him out consistently, and he could never hit me consistently. But if it was one way or the other, he hit me more times than I got him out. He was the best hitter I ever pitched to. Ted didn't hit me as well as Tommy Henrich, who was the toughest hitter for me, but he hit me pretty good. There wasn't a pitch he couldn't hit. He had no weakness.

One of my favorite catchers was Rollie Hemsley. A great catcher and a good friend of mine. He had a drinking problem—that's no big secret—but he could catch drunk better than most guys could sober. He loved to kid around. He set a train afire one time by throwing matches into the upper berths. We were traveling north with the Giants and were going from Richmond to Washington. Hemsley was walking through the car with too many drinks in him and just for the hell of it started throwing lighted matches into the upper berths where the equipment was kept. Yeah, Rollie was quite a Rollie. Slapnicka finally talked him into joining Alcoholics Anonymous. Hemsley did that and went on the wagon and never drank again.

Johnny Allen was another guy who was not exactly a tee-totaler either. He was a rough, tough character. Good pitcher, a real competitor. Hot-tempered. He hated to lose. Sometimes when he lost, he'd take it out on inanimate objects. He lost a tough game one time in Washington and went back and tore up his room at the Wardman Park Hotel. He threw a few chairs and lamps out a window. Then he took a fire extinguisher and went down to the lobby with it and drenched the room clerk and whoever else was down there. That was at three o'clock in the morning. A few hours later the whole ball club was thrown out of the hotel. We all had to go to another hotel. Tough losers are a lot of fun to have on your club.

Fun and games. You always had a few guys around to liven it up. One night in Griffith Stadium we had a rookie sitting on the bench. Just up. Kind of nervous, looking around, not saying anything. One of the guys said, "I see that clock out there is a little fast." Everybody agreed. The clock was fast. And that was that. Well, there was no clock out there, but there were so many signs and so many different colors on those outfield walls that it was hard to be certain. Of course, a rookie is not going to ask too many questions, and for the rest of the game we'd catch him frowning out at the fences, looking for that clock.

In December, 1941, I was on my way from Iowa to Chicago to go to the major league meetings, just to be doing something. It was on a Sunday. About the time I was crossing the Mississippi River at Moline the broadcast came over the car radio about Pearl Harbor. I kept going and checked into the Palmer House in Chicago and called Gene Tunney in California. He was the head of the armed services athletic program, and he'd been hounding me to get in. So he flew out to Chicago, and I signed up at eight o'clock the next morning at the courthouse.

My dad was dying of cancer, and I wouldn't have had to go in. I was what they called 2-C. Farmer. I couldn't have played ball, though; I would have had to stay on the farm. Otherwise there was no way I could have stayed out. But I figured, too, that it was the right thing to do, and so I went in.

I went to war college in Newport, took a gunnery course in Norfolk, went to PT boat school. I was pretty good at antiaircraft gunnery. I ended up in the South Pacific, on the *Alabama*. Battleship. I requested combat duty. I probably could have sat in Honolulu drinking beer, but the hell with that. I figured if I was in, I might as well be in all the way.

The *Alabama* was with the Third Fleet and we got into quite a few of those scrapes. Tarawa, Kwajelein, the Marshalls and Gilberts, Iwo Jima, the Philippines. Our job was to protect the carriers. We'd have those air battles, and the Japanese planes would try to get at the carriers. And sometimes they'd come after us. Torpedo bombers. They'd come in low, to get underneath our shells, sometimes so low they would fly right into a wave or a big swell. I'd be up there on the main deck with a bunch of kids, banging away with Bofors. The one that gets you you never see; that's the scary thing. You can never be sure about anything one minute to the next. Was it as scary as pitching to Jimmie Foxx? I'll say. That's for keeps, that racket. (And anyway, Jimmie couldn't hit me with a paddle.)

I came out of the Navy late in the season in '45 and pitched in a few games, but that didn't amount to much in my mind. I didn't feel like I was really back until spring training in 1946. I got myself into great shape and was looking forward to having a good year.

Right early in the year, in April, I pitched a no-hitter against the Yankees in New York. That's a game that will always stand out in my mind.

We had quite a large crowd that day, almost 40,000. In fact, it was the largest crowd ever to see a no-hitter up to that time. The Yankees weren't going anywhere that year, but it was still a tough lineup. They had Stirnweiss, Henrich, DiMaggio, Keller, Gordon, Dickey, Rizzuto. That was a pretty fair ball club.

In the first inning Boudreau made a great play behind the pitcher's mound on a high hopper by Stirnweiss which was the only tough chance of the ball game. You don't start paying attention to a no-hitter until about the seventh or eighth inning. I knew I had pretty good stuff that day and figured I might go all the way with it. The only problem was we didn't have any runs. You get to thinking about that. Hell, I figured, here goes a whole day's work. I'll probably walk somebody, wild pitch him to second, then watch him come around on an error, and I'll lose a no-hitter. I'd had a lot of oddball things happen to me late in games in Yankee Stadium.

But then in the ninth inning, my catcher, Frankie Hayes, hit one into the left-field seats, and I had a run to work with.

A hell of a lot of tension had built up for that last of the ninth. Stirnweiss led off, and he got on through an error. So there was a man on first, nobody out, and Henrich, DiMaggio, and Keller coming up. Talk about earning your money.

Henrich laid down a bunt and sacrificed Stirnweiss over to second. DiMaggio came up, and I got two strikes on him and then he started fouling them off. Finally I threw him a slider, and he ground out to Boudreau. Keller was next. The tying run was on third now, so I had other things to worry about besides the no-hitter. I threw him a big overhand curve, and he beat it into the ground to second. Ray Mack charged the ball, picked it up, and then slipped and went down to one knee. There wasn't a damn thing I could do but stand there and watch him. He recovered in time and threw to first base for the out. I've got to say that was one of the sweetest moments I ever had on a ball field.

The best stuff I ever had in mylife, though, was in 1947, in a game against the Athletics in Philadelphia. I'd struck out nine of the first eleven, and I hadn't thrown a curveball all night. Then I threw a curve to the next hitter, Barney McCoskey. When I threw my curve, I stepped a little differently from when I threw my fastball. Well, I had raveled up a lot of dirt, and I hadn't knocked it off to get the loose dirt out of the way so my left pivot foot could go into the clay. So, when I threw the curve, I stepped on top of this loose dirt and slipped. My leg went straight out, and I fell hard. When I got up, they were throwing the ball around the infield—I'd struck McCoskey out. But I'd pulled my shoulder and my knee. I was in pretty bad shape. I missed a month of the season at least. I thought I could have struck out 20 that night. They had a lot of hard-swinging right-hand hitters, and I was very fast and had pretty good control. But I had to leave the ball game, so I'll never know how many I could have struck out that game.

I missed the All-Star game that year because of my injury. Some people made a big stink out of my not going. But I didn't want to go because I couldn't throw. Any better reason? But it made a better story for the papers to say I wasn't going because I didn't want to go.

Then in '48 I was having a lousy year. I couldn't get anybody out. But they put me on the All-Star team anyway, probably for sentimental reasons. I didn't belong on the All-Star team that year any more than you did. No way. Bill Veeck, who owned the Indians, told me, "You need some rest. Don't go. Go fishing."

"Hell," I said, "I can't get out of this. I had a legitimate reason not to go last year, and I got hell. What are they going to say this year?"

"If I tell you not to go, don't go," he said. "Tell them you cut your finger on a razor blade."

"Oh, horseshit," I said. "That's not gonna work."

"Well," he said, "I'll figure out something. I'll tell them you got an injury."

"It's not gonna work," I said.

"We'll see," he said.

Well, he was absolutely right, but he shouldn't have done it. I should have gone, told them that I had a bad arm, that I would throw a little batting practice, run around, smile at people, sign autographs, but not pitch. I know a lot of guys that do it. They get on the team, they get the gift, they get the prestige, they have a little fun, a few drinks with the guys, a few laughs. Hell, I know a lot of guys who do that.

Anyway, the Cleveland ball club's publicity department came out with a statement: "Feller has withdrawn from the All-Star game. Reasons unknown." Something along those lines. Made me look great.

When I saw that in the paper, I started trying to track Veeck down. I finally got him on the phone at some nightclub, at about three o'clock in the morning.

"Goddamn," I said, "what in the hell is this anyway?"

"Don't worry about it," he said.

"Look" I said, "I want you to come out with the whole story. You tell them the truth."

Which he did. He released a statement which said, in effect: "Veeck takes blame for keeping Feller out of All-Star game.

Veeck says it was his mistake, that Feller was willing and wanted to go but was not permitted." But nobody ever saw it in the paper. Did you? Neither did I.

Fastest pitcher I ever saw? Koufax was fast. So was Ryne Duren. Rex Barney. Barney could throw as hard as anybody, but he couldn't get the ball near the plate. Anyway, speed alone isn't enough. It's what the ball does that counts, if it hops or sinks or sails. My ball had a hop, and it would rise. When I threw it sidearm to right-hand hitters, it would run in on them.

Walter Johnson? I knew if we talked long enough, you'd mention him. In my opinion Walter Johnson has to be the fastest pitcher of all time, for the simple reason that he didn't have a curveball and he struck out so many hitters. I would say he had to be a harder thrower than I was. People who saw us both in our prime generally say that. I heard somebody say one time that Johnson, after seeing me pitch, said I threw pretty hard but that he thought he threw harder. Well, of course he's going to say that, but I'm sure he was absolutely honest and sincere about it and probably 99 percent correct.

What would my record have looked like if I hadn't lost those years in the service? I think I would have hung around a few more years to see if I couldn't have won 400. I ended up with 266 and could have won 100 easy during those four years. Might have pitched another no-hitter or two, struck out another 1,000 or 1,200 guys. Hell, I was averaging before and after the war 250 a season. So I could've been up to around 3,700 or 3,800 strikeouts lifetime, which would have put me at the top of the list, ahead of Walter Johnson.

But we'll never know, will we?

PETE REISER

HAROLD PATRICK REISER
Born: St. Louis, Missouri, March 17, 1919; Died: October 25, 1981
Major-league career: 1940–52, Brooklyn Dodgers, Boston Braves, Pittsburgh Pirates, Cleveland Indians
Lifetime average: .295

In Brooklyn they called him "Pistol Pete." Branch Rickey called him, "The greatest natural ballplayer I have ever seen," and Leo Durocher said he "might have been better than Willie Mays." He was a National League batting champion at the age of twenty-two in 1941, hitting .343. He could switch-hit, throw with either arm, play infield and outfield, outrun anybody on the field, and hit with power. Until injuries shattered his career, he was on the high road to Cooperstown.

Over the winter of '47 I was invited to talk—for the *fifth* time—to the Missouri School for the Blind, in St. Louis. I was beginning to wonder about it. Every year they were getting me. So I said to the director, "Look, I don't mind coming here, but why do you keep asking me?"

"You're our favorite player," he said.

"But I'm from Brooklyn."

"That makes no difference," he said. "Our children here always have problems with walls, and they hear that you have the same problem. They figure you're one of them."

Actually, you know, I only ran into the wall twice that I *really* hurt myself: in '42 and '47. Hell, any ballplayer worth his salt has run into a wall. More than once. I'm the guy who got hurt doing it, that's all. I remember somebody asking me one time how long I think I would have played and what my averages might have been if I hadn't played as hard as I did. If I hadn't played that way, I told him, I may never have got there to begin with. It was my style of playing; I didn't know any other way to play ball.

Remember, when I was twelve years old, I was playing ball with guys five years older. My brother Mike used to bring me around to play on his team. The other guys would say, "What's this kid doing here?" My brother said, "He'll show you." So maybe it started there, having to try hard, hard, and harder, to prove to them, to live up to the expectations of somebody you admired the hell out of, and to keep on proving it. And I always felt I could do better than I was doing, that there was no limit. I couldn't wait from one day to the next to get out there and prove it.

Late in July in 1942 we went into St. Louis to play a series. In our two series prior to that, in Chicago and Cincinnati, I'd gotten 19 hits in twenty-one at bats. I came into St. Louis hitting .380, and just starting to get warm. Just starting to get the bead on everybody. I could've hit .400 that year. No doubt in my mind about that. And to make it all the sweeter, we had a 13½-game lead.

Whitlow Wyatt, who for a few years there was the finest right-hand pitcher I ever saw, was hooked up in one of his famous pitching duels with Mort Cooper, who was also a tremendous pitcher. We were playing the second game of a doubleheader, and in those days they didn't turn the lights on to finish a ball game. It was getting dark, and this was probably going to be the last inning. We were in extra innings—the thirteenth, I think—and there was no score, and Wyatt is out there pitching his heart out. I know this sounds melodramatic, like I'm making it up, but those were the kinds of ball games we had with St. Louis in '41 and '42.

Enos Slaughter leads off the inning, and he ties into one. It's a line drive directly over my head, and my first thought was that it can be caught. Which is pretty much the way I felt about *any* ball that was hit. I'm a firm believer in positive thinking. I used to stand out there in center field and say to myself, *Hit it to me, hit it to me*. Every pitch. I wanted that ball.

Well, if this ball isn't caught, it's a cinch triple, and Wyatt can get beat, and above all the Dodgers. I caught it, going at top speed. I just missed the flagpole in center field but I hit the wall, hard. I dropped the ball, picked it up, relayed it to Pee Wee—how I did that I'll never know—but we just missed getting Slaughter at the plate. Inside the park home run. Wyatt's beat, 1–0. And I'm out cold in center field. It was like a hand grenade had gone off inside my head.

Was I being foolhardy in going after that ball the way I did? After all, we had a 13½-game lead, didn't we? You can slow up in those circumstances, can't you? No, you can't. You slow up a half step, and it's the beginning of your last ball game. It might take a few years, but you're on your way out. That's how I look at it. You can't turn it on and off anytime you want to. Not if you take pride in yourself.

What kind of kid was I? Ornery. Mean. Nice. A nice mean kid. I had a bad temper. My grandfather, who I never knew, was a professional soldier; he fought in the Civil War. He was a cavalry officer, and we had his sword in the house. I'd get mad once in a while and chase my sisters and anybody else who was in the way with that sword. Just to scare 'em.

Sure, I wanted to be a ballplayer when I was a kid, but it wasn't my first love. Football was. My ambition was to be the greatest football player Notre Dame ever had. When I was ten, I was competing in football against fifteen-year-old kids. Running right over them. Knute Rockne was one of my idols. I heard him talk once on the radio, one of his inspirational talks. I'll never forget it. I'm very emotional. I cry at the movies. I still get the chills when I hear "The Star-Spangled Banner."

I was a hell of a soccer player, too; in fact, I was declared a professional soccer player when I was fourteen years old. I was playing for the Catholic school in St. Louis when some guy came along and offered me $50 to kick soccer one Sunday. He was trying to compete against the pros in St. Louis, and he was signing all the kids from the Catholic schools who could kick soccer and who could run. And he was giving us $50, which was a lot of money. Hell, my dad was making $25 a week and supporting twelve children.

My dad made everybody in the family play ball, boys and girls alike. As soon as you were old enough, he put a ball in your hand. He'd played ball in St. Louis, in the old Trolley

League. You ever hear of the Trolley League? That was quite a league in those days around St. Louis and part of Illinois. He was a pitcher. A printing company saw him pitch. They were part of an industrial league, and they offered him a job, work five days and pitch for them on the weekend. He was married then, already had two kids, so he took the job. He always regretted not taking a crack at professional baseball. He always thought he could have pitched in the big leagues. You know how it is, the older you get, the better you were. But he was a good ballplayer.

I was a nut for the Cardinals, but when I was a kid, my favorite major league ballplayer wasn't a Cardinal, he was a New York Giant—Mel Ott. I don't know why; you just get attached to a guy I guess. Then of course, later on I got to play against him. But idol or no idol, he came into me one time at third base with his spikes kind of high, and I dumped him on his ass.

I was always a pretty good ballplayer, but the real ball-player in the family was my older brother, Mike. He was five years older than I was, and he was my hero. Mike could do everything, and then some. But it wasn't meant to be. He died when he was seventeen—just after he'd signed with the Yankees.

That was around the winter of 1931. Mike got scarlet fever. And I caught it from him. I wasn't supposed to go into his room, but I did, and I caught it. We ended up with throat infections, and the doctor lanced our throats. Operated on both of us right in the house. The doctor was more concerned about my condition than Mike's, and he told my parents to watch me, that I could have a rough night. So I was the one everybody was worried about. About two o'clock in the morning my brother asked me how I was. I told him all right. "Well," he said, "I've got something in my throat. I've got to get a drink," And then he coughed, and the blood just came rushing out. I screamed for my mother, and she came running in. It was terrible. She yelled for somebody to get a priest. I ran out of the house, in my bare feet. It was snowing out. I ran for twelve blocks. I got to the door of the rectory and pounded on it. When they opened the door, I said, "My brother is dying." Then I collapsed.

I woke up the next morning in the hospital—not a damn

thing wrong with me. My throat was almost healed. Perfect health. It was a miracle. It had to be. I was the one who was supposed to have the hemorrhage, not him. That's what the doctor said. We both should have been in the hospital, but there was no money for that. He was some kind of ballplayer, my brother Mike. But I guess it just wasn't meant to be.

When I was fifteen, I went to a Cardinal tryout camp. It was held at Public School Stadium on Kings Highway Boulevard, off of St. Louis Avenue. About 800 kids showed up for it. It was supposed to be for sixteen-year-olds and up, but I lied about my age and went out there. I wanted to see how good the competition was.

It was a Cardinal camp, but scouts from other clubs were there too. Just because the Cardinals had organized the tryout didn't give them exclusive rights.

With so many kids on hand, you didn't get much chance to show your stuff. You ran a 100-yard dash, threw from center field to home plate, and got three swings. That was it. Then they weeded the kids out, asking the ones they liked to come back the next day. I was one of the ones cut the first day. I went home, really feeling bad. I told my father, "Well, Dad, I guess I'm not as good as I thought I was."

"Don't worry about it," he said. "You're only fifteen years old."

A couple of days later this big Buick pulls up in front of the house, and out comes Charley Barrett, the Cardinals' head scout. He knocks on the door and my father answers.

"Reiser residence?" Charley asks. My fathers says yes. Charley introduced himself and says, "I want to talk to you about your son."

"Well, I want to talk to you too," Dad says. "Why'd you cut him?"

"We didn't want anybody else to see him," Charley says. "That's why we didn't ask him to come back. We know who he is."

It turned out they'd been watching me play ball since grade school. They never said anything because they didn't want anybody else to know they were interested in me until they could sign me. You see, in those days if the Cardinals showed any interest in a kid, the other clubs would rush in to try and sign him, simply on the basis of the Cardinals' interest. That's the kind of reputation the Cardinals had in those days.

So Charley Barrett signed me. My Dad was the happiest guy in the world, since he always wanted me to play ball, and especially with the Cardinals. He had to sign for me, of course, because I was underage. But contract or no contract, I still couldn't play for a while because you had to be at least sixteen years old, and I wasn't quite that yet.

What they did was pay me $50 a month to go around with Charley Barrett that summer. Whenever he went out to scout different places, I went along. I was officially listed as his chauffeur, and every once in a while on an open road he'd let me take the wheel. We went all over the map, wherever the Cardinals had a club—and they had tons of them in those days. We went to Georgia, Alabama, Louisiana, Kentucky, Tennessee, Arkansas.

Whenever we went into a town, I'd work out with the club, take infield, batting practice. Then, when the game started, I'd have to get out of uniform. When Charley was ready to leave, the manager would say to him, "Say, Charley, leave the kid here." "Can't," Charley would say. "He's only fifteen." "So what? We'll change his name." "Unh-unh," Charley'd say, and off we'd go again.

I'll tell you how green I was in those days. Our first stop when we left St. Louis was Mayfield, Kentucky. We went into a restaurant, had a nice meal, and left. We were about 25 miles down the road, and I was feeling pretty proud of myself because I thought I'd done Charley a favor. Finally I told him about it. "You know what you did, Mr. Barrett?" I asked. "What?" he asked. "You left some money on the table back at the restaurant. But I picked it up for you." "You did *what?*" he yelled. "I picked up the money you left," I said. "By God, boy," he yelled, "that was a tip!"

Hell, I'd never eaten in a restaurant in my life. How was I supposed to know any different?

Well, you know the story. I never got to play for the Cardinals. You see what happened, in those years the Cardinals were signing every young ballplayer who showed any promise. No bonuses. Just sign 'em. Then let the good ones prove who they were. In doing that, in having so many ballplayers, they had to do a lot of manipulating of contracts, and they broke a lot of organized baseball's rules. Sooner or later that bubble had to burst. The old judge was commissioner then, Landis; he was a sharp guy, and he had a pretty good idea of what the Cardinals were doing.

In the spring of 1938 Landis turned loose about 100 of us. The "slaves" from the Cardinal "chain gang," the papers called us. When that happened, the Dodgers signed me to a contract, for a $100 bonus.

The Dodgers sent me to Superior, Wisconsin. I was a short-stop at the time and a strictly right-handed hitter. Well, I could always run real good, but often I was just getting nipped at first base, and it would aggravate me. I said to myself, "Hell, if I was on the left side of the plate, those would be base hits." So, with the manager's permission, I started hitting left-handed. It took a little time, but gradually I began making contact, and I was beating out some of those grounders. I was the happiest guy in the world, believe me. It cost me some points on my batting average, but I didn't care about that—I'd learned how to hit left-handed.

Charley Barrett lived in St. Louis, and so did I. Over that winter I went to him and said, "Charley, if I could just get down to spring training in Florida early, I could get a jump on some of these guys." He said, "Well, a very good friend of mine has just been named manager of the Dodgers. Leo Durocher. I'll talk Leo into bringing you down."

So I went to Clearwater in the spring of '39, just to shag and run and get the feel of a big-league camp, as a favor to Charley Barrett from Leo Durocher. I was like any young kid. I was eager. Every time somebody was slow getting into the batting cage I jumped in, which I wasn't supposed to do. Made some of the regulars pretty sore. When I wasn't hanging around trying to sneak into the cage, I'd be out in the field someplace, doing something, keeping busy all the time.

Leo took a liking to me. Even though I was just a kid nobody, Leo saw me out there. I'll tell you something: Leo Durocher sees *everything* that's going on on a ball field. He may not be looking, but he sees it.

They had a guy down there, I think his name was Cesar. He was supposed to be the fastest man in the Dodger organization. One day Leo says to MacPhail, "I got a kid that'll beat Cesar by ten yards."

"Bullshit," MacPhail says.

"I've also got," Leo says, "a hundred dollars to back it up."

They would bet on anything in those days.

Next thing I know Leo is calling me over. "I want you to do a little running, kid," he says.

So here all of a sudden I'm running against the fastest guy in the Dodger organization, and the manager and the general manager are betting $100 on it. And all I'd wanted to do was come down there and work out in a big-league camp and mind my business.

Well, I did beat the guy. Yeah, by 10 yards.

So Leo really had his eye on me after that. He liked me. But there was one play that I think really cemented it for him. We were playing Detroit, and I was playing second base that day. I got on first, and somebody hit a ground ball. I took off for second with one thought in my mind: break up the double play. Billy Rogell was playing short for them. A veteran, and rough and tough. I knew damned well who he was and didn't care. I barreled into him and knocked him flying. "You bush son of a bitch," he said, "when I get on that base, I'm gonna cut you from ear to ear." "You've got to get on base first," I told him.

So then he does get on, and everybody knows he's coming. Leo was playing short, and he says to me, "I'll handle the throw."

I said, "*I* want the throw."

"No," Leo says.

"I'm taking it," I said. "So you stay clear." I'm talking to the manager like that.

First pitch, here comes Rogell. He's going to barrel into me. I went over, took the throw, laid it on him, and stepped aside. He threw up a ton of dirt but never touched me.

From that day on I think I became Leo's pet.

On St. Patrick's Day, which is my birthday, we had a game scheduled. I wasn't in the lineup, but just before the game started, Leo came up with a migraine headache.

"How'd you like to play short today?" he asked me.

"Hell, yes," I said.

Well, I played short that day, and I played the rest of the exhibition games after that. I hit something like .485 in about thirty exhibition games. My first twelve at bats I got on base—

three home runs, five singles, four walks. I hit home runs off
Gomez and Tommy Bridges. Was I surprised? Honestly, no. I'd
been doing it all my life, in my mind, and I'd convinced myself
I was going to do it for real when the time came. So I wasn't
surprised. I expected it.

We barnstormed north with the Yankees from Florida, rode
the same train, stayed at the same hotels. One day Joe
McCarthy walks up to me and says, "You're going to be my
third baseman this year." "How do you figure that?" I asked.
"We're going to make a deal for you," he says. A few days later,
the same thing. "It won't be too long now before you're a
Yankee. The deal is almost made." And he emphasized it again:
I was going to open at third for him. Red Rolfe or no Red Rolfe.

I don't know exactly what they were offering, but it was
supposed to be a pretty big deal. The Dodgers needed ballplayers at that time, and the Yankees had those great farm
clubs at Newark and Kansas City filled with first-rate players.

How did I feel about it? Well, in those days anybody who
didn't want to play for the Yankees was crazy. Baseball was
the Yankees, and the Yankees were baseball.

Leo heard about it and said, "No way." He threatened to
quit if MacPhail made the deal.

So I was having a hell of a spring, wasn't I? Now I'm the boy
wonder and what-not, and Leo has got me in the opening day
lineup at shortstop for the Dodgers. I take infield, then batting
practice with the starting lineup; then I go into the clubhouse
to change my shirt. The telephone rings.

"It's for you, Pete," somebody says. "Mr. MacPhail wants to
talk to you."

I took the phone and said hello. That's about all I got to say.

"I don't give a damn what Durocher says," he said. "You're
going to go to Elmira." And he hung up.

I just sat there stunned. Jesus crimminy, I thought, he can't
do that to me. I had a good spring, didn't I?

Leo comes in and sees me sitting there like that and says,
"What's the matter, kid? You scared?"

"Hell, no," I said. "Mr. MacPhail just called and said I was
going to Elmira."

Leo looked dumbfounded for a second, then said, "Like hell
you are!"

So Leo called him, and they argued hot and heavy. Then Leo hung up.

"There's nothing I can do about it," he said. "He won't sign you to a major-league contract, and I can't play you until he does."

So I went to Elmira. Didn't like it, but I went. I had some injuries there—broken elbow, brain concussion—and didn't play a full season. But I did all right anyway. Hit .300.

The next spring, 1940, I go to spring training not with the Dodgers but with Montreal. Clyde Sukeforth was the manager. He kept telling me, "I don't give a damn what they say, you're my center fielder."

"But I don't want to play the outfield," I said. "I want to play the infield."

"Well," he said, "regardless of where you play, you're going to play on my ball club."

So he had me playing all over the place that spring, infield and outfield. Then right after the season opened the Dodgers cut their squad and sent a bunch of veteran players down to Montreal, and Sukeforth was told to play them. I had to sit down. Boy, I'm really mad now. Then, a few nights later, they really laid it on me. Clyde called me up to his room.

"I know you're not going to like this," he said. "I've got some real bad news."

"What?" I asked.

"MacPhail said to send you to Elmira."

"Bull*shit!*" I said. "No way you're going to send me to Elmira."

"Pete," he said, "my hands are tied. MacPhail promised the people in Montreal a winner, that he would not take one player away from the Montreal ball club. He's afraid that you're going to do so well that he'd have to break his promise and take you to Brooklyn. He does not want to offend the people who are supporting a valuable franchise."

Then I get a telephone call from Elmira, from Bill Killefer, who was both the manager and general manager of the Elmira ball club. He gave me some soft soap, and then he said, "You come to Elmira and I'll make you a promise. If you're going good before July 1 and the Dodgers don't bring you up, I'll sell you to the highest bidder."

"How are you gonna do that?"

"You're being optioned outright, and I'm the general manager of this club, and I can do what I want. I don't have more than a year or two left in this game anyway, so the hell with them. You should have been on the Dodgers in '39."

I always liked the guy, trusted him, and so I believed him.

"All right," I said. "But, boy, if I'm not up there—"

"You'll be there, kid," he said. "Don't worry."

So I went to Elmira, and I'm having a great start. It's well into June and I'm hitting around .380. I'm really chomping. Then I hear the Dodgers have made a deal with the Cardinals for Joe Medwick. It was a pretty big deal, involving Medwick and Curt Davis and some other players and a lot of money and a player to be named later. So now they've got Medwick in Brooklyn. The outfield was filled out, and they had Pee Wee playing shortstop and having a hell of a year. Where did that leave me?

So I went to see Killefer.

"Bill," I said, "it's getting pretty damned close to July 1."

He smiled and said, "You're going to Brooklyn tonight. You've been called up." Then he told me, "Do you know why you didn't stay there in '39? Because you were property of the Cardinals."

You see, when I was declared a free agent, I was barred from playing in the Cardinal organization for three years. So there was a gentleman's agreement between the Dodger and Cardinal scouts that I would play in the Dodger organization for three years, and then I was going to be returned to the Cardinals. Killefer was the one who really kicked up the fuss, when he threatened to sell me to the highest bidder. Well, I became the player to be named later in the Medwick deal; I was supposed to go back to St. Louis eventually. Instead, they gave the Cardinals some more money.

So there were two things that could have happened to me in those years. They could've sold me to the Yankees, and I probably would have been the Yankee third baseman for a long time. And if I played for the Cardinals, I probably still would have been an infielder, because they had guys like Slaughter and Terry Moore in their outfield. Plus the fact if I would have been declared a free agent in '39, there's no telling how much money I could have got to sign. So you see how your whole life changes.

Anyway, the Dodgers called me up on June 22, 1940. I felt great. I rode the bus all night into New York. Couldn't sleep a wink, I was so excited. The first game was a night game, and afterward I'm leaving the ball park, and some big guy hits me on the shoulder.

"Hey, Pete," he says in this deep voice.

Here was the meanest-looking son of a bitch you ever saw. I asked myself, "What the hell does *he* want?"

"You don't know me, do you?" he says.

"No, I don't think so," I said.

"Well, I know you."

"From where?"

"Elmira," he says.

"Oh, you from Elmira?" I asked.

"No," he says. "I'm from Brooklyn. But you and the Elmira Pioneers came up there last year and played an exhibition game at the prison. Listen," he says, "I just got out. And I want to tell you I appreciate things like that from you athletes. Listen, anybody gives you any trouble in this town, I want you to know I'm gonna be out there every ball game. You just whistle up to me. Anybody gives you any trouble, they're dead."

Welcome to Brooklyn!

You know, I saw that guy out there as long as I played in Brooklyn. I'd walk out to center field, and he'd stand up and yell, "Everything all right, Pete?" "Great, buddy," I'd yell back.

You know, that Ebbets Field was a hell of a place to play ball. Some of those fans were unbelievable. And they were out there day after day. You got to know them. One who still stands out in my mind is Hilda Chester. She never missed a game, it seemed. She'd sit out in the bleachers yelling in a foghorn voice and ringing this big cowbell she always carried. I remember one time, it was in either '41 or '42, we were in the seventh inning of a game. I was going out to take my position in center field, and I hear that voice: "Hey, Reiser!" Hilda. There could be 30,000 people there yelling at once, but Hilda was the one you'd hear. I look up, and she's dropping something onto the grass. "Give this note to Leo," she yells. So I pick it up and put it in my pocket. At the end of the inning I start heading in.

Now MacPhail used to sit in a box right next to the dugout, and for some reason he waved to me as I came in, and I said, "Hi, Larry," as I went into the dugout. I gave Hilda's note to Leo and sat down. Next thing I know he's getting somebody hot in the bullpen; I think it was Casey. Meanwhile, Wyatt's pitching a hell of a ball game for us. In the next inning the first guy hits the ball pretty good and goes out. The next guy gets a base hit. Here comes Leo. He takes Wyatt out and brings in Casey. Casey got rocked a few times, and we just did win the game, just did win it.

Leo had this rule that after a game you didn't take off your uniform until he said so. Usually he didn't invoke it unless we'd lost a tough one. But this day he goes into his office and slams the door without a word. We're all sitting there waiting for him to come out. Finally the door opens and out he comes. He points at me.

"Don't you *ever* give me another note from MacPhail as long as you play for me."

"I didn't give you any note from MacPhail," I said.

"Don't tell me!" he yells. "You handed me a note in the seventh inning."

"That was from Hilda," I said.

"From *Hilda?*" he screams. I thought he was going to turn purple. "You mean to say that wasn't from MacPhail?"

I'd never even looked at the note, just handed it to him. Leo had heard me say something to MacPhail when I came in and figured the note was from Larry. It seems what the note said was: "Get Casey hot, Wyatt's losing it." So what you had was somebody named Hilda Chester sitting in the center-field bleachers changing pitchers for you. You talk about oddball things happening in Ebbets Field, you're not exaggerating.

There was a guy named Eddie, used to come out to all the games. He owned some apartment houses in Brooklyn. He was a real rabid fan. He came up to Boston with us in '41 when we cinched the pennant, and naturally he came back on the train with the team. Well, there was a big mob to meet us at Grand Central that night and the reporters are interviewing everybody who comes off the train. Somebody asks Eddie how he feels about it. He says, "I'm so happy about this I'm going to put all new toilet seats in my apartment buildings."

There really was no place like Brooklyn.

Anyway, I'm finally there, in June, 1940. And I don't play. Finally I do a little filling in at second base. Then Pee Wee breaks his ankle, and Leo says, "Go to short." So I go to short. I'm there for a few days, and Lavagetto has a busted appendix in Cincinnati. So now Leo puts himself back on the list, and he plays short, and I play third till the end of the season. Bill McKechnie came up to me one day and said, "You're the best third baseman in this league. I think you've found your position." I loved third base.

I figured I could beat out Lavagetto for the job next spring. I went to spring training in '41 figuring I was the Dodger third baseman. One day MacPhail and Leo called me into the office.

"You want to play for the Dodgers this year?" MacPhail asked.

"Damn right I do," I said.

"Well, then you learn to play center field."

Hell, I thought, anybody can play center field. All you had to do was run a ball down. Nothing else to worry about. So, with help from Charley Dressen and Freddy Fitzsimmons, I spent that spring becoming a big-league center fielder. When the season opened in '41, I felt as if I'd never played anywhere else.

I made another big change that spring—I stopped hitting right-handed. The Dodgers almost blew their stacks. But I got hard-nosed about it. The guy who suggested it to me was Paul Waner. He was watching me in the cage one day, and when I got out, he said, "Why in the hell do you switch-hit?"

"Because I'm a natural right-handed hitter," I said.

"Maybe," he said. "But your stroke left-handed is perfect. I know you've got more power right-handed, but you're an entirely different hitter. You uppercut right-handed; left-handed you don't. With your speed, you stay left-handed, kid."

Well, Paul Waner knew something about hitting, to say the least. So, once in a while during an exhibition game, when there was a left-hander out there, I tried it. No problem. Left-handers didn't make a bit of difference. But still I had to convince Leo. We were playing the Yankees one day, and Gomez was pitching.

"I hit him pretty good right-handed," I told Leo, "but I'll hit him better left-handed." You know, I was just a kid, and a little cocky. But I went out and did what I said I was going to do. I made Leo a believer. Then MacPhail was going to fire him for letting me hit left-handed. MacPhail was always firing Leo. But I stayed stubborn and refused to hit right-handed, I didn't care how much dust MacPhail kicked up. MacPhail got so goddamned mad that he came within an ace of trading me to the Cubs in the Billy Herman deal. But I guess by the end of the year MacPhail was a believer, too. What the hell, I hit .343 and led the league. Batting left-handed.

That was some kind of year, '41. Everything happened. I got myself beaned twice, each time pretty hard. Ike Pearson of the Phillies zonked me in Brooklyn early in the year, and then later on Paul Erickson hit me in Chicago. What provoked the Chicago beaning was something that had happened on our previous trip in. I was on first and somebody doubled down the right-field line. I came all the way around, and the catcher thought he had the plate blocked. I knocked him on his ass and scored. Jimmie Wilson was the Cub manager, and he didn't like what he saw. He came up to me and said, "We'll get you for that, bush." I didn't give it another thought.

Next trip into Chicago this big Paul Erickson is pitching. He could fire. I come up. You can hear it coming out of the dugout: "Stick it in his ear."

The old judge is sitting in a box behind the dugout. Landis.

Erickson winds up, and the next thing I know Landis is visiting me in the hospital.

"Do you think that Paul Erickson threw at you intentionally?" he asks.

"No, sir."

"You didn't hear, 'Stick it in his ear'?"

"I heard something like that," I said.

"Then why don't you think he threw at you intentionally?"

"He doesn't have that kind of control," I said. "I lost the ball in the shirts in center field."

"Then you won't accuse him of throwing at you?"

"No, sir," I said.

He was skeptical. He was no dummy, the judge. But he had to accept it. Christ, in those days all you heard was "Stick it in his ear." "Put him in a squat position." "Drill him." "Flip him." If you got hit, you got hit. And nobody ever said excuse me. You wanted to play ball, you played the way it was played.

You know, you wonder sometimes how much of this game is

psychological. I'm not all that highly educated, and I can't explain why certain things happen, but I do know they happen. I remember one time, in '42, we came into Cincinnati for a series. A sportswriter named Grayson met me at the railroad station and asked me to have breakfast with him. I was going real good at the time, and he wanted to write a story about me.

It was an enjoyable breakfast, and as he was leaving, he said, "By the way, what does Bucky Walters do to tip off his pitches?"

"I don't understand you," I said.

"Well, I talked to Bucky the other day about you. He says he throws you everything and you seem to know what's coming. I looked it up and you're hitting eight hundred against him."

"Against Walters?" I could hardly believe it. He was one of the best pitchers in the league. "You've got to be kidding."

"No, I'm not," he said. "Bucky can't figure it out. He says he's done everything to you—knocked you down, come close, thrown his best stuff, done everything he can think of. But you still hit him, like you know what's coming."

I never thought I was having such great luck with Walters. I knew I enjoyed hitting against him because he was a control pitcher, always around that plate, and I loved to swing. I was what they called a Bible hitter: They shall not pass.

"Incidentally," Grayson said, "Walters is pitching tonight."

Great, I say to myself. There's three for four. But you know what happened, don't you? I can hardly remember getting a hit off of Walters after that. The point is, I had great luck against him until it was pointed out to me and I started thinking about it. Maybe I became overconfident, and if you become overconfident with a pitcher as great as Walters, it's fatal. I stopped challenging him the way I had been doing, and from then on the advantage was his.

Well, we won the pennant in '41, and we figured to repeat the next year. And we would have, too, if it wasn't for me. I cost the Dodgers the pennant in '42. I told you about that injury when I hit the wall going after Slaughter's drive. Well, that was the start of it.

I woke up in St. John's Hospital in St. Louis. The Cardinal club doctor, Dr. Hyland, who was a very good friend of mine and of all ballplayers, said I had suffered a severe concussion and a fractured skull. He recommended I not play any more that year.

When MacPhail heard about it, he went through the roof. He began screaming that Hyland was saying that just to keep me out of the lineup. Stuff like that. He said he was going to have his own doctor examine me.

The injury occurred on a Sunday, and on Tuesday I left the hospital. I wasn't supposed to, but I told Dr. Hyland that I had to get back to Brooklyn. I insisted on leaving, whether they liked it or not. I was kind of bullheaded. Probably still am. Instead of going to Brooklyn, I stopped off in Pittsburgh, where the Dodgers had gone to play their next series. What the hell, to get to Brooklyn you have to go through Pittsburgh, don't you?

I got there in about the seventh inning. I was sitting behind the dugout, and when the guys spotted me, they figured because I was out of the hospital I must be all right. Leo poked his head up out of the dugout.

"How you feeling?" he asked.

"I'm feeling all right," I said.

"Go put your uniform on."

"I can't play."

"Put it on," he said. "I'm not going to use you."

So I went in and put my uniform on and sat on the bench. We went into extra innings. By the fourteenth inning we don't have anybody left to hit, and the winning run is on second base. Leo looks at me.

"You want to hit?" he asks.

Now, he didn't ask me if I could. There's no way I could. But I *wanted* to. There's a big difference.

I went up to hit. Kenny Heintzelman was the pitcher. I hit a line drive over the second baseman's head and scored the run. I rounded first base and fell flat on my face. Passed out. I woke up in a hospital in Pittsburgh now.

They took me back to Brooklyn, to Peck Memorial Hospital, and the doctors there suggested I not play anymore that season. Three weeks go by. The club is losing now. MacPhail has blasted the team, accusing them of complacency. He's willing to bet that we're going to blow it. What he was trying to do, of course, was jack us up.

So I volunteer to play. I guess I didn't do that badly for a couple of days, but gradually I kept getting weaker and weaker. I was ducking away from pitches I couldn't see—that were right down the pipe. Babe Pinelli, the umpire, finally told Leo one day. "You'd better get him out of there because he's not seeing them. I know he's not seeing them."

Leo kept me in there, but I probably shouldn't have played. Fly balls I could stick in my hip pocket I didn't see them until they were almost past me. I went from .380 down to .310. But the big thing wasn't the batting average; it was the fly balls that I couldn't run down. That's what hurt us. So we blow the pennant. I say blow—we won 104 ball games! But there's no question in my mind that by being stubborn, I cost the Dodgers the pennant in 1942.

Do I blame Leo for keeping me in there? Listen, if you'd ever played for him, you wouldn't ask that. You have to have played for him. He wanted to win so bad it hurt, and I wanted to win so bad it hurt. I don't blame Leo; I blame myself. I've heard a lot of guys knock Leo about a lot of things. But I've always said this about him: If you didn't know him, you'd hate his guts, but if you knew him, you'd love him. He was the best. He was aggressive, and he fought for you. He always fought for you.

Leo kept things boiling out there on the field. He'd get the umpires riled up, the opposing players, the fans, everybody. There were times I thought we should've got combat pay, playing for Leo. One time in Chicago, this was in 1940, he gets on Claude Passeau something terrible. Passeau was a big guy, and mean. He keeps looking over, trying to catch who's doing the yelling. Joe Gallagher was with us then. He's a big, good-natured guy, strong as hell. He's sitting on the bench, not paying attention to anything. Leo yells something particularly rough, and Passeau has had it. He throws down his glove and starts walking in, yelling, "The guy who made that last crack doesn't have guts enough to come out and back it up." Leo looks at Gallagher, who's still preoccupied with something else, and says, "Joe, get out there and hit." So Joe picks up a bat and comes out of the dugout. Passeau walks up to him. "You need a bat, you big son of a bitch?" he says, and hauls off and belts him. Gallagher doesn't know what the hell's going on. "Claude," he says, "what's wrong with you?" Passeau belts him again, hard, but that Gallagher is like a stone wall. "Claude," he says, "don't get me mad." Passeau winds up to hit him again, and Gallagher drops the bat and grabs him and starts to squeeze. "Claude," he says, "if you don't want to talk about this thing, I'm just gonna keep squeezin' and squeezin'." They both get kicked out of the game, and I'll bet to this day Gallagher doesn't know what the hell it was all about. Next trip into Brooklyn, Passeau finds out who was on him. He winds up from the mound and fires one into the dugout at Leo. Just missed him. Just.

Like I say, Leo kept you alive out there.

We had some great times and some great ballplayers in Brooklyn back in those days. Pitchers? Give me Whitlow Wyatt. He was always one of my heroes. He was nice to me when I was a rookie at Clearwater in '39. What did he do? He said hello to me. That was a rare thing for a rookie to hear from a veteran in those days. And he worked hard and was dedicated and felt the same way I did about baseball.

If I could sculpt a statue of what a pitcher should look like, for form and grace and style, it would look like Whitlow Wyatt. I said it before, for those few years there in the early '40's he was the best right-handed pitcher I ever saw. He could do just about anything he wanted. We'd hold a meeting before the game, going over the other team's batting order. He'd hold the list in his hand and say, "Well, there's twenty-seven outs here." He's telling you he's already won the ball game. "First two hitters, there's no way they're gonna touch me. Third, fourth, and fifth hitters, may get a hit. Sixth hitter, he'll bloop one maybe. The last three hitters, no contest. Get me a run." And that's the way it would be. It was a pleasure to play behind him. A real gentleman, too. A prince of a man. But a hell of a competitor out on the mound. All business, and, oh, he was tough.

He knocked DiMaggio down in the fifth game of the '41 Series, I'll never forget it. In fact, I was talking to DiMaggio not too long ago about that. We were talking about that Series.

"You know who was the meanest guy I ever saw in my life?" he said.

"Yeah," I said. "Whitlow Wyatt."

"You remember that?" Joe asked.

Joe liked to dig in, you know. Wyatt didn't like that. First pitch, Joe goes down. He didn't say anything. He gets up, digs in again. Second pitch—whiz!—down he goes again.

"What the hell are you trying to do?" DiMaggio yells.

"Joe," Wyatt yells, "you do that against me again, you'll be in a squat position the rest of your life. You can hit me, but don't dig in."

He hit Marty Marion once. Marion was in the box, smoothing out the dirt, taking his time. Wyatt's standing out there, watching him with those big green eyes. When Marion's finally set, Whit yells, "You ready?" Wyatt winds up, fires it in, and down Marion goes. I guess he was expecting it, because he got up laughing. Next pitch—wham!—right in the ribs. Marion arches his back; that hurt. "Jesus Christ, Whit!" he yells.

"Don't laugh when I'm on the mound," Wyatt says.

I'll tell you a story you probably never heard before. I believe it's true—I was told by somebody in good authority that it was true—but I've got no way of proving it. MacPhail was so mad at us after we'd lost the '41 Series that he had us all traded to the St. Louis Browns. We were waived out of the National League and sold to the Browns for $3,000,000 or $4,000,000 and the Brown ball club. How'd he get us out of the league? Master waiver. He put the whole club on waivers, and everybody laughed, thought it was a big joke. Time elapsed, and we were waived out of the league. The whole club, lock, stock, and barrel.

Don Barnes was the owner of the Browns. He started running around to the St. Louis banks to raise the $3,000,000 or $4,000,000. The banks thought he was off his rocker. "What do you need these millions for, Don?" "I'm buying the Dodger ball club for St. Louis." They thought he was crazy.

Now I don't know if MacPhail would have gone through with it. I doubt it. But can you imagine what would have happened in Brooklyn if the St. Louis Browns had turned up there one day all wearing Dodger uniforms? Give *that* some thought.

After the '42 season I got to thinking about things. The war was on full blast then. I decided I'd join the Navy. So I went and took a physical. But because of all the injuries I'd had playing ball, I turned up 4-F. They told me no induction center in the country would take me. Then I get a call from the

Army. I go down to the induction center, go all the way through, and I'm told to sit with the rejects.

I waited around for about an hour while they were processing everybody's papers. Then some captain came out and said, "Is there a Harold Reiser here?"

"Yes, sir," I said. I figured he's got my papers all signed up.

"Goddamn, boy," he said, "why don't you use your right name when you come into this man's army?"

"What are you talking about?" I asked.

"Aren't you Pete Reiser, the ballplayer?"

"Yes, sir."

"Goddamn," he said, "your papers have Harold Patrick. Where's Pete?"

"Pete's my nickname," I said.

He gave me a fishy look.

"What are you going to do if we let you go?" he asked.

"Play ball," I said.

He turned around. "Sergeant," he said, "fingerprint this guy and induct him."

I'm in.

January 13, 1943, I'm inducted. I go to Fort Riley, Kansas. First two days there we're put on a 50-mile forced march, full pack. It's 15 below zero. I catch pneumonia. I wake up in an Army hospital; don't know where I'm at and care less. A doctor comes over. He's been studying my case history.

"Feeling better?" he asks.

"Yeah."

"How long you been in the Army, son?"

"Three weeks."

"How'd you ever get in?"

"They told them to fingerprint me and induct me."

"You'll be out in two weeks," he says. Pats me on the shoulder and walks away.

So I'm in the casual outfit—guys who are waiting for their medical discharge. I'm hanging around for about ten days, and then this announcement comes booming over the bitch box: "Private Reiser report to camp headquarters."

I go to camp headquarters, and I'm told to go in to see some officer. He's sitting behind the desk.

"Private Reiser?"

"Yes, sir."

He tells me who he is. Colonel so-and-so. Graduate of West Point, etc., etc. I don't know why he's telling me all this. Then he says, "One of the greatest things in my life is that I'm a sports fan. I've followed all sports, but my love is baseball."

I say to myself: Oh-oh.

"You wouldn't happen to be related to Pete, would you?"

"Yes, sir."

"You're not Pete, are you?"

"Yes, sir. I'm Pete."

"You know," he says, "I've always wanted to meet you."

"Thank you, Colonel."

He looks down at the desk. "I've got your papers right here. They want to discharge you. It's up to me to sign them or not. Tell me, what happens if I sign?"

"I'll probably play center field for the Dodgers," I said.

"I was looking forward to having a hell of a ball club here in Fort Riley," he said. "Now do you really want to go back to Brooklyn? The war's going bad, you know. I think it would be a shame if you left the Army. No, I'm not going to sign this." He picks up the papers and rrrip! Then he says, "You don't like that, do you?"

"I didn't say anything, did I? Just tell me what I'm supposed to do."

"You don't do anything," he says.

He writes out a pass for me, from 0600 to 0600 daily. I can go anyplace I want. I also get a private room in the barracks—which made my hard-assed sergeant turn blue in the face—and no duties. I stayed there for a couple of years, playing center field for Fort Riley, Kansas.

We ended up with a hell of a ball club. We had Joe Garagiola, Lonny Frey, Creepy Crespi, Harry Walker, Al Brazle, Murry Dickson, Rex Barney, Ken Heintzelman. We whomped everybody we played.

One day a Negro lieutenant came out for the ball team. An officer told him he couldn't play. "You have to play with the colored team," the officer said. That was a joke. There was no colored team. The lieutenant didn't say anything. He stood there for a while, watching us work out. Then he turned and walked away. I didn't know who he was then, but that was the first time I saw Jackie Robinson. I can still remember him walking away by himself.

When the war ends I'm in Camp Lee, Virginia. By this time I've got enough points to get out; I don't need a medical discharge. But then they start talking about sending guys over to Europe for a year to entertain the occupational forces. I'm selected as one of the entertainers. Before I could go overseas, though, I had to take a physical. I walk in, and there's a colonel sitting at a desk going over my papers. He's got a chestful of medals and ribbons and battle stars. He's been through it all. I look at that chest, and I figure I'm gone.

He looks at me and says, "How the goddamn hell. . . . For three years you've been putting up with this crap?"

I don't say anything.

"You come with me," he says.

I went with him and he signed some papers and said to a sergeant, "I want this man discharged in twenty-four hours."

I was out the next day. That was in January of '46.

So it was back to the Dodgers. I stole home seven times in 1946. That's still a record. It was really eight, but Magerkurth missed one. It was in Chicago. I had it stolen clean, against Johnny Schmitz. I come sliding in there, and Magerkurth throws his thumb up in the air and says, "You're out!" and then says, "Goddamn, did I blow that!" He looked at me and said, "Called you out, kid. Sorry." Nothing I could say about it.

I'll tell you a great story. Professionalism. Billy Herman. One of the greatest second basemen in National League history, right? Why he isn't in the Hall of Fame is beyond me. Brilliant career with the Cubs and the Dodgers. He comes back from the service in '46 still a great star but with mileage on him now. Rickey has all these young kids coming out of the service, so what's he going to do with this thirty-six-year-old outstanding star? He trades him. Herman gets a call at two o'clock in the morning, right at the trading deadline. "You have been sold to the Boston Braves." This is two o'clock on a Sunday morning. In Brooklyn. Now who do you think played a doubleheader for Boston *in* Boston that afternoon? You're damn right. Billy Herman. He left his hotel at two o'clock in the morning and got right up there. What did Billy Herman have to prove to the Braves? That he could still play? No, it was something else: I *want* to play. That's a pro.

I mentioned Jackie Robinson. I guess you heard the story where some of the Dodgers were getting up a petition against him that first year—'47—to get guys to say they wouldn't play with him. Well, I'd had an experience when I was in the Army. This was in Richmond, Virginia. I'd just been transferred there. My daughter got very sick. So I looked up a doctor in the phone book. He told me to bring my daughter to the office. The office was in a Negro neighborhood. The doctor was a Negro. I didn't think anything of it. What the hell was the difference? He gave her a shot, penicillin I think it was, and cured her.

I told that story to one of the players who wanted me to sign the petition against Robinson. I said, "What would you have done?" He said, "I would have turned around and walked away from that neighborhood." I told him I thought he was a goddamn fool, and then I told him what he could do with his petition. Here's a guy asking me not to play ball with a man because he's black—after I'd just told him that without any doubts or hesitations I'd entrusted my daughter's health to a black man!

In '46 we're fighting the Cardinals down to the wire for the pennant. Just like old times. With two days of the season to go, I was playing with a very bad hamstring pull. I told Leo, "I can play, but I can't run." In the first inning I get on base with a walk. Next thing I know the damn steal sign is on. Jesus Christ. So I get off to take my lead, and the pitcher makes a routine throw over, and I try to slide. My spike caught, and I could hear my ankle crack. Leo comes running out. "Get up," he says, "you're all right." "Not this time, Skip. It's broke." The bone was sticking out.

Then in '47 I had that bad accident in center field, in Ebbets Field. I almost died. I was paralyzed for ten days. You see, Rickey (he was general manager of the Dodgers then) had cut the fences; he took about 40 feet out of center field. So there's this long fly ball to center, and I tell myself, "Hell, this is an easy out." I'm going full speed . . . and oh, my God. I'd completely forgotten about the 40 feet that wasn't there anymore. When I woke up, I couldn't move.

I joined the club after five weeks, in Pittsburgh. I was out in the field during batting practice, and Clyde King ran into me. We bumped heads. I was knocked out, but I didn't feel that bad. That night I was sitting in the Schenley Hotel with Pee Wee. He looked at me kind of funny. "You all right?" he asked.

"Yeah. Why?" I said. "What's that big knot on your head?" I touched it and it felt like a big boil. "Maybe you'd better get the doctor," he said.

The doctor came, had one look at me and called Mr. Rickey in Brooklyn. Next thing I know I'm being flown to Johns Hopkins in Baltimore to be operated on. I had a blood clot. I'd had it from the wall injury, and when King ran into me, that moved it. They told me I'd never play again. But I went back. Played the last two months and hit .309. But I could feel myself getting weaker and weaker and weaker.

We won the pennant. We're in the Series against the Yankees. I slide into second to break up a double play and feel something go in my ankle. The doctor x-rayed it that night.

"You've got a broken ankle," he says. "A very slight fracture."

Boy, was I ticked off! Did it have to happen right in the middle of a World Series?

"Listen," I told the doctor, "don't say anything. Just put a tight bandage on it, say it's a bad sprain, and that I'm through for the rest of the Series. That's all."

I was afraid that if he said it was broken, Rickey would give me a dollar-a-year contract next year—meaning I would have to prove I was physically fit to play before I could sign a regular contract.

Then we get into this game where Bevens is pitching a no-hitter. It's the last of the ninth, two out, and Al Gionfriddo is on first. Shotton sends me up to hit. Gionfriddo steals second, and why he did that I'll never know, because it wasn't on. Then Bucky Harris, who was managing the Yankees, told Bevens to put me on. The winning run. Pretty unorthodox move. Because of the bad ankle, Eddie Miksis ran for me; and then Lavagetto hit that double down the right-field line, and Bevens lost his no-hitter and his ball game all at once.

DiMaggio told me years later that Harris knew I had a broken ankle, but that he still didn't want to pitch to me. "He'll still swing, ankle or no ankle," Harris said. That was a nice tribute to me, but it cost him.

In '48 Rickey didn't want me to play at all. He said he would pay me if I sat down all year. Being bullheaded, I said I wanted to play. But by that time all of those injuries were beginning to take their toll. My record after the war was all right, but nothing like it had been before. Something was gone. It had always been so easy for me, but now it became a struggle. I was only twenty-nine, but the fun and the pure joy of it were gone. When something that you like to do, and that you always did well, becomes hard to do, that's the time to get out of it. No way was I going to go out there and make an ass of myself.

But you know what really bothers me? I meet people today, and they say, "Oh, you're the nut that used to run into the walls." That's a hell of a way to be remembered.

But as I said before, it was my style of playing, the only way I knew how. You can't turn a thing like that off. Why should you? It's born in you, it's part of you. It *is* you.

No, I don't have any regrets. Not about one damned thing. I've had a lot of good experiences in my life, and they far outnumber the bad. Good memories are the greatest thing in the world, and I've got a lot of those. And one of the sweetest is of the kid standing out on the green grass in center field, with the winning runs on base, thinking, Hit it to me. *Hit it to me.*

BASEBALL

BETWEEN

THE LINES

TOMMY HENRICH

THOMAS DAVID HENRICH
Born: February 20, 1913, Massillon, Ohio
Major-league career: 1937–50, New York Yankees
Lifetime average: .282

One of the most popular players ever to wear the Yankee uniform, Tommy Henrich earned the nickname "Old Reliable." Part of the famed Keller-Henrich-DiMaggio outfield of the late thirties and early forties, Henrich was considered one of the game's most intelligent players. He had a career high of 31 home runs in 1941 and in 1947 and 1948 led the league in triples.

I was born and raised in Massillon, Ohio, the middle one of five children. You know what Massillon is—it's a football town. Everybody says, "How'd you get started playing baseball?" Well, my dad didn't like football. He thought you could get hurt at it. So as soon as I was old enough, I was throwing a ball. I had a very natural talent for throwing a ball and catching it and hitting it. It was no fluke. You couldn't have kept me away from baseball. It was all there, right from the beginning.

At that time, growing up, I didn't have any ambition about making baseball a career. Never thought about it. I never dreamed I could be good enough to play professional baseball.

I played a lot of softball. The town seemed to go in for that. I think that was because there weren't enough good fields for baseball, and not enough equipment. Softball was more convenient, and it was an easier game to play. I played all the way through high school and for a year after I was out of high school.

How did I finally get into hard ball? Well, I can tell you just how that happened. I'd been playing softball for a team around here for two years. And we had a great team. We won 80 out of 87 games in 1932. At the end of the year we had a bazaar. We sold chances on Indian blankets and things like that, to get some money together to buy team jackets with. We took in $200, and then the manager told us that by a strange coincidence the expenses just equaled that amount. It left a sour taste, and that was the end of the ball club.

During the winter somebody asked me if I'd like to play hard ball. I said all right, I'd give it a whirl. So I joined this team in the spring and was doing all right. One day in June a scout from Detroit named Billy Doyle showed up. He wanted to see the game against Canton. It was a six-mile ride out to the ball field from town and Doyle wasn't about to go for the cab fare, so some of us invited him to ride along. On the way he told us he'd come down to scout the guy who was pitching for Canton that day.

"What about some of the boys on our team?" somebody asked him.

"I came to see the fellow on the Canton club," he said.

"We've got some good ballplayers, too," we told him.

"Maybe you do," he said. "But I came to see the fellow on the Canton club."

He seemed pretty definite about that.

Well, I hit two screamers in that game and around the eighth inning I'm sitting on the bench and I feel somebody tapping me on the shoulder. I turn around. It's Billy Doyle.

"How would you like to play pro ball?" he asked.

I think my eyes must have popped. "Are you kidding?" I asked. "You're doggone right I would."

"Okay," he said. "I'll send you a contract. You sign it immediately and send it back."

Sure enough, the contract came in the mail. It called for me to report in 1934. Now, this was June of '33. I said to myself, "Gee, I sign up now but don't do anything until next year." I wasn't so sure I wanted to sign it. So I filed it away, and at the same time told myself that maybe I ought to get serious about baseball. I started getting in some batting practice every day and played as much as I could. I figured that after having played softball for so many years I had some lost time to make up.

Then in September down comes Bill Bradley of the Cleveland Indians and he offers me a contract. He stayed around for a while and I got to know him and to like him. So I signed a contract with Cleveland, to go to Zanesville, Ohio. I eventually wound up playing for Monessen, Pennsylvania.

The funny thing was, Cleveland was more or less the local big league club, the closest one to Massillon, but I'd never been a Cleveland rooter. Never rooted for them a day in my life. At that time I was a New York Yankee fan. I'd been a Yankee fan since 1921, when I was eight years old. I was a Babe Ruth man. When I look back now I wonder how lucky a guy can be—to be in love with baseball, to love the New York Yankees and Babe Ruth especially, and to end up not just with the Yankees but playing out there in right field where Ruth had played, and winning pennants every year to boot. What more can a guy ask?

I played three years in the Cleveland organization. At the end of 1936 I was sold to Milwaukee in the American Association. Milwaukee was also a Cleveland farm. In other words, I was being shifted around the Cleveland organization. Now, in my three years in the minors I'd hit .326 in D ball, .337 in C, and .346 in AA. I was hitting better the higher up I went, and I was beginning to ask myself when I was going to get a shot at the big leagues. At that time Cleveland had Jeff Heath in the organization and Heath was a particular favorite of Cy Slapnicka, the general manager. I heard that they were bringing Heath to spring training with them in 1937, even though he'd played only Class C ball. Jeff Heath sure turned out to be a fine slugger, but at that time I felt a little put out, feeling that I'd earned the shot.

Early in 1937, right after the new year, I read in the paper where the Boston Braves are interested in buying Henrich from the Milwaukee Brewers. I also read where the Cleveland Indians are toying with the idea of trading Joe Vosmik to the St. Louis Browns, with Henrich as a throw-in. So at about this time I started saying to my dad, "For heaven's sake, who in the heck do I belong to? Milwaukee wants to trade me to Boston, and Cleveland is talking about trading me to St. Louis."

After thinking about it for a while I decided to write to the commissioner, Judge Landis, and try to get the situation clarified. What the heck, he was a ballplayer's commissioner, wasn't he? I knew I'd get a fair decision from him.

So I wrote the letter. It reached Landis somewhere in Florida, where he was on vacation. Well, I got a telegram back from him, about fourteen lines deep, the biggest telegram I ever saw in my life. I wish I could remember his exact words, but it went along like this: "You say so-and-so. Prove it. You say so-and-so. Prove it. You say this and that. Can you prove it?" And on and on like that.

I went through everything I had, trying to make as strong a case as I could, and wrote back to him. When I heard from him again he told me to report to the Milwaukee training camp, which was at Biloxi, Mississippi, that year. So I went down there. By this time it was around March first. Cleveland was training in New Orleans, not far away.

Landis called a meeting in the Roosevelt Hotel in New Orleans, and over I go, with the top executives of the Milwaukee ball club. I was scared to death. I thought Landis was going to be my lawyer in the matter, but I was wrong; he was the judge, he was taking the evidence. So I had to be my own lawyer.

What I had was mostly hearsay, but Landis was familiar with the kind of shenanigans that were going on and he went after those guys. I don't think he liked Slapnicka, anyway. Nevertheless, he made his decision strictly according to baseball law, as it existed at that time. Cleveland was definitely directing my progress through the minor leagues, which, according to Landis, they had no legal right to do. So it was a clear violation, although hardly an uncommon one. It was an everyday thing in baseball back then. The judge could have let it go, but because he didn't like Slapnicka, and because I think he got a kick out of me writing to him and standing up for my rights, he declared me a free agent.

So I went back to Massillon. I got there on a Thursday night. By Saturday I'd heard from eight clubs, including the Yankees. Jacques Fournier, the old Brooklyn first baseman, was scouting for the Browns, and he kept hammering away. I think he was ready to top the Yankee offer, but I thought to myself, "Gee, I don't want to belong to the Browns." I knew where I wanted to play.

My dad said, "Do you think you can make the Yankee ball club?"

"Well, I don't know," I said. I figured if I wasn't a good ballplayer it wouldn't make any difference where I played; but if I was a good ballplayer, then I wanted to be with the Yankees. And that's where I went.

I joined the Yankees at the beginning of the season in '37, stayed with them for two weeks and then was shipped to Newark. I was there for about ten days and was hitting around .440. Then McCarthy got rid of an outfielder and I was recalled.

On one of our first trips into Chicago I was standing at the batting cage and an usher comes walking up to me.

"Are you Henrich?" he asks.

"That's right," I said.

"Well, the commissioner wants to see you."

I took a look and there's Landis sitting in the front row, staring at me. Oh-oh, I thought, what's this all about? What have I done wrong?

I walked over to him and said, "How are you, Mr. Commissioner?"

He's still staring at me, very sternly.

"How are they treating you?" he asked.

"Just fine," I said.

"Well," he said, "they'd better."

I loved Judge Landis. He was quite a man. I've always said that the two greatest names in baseball are Babe Ruth and Judge Landis. Landis cleaned it up and Babe Ruth glorified it.

I remember right after I joined the Yankees in '37 Al Simmons beat us with a home run off of Lefty Gomez into the right-field seats. That was my first look at Simmons, and what a smasher he was. He's got to be the most vicious man I ever saw at home plate. He was starting to go downhill when I came into the league, but I saw him look real good. Oh, but he was one angry man when he strode up to home plate. He hated that pitcher with a vengeance, and showed it.

Bill Dickey told me a story about Simmons one time. In 1928 the A's were the coming team. Connie Mack had put together that great team and was challenging the Yankees. The A's came in for a big series and the Yankees were wondering what to do about some of those big hitters like Foxx,

Cochrane, Haas, Simmons. Somebody thought it would be a good idea to rough Simmons up, to knock him down a little.

"So we rough him up," Dickey said. "In a four-game series he had eleven base hits, ten of them for extra bases." Yeah, they roughed him up all right, and he returned the compliment. He hated the Yankees, but I liked him. I liked him for the way he would bear down against us.

He hung around as a coach after he was through playing. I used to yell to him during batting practice. "Hey, Al, get in and hit a few." He'd push out his lip and shake his head. "Go on, Al," I'd yell. "Go on and hit a couple." The guys would hear it and they'd let him get in. The reason I'd do that was just to watch him step in there. It was something to see. When Al Simmons would grab hold of a ball bat and dig in he'd squeeze the handle of that doggone thing and throw the barrel of that bat toward the pitcher in his warm-up swings, and he would look so bloomin' *mad*. In *batting practice*, years after he'd retired! I'd watch him and say to myself, "Tom, old boy, *that's* the mood you ought to be in when you go to home plate."

Joe McCarthy? I loved him. One of the greatest men I ever knew. I don't know where in the heck he learned all his psychology about ballplayers. He could handle almost anybody. And if he couldn't handle them he'd trade them, I'll tell you that. Fellows like Ben Chapman and Johnny Allen. He traded them. But I don't think anybody was ever able to handle Johnny Allen. He was a case all by himself.

But that McCarthy, he seemed always to know just how to talk to you. He knew when to jump on you, when to be your friend, when to give you a pat on the back, when to leave you alone. Best manager I ever knew or heard about. That's the way I felt about him, and I know quite a few other fellows who felt the same way.

He had a phenomenal memory for facts and figures and for a ballplayer's strengths and weaknesses. I don't think that guy ever forgot anything. He told me a story one time, after he'd retired. Red Rolfe was managing the Tigers and Joe was managing the Red Sox. The Tigers were doing all right, but they might have been doing better. The Red Sox came in for a ball game and Rolfe invited McCarthy into his office to sit down and talk a little bit. Rolfe idolized McCarthy.

"So I went over to his office," Joe said, "and we sat and

chatted for a while. Then I noticed he had a lot of clipboards hanging around the office. I asked him what they were. He said they were records he was keeping. Records of what? I asked. Oh, he said, various things that had happened in ball games during the year. He liked to keep those records so he could refer back to them."

After telling me that, McCarthy looked at me and said, "That's what his trouble is as a manager."

"What?" I asked

"He's got a lousy memory."

McCarthy didn't need any clipboards; he had it all upstairs, all the time. I'll tell you another story about him. Remember Jimmy Wasdell? He came up to the major leagues with Washington in 1937, in the middle of the season. Now, I knew him; I'd played with him in the Mid-Atlantic League in 1935. He hit .357 that year. That guy could hit. He was a good friend and I was delighted when he came up.

The next time we played Washington, Charley Ruffing was the pitcher. He's sitting in the clubhouse looking at the Senators' lineup.

"Who's this guy Wasdell?" he says. "What do we know about him?"

Well, as far as I knew, I was the only one on the club who had ever played with Wasdell, who knew anything about him. But I'm not that dumb; I'm not going to tell these wise guys how to pitch to Jimmy Wasdell. I've seen too many outfielders give well-meaning advice that exploded in somebody's face. But while I'm keeping quiet, McCarthy says, "I know who he is. He's that kid that pinch-hit against us in Chattanooga when we came through there in the spring. He can't hit a change-up." This is what McCarthy says.

I looked at him. I couldn't believe it. To this day I can't believe he's that sharp, that he could size up and remember a man in one appearance in an exhibition game. The truth was, Wasdell *couldn't* hit a change-up. But I still don't believe a man can have that kind of memory. He *must* have called and got a scouting report on Wasdell when he heard Jimmy was joining the Senators. And if he did do that, then he was shrewd enough to sell us on the idea that he did indeed remember Wasdell from one at bat in the spring.

Anyway, so now we have the lowdown on Wasdell, right?

Change-ups. Ruffing is the pitcher. Do you know what Was-dell did that afternoon? He was 0 for 4. Didn't get the ball out of the infield. After the game I went around to the Washington dressing room to wait for him. When he came out he was pretty upset.

"Let's get out of here," he said.

"What's the matter, Jim?" I asked.

"Big leagues my foot," he said. He was really disgusted.

"What's the problem?" I asked.

"Smart guys," he said. "Big leaguers. I asked those guys before the game, 'Who's pitching?' They say Ruffing. 'What do you look for with Ruffing?' I asked. 'Seven out of eight fast-balls,' they tell me."

Well, they were right, because Ruffing did throw a lot of fastballs. But I haven't told Jimmy to this day what happened over on our side, how he got double-crossed.

That was McCarthy. What a cagey man. He knew every-thing that was going on, and when he didn't want you to know something, well, you just didn't know it. Art Fletcher was our third-base coach in those days and McCarthy would flash signs out to him. And do you know that no Yankee ballplayer ever knew what those signs were? Now, on any ball club, after a while the players know what signs the manager is using with the coaches. Not only did we never know them, but he never told anybody what they were and I don't suppose he ever will.

Now, Gomez was pretty cute. You know all about the Great Gomez. One day he's sitting a few feet down the bench from McCarthy, watching out of the corner of his eye to see if he could pick up those signs. All of a sudden, without even look-ing at him, McCarthy says, "Gomez, pay attention to the ball game. You can't get my signs."

Yes, you look back and talk about those great old names. At one time we had on the team seven guys who went into the Hall of Fame. Do you suppose any other team ever had that? We had McCarthy, Earle Combs, who was coaching; Lou Geh-rig, Joe DiMaggio, Gomez, Dickey, and Ruffing. Pretty good gang, wouldn't you say?

I roomed with Gomez for three years. One of the wittiest men I ever met. He told me a story once that happened when he was just breaking in. He recognized that he pitched like

Grove—a lefthander who got by with a fastball. So he figured he'd talk to Grove.

"Hey, Lefty," he said, "what do you do when you get down to about the eighth inning and you've got to get a guy out?"

"Oh," Grove said, "when it gets down to the eighth inning I just give 'em a little extra."

"Okay," Gomez said, "now what would you do if it was the ninth inning and you really got to get a guy out?"

"Oh," Grove said, "if it's the ninth inning I just blow it by 'em."

Gomez looked at him and said, "Thanks, Lefty. Now I'm a smart pitcher."

Of course when I came into the league Grove didn't have that great fastball anymore. Dickey said he was the fastest he ever saw. He said one day they knocked the Athletics' pitcher out of the game. Dickey was the next batter and he's standing up there looking out to the bull pen to see who they're bringing in. "Wasn't anybody coming in from the bull pen," he said. "Grove walked out of the dugout, threw three pitches and said he's ready. Then he threw three more and I haven't swung at them yet. Don't ever tell *me* about a guy throwing fastballs."

But that didn't happen too many times to Dickey. He was one of your best money players. Take that first game of the 1939 World Series, against Cincinnati. We're tied 1–1 going into the last of the ninth, Derringer against Ruffing. Charlie Keller hits a ball between Harry Craft and Ival Goodman into right-center field. Either one could have caught it, but they couldn't get together and it drops. So Keller's on third, one out, and up steps DiMaggio, followed by Dickey and Selkirk. What do you do? Walk DiMaggio? Never a bad idea, and that's what they did. Then what do you do, walk Dickey to set up a force at any base and pitch to Selkirk? You don't like to pitch to Dickey in a spot like that, but you don't like to pitch to Selkirk, either.

So they pitched to Dickey. When I saw that—and this is the absolute gospel truth—I turned around and picked up my glove, because I knew the game was going to be over right now. And it was. Dickey singled into center field. One way or another, he was going to get that run in. No doubt about that.

Gehrig was still there when I came up, and I saw a pretty good Lou Gehrig for a couple of years before he got sick. What

kind of guy was he? Live and let live. Very, very nice and
friendly man. Always in good humor. Of course, when you can
hit like he could, it's not hard to be in good humor. When I
joined the club in '37 he was in a slump. You could see he
wasn't making good contact. Then one day in Philadelphia he
came out of it. All of a sudden I saw Gehrig hit four line drives
to all parts of the ball field. Four for four. I said to Dickey after
the game, "I never saw such line drives in my life." And
Dickey said, "Wait awhile. You haven't seen anything yet.
Those were *soft* ones." What a smasher! That's what Gehrig
did. He just went up there and smashed that ball to all fields.
A mean, vicious hitter. Like Simmons. Medwick was another
one. They just whacked that ball all over the lot, didn't care
where it went.

Gehrig was the perfect team man. Never created any problems, always hustled. Where McCarthy used to have some
problems with Ruth—who didn't have problems with Ruth?—
he never had any with Gehrig. They respected each other, to
the extent that as sad as Gehrig looked in 1939 McCarthy still
wouldn't take him out of that lineup. It was going to have to
be Gehrig's decision.

Lou was pathetic that spring. He couldn't move, couldn't hit
the ball hard, couldn't do anything. Nobody knew he was sick;
we just thought he was through as a ballplayer. I remember a
game in Clearwater that spring. Gehrig tried to go from first
to third on a single and when he went around second it looked
like he was trying to run uphill at a forty-five-degree angle; he
was running as hard as he could and not getting anywhere.
But he never complained. I never, never heard him complain.

Then finally he had to take himself out. That was in Detroit,
early in May. He went up to home plate to hand in the lineup,
then came back to the bench and sat down and began bawling.
The public-address announcer saw the lineup cards, realized
that here was baseball history in the making, and made the
announcement: "Ladies and gentlemen, Lou Gehrig has taken
himself out of the lineup for the first time in 2,130 games."
There was a tremendous ovation for Lou, while he was sitting
there bawling. Now, what do you do? That's a very sad and
delicate situation. Well, here's what happened. After about
fifteen seconds Gomez got up and walked down past Gehrig,
looked at him and said, "What the heck, Lou, now you know

how we feel when we get knocked out of the box." Everybody laughed, including Gehrig, and that broke the tension.

Lefty Gomez. A sweetheart of a guy and a sweetheart of a pitcher. You know, there wasn't that much difference between him and Ruffing, but for some reason Ruffing was always looked upon as the ace. He seemed to have that stature. But for most of those years in the thirties you couldn't have chosen between them, one was just as tough as the other, the way Raschi and Reynolds were ten or so years later.

You know, you bandy these names around and then you stop to realize why there was such a thing as a Yankee dynasty. Just stop and look at how some of those players came up and took each other's place. DiMaggio's last year was 1951, which was Mantle's first year. Dickey retired in 1946, and Berra came up at the end of that year. When Crosetti began to slow down, Rizzuto came up. They got rid of Lazzeri and replaced him with Joe Gordon. And so on. The farm system was inexhaustible in those days.

I played on five pennant winners in my first six years. The only year we missed was 1940. That 1941 Series stands out in my mind; that was the first one the Yankees and Dodgers ever played against each other, the first of many. Some of the wildest things ever to happen in a World Series occurred between the Yankees and the Dodgers. I was right in the middle of a couple of those things.

I was up at bat when Mickey Owen let that third strike get away. Is that the most famous strikeout in baseball history? I don't know; it could well be. Whatever it was, it wasn't a very good time to strike out, since it was the top of the ninth, two out, nobody on, and we're losing 4–3. Hugh Casey threw me a heck of a pitch. Everybody says it was a spitter, but I don't buy that. I listened one time to Mickey Owen describe what he thought the pitch was and he described it exactly as I remembered it. He said it was the best curveball Hugh Casey ever threw. Casey didn't have a good curve, but this ball exploded.

The count was three and two, and I'm up there guarding the plate—poorly. In comes this pitch, and if I were a Johnny Mize or a Ted Williams or a Paul Waner I would have waited a little longer on it, because they were great waiters. But I had committed myself too quickly and too far and when I realized that was a bad ball I couldn't hold back. It broke down so fast

I knew it was going to be ball four. You see, he didn't start it out chest-high; he started it out belt-high. It looked like a fastball. Then when it broke, it broke so sharply that it was out of the strike zone. So I tried to hold up, but wasn't able to. There's that famous picture you see all the time—that's the end of my swing, right out in front of me; I never wrapped that bat around me; I never finished that swing; I was trying to hold up. But I knew, too, that I'd committed myself and that it was going to be strike three.

But even as I was trying to hold up I was thinking that the ball had broken so fast that Owen might have trouble with it too. Yes, sir, that went through my mind. There's another picture—I'm looking for that ball, I'm looking in a hurry. And I saw that little white jackrabbit bouncing, and I said, *Let's go.* It rolled all the way to the fence. I could have walked down to first.

When people talk about that top of the ninth inning all they seem to remember is Hugh Casey, Mickey Owen, and me. I always say, "Wait a minute. You're forgetting a few guys. What about DiMaggio coming up and hitting a screaming line drive to left for a single? And then what about Keller coming up and doubling off of that right-field screen to score us? And then Dickey walking, and Joe Gordon doubling to left for two more." That's what happened. We won it, 7–4. We beat them again the next day and ended the Series.

I guess one of the nicest things ever to happen to me took place in September, 1942. I was playing my final game before going into the Coast Guard. When I came up for my last time at bat the public-address announcer got on his microphone and told the fans that this was my last appearance for the duration. Well, it was a pretty good-sized crowd and jee-minnies did they let loose! They just rose up and cheered and cheered. It was a tremendous feeling for me, knowing they felt that way; though I'm sure that part of that outpouring was for all the fellows who were in or going in the service at that time.

I was embarrassed. I stepped out and tipped my hat. They kept cheering and applauding. Then I stepped back in and was ready to go. We were playing Detroit and Dizzy Trout was the pitcher. But he wasn't about to pitch. He just stood out there looking at me, saying, "This happens once in a lifetime. Enjoy it." He wouldn't pitch. He was a rough, tough guy, but I guess a sentimentalist at heart.

Finally the cheering died down and I stepped in and got ready. I figured now I've got to hit one to the moon for these people, after that. That's the way it should happen, right? Well, I took a few and missed a few, and the count went to three and two. I said to myself, "Forget about the moon—just hit the ball." Well, the next one came in and I hit a line drive to center for a single. And I'll tell you something—you'll never hear me say a word against Dizzy Trout, because he knew I was a fastball hitter, and he gave me six fastballs. That's some kind of class, isn't it?

Bob Feller once said that I was one of the toughest hitters for him, and I think that's a tremendous compliment, because he had as much super-stuff as I ever saw in my life. Why I got as many hits off of him as I did I'll never know.

As I said, I was a fastball hitter, and I don't know why Bobby gave me as many fastballs as he did, because he also had that remarkable curveball. I never asked him about it. Maybe he was a little bullheaded and was saying to himself, "You son of a gun, I *will* throw this by you." Because if he was, I was saying to myself, "Oh, no you won't."

I'll tell you something else. I'll show you how good Feller was. For two years we knew every pitch he was making with nobody on base. I'm not sure what the record shows for those two years, but I'd say we were around .500 with him. And these were years when he was right at the height of his greatness. You see, when he was going to throw his fastball his arms would be separated; when he was going to throw the curve he'd cover the ball with his glove. So for two years we knew every pitch he was going to make, with nobody on base, and still couldn't do better than .500 against him. That's how good Bob Feller was.

Talking about stealing those little advantages, Detroit had a guy coaching for them in those years who was as skillful at picking off the opposition's signs as anybody you can name: Del Baker. Not every hitter likes to get those signs, you know; they're afraid they might be crossed up and step into a pitch thinking it's a curve and find themselves face to face with a fastball. But Hank Greenberg didn't mind getting the signs when they were available.

One time Hank was in a slump, and at the same time Baker was having trouble picking up on the other team's signs.

"Come on, Del," Hank says to Baker. "What's going on here? You're not giving me any signs."

Del says, "I'll tell you the truth—I'm not getting any."

And Greenberg, who's pretty frustrated by this time, says, "Well, *guess.*"

Hank was a great one. Power to burn. You know, back then, in the late thirties, when there was trouble in the eighth or ninth inning the cry always went up: "Bring in Murphy." Johnny Murphy, our great relief pitcher. One day we're in the bottom of the ninth, it's a tight game, and Greenberg is up. "Bring in Murphy." And that means Murphy is going to curve him, that's all there is to it. So here he comes, walking across the center field grass—in those days the bull pen in Briggs Stadium was out in center field. He passes by DiMaggio, and for the only time in his life that I ever heard of, DiMaggio has a thought for the pitcher. Joe has a brilliant idea.

"Why don't we fastball this guy once?"

Murphy thinks it over and by the time he reaches the mound he's saying to himself, "That's not a bad idea. Change the pattern."

So Johnny changed the pattern. And on the second pitch, *Pow!*, in the seats. That's the end of the ball game. We get into the clubhouse and Murphy's sitting there with his head in his hands, and DiMaggio's saying nothing. All of a sudden, after about five minutes, DiMaggio gets up and walks over to him.

"Let me tell you something," Joe says. "Don't you *ever* listen to anything I ever have to say again."

That was pretty funny, for Joe.

Joe of course was always in a class by himself. A very quiet and unassuming man. His performances out on that field day in and day out were hard-boiled and businesslike, and I don't think he ever looked upon himself as being anything special. In 1941 the team got together and bought Joe a gift, a sterling silver humidor, engraved with all our autographs. It was our way of paying tribute to him. Murphy presented it to him in the Shoreham Hotel in Washington. It came as a complete surprise to Joe and he was deeply moved by it. Joe didn't show emotion easily, but this was one occasion when he did. He said later that it was one of the nicest things ever to happen to him. Joe was surprised that his teammates thought that much of him.

Jimmie Foxx? A wonderful man. I loved him. You know, I saw Jimmie Foxx hit a home run in my hometown of Massillon when he was just a kid, about seventeen years old. He was with the Athletics then; Connie Mack had just signed him up. They were playing an exhibition game against a semipro team, the Massilon Agathons. Must have been around 1925. Well, he tagged one, way out into the left-field corner and sprinted around for an inside-the-park home run.

Many years later, when I came up to the Yankees, we were playing the Red Sox and I got on first base. Jimmie walked over to hold me on. He was a great, good-natured, outgoing man.

"Well, Tommy," he said, "how's everything going?"

"Just fine, Jimmie," I said. Then I said, "You know, I remember a home run you hit in Massillon, Ohio, when you were just a kid with the A's. A home run inside the park."

"I remember that," he said. "Man, I belted that ball, didn't I?"

"You sure did," I said. "And you legged it around pretty good, too."

"Hey, I could run," he said. And he could, too.

In 1938, on Decoration Day, we played the Red Sox a double-header. We had the biggest crowd in the history of Yankee Stadium that day, around 80,000 people. Grove is pitching for them and they're ahead. Then we start to get to him. Lefty began to lose it and was getting wild. He came close to a couple of guys. McCarthy, our master psychologist, wants to get Grove out of there. He turns to Jake Powell and says, "You see what he's doing to us, Jake? You see how close he's coming? You going to let him get away with that stuff?"

Jake, who was a rough, aggressive character, says, "No sirree. He ain't gonna get away with throwing at us."

Now, when it becomes Jake's turn to hit, the Red Sox have taken Grove out of the game and brought in Archie McKain, another left-hander. So Jake is up there full of fire. The first pitch McKain throws is a curveball, inside. Well, now, that's enough for Jake. He's not going to stand for any more of this nonsense. So on the next pitch he's going to bunt the ball; you know, push it down to first, make the pitcher cover and spike him when crossing the bag. That good old play—which I've never seen happen. The next pitch is a curve that breaks too far inside and hits Jake. Well, that's all he needs. Jake drops his bat and goes for Archie McKain. But before he gets there Joe Cronin intercepts him, and they go at each other. They roll around on the grass, and then both of them are thrown out of the game.

McCarthy sends me in to run for Powell. I'm standing on the bag, next to Jimmie Foxx, while Cronin and Powell are leaving the field. In those days you had to leave through the Yankee dugout, which was on the third-base side then. They went through the dugout, and then went at each other again, underneath the stands. Our team found out about it and suddenly the whole bench empties and disappears down the runway. The Red Sox see that and naturally they go storming across the field, into our dugout and down the runway. Everybody is gone. There are two guys left on the field. Henrich and Foxx, at first base. Well, you know what he looked like—he had to turn sideways to get through a door; he was just a mountain of muscles. He looks at me and says, "Well, looks like they're choosing up sides."

For a minute I thought he was serious. Then I said, "Are you kidding? Get out of here, you big gorilla, you." And he laughed. He was a great man, a great, wonderful guy. And could he hit that ball!

Somebody once asked Gomez who hit the longest ball off of him.

"Foxx," Gomez said.

"Where'd he hit it?" the guy asked.

"He hit it in the upper deck of the left-field corner in Yankee Stadium. Way back in the upper deck."

"How far is that?" the guy asked.

"I don't know how *far* it is," Gomez said, "but it takes you forty-five minutes to walk up there."

I'll tell you another one on Foxx. He's out in Comiskey Park one day putting on a show in batting practice, pumping one after the other into the upper deck. Finally somebody says, "Ah, for Pete's sake, you're so doggone big and strong; what would you do if you had to hit-and-run like we do?"

Jimmie was indignant. "I can hit-and-run," he says. "I can hit behind the runner anytime I want to."

The guy is skeptical.

"I'll prove it to you," Jimmie says. "I'll hit-and-run today."

So, sure enough, during the game he comes up with a man on first. Jimmie gets the sign to hit behind the runner. The pitch comes in, the runner takes off, Jimmie chokes up and punches the ball—on a line into the right-field seats. He hit behind the runner all right; he hit behind the outfielder, too.

I remember the year Ted Williams came up, 1939. Early in the season he and I were sitting in Yankee Stadium talking about hitting the long ball. He'd already hit some clouts, one out of Briggs Stadium, one out of here, one out of there.

"Did anybody ever hit a ball out of Yankee Stadium?" he asked.

"No," I said, "and don't get any dumb ideas either."

"Why?"

"It's further than you think."

He looked out toward right field. Sort of measuring it. I just knew what he was thinking.

So the next time they came to New York I was watching them take batting practice. Ted caught hold of one; it was a beauty. Man, he drilled that thing up into the third deck, right into an exit. Quite a shot. But still not out. I yelled, "Hey, Ted." He turned around. "You give up?" I asked. He grinned and yelled back, "Hey, don't tell anybody I said that, huh?" But he had ideas about doing it.

I saw Ted for the first time in spring training. Of course he looked good up there, but you never know how good a guy really is until you've seen him for a while. But Ted was always confident. And to say the least, he knew the strike zone.

We had a clubhouse meeting before our first series with the Red Sox. We talked about Cronin, Foxx, going down their lineup. We get around to Williams. What do we know about Williams? Spud Chandler wants to know. He's pitching. Well, the consensus was pitch him high and tight, low and away. The old words of wisdom. So we went out and played. And Ted had a pretty good day. The next day we're talking again. What did we learn about Williams? Chandler speaks up.

"Well, I'll tell you what I found out," he says. "High and tight is ball one, and low and away is ball two."

Then Bill Dickey, in his own quiet way, said, "Boys, he's just a damned good hitter."

And that sizes up Ted Williams. That's what we found out, after one look. And it stuck.

I'll tell you another great man with that bat—Buddy Lewis of the old Washington Senators. Talk about bat control, he was an artist. I used to drool watching Buddy Lewis handle a ball bat. He could hit a pitch just about anywhere he wanted. They had another guy with Washington at that time, Cecil Travis. My first year up I hear the guys moaning about Travis. Ruffing especially. There weren't too many hitters who gave Ruffing trouble, but you mention Travis and he just shook his head. I'm watching him pitch to that guy and Travis is slicing line drives to left field like it's the easiest thing in the world.

"Hey, Charlie," I said to him one time, "how come you never change up on Cecil Travis?"

He smiled. This was my first year up, remember. "We did that, Tom," he said. "Believe me, we tried it. We pitch him fast balls to get him to single to left; when we change up he triples to right."

The '47 Series? Well, I was the man in the middle again, wasn't I? That's right, I was out there in right field when Cookie Lavagetto hit that line drive to break up Bevens' no-hitter and win the ball game. I would say that those were the toughest five seconds of my life.

Remember now, it's the last of the ninth, the Dodgers have men on first and second, there are two out, and we're winning by a run. On top of that, of course, Bill Bevens has the no-hitter going.

When Lavagetto hits the ball I know immediately it's a good line drive. As an experienced outfielder, I know the ball is tagged very well and that it's going to reach the wall. What I don't know is if it's going to be too high for me to go to the wall and catch, and if it is then I have to get set to play a rebound. But if it's six feet high and I decide to stay off the wall to play a rebound, then I've booted it. Now don't forget, I don't have much time to get there. As it turned out, I couldn't have gotten there anyway; so there's no way for me to second-guess myself. In the meantime, I lose that ball for a fraction of a second—don't ask me how. This is beautiful, right? What a spot. Then I pick it up again, and now I find it's too high for me to catch. But when it comes out and I see it I know I *cannot* get that ball, and I tell myself, "Get the heck off that wall as fast as you can."

It was going to happen fast, you see. I was so close to the wall that I knew the ball was going to rebound to me on the fly. It's going to be bang-bang and my glove had better be there. There wasn't much time, but actually I lined up pretty well. The ball came back and hit my glove—but it hit the heel of the glove while I was pulling toward the infield to get set to throw. So the ball drops down, and now I've got to stop and come back and get it. You know how long that takes? A good three seconds. And that's the second run. If I catch the ball cleanly and throw it in, Eddie Miksis, who's carrying the winning run from first, will have to stop on third. But because I have to turn around and go back for the ball, that's one more base for him. It was no contest for him; he scored easily. That's where I lost it, because the ball dropped.

Now, you might say I should have got off the wall and played for a rebound to begin with. Well, that's fine—but suppose the ball was six feet high? What does Bevens think? I gave away a no-hitter. But as I say, it all happened in five seconds, and I won't second-guess myself. Not in that kind of situation. And I also say those are five seconds I could have lived without.

But I can tell you what happened the next day. We're still in Ebbets Field. Frank Shea has them beat 2–1 in the last of the ninth. There's a man on first and two out, and we know that Lavagetto is going to pinch hit. You wonder: Can that guy do it again? I was standing near DiMaggio in the outfield, and we look at each other. Would you believe that he said to me, "For Christ's sake, say a prayer"? That's exactly what he said. DiMaggio.

Shea strikes Lavagetto out. We run into the clubhouse and I go over to Crosetti. "Get a load of this," I said. "What do you think the big guy said when Lavagetto came up?" And I tell him. Crosetti's reaction is, "Why didn't you tell him to pray?" That's pretty good, right? So I go over to DiMaggio. "What do you think Crosetti said?" And I repeat it to him. And Joe says, "I *was* praying. I wasn't sure if I was getting through."

We won it again in '49, after a heck of a battle with the Red Sox. They came into the stadium for the last two games of the season needing only one to clinch it. We beat them on Saturday, on a home run by big John Lindell. That put us in a tie, so it came down to the last game of the season.

The Red Sox started Ellis Kinder. Rizzuto led off for us with a double, and Williams had trouble on the wall in left field and played it into a triple. So we've got a man on third in the first inning, nobody out, and I'm up. And I can't hit Ellis Kinder nohow. I take a look to see how they're playing me, and they're giving us the run. The right side of the infield is playing back, which means if I can hit a ball on the ground to the right, we've got a run. Well, that was about how good I was against Kinder—about a ground ball's worth. I knew one thing: I was not going to pop up. I made up my mind that I was going to put that ball on the ground. And I did. I hit about a fourteen-hopper to second base and Rizzuto scored.

That run held up to the eighth inning, when they had to take Kinder out for a pinch hitter, because they hadn't scored yet, with big Vic Raschi mowing them down. Now they bring Mel Parnell in to pitch to us in the last of the eighth. I'm the lead-off hitter. And I get lucky and hit one in the seats, so now we're ahead 2-0. Then we get three more and we go into the ninth ahead by five runs.

They got a few base hits and the next thing we knew they had three runs. DiMaggio had been sick with the flu all week, and he took himself out of the game in that inning because he felt he was hurting us in the field. Cliff Mapes took his place in center. Somebody flies out to Mapes for the second out. I'm playing first base and I position myself at the mound to take the throw in. Mapes throws it over my head to Yogi at home plate. Raschi is backing up Yogi. So I'm standing at the mound. Yogi comes out and we wait there for Vic. And here he comes, scowling; he's all business. Vic Raschi was always all business. I know Yogi is going to give him the old, "Come on, Vic old boy, just one more." That's what I'm going to say, too. As Vic gets close to us he says, "Give me the damned ball and get the hell out of here." We left. And as I walked to first base I said to myself, "We're in."

Birdie Tebbetts is the batter. He hits a foul ball in the air down to first base. I didn't have to move more than a few feet. But I hear Jerry Coleman yelling behind me: "I got it! I got it!" Jerry called for everything. "Get out of here!" I yelled. He wasn't taking that one. That was my ball. That was the one I'd been looking for all year long.

So we went into the Series, against the Dodgers again. That first game was as good a pitching duel as you'll ever want to see, Allie Reynolds against Don Newcombe. Nobody got close to a run until the bottom of the ninth. I led off that inning. Newcombe tried a fastball and missed outside. Then he came back with kind of a slider and missed outside again. Now it's two balls and no strikes. He hasn't walked anybody all game, and nobody wants to start an inning with a base on balls. So I say to myself, "This is going to be a good ball." I was ninety-nine percent certain he was going to throw his fastball and that it would be over the plate.

So I'm geared for the right speed now. Everything was my way, right? Hitting the ball was something else again, but at least I knew I had every advantage. If I had been anything less than positive about it I would have sacrificed part of that advantage. Newk came in there with it and I tagged it good and solid. I knew it was hit hard enough, but sometimes that kind of ball sinks before it has a chance to go out. As I ran down the line I looked at Furillo and as soon as I saw his head go up a little bit I said to myself, "*That's all.*" I knew it was going to go out.

That got us going in that Series. We won it in five games. You know, I participated in eight World Series, as a player and a coach, and was never on a loser. Never saw the losing side of a World Series. That's pretty good, isn't it?

EWELL BLACKWELL

Ewell Blackwell
Born: October 23, 1922, Fresno, California
Major-league career: 1942–53, 1955, Cincinnati Reds, New
   York Yankees, Kansas City Athletics
Lifetime record: 82 wins, 78 losses

In 1947 Ewell Blackwell put together one of the most remarkable seasons a pitcher ever had. In addition to leading the league with 22 wins, 23 complete games, and 193 strikeouts, Blackwell startled the baseball world with a 16-game winning streak that included a no-hitter and a near miss of a second consecutive no-hitter. After suffering an arm injury in 1948, Blackwell returned to have several more successful years for Cincinnati.

I was pitching for an aircraft company team in Downey, California, in 1941 and a lot of big-league scouts were coming to my front door. I signed with Cincinnati and I can tell you exactly why. They had a farm club in Ogden, Utah, where my mother originally was from. Well, we thought it would be nice if I went there to pitch. So, when the Reds promised they'd send me to Ogden, I signed with them.

They took me to spring training with them in Florida, and I was throwing the ball pretty good. One day a front office guy walked up to me and said, "Blackie, you're not going to Ogden."

"Listen," I said, "that was the deal."

"It's all changed," he said.

I didn't like the sound of it until they told me they were tearing up my contract and signing me to a big-league contract. Well, I sure wasn't going to complain about that, was I? I got into a few games for the Reds but spent most of my time with Syracuse in the International League. I won fifteen games. Then I went into the service. This was 1942.

I was supposed to go to Norman, Oklahoma, to join the Navy. Had my railroad ticket and was all set to leave. Then that afternoon President Roosevelt came on the air and said all enlistments were canceled. A week later I went into the infantry.

I was in the service for three years, three months, and three days. Went through France, Germany, and ended up the furthest east of any ground troops, in Austria, where we met up with the Russians. I was with the third Army, Patton's army. Old Blood and Guts. Our blood and his guts.

I was discharged in the spring of '46 and headed for Tampa, where the Reds were already in training. I had played a little ball in Europe before leaving, so I was in pretty good shape and had every intention of making the club. Bill McKechnie was managing the Reds then, and he was a man who knew every aspect of baseball, frontwards and backwards. He helped me tremendously. I made the club all right. I won nine and lost thirteen that year, and led the league in shutouts with six.

Even though I'd had a losing record, I still felt pretty good about things. I was confident I was going to do better in 1947.

Things seemed to be happening pretty quickly for me—first year in Triple A and then out of the service and right into the big leagues. But I wasn't all that surprised. I always wanted to be a baseball player, from the time I was in elementary school, out in San Dimas, California. It's hard to believe today, but at that time I wondered if I'd ever be big enough to play ball. When I was a sophomore in high school I was five feet five. In my junior year I went to six-three, and in my senior year to six-six. No, it wasn't so surprising; they seemed to run to height on my father's side of the family. They were all very tall men. I just took my time getting up there, that's all.

My dad encouraged me to play ball. He built a "control box" for me and hung it on the garage wall in the backyard. It was a frame of the strike zone. I'd stand out there about three hours a day and try to throw to spots in it, using old baseballs or a tennis ball, whatever was most handy. I always had pretty good control, and I think all that early throwing helped.

When I was a freshman in high school I went out for the football team, even though I was real small then. They had me playing guard, which I don't think was a very good idea. One day there was a play and some big guy landed on my shoulder and gave me a pretty sound shaking up. Now, I don't know if that accounted for it or not, but I never could get up and throw overhand with any real power. So I pitched sidearm. The so-called "Whip" delivery. I never thought too much about it. It was just my way of throwing, that's all. To me sidearm is more natural, anyway. There isn't as much strain on your arm as there is in throwing overhand.

That delivery was rough on righthanded batters. With the height I had, coming from way around with that ball, it was tough for them to pick up. Some of those righties would come up to me and swear it was the third baseman pitching to them. I've had many guys taking called strikes lying flat on their backs, thinking the ball was coming right at them. But, as I said, that delivery was very natural to me.

When I had my good stuff, before I hurt my arm, I never cared who was standing up there with the bat, righty or lefty. Stan Musial was a great hitter, but he never hit a home run off of me. Neither did Johnny Mize. He still can't understand that. John used to have a liquor store in Florida, you know, and he had the shelves lined with baseballs autographed by the pitchers he'd hit home runs off. I walked in there one day and stood gazing at all of those baseballs.

"John," I said, "where's my baseball?" He growled a little and said, "You don't have one."

Johnny had his laugh on me, though. This happened in the Polo Grounds in 1946. It was two out in the bottom of the ninth and I had a big lead, and at the same time was working on a big old chaw of tobacco in my mouth. I threw a pitch to Mize and he hit a line drive. I never saw it, but I heard it—it whistled right by my ear. I was so startled I swallowed that whole plug. I thought I was going to die, right out there on the mound, in front of all those people. Somehow I got the next man out to end the game, then took off for the clubhouse. That was about five hundred feet away, if you remember. I just did make it, but when I got in there they told me I had more colors in my face than a rainbow.

I'll tell you about another hitter. The best I ever saw. A

fellow I pitched against in a high school tournament. Ted Williams. That's right. I pitched for the high school in San Dimas and Ted for the one in San Diego. That's the first time I ever saw him. He was a pretty good-looking pitcher. But he looked even better with the bat.

I always loved to watch Ted hit. One spring, when I was with the Reds, we were heading north and played an exhibition game against the Red Sox in Birmingham, Alabama. The wind was blowing in from right field at about forty miles an hour. The guys on the bench were saying that you would need a cannon to get the ball through that wind.

Ted was leading off an inning late in the game and I called my catcher, Ray Mueller, out to the mound.

"Let's see how strong he really is," I said. "You tell him I'm going to throw a fastball belt-high right down the middle."

Mueller went back and gave Ted the message. The first pitch I threw was right there. Ted jumped on it and hit a line drive straight through that wind into the right-field seats. I wasn't at all surprised—he had the greatest eyes and wrists of any hitter I ever saw.

As I said, I was confident I was going to have a good year in '47 and I did. On May 10 I had a 2–2 record and started a game against the Cubs. I won that game and then didn't lose again until July 30. In between I won sixteen straight. Every one was a complete game, too, and five of them were shutouts.

The eighth game of the streak was a no-hitter against the Braves. That was a night game at Cincinnati, on June 18. The score was 6–0. Remember Babe Young, the first baseman? Well, we'd just bought him from the Giants and he had just reported that morning. He went right into the lineup. He came up in the first inning with two on and hit a home run. Then around the fifth or sixth inning he hit another home run with two men on. That was my six runs. His first day in town.

He walked up to me in the clubhouse after the game and said, "Blackie, here I am a 'pheenom' tonight, and you had to be a double 'pheenom.'" Here's a fellow joins a team and in his first game knocks in all six runs with two homers and after it's over nobody's paying him any attention. I paid him some attention though, you can be sure.

I had real good stuff that night. I think the closest anybody came to a hit was Bama Rowell. He hit a line drive in the fourth or fifth inning that Frankie Baumholtz caught against the right-field screen. Johnny Hopp tried to bunt his way on in the ninth inning, but Ray LaManno made a great play coming from behind the plate and threw him out.

You know, my third baseman, Grady Hatton, who was also my roommate and good friend, didn't even know I had a no-hitter in the works. I had two men out in the ninth and was really taking my time on that last hitter. You come that far, you *want* it. All of a sudden I look up and here's Grady walking over to the mound, as casual as could be.

"For cryin' out loud, Blackie," he says, "I'm tired. Throw the ball down the middle and let him hit the damn thing. Let's go home."

I thought he'd gone out of his mind or something. I looked at him and there must have been homicide in my eyes, because he turned around and got out of there in a hurry. I can laugh now, but it wasn't so funny then. But I got the last man out and the fans went wild, and the team came running out to pound me around—and Grady still didn't know what was going on. He finally came up to me later in the clubhouse wearing the most sheepish grin you ever saw.

"Next time pay attention," I said.

Well, the next time *everybody* paid attention. It was four days later, on June 22, and I was starting against the Dodgers. I suppose you might say that's the most well-remembered game I ever pitched, more so even than the no-hitter. Were there any thoughts about a second consecutive no-hitter? Yes, there were. I went on a talk show right after pitching the no-hitter and I told the guy I was going to pitch another one next time out. You're not supposed to say that, are you? What made me say it? I don't know. I just felt strong, felt I had real good stuff. Sure, that was a pretty nervy thing to say over the air, but I wasn't talking bigger than I could handle, because there should have been the second no-hitter. Didn't miss it by more than an eyeblink.

I had a good feeling from the moment I began warming up. Just never felt better. I walked out onto that mound with all the confidence in the world.

The way things developed, though, I had a tougher game on my hands than I bargained for. Joe Hatten started for the Dodgers and he seemed to have the same idea I did—through four innings neither one of us had given up a base hit. Eddie Miller finally got a double in the fifth. In the sixth Hatten walked four men and we took a 1-0 lead.

By the top of the ninth we were leading, 4-0, and I still had the no-hitter going. You know, looking back, it was interesting how many coincidences were at work. The only man in major-league history ever to pitch consecutive no-hitters also pitched for Cincinnati—Johnny Vander Meer. He'd pitched them in the same month that I was going after mine—June. And not only that, but he had pitched them against the same clubs and in the same order as I was hoping to do—the Braves and the Dodgers. And to cap it all off, Johnny Vander Meer was still with Cincinnati and was sitting on the top step of the dugout, waiting to come out and shake my hand.

First man up in the ninth was a pinch hitter, Gene Hermanski. He flied out to Augie Galan in left.

Eddie Stanky was next. He took a pitch for a ball.

Then on the next pitch he hit it back to me. I thought he had hit it harder than he actually had; when it's hit straight back at you it's sometimes hard to judge just how fast it's moving. But it wasn't hit as hard as I thought—in fact he'd broken his bat on it—and I made my move too quickly. I went down for it and came up thinking I had the ball. Well, I didn't have it. It went under my glove and right through my legs, rolled through the infield and died on the center-field grass, about twenty feet out.

I just stood there looking at that ball, that little white ball lying on the grass. How did I feel? Well, I figured about $100,000 had gone down the drain, and I felt accordingly.

I won the game, 4-0. That was the ninth win in the streak. I was going for my seventeenth, against the Giants, when I finally lost one. I was leading them, 4-3, with one out in the ninth, with a count of two strikes and no balls on Willard Marshall. I tried to brush him back, but that was one of the times the ball didn't go where I wanted it to; it went right down the middle of the plate, and it went where he wanted it to. He hit a home run and tied it up.

Then in the tenth they got a man in scoring position with two out and Buddy Kerr up. I got two strikes on him, then threw a pitch that, so help me, cut the middle of the plate belt-high. I swear I never threw a cleaner strike. But the umpire missed it. So I had to try it again, and this time Buddy looped it over short for a base hit and that beat me, 5–4.

No, I didn't take that home with me. I left it right there in the ball park. I wasn't the sort to brood over what happened on the field. As they say, it's a game of seconds and inches; it can't be played any other way. You could, if you wanted, brood over everything that happens in a game, it all happens so fast; but there's no sense in letting it get to you.

But while I hated to see the winning streak come to an end, in some ways it was a relief. That sort of thing can become a burden. It got so I felt like I was carrying a piano on my back every time I went to the mound.

You know, some people thought I might be putting too much strain on my elbow the way I whipped my arm around to deliver the ball. But the elbow never has bothered me in my life. When I did hurt my arm it was in the top of the shoulder. It happened in an exhibition game in Columbia, South Carolina. We'd been training in Tampa, in real fine weather, and then broke camp and began heading north. We played a game with the Boston Braves in Columbia. It was a week before opening day. I hadn't gone more than six innings in a game in Florida, but Luke Sewell, who was managing, said I had better try to go nine in that game. It was a miserable day, wet and cold and windy. In the eighth inning something just popped in my shoulder. I finished the game all right, but I had torn some kind of a nerve in my shoulder.

It became painful for me to throw a ball. I'd wind up and begin to deliver and halfway through my delivery it would suddenly feel like somebody was sinking his teeth into my shoulder. I tried to pitch out of it but couldn't. My wins dropped from twenty-two in 1947 to seven the next year. Then, in January of '49, I had a kidney out. I just couldn't throw right and won only five games. But in '50 I came back strong and won seventeen and in '51 I won sixteen. Then in '52 I had a bad year and went to the Yankees. I was just about through then.

I started one game at Ebbets Field early in 1952, I never will forget it. In the bottom of the first I walked a few and then gave up a few hits. Sewell came out.

"Blackie," he said, "it's not your night."

"I'm getting the same idea," I said.

Bud Byerly came to relieve and I left. I went into the club-house, took a shower, then left the ball park and took a cab back to the Commodore Hotel over in Manhattan. I went into the bar and sat down for a drink. They had the game on television and when I looked up at it I heard the announcer say Brooklyn was still hitting in the bottom of the first inning. I thought he had to be mistaken, but he kept saying it over and over. The Dodgers were going around those bases like they were on a merry-go-round. They scored fifteen runs that inning. I couldn't believe that I was sitting in a bar in Man-hattan looking at the bottom of the first inning of a game I'd started over an hour and a half ago in Brooklyn.

Then the next thing I know Bud Byerly comes in and sits down next to me.

"What inning they in?" he asks.

"Bottom of the first," I said.

He didn't say anything.

"Don't you want to know what the score is?" I asked.

"Frankly," he said, "no."

"Don't feel so bad," I said. "At least they can't blame it *all* on us."

But the pitching did tighten up a bit after the first inning and the final score was only something like 19–2.

I remember at the end of one season, it must have been around '49, we had the wildest train ride home. We ended the season in Pittsburgh and the club had arranged to have two Pullman cars to take the players who wanted to go, back to Cincinnati.

After the game we got on the train. They had those Sunday blue laws in Pennsylvania, which meant you couldn't buy beer or liquor or anything else to celebrate the end of a base-ball season with. So we arranged with the railroad people to have the men's rooms in our private cars all filled with beer and about three cases of liquor.

We sat on the train for about an hour before it took off and by that time the beer and liquor were all gone. So when the train began rolling everybody was feeling real good. There was a lot of noise and some hijinks. About an hour later the conductor came back and said they were going to disconnect us from the train and put us on a siding because we were causing too much trouble. Just leave us there. Walker

Cooper—he was just about the strongest man I've ever known—went up to him and said, "I don't know what your name is today, but it's going to be shit tomorrow if you try that." The conductor went away.

Then we stopped someplace in West Virginia. It was supposed to be a thirty-minute stop. Cooper and our trainer, Doc Bohm, got off to get some more beer. No sooner were they off than the train started up again. Well, we figured we'd see them again in the spring.

We cruised along for about thirty minutes and then all of a sudden came to a screeching halt, in the middle of nowhere. Pitch black outside. We looked out and couldn't believe it—here's Cooper and Doc Bohm walking up the tracks, each of them carrying two cases of beer.

What those guys had done was hailed a cab and told the driver he had to beat that train to the next crossing. When they got there they made the driver straddle the tracks with his cab, to make the train stop. So they got back on, the cab went away, and here we go again.

It was still quite a way to Cincinnati and things kept getting wilder. Soon nobody had any buttons left on his shirt. I didn't have any buttons or any sleeves either on mine. Then Cooper started going around and reaching back into your pants and ripping your underwear off. He'd take the top of your shorts in his hand and just rip them right off you. Grady Hatton tried to go to sleep and somebody poured a bucket on water on him. A good time was had by all.

When we pulled into Cincinnati we were in good shape. We came rolling off of that train without buttons, without underwear, half of us without shirts. We were the drunkest, happiest, noisiest baseball team that ever got off a train. But then all of a sudden you could have heard a pin drop. There wasn't a sound, because there they were—our wives, standing in a group waiting for us. I don't think we realized what we looked like until we saw the expressions on their faces. My wife said we were the sorriest-looking bunch of people she ever did see.

Very quietly we all shook hands, wished each other a good winter, promised to meet again in the spring, and then went home to face the music.

BUDDY HASSETT

JOHN ALOYSIUS HASSETT
Born: September 5, 1911, New York, New York
Major-league career: 1936–42, Brooklyn Dodgers, Boston
  Braves, New York Yankees
Lifetime average: .292

A first baseman in the Yankee farm system in the days of Lou Gehrig, Buddy Hassett came to the big leagues with the Brooklyn Dodgers. His career was marked by quiet consistency; only once did his batting average slip under .284, and three times it was better than .300. He entered the Navy after the 1942 season and did not return to the big leagues when the war was over.

I got started playing ball right on the sidewalks of New York, in the 1920's. Played a lot of semipro ball around the city. Semipro was a big thing in those days. We'd pass the hat during the game and this was how we helped keep the team going. If there was some rain during the game the manager would hand me a megaphone and I'd sing "When Irish Eyes Are Smiling" and other songs to the fans, to keep them entertained until the rain passed. I always had a pretty good voice.

    I was attending Manhattan College when Paul Krichell, the old Yankee scout, had a look and decided he liked what he saw. Upon graduation in 1933 I signed a contract with the Yankees, and they sent me down to Wheeling in the Middle-Atlantic League. I had a good year, then had a couple more good years, at Norfolk and Columbus, where I played on option. I hit .332, .360, and .337, but I wasn't any closer to playing first base for the Yankees than I was on the day I started. They had a roadblock up there named Lou Gehrig; so it didn't make much difference how well you did. George McQuinn was in the organization the same time I was, and we shared the problem.

So I asked to be traded and they accommodated me, selling me to Brooklyn in '36. I went over there and that was my first exposure to Charles Dillon Stengel, who was managing the Dodgers then. He was a great person and a good baseball man. Playing for him was a memorable experience.

Stengel was a vivid character, but so were a lot of the fellows we had with the Dodgers in those years. Van Lingle Mungo was one. Gee, he was a great pitcher; but he could do some funny things too. Now and then he'd jump the ball club and get lost for a couple of days. Frenchy Bordagaray was another one. Good-natured guy. Always happy. He came to spring training in 1936 with a goatee and mustache. What a fuss it caused! Today it wouldn't mean anything, but in 1936 it was really something different.

I remember one day we were playing an exhibition game. A ball was hit over Frenchy's head; it wasn't a matter of him catching it, it was a matter of him running it down. He wheeled around and started running, and as he ran his cap flew off. Well, most people would run the ball down first, wouldn't they? But Frenchy wasn't most people. He went back, got his cap, and then went after the ball. Stengel stood in the dugout with his arms hanging and his mouth open. He couldn't believe what he was seeing. When Frenchy got back to the bench Stengel asked him what he thought he was doing out there. "The cap wasn't going anywhere, Bordagaray," Casey said, "but the ball was." "I forgot," Frenchy said.

Another time Frenchy got into an argument with an umpire and in the course of it spit in the umpire's face. Of course the umpire ran him out of there, even though Frenchy claimed he had simply been talking fast and that you can't help spraying a little when you do that. Then the league fined him fifty dollars and when he heard about it, Frenchy said, "That's more than I expectorated."

Once Frenchy was on second with two out and we're down a run. Stengel was coaching third and he kept yelling at Frenchy not to come over, to stay there. Sure enough, on the next pitch here he comes, stealing third, with two out. He slides in and makes it. Stengel walks over and looks down at him.

"I ought to fine you for that," Casey says.

"With the lead I had," Frenchy says, "you ought to fine yourself for not inviting me over."

But that was the way we did things in Brooklyn in those days. We had Max Butcher. I don't know if you recall Max or not. He was a pretty fair pitcher. Max's eyes were always blinking, and the guys used to say that he pitched between blinks. In 1937 Burleigh Grimes was managing the club. We were playing an exhibition game and Burleigh was coaching first base. The steal sign was when he winked at us. "When I wink, you go," he said. Then in the middle of the game he gets a long-distance phone call and has to leave the field. They put Max in to coach first base. Gibby Brack gets on. Gibby, Lord rest his soul, wasn't the brightest guy in the world. He looks at Max, Max's eyes are blinking away, and Gibby lights out for second. He's shot down by about fifteen feet, just as Grimes is coming back. Burleigh starts roaring. "Who gave that steal sign?" And somebody says, "Nobody gave it, but look who's coaching first base." And there's big Max Butcher standing there, blinking away.

We had Babe Phelps, too, in those years. Great hitter. Wonderful fellow. They tell a story about Babe—I don't know if it's true or not—that he built a home in Maryland and forgot to put a toilet in it. Then we had Freddy Frankhouse, the pitcher. Freddy was always looking out the window hoping it would rain. He loved rainy days. I asked him once what he did on rainy days. "Nothing," he said. He just liked having the day off.

We were always scrambling for players back then, signing anybody we thought might help, no matter how much mileage they had on them. We had big George Earnshaw for a while. Heinie Manush was with us for a year or so, too. He used to call me "The Red-necked Thrush." "You're always either singing or you're mad," he said. Great line-drive hitter. He came up under Cobb, and Cobb worked with him and taught him an awful lot. Now there, as far as I'm concerned, is probably the greatest of them all, Ty Cobb. When you look at that average of .367 over twenty-four years it's just phenomenal. They say he was a driving, slashing player. Never went out onto the field to make friends. I met Cobb only once. I was coming out of Yankee Stadium after a World Series game with Paul Krichell and we bumped into Cobb. Paul introduced me and then they stepped aside to talk. Later, when we were driving out, Paul said, "Now there's a funny one."

"What's that?" I asked.

"What do you think he wanted to talk to me about?"

"I don't know, Paul," I said.

"He told me that he would give up all his money and just about everything he's got if the fellows he played with and against would only accept him and talk to him today."

That's a pretty sad commentary; but at the same time it gives you some idea what he must have been like out on that field.

We had Waite Hoyt and Kiki Cuyler, too, for a while. And Freddie Lindstrom was with us in '36. I saw Freddie play his last game. He was out in left field. We were playing the Giants in the Polo Grounds, it was the last of the ninth, the tying run was on second base, and I think Mel Ott was on first with the winning run. Somebody hit a pop fly into short left and Lindstrom came running in, the shortstop went running out, and it was "I got it, you take it, who's got it." The ball dropped in and both runs scored and we lose the game. Lindstrom came into the clubhouse and said, "I'm a son of a gun. I heard about these things that happen in Brooklyn. I never thought it would happen to me, and I'll tell you, it's never going to happen again." He took off his uniform and never put it on again.

In 1939 I was traded over to Boston. Stengel was managing up there then, so it was a reunion. We had a situation there one day which, to say the least, was highly unusual. There was a certain guy on the club whose ambition it was to drive in a hundred runs that year. That's very commendable, of course, and every hitter would like to do it; but with this guy it became an obsession. Every time he came up with a man in scoring position you'd see him grinding the sawdust out of the bat handle. Listen, I'd rather not mention his name; let's just call him "RBI."

We were playing the Phillies this day and beating them about 12–5. I always used to say thank the Lord for the Phillies, because they kept me out of eighth place just about every year I was in the National League. Frank Demaree led off with a single, and I'm the batter. Well, as I always said, the pitcher had good control and he hit my bat, and the ball fell over the third baseman's head for a double. Up comes RBI. You could see the gleam in his eye—men on second and third and nobody out.

The first pitch is right down the middle, and he pops it up. You never saw a guy so disgusted. He flung his bat away and went through the motions of running down to first. He gave the bag a kick, turned around and began walking back to the dugout, which was on the third-base side. He's got his head down and he's muttering to himself. While he's walking, the pitcher is beginning to work to the next hitter, who happened to be Paul Waner.

They liked to work inside to Paul in those years, figuring he'd have trouble getting around on those pitches. Well, the first pitch is way inside and off the catcher's glove and rolls right across RBI's path—he's still looking down and muttering. Frank Demaree's on third and he starts storming down the line. The catcher—it was Bennie Warren—for some reason never left the plate. RBI sees the ball, doesn't know what's happening, picks it up and flips it to Bennie Warren who then whirls around and tags out Demaree sliding into home plate. This actually happened.

I go over to third base on the play and say to Stengel, who's coaching there, "Casey, do you think they'll give him an assist on the play?" I don't think he heard me; he was fit to be tied.

The next pitch is another wild one and now I come in to score—successfully, what with no teammate hanging around the plate to throw me out. I go into the dugout and there's RBI, walking up and down, mortified and miserable; not only did he pop up with ducks on the pond, but now he's pulled this boner. He's walking up and down, still not paying attention. All of a sudden Waner fouls a screamer right into the dugout and hits RBI on the side of the head. He goes down like he was poleaxed. Naturally we ran to pick him up, but Casey comes running over from third base yelling, "Don't anybody touch the son of a bitch; let him lay there—it might drive some sense into him."

You know, I roomed with Paul Waner for a while. He could drink pretty good. That's no secret. But he could also sober himself up in a hurry. He would do backflips. He had remarkable agility, like an acrobat. Fifteen or twenty minutes of backflips and he was cold sober, ready to go out to the ball park and get his three hits.

Paul was a very serious-minded person. He studied the writings of Seneca. This is what he read. And he had his little sayings. We were playing a game of pepper one time and right out of the blue I hear Paul saying to me, "You know, they say money talks. But the only thing it ever says to me is 'Goodbye!' "

Jimmie Wilson, the old catcher, told me a story about Paul. They were playing against each other one day and each time Paul came to the plate he asked Jimmie where he wanted the ball hit. "I called the right and left-field lines four times," Jimmie said, "And he hit four doubles right where I said, and of course we're pitching him exactly opposite."

Paul and I would get to talking hitting. Of course when you're in close proximity to such a fine hitter you want to talk to him about it, hoping that somehow something might rub off. But he had no great theories. He said he just laid that bat on his shoulder and when he saw a pitch he liked he threw it off. That's all. Simple, isn't it? Lay the bat on your shoulder and then throw it off.

I'll tell you about a guy who was a great ballplayer and who should have been one of the greatest: Pete Reiser. He came out of nowhere in 1941 and in his first full season led the league in batting. He had everything—speed, power, good arm, good fielder. I always felt that he played *too* hard. He was a very intense kid. He suffered those injuries—running into walls, breaking bones—that he might otherwise have avoided. But it was his style of playing, I guess. He was an awful tough man to play against because he could be explosive in any situation, whether it was in the field, at bat, on the bases.

Now, let's talk about Arky Vaughan. This is one of my pet peeves. Why isn't he in the Hall of Fame? Here was another guy who could do it all. A .300 hitter, year in and year out, and he could run and field with the best of them. You know, there was a time when I bore a slight facial resemblance to Arky. One day I was coming out of Ebbets Field after a game with the Pirates. When I hit the street a dirty-faced little kid came up to me and said, "Hey, Arky, will you give me your autograph?" I thought it over for a second, then took his scorecard and signed Arky Vaughan. It felt nice.

In the winter of '41 I was working as a plumber in upstate New York when I heard I'd been traded to the Yankees. It was a surprise, a very pleasant surprise. That year, 1942, was my last in the big leagues, and it's nice to say I went out a winner. After all those years in the second division in the National League I finally got into a World Series, against the Cardinals. I played in only three games because in that third game I was trying to bunt against Ernie White and the ball came in on me and broke my finger. That finished me for the Series, and as a matter of fact, I never played major league ball again, because I went into the Navy after the season. But the nice thing was that after having signed with the Yankees so many years before, and after having spent all of my career with the Dodgers and Braves, when I did get into a World Series it was with the Yankees. So it finally came full circle, you might say.

A few years ago I attended a B'nai B'rith gathering where a lot of the old Dodgers were being honored. It was a nice, nostalgic evening. When I came up to be introduced the band started playing "When Irish Eyes Are Smiling." So instead of saying thank you, I asked the band to strike it up again and I sang "When Irish Eyes Are Smiling." One more time.

GEORGE CASE

GEORGE WASHINGTON CASE
Born: November 22, 1915, Trenton, New Jersey
Major-league career: 1937–47, Washington Senators, Cleveland Indians
Lifetime average: .282

Although he was a fine outfielder and a steady hitter, George Case will always be remembered as one of the greatest basestealers of all time, despite a career prematurely ended by injuries when he was thirty-one. Between 1921 and 1961, no major leaguer stole more bases in a single season than Case. He led the American League five consecutive years in stolen bases, between 1939 and 1943, a feat at that time unprecedented in major league history. His single season high was 61, in 1943.

I could always run. When I was in high school I ran against the track stars in my baseball uniform. It was always a challenge to me because I used to feel I could have been a track star if I'd wanted. And more times than not I did beat them. But I never did have a reputation for being that quick until my second year in the minors, when I led the league in stolen bases. From then on that was my reputation. Still is, I guess. I still meet people today who say to me, "Oh, yes, you're the fellow who stole all those bases."

During the war years I ran more match races than anybody that ever put on a uniform. One year I ran five races for purses, and the only guy that ever beat me was Jesse Owens. That actually was in '46, when I was with Cleveland. It was Bill Veeck's first promotion in the big leagues, matching me against Jesse Owens.

Sometime in July 1943, Clark Griffith got hold of me and said, "George, our publicity man has arranged for you to try and beat Hans Lobert's record for circling the bases. I'm going to give you a thousand dollars for doing it." He thought it would be a good gimmick and would draw some people, which we needed to do; we weren't drawing flies at that time.

Lobert's record for circling the bases was 13.8 seconds. Evar Swanson, an outfielder who played in the early thirties, had done it in 13.2, but while that was considered the official time it really shouldn't have been, because they held only one watch on him. A lot of people considered Lobert's mark to be the official one, and that was the one I was trying to better.

The ball club made a big thing of it, the newspapers played it up, and sure enough we pulled a good crowd that day. When it was time to make that run all the players left the field and I went up to home plate. There were three AAU officials there as timers; in the event I set a record it would be official.

Well, I beat Lobert's record, circling the bases in 13.5. Now, Swanson's record is still regarded as official, but it really shouldn't be. I feel I hold the record and ought to be given credit for it because I had three AAU people holding the clock on me.

Remember Gil Coan? He came up from the minor leagues with the reputation of being tremendously fast. After I was sold to Cleveland in 1946 some of the Washington writers seemed to think he could take me. One day I got a phone call from one of them.

"George," he said, "next time you come to Washington I can get you a thousand dollars if you'll run against Gil Coan. We think it'll draw a lot of people, and Mr. Griffith's all for it. What do you say?"

"Hell, yes," I said. A thousand bucks was a lot of money in those days.

So the race was announced and the next trip into Washington I ran against Coan. Just before the race was to start somebody came over to me and said, "George, step over to the boxes for a minute, somebody there wants to shake hands with you."

I was concentrating so intensely on what I was going to

have to do that I didn't look up until I reached the box-seat railing. Well, I'll be darned if it wasn't General Eisenhower, standing up with that big grin and his hand stretched out.

"Hello, George," he said, and we shook hands. "I want to wish you luck. I've come a long way to see this."

I found out later he'd come up from Virginia especially for the race. Well we gave him a good one. Gil Coan was very fast, but I beat him. It was a darn good promotion and pulled a lot of people into the ball park—including General Eisenhower.

You know, you don't see that sort of thing anymore in baseball—no field days, no match races, no attempts to circle the bases. They're all afraid today that a ballplayer will pull up lame. I think that's nonsense; hell, a ballplayer is used to running, it's his living. It's too bad they've done away with those things, because the fans love that sort of competition. There's always some question in everybody's mind about who is the fastest man in baseball. Everybody has their candidate, whether it be Bobby Bonds or Lou Brock or whoever. Why not have that as an added attraction at the all-star game? Pick your three fastest from each league and let them run it out, for a purse. The fans would love it.

I never ran from signs; I ran on my own. Any good base runner has to be on his own. Of course you have to earn the privilege. The manager will watch you for a while and then pull you aside and tell you, "Look, you have the speed, you know when your timing is right, and you know the pitchers better than I do. Just use good judgment. Don't run us out of an inning." They play it differently today, but back then if you ever tried to steal third base with two out or second base when you were three or four runs behind, you'd get the hell chewed out of you. I remember one time I'd stolen twenty-one bases in a row. We were playing the Browns in St. Louis and were down by three runs in the middle of the game. I led off an inning with a base hit and then decided to steal second. I stumbled breaking away and was thrown out. And before I'd even gotten back to the dugout Bucky Harris had already told somebody else to get ready to go out and replace me; he was taking me out of the game.

I went into the clubhouse, took a shower, and sat around. Harris came in after the game and never said a word to me. But that night I was sitting in the lobby of the Chase Hotel, and he came up to me. I can still see him standing there. He had a rolled-up newspaper in his hand and he hit the paper lightly in the palm of his hand a few times, then said. "You got a pretty good idea why I took you out of there today?"

"Obviously because I ran at the wrong time," I said.

"That's right," he said. "And as long as I'm managing the ball club, don't you ever run like that when we're down."

And I never did. But that took away from my stolen bases.

So you can see how they played it then—a bit more conservative. Nevertheless, I still stole 61 bases one year and 51 another. If I was running today, the way they're playing it, there's no doubt in my mind I'd be stealing a hundred bases, too. No doubt at all. One year I stole 44 bases and was caught only six times, and three of those I was thrown out of the game for arguing the decision. Were they that close? Hell, no, they weren't close—that's why I was arguing. They were bad calls; I had the damned base stolen, and I told the umpire so, which was why I was run out of there.

You know, sometimes I was able to steal a catcher's pitch-out sign. The pitch-out, of course, is the one thing a base runner has to fear more than anything else, because in that situation you're running against a ball thrown to a catcher who's trying to throw you out. But I came to realize that most catchers signaled for a pitch-out by either wiggling their fingers or making a fist. Well, when I got on first base I would watch their arms. If a guy made a fist you could see the muscles tighten in his forearm, or if he was wiggling his fingers you could see that action by his arm, too.

The toughest catcher for me to steal on was Paul Richards. I had a hell of a time running against him. He always seemed to be guessing right along with me. Now I'll tell you something funny about that, just to give you some idea what goes on inside of a ball game. I had a bad left shoulder, it bothered me for about four or five years until I had it operated on. One spring during the war, when we were training at the University of Maryland, Bill Dickey stopped by to visit. Bill was in the Navy then. He sat down next to me on the bench.

"You don't have too much luck running against Richards, do you?" he said.

"Tell you the truth, Bill," I said, "he gives me a fit."

"Well, I'll give you a tip," he said. "Whenever you're about to run you tuck your left arm into yourself. Richards has spotted that."

Well, I'll be a son of a gun, I thought to myself. Dickey was right. Whenever I knew I was going to run I became conscious of that bad shoulder and protective of it; so I used to bring that arm in against myself. And Paul Richards, being a very shrewd man, picked it up.

In 1939 I stole 51 bases, which was quite a few steals for those years. That winter, just before I was going to leave for spring training, I get a call from Tampa, from a guy I'd never heard of. He's the representative of the Camel cigarette people, through an advertising agency in New York. "I understand you smoke Camels," he said.

Well, it so happened I did.

"Would you be interested in endorsing them?" he asked.

"Sure," I said. "What's in it?"

"When are you going to be in Florida?" he asked.

"I'll be down in Orlando in a week," I said.

So we arranged to meet down there and talk further about it. I arrived in Orlando a week later, and this fellow meets me in the hotel lobby.

"This is the deal," he said. "If you'll endorse Camels for one year I'll give you a thousand dollars and a carton of cigarettes every week for fifty-two weeks."

Now, this was only my second year in the big leagues, remember. I was flattered, but curious.

"Why me?" I asked.

"Listen," he said, "you don't know it, but I followed you around the league last year. I went into every town that you played in on the road and was impressed with the fan reaction to you. You're the kind of person we want to advertise our product because the fans come out to see you play. Your style of play excites them."

Frankly, I was surprised. A ballplayer doesn't really know how the crowd is reacting to him; he's so busy concentrating on his game he just can't pay attention. But apparently the base-stealing had caught the fans' imagination and this fellow was aware of it and wanted to capitalize on it.

So they chartered a DC-3 and brought down a whole production crew to shoot the pictures. They trucked in three tons of sand, spread it out around second base, set up platforms for

angle shots, and were otherwise very thorough in their prep-
arations. I spent a whole afternoon being photographed sliding through that sand into second base.

The advertising campaign was keyed to the opening of the
season. I was on the back of *Liberty* magazine, *Saturday
Evening Post,* and other publications. "George Washington
Case. I smoke Camels." That's what it said. It was quite a
campaign. But then do you know what happened? One week
after it was launched I started to get very indignant letters
from parents all over the country, saying I was a bad influence
on American youth. What's more, Will Harridge, the president of the league, was getting the same kind of mail. So he
called me on the phone and asked me to stop in and see him
the next time I was in Chicago.

First trip into Chicago I went up to his office. He opened up
a desk drawer and it was stuffed with mail. I read a few of
them and they were awful.

"Mr. Harridge," I said, "I've been getting the same thing."

"Well," he said, "we can't have this."

So he called the advertising agency and told them that no
American League ballplayer was ever to be photographed
endorsing a cigarette in their baseball uniform. The advertising people called me.

"Look," they said, "we've got a lot of money invested in this
and we don't want to drop it."

A compromise was reached—I would pose for a new series of
photographs in street clothes. That's what happened. I think
I was the last baseball player ever to endorse tobacco in a
baseball uniform. There had been a few before me, but they
had mostly been pitchers. I think it was because my name was
associated with running speed that upset so many people.
Kids were probably saying to their parents, "Hey, George
Case smokes cigarettes and he can run like the devil."

But that wasn't the end of it. As a result of that Camel
advertisement these three guys used to get on me whenever
we came to Fenway Park. They'd parade around the stands
during batting practice yelling, "George Washington Case. I
smoke Camels. *You stink!*" Over and over. Every time we
went to Boston. Finally I couldn't stand it any longer and
went up into the stands after them. You're damned right I did.
And I went in swinging, in full uniform. The cops came over

right away and broke it up; but I was ready to take on all three of them.

That was some deal I made with Camels.

You know, I almost went with the Philadelphia Athletics instead of the Senators. After I graduated from prep school in New Jersey I was invited to Shibe Park to work out with the A's. Connie Mack liked me but said he didn't have an opening for me in his organization. But he did help get me placed in the New York–Penn League. This was in 1936. In '37 I led the league in batting and that fall went up to the big leagues with the Washington Senators.

The Senators were a chronic second-division team, but at the same time their lineup was chock-full of .300 hitters. They had Buddy Myer, who was always a good hitter, and one of the most rugged competitors I ever saw. Off the field he was the nicest, most placid guy in the world; but the moment he put on his baseball uniform his personality changed; he became aggressive and pugnacious. It was the most amazing thing; you wouldn't think it was the same person. And they had Cecil Travis, who was certainly one of the best hitters I ever saw. And Buddy Lewis was a good one, too.

The ball club also had a lot of old and established players. Let's see, in addition to Myer, there was Goose Goslin, Rick and Wes Ferrell, Sammy West, Al Simmons.

When I joined the team in the fall of '37 those old guys didn't want to know that I existed. The only ones on the club who came up to me and introduced themselves were Buddy Lewis and Cecil Travis. The next spring when I went south with the team Al Simmons didn't remember me from the previous fall; he didn't even know I was on the ball club. I had to reintroduce myself to him.

At that time Al was on his way out; still a good hitter but no longer the devastating one he had been. They'd play him a couple of days, then rest him a couple of days. He was at that point in his career.

One evening in Boston I was sitting in the lobby of the Copley Plaza after the ball game. Simmons came in at about nine-thirty with a newspaper under his arm. He stopped, looked around, then looked at me. He was never particularly friendly to me, but I was the only ballplayer sitting there, so he came up to me.

"Young fellow," he said, "come on and have a drink with me."

Here's the great Al Simmons asking me to have a drink with him, and all I could get out was, "Al, I don't drink."

"Hell, you drink ginger ale, don't you?"

"Sure," I said.

"Then come on in," he said.

They had a merry-go-round bar in the Copley Plaza; you know, one of those bars that go around and make a full circle every sixty minutes. We had an off-day the next day and I sat at that bar with him until two-thirty A.M. drinking ginger ale until it was coming out of my ears, while he was drinking Scotch and water. For some reason, he told me the story of his life, practically from the day he was born. One of the things he said was, "You know, I've got a reputation for being coarse and a little bit ornery, but believe me, enough things have happened to me in my lifetime to account for that."

He told me about his boyhood, about what a rough time he'd had, how poor his family was, how hard he had to work when he was a boy. It was all very interesting and sad, and I got to know Al Simmons that night.

After that, he was my closest friend on the ball club. He took me under his wing, gave me an awful lot of good advice and encouragement. I considered it a privilege to be on the same team with Al Simmons. He turned out to be, under that gruff exterior, a very kindly and thoughtful man. Of course he was one of the greatest right-hand hitters that ever lived, a man of tremendous achievement and tremendous pride. Bearing that in mind now, you can imagine what it was like one day when Bucky Harris took him out for a pinch hitter.

Al was having some difficulty making contact and we were in the late innings of a game, with a chance to win. We had a couple of men on base and Al's turn was coming up. He picked up his bat and headed for the on-deck circle. All of a sudden Harris called him back. Frankly, I was stunned, and not because I thought Harris was making the wrong move, but because it was happening. We all looked at one another on the bench, but nobody said anything. Those few seconds were highly charged; the moment Bucky called out to him we knew what it was, and when Al turned around there was a look of puzzlement on his face; he couldn't believe it. It was the first time he had ever been hit for. He stared at Harris for a few seconds, then took that bat and threw it up into the air about fifteen feet, let it drop, and walked back to the bench, right on through the dugout and into the clubhouse without saying a word.

Hank Greenberg is another guy I always think of when they talk about the great right-handed hitters. Hank was a very fine person, and I can tell you a little story to illustrate what I mean. We were playing Detroit one time, and I was on first base. I guess my mind must have been wandering a bit because I'd lost track of how many outs there were. Somebody hit a long fly ball and Hank said, "Two out, get going." I took off. Well, there was only one out and I was doubled off the base. Boy, was I mad! I was in the league just about a year or so and I was a pretty hot-tempered kid. When I realized what had happened I yelled at Greenberg, "You big so-and-so, I'm going to cut your leg off next time I come down there." That was me, rookie George Case, talking to Hank Greenberg that way.

Next time up I pushed a ball between first and the pitcher. The pitcher had to field it and shovel it over to first. It was going to be a close play and Hank was stretched way out to pull it in, and there was his leg, right where I could get at it. I hit him on the heel and tore his spike off. Fortunately it was nothing more than that. When I turned around I saw him standing there looking at his shoe. As I walked back past the base—I'd been thrown out—Hank said, "Well, young fellow, I hope you're satisfied." That's all he said. Just that and nothing more. Well, that sank in. Taught me a lesson. Something like that impresses you more than a guy coming at you. He let me know in a quiet way that I'd done something foolish and I never forgot it.

By the time I came into the league Lefty Grove was strictly a one-day-a-week pitcher. His fast ball was pretty much gone, but that crusty personality I'd heard so much about hadn't mellowed one bit. On the day he was going to pitch his teammates on the Red Sox wouldn't talk to him and he wouldn't talk to them. He would come into the clubhouse and lay down on the trainer's table, and take a nap. If you wanted a rubdown you were out of luck—Lefty was snoozing there. Then he'd get up, take a shot of whiskey and get ready to pitch. This was his ritual.

Lefty was along in years then and he had a hard time fielding bunts. As a matter of fact, he couldn't field a bunt worth a damn. He never shut me out in his life, because if I went up a couple of times without a base hit all I had to do was bunt and I was home free. And of course he hated when you bunted on him. One particular ball game I pushed one up along the first-base line and Lefty came after it. I was really flying down there, outrunning the ball and Lefty both. When he saw he couldn't get me, he got mad as hell and out of frustration kicked the ball over to first base. Then he stood there jawing at me a mile a minute, calling me a "bush bastard" and giving me an awful going over. Lefty Grove was all by himself as a character. But when you talk about colorful characters I think you have to put Bobo Newsom on top of the list. If he were living today and pitching today, on television, he would have to be one of the greatest attractions in the game. There was only one Bobo Newsom and there will never be another one. Some people might say amen to that but not me; I thought he was great.

He was with the Washington ball club on four or five different occasions—he was always being traded. On one of those occasions, in 1942, we got him from Detroit. Well, on our first trip into Detroit he went to his bank to draw out his money. He showed up later in the lobby of the hotel, where a few of us were sitting. He spotted Bob Repass, who was his roommate, and went up to him and said, "Bob, you got change for ten?"

Repass went into his pocket and pulled out a couple of fives. Bobo handed him a ten, but it wasn't a ten-dollar bill, it was a ten-*thousand*-dollar bill. In typical Newsom fashion, instead of getting his money in a bank draft, he got it in cash, and then walks up to Repass and asks for change. We all just stood around with our mouths open, looking at that piece of paper. I'd never seen one before and I've never seen one since. I don't think they even circulate them anymore.

Newsom was one of the best natural comedians I ever saw. Once in a while on those long train rides he'd suddenly get up and begin preaching a sermon. He would stand on a suitcase in the club car, holding one of those Gideon Bibles in his hand, with a pair of glasses pushed all the way down the end of his nose, and preach a hellfire sermon in the style of a Southern Baptist minister. He'd have us rolling in the aisles. Just about everything he did or said was funny; he was a natural.

Ted Lyons was another veteran in the league when I came up. He was just as tough and unforgiving a competitor as Grove. I'll never forget the time I pulled something on him— I was just a rookie at the time—which I don't think has been done since: I got two bases on a base on balls. He walked me on a three-and-two pitch and I trotted down to first base. When I got there I glanced at second; Luke Appling wasn't paying attention, he had his back to the infield; and Jackie Hayes, the second baseman, was away from the bag. So I lit out for second, and I don't think there was even a play on me.

Lyons, being the competitor that he was, didn't like that one bit. He stood on the mound growling at me, calling me every name in the book. Then he turned around and took off his glove and began to rub up the baseball, I guess trying to work off some of his steam. When he turned his back I lit out for third—Marv Owen, the third baseman, was away from the bag. They yelled at Lyons and he whirled around and fired the ball and Owen made a great play on it, catching the ball and making a diving tag on me. Just did get me.

In the process of sliding I threw my shoulder out. So there I am, lying on the ground in great pain and all of a sudden there's Ted Lyons standing over me, chewing me out again. Oh, he was steaming! Called me a busher and a show-off and a lot of other things, none of them complimentary. Even while they were helping me off the field, Ted was following me, still yelling at me. But I damn near wound up on third base on a base on balls. Ted Lyons and I became good friends later on, and he'd often remind me of that base on balls and we'd laugh about it; but he wasn't laughing that day.

Right after Pearl Harbor the country was in a turmoil. Nobody knew what was going to happen. But the owner of the ball club, Clark Griffith, who was a friend of President Roosevelt, kept telling us that baseball was going to continue because the country needed it as recreation and diversion.

Nevertheless, ballplayers were no different from anyone else and whoever was eligible was soon drafted. Little by little guys began being called into service. The personnel changes during the war went on all the time, almost from week to week. And I'll say one thing—everybody that played during those war years were legitimate rejects from the service. Most of them were either color blind, or had bad cartilages, bad shoulders, bad stomachs. Our center fielder, George Binks, was hard of hearing in one ear; as a matter of fact, I ran into him a half dozen times one year because he couldn't hear me calling for the ball.

In my own case, because I was a professional baseball player, I was examined three times in one year to see if I was eligible for the service, but I was a reject because I'd had a serious shoulder operation and had limited movement in my arm.

A lot of people won't remember this, and most will find it hard to believe today, but during the war years the fans used to throw balls that were hit into the stands back onto the field, because it was announced that those balls would be sent to service bases. Anybody who didn't throw a ball back was looked upon as unpatriotic, which was no light accusation to have made against you in those days.

Baseballs were scarce as hell, and after a while we began running out of bats. Louisville was having a difficult time manufacturing bats, and believe it or not, we used some bats that were designed by the Glenn Martin Company, the aircraft manufacturers in Baltimore. Glenn Martin was an avid Washington Senator fan and when he read in the papers that we were having bat problems he had his engineers design a bat for us that looked like an airplane wing. It was tapered at the hitting end, and actually the principle of it was very sound. The swing weight was excellent. I don't know why none of the bat manufacturers ever followed up on that. Martin made us ten or twelve dozen of those bats and we used them. They did break easily, which was one of the problems.

There were shortages of everything in those days, and rationing. We had trouble getting gasoline, sugar, meat, and a whole lot of other things. Dutch Leonard was on our ball club at the time and he was a shrewd fellow. He seemed to know of every service station in the Washington area that had gasoline, and he seemed to know what meat markets were getting deliveries. Naturally, in order to be able to receive this information, Dutch had to give something in return, and what he gave were autographed baseballs. He was always swiping them from the ball bag. There's a certain magic about an autographed baseball, isn't there?

Buddy Lewis was one of the first to go into the service. He joined the Air Corps and became a pilot, stationed in Georgia. One of his first assignments after he got his wings was to fly some VIP's up to Washington. He happened to come into town on a Sunday, when we had a double-header scheduled, and as soon as he could he came out to the ball park. Just before he had to leave, he said, "It's been great seeing you guys. I'll be leaving before the double-header is over, but I'll tell you something—I'm going to split this ball park in two with that airplane when I leave Washington. I'm going to come right down center field."

Well, right after the second ball game started here comes a low-flying airplane over the top of the stands, heading straight for the flagpole in center field. As it so happened, I was just getting ready to hit when it came roaring over. It was Buddy, flying at a ridiculously low altitude, breaking God knows how many laws and regulations. I got so excited I threw my bat up in the air as if to say, "Hi, Buddy, we know it's you." He wiggled his wings a little and went soaring over the center-field bleachers and off into the blue sky. We didn't see him again until the war was over.

We finished second in 1945, a game and a half out. Detroit beat us out on the last day of the season. I think that was one of the most unusual pennant races there ever was. You see, we had finished our season a week before everybody else. So we had to sit around and watch it happen, to see if we were going to win it, or get a tie, or whatever. The Tigers were playing the Browns a double-header in St. Louis that last day, and if the Browns won we were going to have to go to Detroit for a play-off. We were sitting in the clubhouse in Griffith Stadium with our bags packed, listening to the radio. It was a tie game until the ninth inning, when Hank Greenberg hit a grand-slam home run for the Tigers that won it for them. So instead of going to Detroit for a play-off we all said good-bye to each other and went home for the winter.

The reason we had finished our schedule a week earlier was because George Marshall, who owned the Washington Redskins, had made arrangements with Mr. Griffith to have the ball park for the football team a week before the baseball season ended. Well, we had finished seventh the year before and nobody expected us to rise up and get in a close pennant race. But we did, and almost won it, and that was as close as I ever came to a World Series.

I was fortunate enough to play on the same team with Bob Feller after he came back from the service. I was in left field when he threw that no-hitter against the Yankees in April of '46. That was the greatest game that I've ever seen pitched. After it was over I said to one of the Yankees, "Bob had pretty good stuff today, didn't he?" And the guy said, "He was all right. But I think if we'd gone another eight or nine innings we might have got a hit off of him."

I'd batted against Bob before the war, of course. He was just a big, rawboned kid then, in 1937 and '38. He'd scare you throwing that ball, he'd scare the hell out of you. He had a little nervous twitch in his eyes and he'd stand out there on that mound with those eyes twitching and you'd be up there saying to yourself, "I hope the son of a gun sees me all right."

You talk about a ballplayer having magnetism, Bob Feller had it, with plenty to spare. He was continually hounded by the press, by well-wishers, by fans, by people wanting something from him. There were times when you simply couldn't get out of the ball park after a game because there were so many people waiting to see Bob. But I'll say this, with it all, he kept a pretty level head. There weren't many ballplayers who had that kind of magnetism. Williams had it, of course, and sometimes it worked against him, because the fans could react very violently to him. He had some people who used to sit out in left field in Fenway Park for no other reason, it seemed, except to boo the hell out of him.

Ted was an incredibly endowed athlete. I remember one time we went out to Fenway Park early, even before the Red Sox got there. We got outside of the ball park and we hear Bang! Bang! Bang! Bang! Shooting. We couldn't imagine what was going on in there. We walk into the ball park and there's Ted Williams in the bull pen with a case of shotgun shells, shooting pigeons. Shooting the hell out of them; they were lying all over the outfield. It seems the pigeons were a health menace in Fenway Park, because of their droppings. So Tom Yawkey gave Ted permission to shoot them, and that's what he was doing.

Along those same lines, Ted was certainly one of the best trap shots I've ever seen; also he's probably one of the best fly fishermen in the world. When it comes to anything that involves coordination between the hand and the eye, Ted is in a class by himself.

To all of us who played back in the thirties and forties it's a new era in baseball. You've got new ball parks, a different kind of playing field, a new set of standards. And of course the money is so much bigger today in baseball, it makes us look like we were playing in a stone age. I can vividly remember coming back from a western trip on the same train with the Red Sox; this was around 1939. About a half dozen players from each team were sitting in the club car that night and the talk got around to salaries.

"You know," somebody said, "I'd like to know how many guys in the American League are making more than ten thousand dollars."

We started naming some names and wound up with about eight or ten guys who were making more than ten thousand dollars, as far as we could determine. There might have been more, but not many. Can you imagine that? And this was during an era of some mighty good players.

One picture stands out in my mind which illustrates to me how different it was then. We had a kid pitcher join the ball club in the late thirties. He walked into the clubhouse one day and I swear, he looked like something out of a painting by Norman Rockwell. He was from a farming community in the deep South, and he was carrying a cardboard suitcase with a belt wrapped around it.

A day or two later we put him in a game to relieve. He walked out there—I wish I could remember his name—and the first thing he did before he began to warm up was take off his cap and put it down alongside the mound. Of course that's not permitted—you have to play in full uniform. The umpire came out and said, "What the hell's going on?"

"I can't pitch with my hat on," the kid said.

"Listen," the umpire said, "You've got to pitch with your hat on. You're in the big leagues."

A grand place to be, too.

DICK WAKEFIELD

RICHARD CUMMINGS WAKEFIELD
Born: May 6, 1921, Chicago, Illinois; Died: August 26, 1986
Major-league career: 1941–52, Detroit Tigers, New York Yankees, New York Giants
Lifetime average: .293

Dick Wakefield was baseball's first big bonus recipient. He paid immediate dividends for the Tigers, hitting .316 and .355 his first two seasons. In 1943 he led the American League with 200 hits and 38 doubles. Returning to the big leagues in 1946 after serving in the armed forces, Wakefield hit well for several years, but never quite fulfilled the promise implied by his first two seasons.

I stepped up to the plate on opening day in 1949 and fifty thousand people booed the hell out of me. Why? It was the press. I had a bad press in Detroit. It was brutal. I couldn't get away from it. Part of it started with the bonus. Some of those writers were making $8,000 a year and they resented an untried kid getting a $52,000 bonus. Who the hell is he to get so much money? they asked. Greenberg—the star of the team—was only making around $40,000 a year. Who the hell is Wakefield? But *Greenberg* didn't care how much money I'd gotten. Hank didn't give a damn. More power to you, kid— that's the way he felt about it.

They said I had the wrong attitude. They figured because a guy could smile when things went bad he had the wrong attitude. Hell, everybody isn't built the same, you know. But once you get a bad press in baseball, no matter how unjustified, it lives with you. I can give you a good example of how these things sometimes happen.

I had a tryout with the Giants in the spring of 1952. The day after I joined them in Phoenix one of the writers filed a story back to New York that cut me up and down. Now, I didn't know anything about it at the time—in fact, I'd never even met the guy before. Meanwhile, I'm out there every day breaking my back trying to make the club.

Then we break camp and start heading East. We arrive in Evansville, Indiana, before jumping off to New York. By this time this particular writer and myself have become inseparable. Now, I still don't know about that story, and he's starting to behave strangely. He knows sooner or later I'm going to find out about what he wrote. He's getting morose.

He got loaded in a bar in Evansville just before we're supposed to leave. Nobody could get him out of there. Finally they send me in to get him—because we're such good pals, right? I find him in there, loaded, stiff, and he's crying. I don't know why, and he's in no shape to tell me. But I induce him to leave and get him on the bus and we begin heading for New York. The morning after we arrived in New York, he calls me. "I've got to talk to you," he says. We get together and he shows me the story. God, it was the most derogatory thing, about my attitude, and a lot of things like that.

"How the hell could you write that?" I asked. "We'd never even met."

"I know, I know," he said. He felt miserable.

"Who gave you that information?" I asked.

"One of the Cleveland writers," he said, and told me the guy's name. It was somebody who had never liked me.

"And you took his word on it?"

He nodded his head. Not only did he feel guilty and embarrassed, but his pride was hurt, too. "Now that I know you," he said, "I see that there's not one word of truth in that story. If that ever happens to me again I ought to get out of the business."

Well, it was too late then, wasn't it? It was already in print, people had read it and formed their judgments. I've always felt that if you hear something negative about a person you ought to first think about who you're hearing it from. What's the source? How well informed is the person, and what might *his* prejudices be? Too often it turns out that your worst enemy is some other son of a bitch's best friend.

When people talk today about the astronomical salaries in baseball they sometimes point back to me as the cause of it all. I was the original bonus baby. But that was an economic development which had to come sooner or later, and I happened to be there at the time.

As always in human nature, there was a certain amount of envy, which is I guess a natural thing, and I had to overcome that. But you can do it as you become one of the guys. They recognize the fact that you're doing the best you can and if things work out, fine; if not, you're gone. It's all cut and dried.

But most of the resentment came from the newspapers. Fifty-two thousand was a sockful of money in 1941 and the papers made a big deal out of it. They were writing about me every day. Today a kid receiving that kind of money barely rates a mention. But I got all the attention because I was the first. The first in anything gets the attention and is remembered, whether it's the first man on the moon or the first kid to get a big bonus.

The scouts started taking notice of me when I was in high school in Chicago. I was a big skinny kid who could hit. I heard later that some of the scouts were talking to my father about me when I was a junior in high school, but he never mentioned it to me because he wanted me to go on to college.

My father had been a major-league ballplayer, too, you know; he caught for the Washington Senators just after the turn of the century. The fact that my father had played big-league ball was an important factor in my life. His contribution to my development as a ballplayer was enormous.

Once I got into college at Michigan State the scouts started coming around in earnest. I went to Brooklyn, Chicago, Cincinnati, Cleveland, Detroit. There was a lot of interest. My criterion was the highest offer; they were all great organizations and great people and I had no particular preference.

Wish Egan, the Detroit scout, convinced Mr. Briggs, who owned the Tigers, to sign me, that I was worth the money. So they signed me, giving me a bonus of $52,000 and a brand-new car.

The first thing I did after signing was to go out to a place on Woodward Avenue that sold Lincoln Zephyrs. I'd made up my mind that was the car I wanted. I walked into that place wearing a pair of corduroys and an old shirt, just like any average university kid. A bunch of salesmen were sitting around talking; they glanced up at me and went right on talking. Not one of them got up. I stood around for a while admiring my car—as I said, I knew just which one I was buying. Finally I spotted a kid about eighteen years old sitting at a desk. I called him over.

"Say," I said, "can you sell me a car?"

"You'd better get one of the salesmen," he said.

"I don't want one of the salesmen," I said. "I want you."

"Just a minute."

He brought out the general manager, who walked toward me looking kind of skeptical.

"I want to buy this car," I said, "but I want this young fellow to sell it to me and get the commission."

"Whatever you say," he said.

So I bought myself that Lincoln Zephyr and paid $1,400 for it. When I signed the papers the general manager looked at my signature and said, "Well, by God, you're Dick Wakefield."

"That's right," I said.

"Been reading about you," he said.

Then all the salesmen came over and shook hands and made a big fuss. When that was all over with, I said, "Now I'd like somebody to take me down to the Leland Hotel, because I don't know how to drive."

One of the guys drove me to the hotel and I watched carefully everything he did. By the time we got there I knew how to drive.

"You sure you can handle her?" he asked.

"Are you kidding?" I said.

Then I drove out to the ball park. Wish Egan spotted me as I was pulling in. He came running over looking like he was going to have a heart attack.

"Dick, for God's sake," he said, "what have you done?"

"What's the matter?" I asked.

"Do you know what kind of car you've got there?"

"Sure," I said. "A Lincoln."

"Well," he said, "*Ford* makes that. Don't you know that Mr. Briggs makes Chryslers and Packards?"

"So what?" I asked.

"Mr. Briggs and Henry Ford are having a feud," he said. "They hate each other."

Well, how was I supposed to know that? Welcome to Detroit.

I stayed with the Tigers for a while in '41, not playing much, but getting a chance to rub shoulders with guys like Rudy York, Charlie Gehringer, Barney McCosky, Pinky Higgins, Schoolboy Rowe, Bobo Newsom. Then I went down to Winston-Salem and played there a half year.

The next season, 1942. I played at Beaumont in the Texas League and was voted the Most Valuable Player there. I came up to Detroit in '43 and hit .316. In '44 I hit .355 and then went into the service.

I was in Hawaii for a while and played some ball there. I met Ted Williams in Hawaii. Did you ever hear about the bet I made with him? That was the craziest thing. After hitting my .355 in 1944 I guess I was feeling kind of cocky. So I told Ted that when we got out of the service and back to baseball, I'd outhit him in several offensive categories. I was some kid, huh?—telling that to Ted Williams. We bet a thousand dollars each on RBI's, home runs, and batting average. But I wasn't altogether crazy, because I also told him what I thought I was going to be getting by way of salary.

"You'll never get it," he said.

"All right," I said, "then let's bet on that, too."

What we did was split the bet in two—half on the batting departments, half on the salary. The total bet added up to something like five thousand dollars.

Well, when we got back in 1946, the first thing that happened to me was Joe Page broke my wrist with a pitch in April. Then a few weeks later I broke my arm running against the wall in Boston. I had one of my worst years. Williams hit .342 and had a great year all around. But I made the money I'd told him I would, so I didn't have to pay off. We broke even on it.

Toward the end of my career I got into a row with baseball. I had always felt that the relationship I had at Detroit was good, but when I needed the old man—Mr. Briggs—he wasn't there. The net result was that in the final run baseball beat me down.

What happened was, the Tigers traded me to the Yankees and then the Yankees traded me to the White Sox, for a pitcher named Joe Ostrowski and $100,000. Well, I refused to report to the White Sox without an adjustment in salary. When that happened, the White Sox said I belonged to the Yankees and the Yankees said I belonged to the White Sox. So I sat back and belonged to myself while I waited for them to settle it.

About a month later, after a lot of hand-wringing about who owned me, I was waived to Oakland in the Pacific Coast League, *waived,* by both leagues, for the price of $7,500. Which meant that Chicago could have gotten me on waivers for $7,500 and saved $92,500 and a pitcher. But you see what was happening—they were trying to ease me out, simply because I had asked for what I believed to be equitable treatment. I wanted them to be fair with me, that's all. Well, they weren't.

I went back to my home in Ann Arbor thinking about suing. I did in fact go to a very prominent attorney and told him the story.

"Dick," he said, "do you still want to play baseball?"

"Yes," I said.

"Then forget about the suit. Go to Oakland."

"What if I wanted to sue?" I asked.

"If you want to sue," he said, "I'll give you my services free of charge."

In other words, I had a pretty strong case against baseball. But I went to Oakland. Probably it was the worst mistake I ever made; but at the time I didn't want to hurt a game that was so good to me for a few years.

I played in Oakland in 1950 and came back again in 1951. Mel Ott was managing the team then and he wasn't playing me. One day he put a second baseman in the outfield, while I was sitting on the bench. I saw that, got up and walked into the clubhouse, packed up and left.

In the spring of 1952 Monte Irvin broke his ankle and the Giants were hurting for an outfielder. I was home in Ann Arbor at the time, just sitting around. So my landlord, completely on his own, mind you, picked up the phone and got hold of Durocher.

"Mr. Durocher," he said, "I've got a fellow here who's as good or better than what you've lost." This is my landlord talking, remember.

"Who?" Durocher said.

"Wakefield."

"Wakefield. What's he doing?"

"He's waiting for a chance," my landlord said.

"All right," Durocher said. "Don't let him leave the house. I'll call you back."

Meanwhile, I get up and go downstairs to have coffee. The phone rings and my landlord says, "That's for you."

"What have you got, ESP?" I asked.

I pick up the phone and it's Durocher.

"Get the first plane out here," he says.

So I joined the Giants in Phoenix. We played Cleveland all the way to New York. By the time we got to New York my batting average was .556. But I still hadn't signed a contract.

I was sitting in Toots Shor's with Bob Elliott. Toots came over and said that Chub Feeney was looking for me. I went upstairs to a room and a few minutes later Feeney came in. He was Mr. Stoneham's nephew. I knew he had to sign me. He had to. You can't release a guy who's hitting .556—especially not when one of your big guns is laid up for the year with a broken ankle.

He told me they'd give me $15,000 salary and that if things worked out they'd adjust it later. Now, I'd just been through a lot of grief, with the Yankees, the White Sox, Oakland, that whole thing. I wanted to get back in baseball. I knew I'd been barred. You know those things. You can sense them.

"Chub," I said, "do me a favor. The salary is fifteen thousand. What's the minimum?"

"Six thousand," he said.

"I'll tell you what," I said. "Give me six thousand in salary and a nine-thousand-dollar bonus."

I figured if they had that much money invested in me I might get a chance. He refused. Wouldn't do it. So I knew I was gone. I had two at bats for the New York Giants. I was released in May. They asked me to fill in at Minneapolis for a while. I did that, and then I quit.

Things like that probably happen today. I don't know. But if they do, if this kind of thing is still around, I think the answer to individual problems in any professional sport has to be in the hands of a very compassionate, intelligent, and shrewd commissioner who will not show favoritism to anybody but see that there is equal justice in all situations.

Money was only part of my problem with baseball. There were other things. I was one of the original founders of the baseball player's pension fund. A lot of strife and effort went into that thing. I guess a lot of the owners didn't like what I was doing, didn't like the way I thought about things. The idea of a pension fund was anathema to them. Why? Because it involved dollars. You see, every dollar we put in, they put in. They didn't like that.

I suppose in the owners' estimation I was something of a radical, although everything we started out to do in those days is part of the baseball structure today and nobody thinks twice about it. Baseball has always been kind of conservative when it comes to new ideas. I think one of the reasons is they're on very thin ice when it comes to contractual involvement. You have no freedom to sell your services where you want to. I think the owners have a right to protect what they've developed, but at the same time they have an obligation to be fair and equitable with the people with whom they do business. In too many cases they haven't been. And what can you do in those cases? Who are you going to talk to? In a tight-knit organization a powerful voice is inordinately strong.

I remember one time, when I was with the Yankees, I'd had it up to here with George Weiss. It was over contract negotiations, his inflexible attitude, and one thing and another. I just couldn't take it anymore and I called him up and gave him my thoughts over the phone. I'm sorry now that I did, but I really told him off. I told him what I thought of him and people like him. I told him where he should be rather than where he was. And later on I think that he, being one of the major-domos, got the word out at their little meetings and I was done. In those days there were only eight teams in the league. Eight owners. A very tight little group. All thinking alike to protect what they had. If a little bug comes into the ointment, get rid of it.

But there were some laughs along the way, too. One night in Seattle I faked a catch. I went back to the fence on a drive, leaped up and pretended I caught it for the third out. The ball went out for a home run, but I came trotting in very nonchalantly, pretending I had the ball. Artie Wilson, the shortstop, came out to get it while the pitcher and the rest of the team all headed for the dugout.

"Give me the ball," Artie said.

"Artie," I said, "I don't have it."

He flicked his glove around in the air and said, "Come on. Throw it."

Now we were standing next to one another at the edge of the outfield grass.

"Give me the ball," he said.

"Artie, I don't have it."

The umpire walked over.

"How about getting off the field, boys?" he said. The other team was out on the field now.

"Just a minute," I said. "That last batter is out, isn't he? He left the field of play, so he's out. Isn't that right?"

"Sure he's out," the umpire said. "Let's go. Come on, get the ball in play."

"I haven't got a ball," I said.

"What are you talking about?" the umpire asked.

Artie looked in my glove and then looked at the umpire. "It's true," Artie said.

There followed one of the longest arguments I think there ever was on a baseball field. Was the guy out for leaving the field, or was he entitled to a home run? All over the field there were little knots of guys trying to explain the rules to each other. Well, they finally gave the guy the home run.

That was one of those goofy things I did for no reason other than curiosity. I'd always wondered what would happen if something like that occurred. So I tried it out and now I know. Why didn't I simply read the rule book? Well, I could have, I suppose; but I felt that my way of doing it was more interesting.

I find now at this stage of the game that if I had my life to live over again, I'm inclined to think that I'd have to try and do something that's more fundamental for humanity than a professional athletic career. That probably sounds like middle-aged wistfulness, doesn't it? I don't say I feel I've wasted my life, because I've had a wonderful time of it. But I think a man ought to try and contribute more than just an athletic career. I twice ran for Congress, you know, but without success. I wish I could have been elected. I'd like to go to my grave thinking I passed just one law that helped a whole segment of society. To think that you might have had the ability to have done something, and never done it, can be rather frustrating.

KIRBY HIGBE

Walter Kirby Higbe
Born: Columbia, South Carolina, April 8, 1915; Died: May 6,
   1986
Major-league career: 1937–50, Chicago Cubs, Philadelphia
   Phillies, Brooklyn Dodgers, Pittsburgh Pirates, New York
   Giants
Lifetime record: 118 wins, 101 losses

*One of the fine fastball pitchers and colorful personalities of
his day, Kirby Higbe was a 22-game winner with the pennant-
winning 1941 Dodgers. That same year, starting and relieving,
the rubber-armed Higbe led National League pitchers in ap-
pearances. In 1940 he led the league in strikeouts.*

I've had a lot of people say to me over the years, "Hig, why
aren't you coaching somewhere, with all you know about the
game?" Well, I had a reputation for doing what I wanted to do,
if it was drinking or whatever it was. I did it and never tried
to hide it. I'd say that ninety percent of them in my day did the
same things I did, but they hid it. They were discreet. That's
the way I ought to have been, I reckon. But that was my
attitude and it was wrong, I can see that now. There are
fellows who became managers, coaches, batting instructors—
some still around today—who did as much as I did, or more,
but were always on the sly about it. So that's the difference.

I came up with the Cubs in 1938 and the first man I ever
roomed with in the big leagues was Dizzy Dean. One of the
greatest guys that ever lived. A lot of people say he bragged,
but as far as I'm concerned he didn't brag, he just told you
what he was going to do and then went out and did it. If he

said he was going to shut them out, he shut them out. I don't call that bragging, not when you can back it up.

I don't know if it's true or not, but my guess would be that there's nobody out there on that field with as much confidence as the pitcher who can throw the real good fastball. You know that when you're right you can just overpower those hitters and that's all there is to it. Greatest feeling in the world, to rock back out there and fire that thing in, especially with those big sluggers, those guys who swing from the heels.

I knew that feeling, and Dean knew it, too, until he hurt his arm. Then he pitched on heart alone, and he had plenty of that, buddy. You know what happened: Earl Averill hit a line shot off of Diz's toe in the 1937 All-Star game. When Diz went back to St. Louis he told Branch Rickey he couldn't pitch for a while, until that toe healed up. But Rickey told him they'd been advertising Dizzy was going to pitch, that there was going to be a full house, and that Dizzy was going to pitch, bad toe or not. So he went out and worked six or seven innings, favoring his toe, throwing off stride, and his arm just snapped on him. Right then and there he lost it all.

Do you remember Burgess Whitehead? Well, he and Dean roomed together in the minors. Later on Whitehead was traded to the Giants. Diz, being the kind of guy he was, would let Whitehead get a few hits off of him whenever he pitched against the Giants. He would say, "Hey, little bitty buddy, I'm throwin' it right over, so you get your hits. You got to get your hits off of Ol' Diz." One day in St. Louis he did that and Whitehead whacked a line drive, it hit Diz right between the eyes. Diz got up and looked over at Whitehead and said, "Little bitty buddy, you got to start pullin' that ball."

But that's the way Dean was. He could afford to let you get a hit off of him, because when it came right down to it and he had to get somebody out, there was no way you were going to hit him. He was colorful and unpredictable and a hell of a pitcher.

But there were a lot of good old boys back in those days. The Dodgers in particular had a reputation for employing characters. I used to hear stories about them from some of the old-timers. At one time there in the early thirties they had Babe Herman. Now there was a real buster. They were playing a game down in Florida one spring and Boom-Boom Beck was pitching, trying to make the club, but not doing too well this particular afternoon. He was throwing a lot of line drives, and back in those days there weren't any fences in the outfield down there. Every time a ball went between the outfielders it would go way on out and, hellfire, those guys had to run it down. After Babe had chased about five of those balls, Boom-Boom threw another one and Babe took off after it again. This time he picked up the ball and carried it all the way back to the mound.

"Boom-Boom," he said, "do us a favor, will you, and walk a couple of men while we catch our breath?"

But I'll tell you the best Babe Herman story. Babe, you know, had made a name for having unusual things happen to him on a ball field, like getting hit in the head with a fly ball and doubling into a triple play. Well, he actually was a good ballplayer and a hell of a hitter, and he finally got sensitive about what they were saying about him. So, the way I heard it, one day he walked up to one of the Brooklyn sportswriters.

"Listen," Babe said, "this is my livelihood and you know I'm pretty good at it. So I'm asking you to do me a favor: Lay off of me. Don't ride me about those oddball things, because you know darn well I'm not really that sort of a guy. I'm a serious-minded ballplayer."

The sportswriter was sympathetic to this, and said, "Okay, Babe. I'll tell you what, buddy, I'm not going to write anything belittling about you again."

They shook hands on it and then talked a few minutes more. Then Babe reached into his jacket pocket, pulled out a cigar stub, put it in his mouth and began puffing on it. The sportswriter took one look at that and said, "Forget what I just said. It's all off."

"What's the matter?" Babe asked.

"By God, you're walking around with a lit cigar in your pocket, that's what's the matter."

I think overall there was more color in baseball back in those days. We played for the love of the game. It had to be that, since there wasn't much money in it then, was there? I remember something Paul Waner told me once. "Kirby," he said, "I used to hold out every year, but if they'd known the truth of it, I would have played for nothing."

But it sure as hell could be frustrating sometimes. You can

believe that, buddy. I was traded over to the Phillies early in 1939 in a deal for Claude Passeau, who at that time was an established pitcher. I guess we had one of the worst ball clubs that was ever in the history of baseball. Gerry Nugent, who owned the team, didn't have any money; whenever they had themselves a good ballplayer they had to sell him just to break even.

Doc Prothro was the manager. He was a good guy and a good baseball man, but there wasn't much he could do with that team. We won 45 games one year and 50 the next. That's 95 wins in two years, and I won 24 of them myself. I lost a few, too, but that was no trick with that team. I lost two games in one day in the Polo Grounds, the first one, 1–0 in eleven innings when Harry Danning plunked one down the right-field line for a home run. Then midway through the second game Doc said, "Kirby, let's try and win a game today. How about relieving if I need you?" I told him I'd be glad to.

Sure enough, we go into the bottom of the ninth and the score is tied. I come in. First guy hits one to short, the short-stop fields it cleanly and throws it into the lap of Mayor LaGuardia, who's sitting over there in the box seats. The runner goes to second and I walk the next guy on purpose. Next man bunts them over, so I have to walk another guy to load the bases. Force at any base now, right? Next guy flies to Joe Marty in short center. Joe's got a great arm, and the runner isn't even tagging up. But Joe decides to uncork one anyway, and he throws it up on the screen and I'm beat again.

There was a time in the 1940 season when we hit a real bad streak, even for us. We'd lost eight or nine in a row, and I mean losing them, not even coming close. "We've got to win a ball game," Doc says. He was all wrung out from losing and getting desperate. We went up to the Polo Grounds and I pitched a good game against the Giants, but lost it, 3–1. That made it about ten in a row. The next day Doc is in the club-house. "We've got to win this one," he says. I've been in close pennant races and never saw a manager more determined. Well, the Giants tore us up that day.

After the ball game Doc says, "I want all you sons of bitches to go out tonight and get drunk. You can't be any the worse for it." So everybody took him at his word. But I didn't go out and get drunk; I had a friend out on Long Island and I went there and spent the night. I got back to the hotel the next morning at ten o'clock, and goddamn, Prothro is sitting in my room. His eyes are red from not sleeping and he's got miles and miles of wear and tear in his face.

"Oh, God, Kirby," he says, "am I glad to see you. I thought you'd jumped the ball club." He shook his head. "Wouldn't have blamed you either," he said. Man, he was glum.

Remember Hugh Mulcahy? Well, old Hugh was with us and he was a good pitcher. But there was a stretch in there when he lost about ten in a row. Every four days, there it was in the box score: "Losing pitcher: Mulcahy." It finally got to the point where that became his nickname and people started in calling him Losing Pitcher Mulcahy. And Hugh was a damned fine pitcher. But that's the way it was. Giving up two or three runs was just as good as a forfeit.

I think whatever money old Prothro earned in salary he spent up buying aspirin. I remember one time the Cardinals were in town. I beat them on Friday, and then we beat them on Saturday. Then up comes the Sunday double-header and we've got fifteen thousand people in the stands. That was a hell of a crowd in Philadelphia in those days, buddy. There used to be days when I could've whipped everybody in the stands. So here's this big crowd out to see us and Doc says, "Kirby, you've got to be ready to relieve in both games. I don't want to look bad today." "Good God, Doc," I said, "*both* games?" "Do it for me, Kirby," he says. So I said okay.

Well, so help me, in the first game they had scored seven runs before I could get to the bull pen. Doc said, "Okay, I won't use you; I'll save you for the second game." The second game starts and it's the same thing—the Cardinals are rattling the walls with line drives in the first inning. Doc looks at me and says, "Get down there, Kirby. But this time *run*, don't walk." So I ran down there, but by the time I got warmed up it was too late again. We were massacred in both games. Those fifteen thousand people got a hell of an impression of the Phillies that day, though I can't honestly say it was the wrong one.

In the winter of 1940 I went up to Philadelphia to talk contract with Mr. Nugent. He told me he was going to give me $7,500.

"You'll be the highest-paid man on the team, Kirby," he

said. I must have looked skeptical about it because he showed me everybody else's contract, just to prove it to me.

"See that," he said. "You're making more than any of them."

"Okay," I said. "I'll sign. But there's one stipulation—I won't be traded or sold." The reason I said that was I wanted to have the opportunity to negotiate a contract with the new ball club.

"Kirby," he said, "if I sell you I don't have any pitching."

So I signed the contract. I left Philadelphia and started driving back home. Around midnight I put on the radio in the car and heard the news that Kirby Higbe had been sold to Brooklyn for $100,000 and three ballplayers. When I got home I called Mr. Nugent.

"Say, Mr. Nugent," I said, "you ought to give me at least ten thousand of that money anyway."

"Kirby," he said, "it was all spent before I ever got here." Which it probably was; they were always in debt in Philly in those days.

So I went to Brooklyn in 1941. You couldn't have picked a better ball club to be with in those days than the Dodgers. I thought Brooklyn was the best place in the world to play baseball. And the team was just right, too. It was a rough-and-tumble club, getting set to win that pennant. We had the right manager, too: Durocher. He was a gambling man on that field; he wasn't afraid to take chances. Leo hated to lose as much as anybody I've ever seen. He was strictly right for Brooklyn. He fit perfectly into that situation and became the best manager in baseball, in my opinion.

MacPhail had asked Leo that winter, "What do you need to win it?" And Leo said, "Owen and Higbe." So MacPhail went out and got Owen from the Cardinals and me from the Phillies. That gave Leo his team and we knew in spring training that we had a shot at it. Hellfire, look at the ball club we had: Mickey Owen, Dixie Walker, Joe Medwick, Pee Wee Reese, Dolph Camilli, Cookie Lavagetto, Pete Reiser, and then right after the season started we traded for Billy Herman. Pitching, besides myself, we had Whitlow Wyatt, Curt Davis, Freddie Fitzsimmons, and Hugh Casey.

Hugh Casey was just about the best friend I ever had in baseball. He was some pitcher, buddy. And I'll tell you another thing about old Hugh: he could drink more liquor and look better the next day than any man I ever saw. He'd go back to his hotel after a game—it was practically all day ball in those years—and start drinking and not stop until he fell asleep. Next morning he'd get up at six A.M., take a shower, light that big cigar and you'd never know he'd had a drop. And he wouldn't take another drink again until after the game. Then he'd go back to the hotel and start over again. Late in the season in '41, when we were fighting for the pennant, MacPhail said to him, "Hugh, are you going to last the season out?" And Hugh said, "If you buy me two cases of Canadian Club I'll finish up in grand style." MacPhail, being a hell of a man himself, sent him two cases of Canadian and Hugh finished up in grand style, just like he promised.

That Reiser was a ballplayer to remember, too. If he hadn't had those injuries he might have been one of the greatest that ever lived. There wasn't a thing that boy couldn't do on a ball field, and do it better than most anybody else. He had speed, power, could field, throw, and he had it inside, too. You know, in those days they'd throw at you. Well, Pete never cared. Didn't bother him at all. They'd knock him down and he'd get up and bang a line drive somewhere.

You just can't believe what a difference there was in playing for the 1940 Phillies and then for the 1941 Dodgers. One of the most memorable games I ever pitched in was against the Cubs that year, at Ebbets Field. Hooked up with Johnny Schmitz. Remember him? Good lefthanded pitcher. We each had a two-hitter going into the last of the ninth and there was no score. Mickey Owen leads off with a triple. He's batting seventh. Next hitter pops up. I'm next. Leo comes in to pinch-hit for me. He was a great bunter, and he squeezed the run in and we win, 1–0. Boy, Leo was proud of that. Next day he says, "You see the importance of being able to do that," and tells us we're going to have a little bunting practice. He gets in the cage and lays down four or five perfect bunts. The next few guys don't do too well, and Leo says, "Christ, you guys don't know how to bunt." And Herman says, "Hell, Leo, you ought to know how to bunt—that's all you did for fifteen years."

We fought all year for the pennant, against the Cardinals. Half game ahead, half game behind. That's the way it seemed to go, week after week. And everybody hated the Dodgers, on account of Durocher. He stirred them up. One year Cincinnati had a chance to break the double-play record. Well, Durocher stole every time somebody got on. He said, "Nobody's going to break any records at my expense." That was Leo, all the way. So as a result they were always lined up waiting for us. Go to Cincinnati, there's Walters, Derringer, Vander Meer. Go to Chicago, Passeau and Bill Lee. Everybody wanted to beat us. Brother, if anybody ever won a pennant, the Dodgers won it in '41. Nobody gave us anything.

Durocher liked to play hunches, you know. More times than not they'd pay out for him. Sometimes they didn't. One time we're in the bottom of the ninth at the Polo Grounds, up one run, they have a man on and Johnny Mize is up. I'm pitching. I hear something from the bench, look over and Leo's giving me the curve-ball sign. I shake my head. He gives it to me again—emphatically. I shake my head again. Man, he comes flying out of there to the mound.

"I told you to throw the big son of a bitch a curve and I mean throw him a curve," he says.

"Leo," I said, "he's the best goddamned low-ball hitter in baseball and you want me to throw him the curve, right?"

"Right," he says.

"Okay," I said. "Good enough."

Leo goes back to the bench. I throw Johnny the curve and he hits it over those right-field stands clean out of the ball park. Back in the clubhouse Leo comes up to me.

"Hig," he says, "I lost this one, not you."

"Oh, yeah?" I said. "You look in the papers tomorrow and see who's the losing pitcher, Durocher or Higbe."

You don't get cute with guys like Mize up there. I'll tell you what my philosophy was when I was pitching: I never tried to outsmart a hitter; I always tried to out-dummy them.

I'll give you another example of the way Leo thought. We were in Chicago. This was in '42. Around the fifth inning we were up, 5–0. They'd loosened up a few of our hitters, but nothing serious. The Cubs had just got Jimmie Foxx, and he was leading off the inning. I did a dumb thing and threw him a change-up—you shouldn't throw a guy as old as Jimmie Foxx was then a change of pace. He hit it by my ear, it sounded like a bee going by. It ended up in the center-field seats. I mean, he branded that ball. Then up comes Lou

Novikoff. He hits one in the same spot. Leo comes charging out to the mound.

"What the hell are you going to do?" he asks. "You going to let them take the bread and butter out of your mouth?"

"Don't worry," I said. "I'll take care of it." I knew what he meant. So I flattened a few of them.

Next inning they bring in Paul Erickson. He could throw hard, buddy. Real hard. Old Paul went out on that mound and flattens Mickey Owen four times. I'm the next hitter. I hear Claude Passeau yelling, "Knock this cocky son of a bitch down." I yelled back, "He doesn't have the guts." Smart thing to say, right? The next pitch was right on target. I went down so fast the ball passed between my hat and my head. When I got up I looked out at Erickson and he's standing there staring at me. He's not finished with me, I could tell. He knocked me down three more times. Then Reese comes up, and down he goes four times. Bases loaded now. Billy Herman comes up and cleans them. It was just beautiful to see.

We went into the bottom of the sixth inning leading, 9–2. I'm so damned mad I can't see. I figure I'm going to straighten them out now. Leo says to me, "You throw at one man it'll cost you five hundred."

"What the hell are you talking about?" I asked.

"We got what we wanted," he says.

And, by God, he was right. They'd handed us four runs. For the rest of that game they came up with their tails in the dugout, waiting to be knocked down. But I just kept throwing that ball right over the plate, and I don't think they got a base hit the rest of the way. Later on, when it was over, Leo comes up to me and says, "See how easy it is when you know how to play this game?"

Remember George Magerkurth the umpire? He was a character. Mage used to chew tobacco during a game, and he had this gap between his front teeth and when he got excited he'd just shower you with tobacco juice. One time there's a close play against us and everybody knew it had been called wrong. Everybody except Mage. Leo comes barreling out and they start yammering away at each other. Every word Mage says is soaked with tobacco juice. Finally Leo starts spitting back at him. "That'll cost you five hundred," Mage says. Leo wipes some of that juice off his face and says, "What the hell do you call this—snow?" It cost Leo fifty. That's the time the fans in Brooklyn collected five thousand pennies in a sack and put it on home plate to pay the fine for Durocher. Those were some fans in Brooklyn; they were just about on the roster.

Charley Dressen was a hell of a guy, too, in those days. He was our third-base coach. Smart baseball man, old Charley. One day I was pitching in Cincinnati, and they were hitting some line drives off of me which they had no business hitting. Charley comes up to me and says, "They're getting the catcher's signs."

"I don't believe it," I said.

"Well, they are."

"Let's see about it," I said.

Frank McCormick led off the next inning for them. I told the catcher to signal for a curve on the first pitch but that I'd throw the fastball. He did that and I fired the fastball at McCormick's head. Well, damn if he didn't stride into it, thinking the ball was going to break. Hit him right in the ear. So Dressen was right—they *were* getting the catcher's signs.

I went to the hospital that night to apologize to McCormick.

Cincinnati had another guy in the lineup in those days—Ernie Lombardi. I guess Lombardi is the greatest hitter I've ever seen. How he hasn't made the Hall of Fame is beyond me. He couldn't run—I could outrun him with an elephant on my back—and the infielders played him back on the grass. But he still hit. You'd see the infielders' lips moving in silent prayer when old Ernie came up. He's got one of the highest lifetime batting averages of any catcher. Look it up and see if it isn't so. And a great receiver, too. Biggest hands I ever saw on a man. The umpire would give him a new ball to put into play and Ernie would rub it up with one hand. You ever see anybody do *that,* buddy?

We took part of our spring training in 1942 in Havana. I think that was probably the wildest spring training any ball club ever had. Unbeknownst to all of us, MacPhail had private detectives following us around. I guess he had an idea there'd be some monkey business and he wanted to know about it. That was a different Havana from what you've got today, you know; it was wide open then.

Everybody had one of these damned Cuban detectives assigned to him. They didn't know our names, we were numbers to them, the numbers corresponding to our uniforms, you see. You'd walk out the front door and they'd start following you. But Casey sniffed them out right off. So we had that advantage. What we did, Hugh and me, we used to climb out the window at night and go our merry way. Nobody ever saw us. Then at about three or four in the morning we'd come back and climb back through the window. This goes on the whole time we're there.

Where was everybody going? To a place at 258 Colon. You never saw anything like this place at 258 Colon. The most beautiful girls in Havana. They had music, soft lights, drinks, and about fifteen rooms. Guys would come back from the ball park, have a drink at the hotel, and head straight for 258 Colon. Some of them just about had their laundry sent out from there. They'd stay till four or five o'clock in the morning and then go back to the hotel, with those Cuban detectives tailing them every step of the way.

Then it's over and we fly back to Miami. We land there and the damnedest thing happens—they don't want to let us through customs. You see, the war had just broke out a few months before and everybody was a little touchy, I guess. What happened was, when they started going through everybody's luggage they found the detectives' reports in the traveling secretary's bag, with all those numbers and information about mysterious moving around. "Number so-and-so: Returned to the hotel, had a few drinks, and went to a house of ill-repute at 258 Colon." All these reports, one after the other. The Customs people must've thought we were spies or something, and they held us up there for quite a while. Finally they realized we were the Brooklyn Dodgers and let us back into the country.

The real thunder and lightning came the next day, though, when Leo started reading those things. He was slapping fines everywhere. Johnny Allen got hit for a thousand bucks. Johnny said if he would have known it was going to cost him that much he would have killed the detective. And if you knew Johnny Allen, he wasn't just a-tootin' his horn.

Then Leo comes to the reports on Casey and me. "Numbers so-and-so: Returned to the hotel, went to their room, and never left." Night after night. Leo crumpled those pages in his hand and looked at us. "You two guys," he said. "I don't understand it and I never will." We never told him we were going in and out of the window.

I went into the service after the 1943 season. I was in the 342nd Infantry, part of the 86th Division, the Blackhawk Division. Went through all the hell and thunder in France and Germany. No, I didn't play any ball over there; kept my arm in shape throwing hand grenades.

After the war was over in Europe they brought us home for thirty days and then shipped us out to the Pacific. We were halfway across when we heard the war with Japan was over. "Well," I told my colonel, "that's it. I'm not mad at anybody anymore." He said that was fine, but that we still had to go to the Philippines and tell the Japs there the good news that it was over.

We landed in the Philippines and sure enough, the Japs were still shooting at us. They were holed up in those hills and caves, popping away. I thought it would be a hell of a thing to get killed after the war was over. I finally ended up in Manila coaching an Olympic team. I was the only PFC in the army who had a sergeant driving him.

I came out of the service and had a good year in '46. Then in the early part of the year in '47 I was traded over to the Pirates. Billy Herman was managing the Pirates then and he wanted me. As far as being a student of the game is concerned, I'd say he was just about the smartest man I ever knew. But I think he made one mistake when he took over the team. He told them, "Fellows, there aren't going to be any rules, because rules are made to be broken." Well, there are some ballplayers who can handle that and some who can't. We had a lot of "can'ts" on that ball club.

We were playing the Dodgers in Ebbets Field one day and one of our guys had the shakes so bad his teeth were rattling. He hid out down in the bull pen the whole game so Herman wouldn't see him. After the game he grabbed me and said, "Kirby, I got to have a drink." I had to help him out of the ball park to a bar across the street. He ordered himself a triple shot, but he was shaking so bad he had to reach down and pick up the glass with his teeth and drink it that way. He did that twice and then was steady as a tree.

The next year we had the ball club they called "the casino on wheels." Ernie Bonham was with us that season. You remember Ernie Bonham, the old Yankee pitcher. One of the greatest guys I ever knew. Of course Ernie had come from a pretty straitlaced and businesslike organization and he wasn't prepared for what he found on the Pirates. After the train pulled out of California, where we'd gone for spring training, Ernie came up to me and said, "Hig, this is the damnedest ball club I've ever been on. You get on the train and the next thing you know the girls come back into the club car and the fellows start pairing off with them. And then it's not long before they start going back to the Pullman. And then the rest of the team begins playing high-stake poker and hearts. And when we pull into Las Vegas nobody gets off because there's more action on the train."

Ernie used to say that the ball had a rabbit in it. "Hig," he'd tell me, "it's just got to have a rabbit in it, the way it travels." One day he brought a stethoscope into the clubhouse, fixed it in his ears and put it on a ball. "Hig," he said, "I can hear the rabbit breathing in there." Then one night we were playing an exhibition game somewhere out in the boondocks. They'd roped off the outfield because it was standing-room-only out there. Somebody hit one into the crowd and goddamn if a rabbit doesn't come running out. You should've seen old Ernie jump and yell, "I told you, Hig! Told you there was a rabbit in the son of a bitch. They've knocked him right out."

Looking back, it seemed like it was all good times. Some people don't like to look back, but I don't find the view all that bad. One night in the winter of '41 I was in a nightclub in Camden, South Carolina, drinking with a good friend of mine. There was a little combo playing on the bandstand. One of the drums was resting on the floor, facing in my direction.

"Tell you what, Hig," my friend says. "I'll bet you fifty dollars you can't throw a glass through that drum."

I don't know how far it was, maybe forty feet. I picked up a shot glass and threw it right straight through that drum. So never mind those stories about Old Hig not having control. Anyway, a guy walks up and says, "That drum cost a hundred dollars, buddy." I collected my bet, added another fifty of my own and paid the guy. So I lost half a hundred on the deal, but what the hell, it gave everybody a laugh.

RALPH KINER

RALPH MCPHERRAN KINER
Born: October 27, 1922, Santa Rita, New Mexico
Major-league career: 1946–55, Pittsburgh Pirates, Chicago
  Cubs, Cleveland Indians
Lifetime average: .279

One of the greatest home run hitters of all time, Ralph Kiner led, or was tied for the lead, in home runs his first seven years in the major leagues, which is an all-time record. Twice he hit over 50 in a season, reaching a high of 54 in 1949. Holder, or co-holder, of numerous home run records, Kiner also had six seasons of over 100 runs batted in. In percentage of home runs per at bats, only Babe Ruth and Harmon Killebrew top him.

Kiner was elected to the Hall of Fame in 1975.

I've always been given credit for the line, "Home run hitters drive Cadillacs, singles hitters drive Fords." Well, I never said it, although it was said about me, by Fritz Ostermueller, who was a pitcher on our ball club. And I think there's probably a certain amount of insight in what Fritz said. People enjoy the big pass play in football, the heavy punchers in boxing, and the home run in baseball, but not simply the home run—they want to see that ball go a long, long distance.

When people talk about home run hitters the landmark names are Babe Ruth, Jimmie Foxx, Mickey Mantle, Ted Williams—the men who could put that ball out there a long way. Ironically, you don't often hear mentioned the name of Hank Aaron, and the reason for that is simple: Hank as a rule does not hit for tremendous distance; he hits steadily and well, but it's that long ball, that 500-foot clout, which seems to capture the imagination of the fans.

I guess I was always a power hitter, to the extent that I was always able to hit the ball further than anyone of comparable age, going all the way back to when I was eleven or twelve years old. It just so happened that I always set myself up to go for the long ball; this was my style, what I was capable of doing, and what the game is all about anyway—putting solid wood on the ball, scoring runs, and winning games. I was always a fellow who hit tremendously high, long fly balls. I don't know why I sent them that way; it was just a natural part of my swing.

No, I didn't consciously go for home runs. Not after my first year in the big leagues anyway. When I first came up I would swing with one hundred percent of my velocity. But that wasn't the answer. I soon learned that you set yourself up to cover the strike zone, give yourself the best possible opportunity of meeting the ball, and that if you hit it correctly with about eighty percent of the velocity you need, that was enough to send it out of the ball park. So I stayed well within myself. The secret of home run hitting is not the distance the ball goes. Sure, it was great for the ego to rock it 500 feet, which I was fortunate to do on occasion; but Johnny Mize used to say that a home run was a home run whether the ball went a mile or whether it scraped the back of the wall going over.

I was raised in Alhambra, in Southern California. I moved there from my birthplace, Santa Rita, New Mexico, with my mother after my father died. The weather being what it is in Southern California, we were able to play ball all year round, which was great. I think I must have averaged around 190 or 200 games a year when I was a kid, counting the pick-up games.

I loved all sports. Going back to when I was seven or eight years old, I wanted to be whatever the sport in season was. When the football season started I wanted to be a football player; same thing with basketball. During the Olympic Games of 1932 I wanted to be an Olympic track star. I went with the tide, and I think it was standard behavior for the average kid growing up. You like to identify with what's going on.

It wasn't until high school that I started to get seriously

interested in baseball, and I think from around the time I was thirteen there was no question in my mind that I was going to be a professional baseball player.

The scouts were watching me play ball all through high school. Although the scouting system was not as elaborate and sophisticated then as it is today, there seemed to be a lot of them in the Southern California area. I had a very good offer from the Yankees, but finally decided to sign with Pittsburgh. Their offer was three thousand dollars to sign, another five thousand if I made it to the major leagues, and that they would sign me to a Class A minor league contract.

That Class A contract probably put the clincher on the deal, as far as I was concerned. That meant something in those days, because this was back when they had the sprawling minor-league organizations, and it was not unusual for it to take six or seven years to get to the major leagues. Because of the legalities involved in baseball contracts at that time, signing a Class A contract assured me of getting a chance at the major leagues in no less than four years.

The scout who signed me was Hollis Thurston, an old-time pitcher. They called him "Sloppy." The reason they called him that was because he was always impeccably dressed and indeed was a high-class man. The fact that he was the scout involved played a very influential part in my decision to sign with Pittsburgh. But I can tell you, when I saw the Pittsburgh ball park for the first time I wanted to wring Hollis Thurston's neck. It was probably the biggest ball park in the major leagues. It was 365 feet down the left field line and 457 in left center. When I saw that I was really downhearted.

I went to spring training with the Pirates in 1941 and in my very first game, against the White Sox, I hit two home runs, one off of Bill Dietrich and the other off of Thornton Lee. Later in the spring they shipped me to Albany, New York, in the Eastern League. I played there for two years, in '41 and '42. I started the 1943 season with Toronto in the International League, but after five weeks went into the Navy.

I was discharged in December, 1945. As soon as I got home I began working out. I worked out every day for two months before spring training started, so when I joined the ball club in San Bernardino I was in great shape. I was ready. I'd heard that I was slated to go to the Pacific Coast League and play with the Hollywood Stars, which was then a Pirate farm club; but I was confident I could make the big team and had made up my mind that I just wasn't going to let them send me back to the minors.

Well, I had such a tremendous spring that I think I even surprised myself a little. I hit at least a dozen home runs, some of them for real distance, knocked in a ton of runs, and won a job that nobody ever expected me to win. I opened the 1946 season in center field for the Pirates and that was the start of my major-league career.

Just to prove that that good spring I had wasn't a fluke, I went on to lead the National League in home runs that year, and I don't think any rookie, before or since, has ever done that. So it was a good beginning—but the next year I almost ended up back in the minor leagues, which tells you something about how quickly fortunes can change in baseball.

Hank Greenberg joined the ball club in 1947. Hank had been one of my first idols in baseball. The year before, 1946, he had led the American League in home runs and runs batted in. One of the great right-handed power hitters of all time. During spring training he used to spend a lot of time taking extra batting practice, after the day's session was over. I was impressed by the fact that this great star, who certainly didn't have to prove anything to anybody, was working that hard. I asked him if I could join him, and I ended up shagging balls for him and he'd shag balls for me. Later on we became room-mates, and to quote Yogi Berra on Bill Dickey, Hank "learned me his experience." I got some very sound advice from him. You see, even though I'd led the league in home runs, I'd also led in strikeouts and hit only .247. So I still had some distance to go.

Hank got me in a better position in the batter's box, right on top of the plate, which enabled me to start pulling outside pitches for home runs. I changed my stance and my whole approach to hitting. Those were the right changes for me to make but they were also very tough to adapt to.

I got off to a horrendous start in 1947 and for a month and a half I was really struggling. By the end of May my record was still dismal. I was confident I'd straighten out in due time, but the ball club was beginning to have its doubts. I hit rock bottom in a game against the Cubs when Hank Borowy struck me out four times. That was the low point of my career, and I was right on the verge of being sent out to the minors.

But Hank Greenberg went to Frank McKinney, who owned the Pirates, to speak up for me.

"Don't send this boy out," Hank said. "He's going to make it. He's got a great swing, he's very determined, and he's going to make it."

Well, they didn't send me out, but it was a close call. At the end of May I started to put it together and the turnaround came. At that point I had hit only three home runs, but starting June 1 I hit forty-eight and ended up the season with fifty-one home runs, tying Johnny Mize for the league lead.

Well when you hit fifty-one home runs in the big leagues, you get your name in the newspapers, to say the least. And it had all happened very quickly. But one thing that made it tolerable was that I don't think we had the pressures then that ballplayers have now, because there was no television. Because of the nature of the medium, television can make you very conspicuous and bring an awful lot of pressure to bear.

So while I don't think the pressures were anything like they would be today, I did get what was probably the maximum amount of exposure at the time. Frankly, I kind of liked it. I'm sort of a gregarious type person anyway. I wasn't like a country boy suddenly hitting it big in the city. Bing Crosby had bought into the Pirates in 1946 and through Bing's interest in the club and in baseball I had gotten to meet a lot of Hollywood celebrities, played golf with Bing and Bob Hope and people like that; so when I made my own way into the limelight I wasn't a total stranger to it and that helped a lot.

The Pirates in those years had a reputation for being a pretty loose and freewheeling ball club, and I guess there was some justification for that. One incident always stands out in mind. Vinnie Smith, who was one of our catchers, got married. The wedding took place on the afternoon of a day when we had a night game scheduled. Some of the ballplayers served as ushers, and after the wedding they all came out to the ball park still wearing their tuxedos, their pockets filled with cigars. When the door opened and they walked in we knew right away they'd been in champagne about as deep as you can get.

"Who we playing tonight?" they asked.

"Cincinnati," somebody said.

"Who's pitching for them?" they asked.

"Blackwell."

Their faces dropped. Ewell Blackwell was at that time just about the toughest pitcher in the league; it was bad enough to go up against him when you were sober; in the condition they were in, it could be frightening. So they marched over to the Cincinnati clubhouse, still in their tuxedos, and gave Blackwell all of the cigars and asked him not to throw too close. I don't think Blackwell had too much trouble beating us that night.

Another time, one of our pitchers got into the sauce pretty good before a game at Ebbets Field. When he got to the ball park he had the good sense to stay out of the way. During batting practice he went down the foul line and crawled into the big cylinder that held the tarpaulin which they used to cover the field with when it rained. That would have been perfect for him, he could have slept in there all day, except for one thing—it rained. The ground crew came running out and began rolling the tarpaulin out into the field and in so doing they rolled him right out of the cylinder. He was the most surprised man you ever saw, and you can be sure it sobered him up in a hurry.

I had a reputation for hitting home runs in streaks, but I think every long-ball hitter is that way. You just don't consistently get the good pitches; but then suddenly you find yourself in a groove when you are getting them, and if your timing happens to be exceptionally good on those occasions you're going to fatten up. I connected for eight home runs in four games and twice had four home runs in four consecutive times at bat, and those were both instances when I suddenly found myself getting just the right pitches to swing at. You've got to have those streaks, because it's nearly impossible to hit home runs consistently.

There's no question that the toughest pitcher for me was Ewell Blackwell. I wouldn't rate him as the fastest I ever saw, but his delivery was the toughest to fight. The fastest might have been Rex Barney, but he never had the success he might have had because he always had problems with his control. Probably the best fastball I ever saw was Robin Roberts'. Robin didn't throw as hard as Barney, but his ball would rise around six or eight inches, and with plenty on it. And he had great control, which made him very difficult to hit.

When I joined the Pirates Honus Wagner was still there as a coach. The greatest ballplayer of them all, some people say, and really a fantastic character. You know, he was one of the few old-timers who didn't knock modern-day ballplayers. He was quick to admit that the game was played better in the 1940's and 50's than it was when he played.

He used to carry an old silver dollar and after a game he would go to a saloon and throw that big coin on the bar so it made a loud ringing noise. People naturally looked around to see who it was and invariably they'd recognize him—everybody in Pittsburgh knew and loved Honus Wagner. So somebody would buy him a beer, Honus would drink it, thank the fellow, pick up the silver dollar and go to the next place and do it all over again.

We always enjoyed sitting around and listening to Honus tell stories, and he seemed to have an inexhaustible supply of them. One time he was playing shortstop, he said, and it was the top of the ninth, two out, and the tying and go-ahead runs on base. It had been a long game and it was quite dark out—this of course was long before the ball parks had lights. Somebody hit a hard smash at him and it went right through his legs. This was very embarrassing for the great Honus Wagner, but fortunately, he said, at that moment a rabbit ran by and he picked it up and threw it to first base and got the runner by a hare.

He could go on for hours with those stories. Another time there was a fight on the field, he said, and somebody got a lucky punch in against him and knocked him kind of dizzy. He was the first batter up in the bottom of the ninth and the score was tied. He hit one out of the ball park, but he said he was so dazed from the blow he'd taken that he ran the bases backwards. When he touched home plate they subtracted a run from the scoreboard and the Pirates lost the ball game.

He was a marvelous old man, and it was always a pleasure to be around him.

When Branch Rickey took over the ball club in 1952 I knew I was gone. He had a reputation for not having high-salaried ballplayers; he also had a reputation for trading players whom he felt had reached their peak and might begin to decline. I fit into both categories, so it seemed a foregone conclusion that I would be traded.

Rickey was extremely difficult to deal with when it came to signing a contract. One year I hit thirty-seven home runs and took a twenty-five percent cut. But that wasn't unusual in those days. You can't compare today's salary structure to what it was back then. But I was very fortunate in that salaries did begin increasing after the war. Before the war most of the stars made nothing compared to what we were getting. Fellows like Medwick and Dean were lucky to be getting $15,000 in their heydays. I was the highest-paid player in the National League at one time, so when Rickey took over I knew my Pittsburgh days were numbered.

Throughout most of my years with the Pirates we were a second-division club, and there's no question about it, the hardest thing in the world is to play on a losing team. The mistakes and the failures are all the more glaring and frustrating. It's an altogether different game when you're winning; it's easier to play and, obviously, more enjoyable. I always had a strong competitive drive and I hated to lose. I took an awful lot of pride out on that field with me. As far as I'm concerned, that's an important element in the makeup of a big-league ballplayer. It has to be, if you're going to get the maximum out of your ability. I could have played a few years longer than I did, but I had a bad back, and when I couldn't reach the performance level I was used to, the high standards I always set for myself, I didn't feel it was right to continue. So I quit.

MICKEY VERNON

JAMES BARTON VERNON
Born: April 22, 1918, Marcus Hook, Pennsylvania
Major-league career: 1939–60, Washington Senators, Cleveland Indians, Boston Red Sox, Milwaukee Braves, Pittsburgh Pirates
Lifetime average: .286

One of the most durable first basemen in big league history, Mickey Vernon was also a two-time batting champion, leading the American League in 1946 and 1953 with averages of .353 and .337. He also led the league three times in doubles. He holds lifetime records for most games by an American League first baseman, as well as most putouts, assists, chances accepted, and the major-league record for double plays.

Yes, I guess it's true that I was President Eisenhower's favorite ballplayer. He was quoted in the papers as having said that. The year after I'd led the American League in batting for the second time, he came out to the ball park to present the Silver Bat to me. I don't think any President ever did that, before or since. Naturally I was pleased and highly honored.

I'll never forget what happened one opening day, I think it was 1954. The President was there, having thrown out the first ball. We were playing the Yankees and the game went into extra innings. Allie Reynolds was pitching. I came up and hit one over the right-field fence to win the ball game. As I rounded third I saw some of the players waiting at the plate to congratulate me, and there was one civilian there. As I crossed the plate he grabbed my arm. I figured he was just an overly enthusiastic fan and kind of pulled away from him.

"It's okay," he said. "I'm a Secret Service man. The President wants to see you over at his box."

So I went over there and Mr. Eisenhower was standing up with a big grin on his face and his hand outstretched.

"Nice going," he said.

That was a great thrill, hitting the home run to win on opening day and then being congratulated by the President. I met him on a few other occasions and was always impressed by how much he knew about the game; he was a real fan.

I grew up in Marcus Hook, Pennsylvania. It was an industrial town. Sun Oil has one of their largest refineries there—my dad worked for the company for over forty years—and there's also a British properties refinery, a rug mill, and a lot of other industry. When all this talk about pollution started, it wasn't anything new to me; I'd grown up in it.

I always wanted to be a ballplayer. Living near Philadelphia, I used to go to Shibe Park and watch those great Athletic teams that Connie Mack had. Some of my idols back then were Lefty Grove, Mickey Cochrane, Jimmie Foxx. I used to wait outside the ball park hoping to get Grove's autograph, but I never did get it. He'd come storming out and brush right past you. Seemed like he was always mad. Of course, later on I played against some of those men. The first time I hit against Grove my knees were shaking so bad they wouldn't stop. As luck would have it, I singled to center and when I got to first base I just couldn't believe it. Here was a guy who was already a legend, whom I'd watched pitch so many times from the bleachers. It's a peculiar experience to suddenly be in there against somebody like that, who was always bigger than life. I guess once you've been a fan a little of the awe and wonder stays with you forever.

I went to Villanova for a year, where I played freshman ball, but then I had a chance to play pro ball in the Eastern Shore League and I jumped at it. The club had a working agreement with the St. Louis Browns. Bill DeWitt was running the Browns at the time and he came down to look the team over, decided there were no prospects, and didn't pick up my option or anyone else's. So I was sold to the Washington club. That's how I got to the Washington Senators.

You've heard the old saying, "Washington, first in war, first in peace, and last in the American League." Well, it wasn't true during the period I played there. We always had the Browns and the Athletics underneath us. As a matter of fact, when I first joined the Senators they had a pretty good ball club, with guys like Cecil Travis, Buddy Lewis, Taft Wright, Buddy Myer, George Case. They were all good hitters. We were a bit thin on pitching; that was our problem.

Cecil Travis was a really outstanding hitter. You know, the year Ted Williams hit .406, Cecil hit .359, but nobody noticed it. He hit .300 as steady as clockwork, until he went into the service. He went through the Battle of the Bulge, where he had his feet frozen, and when he came back after the war he was never the same again.

I went into the Navy after the '43 season. I spent the summer of '44 at Norfolk, playing ball. After the season they rounded up a bunch of ballplayers, put us on a ship in San Francisco and sent us over to Honolulu. That's when I found out I shouldn't have gone into the Navy. I got seasick even before the Golden Gate Bridge was out of sight. I think it must have been one of the most monumental cases of seasickness anyone ever had. It was supposed to be a ten-day trip to Honolulu but it took us eleven because of a submarine threat that cost us a day stalling around. That was around the fifth day of the trip and I'll tell you, by that time I was so sick I was almost hoping that baby would come around and sink us.

On about the third day out I was lying in my bunk absolutely dead to the world. Big Mike Budnick, who pitched for the Giants, picked me up and threw me over his shoulder and carried me to sick bay where they kept me for a day or so, giving me pills and trying to cheer me up. Then they turned me out and I spent the rest of the trip up on the deck, which helped a little but not enough to make much difference.

I was too weak to shave, and by the time we got to Honolulu my beard had grown, and I had become so gaunt in my misery that the other players started calling me "Abe"—they said I looked like Abraham Lincoln. For years after the war anytime I met any of the guys who were on that trip they called me Abe. We had Elbie Fletcher, Johnny Lucadello, Pee Wee Reese, Pinky May, Johnny Mize, Barney McCosky, Tom Ferrick, Virgil Trucks, Johnny Rigney, Johnny Vander Meer, Gene Woodling, and some others.

Del Ennis was with us too out in the Pacific. Del had played just one year of minor-league ball, but he did very well against the big-league ballplayers. He was really impressive. There was a story to the effect that Dan Topping, who had recently bought the Yankees and who was in the service himself, saw Del playing in Hawaii and offered him a twenty-five-thousand-dollar bonus if he would sign with the Yankees.

"I'm already signed," Del said.

"With who?" Topping said.

"The Phillies."

"You get a bonus?" Topping asked.

Del smiled and said, "Fifty dollars."

After about five months in Honolulu they got us together and sent us out to the islands to play ball for the guys stationed out there. The deal was we were supposed to come back to Honolulu when the tour was completed; but when we got to Guam they separated us and assigned us to different islands for duty. Elbie Fletcher, I remember, went to Peleliu and I went to Ulithi, while the rest of the guys stayed on the three big islands, Guam, Saipan, and Tinian. Fletcher and I always wondered how in the heck they decided to ship us out. As far as we could tell, Peleliu and Ulithi really didn't need left-handed hitting first basemen. I ended up on an atoll about a mile long by a quarter mile wide. I stayed there about ten months and by then I had the thousand-yard stare.

We organized a softball league on Ulithi and two of the young fellows we had in the league were Larry Doby and Billy Goodman. Doby was a great athlete. We got to be good friends. Many a night he'd come by my tent and we'd spend hours and hours talking. He was planning to go back and play for the Newark Eagles in the Negro League after the war. This was before the color barrier had been broken, of course. He never talked about that, though I'm sure he was hoping the situation would change. I remember I wrote a letter home to my father saying that if they ever did accept Negro players that here was a fellow I was sure would be in the big leagues someday. And sure enough, he was the first one in the American League, and he had a great career.

I guess a lot of people were surprised when I led the league in 1946. And I'll confess, I was one of them. I hadn't had a .300 year before the war and suddenly I come out and hit .353. I don't think you can explain what the difference was. Luck was part of it. Most every time I hit a ball well it went in. Sometimes you can have a year like that, when you just stay sharp and healthy and lucky all the time.

When I tell you a lot of people were surprised, I'm not kidding. At the All-Star game in Boston that year Bob Feller was going around talking to fellows to see if they were interested in going on a barnstorming trip after the season. He was guaranteeing them so much a game. I was leading the league at the time, and I don't think he thought I would still be on top at the end of the season, because when he made his offer to me he said, "I'll give you so much extra if you lead the league." Now, Bob can be pretty conservative with a buck, so I'm sure he never expected me to finish up on top. When I was traded over to Cleveland in '49 we talked about that and he laughed and said, "You got one on me, didn't you?" But it was a wonderful trip. Bob let me bring my wife along and he couldn't have been nicer.

Bucky Harris used to have a saying every time Feller would pitch against us: "Go up and hit what you see, and if you don't see it come on back." That first half year I was up, in '39, I faced Feller about fifteen times and I think he struck me out nine of those times. He was tough, the toughest pitcher I ever faced. He didn't just have the best fastball, he also had the best curve I ever saw.

Ted Lyons was still going strong when I broke in, and he was another tough pitcher to hit. He had a good knuckleball, and he was quick, and had an outstanding change-up. I used to hear stories about how physically strong he was. I didn't see this, but I heard about it: The A's and the White Sox were on the same train going somewhere. Ted was walking through one of the cars and Jimmie Foxx was standing in the aisle. Jimmie was a playful guy and he wouldn't move out of the way. So Lyons just took hold of him, lifted him up and sat him in an upper berth and then walked on.

Satchel Paige was on the club with me in Cleveland. I remember one day in spring training in Arizona some of the guys were kidding him about his control. "I'll show you some control," he said. He took a chewing gum wrapper and put it down in front of the catcher and threw about eight out of ten right across it. And he wasn't lobbing them in either, he was putting some zip on them.

I had a bad year in '48 and so did Early Wynn, and we were both traded to Cleveland. I did all right in '49, but at the same time they had Luke Easter having a great year in Triple-A. Luke was ready to come up and become the first baseman in 1950. So Hank Greenberg, who was general manager at the time, asked me during contract negotiations if I would like trying to play the outfield.

"Well," I said, "if I try it I'm going to have to have more money on my contract."

"I can't do that," he said.

"Why not?"

"It just isn't done," he said.

"Well," I said, "I remember a first baseman with Detroit in the thirties who moved from first to the outfield and got x number of dollars for doing it."

I was talking about Hank himself, of course. He kind of grinned, but he didn't give me the money.

They tried Easter in the outfield for a while, but that didn't pan out, and they put him back on first. That made me expendable, and I was traded back to Washington in June, 1950. It would have been nice to have gone to a contender, but I really couldn't complain too much. You had to look at it this way: there were only eight first basemen in the American League at that time, and you were one of them.

Early Wynn and I sort of grew up together in the Washington organization. When he was with Washington he was still pretty much of a thrower, a guy with a good arm and a good fastball. But when he went to Cleveland in that deal Mel Harder began working with him and Early developed some good breaking stuff and became a great pitcher, a 300-game winner.

He was a tough competitor and wasn't shy about bearing in on you. When we were together with Cleveland we were roommates and good friends. After I was traded back to Washington I got four hits off of him the first time I faced him, the last one knocking the glove off his hand. He hated when anybody hit back through the middle. When I got to first base I turned around and I could tell he was steaming. He looked over at me and said, "Roommate or not, you've got to go in the dirt next time I see you." Sure enough, next time I faced him the first pitch was up over my head—not at my head—to let me know he hadn't forgotten.

In 1953 I got lucky all over again and won the batting crown for a second time, with an average of .337. Beat out Al Rosen by one point. Al is a very good friend of mine and I would have liked to have seen him win it because it would have given him the Triple Crown; but naturally I wanted to win it, too. I was leading the league most of the year, but then coming down the stretch he got hot, getting two or three hits a game. I think if the season had been just a few games longer he might have passed me.

I had a few points cushion that last game, which it turned out I needed, because Al got three hits and still didn't catch me. I heard that he missed another hit when he grounded to third and beat the throw but then ran over the bag at first without touching it and was called out. That sometimes happens, you know, when the runner thinks he's an easy out; but in this case the third baseman was a little slow coming up with it and Al just didn't step on the bag. I guess that made the difference, since I beat him out by just a point, even though I had a bad game.

I could have won the batting crown by sitting down that last game, but I just couldn't do it. I wanted to win it swinging, or lose it swinging.

You know, in my first full year in the big leagues we came into New York to end the season against the Yankees and I was hitting .302. This was my rookie season and I would loved to have hit .300. Before the series Bucky Harris said to me, "You want to hit three hundred?"

"Sure I do," I said.

"Okay," he said. "I'll sit you down."

"No," I said. "I want to play." I thought he might be testing me, to see what kind of guy I was.

By the last game, on Sunday, I was down to .299. In those days the visiting club came onto the field through the Yankee dugout. I was coming along the runway and Red Rolfe stopped me.

"I see you need a few hits to get three hundred," he said. The New York papers printed both teams' batting averages in the box scores and I guess that's where he'd seen it.

"That's right," I said.

"Well," he said, "if you drop a bunt or two I'll be back on my heels." The Yankees had long since clinched the pennant, of course, so this game didn't mean anything.

The first three times up we had men on base, so I didn't have a chance to bunt. But I did get one hit. I came up for the last time, needing one more hit for .300. There was nobody on base. I looked down at Rolfe and he was playing way back. Okay, I thought, here's my .300. I dropped one down and Rolfe barely moved. But I'll be a son of a gun if Dickey doesn't come charging out, pick up the ball and throw me out. We'd forgotten about him. And I ended the season with an average of .299.

I've heard about guys sitting down on the last day of the season to clinch a batting title or freeze an average. Well, I don't like to criticize anybody, but I would think that that standard was set once and for all by Ted Williams in 1941. He came into the last day of the season hitting .400 on the button and had a double-header scheduled. Ted could very easily have sat down and taken it. But he wouldn't think of it. He played both games and rapped out enough hits to end up with .406. Now *that's* the way to do it.

I was on the Red Sox when Ted hit .388. That was in 1957, when he was thirty-eight years old. Was I surprised at what he was doing? Not in the least. I'd been watching him for more than fifteen years by that time, so I was never surprised at anything he did with the bat.

I was hitting right behind him that year. You know, if he was leading off an inning he couldn't wait to grab his bat and get up to the plate to watch the pitcher take his warm-up throws. Or if he was the hitter and they were changing pitchers he would move up to watch the new pitcher warm up, to see what the ball was doing. He was always studying. Well, one day we've got the bases loaded against the Yankees and they're making a pitcher change, Ted's the hitter, and I'm on deck.

The Yankees bring in Tommy Byrne, a good left-hander. Tommy was something of a character; a well-educated guy, but he would do some quirky things now and then. When Tommy reaches the mound Ted turns around and calls me over. "Have a look at this guy," he says. "See what his ball is doing." So I walk over and we're standing together about seven or eight feet from the plate, watching Byrne get ready. Tommy didn't like that. He winds up, watching us out of the corner of his eye, and the first pitch is right at us, with something on it. We ducked under it, and Williams says, "Flaky left-handed bastard. If that ball had hit us I would have gone out there and pinched his head off." And then Ted stepped in and hit one right back through the middle for a base hit.

When I first came into the league in 1939 the Red Sox had Williams and Foxx in the lineup. That was a one-two punch to match anybody's. I can remember, when I was a rookie, whenever somebody would hit a real long ball and there was some comment about it on the bench, one of the older players would say, "You think that was long? Well, there's where Foxx hit one," and they'd point much further, much deeper. And that was in every park.

I'd put Mantle right there, though. He hit some of the longest balls I ever saw. He hit one off of Chuck Stobbs that went over the bleachers in Griffith Stadium. That was one time when nobody stood up and said, "You should have seen the one Foxx hit." That was a blast all by itself. They said it went around 560 feet and I can believe it.

My all-star team? Well, that's not as easy to answer as it seems. I'll try, but I think we'd better confine it to the American League, to the era I played in. Dickey was just finishing up, so I won't put him on, even though everybody knows how great he was. So my catcher would have to be Berra. I didn't see that much of Foxx, so I'll pick George McQuinn for first base. The rest of my infield would be Joe Gordon, Luke Appling and Brooks Robinson. The outfielders are Williams, DiMaggio, Mantle. My right-handed pitcher is Feller and my left-hander is Whitey Ford. That's my team. And when people read this I'll probably get some letters, right?

JOHNNY VANDER MEER

John Samuel Vander Meer
Born: November 2, 1914, Prospect Park, New Jersey
Major-league career: 1937–51, Cincinnati Reds, Chicago
 Cubs, Cleveland Indians
Lifetime record: 119 wins, 121 losses

Johnny Vander Meer will, of course, be remembered primarily as the only man in major-league history to pitch two consecutive no-hit games. However, for many years after that unprecedented and unequaled feat, Vander Meer reigned as one of the National League's premier left-handers. He led the league in strikeouts in 1941, '42, and '43.

I do a lot of traveling today in my work and I'd say that at least once a day I hear about my no-hitters. Somebody will hear the name—my name isn't all that common—and ask me if I'm *that* Johnny Vander Meer. Nobody else, before or since, has ever pitched consecutive no-hitters and I guess it's just something that's caught the public's imagination. Some of the people who talk to me about it weren't even born when I pitched those games back in 1938; but that doesn't seem to make any difference, they still like to ask me about them. No, I don't mind. It's no burden when they remember you for something you're proud of having done.

Did I want to play big-league ball? Well, kids always have had their dreams, haven't they? I played ball all the time, in the streets, in the fields, at school; that's all I did. Ate it, drank it, slept it. I think most of the boys at that time wanted to be big leaguers. What do they want to be today? Astronauts maybe. I don't know. But the thinking is the same.

I grew up in Midland Park, New Jersey. That's not too far out of New York City. Carl Hubbell was my idol in those days. Whenever I could scrape together the money I'd make the trip into New York and go up to the Polo Grounds to watch him pitch. He was the greatest left-hander of his day, so naturally I tried to imitate him. Of course we were direct opposites in our pitching styles. He relied on that marvelous screwball and a great curve, and sharp control—when Hubbell was wild he threw the ball over the heart of the plate. I was a power pitcher, trying to get the ball over the plate, and when I did I was all right.

Ironically enough, my first big-league start was against Hubbell at the Polo Grounds. I pitched the first nine innings of an extra-inning game and wasn't involved in the decision. But there I was, pitching at the Polo Grounds against Carl Hubbell. So when you hear about kids chasing rainbows, don't laugh, because we live in the kind of world where they can catch them. It happened to me.

You know, I was originally signed by the Brooklyn Dodgers. I was pitching semipro ball in New Jersey at the time. This was in 1932. We had our own team, our own little organization. You got thirty cents an inning when you pitched. That's right, paid by the inning. You never heard of that, huh? If you didn't go nine you got paid only for the innings you pitched. There was always a guy down in the bull pen waiting for you to get knocked out. This was back in the Depression, remember, and everybody was scrambling for whatever they could get.

The Dodgers sent me out to Dayton, Ohio, in 1933. I was supposed to be getting $125 a month, which wasn't bad money in 1933. But things were a little tough. When payday came around they'd say, "How much do you need to get by?" They might give you a third of your money, or two-thirds. At the end of the season they owed me $250. Everybody was at the bottom of the barrel in those days.

The next year I was assigned back to Dayton. I went, but I wouldn't sign a contract until they paid me what they owed me from the previous year. Halfway through spring training the Dayton club made a deal for me with Scranton, in the New York–Penn League. So I was now the property of the Scranton Miners, and the deal there was if I was sold they were going to split the money with the Dodgers. Then the Dodgers stepped in and wanted to know what I was doing at Scranton; they claimed they still owned me. In those days there was a lot of manipulating of minor-league players, contrary to existing baseball law.

I finally wound up in front of Judge Landis. He held a hearing and awarded me to Scranton. He also got me my back money. The following year the Boston Braves bought me from Scranton. Then they traded me to Nashville and Nashville sent me to Durham. That's where I pitched in 1936 and I had a good year. I won *The Sporting News* Minor League Player of the Year Award for 1936. The Reds had a working agreement with Durham and they bought me. That's how I ended up with Cincinnati.

In 1937 I went to spring training with the Reds and split that year between Cincinnati and Syracuse.

Bill McKechnie was managing the Reds at that time. I can sincerely say that I was proud to play for him. He was one of the greatest individuals I ever met in my life, either on the field or off. Ballplayers never feared McKechnie; they respected him. He had a remarkable ability for evoking respect; a great handler of men. He was the most outstanding defensive manager I ever saw. We were not noted as a heavy hitting team, so all of his skills and insights were directed toward defense, from handling his pitchers to positioning his men in the field. He was so skillful at doing these things that we never had to score too many runs to win. McKechnie knew how to hold onto a one- or two-run lead better than any other manager.

If you're willing to listen and learn in baseball you'll find there's an awful lot of experience around you all the time. One spring, it was either '37 or '38, we traveled north with the Red Sox. Grove was on that ball cub, near the end of his career now, but still the greatest mechanical throwing pitcher I've ever seen. He threw easily, with a tremendous amount of rhythm, which probably is the one reason he was able to pitch for so many years. When I wasn't in the game I'd go and sit in the Red Sox bull pen with Grove and just listen to him. He always had that great will to win and he helped fix that in my mind. I absorbed as much as I possibly could and became a real Lefty Grove fan.

I always had a tendency to walk a lot of men, but at the same time I always struck out a lot—I led the league in strikeouts three years in a row. You can minimize the disadvantages of wildness if you can strike them out. If you can pitch yourself out of trouble after you've pitched yourself in, the manager will leave you in there. I always had the ability to strike somebody out in a jam. So wildness never bothered me mentally. Neither did three-and-two pitches. I followed Grove's philosophy in that. He always said that if you had good stuff, then on a three-and-two pitch the batter was hurting more than you were.

You see, you have to understand your abilities in relation to the job you're being asked to do. I knew I was wild, that I was going to throw more pitches in a game than the average pitcher. So I trained harder, worked harder to stay in condition. As far as I was concerned, I was going out there to pitch eleven innings, because my nine innings were equivalent to somebody else's eleven.

On Saturday, June 11, 1938, I started against the Boston Braves. I had pretty good control that particular ball game, though I wasn't real fast. But I had good stuff and my ball was tailing. I was hitting that low and outside spot consistently all day and a lot of balls were hit on the ground. Harry Craft made a nice catch in center field during the game to rob somebody of a base hit, otherwise it was pretty much a routine ball game. I was in control all the way; never in trouble at any time. I shut them out without a hit, 3–0.

That was the first no-hitter, the one that nobody remembers. But without that one there wouldn't have been a second. The second one was an entirely different type of ball game. First of all, the game was a festive occasion even before it started. It was June 15, 1938, the first night game ever in Ebbets Field. Larry MacPhail made a big thing out of it. The ball park was jammed. The game was held up for about twenty-five minutes, as a matter of fact, because they were still selling tickets. People were sitting in the aisles and were standing all over the place. The fire department had to come and remove some people from the park because of overcrowding, and naturally they didn't want to go, and this took some time. So it was quite a background for what was going to happen.

And on top of all that, I figured I was going to be jinxed that night. You see, a whole contingent of friends and relatives from New Jersey came out for the game. Around seven hundred of them. There was a little ceremony prior to the game and they gave me a watch. According to baseball tradition, anytime you're honored like that by your friends you're supposed to have a bad game. I was sure I'd be out of there by the third inning.

I started the ball game and I was quick. I was real quick that night. I don't think I threw more than five curveballs over the first seven innings. The curve was hanging; for some reason, when I had the exceptionally good fastball I didn't have the real sharp curve. But the fastball was moving and I wasn't having any trouble. Along about the seventh inning the fastball was easing up a little and I began throwing more curves. The curve started to work for me and that was a break because everybody was looking for the fastball and that made me a little more effective.

In the last of the eighth I put them down in order. I got Woody English, Kiki Cuyler, and Johnny Hudson. So you can imagine what that ninth inning was like. The Brooklyn fans were pulling for me by that time; they wanted to see it happen. We were winning the game 6–0, so that wasn't a factor. Frank McCormick had hit a big three-run homer in the third inning, and that lead made things a whole lot easier.

No, in neither game did I consciously go for a no-hitter until the last inning. By that I mean I just pitched along as I would have under ordinary circumstances. I'd been involved in too many ball games with no hits for six or seven innings. You've got to wait for the big inning, the ninth. So in the ninth inning I started pressing.

Buddy Hassett was the first man up. He hit a little grounder along the first-base line and I fielded it and tagged him out myself.

One out.

Then I got wild. I walked the bases full—Babe Phelps, Cookie Lavagetto, Dolph Camilli. Three pretty good hitters. Maybe it was a good thing I walked them. What I was doing was forcing myself, trying to throw the ball harder than I could. I wasn't holding anything back.

McKechnie called time and came out to the mound.

"You're trying too hard, John," he said.

I knew exactly what he meant. And he was right.

"Just get it over the plate," he said. "For all you know somebody will hit it right back to you and you'll get a double play out of it."

Then he went back and I was alone out there again.

So I concentrated on throwing strikes. Ernie Koy was the batter. I ran the count on him to one and one and then he hit a ball down to Lew Riggs at third base. Lew had the option of going for the double play, but it was a long double play, and Ernie Koy was one of the better runners in the league. So Lew went home with it, to Lombardi. Lom took the throw and wheeled around to try and get Koy at first. But Koy was a smart baserunner and he was running inside the line, blocking Lombardi's line of vision, and there was no throw.

But that was two out and now Leo Durocher was up. I got two strikes on him and then something happened that I'll never forget as long as I live. The umpire was Bill Stewart, and incidentally, he was a good one. But Stewart was kind of short and occasionally had trouble seeing over big Lombardi. Well, I hit that outside corner with about two inches to spare, and he missed it. He called it a ball. Lombardi gave him a little blast, but I didn't say anything. There was no sense in upsetting myself, not in that spot.

On the next pitch Durocher lifted an easy fly ball to Harry Craft in center field, and that was it. And do you know who was the first guy out to the mound? Bill Stewart. He came running out and he said, "John, I blew that pitch. If you hadn't got him out I was the guy to blame for it." That was real nice of Bill to say that; but I'm just wondering: if Durocher had got a base hit, would he have come out and said it anyway?

Of course there was chaos after it was over. The fans spotted my dad in the stands and mobbed him to congratulate him. The police had to take him through the dugout to get him away. The funny thing was, Dad didn't know very much about baseball and was probably the only person in the ball park who didn't know I'd set a record. He was wondering what all the fuss was about.

Four days later I started again, up in Boston. Casey Stengel was managing the Boston club then. Well, I started off with three more hitless innings. That was 21⅓ straight no-hit innings. You could just feel what everybody in the ball park was thinking: *What gives with this guy?* To tell you the truth, I was beginning to wonder myself.

In the bottom of the fourth Stengel switched from coaching third and went over to first. Of course, Casey is Casey, and I think he tried to psyche me a little. As he was crossing over to first he made sure he passed in front of me as I was beginning to loosen up. He looked down so nobody could see he was talking to me, and said, "John, we're not trying to beat you, we're just trying to get a base hit." And they did, that inning. Debs Garms got it; he hit a three-and-two pitch right back through the box. To be honest about it, I was relieved; the pressure had become too much and I was glad to get out from under it. Enough was enough.

In 1939 I was going along pretty good. Then one day I was pitching a ball game in Pittsburgh. There was a rain delay for about an hour, and then we started up again. I went back out to the mound, and as I was throwing a ball my foot slipped as I came down on it, and I heard something in my shoulder make a noise. I finished the ball game all right, but the next day the pain set in. I had torn all the muscles underneath my shoulder blades into my back.

I had to go down to Indianapolis in 1940 to work it out and finally came back to Cincinnati at the end of August. That was in time for the September drive. We'd won the pennant in '39 and were about to win it again. We were in Philadelphia and needed one more win to clinch it. McKechnie gave me the ball and told me to go out and win us a pennant.

The Phillies were not a very strong club in those days, but they had a first-rate pitcher going for them that day, Hugh Mulcahy. This was an important game for me, very important. Not only was I anxious to nail it down for the club, but it was going to be a good test to see how far I'd come back from that injury.

In the seventh inning the score was 2–2. It went into the tenth inning. We scored a run in the top of the tenth, but darn if I didn't let them tie it up. So we kept going, into the thirteenth. I led off the inning and got hold of one and whacked it for a double. They sacrificed me to third, and then Ival Goodman brought me home with a fly ball. McKechnie brought in

Joe Beggs to pitch the last of the thirteenth and Joe held them. That gave us the pennant.

That was a tremendous game for me. I had pitched twelve strong innings without tiring. It gave me back all my confidence. I knew I hadn't done any permanent damage to my arm and was going to be able to continue playing ball.

What's the greatest game I ever pitched? That was in Brooklyn. No, it wasn't the second no-hitter. It was in September of '46. The Dodgers were deadlocked at the time with the Cardinals, fighting for the pennant. The game meant an awful lot to them. It went nineteen innings and ended in a 0–0 tie. They finally had to call it because of darkness because at that time you weren't allowed to turn the lights on to complete a game.

I went the first fifteen innings and gave up only seven hits. I struck out fifteen and walked only two. I was still going strong, too, and probably could have kept pitching, but I was thrown out at the plate trying to score in the top of the fifteenth and McKechnie was afraid I might have tired myself out. Harry Gumbert came in and finished it. I don't think I made a bad pitch that whole game. Branch Rickey said later it was the greatest game he ever saw pitched. I thought it was pretty fine myself, but I wish I could have won it.

BILL WERBER

WILLIAM MURRAY WERBER
Born: June 20, 1908, Berwyn, Maryland
Major-league career: 1930, 1933–42, New York Yankees, Boston Red Sox, Philadelphia Athletics, Cincinnati Reds, New York Giants
Lifetime average: .271

A scrappy, aggressive player, Billy Werber was one of the game's most consistent third basemen during his ten years in the big leagues. Three times he led the American League in stolen bases, and in 1934 hit .321 for the Red Sox, his finest season. In 1939–40 he anchored third base for two pennant-winning Cincinnati teams.

I signed a contract with the New York Yankees after graduating from Duke University and I joined them at the Chase Hotel in St. Louis. I made the tour of the western cities with them and we came back to Yankee Stadium. This was in early July, 1930. Then Lyn Lary, the regular shortstop, was hurt in a ball game, and George Wuestling, the utility man, played the first game of a double-header and became ill. So they put me in at short for the second game. That was my introduction to professional baseball.

No, I wasn't awed by it at all, even though I was out on the field with some remarkably gifted ballplayers. The Yankees had a tremendous ball club. They had Bill Dickey, Lou Gehrig, Ben Chapman, Tony Lazzeri, Earle Combs, Babe Ruth. All of those fellows hit over .300 that year. In fact, the low man among the regulars that year was Lyn Lary, and he hit around .290. But I was a very confident young man and I expected to go out there and take over the shortstop job. I really did. After all, I'd hit .450 at Duke, hadn't I?

But you live and learn. I soon realized that I really didn't have enough experience as yet to go right in and play major-league baseball. There are a lot of tricks you think you know when you're a collegiate star, but it's a far cry from the major leagues.

The coach at Duke when I got there was an old-time major-league ballplayer named George Whitted. I think George saw in me a good major-league prospect and the possibility of his earning some additional money if he could sell me to a big-league club. So there were a lot of scouts that looked at me in my freshman year at Duke. At the end of that year I had made a verbal agreement with Paul Krichell to play with the New York Yankees when I was through at Duke. There were certain sums of money to be paid for my education the remaining three years at the university, plus a certain bonus amount to be paid when I graduated.

I had always been interested in baseball and I worked awfully hard at it, but that was primarily for personal success and satisfaction and not necessarily to make a career. I went to Duke with the idea ultimately of going into law; I had taken a prelegal course and intended to practice law. The Yankees finally asked me whether I meant to go on with my educational pursuits or play ball. By that time I was married and had a young child and had to go to work for a living. So I got into baseball, was reasonably successful at it and began earning pretty good money.

As I said, that was a tremendous Yankee ball club I joined in 1930. And right at the heart of it was Babe Ruth. Babe was a loud, gregarious person. I played a lot of bridge, with Dickey as a partner, against Ruth and Gehrig. Babe used to drink quite a bit on the trains, and he was a good bridge player until he had put away some of that liquor, and then he'd begin giving Gehrig bad bids, at which point the game usually broke up.

Ruth never knew who you were. He called everybody "Keed." One day at Back Bay Station in Boston Tony Lazzeri brought Myles Thomas up and introduced him to Babe as a new pitcher who had just joined the ball club from Yale. Babe stuck out his big mitt and said, "Hi, Keed. Glad to have you on the club." The fact was, Myles Thomas had been a relief pitcher on the Yankees for three or four years.

Ruth was a friendly man, always kindly toward strangers. He would sign autographs by the hour. He was much more responsive to people than Gehrig was. Lou didn't like to stop and sign autographs when leaving the ball park. He was a loner, never had much to say to anybody. But on the other hand, unlike Ruth, he was a clean-living fellow, didn't smoke, didn't drink. He seemed to have a great deal of tolerance for pain. I saw him play a whole series of ball games with a broken finger on his glove hand. This was before his consecutive-game streak had reached unique proportions and there was no special reason for him to be in there, except that he was that kind of man and that kind of ballplayer. He was a tremendously powerful man physically, extremely muscular, very determined, a great hustler.

Babe and Lou were total opposites in personality, and they didn't hit it off too well, actually. Babe would needle Lou a great deal. Ruth didn't have too much regard for anybody that had gone to college, and he would call Lou a kink-head college kid, and things like that. Gehrig ignored it. I guess he considered the source.

Well, the Yankees farmed me out to get that experience. I was out for two years and came back in the spring of 1933. I had a very fine spring and under ordinary circumstances would have been the Yankee shortstop. But at that time the Yankees were well stocked at short; they also had Lyn Lary and Frank Crosetti. So I was sold to the Red Sox.

I was disappointed about leaving the Yankees, but at the same time I was glad to have the opportunity to go to Boston and play regularly. I had heard good things about Tom Yawkey, that he was determined to build a winning club in Boston. And he did go out and buy a lot of good ballplayers over the next few years. The same year I joined them they got Rick Ferrell from the Browns, and later on they got fellows like Jimmie Foxx, Lefty Grove, Rube Walberg, Doc Cramer.

We had both Ferrells there for a while with the Red Sox. Wes came over from Cleveland in 1934. He was a good pitcher and possessed a world of confidence. For example, in spring training in 1935 everybody was hitting him. He just couldn't get anybody out. But each time he was knocked out of the box he'd go to Cronin and say, "Joe, don't worry about it, I'm going to be just fine. I want opening day. I want to pitch against Gomez at the Stadium. I'll be ready." And Cronin would say to me, "How in the world can I start that guy on opening day? He hasn't gotten anybody out in spring training."

Well, he started Wes on opening day in Yankee Stadium, against Gomez. Wes walked the first man that faced him on four pitches. And then he tore the mound up with his spikes, pulled his cap down tight on his head, and went ahead and pitched a whale of a ball game. He beat Gomez, 1–0.

Wes was a marvelous character. I've seen him, after being removed from a ball game, hit himself in the jaw with both fists and nearly knock himself out. I've seen him jump in the air and crush the face out of an expensive watch. I've seen him tear card deck after card deck to pieces because he wasn't getting good hands. He hated to lose, at anything. He was a very determined competitor, the kind you like to have on your side.

Jimmie Foxx joined us in '36. Jim could hit a ball so far that it's just a pity they weren't putting tape measures on them in those days. I saw him hit one in Cleveland one day, I never will forget it. It went beyond the left-field bleachers, which was 417 feet. The bleachers ran up to a big Lux soap sign and beyond the sign was a very tall white oak tree. Foxx hit the ball through the top of that tree. We all jumped up in the dugout the moment he hit it to see where it was going. Dusty Cooke stood on the top step of the dugout gazing out toward left field for a few moments, then turned to me and said, "It's a damned lie." That ball must have gone close to 600 feet.

Jimmie was a very pleasant fellow. Happy-go-lucky, always smiling. Never saw him mad. And as strong as he was, it was a good thing he had that sort of disposition. He could wrap his hands around my ankles and lift me straight up off the floor —and I weighed 178 pounds. We called him "The Beast." Amazing calves, forearms, biceps, shoulders. Unbelievable strength. And he showed it the way he hit those long balls. There wasn't a ball park in the league that could hold Jimmie.

I played for Bucky Harris my second year at Boston. Harris was a great practical joker, you know. One time on a long train ride to St. Louis he decided to liven things up. He had a cigar and I got some bluehead matches and we pushed them into the cigar. There was a very intense poker game going on around a table in the men's room. We went in there and Harris lit the cigar. The moment those matches began to flare up he threw the cigar onto the table. Well, those guys thought it was a giant firecracker and they jumped up and went barreling out of there so fast that the table flew up and the cards and the money all went flying into spittoons and wash basins and all over the floor . . . while that cigar just lay there smoking harmlessly away.

You always had practical jokers on ball clubs in those days. We had another fellow, Tom Daley, who could knock your eye out with a bamboo toothpick and a BB. He'd take a BB shot and press it down hard between his teeth and with a flick of this hard tensile bamboo sliver shoot that BB with great velocity and uncanny accuracy. He would go into a movie theater and always find himself a baldheaded man and drive him crazy, sitting there in the dark quietly bouncing BB's off of that man's bald head.

One year down in spring training they found out that Oscar Melillo had a fear of animals. So somebody went and got a baby alligator and put it in Melillo's locker and covered it with a shirt. When Oscar came in to dress after the game and picked up the shirt he uncovered the alligator. He took one look at it, whirled around and, in an advanced state of undress, shot out of that clubhouse and wouldn't come back until somebody had got rid of the alligator.

Another time Melillo went to the movies with Heinie Manush. As they were going through the lobby Manush spotted a cat sitting there and picked it up, without Melillo knowing it. When they got inside and were going down the aisle through the dark, Manush suddenly threw the cat onto Melillo's back. Well, Oscar didn't know what it was; all he knew was that something furry and alive was digging its claws into him. He started running down the aisle and screaming, making such a racket that they stopped the movie and put the lights on to see what was happening.

One day Rollie Hemsley went out and got himself a bullfrog. He put it inside his shirt and went up to the batting cage where Melillo was standing. Rollie put one arm around Melillo's shoulder and started talking, and while he was doing that he reached into his shirt and pulled out the bullfrog and sat it on Melillo's other shoulder and took his hand away. So there was the frog, sitting on Oscar's shoulder, about two inches from his face. He didn't notice it right away—he probably thought the pressure he felt was still Hemsley's hand—but then he turned his head and looked the frog right in the eye. Boy, he took off; ran right out from under that thing.

One spring in Sarasota Wesley Ferrell rented a car. Well, the car was sitting outside of the hotel one afternoon. Some of the guys went around to the back of the hotel where the garbage was put out and got a pile of crab guts and fish heads. Then they went to the car and lifted out the seat and dropped this filthy, foul-smelling stuff in there and replaced the seat. And of course that car stayed out there in a broiling Florida sun, all that day and the next day too.

The following night Roy Johnson had a date and asked Wes if he could use the car. Wes, always the good fellow, said sure. When Roy opened the door the stench almost blew him over. There were some old clothes lying in the back that Wes used to wear when he fished, and Roy thought they were the cause of it. So he got rid of them and went along. He drove past the hotel later that evening with his date and she had her head stuck out the window on one side of the car and Roy had his head stuck out the window on the other side. When we asked him about it the next day, he said, "It was the most horrible experience I've ever had. She thought it was me and I thought it was her."

The next day in the clubhouse before we went out on the field Wes got up on a stool and called everybody to order. "If the man who put those fish leavin's in my car will come forward I'll whup him right here and now. And if it was three or four of you, then I'll whup all of you." But of course nobody knew anything about it. Wes was talking to a room full of innocent men.

That same year we had a fellow by the name of Dib Williams. He was a country boy from Arkansas. One night we were coming back from the movies and an opossum was going across the street. Dib picked it up and took it back to the hotel. We took it up to the room of Johnny Orlando, the clubhouse boy, and put it under the washbasin in his bathroom. Then we unscrewed the bulb in the bathroom and closed the door.

We asked the front desk to dial a certain room and let us

know when Orlando came in. When the phone rang and the clerk told us Johnny was back, we went out into the corridor and watched him go into his room. Then Dusty Cooke went to the door and took hold of the doorknob and held onto it. Meanwhile, Orlando undressed and got ready for bed. When he opened the bathroom door and the light from the bedroom hit that opossum's eyes they lit up like fire and the opossum hissed.

Well, we were out in the corridor and we heard the yell. The next thing we heard was John hitting the door, but Cooke was holding the knob. There was a lot of yelling and scrambling and then we saw John up at the transom, glaring out in horror and screaming that there was a sewer rat in his room. Then Cooke opened the door and we went in to try and calm him, but that wasn't going to be so easy. As soon as the door opened, John dropped from the transom and pushed through us and took off down the corridor, stark naked. We went after him to bring him back, but you know what a naked man does in public—he runs, fast. There was a good deal of yelling and excitement and I guess a certain amount of misunderstanding on the part of some of the other guests until we caught John and calmed him down.

In 1937 I was traded to the Athletics for Pinky Higgins and there I had the opportunity to get to know Connie Mack. I was very fond of him. He was a wonderful gentleman. He was over seventy years old when I got there, but he was still an extremely perceptive and intelligent baseball man. I enjoyed talking to him and, whenever I could, would sit down and have dinner with him when he was eating alone. He would reminisce quite a bit. His favorite ballplayer, of all the stars who played for him, was Rube Waddell, the great left-hander who pitched for Mr. Mack around the turn of the century.

He would sit there and chuckle away while telling stories about all the problems he had had with Rube Waddell. Rube, it seemed, would disappear for three or four days at a time and Mr. Mack would have to hire detectives to go out and find him. The detectives would fan out and go to all the firehouses in and around Philadelphia, because firehouses had a fascination for Rube. And ultimately that's where they would find him, sitting in a firehouse, and bring him back. Mr. Mack said that if Rube was sitting on a bench during a game and a fire engine went past, Rube was apt to run out of the ball park and follow it. But that was Mr. Mack's favorite ballplayer of all time—Rube Waddell.

In 1939 I was traded to Cincinnati and walked into two pennants. I recognized immediately in spring training that we had an exceptionally good ball club. I felt we could win it and we did win it. It was a beautifully balanced team. We had fine pitching, good defense, and pretty good power. We had Ernie Lombardi, who could hit with anybody; if he hadn't been so slow afoot I don't think he ever would have hit much under .400. Frank McCormick was another strong hitter, and so was Ival Goodman. Then we had Wally Berger, Lonny Frey, Billy Myers, Harry Craft. And a good bench.

We were particularly strong on the mound. Bucky Walters and Paul Derringer won fifty-two games between them that year, and in addition we had Whitey Moore, Junior Thompson, Lee Grissom. We beat out a good Cardinal ball club by four and a half games.

But that Ernie Lombardi was something special. He wasn't just a hitter, he was a great catcher, too. Enormous hands; he could wrap his fingers completely around a baseball so that you couldn't see it. Twice I saw him do something I never saw another catcher do, or even try to do. Once it was with Vander Meer pitching, the other time I think it was Derringer. They threw balls outside that were going to be wild pitches. Lombardi couldn't get his glove across in time, so he just stuck out that big hand and plucked the ball right out of the air as easily as you'd pluck an apple off of a tree.

We didn't have much success in the Series against the Yankees in 1939; they took us four straight. The 1940 Series was a better one, for the ball club and for me personally. We won a tough, well-played seven-game Series and I hit .370.

We came down to a seventh game that was a classic pitching duel between Paul Derringer and Bobo Newsom. Going into the bottom of the seventh inning we were losing, 1–0. Then Frank McCormick doubled. Jimmy Ripple came up and hit a drive to right field that Bruce Campbell had a chance to catch. But Campbell didn't catch it. McCormick, however, had to hold up and when he saw the ball falling safe he got a late start. When the relay came in from the outfield to Dick Bartell at short I don't think McCormick was halfway home yet.

Bartell, with his back to the plate, had made the assumption that McCormick would score easily. The place was in an uproar; it was a hometown crowd, remember, and they were up on their feet yelling—I'll never forget that uproar. We were all on the top step of the dugout yelling, "Run, run, run!" to McCormick. If Bartell had turned around Frank would have been a dead duck. Charlie Gehringer was yelling to him to throw it home, but Bartell couldn't hear him above all the noise. By the time he turned around McCormick had scored.

That tied the game. Ripple was sacrificed over to third and then Bill Myers hit a fly ball to center that scored Ripple. Derringer shut them out over the last two innings and we were World Champions. And that was a great feeling.

We had Al Simmons with us at Cincinnati as a utility outfielder in 1939. Al was near the end of his career and he didn't play much. He was an entirely different fellow than he was when he was hitting .380 and .390 in his heyday with the Athletics. He hardly spoke to you then; he was a swashbuckling pirate of a man. But over at Cincinnati he was going the other way and he was extremely pleased if you invited him to go to a movie with you. He had become a very decent, quiet, humble guy. When I joined the Yankees out of college, Herb Pennock told me in a conversation, "Bill, in this business be awful nice to people on your way up, because you're going to meet a lot of them on your way back down." Well, you've probably heard that before; it's a shopworn piece of wisdom but nonetheless valid for that. You know the day you begin that inevitably you're going to start losing that stamina and resilience, that your talent is going to fade. So you don't want to be overly impressed by it.

Did I look ahead when I was playing? I'll say I did. I quit baseball twice before I left it for keeps. I quit after the 1939 World Series. I didn't want to play baseball any longer. But Mr. Giles, who was general manager of the Reds, persuaded me to play another season. I quit again after the '41 season, but Mr. Giles called me and told me he had the opportunity to sell me to the Cubs, the Giants, or the Pirates.

"They'd all like to have you," he said. "I'll sell you to whichever club you prefer and I'll pay you ten percent of the purchase price."

I chose the Giants, and he sold me there for $35,000. So I

played for the Giants in 1942. After that season I retired and this time made it stick. You see, I was making as much money in the insurance business as I was playing baseball. I felt that if I devoted full time to my business I could do even better.

I still had some good years ahead of me, but I never had any regrets about retiring when I did, just as I never had any regrets about playing. I'll always be a strong advocate of baseball and am very appreciative of what it did for me. But I had realized as far back as 1934 that baseball was not going to be part of my future and so I worked to get out of it.

I can tell you exactly when and why I determined that I would get out of baseball just as soon as I was able to. We were playing the Yankees in Boston and I hit a low line drive out to Babe Ruth. He came in for it but couldn't make the play and the ball went through his legs to the wall for a triple. Babe had a bad game generally and the people that day in Boston booed that man unmercifully. Babe was nearly forty years old then and obviously near the end of his career, and I said to myself, "If this game can be so unkind to a man who's done so much for it, maybe it's not for me."

But I enjoyed my years in baseball and, as I said, I have no regrets. There was always a great deal of enthusiasm on the part of the players. I can remember sitting in the dugout one day and Rick Ferrell turning to me and saying, "Can you imagine getting paid for doing this?" There were an awful lot of fellows back then who would have played for nothing, because they loved the game.

Of course, you've got a different breed of player today. I don't know them, I don't profess to understand them, so I can't fairly criticize them. But when I read in the newspapers about a .210 hitter asking for a raise, I can't help but to wonder. In my day a ballplayer who hit .210 would pray all winter that he was going to be invited to spring training the next year, much less demand an increase. Why, back then if you hit .210 you would have been ashamed to go back to your home town after the season.

BOBBY SHANTZ

ROBERT CLAYTON SHANTZ
Born: September 26, 1925, Pottstown, Pennsylvania
Major-league career: 1949–64. Philadelphia and Kansas City
   Athletics, New York Yankees, Pittsburgh Pirates, Houston
   Astros, St. Louis Cardinals, Chicago Cubs, Philadelphia
   Phillies
Lifetime record: 119 wins, 99 defeats

Bobby Shantz put together his finest year in 1952, when he won 24 games and lost only 7 and was voted Most Valuable Player in the American League. In spite of an injury suffered the next spring, Shantz remained in the big leagues for many more years, leading the American League in earned-run average in 1957. Often described as a "fifth infielder," Shantz was considered by many to be the greatest fielding pitcher of his era.

I was playing in a semipro league on the sandlots around Philadelphia and a few scouts from the Phillies were looking at me. Not saying anything; just looking. They'd show up, watch, then go away. I was getting curious about what they were thinking. Then one day I found out. After a game one of them walked up to me and shook hands.

"We've been watching you," he said.

Well, that much I knew.

"You've got a good arm," he said. "You've got a hell of a good arm. But I don't know if you could make it in pro ball."

"Why not?" I asked. I knew what he was going to say.

"You're too small," he said.

That was in 1947. Five years later, after I'd won the Most

Valuable Player Award in the American League, I met him and he laughed and said he'd made a big mistake.

To tell you the truth, at the time I was half convinced he was right; I really thought I was too small to ever get anyplace in baseball. I was only five feet six and a half.

But then after that season in '47 a scout from the A's, Harry O'Donnell, came around and asked me if I'd be interested in going away. I didn't know what to do. I was working in a sawmill, making seventy-three cents an hour, which was decent money at that time. You know the saws they use to cut the wood with? Well, my job was to glaze them. I was called a handsaw glazer. I'd put emery dust on them and put them through a machine and all this black dirt would come out in my face. I had to wear a mask and goggles all day. It was a terrible job, but I had to make a living somehow.

But as much as I disliked the job, still I hated to quit it. I kept remembering what the Philly scout had said and couldn't help wondering if maybe he was right, that I was too small for pro ball. My parents saw I couldn't make up my mind, so my father talked to me.

"Do you want to stay in that sawmill for the rest of your life?" he asked.

"No," I said.

"So, why don't you sign that contract?"

"I don't know if I can make the big leagues," I said.

"Why not?"

"I'm too small," I said.

"How do you know?" he asked.

Well, that was the point: I *didn't* know. Whenever, wherever, and whatever I played, the competition was always taller, and I'd always done all right. My parents were all for me taking advantage of the opportunity, for getting out of the sawmill; and the Athletics certainly didn't think I was too small. So I quit my job, signed the contract and went away. Best thing I ever did in my life.

The A's started me off in Class-A ball, in Lincoln, Nebraska. I had a pretty good year there, winning 18 ball games. The next year, 1949, I went to spring training with the Athletics. I had a good spring and it looked to me like I'd made the team. They brought me back to Philadelphia with them and I'd no sooner unpacked my bags than they told me they were sending me to Buffalo.

A little disappointed, I packed up again, got in a car with another guy and took off for Buffalo. Well, a few hours after we left I was recalled. But I didn't know that. I was driving to Buffalo, bemoaning my luck all the way. The Athletics called the state troopers and the local police and asked them to try and head us off, but they missed us. We just kept going. That's a long, long drive, especially after you thought you'd made the ball club.

When we arrived in Buffalo word was waiting for me: Get on a train and go to Detroit—that's where the A's were playing. I thought somebody was kidding.

"Why'd I drive all the way up here?" I asked.

"To get the good news," they told me.

They handed me a train ticket and I was on my way to Detroit. You know that song, "Shuffle Off to Buffalo"? Well, don't sing it around me.

So it was all kind of roundabout, but I got there, and once I did I stayed for sixteen years.

A day or two after joining the club I relieved Carl Schieb in a game. I came in with nobody out in the third inning and pitched nine consecutive innings of no-hit ball. I think I must have been half unconscious out there. Honestly. I mean, this was my first big-league game and I'm pitching the equivalent of a no-hitter. We finally scored in the top of the thirteenth. In the last of the thirteenth I gave up a hit, but it didn't mean anything. George Kell got the hit. He was the first big leaguer to get a hit off of me.

When I walked off the mound after that game I don't think my spikes touched the grass. I was really floating. I think that game was what kept me in the big leagues that year. I finished up 6 and 8.

Connie Mack was still managing the A's at that time. He had been managing them for a long time when I was born, and he was still at it when I joined them. He was around eighty-five years old and the years were beginning to tell on him. He wasn't able to handle the ball club very well. His son Earle sat on the bench with him and helped him out. Mr. Mack still moved the outfielders around with his scorecard, but he had difficulty staying with the ball game. Sometimes you'd have to wait and wait for a sign to come.

He managed the first two years I was there, '49 and '50. He was very nice, but didn't say too much; tell you the truth, I don't think he even knew my name. All the same, I think I was very fortunate to have played for him. I grew up in the Philadelphia area and of course he was a legend there, and it's nice today to be able to say that I played for Connie Mack.

You know, I never really followed the big leagues all that closely when I was a kid. I loved baseball and now and then my dad used to take me down from where we lived in Pottstown to Philadelphia to see a game, but I didn't keep up with it that much. I sure never expected to be there myself. Naturally I knew about Ted Williams and Joe DiMaggio, that they were supposed to be the greatest, and they were. And then all of a sudden, holy mackerel, I'm competing against them.

Did they tell me how to pitch to Williams? Sure they did. It was great advice, very encouraging. They said he has no weakness, won't swing at a bad ball, has the best eyes in the business, and can kill you with one swing; he won't hit at anything bad, but don't give him anything good. Good luck. Man, I threw him some wicked curveballs that didn't miss by more than a fraction, and he'd just stand there and look at them, and that bat would stay right back, not budging an inch. You'd just do the best you could with him and hope your number wasn't up when he swung.

In 1951 I won 18 games and I think that really built up my confidence. I began to move that year; I got the feeling I could start getting them out consistently. I remember one of our catchers, Joe Tipton, pulled me aside one day and said, "You've got a hell of a curveball, but you're going to have to learn to change speeds on that fastball. You learn to do that and I think you can win some ball games." That sank in. I began practicing taking something off the fastball. I finally learned how to throw that darn thing without slowing up on my arm motion, and boy, I started winning. Wow, did I start to win!

I figured I'd have a good year in 1952, but never expected it to be that good. I was 24 and 7. I was surprised. You'd better believe I was surprised. I kept asking myself, "What the hell is going on here?" I couldn't lose a game. But, say, don't forget, I had some pretty good guys behind me, and that really helped.

We had guys like Ferris Fain, Pete Suder, Eddie Joost, Dave Philley, Gus Zernial, Elmer Valo.

I got to a point where I could do just about anything I wanted to out there on the mound. Everything seemed to go right. I was changing speeds when I was behind the batter and throwing the ball right on the corner. You sometimes get into ruts where everything goes wrong, but this was the opposite— everything was going right. And of course the confidence keeps building.

I pitched an inning in the All-Star game that year, which turned out to be the last inning. The game was called after five because of rain. It was played in Philadelphia, in front of the hometown crowd. Boy, I was nervous as the devil out there. The first man I faced was Whitey Lockman, and I struck him out. Next was Jackie Robinson, and I struck him out. Then came Stan Musial, and I struck him out. Then the rain started to fall and it washed away the rest of the game. It was too bad, because I felt good and would liked to have kept going.

After the game the writers crowded around me in the clubhouse.

"Do you think you might have broken Carl Hubbell's record if it hadn't rained?" they asked.

"What record?" I asked. I wasn't too sharp on baseball history.

"What he did in the '34 All-Star game."

"What'd he do?" I asked.

"Struck out five in a row—Ruth, Gehrig, Foxx, Simmons, and Cronin."

Well, I'd never known that. And I guess I'll never know, either, how far I could have gone in that game. But I'll settle for the three.

Jimmy Dykes was managing the A's that year. He'd been after me to switch from batting right-handed to left-handed, because he didn't like the idea of my left arm being exposed to the pitcher when I stood at the plate. I tried switching but it didn't work out, so I went back to hitting righty. I loved to hit.

Toward the end of the season, with still a couple of weeks to go, I was batting against Walter Masterson. A pitch got away from him and sailed in at my head. I threw up my hand to protect myself and the ball hit me in the wrist and broke two bones. That's my left wrist I'm talking about. The pitching one. I was through for the year.

I went to spring training the next year and felt pretty good. My wrist didn't bother me. Then the season started and I was making my first start, against the Red Sox in Fenway park. I threw a ball and felt something pull in my shoulder. It felt just like somebody had stuck a knife in there. I'd really torn up that shoulder muscle. The doctor said I might have been favoring the wrist. I don't know if that's true or not. I know, though, that I never did seem to have the good snappy curve that I used to have. Something was gone.

I wasn't worth a damn all year. Won only five games. I just couldn't throw. Frustrating? I'll say it was. You talk about a roller coaster ride from the top to the bottom in a hurry, that's what that was. I'd received a pretty good raise, from $12,000 to $25,000. I hated even to take the money.

The following year I did the same damn thing, in the very first game of the season. Tore something back in there again. I didn't pitch another game for the rest of the season.

It was depressing. It looked like baseball was all over for me, and I didn't know what else I could do. I didn't have a real good education and didn't see many opportunities for myself away from baseball. You're just not prepared for an injury like that early in your career. So I kept hanging in there, taking shots of cortisone, taking pills, all kinds of treatment.

Baseball can be a lot of fun, but, boy, you never know what can happen all of a sudden, do you? Look what happened to Herb Score. I was there when he got hit in the eye with that line drive. Man, did he get belted. You heard the crack of the bat and he was down, just like that. Never had a chance to protect himself.

Before he had that injury Herb could fog that ball. But you know, as fast as he was, I don't think he was quite as fast as Koufax. It's hard to tell, really, but I'd say Koufax was just a little quicker. I pitched against Koufax when I was in the National League. He was in his heyday then, and he was tough. Exceptionally tough. Best pitcher I ever saw. I never say anybody throw harder, and he had a great curveball, too. He threw everything straight overhand, right out of the same motion. That fastball used to rise. You'd think it was going to be low and all of a sudden it just shot up at you. And the way he came over the top with that curve, it broke straight down, with tremendous speed. Even if you got your bat on it, where were you going to hit it?

In the winter of '56, after a couple of mediocre seasons, I was traded to the Yankees. How did I feel about that? Are you kidding? To go with that ball club? I was delighted. My only concern was if I could win for them. And I did have a pretty good year in '57; won 11 and lost 5 and led the league in ERA.

You know, I never thought I'd ever get into a World Series, but with the Yankees in those years that's about all I did. Winning pennants was part of their routine. I was with them four years and we won it three times. The White Sox beat us out in '59. I still don't know how that happened.

You remember that Series against Pittsburgh in 1960, don't you? That was something. We did all the hitting but they came out on top. I can't figure out how we lost it. We hit .338 as a team for the Series. But the whole thing turned around in the seventh game because of a damned pebble or something.

Everybody remembers the ball that hit Kubek in the throat. But do you know who was pitching for the Yankees when it happened? Yours truly. I came in in the third inning and was really mowing them down. Shut them out for five innings while we caught up and went ahead. We were winning, 7–4, going into the bottom of the eighth. Gino Cimoli came up to pinch-hit and he got a single. Still nothing to worry about, right?

Bill Virdon was the next hitter. I threw him a good pitch and got him to hit it on the ground to Kubek at short. A sure double-play ball. Richardson was running over to cover second. I turned around and could just see that double play being executed. But it never happened. The ball hit a pebble or a clod of dirt or something, took a wild bounce and got Tony right in the throat. He went down and lay there gagging. I'll never forget it. He had to leave the game.

Boy, that was a lousy break if there ever was one. Instead of two out and nobody on, they had two on and nobody out. I left the game at that point and Jim Coates came in. He gave up a base hit to Dick Groat, but got the next two guys out. Then Clemente hit a little roller down the first base line and beat it out when Coates didn't cover the bag. Skowron fielded the ball okay but Coates just didn't get over there. Skowron was mad as hell. That should have been the third out. Instead, Hal Smith came up and he hit a home run and we were down, 9–7.

We came back and tied it in the ninth, but all that did was set the stage for Bill Mazeroski. He was a fastball hitter and Ralph Terry, who was in there then, threw one right up his alley and he really tagged it. I felt sorry for Ralph. I felt sorry for me, too. As soon as I saw Mazeroski hit that ball I knew it was going to be a long winter.

ENOS SLAUGHTER

ENOS BRADSHER SLAUGHTER
Born: April 27, 1916, Roxboro, North Carolina
Major-league career: 1938–59, St. Louis Cardinals, New York
   Yankees, Kansas City Athletics, Milwaukee Braves
Lifetime average: .300

Despite the loss of three prime years in the Air Corps during World War II, Enos Slaughter still compiled a hit total of nearly 2,400. A nonstop hustler, the remarkable Slaughter hit .304 as a part-time player at the age of 42. His finest year was 1949, when he hit .336. He led the National League in hits once, doubles once, and triples twice.

I think the game of baseball is just like any other sport, in that you've got to keep your legs in shape. I was able to play for so many years because I took care of my legs. I've always been fond of hunting, and every winter I tried to do as much of it as I could, to get in all that walking. Even though I was living in St. Louis then, I'd still come back to North Carolina in the spring of the year and get out on a farm for two or three weeks and cut wood and maul wood and get shaped up that way, because, boy, I loved that farm life.

We used to have these good old wood choppin' contests; get up on the log with that ax and chop away. I can see the danger in that now—I could've cut off my foot as easy as not. One glance of that ax would have been enough. But nobody thought of that. We had a lot of fun cutting wood in those days.

You see, we used wood at that time to cure tobacco with. That was before your oil burners and gas burners came in to cure the tobacco. We'd cut the wood to about six- or eight-foot lengths and then take maul wedges and bust it open and stack it to dry. Later we'd put it in these big concrete and brick flues to cure our tobacco with. You could run that heat up to two hundred degrees in the barns, just throwing those good old logs into the fire. I tell you, that kind of work kept me in shape. I played ball until I was forty-three years old and was still doing a capable job.

I was born in Roxboro, North Carolina. I guess it was what you'd call a textile town, though there was also quite a bit of farming done around there, too.

My father owned a farm and we raised a little corn, some wheat, and tobacco, of course; tobacco was our money crop. There were five boys in our family and we took turns milking cows. I used to walk to and from school, and when it was my turn to milk the cows I'd come home and get my pails and go down to low ground where we kept the cows, and milk them until it got dark. Next morning I'd get up early and do my milking and then head for school. I was doing that until I got out of high school. You know the old saying: "You can take the boy out of the country, but you can't take the country out of the boy." I guess that's how you'd have to describe me. In fact, you know the nickname I had all through my baseball years—Country. Country Slaughter. I was strictly a country boy, and still am.

I was playing semipro ball with a team sponsored by one of the textile mills when I was recommended to a sportswriter for the Durham *Morning Herald*. He in turn contacted somebody in the Cardinal organization. Soon after, I got a letter from the Cardinals inviting me to Greensboro for a tryout that September. They said if I made good and they signed me up they would pay my expenses; otherwise I'd have to pay my own. That was all right with me; I just wanted the chance, because I was confident I could make good. So I went to Greensboro and was hitting the ball real well, but they said I was too slow and too clumsy to be a second baseman, which I fancied myself at that time. So they moved me to the outfield and I was signed up as an outfielder. This was in 1934.

Money? Never crossed my mind. I just wanted to play baseball. I signed a contract calling for $75 a month that first year. Coming off the farm, that looked like great money. Remember, this was during the Depression and there wasn't too much money stirring. The important thing to me was that I was getting the opportunity to play professional baseball.

I played at Martinsville, Virginia, in 1935. I had a little trouble with the strike zone—I struck out over a hundred times. I hit .273, but almost half of my hits were for extra bases. Mr. Rickey, who was general manager for the Cardinals then, noticed that. He noticed everything, that son of a gun. So he sent me to Columbus, Georgia, the next year, which was Class-B ball. Eddie Dyer was the manager there.

I got off to a poor start that year. I was hitting something like .220 for the first half of the season. Still having a tough time keeping my bat in the strike zone. I'll never forget one night, we were losing by a run and I was up with the bases loaded and the count was three and two. I swung at a pitch around my ankles and struck out. Eddie Dyer came up to me later.

"Kid," he said, "if you can learn where the strike zone is you've got a chance to go to the major leagues."

Well, hearing that must have done something for me. I found myself laying off the bad balls after that and wound up the season hitting .320. Another thing happened that year. You know, I always had this reputation for running on and off the field. In fact, it flatters me no end when I hear a young kid described as being an "Enos Slaughter type" because of his hustle. Well, that came about in 1936, at Columbus, Georgia. I used to come running in from right field and when I reached the third-base line I'd stop and walk the rest of the way to the dugout. One day Eddie Dyer said to me, "Son, if you're tired I'll get you some help." Don't ask me why, but those words made a tremendous impression on me, and from 1936 until I finished my career in 1961, I never walked on a ball field. I left the dugout running and I hit the top step running coming back. And I always ran out everything I hit; I put on the same speed whether I was running out a triple or a one-hopper to the pitcher. Didn't know any other way to play. And I trace it all back to that one remark Eddie Dyer made to me.

In 1937 they promoted me to Columbus, Ohio, in the American Association. That was Triple-A ball, one slice away from the top. I got off to a good start there and kept going. Ended up leading the league with .382. I was making all of $150 a month then. Branch Rickey, you know, was probably the most knowledgeable man that was ever in baseball, when it came to spotting talent. But he didn't like to pay out money. He'd go into the vault to get you a nickel change.

They had a big party for us at the end of the season, and I eased up to Mr. Rickey and asked him for a little bonus. He stared at me from out under those big bushy eyebrows, chewed his cigar a little, and said, "The older boys have been talking to you, haven't they, Slaughter?" So I didn't get a bonus.

I went up to the Cardinals the next year and wasn't exactly overpaid there either—$400 a month. This is the big leagues now. Around midseason they raised me to $600 a month, because I was hitting. In 1939 I hit .300 and led the league with 52 doubles and they were paying me $750 a month. That's not much more than they get in meal money today, I reckon.

When I joined the Cardinals in 1938 Frankie Frisch was still managing—it was his last year there—and he was a tough man to play for. Very critical, very demanding. From the McGraw school you know. But that didn't bother me. I didn't care who I played for, just so long as they gave me the chance to play, because I knew I could do the job. So I just kept my mouth shut—I was too scared to say anything anyway—and kept my eyes open.

Pepper Martin was with the Cardinals then, and so was Joe Medwick, Johnny Mize, Lon Warneke, and a lot of other good ones. Pepper Martin was quite a character. You never knew what to expect from him. We were in Boston one time and Frisch had him playing third. Pepper didn't like to play third because he hated to field bunts. Casey Stengel was managing the Braves then and before the game Pepper went up to Casey and said, "You'd better tell your guys not to bunt on me, because if they do I'm gonna hurt 'em." So naturally they started bunting. After a while Pepper got so mad that when he charged in and picked up the ball he'd throw it at the runner going down the line instead of to first base. He was zinging that ball right over their heads. He figured that was the best way to stop them.

Then Elbie Fletcher dropped one down the line that Pepper got a good jump on and when Elbie saw how quick Pepper had got that ball and saw him winding up with it, Elbie cut away

from the line and ran straight for the Cardinal dugout, ducking his head between his shoulders. I tell you, that ball came
like a bullet right over the button of his cap and smack into
the dugout and damn near cleared our bench. That ended the
bunting.

I'll never forget one day that spring, just before the season
opened. We were in Springfield, Missouri. Dizzy Dean came
into the clubhouse and started going around shaking hands
with everybody. He had just been sold to the Cubs. His arm
was bad, but everybody told me that Mr. Wrigley knew that
when he bought him. The Cubs wanted Dizzy, sore arm or no,
because every time he pitched there was a full house. But
even with the bad arm Dizzy went out and did a fine job for the
Cubs that year and helped them win the pennant. When he
came up to me that day he said, "Well, I'm not going to say
good-bye to you, because I'll be seeing you again soon." It
seems the Cubs had offered $100,000 for me—which the Car-
dinals turned down. That gave me something to think about:
The Cubs were willing to give $100,000 for me, and I was still
only making $400 a month at that time!

I can recall quite well the day Medwick got beaned. He had
been traded to the Dodgers and not long after the deal we
went into Ebbets Field. We had a young pitcher named Bob
Bowman on the mound, and he hit Joe in the head just about
as hard as I've ever seen anybody get hit. Some people thought
it was done intentionally, but I never believed that.

Chuck Dressen was coaching third base for the Dodgers at
that time, and he was great at stealing signs and letting the
batter know what was coming. Every time Bowman threw the
curve Dressen picked it off and whistled up to the batter. So
Don Padgett, who was catching, went out and told Bowman to
hold the ball like he was going to throw a curve and then
throw the fastball. That's one way to put a dent in somebody's
head, but that's the batter's lookout. Anyway, Bowman faked
the curve, Dressen whistled, and Medwick stepped into a fastball and got hit. Hit hard.

A big free-for-all broke out. That was always happening
with the Dodgers in those days. I remember it well because I
came running in from right field and grabbed the first guy I
saw—and who do you think I wound up with? Big Van Mungo.
And then Freddy Fitzsimmons collared me, and there I was,

caught between two of the biggest guys on the field. I was lucky to get out of there with my head on straight.

In 1941 we battled the Dodgers for the pennant. There was lots of low-bridging, lots of brawls. Whit Wyatt would throw in tight and so would Mort Cooper. And those guys could scorch that ball. We might have won it that year, but we had bad luck with injuries. Jimmy Brown had a broken nose, Terry Moore got hit in the head, and I broke a collarbone.

I can recall it so well. We were playing in St. Louis, the second game of a double-header against Pittsburgh. In the first inning Stu Martin, who used to be a Cardinal, hit a line shot to right-center and Terry Moore and I both went after it. We were both hollering for it and at the last second I saw Terry leave his feet. He dove and caught the ball and skidded right between my legs. I tried to jump him, and as I went over I hit his shoulder and flipped and broke my collarbone.

I was in the hospital for four weeks. Dr. Hyland, who was the team physician, wired my shoulder up, because I had a compound fracture. He said if I hadn't been an athlete he would have left the wire in permanently, but Dr. Hyland was the type of physician who made every effort to keep from putting bolts and wires into you because he was afraid it would cause you trouble later. So after four weeks he pulled the wires out of my shoulder. I went from the hospital right out to the ball park, where we were playing the Dodgers. Wyatt was pitching against Cooper, and beating him, 1–0. Billy Southworth sent me up to pinch-hit. Well, it would be nice to say I came out of the hospital and hit a home run. Unfortunately I didn't. Wyatt struck me out. It doesn't always happen the way it does in the storybooks, does it?

Because of all those injuries we found ourselves short of ballplayers. In September Mr. Rickey brought Stan Musial up from Rochester. We didn't catch the Dodgers that year, but it wasn't Musial's fault—he hit around .420 for the few weeks he was there.

You know, I hit at Musial when he was a left-handed pitcher in the Cardinal farm system. He started as a pitcher, but he came up with a bad arm and since they saw how well he could move that bat they converted him to an outfielder. But I don't think anybody knew what a great hitter he was going to be, because of that odd batting stance he had. I know I heard a lot of pitchers say he could be pitched to, but I never saw anybody do it successfully.

There were a lot of times when they would pass Musial to get at me. How did I feel about that? Well, I always loved to hit with men on base. And when they'd walk him to fill a base and pitch to me, it put another man on and just made me more determined to do something with that ball.

I'd have to say today that the 1942 Cardinals was the greatest club I ever played on. There was tremendous team play and desire; we felt like we just couldn't be beat. Never seemed to matter how many runs we were down in a game, we were always confident we could come back. You know, we didn't miss that pennant by much in '41, losing to the Dodgers by just a couple of games. So we were hungry. Young, talented, confident, and hungry. That's a combination hard to beat.

We had Johnny Hopp and Ray Sanders alternating at first base, Jimmy Brown on second, Marty Marion at short, Whitey Kurowski at third, and one of the best behind the plate, Walker Cooper. He'd be catching and a guy would come up to hit and Cooper would spit tobacco juice across his shoes. The guy would back out of the box and look at him, and Cooper would say, "Well, what are you going to do about it?" Here's this six-foot-four, 220-pounder, wearing a mask and chest protector. What were you going to do about it? Nothing. You got back in there and hit. He was a great guy though. Wasn't mean. Really very good-natured.

In the outfield we had Stan Musial, Terry Moore, and myself. And we had Mort Cooper and Johnny Beazley winning twenty games for us, and we had Max Lanier, Ernie White, Howie Pollett, Howie Krist, and some other good pitchers.

It was another tight pennant race with the Dodgers that year. You know, we were something like ten games behind in August, and we caught them and passed them. They won 104 games and we won 106.

That was my first World Series, in 1942. Anybody who tells you he's not nervous going into his first World Series is lying to you. Why, being nervous is part of it. If you're not nervous, then it isn't important, and to a ballplayer the World Series is the most important thing there is.

We opened in St. Louis, against the Yankees. Red Ruffing was pitching for them, and he showed us something. He had a no-hit, no-run game for seven and two-thirds innings before Terry Moore finally got a base hit and broke it up. We went into the last of the ninth getting beat, 7–0. Well, something happened then. We knocked Ruffing out and scored four runs and had the tying run at the plate before they stopped us. That rally, even though it fell short, was the turning point for us. It made us feel real good. We went into the clubhouse and said, "Well, we gave them one hell of a scare."

The next day Johnny Beazley went out and beat them, 4–3. I can recall that quite well. In the last of the eighth it was tied, 3–3. I came up and doubled and on the throw to second Rizzuto bobbled the ball and I went into third. Then Musial singled to center to put us ahead. In the top of the ninth, they had a man on first and Buddy Hassett singled to right field. I came running in and scooped it up and threw the man out at third. That broke the back of the inning and we won the ball game.

Then we went to New York and played them three games in Yankee Stadium. Ernie White and Spud Chandler hooked up together, and Ernie shut them out, 2–0. We beat them a wild ball game the next day, 9–6. Beazley came back in the fifth game. Johnny was just a rookie, you know, and he had a great season and a great Series. We were down 1–0 in the fourth inning, and I came up and hit one into the seats off of Ruffing to tie it. We went into the top of the ninth tied, 2–2. We got a man on and Whitey Kurowski hit one into the left-field seats. That gave us the game and the World Championship.

Everybody said what a great upset it was, us beating the Yankee team. But I don't think it was such an upset. Those 1942 Cardinals were a great ball club, that's all.

It was a happy moment for me, and a sad one at the same time, because on August 27 of that year I had enlisted in the Air Corps and I knew I'd be gone soon. I was finally called into service the twenty-third of January, 1943, and was gone for three years.

I wanted to be a pilot, but they said they wanted me to be a bombardier. Well, I didn't care anything about pushing a button, and I was grounded. They were going to ship me out then, but one of the colonels said they wouldn't have much of a team if they let me go. You see, we had a service league down there in San Antonio, with eight teams in it, and those officers took it very seriously. I was all set to go, had my bags packed and everything, when they got a wire the night before from the Eighth Service Command saying that they could keep me there.

I stayed at San Antonio for the next two years as a physical training instructor. I was fortunate in that I was able to continue playing baseball, keeping myself in pretty good shape. Hit .498 the first year in the service league, then the next year I fell to .420. The pitching started getting better, you see—fellows like Tex Hughson and Howard Pollett were showing up.

Then it turned out that the Navy was beating the Air Force pretty badly over in Honolulu. That didn't sit too well with Larry MacPhail, who had gotten himself a commission in the Air Force. So he had a hand in getting us shipped out to Honolulu. About forty-five ballplayers, mostly major leaguers and Triple-A players, were assembled in Kerns, Utah, and then sent up to Seattle where they put us aboard a ship and we all wound up in Honolulu.

Right after we got there, however, the Navy disbanded their team. That's the way things go in the service, I guess. So we never did get the chance to challenge them in Honolulu. I was stationed at Hickham Field, and on the team there we had Birdie Tebbetts, Billy Hitchcock, Pollett, Joe Marty; and then there was a team at Wheeler Field, with boys like Taft Wright, Max West, Lew Riggs, Ferris Fain, Sid Hudson, and Hughson. We played a lot of ball over there for the servicemen.

Then one day they called us all together and an officer spoke to us.

"Boys," he said, "if you'll volunteer to go out to the islands and play some ball for the fellows out there, we'll see you get shipped home real fast when the war is over."

We said we'd go. We were all willing, and anyway nobody wanted to take a chance on saying no. So we got our shots and they boarded us onto a ship—the PA-101, I'll never forget it—and we landed in Saipan on July 4, 1945. Then they divided us up. I was assigned to the B-29's of the 58th Bomb Wing on Tinian. We had two teams there and one over at Saipan, in the Mariana Islands. A long way from Roxboro, North Carolina. I'll say.

The first thing we had to do was build diamonds. I got in working with the Seabees, running a bulldozer, helping to carve out the ball field. They did the same thing on Saipan, and we played back and forth. The bleachers were built out of empty bomb crates and sometimes we had as many as 15,000 troops at a game. We were drawing better crowds on Saipan than they were in Philadelphia.

You've heard what great baseball fans the Japanese are. Well, when we got to Saipan there were still quite a few of them holed up in the hills. I'll be damned if they didn't sneak out and watch us play ball. We could see them sitting up there, watching the game. When it was over they'd fade back into their caves. But they could have got themselves killed for watching a ball game. Talk about real fans!

A lot of times we'd go out and sit on the edge of the runway and watch those B-29's taking off, one after the other. You know, we were on Tinian when that plane took off to drop the atomic bomb on Hiroshima. Of course nobody knew what was up. That was the best-kept secret of the war. Later on we met the crew that had dropped the bomb. They were a pretty quiet bunch of boys.

Well, after the war they kept their word to us. They assembled us together at Guam and we got aboard a ship and headed for home. On the way back we ran into the tail end of a typhoon; our ship was supposed to be eleven days back but we wound up taking nineteen. Three of those days they kept us locked down under because the ship was doing a thirty-nine-degree angle. You never saw so many pale and sickly faces. The ship was creaking and crying and we were just praying she'd hold together. Finally when we got up out of the hole the ocean was still wild. It looked like a blue mountain that wouldn't stand still; it would be so high, and the next thing you knew you'd be looking down and not seeing bottom—that's how much that old ship was tossing and pitching. But it was okay, because we knew we were headed home.

So I came out of the service in pretty good shape, and a good thing I was, too. They were calling me an old man—I was thirty years old then. That was a laugh; hell, I had fourteen more seasons ahead of me in the big leagues. Led the league in RBI's my first year back with 130. Then we got into that play-off with the Dodgers. Ended up in a flatfooted tie. First time in baseball history that had ever happened.

It was a best two-out-of-three series. The first game was in

St. Louis, and we beat them there, 4–2. Then we took that long train ride back to Brooklyn, to play the second game at Ebbets Field. We jumped out to a big lead and were ahead, 8–1, going into the last of the ninth. Murry Dickson was pitching for us. They got a rally going, knocked Dickson out and the next thing we knew it was 8–4 and the bases were loaded and their big first baseman, Howie Schultz, was the batter.

Eddie Dyer was managing the Cardinals then. He brought in our lefty screwball pitcher, Harry Brecheen. Well, that Ebbets Field was a madhouse. You can imagine, in a situation like that. But that Brecheen, nothing bothered him. He worked the count full and then threw the prettiest screwball you'd ever want to see and struck Schultz out. That gave us the ball game and the pennant.

We got on the train and went back to St. Louis to open the Series against the Red Sox. They beat us the first game, 3–2, when Rudy York hit a home run in the tenth inning. Then we battled them around and after the fifth game we were down three to two. We played that fifth game in Boston and Joe Dobson beat us, 6–3. So we were in trouble. And I was in trouble myself. You see, in the fifth inning Dobson hit me with a pitch on my right elbow. It really gave me a sting, but I wanted to stay in there. I went ahead and tried to hit one more time, but the elbow had swelled up so much that I couldn't even swing the bat, and I couldn't throw a lick. So I went to Eddie Dyer and for the first time in my career asked to be taken out of a ball game.

"Skipper," I said, "I can't do you any good. I can't throw and I can't swing a bat. Better get me out of there."

Doc Weaver, the club trainer, took me into the clubhouse and put ice packs on the elbow, but it didn't feel like it was doing much good. We had to go back to St. Louis that night to finish the Series. When I got on the train Doc wrapped my arm up with a towel and epsom salt and I put on an electric jacket that the pitchers wore in the bull pen on cold days, plugged it in and stayed put on the train all the way back to St. Louis.

When we got to St. Louis Doctor Hyland took me right to the hospital and x-rayed my arm. Then he came to me with a sad look on his face.

"Eno," he said, "I'm sorry to say, but you've got such a bad hemorrhage that if you get hit on it again the chances are I'll have to amputate your arm."

"Doc," I said, "I guess we'll have to take that gamble."

So I played in the sixth game and Brecheen beat Mickey Harris to even up the Series. No, I wasn't worrying about my arm. I just played my game, that's all. Took my chances.

Then we went into the seventh game. The seventh game of the World Series. Say it aloud—it's got a *sound* to it, doesn't it? The first game is all nerves and excitement, but that seventh game, that's in a class by itself. By the time that game comes up you're a bunch of battle-scarred veterans.

We had them down 3–1 going to the top of the eighth and they got two runs. So we went into the bottom of the eighth tied up. Bob Klinger was pitching for them, a former National Leaguer. I led off the inning with a base hit. Whitey Kurowski tried to sacrifice but popped up. Then Del Rice flied out. Harry Walker was the next batter. With two out and Harry not being a long-ball hitter, I figured it might be good strategy to try and steal; then if Harry poked a hit I'd be home. I took off to steal second and Harry hit one into left center, not too hard. I had got a good jump and when I got to second and saw where the ball was going I said to myself, "I can score."

You know, there was some background to that play. In an earlier game in the Series Mike Gonzales, our third-base coach, had stopped me at third on a bad relay throw and we lost that ball game. I went to Eddie Dyer and told him I thought I could have scored easily if I hadn't been held up.

"Well," he said, "from now on if you think you've got a legitimate chance, with two out, you go ahead and try it and I'll back you up."

So that was in the back of my mind when I went around second base. I kept going. I never broke stride. I had it in my head that I was going to score. Sometimes you just make up your mind about something and everything else gets locked out. I still don't know to this day if Mike Gonzales ever gave me the stop sign or not. It wouldn't have made a lick of difference if he'd had. I rounded third and kept going. When I got ready to slide into home I saw Roy Partee, the catcher, take about two or three steps up in front of the plate and I slid across easily.

You know, they've made Pesky the goat of that Series because when he took the relay from the outfield he hesitated for a second before pegging it home. Well, I don't go along with that. Anytime an infielder has to go out to take a relay his back is to the play and it's up to his teammates to let him know where the runner is. Bobby Doerr, who was playing second for the Red Sox, told me later that with 36,000 people up on their feet yelling, nobody could hear anything. So Pesky didn't know where I was or what I was doing and nobody could tell him, because of the noise. If somebody would have told him where I was he probably could have thrown me out by ten feet. I've seen the films, and what he did after he caught the ball was turn toward second base because Walker had rounded the bag and was coming toward second; then he saw me out of the corner of his eye coming home, and he had to turn again and threw off stride to home, and I was able to slide in safely.

They called it "Enos Slaughter's Mad Dash Home." I guess I'll always be remembered for that more than for anything else, and that's just fine with me, because it was right in my style of play.

You know, a few years ago they had us back to St. Louis for the twenty-fifth anniversary of the Series between the Cardinals and Red Sox. The public relations people asked me if I could re-enact the "Mad Dash."

"I'll try," I said. "I don't know if I can make it or not, but I'll try."

They had made every effort to get as many of the original players back on the field as they could. Pesky was there at shortstop, Roy Partee was behind the plate, and they had Joe Dobson pitching this time. They couldn't get Harry Walker to hit the ball because he was managing Houston at that time, but they did get his brother Dixie. So I'm on first and when Dobson delivered the ball I broke. Well, you wouldn't believe it, but Dixie hit the same type of ball to left center that Harry had hit twenty-five years before. And I'm going. Huffing and puffing, but going. Heck, I'm fifty-five years old now. I barrel around second. Then I come into third, and I go around third. Pesky takes the relay and throws to the plate, and doggone if his peg doesn't pull Partee up the line again and I slide in and score, twenty-five years later. Exact same thing. If we'd rehearsed it for a year we couldn't have done it any more perfect. But, boy, I'll tell you, I was pooped.

Later on I told Pesky, "We'll do it again twenty-five years from now."

He said, "You'll never make it."

You can't tell. I'll be only eighty years old then, and you know I keep my legs in shape.

In 1954 I'd been in the Cardinal organization for nearly twenty years and loved every minute of it. I loved the Cardinals. When Mr. Busch took over the team, my contract was the first one he ever signed. "Enos," he said at that time, "you're a credit to the game and you'll always be with us."

We go to spring training and I have a good spring. Then we come back to St. Louis and are playing a preseason series with the Browns. On Saturday I help beat Bob Turley with a double. On Sunday I'm not in the lineup, which felt strange to me. In the latter part of the game I'm sitting on the bench and Eddie Stanky, who was managing then, looked at me and said, "Slaughter, go on and get dressed. The general manager would like to see you in his office." It never dawned on me about being traded.

So I went and got dressed and went on up to see Dick Meyer, who was the general manager.

"Eno," he said, "all things have to come to an end. We've sold you to the New York Yankees."

Well, it floored me. It cut my heart out. I cried. I cried like a baby. I couldn't help it. I'd been a Cardinal since 1935, and I don't think anybody who's ever worn a Cardinal uniform was ever more loyal to it than I was or put out as hard as I did or gave as much. But you go. Of course you go. You have to. Somebody says to you, "That's baseball." You get a few handshakes and walk away from twenty years of your life.

So I joined the Yankees and, believe me, I gave them the same one hundred percent that I had given the Cardinals. In fact I even gave them some of my blood. There was a brawl one day, I think it was the worst I ever saw on a ball field. We were in a tough race with the White Sox and tempers were running a little high. In this one game Art Ditmar was pitching and Larry Doby was hitting. Elston Howard was the catcher, and Nellie Fox was on first. Doby was a low-ball hitter and we were trying to pitch him high and tight. So Ditmar brushed him back on a couple of pitches. Then the next one got away from Howard and went all the way back to the stands. Fox rounded second and went to third, and Ditmar went in to cover the plate. I don't know what was said, but he and Doby had a few words. Then Ditmar came back to the mound and Doby stepped in to hit.

Billy Martin was playing second base, and he came in to the mound and asked Ditmar what Doby had said. Next thing that happens Billy Martin is yelling at Doby. So Doby starts for the mound and Ditmar starts for home plate. A couple of punches were thrown. Well, you know what happens then. Both benches flared up and everybody is on the field. Bill Skowron came over and tackled Doby. Then big Walt Dropo, and I mean big—six feet six, 240 pounds—comes over and jumps on Skowron. So they're three deep on the ground there.

Well, along with everybody else, I'd run off the bench and tried to get in there. Wasn't mad at anybody, just trying to help out. You know how it is when a fight's swarming over the field. Jim Rivera grabbed me by the belt and said, "Hey, Enos, you don't wanna get in there." That was good advice and I should have listened.

Finally I got in the middle of that thing and took hold of Walt Dropo's collar and said, "Walt, get up off of them." Then somebody got hold of me and jerked me backwards while I was still holding Dropo by the collar. So now I'm choking Dropo. Man, that didn't rile him! He got up snorting and ran over the top of everybody and grabbed my uniform and tried to measure me off. He never did land a lick, fortunately, because I was like a little bantam rooster, darting around under those big arms while he was swinging. He ripped my whole jersey right off of me. Then I look up and there's my roomie, Whitey Ford, up on Dropo's back, and Dropo is carrying him along like a little old bumblebee, still trying to get at me.

Well, finally we all cooled off. A couple of policemen came and took Billy Martin and me off the field. As I was going off, one of the umpires picked up my cap and put it on my head backwards. Billy and me went into the clubhouse and had a beer and sat there and watched on television while the Yankees went ahead and won the ball game.

I didn't play all that much for the Yankees; Stengel had me alternating against right- and left-hand pitchers with Hank Bauer. Then early in 1955 they traded Johnny Sain and myself over to Kansas City, which at that time people called the

Yankee farm team in the American League because of all the deals that went back and forth between those two clubs. I had a good year for Kansas City, hitting over .300. Then a year later the Yankees bought me back. This is 1956 now. We won the pennant that year and went into the World Series against the Dodgers. We played a few games that Series that I'll always remember. One of them, of course, was the perfect, no-hit, no-run game that Don Larsen pitched. I was in left field in that one. That put us up three to two and we went over to Ebbets Field for the sixth game.

The sixth game was one of the finest pitching duels ever in a World Series. Bob Turley and Clem Labine hooked up and it was 0–0 all the way to the bottom of the tenth inning. The Dodgers got men on first and second with two out and Jackie Robinson was the batter. Well, what I figured I ought to do was play a medium left field, where I had a chance to throw the man out at the plate on a base hit, and still have time to go back for a fly ball. But what Robinson did was hit one of those line drives that come out there like it's shot out of a rifle. I went back as quick as I could and jumped against the wall, but the ball hit up there and the winning run scored. Some of the newspapermen wrote that I'd misjudged the ball, but that was wrong; it was hit just too quick for me to get back on it.

Anyway, Johnny Kucks shut them out in the final game and we won the World Series. We won pennants again in '57 and '58. So I got into three World Series with the Yankees. I enjoyed my years with the Yankees very much. But I guess deep in my heart I was a Cardinal, and always would be, even though they'd hurt me awful bad.

VIC RASCHI

VICTOR JOHN ANGELO RASCHI
Born: March 28, 1919, West Springfield, Massachusetts
Major-league career: 1946–55, New York Yankees, St. Louis
    Cardinals, Kansas City Athletics
Lifetime record: 132 wins, 66 losses

In his prime years with the Yankees, Vic Raschi was known as one of baseball's finest clutch pitchers. The three-time 20-game winner also posted five World Series victories and in 1951 led the American League in strikeouts. Since 1900 only Spud Chandler, Whitey Ford, and Lefty Grove have posted a higher winning percentage than Raschi's .667.

There was something special about being a Yankee back in those years. We believed we were the best and that we couldn't lose. It wasn't arrogance, it was pride. We used to go out there each day with every expectation of winning. And when we didn't win, then it was more than just losing a ball game, because it hurt our pride.

They began cultivating it in the minor-league system. They let you know that you were part of a great winning tradition that began with Babe Ruth and Lou Gehrig. It was drilled into you that once you made the Yankees you would be entering that tradition, that playing for the New York Yankees was the height of anybody's baseball career.

In 1949 the Red Sox came into New York to close out the season with a two-game series, leading us by one. All they had to do was win once to take the pennant. They had a rookie pitcher, whose name I forget at the moment. Well, just before the Saturday game we overheard some of the Red Sox talking about starting this rookie on Sunday. In other words, they were so confident of beating us on Saturday that they were looking forward to relaxing in the last game, figuring they'd have wrapped it up by then. This was the way they felt. I suppose they were entitled to feel confident; but it made us kind of mad and gave us some added incentive—not that we weren't primed for those games to begin with.

Well, they did jump off to a 4–0 lead in that game. But we tied it and then won it on Johnny Lindell's home run and some great relief pitching by Joe Page. So we went into Sunday's game tied for first place and I guess they forgot about starting that rookie.

Ball games just don't come any bigger than that, do they? Not only are you tied for first place on the last day of the season, but you're playing the team that you're tied with.

To make things just a little more difficult for us, Joe Di-Maggio had been sick for about a week with a virus and wasn't up to full strength. He couldn't run too well, but he was in there, and we wanted him in there.

I had a pretty good idea that I would be pitching that game and I was pleased about it. You have to get back to pride again; everything was riding on this one game and the team was entrusting me to win it for them. I knew that as long as I stayed in baseball, no matter how many times I went to the mound, I would never pitch a game bigger than this one.

I never talked too much before I pitched, because I had a lot of thinking to do. You've heard of pitchers psyching themselves before a game; well, it can help quite a bit, but I think it helps even more if you get a kind of sweaty feeling in the palm of your hand. That's anticipation. I had never experienced a build-up and an anxiety before a game to such an extent. And they can say what they want to, but they all get it. I wouldn't give one penny for any ballplayer who didn't get that anxiety; I wouldn't want him playing beside me.

I think it was fitting that it turned out to be a close, hard-fought game. We scored a run in the bottom of the first inning. Phil Rizzuto hit a triple and Tommy Henrich brought him in with a ground ball. After that it was nip and tuck all the way. Nothing but zeroes up on the scoreboard, and that big, big Sunday crowd sitting back and watching.

Ellis Kinder was pitching for them and he was going beautifully. But then in the top of the eighth they had to take him out for a pinch hitter. Mel Parnell came in. Henrich hit a home run and then we loaded the bases off of Tex Hughson and Jerry Coleman cleared them with a double that Al Zarilla just missed catching in right field.

So we went into the ninth inning leading by five runs. It should have been easy, but it wasn't. The Red Sox still had some kick left in them. They got two men on and Bobby Doerr hit one into deep center. Normally, DiMaggio would have caught that ball, but he was so sick and worn out that he couldn't catch up with it. It fell in for a triple. Joe took himself out of the game, right then and there. Cliff Mapes went into center and the next batter flied out to him. That was two out. But Billy Goodman singled and that made it 5–3. Birdie Tebbetts was up next, and he was the tying run.

When the ball came back into the infield after Goodman's hit, Henrich got it and walked it over to the mound. I knew he wanted to say something encouraging, but before he could open his mouth I said, "Give me the goddamned ball and get the hell out of here." Poor Tom wasn't expecting that. He handed me the ball and scatted out of there.

Well, a moment later Tom had the ball back in his hand when Tebbetts fouled out to him. We'd won a pennant.

I started the second game of the Series that year, against the Dodgers. We had won the first game, 1–0, behind Allie Reynolds. The score of the second game was 1–0 again, but we didn't win it. Preacher Roe beat me, and it was my own fault.

In the second inning Jackie Robinson doubled and got over to third, and Gil Hodges was the batter. Right here is where I made my mistake. One of the things they teach a pitcher is how to work when there's a fast man on third base. If you decide to pitch out of a windup you've got to make up your mind that the runner on third isn't going to bother you; you keep your concentration fixed on the batter. If you can't do that, if you're going to worry about the man stealing home, then you work out of a stretch position.

So Jackie Robinson was on third, and he was just about the best base runner I've ever seen. He could get away from a standing position in a flash; by his second or third stride he was going at full speed. I'd never pitched with him on base before and I was going into a full windup. But his movements were distracting me—remember how he used to agitate on the bases? You never knew what he was going to do, and he was fully capable of doing almost anything he wanted. So I decided I had better switch over and work from a stretch position. But you can see right there what happened—Robinson had broken my concentration. I was pitching more to Robinson than I was to Hodges, and as a result I threw one up into Gil's power and he got the base hit that beat me.

When I went into the dugout nobody dared say a word. I knew what had happened and everybody else knew what had happened. That was the only run of the game, and it was my own fault. I think that was the only mistake I made in that game; but you don't have to make too many when you lose 1–0, do you?

I guess I began to take baseball seriously when I was a freshman in high school in Springfield, Massachusetts. We were playing in a scholastic tournament and a Yankee scout by the name of Gene McCann was scouting it. He came up to me after the game and said he would like to talk to my parents and me about a career in professional baseball.

He visited the house one evening and told us what he had in mind. After I graduated high school the Yankees would get me a scholarship at a college and pay my way through. My only obligation was to give the Yankees first crack at me after I had completed my college education.

Well, I wanted to go on to college, but this was during the Depression and my family didn't have much money. So, with my father's blessings, I accepted the Yankees' offer and they arranged for me to go to William and Mary, down in Virginia.

I'd had a few other offers at the same time. The St. Louis Cardinals wanted to sign me, but they would have put me right into their minor-league system. The Cleveland Indians were also interested. As a matter of fact, they invited me up to Boston to work out with them at Fenway Park.

I took the train to Boston, feeling pretty excited about it. Steve O'Neill himself, who was managing the Indians, met me at the station and took me out to the ball park. In the clubhouse they gave me a Cleveland uniform to put on and then I went out onto the field. I was only sixteen years old and there I was, wearing a big-league uniform, working out in a big-league ball park, and keeping my eye on fellows like Mel Harder, Earl Averill, Hal Trosky, Johnny Allen.

Steve O'Neill told me to loosen up my arm easily, that he wanted to see me throw to a catcher. In a little while he brought a catcher over and I pitched to him. I cut loose and threw as hard as I could and felt pretty good about myself.

Then this kid walked out and started to warm up. You couldn't help but notice him because he had this big, flashy windup. He started throwing harder and harder. Each pitch seemed so much faster than the previous. I'd never seen anybody throw a ball like that. Pretty soon it sounded like it was exploding when it hit the catcher's mitt. He was throwing bullets, just plain bullets. "Good God!" I said to myself. No way was I going to compete with this guy.

It was Bob Feller, of course. I hadn't heard of him yet at that time. But it was marvelous to watch him throw that ball, and demoralizing, too. Heck, we were about the same age.

You know, I had the reputation for staring hitters down, for standing out there and glaring at them once they got set in the batter's box. Well, that was true, and it was all very carefully calculated. I figured if I could break their concentration when they came up to the plate I had them beat, or at least gained an advantage. Once you had made them turn their eyes away you had a slight psychological edge, in my opinion. But there was one guy you couldn't do it to. Want to take a guess who? That's right—Ted Williams. Well, what do you do with a guy that's been staring at *you* from the moment he's left the dugout to go out into the on-deck circle, and keeps his eyes on your eyes when he steps into the batters' box. How long can you stand out there and stare at a guy? The ball game's got to go on, doesn't it? He was the one man I couldn't stare down. You see, Ted's concentration up at the plate was so intense I don't think he even knew what I was trying to do.

I don't know how I would have fared trying that on Joe DiMaggio. I was fortunate in having Joe as a teammate and so never had to face him. He was the greatest all-around ballplayer I ever saw. He was a quiet leader on a ball club. Never said much, never argued. But at the same time he evoked tremendous respect and inspiration. A great team man.

You almost never saw him say anything to an umpire, and if he did, it was usually quietly, so that the fans never knew it. When he got mad he would give the dirt a little kick—that was the extent of it, that little kick at the dirt. When they threw at him he'd never say anything. He wouldn't come back to the dugout cursing, asking our pitcher to deck somebody in retaliation. Did they throw at him much? Sure they did, especially in Detroit. Detroit had some pretty mean guys on their staff. Dizzy Trout would throw at you, and so would Virgil Trucks and Freddy Hutchinson. But Joe never complained. Personally, I never thought it very good strategy to throw at guys like Joe or Ted Williams. They could beat you when they were happy; get them mad and they'd kill you.

We talked about Bob Feller before. Well, of course I got to pitch against Bob later when I was with the Yankees. One game will always stand out in my mind. It was a night game in Cleveland, back in 1950, in August. Bob and I hooked up in a real duel. We were leading, 1–0, in the eighth inning, and I was on third base with one out and Phil Rizzuto was the batter.

They put the squeeze play on. Phil laid the ball down just right, and I was slow getting away from third—I wasn't the fastest thing on two feet anyway. Luke Easter fielded the ball and threw home, and there's Jim Hegan waiting for me. Well, I slid in and all I could see was shinguards—Hegan knew how to block the plate. I was out, but we won the game anyway, 1–0.

At about three o'clock in the morning I woke up with a terrific pain in my right knee. It turned out I had torn the cartilages on the outside of that knee. We didn't tell anybody, though. We kept it quiet for two years because they didn't want anybody bunting on me and taking advantage of the bad knee.

I had a lot of trouble running and tried to stay off the bases as much as I could. But finally they had to operate on that knee, and it was a successful operation. A few years later, during the winter, I slipped and sure enough, tore it up again. It finally led to my giving up baseball.

George Weiss was the general manager when I was with the Yankees and he was a tough man. A little while ago we talked about staring a man down; well, here was someone who would never look at you. You'd talk to him and he would be looking everywhere but at you. You always got the impression he was thinking, *What's this guy want and how can I get rid of him in a hurry?*

When it came to negotiating a contract he would let you know that the whole Yankee organization had had a hand in winning the pennant. Talking to him, you felt your own contribution getting smaller and smaller. What used to irritate him when we talked salary was my not quibbling over my earned run average, my wins, my shutouts, etc. I never talked to him along those lines. The only thing I would ever discuss with him was my value to the ball club. Was I valuable to the Yankees or wasn't I? This irritated him, because he had nothing to come back on, no counterarguments to make.

After winning 21 ball games three years in a row I dropped down to 16 in 1952. That winter I went in to talk contract with Mr. Weiss.

"Didn't have such a good year, did you?" he said.

"Yes," I said. "I know that."

"I think we'll have to cut your contract," he said.

"I don't think that's fair," I said. "Look at the years I've put in. I've had a bad knee and still went out there. I had a bad knee last year and still won sixteen ball games, and we won the pennant."

We argued back and forth and didn't get anywhere. Finally I left, telling him I'd see him down in spring training. This made him mad; he liked to have everything settled before camp opened. When finally we agreed and I signed a contract, it was on terms that were more satisfactory to me than they were to him. After I had signed, he said to me, very sternly, "Don't you *ever* have a bad year."

I won 13 games that year and he sent me a contract calling for a twenty-five percent cut. Same thing. I told him I'd see him in spring training. I went down to St. Petersburg and never saw him. The next thing I knew, newspapermen were coming out to the cottage where I was staying.

"You've just been traded to the Cardinals," they said.

That's how I found out about it. Weiss never told me. I'd had the bad year he had warned me about—if you want to call 13 and 6 a bad year—and he got rid of me. I was awfully disappointed about it. I'd been a Yankee for a long time.

I decided I'd better call my mother and tell her, rather than have her hear it over the radio. When I got her on the phone,

I said, "Mom, I've got something to tell you. I was just traded from the Yankees to the St. Louis Cardinals."

"That's wonderful," she said. "I'm happy, really happy."

I was dumbfounded. "What do you mean, you're 'really happy'?" I asked.

"I never wanted you to be a Yankee," she said. "I never liked the Yankees."

"You didn't?" I asked.

"No," she said. "I always wished you could be a Boston Red Socker."

How do you like that? All those years my mother was wishing I was with the Red Sox.

MONTE IRVIN

MONFORD MERILL IRVIN
Born: February 25, 1919, Columbia, Alabama
Major-league career: 1949–56, New York Giants, Chicago
  Cubs
Lifetime average: .293

Because of the color barrier, Monte Irvin did not reach the big leagues until he was thirty years old. In a few short years, however, he established himself as one of the National League's premier right-handed hitters. In 1951 he was the power hitter behind the Giants' remarkable drive to their "miracle" pennant, batting .312 and leading the league in runs batted in with 121.

In 1973 Irvin was elected by a special committee to the Hall of Fame in recognition of his outstanding play in the Negro Leagues.

I got out of the service in September, 1945. I had been away from baseball for a few years, so I went down to Puerto Rico to sharpen my skills a little bit. A few months later we heard that the Dodgers had signed Jackie Robinson.

Yes, it came as a surprise. Originally we had heard that Branch Rickey had signed Jackie to play for a team called the Brown Bombers in Brooklyn, to play in Ebbets Field when the Dodgers were on the road. But then the straight story came out, that he would be given a chance to play for Montreal and that if he was good enough he'd move up to the parent club. I was delighted for Jackie, and it gave hope to a lot of us. Hopefully he was going to open the door for other black players to follow.

So we followed Jackie's progress very carefully. There was a lot at stake, and not just for Jackie, not just for the other black ballplayers, not just for baseball; it went beyond that. We knew, of course, that he was going to have to take an awful lot. I guess we knew better than anybody else what he was going to have to put up with.

It was nail-biting time. If Jackie had not been able to stand up under the pressure, I don't know what would have happened, I don't know where it would have gone from there. But you know the story. Under all the pressure—and the pressure was tremendous—he handled himself well. He was a great ballplayer, a dynamic ballplayer, and every day that he played he pushed that door open just a little bit wider for the rest of us who were waiting to get through.

The amazing thing about Robinson was that during those first few years he was very stoic about what he was undergoing, accepting the abuse and the insults without saying a word. Then, after he had made it and been accepted, you found out what kind of fires he had inside him, how explosive and aggressive he really was. Those first few years must have been hell for him. I understand that Branch Rickey was talking to him all the time, telling him to keep that temper under control, not to provoke any incidents.

As I said, I followed Jackie's progress very carefully. I was only twenty-seven at the time, and I was hoping that the opportunity to go into organized ball might come my way.

I was born in Columbia, Alabama. My family moved to New Jersey when I was about eight years old. So I remember very little about Alabama; all my memories are, for the most part, about New Jersey. We were sharecroppers in Alabama and we couldn't make a decent living there. My older brother and sister had come to New Jersey and they found out how much better the opportunities were. So the rest of us decided to follow. This was around 1927.

It was great growing up in New Jersey. There were ten of us, living all together in the same house. Of course we were as poor as everybody else, but we were healthy, hard-working, and just one big happy family.

It was rough making a living during the Depression. We had just the bare necessities. But my father and brothers worked at a dairy, so we had plenty of milk. And my father had a green thumb, so we had a garden and lots of fresh vegetables. We all pitched in. When I was old enough I worked in a bowling alley, setting up pins. Later on I got a job helping to deliver milk. In those days they delivered milk by horse and wagon. I liked that, because not only was I earning money, but I was building up my legs, going up and down that wagon all day. I was about twelve or thirteen years old then.

I was always interested in athletics. My best sport when I was growing up was football. But at that time the door hadn't been opened in football either. Also, I knew that as far as injuries were concerned, you were less likely to hurt yourself at baseball. So I took the baseball route. I'll tell you, I had a lot of confidence in myself. I didn't think anybody could beat me at playing baseball. I could run, I could throw, I could hit the ball as far as anybody. In fact, they still talk about some of the balls I hit when I was playing around New Jersey. I was a shortstop then, and I had a real good arm; sometimes, if the pitcher didn't show up, they'd send me out to the mound. I remember pitching against Hank Borowy when we were high school kids. But I loved to hit. I always had a lot of power.

There was a man operating a team in Newark, named Abe Manley. He'd heard about me and thought he would come up and take a look. I guess he liked what he saw, because he said he wanted to sign me. There was no bonus, of course. In those days you had to consider yourself lucky if you were asked. So I jumped at the chance. This was in 1937. I had to play under an assumed name and only on the road, because I was attending college at the time—Lincoln College, in Pennsylvania. I was majoring in history, with hopes of teaching someday. Actually, what I wanted to do was become a dentist, but I didn't have any money and didn't have any hopes of getting any. So in 1939 I left college after two years and became a full-time member of the Newark Eagles.

I didn't know back then whether or not I'd ever get the chance to play in organized ball. I was always optimistic, but I couldn't be sure, because if you weren't around at that time, you don't know how intense feelings about it were. The mood of the country was completely different then. You know, I starred at Orange High School for four years. High school athletes generally are regarded fondly in their hometown, right? Well, the night I graduated I went with a date and another fellow and his date to a restaurant two blocks away from the school—and we were turned away. They wouldn't let us in. This is pretty hard to take. But there wasn't anything we could do about it.

After the war things began to change for the better, particularly in organized baseball. But before that happened, there were a lot of good black ballplayers who passed from the scene without ever having had the right opportunity. I'm not talking about just the men we've put in the Black Hall of Fame already, but many others, men like Willie Welles, Oscar Charleston, John Henry Lloyd, Ray Dandridge, Leon Day. These men would have been outstanding, if those barriers hadn't been up against them.

Sure, there was a lot of talk among the players at the time about the color barrier. We just couldn't understand why the feeling against us was so intense. Everybody had gone to school together, done a lot of things together—so why couldn't we play professional baseball together? We hit the same ball, ran the same way, threw the same way, played by the same rules—so what was the difference? When we weren't playing league games we played exhibition games against white teams, and a lot of the white players used to tell us that some of us should be in the major leagues. They knew the barrier was wrong, an awful lot of them did. But it wasn't time yet.

In 1947, a short while after Jackie made the big leagues, I signed with the Dodgers. But then Branch Rickey couldn't get together with the Newark ball club for compensation. Mrs. Manley, who pretty much ran the club's business, wanted a certain amount of money for my contract, and Rickey didn't want to give it. She raised such a fuss about it that the whole thing was dropped. Then Horace Stoneham came along. He'd seen that the Dodgers were signing black players, so I guess he figured he had better start thinking in those terms, too.

This wasn't until early in 1949. I was playing ball in Cuba that winter. A Giant scout named Alex Pompez approached Henry Thompson and myself. He told us we'd get the minimum salary—about $5,000 then—but that the Giants thought we had the ability to play in the major leagues. He wanted to know if we were interested. We sure were.

I was excited, naturally, but at the same time a little apprehensive. I didn't know what it was going to be like. Jackie had had a few unpleasant incidents, which we knew about, of course. We figured it was going to be rough, but it was an opportunity and at the same time something new was happening and we wanted to be part of it. There were some rough moments, especially in the South, but we were young, and we so badly wanted the opportunity to play in the big leagues that we were willing to put up with whatever came our way.

I started off the 1949 season with Jersey City and did all right. After about a half season I was hitting .373 and they brought me up, along with Hank Thompson. Leo Durocher was managing the Giants then. He couldn't have been nicer. He welcomed us very warmly and introduced us around. Then he talked to us privately.

"Fellows," he said, "it's no different from what you've been doing everywhere else. Just go out and play your own game and you'll be all right."

The following spring the Giants decided to go with Don Mueller as their right fielder and sent me back to Jersey City for a little more seasoning. I played there for about a month and was hitting .510. I guess they figured that was seasoning enough and brought me back up. I went into the regular lineup then and stayed there.

Willie Mays? I think most anybody who saw him will tell you that Mays is the greatest ballplayer that ever lived. He could do everything: run, field, throw, hit, hit with power, steal bases. I don't think there was ever a center fielder, be it Tris Speaker or Joe DiMaggio or Terry Moore or anybody else, who was better than Willie in going and getting a ball. He would play shallow, catching the line drives and would-be Texas Leaguers, and at the same time you couldn't hit anything over his head. At the crack of the bat he was gone. And of course he had an arm like a cannon; you could never take an extra base on him.

Willie joined the club a month or so into the season in '51. They brought him up from Minneapolis, where he was hitting .477. Leo assigned him to room with me and we became good friends. He was a fine young man, with a wonderful, happy-go-lucky disposition. No inhibitions. All he wanted to do was play ball. He was a tonic to have around, and not just for his great ability. Everybody was extremely fond of him.

Playing alongside Willie every day was exciting. He kept

pulling one miracle after another and as many times as you watched him you still never quite got used to it. One day he made this unbelievable catch in Pittsburgh, off of Rocky Nelson. He was playing in close and Rocky got hold of one and drove it way out into that big center field they had in old Forbes Field. Willie whirled around and took off after it. At the last second he saw he couldn't get his glove across his body in time to make the catch, so he caught it in his bare hand.

Leo was flabbergasted. We all were.

"I've never seen anything like that in my life," Leo said.

Then Leo decided to have a little fun with Willie. He told us to give Mays the silent treatment when Willie came in after the inning. You know, you do that sometimes, after a guy has done something spectacular on the field and is expecting the big noisy reception when he comes in. So when Willie came back to the dugout nobody said a word. We just sat there with our arms folded and stared out at the field, ignoring him completely. Willie was puzzled. He sat there looking around waiting for somebody to say something. Finally he couldn't contain himself any longer.

"Leo," he said, "didn't you see what I just did out there?"

Durocher didn't say anything.

"Leo," Willie said. "Didn't you see what I did?"

Leo turned around and looked at him, poker-faced. "No," he said, "I didn't see it. So you'll have to go out and do it again before I'll believe it."

And then there was that great catch he made on Vic Wertz in the 1954 Series. I never thought he had a chance to get even close to it. You know, he likes to play that catch down. But let me tell you, that's one of the greatest outfield plays I've ever seen. I was going out there to play the rebound, hoping to hold Wertz to a triple. That ball was *hit*. But Willie caught it. Don't ask me how. But there he was, going a mile-a-minute, his back to the plate. When the inning was over and we were on our way in, I said to him, "Nice going, roomie. I didn't think you'd get to that one." Very casually, he said, "I had that one all the way. Had it all the way." And I said, "Oh, you did, huh? Well, okay."

But you talk about World Series games, why, we played twenty-two of those each season—every time we played the Dodgers. Those games were always something special. It didn't matter where we were in the standings—though in those years we were usually both right around the top—it was always a battle.

We'd look at the schedule, see the Dodgers were coming up and a terrific sense of anticipation would begin to build. We were always up for those games. You couldn't help it. It was a traditional rivalry, and if you ever forgot it, then the fans reminded you in a hurry. If we didn't win the pennant, then beating the Dodgers was the next best thing.

In 1951 we did it all—won the pennant and beat the Dodgers head-on in doing it. That was the strangest kind of season, 1951, any way you look at it. We won our opener and then lost the next eleven. We just couldn't seem to do anything right. It didn't look like we'd ever get squared away. But then we did; we started playing good ball later in the summer, but by that time it looked like it was too late, that we'd given away too much ground to make up. It was the middle of August now, and we were 13½ games behind the Dodgers.

We had just lost three in a row to the Dodgers in Ebbets Field and were in the clubhouse after the game. The clubhouses there were pretty close together and we could hear some of the Dodgers yelling through the wall at us. They were on Leo particularly; some of them didn't like him and were really giving him a raking. They were letting him know that it was all over as far as they were concerned.

Well, somehow that struck a chord in the whole team. I can't explain what it was; maybe it simply was pride. It was like right then and there every man made some private decision—the same decision—that we were going to make a run at it, no matter how hopeless it looked. From then on we really started to play some ball.

We were a good ball club. There was nothing flukey about what we did. Willie had joined us after the season was underway and went to center field, and Bobby Thomson switched from center field to third. Then Leo made a key move; he took me off of first base and put me in left field, and took Whitey Lockman out of left and put him on first. Also, we had Alvin Dark, Eddie Stanky, Don Mueller, Wes Westrum, Henry Thompson. And those good pitchers—Sal Maglie, Larry Jansen, Jim Hearn, Dave Koslo, George Spencer. It was a very well-balanced ball club. I think the Dodgers might have had a better team, man for man. Why, they practically had an all-star club, with Robinson, Duke Snider, Pee Wee Reese, Roy Campanella, Gil Hodges, Billy Cox, Carl Furillo, Andy Pafko. And that made it all the sweeter, of course, beating a club as good as they were.

We had great leadership and inspiration going for us. We were coming from behind, all season long. I think that probably makes a difference. You can't let up for a minute, not for a game or an inning or a pitch. Every day you go out and you know you've got to make up ground. Somehow we never really got discouraged. I've got to go back to that kid we had in center field: he was one of the big things we had going for us. Day after day he kept coming up with those great plays and throws to save a game, or the hit that won it. And remember, he was just a rookie that year, playing in the biggest baseball pressure-cooker of them all—a Dodger-Giant pennant race.

In addition, Durocher was making fantastic moves, taking the pitcher out at just the right moment, putting up the right pinch-hitter, moving men around in the field as if he just *knew* where the ball was going to be hit. He was uncanny. Personally, I think he must have won six or seven games for us by his strategy.

Leo kept prodding us on. We didn't know if we would ever come close or not. We never mentioned winning the pennant. We just didn't like the idea of letting them run away with it. So we figured we'd give them a fight for it, let them know we were in the league. Then they started to lose and we started to win. The Dodgers didn't play bad ball coming down the stretch—they were around .500, I think, which isn't championship baseball, but isn't a total collapse either. But the thing was, we hardly lost a game after the middle of August. We won 39 of our last 47 games. At one point we put together a sixteen-game winning streak.

We finished the season in Boston, winning our games there. When our game was over we were in first place by a half game and the Dodgers were battling the Phillies in Philadelphia. We were listening to that game on the radio. They went into extra innings, and I remember one spot when the Phillies had the bases loaded with one out and Del Ennis was up. "Hit it, Del," we were yelling. "Hit it anywhere." Hell, we were a fly ball or a ground ball away from a pennant. But Newcombe struck him out. Then Eddie Waitkus lined one that looked like a sure hit, but Jackie made that great diving catch on it. Then Jackie came up in the fourteenth inning and hit the home run to win it. We were on the train back when we heard about it.

So there was going to be a play-off. The first game was in Ebbets Field, and Jim Hearn won it for us, 3–1. I hit a home run and so did Bobby Thomson. We beat Branca. Not many people remember that Bobby hit two home runs off of Branca in that play-off, and each one was a big one.

Then we moved over to the Polo Grounds and Clem Labine shut us out, 10–0, throwing that great sinker and that jug-handled curve ball.

So there was one more game to play. It was inevitable I guess, typical of what we'd been going through—always that one more game to play, the one we just *had* to win. And it was true; they'd all been big games. But this was the biggest one of them all.

Big Newcombe started for them, and he came out throwing bullets. He went along strong for eight innings, and going into the last of the ninth we're down, 4–1. Well, I don't have to look in the record books to tell you how it happened. Dark was up first and he singled. Then Mueller got a base hit. Two men on. And I'm up. The tying run.

Now, I'd had a good year, and a particularly good second half. Got a lot of key hits. Hit over .300, had twenty-four home runs, led the league in runs batted in. Mr. Clutch. But what did I do? Popped up to Hodges in foul ground, right near the railing. Well, I *could've* hit into a double play.

Whitey Lockman was up next. He hit one down the left-field line for a double. That made it 4–2, and put the tying run on second, with one out. When Mueller slid into third he hurt his ankle and they had to take him out and put in a runner. While that was happening, Charley Dressen, who was managing Brooklyn, got on the phone to the bull pen, where they were throwing. He asked who looked good down there. Well, Erskine was warming up, but it seems he was kind of wild; he'd bounced a few curves. Branca was throwing strikes and was really popping the ball. So Dressen asked for Branca, and Ralph took that long walk in.

Branca's first pitch to Thomson was a fastball for a strike. It was just the kind of pitch Bobby liked to hit, inside and a little high. But he took it. Now let's just hold it there for a second while I tell you where, in my opinion, we had got a good break. Campanella had injured himself in that last game in Philadelphia and wasn't playing. Rube Walker was behind the plate. But I'll tell you what I think might have happened if Campy had been in there. He would have called time, even though the pitch was a strike, and gone out to Branca and said, "Hey, wait a minute. We've got to keep this ball down. Don't let him hit a home run. Keep it down." But Campy wasn't there.

So Ralph threw him the same pitch. And Bobby was ready for it, and he whacked it. You know what happened. Would I say it was the biggest single moment in baseball history? Well, I don't know. What would you say?

We were stunned for a moment. Nobody said anything, nobody moved, even though we saw that the ball had gone in the stands. Then it struck us: We'd won. It sank in. We began jumping up and down and yelling. All that joy and excitement flooded into us like so much nervous energy and I think if we hadn't started yelling and jumping we would have exploded. We started grabbing each other and laughing; we just couldn't find words. It was chaos. Happy chaos. And then pandemonium broke loose throughout the whole ball park. One thing I'll always remember though: Jackie Robinson was standing there watching Bobby circle the bases, making sure he touched each one.

Then we were all at home plate, waiting for Bobby. Our next problem was getting from home plate to the clubhouse in center field. The fans were swarming all over the field, patting us on the back, shaking our hands, pulling at us. Too many well-wishers can be scary. Finally the police came and helped us get through.

We celebrated in the clubhouse with warm champagne. Somebody had forgot to chill it. I guess when we fell behind in the game they figured we were licked. Can you imagine that?

GENE CONLEY

DONALD EUGENE CONLEY
Born: November 10, 1930, Muskogee, Oklahoma
Major-league career: 1952–1963, Boston and Milwaukee
Braves, Philadelphia Phillies, Boston Red Sox
Lifetime record: 91 wins, 96 losses

An unusually endowed athlete, Gene Conley was the first man to play two major sports in the same city—basketball for the Boston Celtics and baseball for the Boston Braves and Boston Red Sox. Conley's best year was 1962, when he won 15 games for the Red Sox. Two years later a bad arm forced him into retirement.

I went to Washington State College and played a couple of years of baseball and basketball. During the summer in my sophomore year I started pitching for a semipro team in Walla Walla and was going real well; there were scouts out at just about every game. I knew they were there to watch me and I guess I liked the idea. It made me bear down harder.

My family didn't want me to sign a contract until I had finished school, but you know how it is—a career in professional baseball looks very glamorous, and in addition you can't help wondering just how good you really are. So when the Boston Braves offered me a $3,000 bonus, I took it.

My first year in the minors was 1951. I pitched for Hartford, in the Eastern League. I was making only $300 a month, was married, my first child was on the way, and I needed some money. One day I got a call from Bill Sharman, who had just joined the Boston Celtics. He said he'd seen me play basketball out in California, against UCLA, told Red Auerbach about me and that Red said to ask me if I was interested in trying out for the Celtics.

"Since your graduating class is '52," he said, "the Celtics would be able to draft you."

"Well," I said, "that's very interesting. Can you make any money?" That was my chief concern.

"You can," he said, "if you make the team."

So the Celtics drafted me and after the baseball season was over in '52 I went up to Boston and tried out. And I made it; I wasn't on the first team, but I made it. I was delighted and a little bit surprised; after all, I'd had only one year of varsity basketball in college. The salary was $4,500, which was a big-league basketball salary in those days.

The Braves didn't seem to mind my playing basketball then. I was still nothing more than a minor-league prospect and they weren't particularly interested in what I was doing.

Then I had a good year pitching for Toledo in the American Association—I won the Minor League Player of the Year Award—and got set for another year of basketball. That was when the Braves wanted to know what was going on.

"Look," they said, "we're thinking of bringing you up next year. We're concerned about your getting injured."

"I played with the Celtics last year because I needed the money," I said, "and I have to play again this year for the same very good reason."

"Well," they said, "if you won't play we'll give you a thousand dollars."

I thought that was pretty nice. Same as getting a thousand-dollar bonus. And since the chance to make the big club was what I was after, I decided to take the thousand, get a job that winter and not play basketball.

I came to stay in 1954. Had a good year and was runner-up to Wally Moon for Rookie of the Year. Once I'd made the big leagues I gave up basketball.

You know, spring training had been kind of rough. The Braves had some hard-nosed veterans who weren't overly cordial to rookies. Every rookie was a potential threat to somebody's paycheck; that was how they looked at it. Some of the fringe pitchers in particular, guys who were battling to hold their jobs, surely weren't going to give you any help. Sometimes the resentment was quite open. When they saw you were scheduled to pitch, you heard remarks like, "Let's see what the pheenom is going to do today." It was understandable, I suppose; after all, I was there to try and take somebody's job. If you pitch a good game or two you're going to send some guy to the bull pen, or even off the team. This inside competition on a ball club is a real thing, especially in spring training and during the first few weeks of the season. That's when jobs are at stake.

So there wasn't much support or encouragement from anybody, except the coaches. Charlie Root, the old Chicago Cub pitcher, was the pitching coach when I joined the club. He was a real rough, tough character. "Don't worry about those other guys," he'd say. "the hell with them. Do your job, take their bread and butter away from them. They've been there long enough." And knowing Charlie, he probably went up to those older pitchers and told *them*, "Don't let that kid take your job. He doesn't know anything. Bear down. Keep him outa there."

Charlie always had a chip on his shoulder anyway, because of that Babe Ruth episode in the 1932 World Series. Charlie was pitching when Ruth supposedly pointed to the center-field bleachers and then hit the ball there. He used to tell me that there was no way Babe Ruth could have done that to him and gotten away with it. "He was raising his arm to straighten out his sleeve or something," he said. Charlie Grimm told me the same thing. "Root would have put that next pitch right into Ruth's ear if Babe had tried that on him," he said. Root was that way. He had a reputation as a head-hunter. And he would tell us young pitchers to be the same way. "Don't let these guys take the bread out of your kid's mouth," he'd say. "Don't let them dig in at home plate. Knock 'em back, knock 'em down."

Generally, I never threw at hitters. Disposition is part of it; I never liked doing it. It just wasn't my style of pitching. But when I was told to do it, naturally I did. I remember a time when we were playing a game in St. Louis. I'd been hit pretty hard my last few times out and just before I went out to warm up Charlie Root came over to me.

"Now, Gene," he said, "your stuff is all right, but they've been digging in on you. What I want you to do tonight is set a couple guys down on their butts."

"Okay, Charlie," I said.

"I'll give you a word of advice," he said. "When Musial gets up there, sit him down and that'll straighten out the whole bunch."

Then he walked away, and I'm standing there thinking to myself: I'm going to knock down Musial, in *St. Louis*, in front of thirty thousand people. I couldn't believe it.

Around the third or fourth inning Musial is leading off. Perfect time to knock him down. I stood out there telling myself how foolish this was. Then I turned around and happened to glance out toward the bull pen and I could see Charlie standing up with his hands cupped around his mouth, yelling something at me. I couldn't hear him, but I had a pretty good idea what he was saying.

So Musial got in there and, boy, did I flip him. I really flipped him. As a matter of fact I thought the ball went through him. I really did. Del Rice was catching and he came out to the mound. "Gene," he said, "I thought the ball came out through his ear, I swear." So did I, and I was scared stiff. I had to take a minute or so to regain my composure. The fans were booing and yelling. Musial? Never bothered him a bit. He got up, dusted himself off, went into that funny little stance and stood there peeking out at me just as if nothing had happened.

Remember when Joe Adcock hit four home runs and a double in one game against the Dodgers in Ebbets Field? Well, Joe had been blasting the Dodgers all year, and we sort of expected they'd come bearing in on him sooner or later. Sure enough, a day or two later somebody hit him in the head. I was starting the next day and Adcock came up to me and said, "Get one of them for me, will you?" I said okay.

For some reason or other the guy I picked out to floor was Jackie Robinson. I knocked him down a couple of times. Then he started dropping bunts along the first base line, but they went foul. I didn't even realize what he was trying to do until I picked up the paper the next day and saw Jackie quoted as saying he wished he could have got one fair so he could have stepped on me at first base. And all the while I thought I was getting a break because Jackie was trying to bunt instead of swinging away. I didn't realize that I was getting an even bigger break when those balls rolled foul. But Robinson played that way.

Jackie was a remarkable ballplayer in so many ways. He was always a factor when he was in the ball game. One night I was pitching against Carl Erskine in Ebbets Field and we went into the bottom of the twelfth in a scoreless tie. It was one of the finest games I ever pitched in the big leagues. With one out Jackie got on first base and Carl Furillo came up. I figured in that situation Robinson was almost certainly going to try and steal. I threw over there a few times, but he kept getting right back off again, not cutting his lead at all.

Then I got set to throw a curve to Furillo, but even as I went into my motion and began my delivery I was watching Jackie, to see what he was going to do. The moment I released the ball I realized I didn't get a good snap on it and I could just see it doing nothing as it went up there. You seldom get away with that kind of mistake, and I didn't get away with it that night. Furillo jumped on it and hit a line drive into the lower deck in left and I'm beat, 2–0, in twelve innings.

Carl Furillo got all the headlines the next day, and he deserved them, because he did the job. But *I* knew that it was Robinson who had distracted me just enough to get me to hang that curve.

We won pennants in '57 and '58. Spahn and Burdette were our big guns those years. Lew had ice water in his veins. Nothing bothered him, on or off the mound. He was a chatterbox out there. I've never seen anybody like him. He would talk to himself, to the batter, to the umpire, and sometimes he would even talk to the ball. Lew would throw at a batter on occasion, and sometimes just as he was delivering the ball he would yell, "Look out!" and then throw one of his dinky little sliders on the outside corner while the batter fell back. He didn't have what you would call great stuff—he threw sliders and sinkers and spitters, but he had great control, and he would battle you. He always knew what he was doing out there.

Sure he threw spitters. Everybody knew it but they could never catch him at it. He would drive the third-base coaches crazy, loading up the ball so that they could see him doing it and then wiping if off when they yelled, or sometimes pretending to wipe it off and throwing a loaded pitch up there. Then he'd turn around and grin at them. He knew how to agitate.

One time in Cincinnati they kept a movie camera fixed on him throughout the whole game, trying to catch him in the act of loading up the ball. I'll bet it must have cost them a few thousand dollars. Lew really enjoyed himself that night, going through all his motions, touching his cap, face, mouth. I believe he shut them out. I asked him later in the clubhouse if he'd thrown many that game. "No," he said. "Only about sixty percent." And that camera didn't catch one of them.

Spahn loved baseball and he loved to pitch; you got the feeling sometimes that pitching was his whole life. I always thought he got kind of a raw deal after he retired by not getting a job as a big-league manager. With his knowledge of the game, he would have been a good one. But as a rule, it seems that not too many former pitchers become managers; certainly not in recent years anyway. I don't know why that should be so. When you figure that approximately two-fifths of every big-league club is composed of pitchers, you begin to wonder why the percentage of former pitchers managing is so low.

Spahn hated to miss a turn. He expected to pitch every fourth day no matter what. If your turn was rained out and he was due the next day, then you sat it out and he pitched. I remember one time it didn't work out that way and they started me and held Spahn back a day. He didn't like that at all. I heard he went up to the front office and got it squared away. He didn't want to miss a turn. And I'm not being critical of him; to the contrary, I think his attitude was great. He knew what he wanted to do, he knew he could pitch and win, and he wanted to do it, without having anybody step on his toes.

Spahn once told me something about Yogi Berra that I thought was interesting. He pitched to Yogi quite a bit over the years and he used to deflate the legend about Berra being a bad-ball hitter. "He guesses with you," Spahn said. "That's what he does." So if a guy is guessing on a pitch and he gets it, then it doesn't matter if he's hitting at a bad ball, because he's ready for that pitch, he's already timed it.

I remember the scouting reports we had on Yogi in the World Series. They said he'd swing at anything, a ball in the dirt, or over his head, or wherever, and that to be careful when you got ahead of him, because he'd go after the bad pitch. But

Spahn said, "I don't want to listen to that story." He said that in a tight spot, when Berra was really bearing down at the plate, he wouldn't offer at pitches that were just off the corner, that you had to throw him strikes.

I believe Spahn was right about Yogi being a guess hitter. I pitched against him in a Series and I threw him a curveball that dropped around his feet, and he hit it for a single that drove in a run. Well, as far as I'm concerned, there was no way he could have hit that pitch if he wasn't guessing on it and was set for it.

The only basketball I played in those years was in the Y in the wintertime, just scrimmaging. I did this until 1958. I had a real bad year in '58. I didn't pitch all that much and when I did I wasn't very effective. When I say a bad year, that's putting it mildly: I was 0–6. It wasn't a matter of arm trouble, it was just that I started off poorly and never got the chance to get squared away. You see, we had a very strong staff and once I was dropped from the rotation I couldn't get back in. We had Spahn and Burdette, plus Bob Rush, Carl Willey, Joey Jay, Juan Pizarro. So they put me in the bull pen and forgot about me. I got lost down there. How can a guy who's six feet nine get lost? Easy.

Then I got into the doghouse. Deep. One night in Los Angeles I went to one of these fancy poolside Hollywood parties, with Red Schoendienst, Burdette, Frank Torre, and another guy, whose name escapes me at the moment. Frank Torre threw somebody into the pool; there was a little heat about it and a couple of tables were broken and a few people went flying around here and there. The next day in the Los Angeles *Times* there was the headline: FIVE MILWAUKEE BRAVES PLAYBOYS INVADE BEL AIR HOME. Under it were our pictures.

Well, there wasn't much they could say to Schoendienst, or Burdette, or Frank Torre, who was having a good year at first base. But I'm sitting there with an 0–5 record. Fred Haney, who was managing the club then, came up to me and said, "Gene, you can't afford this." So that put me even deeper into the doghouse, so deep I never got out.

At the end of the season they told me I was going to get a salary cut, which didn't surprise me. So I started thinking about the Celtics again. They'd just got Bill Russell and some of those other outstanding players and were beginning to launch that great dynasty. I'd been away from it for a long time, but I got to thinking about what would happen if I got in touch with them to see if I could get started again. I called up Red Auerbach and asked him if he could use an old washed-up pitcher.

"You think you can still play?" he asked. "You know we play it a little differently now." He reminded me about the twenty-second rule and some of the other changes. He reminded me, too, that they had a pretty good team, with Russell, Bob Cousy, Tom Heinsohn, and guys like that. I told him I'd like to give it a whirl and he said I was welcome to come up for a tryout. I did that and doggone if I didn't make the team again, five years later.

They got into the play-offs that year and those games overlapped with spring training. Birdie Tebbetts, who was general manager of the Braves, called me up.

"Play-off or no play-offs," he said, "you're going to have to leave the Celtics. You're still a baseball player."

He said that even though I'd had a lousy year they felt I could still pitch. Then he told me they were cutting my pay twenty-five percent. That seemed like an awful lot.

"I realize you've got to cut me," I said, "but I don't appreciate the dimensions of it."

"Listen," he said, "you're going to take the cut and you're going to come to spring training." Birdie could be a pretty tough guy.

"I don't know if I can make it to spring training," I said. "We're into the play-offs now and I can't leave them. It wouldn't be right."

We left it at that, and when I mentioned it to Auerbach, he said, "Oh, no, you can't leave this club now. You're playing a little and you're good relief for Heinsohn and you're helping us. We've got a championship team here. Stick around and enjoy it." Then he gave me a few thousand to help me make up my mind.

So I kept writing Birdie, telling him I'd be there, but that I'd be a little late. I stayed with the Celtics right to the end and we won the championship, we won the whole works, which was a tremendous thrill. I'd been on pennant winners with the Braves in '57 and '58 and then on a championship team with the Celtics right after that. So I was pretty excited.

The day after the Celtics had won it all I joined the Braves in spring training. And there was Birdie.

"Forget it," he said. "You've been traded to the Phillies."

At first the Phillies didn't seem to care if I played basketball or not. Then one day Bob Carpenter, who owned the ball club, called me in and said, "Gene, I don't think I want you to play basketball."

"Mr. Carpenter," I said, "you don't know how much fun I'm having. The Celtics are a great bunch of guys, plus we're winning championships."

"That may be so," he said. "But we're paying you pretty good money, and I think you ought to give up basketball."

"I can't do that," I said.

"What will it take to keep you from playing?"

"Well," I said, "I'll have to think that over. After all, I've played two years with them and I'm helping them and they want me."

"Name a figure," he said.

"Twenty-five thousand," I said.

"I'll give you twenty."

"Make it twenty-five."

"Twenty," he said.

"Twenty-five and I'll quit," I said.

That made him mad. "You'll either take what I offered you," he said, "or get out."

"Then I'll get out," I said.

I went to Auerbach and told him what I'd done.

"Good for you," he said. "Now you're talking like a champion. Stick with us and you'll have a lot of fun."

"That's all right," I said. "But the least you can do for me now is give me a two-year contract."

"No problem," he said.

Frankly, I was astonished when he said that. They just weren't giving two-year contracts to anybody at that time. Russell, Cousy, none of them had two-year contracts. I was the only one.

Then the Phillies traded me to the Red Sox and the Red Sox—always generous with salaries—gave me a five-thousand-dollar increase over what I'd been making with the Phillies. As luck would have it, Dick O'Connell, the Red Sox general manager, was a red-hot Celtics fan and he was delighted that I was playing for them. I guess that's what I'd needed all along—a general manager who was a basketball fan.

The differences between baseball and basketball are tremendous. In baseball there's much more individual responsibility, especially if you're a pitcher. You're alone out there on the mound, really isolated, and nobody can help you throw the ball over the plate. The only comparable moment in basketball is the free throw; that's when you're really on the spot. Otherwise you're always working as part of a unit every moment, hitting the open man, looking for an opening, always playing together. Also, I'd say there's more room for error in basketball, more room for making a mistake and getting away with it.

Conditioning in basketball is harder. It's unbelievable the shape you have to be in. That's because you're always in motion when you're out there; there's no standing still. But at the same time don't underestimate the stamina you need, say, to pitch a nine-inning game in St. Louis in the middle of August when it's over a hundred degrees on the field. That is simply an incredible ordeal. You lose from twelve to fifteen pounds and for the next day or two you feel sick.

So playing both sports I was always in top condition. There was no way I couldn't be. And since those seasons overlapped by three weeks at each end I used to get the feeling I was playing some kind of ball for thirteen months each year.

I roomed with Robin Roberts for a while when I was with the Phillies. He was something like Spahn, in that he'd pitch all day and all night, throwing out of that easy motion. Fast ball across the knees. That was Robby. Speed, control, stamina. Sometimes I got the feeling he had only two signs: fast ball and pitch-out. But what a great pitcher! He was something special out there. You give Robin Roberts a run or two lead in the late innings and there was no way anybody was going to take it away from him. He could reach back when he had to.

I asked him one time, "Robby, when you've got a runner on third and you need some extra on the ball, do you find yourself pushing off that mound a little harder?"

"No, Slim," he said. He called me Slim. "I pitch the same all the time. The first pitch goes in the same way as the last one."

"That can't be true," I said, "because I notice when there's a man on third and less than two out, that ball pops a little better."

"Well," he said, "you can't see what I'm doing, Slim. That comes from within."

That was his way of saying it, and I think what he was saying is the very essence of the great pitcher, or the great athlete in any difficult situation. He didn't *look* like he was doing anything different, but, boy, he was doing it when he had to. Bill Russell was like that. He was the type of guy, in a basketball game, who was always involved in the key moment. If it meant a blocked shot, a shot that might beat you, his timing seemed always to be just a little better. He'd be in the right spot, getting just high enough to get a piece of the ball. Jackie Robinson was like that too. Doing it when it had to be done. You'd look back later and ask yourself: How the devil did he do that? You couldn't answer it. I don't think they knew themselves. They just did it.

Ted Williams had just retired when I joined the Red Sox, so I never had the opportunity to be a teammate of his; but I did pitch against him a couple of times here and there. There was no better swing. I pitched against him in 1952, when the Braves were still in Boston, in a city series. I'll never forget Ted coming to the plate. You talk about a guy putting you back on your heels on the mound. He dug in, and he looked so *big* up there and the bat looked so light in his hands, and he didn't swish it around, he *snapped* it back and forth, and he looked so darned anxious, as if he was saying, "Okay, kid, let's see what you've got." Confidence just oozed out of him. He took something away from you even before you threw a pitch.

You know, he claimed that no one could hit him with a ball. He could pick up a pitched ball that quick and his eyes and reflexes were so good that he never had a problem getting out of the way. Speed never bothered him; you couldn't throw a fastball by him, so you have to believe he was seeing that ball the moment it was released. I've heard a lot of guys say that a pitcher who was particularly fast and a little wild, like Herb Score, for instance, never bothered Ted. If a ball came at his head all he did was step back easily and let it fly past, that he never staggered or fell away, the way most batters do when the ball is at their head. Ted knew right away what it was and where it was going.

I had arm trouble off and on for several years. My last year with the Red Sox was '63. I went to spring training in '64 but could hardly throw the ball. My arm was completely gone. A few days after the season opened, Pinky Higgins, who was the general manager then, called me up and gave me the bad news. It came as no surprise, of course, but still it hit me pretty hard. I'd been in baseball for fourteen years and suddenly with a one-minute phone call it's all over.

My arm was dead, there was no question about it. But I thought that maybe I could fool myself. So I made a phone call to Gabe Paul in Cleveland.

"Gene," he said, "we're fixed for starters, but we could use a guy who can go a few innings in relief. Do you think your arm might come around?"

"I think it just might," I said.

"Would you like to come to Cleveland now and do some throwing?"

Well, at that very moment my arm was hurting so bad I could hardly hold on to the telephone.

"I'd better work out some more before we do that," I said.

"All right, Gene," he said. "I'll tell you what. I'll pay your expenses if you want to go down to Burlington, North Carolina."

They had a club there and he suggested I go down into that warm weather, pitch a few games and see how I felt. I said okay. Still trying to fool myself. So I went to North Carolina, to a bush league, after spending ten years in the big leagues. It was like going from the top shelf to a dusty old drawer at the bottom of the bin. I tell you, sometimes you can't get out until you've been humiliated and embarrassed and gone right down to the very dregs of your pride.

They gave me a uniform that made me look like something out of the 1920's, with the pants reaching only to the knees, like knickers. There were holes in the socks. But it was the best they could do. And I was riding that rickety bus, going to ball parks where the fields were lumpy and the lights were unbelievably bad. But I figured I'd make the best of it.

I took cortisone for the pain in my arm and did some throwing. After a few days the manager asked me if I wanted to try it in a game.

"Do you think I ought to?" I asked. I was dreading the idea of it.

"Why not?" he asked. "Does your arm feel all right?"

"It feels as well as it's going to," I said. The pain was killing me.

So I started a game. We were playing Greensboro, North Carolina. Those kids came up to the plate and started knocking line drives all over the place. I tried flooring a few of them, but they weren't impressed; I didn't have enough on the ball to scare anybody. After four or five innings they had to take me out.

I called Gabe Paul the next day.

"Gabe," I said, "I tried but I can't do it."

"I thought that might be the case," he said. "I guess you just had to get it out of your system."

"Well," I said, "it's out."

When I walked away from that telephone I was really shocked. There was no more fooling myself. It was all over and I knew it. Not only that, but I didn't have a job, nothing to go back to. The basketball was about over, too. So I was pretty depressed.

I wandered around for a while, a lost soul on the streets of this town in North Carolina. Then I walked into a church and sat down in the back, all by myself. There was a service going on. After the singing this Baptist minister started preaching. All of a sudden it hit me real hard and I caved in and started crying. I just sat there in that last row and cried and cried, trying to keep my head down so as not to upset anybody. Then I felt a hand on my shoulder and I looked up. An elderly Southern gentleman was standing there gazing down at me.

"What's the matter, son?" he asked. "Did you lose your mother?"

I shook my head, the tears still running. "No, sir," I said. "I lost my fastball."

TOMMY HOLMES

THOMAS FRANCIS HOLMES
Born: March 29, 1917, Brooklyn, New York
Major-league career: 1942–52, Boston Braves, Brooklyn
  Dodgers
Lifetime average: .302

In 1945 Tommy Holmes set a modern National League record that stood for over thirty years: He hit safely in 37 consecutive games. In addition to the streak, that year Holmes led the league in home runs, doubles, hits, and slugging average, and had a batting average of .352. In 1947 he led the league in hits for a second time. From 1944 through '48, Holmes' batting average never went below .309. His batting eye must be rated among the best of modern times, for even though he often went to bat over 600 times in a season, Holmes never struck out more than 20 times in any one year.

I grew up in the Borough Park section of Brooklyn, which was a hotbed of baseball. But even though I played a lot of baseball as a kid, I began training early on to be a professional fighter. I loved the ring and really thought I could make a go of it. I could spend hours on the punching bag, and even when I was a kid I won all kinds of prizes for my skill on the bag. But my father, who had been a second for a lot of great fighters, put a stop to all that. "My son will never be a prizefighter," he said. He was pretty definite about it, and so that was that.

I started to draw some attention as a ballplayer when I was going to Brooklyn Tech. I had a few good years there when I hit for averages like .613 and .585. That can't help but to attract the scouts, even if it's only high school. Then I started playing semipro ball on Sunday for five dollars a game.

Living in New York City I wanted to be a New York ballplayer. Being a Brooklyn boy, the Dodgers naturally were my team, but they never did show much interest. It was the Yankees who came around with a contract. In fact it was Paul Krichell, their top scout, who signed me. Even though I was a Dodger fan, I found it flattering to be offered a Yankee contract; they were the glamour team back then.

I went to Norfolk, Virginia, in 1937 and began my professional career. I managed to hit the ball and always had good percentages. I played five years in the Yankee farm system and my averages were .320, .368, .339, .317, and .302. Pretty good hitting, right? But you never saw me in a Yankee uniform, did you? It was murder playing in that organization then.

I'll tell you what my problem was. I was a center fielder and the Yankees already had a guy out there named Joe DiMaggio. And to make matters worse, they had a couple of other guys in the outfield named Tommy Henrich and Charlie Keller. But Mr. Weiss, the Yankee general manager in those days, said to me, "Tommy, if we see we can't use you we'll send you to a club where you'll be able to play." That was the promise he made to me and he kept it, because they finally sold me to the Braves and I had a chance to be a regular.

Casey Stengel was managing the Braves at that time, and even though we weren't a winning team we had some good veteran ballplayers on that club. Paul Waner was one of my teammates on the '42 Braves. We talked hitting a lot, naturally. He used to tell me, "Look, there are three men in the outfield; why should we hit it where they are?" He used to preach shooting for the foul lines. If you missed, he said, it was just a foul ball; if you got it in, it was a double. "And if it goes in the stands," he said, "don't worry. We don't pay for the baseballs." If they tried to cover the lines on him, then they were opening gaps in right- and left-center and he would put the ball out there. This is what he taught me. And while I wasn't a power hitter, I used to get around thirty-five or forty doubles a year, from following Paul's advice.

Paul had his habits, as everyone knows. It's no secret that he drank. One day during the war the ball club traveled to an army camp somewhere in New England to play a game for the soldiers. The whole ball club went. We were riding in army trucks, standing up and holding onto the straps in the back. It was a hot day, a real scorcher. The perspiration was running off of us. One of the guys said to Paul, "Say, Paul, what would you give for a shot right now?" Paul smiled. He had a fountain pen clipped to his breast pocket and he took it out, opened it and darned if he didn't have a shot of whiskey in it. He drank it, screwed the pen together again and clipped it back onto his pocket, and I think that truck must have been shaking, everybody was laughing so hard.

Ernie Lombardi was there too. What a hitter! You know, that poor guy was severely handicapped by being terribly slow afoot. How he ever hit for those .320 and .330 averages I'll never know. Stengel loved him, and loved to kid him. One time we had a big lead in the late innings and Lombardi is on first. Stengel stands up in the dugout and yells, "Steal it, Lom!" Everybody starts to laugh. But on the next pitch, Lombardi starts moving. He was going to prove something. I think everybody in the ball park, fans and players alike, froze. Nobody could believe it. Here's big Ernie Lombardi heading out to steal second. The catcher was so startled he couldn't throw, the second baseman was so startled he was late covering. Lombardi could have taken it standing up, but he went in sliding, in a triumphant cloud of dust. When he stood up he had the biggest grin of satisfaction on his face. He played seventeen years in the big leagues and in all that time stole only about a half dozen bases, and that was one of them.

I remember one time we got on the train to take our first western trip of the year. We had a few rookies on the team and in those days they weren't making much money, maybe six hundred a month. They were pretty excited about making their first western trip. Well, Lombardi—bless him, I'll always remember him for this—went around to all the kids and said, "Hey, kid, got enough money?" And without waiting for an answer he'd push a twenty on them. Just wanted to make sure they had a few extra, to tip porters and waitresses, or buy themselves a beer, and so on. He wanted them to be able to feel like big leaguers. That was the kind of guy Ernie Lombardi was.

You look back and you remember those things, those acts of

kindness, the men like Ernie Lombardi. And you remember, too, the men who taught you and who helped you and you realize that this is what the game is all about—one man passing along his advice and his insights to the next. This is what helps make baseball a tradition, along with the memories and the base hits and all the marvelous things that take place out on that field. Do I sound like a sentimentalist? Well, maybe I am. But I'll always remember the Paul Waners and the Casey Stengels, and all the others who did so much to help me. And I suppose that in a way I'm remembering the men who helped *them,* men I never knew. Today I try to help young players whenever I can, passing along whatever helpful tips and advice I can. And so it goes along, it never stops.

But talk about great ballplayers, what about Pete Reiser? There wasn't a thing he couldn't do on that ball field. When I came up in '42 he had already led the league and was well on his way to doing it again when he suffered that injury, running into the wall in St. Louis. I always admired him, from the first moment I saw him. We were both center fielders, both built about the same. But I'll be frank—that's where the resemblance ended. He could hit a ball twice as far as I could, he could run twice as fast as I could. It's just a sin that he never became the .340 lifetime hitter that he should have been, or the base-stealing champion that he should have been. The feeling about him in 1942 was that he was as great a star as there was in the game.

Nineteen forty-five was a year when everything I tried, everything I did, worked out. I led the league in home runs, hits, doubles, slugging average, and just missed winning the batting crown by a few points. Phil Cavaretta edged me out, .355 to .352. Later on, somebody pointed out something else that I wasn't aware of: I was the only man ever to lead the league in home runs and also have the least strikeouts for a regular; I struck out only nine times that year.

Also in that year I got real lucky and went on a tear throughout the month of June and into early July, hitting in thirty-seven consecutive games. That set a National League record and I'll be darned if it hasn't stood up now for more than thirty years. The previous league record was thirty-three straight games, by Rogers Hornsby.

I had thirty-two straight games when the Pirates came into

Boston for a double-header. I needed hits in both of those games to set a new record. Frankie Frisch was managing the Pirates then and he came up to me before the first game and said, "Good luck, Tommy—I'm throwing two left-handers against you." What he was telling me was there was no sentiment in our business. The lefties were two good ones, too— Al Gerhauser and Preacher Roe. Frisch wasn't giving away anything that day.

But I was hot. I didn't waste any time. First time up in each game I doubled, on the first pitch from Gerhauser and on the second pitch from Roe. A photographer snapped a picture just as I was hitting that double off of Roe and setting a new record. Later on I asked everybody on both teams to autograph it for me.

You know, it wasn't until after I'd broken the record that I realized how much tension and pressure I'd been under. A sigh of relief went out of me so huge that I felt like a collapsing balloon. Up until that moment it had never bothered me; but, boy, it had been building.

It finally stopped at thirty-seven, in Chicago. Hank Wyse shut me out. I didn't even come close to a hit. But I guess that hitting streak is the thing I'm proudest of, and do you know why?—because when they talk about hitting streaks they say DiMaggio in the American League and Holmes in the National. Anytime they link you up with Joe DiMaggio, you know you're in with the big leaguers.

In 1948 we won the pennant and went against Cleveland in the World Series. That opening game is one that people still remember. Bob Feller pitched for the Indians and Johnny Sain for us, and they hooked up in a beauty. There was no score going into the bottom of the eighth and Feller was pitching a one-hitter. It looked like we were going to be playing all day and all night before somebody scored.

Then Feller walked Bill Salkeld to open the inning. Phil Masi went in to run and we sacrificed him over to second. Johnny Sain was the next batter and he made out. That left it up to me. There then occurred one of the most controversial plays ever in a World Series, one that you can still get an argument about today.

Johnny Cooney was coaching third base for us and he was yelling to Masi to be careful with his lead; at the same time he wanted Masi off the bag in order to get a good jump if I happened to get a base hit.

Now, Johnny Cooney told me this. He was watching Lou Boudreau, who was playing shortstop and who was trying to keep Masi close. Boudreau was crouched over, his hand on his knee, his fingers spread. He turned around and looked at Walter Judnich in the outfield. Nothing happened. Then Boudreau did the same thing, turned around to Judnich, but this time his thumb closed against his finger. Cooney spotted that and yelled to Masi, "Back!" You see, they had put on a timed pickoff play. From the moment Boudreau brought his thumb in, a count was on—one, two, three. At the count of three, Boudreau was at the bag and Feller was wheeling to throw. Masi broke for the bag when Cooney yelled, Boudreau was breaking with him, and Feller was turning and throwing. Masi hit the dirt and it was a close play, and Bill Stewart, the umpire, called him safe. Boudreau argued long and loud, but the decision stood, of course.

Phil Masi was my roommate and I asked him later, "Phil, were you safe or were you out?"

"Tommy," he said, "he tagged me behind the shoulder, but my hand was touching the base. I was safe."

Now, someday I'd like to ask Lou Boudreau if that was in fact the sign, that movement of the thumb, because that's what we believed it was, and when Cooney saw it he yelled. That made the difference, that enabled Masi to get back, on a very close play.

So then play resumed. I'm still up, remember. Now, if I had made out, that whole thing would have been forgotten. But I didn't make out. Feller threw me a fastball high and outside— one of the few he put out there on me all day. I hit a low line drive past Kenny Keltner into left field; two skips and she was out there. Masi scored easily. Biggest hit of my life. Sain held them in the ninth and we won the game, 1–0.

Whenever I tell people about the 1948 World Series they say, "That was the one with the pickoff play, wasn't it?"

"That's right," I tell them.

"When Bob Feller lost the heartbreaker."

"That's right," I say. "But never mind that; let's talk about who got the hit."

HERB SCORE

HERBERT JUDE SCORE
Born: June 7, 1933, Rosedale, New York
Major-league career: 1955–62, Cleveland Indians, Chicago
  White Sox
Lifetime record: 55 wins, 46 defeats

Herb Score was one of the most brilliant young pitchers ever to come to the major leagues. In 1955 he set an all-time record in strikeouts for first-year men: 245—it was also a league-leading figure. The following year he struck out 263 to lead the league again, coupling this with a 20–9 won and lost record. Score's future seemed limitless, but his career was aborted by a series of injuries, leaving baseball fans to speculate upon "what might have been."

One night in the spring of 1957—my third year in the big leagues—I was heading back to the hotel. It was just at curfew time. When I walked into the lobby there seemed to be something going on—it was awfully crowded, with lots of people standing around, including newspapermen. Hank Greenberg, the general manager of the Cleveland ball club, was there too. Boy, I said to myself, am I glad I'm getting in under curfew.

When they saw me they all came running over and I got concerned because I thought something had happened.

"Herb," somebody said, "what do you think of it?"

"What are you talking about?" I asked.

"You haven't heard?"

"Heard what?" I asked.

By this time everybody was standing around me. I couldn't

for the life of me figure out what was going on. Then somebody said: "The Red Sox have offered a million dollars for you."

"What?" I said. I thought they were kidding me. A million dollars is a lot of money today, but in 1957 it was really a ton.

"It's true," somebody said. "A million dollars. Cash."

Greenberg told me later that it was a bona fide offer, that Tom Yawkey was ready to sit down and write out a check for a million dollars. "We told them no," Greenberg said. And that was that.

A few weeks later, though, I'll bet they wished they'd taken it.

I can honestly say the only thing I ever wanted to be was a baseball player. I was just fortunate in being physically able to do it. That physical ability is the whole thing, of course—you either have it or you don't, you either can do it or you can't. An athlete is endowed by the good graces of mother nature; after that it's simply up to him to polish that talent.

I was born in Rosedale, Queens, in New York City, but when I was in high school we moved to Lake Worth, Florida. That's when the scouts started to take notice of me. I pitched a no-hitter in my freshman year and that caught some attention. Then I began averaging pretty close to three strikeouts an inning, and that made them curious.

Cy Slapnicka of the Cleveland Indians wintered in Lake Worth, and one day somebody suggested he come out to see me pitch, and he did. He began showing up at the games, watching me. By my senior year in high school there were a lot of scouts coming out to the games. We got to know who they were and we'd spot them and everybody would start buzzing. No, it didn't make me nervous to know they were out there watching me; nothing ever made me nervous out on the mound; I was never happier or calmer than when I was standing out there. I loved it and I enjoyed it.

The scouts weren't supposed to talk to a kid about signing until he was out of high school. But some of them, especially the older ones, were very ingenious when it came to getting around the rules. In my case, Slapnicka used to take my mother, my sisters and me out to dinner, and never once would he talk to me about signing or do or say anything he wasn't supposed to. But he did talk about the Indians and their organization. Very quietly and effectively he sold me the idea that Cleveland had a good organization with a history of fine pitchers; at that time they had Lemon, Wynn, Garcia, Feller.

Slapnicka had signed Feller, you know, and I'm sure that fact impressed me. He talked a little bit about it, about how he had gone out to Iowa to see this unknown farm boy pitch, and how exciting it had been the first time he saw Bob kick and fire that fastball. There's no getting away from it—when you're talking with the man who signed Bob Feller, and he's interested in signing you, you pay attention.

So after high school, when it came to deciding with which club to sign, I chose Cleveland. I wanted to go with them. They gave me a bonus of $60,000, while I had three other offers that started at $80,000, and one club in particular that told me to come to them last and they would top any offer I had received. But I didn't want to do that; I didn't want to make it seem like an auction; and anyway I had pretty much made up my mind to go with Cleveland, and I don't think I made a mistake.

I would say that the two men who had the greatest influence on my playing career were Mel Harder and Ted Wilks. Mel taught me how to throw the curve, and Wilks was the pitching coach at Indianapolis, where I played in 1954. He really turned me around and got me to the major leagues. I was wild, just as wild as a pitcher could be. There was no question, I could throw hard, but that wasn't doing me much good if I wasn't getting it over.

In the spring of '54 I was pitching an exhibition game for Indianapolis and threw 44 pitches and only four of them were for strikes. Hank Greenberg was at the game and later on he pulled me aside.

"Look," he said, "there's no reason for you to be this wild. I know you're willing to work hard, and with the stuff you have, if you can't get it over the plate it's just going to be a waste."

Then he told me that Ted Wilks, who used to be with the Cardinals, was coming to the club to work with the pitchers. Hank gave me strict orders to listen to Wilks.

Ted was a garrulous type of guy. He also was very tough-minded and stubborn. The first thing he said to me when we got together was, "Now, don't tell me you can't. Whatever I tell you to try, I want you to try. I don't want to hear you say 'I can't.'"

"Okay," I said.

"The first thing I want you to do is cut down on your leg kick."

"I can't," I said.

We looked at each other and laughed.

Ted worked with me every day, even when I was in a game. I'd be out there pitching and I'd hear him in the dugout calling me every conceivable name, cursing me out when I wasn't doing what I was supposed to. I'd hear that voice: "You dumb so-and-so. Bend your back. Keep your head still." He never let up. He never stopped drilling those lessons into me. I'll always be grateful to him. Thanks to Ted Wilks I had a good year, winning 22 games and chalking up 330 strikeouts.

I came up to the big leagues in 1955. In spite of the great year I'd had at Indianapolis it still wasn't easy breaking into that pitching staff. They had Bob Lemon, Early Wynn, Mike Garcia, Art Houtteman, and the best one-two punch I've ever seen coming out of the bull pen, Don Mossi and Ray Narleski. Feller was still there, it was his next-to-last year. Meeting him and becoming his teammate was a great honor.

When I came up Feller had lost that tremendous speed, but he still had the great curveball. His curve was really remarkable. He had terrific spin on it—that's what makes the curveball. You could almost hear the seams biting into the wind.

Of course people would start trying to make comparisons between my fastball and Bob's. They would ask him about it, and what could he say? What can anyone say? As far as I'm concerned, you take the real hard throwers, like Feller, Koufax, Nolan Ryan—there's not that much difference between them. But you take guys like Feller and Koufax, they also had outstanding curveballs. Thanks to Mel Harder, I had the good breaking ball, too. You strike out as many batters with your curve as with the fastball because when you can throw that hard the batter has to be geared up to get around on it, and so you can catch them off stride with the breaking ball.

I had a big follow-through; I really drove off of the mound when I delivered the ball. In fact, I used to wear a basketball players' kneepad on my right knee because when I'd follow through, very often I would hit my left elbow against my right knee. That's how hard I was throwing; I used to put so much behind each pitch that my body was swung way out of position after I delivered the ball. I used to throw balls that I never saw reach the plate, and when they were hit I had to look around to see where they were going. Very often I simply didn't see the ball after I'd let it go.

I suppose that's what happened when I was pitching to Gil McDougald that night in Cleveland. I had retired Hank Bauer and Gil was the second batter of the game. He hit through the box a lot, but I never worried about a ball being hit back at me; I just never allowed myself to.

So I fired it in there, heard the crack of the bat, looked up and I can remember seeing the ball coming right into my eye. Boy, it had got big awfully fast and it was getting bigger. There was really nothing I could do about it. It hit me flush in the eye and as soon as it hit I remember saying to myself, *Saint Jude, stay with me.* I went down and I knew enough not to move; I just lay there. I never lost consciousness. I could hear everybody around me. I knew I was bleeding because I could taste the blood. I remember putting my finger in my ear to see if I was bleeding out of the ear, since I knew that if you had a concussion or a fractured skull you'd be getting blood out of your ear. My nose and my mouth were filled with blood and I remember somebody sticking a towel in and I said, "Hey, get that towel out, you're going to choke me." I was conscious the whole time, and lucid, and calm; I think I was the calmest one out there.

They carried me to the clubhouse and put some ice wrapped in a towel over my eye. The team doctor came in, took the towel away and looked in the eye with a light. While he was doing that I closed my other eye and couldn't see the light.

"Do I still have an eye?" I asked.

He didn't say anything. The clubhouse was very quiet. The grandstands were pretty quiet too, even though there were a lot of people in the ball park. Play had been suspended while another pitcher warmed up to take my place.

"I can't see that light, Doc," I said. He had it right in my eye.

"Look," he said, "you've got so much bleeding and swelling in there I'm not surprised."

Then he covered up the eye with a bandage and I went to the hospital. When I got there they still couldn't tell me if I'd lose the eye or not; there was too much hemorrhaging in it for them to be able to determine the extent of the damage. They told me it would take a few days.

Fortunately, I didn't lose the eye, but I had to lie absolutely still for eight days, with both eyes covered. It was while lying in the hospital those days, in the darkness, that I had a chance to reflect a little about myself, about life, about all the things that were important to me. In many ways it was a maturing experience. You learn something about values, yours and other people's. That eye injury was not the worst thing that ever happened in my life.

You know, people think what happened to me that night cost me my career. But they're wrong. That had absolutely nothing to do with me losing my effectiveness. The following spring I was pitching as well as I ever did. Then I was pitching in Washington. In the third or fourth inning my arm started to bother me. I didn't say anything. I figured it would work out. These are the mistakes you make when you're young.

Then in the seventh inning I threw a pitch to somebody and it actually didn't reach home plate. I called out Bobby Bragan, the manager, and told him I thought I'd hurt my arm, and he took me out. The next day the thing had swelled up so much I couldn't get it through the sleeve of my coat. It turned out I had torn the tendon in my elbow. I was advised to rest for thirty days. They thought that would help, but it didn't.

I pitched the rest of the year with a bad arm. I'd missed a whole year in '57 because of the eye injury and didn't want to miss any more time. So I kept throwing with a sore arm. I used to tell myself not to change my delivery to compensate for the soreness. But you do change your delivery; what once was natural becomes unnatural. After the soreness went away and I could throw without pain again, I never had quite the same motion.

I could still throw the good curve, but I couldn't throw the fastball like I used to anymore. It was gone, and with it a lot of the fun of the game went for me.

The last couple of years I pitched I was terrible. I just couldn't put it all together anymore. I went back to the minor leagues for a while and tried it there. The reason I did that was to prove to myself, once and for all, what I could do or what I couldn't do. I didn't want to go into middle age later on saying that I could have pitched some more if I'd tried. I tried. I probably worked harder in those last years than I ever did, until I had finally proved to my own satisfaction that I couldn't pitch anymore. Some people asked me why I went back to the minor leagues; they felt I was humiliating myself. But I never felt humiliated. There was no disgrace in what I was doing. The disgrace would have been in not trying.

BILLY GOODMAN

WILLIAM DALE GOODMAN
Born: March 22, 1926, Concord, North Carolina; Died: October 2, 1984
Major-league career: 1947–62, Boston Red Sox, Baltimore Orioles, Chicago White Sox, Houston Astros
Lifetime average: .300

Billy Goodman must rank as baseball's greatest utility man. In his career he played 624 games at second base, 406 at first base, 330 at third base, and 111 in the outfield. But wherever he played, he hit. Five times he hit over .300 and six times over .290. In 1950 he led the American League in batting with a .354 mark—while getting into games at a half dozen different positions.

In 1950 I led the American League in batting with a .354 average and when I came to spring training the next year I was considered a utility man. No, I didn't complain about it. That never bothered me. I knew I'd be playing someplace, be it first base, second base, or the outfield. I had a contract and that's all that mattered.

You see, you have to remember what kind of ball club the Red Sox had in those years—an all-star at just about every position. If I had been strictly an infielder or strictly an outfielder I may never have got a decent opportunity to show what I could do. But by being willing, able, and eager to play anyplace they asked me to I was able to get that opportunity, and I made the most of it.

I remember one time Mr. Yawkey called me into the office and asked me if I had a preference where I wanted to play.

I told him, "Wherever they need me." That's about how I felt.

Going way back to when I was a kid, when we had these little old pickup teams back home, playing on Saturdays in the cow pasture, you didn't have a regular position. Sometimes you'd play infield, sometimes you'd play outfield. You shifted from one place to another. Hell, I figured if you can do it, do it. In baseball you're supposed to use to the utmost what abilities you have. A fast man steals bases, a power hitter goes for the long ball. And if you have the ability to be versatile on a ball field, then you use it. Am I right or wrong?

I was born on a dairy farm, in Concord, North Carolina. I milked the cows, chopped cotton, plowed cotton, did just about a little of everything. That old versatility again, huh? I don't know if I would have stayed a farmer if it hadn't been for baseball. I just never thought about doing anything else except playing baseball. It was an ambition of mine right from the beginning.

A scout from the Atlanta Crackers saw me playing semipro ball in Concord and signed me to an Atlanta contract. It was an independently owned ball club then. I played in Atlanta in 1944, went into the service for a year, then played there again in 1946. Earl Mann, who owned the team, told me if I had a good year he would sell me to a big-league club and give me a little of the money. Well, I had the good year—hit .389—and he sold me to the Red Sox, and sure enough I got a check in the mail from him. Earl Mann is the only man I ever played for who kept every verbal agreement he ever made with me. That's not much of a commentary on human nature, is it?

I went to spring training with the Red Sox in '47 and there he was, Ted Williams. Best hitter I ever saw, period. No, I didn't talk to him then. I was a rookie and wasn't supposed to say anything.

I stayed with the Red Sox until June and then finished up the season at Louisville. I'd played first base and the outfield in Atlanta, then shortstop and outfield at Louisville. In 1948 Joe McCarthy made me the regular first baseman. I played under a lot of good managers, but McCarthy was tops. He was first class. He treated me great. A great handler of men.

That was my first full season in the majors, 1948, and I stepped into a terrific pennant race. We tied with Cleveland at the end of the regular season and played them in the first pennant play-off ever in the American League. It was a one-game play-off, in Fenway Park.

McCarthy started Denny Galehouse in that game for us. A lot of people were surprised by the choice, myself included, I guess. Denny was a good pitcher, but he wasn't our ace that year. But I don't think we had a hell of a lot of options; we were up against it for pitching that day. Remember, we'd just come charging down the line to get into a tie and we had a lot of tired arms. Mel Parnell, Jack Kramer, and Joe Dobson were our aces and they were about worn out. So I think that no matter who McCarthy started in that game he would have drawn criticism. What he did was his decision and it was good enough for me, then and now.

Gene Bearden started for the Indians. He had a great year for them. He won twenty games, which he had never done before and which he never did again. He was a left-hander and his best pitch was a knuckleball. The next year the hitters started laying off the knuckler, which wasn't always a strike, and he had to start coming in with other pitches, which didn't work too well for him and he never had much success again. But in 1948 he was great. He beat us in that play-off game, 8–3. Lou Boudreau hit two home runs for them.

We might have done better that year, but it was just about then that Tex Hughson's arm went bad and Dave Ferriss' arm went bad. You lose two pitchers like that at the same time and you're going to hurt. Hughson was some pitcher when he was right. He had a good fastball, and he could throw just about any pitch you can name. We thought we were fixed for pitching for at least five years, but then those two hurt their arms.

The next year wasn't much different. It came down to the last game of the season at Yankee Stadium. We'd come in there with two games to play and needing just one to clinch it. We lost the Saturday game and that put us in a tie with the Yankees. We started Ellis Kinder in that last game and they went with Vic Raschi.

I remember something Ellis Kinder said on the bus after the Saturday game: "You get me three runs tomorrow and you've got yourselves a pennant." Well, if we would have done that for him we would have won. We went into the top of the eighth inning losing, 1–0, and had to take Ellis out for a pinch hitter. Then in the bottom of the eighth the Yankees scored four more. In the top of the ninth we scored three off of Raschi. Those were the three Ellis had asked for, and if we would have done that while he was still in there we would have taken it, because he was pitching great ball. But it wasn't enough and we lost, 5–3.

So that was two of them we'd lost on the last day of the season. I was beginning to wonder if there was such a thing as a pennant. It's really frustrating to come so close and go away empty. Look at it this way; in 1948 we tied, in 1949 we lost by a game, and in 1950 we lost by four games. That's missing three pennants by a total of five games. We just didn't have that little extra in pitching. Cleveland had Lemon, Wynn, Garcia, Feller. The Yankees had Raschi, Reynolds, Lopat, and then Ford. We never seemed to have that extra depth, particularly that big man coming out of the bull pen to put the cork in the game.

I had my biggest year in 1950. Everything broke right for me. It happens like that once in a while. I woke up in the morning feeling great, went out, got my base hits, and kept it going for a whole season. Ended up hitting .354 and leading the league. The funny thing about it was that we had such a powerful club in 1950 that I still had a problem breaking into the lineup.

I opened the season at first base but then chipped my ankle and was out for three weeks. So they brought up Walt Dropo and he got hot and stayed hot all year. When I was ready to play again there was no place to put me, even though I was able to play almost any position on the field. We had Dropo, Bobby Doerr, Vern Stephens, Johnny Pesky, Williams, Dom DiMaggio, Al Zarilla. And every one of them was hitting hard. Doerr was low man among the regulars that year, and he hit .294. The club average was over .300. I think it's going to be a while before you see that again.

Then Williams broke his elbow in the All-Star game and I went into left field. When Ted came back I started filling in wherever they needed me. I played outfield, third base, second base, first base. But I still can't break in regularly anywhere— and all the while I'm leading the league! But it really didn't bother me. I didn't think that much about it. I just tried to do whatever they wanted me to. When you're on a great ball club you tend not to think about yourself that much; there are too many interesting things going on, like every time Ted Williams comes to bat, for instance.

We lost Williams for nearly half a season in 1950 but still made a run for the pennant. We missed out by just a few games. But that's a hard man to replace. Ted was some kind of man to have in that lineup, especially in a close game. You were always in it as long as you knew Ted was coming up. He could rock it all of a sudden and everybody knew that. It had to be on the mind of the opposing pitcher; he just had to be giving some thought to Ted's coming up. It's hard to measure that kind of advantage, of course, but it has to be a factor.

With Ted in there we often had to play a different game; the guys batting ahead of him did, anyway. We never did steal much, because with him hitting behind you you didn't want to take a chance on getting thrown out, and neither was it always a good idea to open up a base because they were apt to put him on. Also, you had to have your wits about you when it came to taking an extra base; you never tried it unless you could put it in your hip pocket, because again you were leaving an open base and didn't want to tempt them into walking him. I'll tell you another thing you had to think about when you were on first and he was up: You had to keep your eye on him, because he could scald that ball, and not just in the air either. I've never seen anybody hit a ball on the ground the way Ted did. It seemed to pick up speed every time it bounced, like there was a little rocket in it trying to take off.

When you're talking about Williams' hitting there's another thing you've got to remember—he was doing it in what was probably the most difficult park in the big leagues for a left-handed batter. The stands break away sharply from that foul line in right field and the power alley is a long way back. And when that wind was blowing in it was really rough. When he got hold of the ball it usually didn't make much difference; he could ride it out. But you had to be as strong as Ted was to do it consistently.

I'd have to say that Herb Score was the hardest-throwing left-hander I ever batted against. It was a damned shame what happened to him, getting hit in the eye the way he did. He seemed to lose something after that. He and I were teammates for a while, on the White Sox. I remember one time, he was pitching and I was playing third. A guy swung at the ball and rolled one up on the grass off to the side of the mound. Score never moved. I had to come way in and field it, and of course by that time the man was on first base.

I said, "Herb, you've got to field that ball. You've got to come off that mound for those."

He said, "I didn't see it."

Well, I knew then that there was something the matter. Either he was throwing the ball so hard that he couldn't pick it up after it was hit, or he was having a problem seeing. Whenever he was pitching I was scared to death somebody would hit another one back at him. If he wasn't seeing those little rollers, then you knew he wouldn't see one that was shot back at him.

Bob Feller was another guy who could throw that ball. I don't have to tell you that. I'll never forget the first time I saw him pitch. That was in '47, first year I was up. Cronin sent me in to pinch-hit. "Make him throw you a strike," he said. I did better. I made him throw three of them, all in a row. I went back and sat down and said to myself, "Man, you're in the wrong league." I'd never seen anything like that. Then after the game I hear some of the guys saying in the clubhouse, "He's lost it. Doesn't have it anymore." I thought, *Lost it?* If he's lost it then he sure as hell doesn't miss it. If he had more stuff before the war, as some of them told me he did, then I'd hate to have seen him. As Satchel Paige used say, "If anybody threw that ball any harder than Rapid Robert, then the human eye couldn't follow it."

But I'll tell you something—Feller wasn't the toughest pitcher I ever batted against. At least when he threw that fast ball you knew it was coming, you had some idea where it was going to be, and now and then you'd get your bat on it and it would go. You'd get your shots off of him. But if I had to pick myself one guy that I wouldn't want to hit against when he was right, it would be Hoyt Wilhelm. It was a battle just to get the bat on that knuckleball. You know good and well, how in the hell is a man going to hit a ball that the catcher can't even catch? I've heard guys pumping somebody up about how Wilhelm knew which way the ball was going to break. Well, I thought if that was so, then Wilhelm would have got together with his catcher now and then and let him in on the secret, especially with a man on third base.

In June '57 I was traded to Baltimore and after that season I was traded again, to the White Sox. Then all of a sudden, after so many years, I got lucky. Found myself on a pennant winner. The 1959 White Sox. We had a good bunch of boys there. They played together, as a unit, better than any club I ever played on. We were a fine defensive team and we had phenomenal pitching. Four good starters—Early Wynn, Bob Shaw, Billy Pierce, and Dick Donovan. And then there were those two guys coming out of the bull pen all year, Turk Lown and Gerry Staley. They were exceptional.

They called us the Go-Go Sox. Remember that? We had a lot of Punch-and-Judy hitters. Now and then somebody would hit one hard, but not too often. But we did everything that the book says you're supposed to do, bunt them over, hit and run, make the good plays in the field. We hit fewer home runs than any other team in the league and had one of the lowest batting averages. But we had the great pitching, the good defense, and speed—we were way ahead of everybody else in stolen bases. A completely different team from those great Red Sox teams. And we won ourselves a pennant.

We won it because we were able to dominate our chief contenders—Cleveland. We worked the Indians over real good. We played them a four-game series in Cleveland at the end of August and swept them four straight. I think that broke their backs. But you talk about a team doctoring an infield. They knew we were a running team—we had Luis Aparicio, Nellie Fox, Jim Landis, and a few other guys who carried that mail around the bases for you. Well, the Indians had that infield plowed up with loose sand lying around, I swear it was a few inches thick, to stop us from running. Didn't do them any good. After we took Cleveland those four straight nobody could stop us. The feeling on the team was, *We's in business.*

Along with Aparicio, Fox, and Landis, we had Bubba Phillips, Earl Torgeson, Jim Rivera, Al Smith, Jim McAnany, Sherman Lollar. That Lollar was a great guy. You know, you've generally got one guy on a club that fixes gloves. He'll restitch them or lace them if somebody asks him to. Sherm Lollar was the guy who did it on our club. One time Clint

Courtney, the catcher, came into Chicago. He wanted some work done on his mitt. Lollar took it and worked on it. Then, just for the hell of it, when he was finished Sherm took a big block of limburger cheese, cut off some pieces and stuffed them up into the glove. When he went into the dugout to hand Courtney the glove, he had the rest of the cheese concealed in his hand.

"Here you are," Sherm said. "Go get 'em now."

While Courtney was examining the job Lollar had done, Sherm gave him several friendly pats on the back, smearing that cheese all over Courtney's shirt.

Then the game started and Courtney went behind the plate. It was a hot day and that stink started rising off of his shirt. You couldn't get within ten feet of the plate without smelling it. If I'm not mistaken, the umpire finally made him go in and change it.

Ted Kluszewski joined us late in the year and without him we would have been hurting. They tried to stop him with left-handed pitching, but he damn near killed some of them. Ted was right on top of the plate and they tried to burn him inside, but, boy, did he hang some out. He hit some line drives through the box that I'll bet are still giving some pitchers nightmares. Of course Ted is big and strong; he's got to be one of the strongest men I ever met, and also one of the nicest.

When he joined the team they assigned him to room with me. "Bill," he said, "sometimes I do some heavy snoring. If it bothers you, just give me a kick."

Sure enough, that first night he starts snoring, real loud. I can't sleep. I'm lying there looking over at him, at this big, big guy. He had told me to kick him. And I'm thinking: *Kick Ted Kluszewski?* Suppose it just happens that tonight he doesn't feel like being kicked? I thought it over for a long time, and then wrapped that pillow around my ears and went to sleep.

Getting into the Series finally after so many years was a real thrill. Boy, you don't know what that's like until you're in it. The phone was jumping off the hook with everybody calling for tickets. I never knew how many third and fourth cousins I had. "Hey, Billy old buddy, don't you remember me?"

We bombed the Dodgers, 11-0 in the first game. Then they beat us some tight ball games. Drysdale beat us one game, but the guy who really stopped us was their relief pitcher, Larry Sherry. He won two in relief and snuffed us out in two others.

The Dodgers were using the Coliseum out there as a home park, and that was the worst place I ever played in, as far as seeing the ball was concerned. In fact I got hit with a ball I didn't even see. Sherry hit me in the knee with one, I never saw it.

They beat us in six games, but we never disgraced ourselves. We weren't the greatest team in baseball history, but we played ball together like we thought we were. And I'll never forget those pitchers. What a staff! I'll tell you, if we would have had those guys in Boston during those big years we would have had some fun. We could have closed shop in August and gone fishing.

ROBIN ROBERTS

ROBIN EVAN ROBERTS
Born: September 30, 1926, Springfield, Illinois
Major-league career: 1948–66, Philadelphia Phillies, Baltimore Orioles, Houston Astros, Chicago Cubs
Lifetime record: 286 wins, 245 losses

Robin Roberts was one of the greatest pitchers in National League history. A power pitcher with remarkable control, he hit his peak in 1952, winning 28 and losing 7. From 1950 through '55 Roberts was a 20-game winner; he led the league five consecutive years in complete games, five consecutive times in innings pitched, twice in strikeouts, twice in shutouts, four times in victories.

Roberts was voted into the Hall of Fame in January, 1976

When I was in grade school in Springfield, Illinois, I went to a little two-room school called East Pleasant Hill. There were two teachers; one taught the first four grades in one room and one taught the next four grades in the other room.

In my eighth-grade year, when we were graduating, we had a sports night. At that time Grover Cleveland Alexander was living in a hotel in Springfield. I guess he was sort of down and out at the time. One of the teachers asked him to come to the sports night and talk to us, and Alex said he would. We had our dinner and afterward Alexander got up to speak. We knew who he was, of course, that he had pitched for the Phillies and the Cardinals and was one of the greatest that ever lived. So when he stood up to say a few words you could have heard a pin drop. This is what he said: "Boys, I hope you enjoy sports. But I will warn you about one thing: Don't take to drink, because look what it's done to me." And he sat down. That's all he said. That's all the man said.

That was a long, long time ago. I've never forgotten the sight of that man, that great pitcher, standing up and baring his soul in front of a bunch of awestruck kids. If anybody had told me that night that I was going to grow up and become a pitcher for the Philadelphia Phillies and break a lot of the club records that Grover Cleveland Alexander had set, well, you can imagine what I would have told them.

I grew up just outside of Springfield, in farming country, though not on a farm. But we did have two acres and wherever we had dirt we grew something edible. I was one of six children—four boys and two girls. My dad was a coal miner. He came over from Wales after the First World War and settled in Springfield.

I guess you might descibe us as poor, but we never thought about it; we were a close family and we had a good time together. We used to take Dad's Bull Durham tobacco sack and fill it full of grass and hit it with a cricket stick that he had for some reason brought over with him from Wales. That was the first bat we used. That's really how I started playing baseball.

I always thought about playing sports, but never particularly about a career in professional baseball. In those days we didn't have television; we listened to the games over the radio and baseball seemed out of reach for most kids at that time. It was all a dream. We just couldn't imagine ourselves as major-league ballplayers, whereas today you can see it on television and it has greater reality to kids. I think, too, that in a curious way it was a little easier to be a ballplayer in those days because it *was* all a dream, and so you stayed natural and enjoyed yourself. Today kids of twelve and thirteen start trying to make it and I think they run the danger of becoming too self-conscious and lose some of their naturalness.

When I was nineteen I went to Michigan State on a basketball scholarship. After my freshman year I went into service, then I came back and played basketball at Michigan State in my sophomore year. I had always played a lot of football and a lot of baseball, too. When I went out for baseball at Michigan State they were surprised that I could play, because I was there on a basketball scholarship. I had played third base and the outfield in high school and on the sandlots. I pitched only when they needed somebody; I could always throw the ball hard, but I had never given much thought to pitching.

So when I came out for the baseball tryout the coach was a little surprised and said to me, "What are you doing here?"

"I think I can play baseball," I said.

"What do you play?" he asked.

"What do you need?"

"Pitchers."

"That's what I am," I said. "A pitcher."

I figured it made sense to go out for what he needed. So from age nineteen on I concentrated on pitching. As I said, I could throw hard, and I could throw strikes; even as a kid I could always throw strikes, and I seemed always to have that smooth delivery.

So I started pitching for Michigan State. Then I played college-league ball in Vermont for two summers, for Montpelier. The scouts started coming around in Vermont that second summer, in 1947. I received six invitations to come and work out in September. Let's see, there was the Phillies, of course, and the Yankees, Red Sox, Tigers, Athletics, and Braves. I had a schedule mapped out to meet these clubs in different towns. The Phillies happened to be first, and I worked out with them in Chicago.

After the workout they said they would give me $10,000 to sign. Now, I had no great understanding of bonuses then, although Curt Simmons had received a big one that May from the Phillies. I just didn't figure myself for a big bonus. I was so anxious to get into baseball that I didn't worry about that. I would have been happy to sign for two thousand.

I told the Phillies, however, that I felt a loyalty to my promise to work out with the other clubs, who had made arrangements for me. The next day the Phillies said they'd pay me $15,000. Well, I was still loyal, but loosening up now. The third day they pushed it up to twenty-five thousand.

Now, that was a lot of money, particularly back in 1947. So I had something to think about. You know, when I was a kid my parents were often on me for playing baseball and not helping my brothers work. I'd read where Lou Gehrig had bought his mother a house out of his baseball earnings, and I'd always thought what a nice thing that was and wished I could do the same for my mother someday. So when Babe Alexander, the Phillies' traveling secretary, told me they would give me twenty-five thousand, I said, "That would buy a nice house, wouldn't it?"

"It sure would," he said.

"Okay then," I said. "Let's go."

So I never did work out with the other clubs, and you can't help but to wonder how high it would have gone if I had—the big-league clubs were throwing around some mighty fancy bonuses in those years. But I signed with the Phillies and have never regretted it.

The first thing I did was buy my mom that house. I think it cost around $19,000. Then I bought myself a car and a couple of new suits. It was great. I was on top of the world. The problem was, I didn't know anything about money, specifically about taxes. I ended up having to borrow from my father to pay my income taxes. It took most of what he'd saved all his life. Everybody thought I was so rich, but I wound up owing money. I paid my father back with my Series check in 1950. It took me two years to get even.

I started the 1948 season with Wilmington. I pitched there for two months, compiled a 9 and 1 record and was called up. The date was, I think, June 17, and I pitched against the Pirates the day I came up. I pitched against Elmer Riddle and he threw a low-hit shutout against me and I lost, 2–0. This was a little more than two years after the coach at Michigan State asked me what position I played.

Naturally I was thrilled about coming up. Surprisingly enough, and I can't explain this, I felt I belonged, right from the beginning. I felt I could pitch in the major leagues. I think it was knowing I could throw knee high and that I could throw hard. I'll tell you though, I might have had second thoughts after facing my first batter. He was Stan Rojek. I was very nervous and threw four of the wildest pitches you've ever seen. The next batter was Frankie Gustine. I went to a full count on him, and then struck him out on a bad pitch. From that moment on I was never nervous in the major leagues again.

I don't think anyone was ever able to concentrate in a baseball game any better than I was. I stood out there in total isolation, just throwing that ball as well as I could. Nothing bothered me. I can remember those good ball games in the early fifties when we played the Dodgers in Philadelphia. Generally it was Newcombe and me, and there would be around 35,000 people in the stands. After the game I would be driving home with my wife and I'd say, "Was there a big crowd tonight?" "It was jammed," she'd say. Not once, not warming up, not pitching, had I ever looked at the crowd. Nor did I ever hear them. That's how intensely I concentrated.

In fact, I would concentrate to the point where I would not even see the batter; I would only see the bat as he swung. When I was pitching well I saw only the catcher. I was telling some young pitchers that once, in spring training. They thought I was kidding; couldn't convince them. Well, that fall in the World Series Spahn pitched a two-hitter against the Yankees, and in the write-up the next day Spahn told the reporters, "I knew I was going to be good because I didn't see anything but the bat early in the game." I cut that baby out and the next spring showed it to those kids and said, "Look, Spahn and I say the same thing."

I guess it's hard for anyone to imagine that kind of concentration. But I'm sure there were other pitchers who worked the same way. Did you ever watch Vic Raschi pitch? I'm sure he concentrated like that. Most guys that are fastball pitchers must concentrate that way, because if you don't follow-through all the way it takes just a little bit off your fast ball. You've got to finish throwing the ball, you've got to throw it by them; you can't stop at the batter, you've got to go on to the catcher. I was always pitching the full way to the catcher; as far as I was concerned that was where the ball was going—to the catcher, not the batter.

Whenever I threw a home-run ball, and Lord knows I threw plenty of them, I usually knew as soon as I saw that full swing what I had done wrong. Of course, when they hit them to opposite fields or over my head to center field I never felt bad. I'd tell myself, "Well, he hit a good pitch." But whenever they would pull them, I'd know I'd made a mistake. That's why I was never upset by a home run, because I knew immediately what had happened and was able to correct it; because as soon as I saw a guy getting his full body into a swing I knew I hadn't finished throwing the ball the way I should have. It was never a mystery to me what had happened.

I was never impressive as a pitcher. I just got them out. I wouldn't strike out more than three or four in a game, but two of them would be with a man on third and one out. Listen, that's when you'd *better* strike them out. I could always throw the ball just a little harder when I had to.

Was I ever sorry I hadn't signed with the Yankees? No. I think one of the most unfair things is people belittling the ball club with which I compiled my record. From 1948 until 1956 the Phillies were a real solid baseball team. A lot of people say I won 286 games pitching primarily with an inferior Philly club, and that's not only unfair, it's untrue. You don't win that many games without getting a lot of help, I don't care how good you are. I won 28 one year; you don't do that with a bad ball club. We had fellows like Granny Hamner, Willie Jones, Richie Ashburn, Del Ennis, Andy Seminick, Eddie Waitkus. They could play ball.

Being with the Yankees wouldn't necessarily have meant that many more wins, because how many can you win? Beginning with my second full year my win totals were 20, 21, 28, 23, 23, 23, 19. Remember, I led the National League six years running in games started; if I'd been with the Yankees I might not have gotten the opportunity to pitch that often. I was so happy to be with who I was with that I never had any regrets. Of course from '56 on we were not a good ball club, and to be frank, I was part of that decline, I was not as good a pitcher as I had been. So those years are not good memories. But as far as those early years with the Phillies are concerned, I wouldn't want to trade them for anything.

When I joined the team Schoolboy Rowe was still there. He was about through then, but still a beautifully coordinated athlete. Big, graceful guy. We were on the staff together for only about a year or so and then they released him. I was working out in the outfield before a night game, and I look up and here he comes, carrying his bag. He was leaving.

"Robin," he says, "I've been released. I'm leaving. But before I go I just want to tell you that you're going to be some pitcher; though there's something you want to look out for— you give your curveball away. I thought I would tell you that before I leave."

I thanked him, wished him well, and watched him walk away. But wasn't that curious? As long as I was on the staff with him, in a sense competing with him, he wouldn't tell me I was tipping my curve. But when he knew he was leaving, he told me. I guess baseball was that way in his day—he came up in the early thirties, remember. When you were on a pitching staff you were rooting for your team of course, but at the same time you were competing with other pitchers to stay there. That was a good illustration, I think, of the old-time attitudes.

The Eddie Waitkus incident? Sure I remember it. It happened in July of '49. I'd been with the ball club a little over a year at the time. I didn't know anything about it until the following morning. I was having breakfast in the hotel dining room and somebody came up to me and asked how Waitkus was.

"I guess he's all right," I said. "Why?"

"He was shot last night," the guy said.

That was the first I heard about it. I'll tell you exactly what I was told and what I believe. Eddie roomed with Bill Nicholson. Eddie was a bachelor. He was out on a date that night—this was in Chicago—and he came in at about a quarter to twelve. While he was out a girl had called the room. She asked for him and Nicholson told her he wasn't there. She left a message, asking Nicholson to tell Waitkus that so-and-so from his hometown was there in the hotel and wanted to say hello. She even gave a street address that was near Eddie's home.

When Eddie came in Nicholson gave him the message. The room number was included. So he went up to her room. This is the way Waitkus told me what happened: He knocked on the door and the girl said "Come in." When he walked in there was nobody in the room. He looked around, and all of a sudden the girl jumped out of a closet with a rifle and shot him. Just like that. She just missed his heart.

You could make a different story out of it, but how does a guy get shot with a rifle if there's anything going on? It had to happen the way Eddie said it did. It turned out that the girl wasn't from his hometown at all. They say she used to hang around the ball park in Chicago all the time.

Waitkus was injured very seriously; I believe he was on the critical list for a while. But he recovered and came back to play the next year and helped us win the pennant.

We finished sixth in 1948, then third in '49. So while a lot of people may have been surprised when we won the pennant in 1950, that didn't include us. We were an improved club. We were a relaxed, cocky bunch of guys; we knew we could play ball. Bob Miller joined us, Curt Simmons became an outstanding pitcher that year, Bubba Church had a good year. Mike Goliat came in and became the second baseman we'd been needing. And of course Jim Konstanty had a big year coming out of the bull pen. We just put it together in 1950. But more than anything else, and I don't think we appreciated it until later, was the leadership given by Eddie Sawyer, our manager, and a wonderful person.

They called us the "Whiz Kids." But that was a little misleading. Although a lot of us were young, we had our share of experienced players, like Seminick, Waitkus, Ken Heintzelman, Konstanty, Dick Sisler.

Coming down to the end of the season it looked easy for us. We had a seven-game lead with nine days to go. But before we knew what was happening we were in Ebbets Field on the last day of the season, having to win that game to avoid a play-off with the Dodgers. People talk about a collapse, except they don't know what they're talking about. We got hurt badly in September. Church got hit in the eye with a line drive off the bat of Ted Kluszewski and was out for the rest of the year. Then Miller suffered a back injury. And to cap it off, Simmons left in the middle of the month to go to military service. So we wound up playing our last ten games with one regular starter available—me.

The lead began to melt away, until that last day. We have to win it, or else we're tied with the Dodgers. It was going to be my fourth start in eight days, and for some mysterious reason, whether it was youth or enthusiasm or whatever, I had as good stuff on that eighth day as I'd ever had. I should have been worn out, but I wasn't.

That was the biggest game I was ever involved in. As I say, I had good stuff all the way, and, incidentally, so did Don Newcombe; it was just one fine baseball game.

We were ahead 1–0 until around the last of the sixth. Then Pee Wee Reese came up and hit one out to right field. Talk about oddball things happening. On top of the right field wall was a screen and where the screen came down to the wall there was a ledge. Well, he hit one against the screen and it dropped straight down to that ledge and just lay there. After that game they changed the ground rules and made it a double; but at that time it was all you could get and naturally Reese, with the ball just sitting up there, got four bases. I'll never forget the sight of Del Ennis standing there looking up at it, waiting for it to come down. But it never did. That tied the game at one apiece.

Did I get the feeling the gods were against me when that happened? No. I can honestly say that I never let anything upset me on the mound. Not errors, not bloop hits, not anything. And I think that good disposition probably helped me as much as the good throwing arm. After Reese had circled the bases I simply got another ball and went back to work.

We went into the last of the ninth still tied. Let's set the inning up. Cal Abrams led off and I went to three and one on him. I threw him a pitch inside, low and inside. Larry Goetz was the umpire, one of the two or three best umpires I ever saw. Larry called it a ball. I remember my reaction at the time—I didn't think it was a ball, but it was close. So I walked Abrams. Reese came up. Twice he tried to bunt and fouled them off. Now, in a situation like that you go inside, to keep the guy from hitting behind the runner. I went inside and Pee Wee hit a rope to left field, a real shot. So now they're on first and second and Snider is up, and Robinson is next. This is getting serious.

Snider's got to bunt, right? That's the way you're supposed to play it, aren't you? Now, I don't know if Ashburn was moving in a little bit in center field. If he was it was because he, like me, was anticipating a bunt and wanted to be ready to back up a play at second base. But there was no pickoff on; that's all story. If there was a pickoff on I didn't know about it, and I had the ball. So I think Richie probably thought Snider was going to bunt, and so did I. Consequently, I didn't throw the ball hard. I was more intent on getting off the mound and fielding the ball and trying to keep Abrams from getting to third.

To my surprise, Duke swung away. I'll never forget it. When he hit it I thought it was a line drive to Goliat at second; but it was to Goliat's right, into center field. I think Abrams might possibly have got a little bit of criticism that was unjust, because I can remember turning and seeing him holding up, and I think he thought too that Goliat might catch it. It was a vicious shot, but it wasn't high in the air. So Abrams had that late jump and Ashburn was in close and caught the ball on the first or second hop in running stride. Richie was not known for his throwing arm, however, so the third base coach sent Abrams in. As it turned out Richie threw a one-hopper to Stan Lopata and Abrams was out by fifteen feet. It wasn't even close.

The runners had moved up, so now it was men on second and third and one out and Robinson was up. Sawyer came out and said put Robinson on. Which made sense. So we walked Jackie to load the bases and that brought up Furillo. Sawyer told me to keep the ball down because Furillo was a high-ball hitter. My first pitch was eye-high, but I got away with it because Carl popped it straight up. The next batter was Hodges and he hit an easy fly to right field. Del Ennis came in, and a lot of people don't know this, but the ball got into the sun and Del had to fight it a little and caught it right against his chest for the third out.

It wasn't until I walked off the mound after that inning and sat down that I realized how petrified I'd been.

So we went into the tenth inning. I was the leadoff hitter. And I singled up the middle, which not many people remember. I started that tenth inning with a base hit. It wasn't a hard-hit ball, it was a seeing-eye baby that went through the middle. Waitkus came up and Sawyer let him hit away. He hit a looper to right center that dropped in and I went down to second base. Ashburn tried to sacrifice but I was thrown out at third.

So now we had men on first and second and one out. Dick Sisler came up. He'd already had three hits. Well, he tagged one very hard, a line shot into the left-field seats. That puts us up, 4–1. I still had to get three more outs in the last of the tenth, and there was no doubt in my mind then that I would. I got them, one, two, three, and Philadelphia had its first pennant since 1915—thirty-five years.

After pitching four games in eight days they couldn't start me in the World Series opener because I'd had only two days rest. Konstanty started and he lost, 1–0. I pitched the second game. I was a little shaky at the beginning and gave up a lot of hits, but they got only one run. Then we tied it up. We went into the tenth inning and DiMaggio came up. He had popped out four straight times. When he came up in the tenth it was the only time that day that I wasn't leery of him. I assumed after getting him out four straight times that I was handling him all right. I think I might have been just a little bit overconfident with him that last time. The moment I saw the pitch going in I knew it didn't have the drive it should have had and I saw DiMaggio's whole body moving into it, and he hit it upstairs. That was the ball game.

They beat us four straight, in four low-scoring ball games. They scored only eleven runs in the Series, but that was enough.

You know, in 1951, for the third year in a row the Dodgers and the Phillies played extra innings on the last day of the season to decide the National League pennant. In 1949 they beat us in ten to win it over St. Louis; in '50 we beat them in ten to win it; and while we weren't in it ourselves in '51, they had to beat us to gain a tie with the Giants. That was the year the Dodgers lost a 13½ game lead in the last six weeks. When they came into Philadelphia for that final series they were in trouble.

On Saturday night I pitched nine innings against Newcombe and he whipped me, 5–3. When I lost a ball game I really took it home with me. I brooded. I couldn't sleep. So, not being very good company and not wanting to bother my family, I lay down in a hammock in my backyard with a half dozen cans of beer and just sipped and rocked all night and watched the sun come up.

When I went to the ball park on Sunday I figured I'd be the last guy they'd want to call on; what the hell, I'd pitched nine innings the night before. So I sat down in the bull pen and relaxed. The game was back and forth all the way. By the eighth inning, in spite of all the excitement, I was getting awfully sleepy. Then Sawyer called down and said, "Tell Roberts to warm up." So I got up and started throwing. Then they brought me in. We were leading by a run, the tying run was on second, and Furillo was the batter. He hit a shot to left field that tied it up. Then I got them out.

The game went on into extra innings. By this time Newcombe was back in it. In the last of the twelfth we loaded the bases with one out. Ennis came up and Newk reached back and struck him out. That brought up Waitkus, and he hit a low screaming liner. Jackie Robinson went in back of second and dove for it. Now, I was on third base, looking back as I ran. I saw Jackie dive for it, get it and then throw it back over his head. I still to this day think he trapped that ball, and he knew it, and in desperation was trying to get a force play at second. When I touched home plate I thought the game was over, but then I looked back again and the umpire was sig-naling that the ball had been caught. I've always wondered why Jackie, if he'd caught it on the fly for the third out, tried to throw the ball to second. Years later I met him at some function or other and I said, "Jackie, did you really catch that ball?" He laughed and said, "What'd the umpire say?"

Then in the top of the fourteenth Jackie hit one upstairs. After saving the game for them, he won it. That put them in the play-off, and set it up for Bobby Thomson. Not even Jackie could do anything about that.

But Robinson had that flair. He was something special on a ball field. I remember something that our coach, Cy Perkins, said to me once. After he'd watched Jackie for about five years, he came up to me one day and said, "You've heard all those stories about Ty Cobb, Robin?" I said yes. Cy had played against Cobb for quite a few years. "Well," he said, "that's the closest thing to Ty Cobb I ever saw. Jackie Robinson."

Jackie was probably as fine a baseball player as I ever saw. Sometimes he looked a little stiff and awkward out there—he was not a graceful performer—but what a base runner, what reflexes, and what a competitor! And he was tough. Nothing describes him better than just plain tough.

Cy Perkins, our coach, who I just mentioned, was a tremen-dous person. He was a wise and compassionate man who'd been around baseball a long time—he came up with Connie Mack's Athletics around the time of the First World War. He worked quietly with us and was always honest with us.

He was there when I first worked out with the ball club in Chicago. When I was working out that first day I heard some-body behind me say, "Don't let that kid get out of this park." I turned around and it was Cy Perkins, and that was the first time he had ever seen me.

In 1950 while I was warming up for a spring training

game—after just one and a half years in the big leagues—he said to me, "Kid, you look great." He always called me "Kid."

"Well, I feel fine," I said.

"I want to tell you something," he said. "I've been in baseball for thirty-five years and the five best pitchers I've ever seen are Walter Johnson, Lefty Grove, Herb Pennock, Grover Cleveland Alexander, and you."

I laughed. My lifetime record at that time was 22 wins and 24 defeats.

"I'm not kidding you," he said. "You've got the best baseball delivery I ever saw. You're our next three hundred game winner."

He never told me how to pitch, he never told me how to do anything. "Do it your way," he used to say. Occasionally I would get knocked out in the first inning and he would say, "Hey, don't worry; they're big leaguers. They're going to do that to you now and then." There was never criticism, always the attitude that he considered himself lucky to be able to work with us.

But he never looked upon me as being a special person because I was a good pitcher; I was a good pitcher by the accident of natural endowment. He felt it was ninety percent gift and ten percent effort. And he would make sure you knew that. He kept it all on a beautiful keel.

When I won a game I never saw him. He felt that I had the stuff and should have won the game; he'd never come over to congratulate me. But when I lost he'd always be there and never let me get morose or despondent about it. As I said, I never slept when I lost. I'd see the sun come up without ever having closed my eyes. I'd see those base hits over and over and they'd drive me crazy.

One night I got knocked out in the first inning. We left town that night and I was in a roomette on the train. I knew I was in for a rough night.

Perkins knocked on the door and came in.

"How are you doing?" he asked.

"Cy," I said, "how can I be doing?"

He sat there for a while and then started to reminisce. Very casually, in a detached sort of way. He went back to the days when he was playing with the Athletics, when they were battling the Yankees. Mr. Mack—they all called him Mr.

Mack—had Lefty Grove primed for this big game. Watching Grove warm up, Cy said he'd never seen him throw harder, which must have been something, because Grove could really fire. The A's went out in the top of the first and Grove walked to the mound. Well, the Yankees ripped him for seven runs in the bottom of the first. Perkins said he couldn't believe it. *Nobody* was supposed to hit Lefty Grove like that. Finally Mack had to take him out.

That's the story Cy told me that night while the train was barreling along and I was lying there feeling sorry for myself. Then he left. And I began to think: "Lefty Grove got knocked out in the first inning. What the hell am *I* worrying about?"

But that's the way Cy Perkins was. He didn't say, "Look, if it happened to Grove it can happen to anybody." He just went away and let it sink in on its own.

He was a very quiet man. He did the same thing for all the guys that he did for me, but always very quietly. The players all had tremendous respect and affection for him, but the owners barely knew he was there; they couldn't appreciate what he was doing.

One day in September, 1954, he came up to me and said, "They're getting rid of me." I thought he was kidding. But he wasn't. So the next day I went to see Bob Carpenter, who owned the club.

"Mr. Carpenter," I said, "Cy Perkins told me you're getting rid of him."

"Cy's getting old," he said.

"Don't get rid of him," I said.

"What do you mean?"

"I don't think you appreciate how much help he gives us," I said.

"You're kidding," he said.

"What does he make, Mr. Carpenter?"

"Why?"

"I'll pay his salary," I said. "That's what he means to me. And I know he means the same to the other guys."

He didn't believe me. They wouldn't listen and they got rid of him.

I had a reputation for not throwing at hitters. That was not entirely true, but most of the time it was true. If they knocked our guys down I would throw at their guys. But generally I didn't throw at anybody. Perkins said to me one day, "Robin, they've been getting on you for not knocking hitters down, haven't they?"

"Yes," I said.

"You never think of it, do you?" he asked.

"No," I said. "It never enters my mind."

He said, "It never does to the good ones."

Why should I have knocked them down without provocation? Here's a man I respect, a man who respects me, telling me not to worry about it. I just never gave a thought to getting involved with that stuff.

So Cy left in 1954. I stayed with the Phillies until 1961. I went to the Yankees in '62, but never pitched for them. They released me at the end of April, which is a bad time to get released, since everybody is pretty much set. So I came home. I didn't know what to do. I was thirty-four years old.

I get a phone call. It's Cy.

"What are they trying to do to you, kid?" he asks.

"What do you mean?"

"Don't you let them drive you out of this game. You'll be pitching shutouts when you're forty."

"Cy, you son of a gun," I said.

"I'm telling you, kid, don't you quit. There's no way that you can't keep pitching."

So I went to Baltimore and had some fine years there. My first year in the American League I was second in earned-run average. I pitched another five years in the big leagues—thanks to Cy's phone call.

Cy passed away a year later, but his encouragement had helped get me back into the big leagues, so I guess you could say he was still influencing my life.

I guess there are times when you do worry a little about getting old. Well, I'm nearly fifty now, but if I would have known how much I was going to be enjoying life at this age I would never have worried about getting old. But it would have been a great help, knowing at twenty-five how much I was going to enjoy being fifty. I don't have any reason whatsoever to look back with any regrets. What happened, happened, and I'm very proud of it and disappointed in some of it. But I wouldn't change any of it.

Regrets about not winning 300? No, not really. A lot of

people thought I was striving for 300 wins. But what I was really striving for was to pitch until I was forty-four or forty-five years old. I knew if I could do that the wins would take care of themselves.

I stayed with Baltimore until August of '65, when I went to Houston. I pitched well there, but found my arm swelling up when I threw curveballs. I had an arm operation that winter to correct the problem. The next year I tried to pitch but the arm wasn't right. So they released me and I went to the Cubs and finished out the year as a pitching coach. They wanted me back the next year, but I didn't go.

After resting all winter, my arm felt good. So I decided I'd go to Reading in the Eastern League and pitch until June 1 and if nobody picked me up, then I'd go home and pack it in. I was forty years old now. I did all right, won five, lost three, pitched a shutout. But June 1 came and nobody had picked me up. So I quit.

As I was driving home that night I knew it was over. I thought about Cy. I thought, "Well, Cy, you son of a gun, you said I'd pitch a shutout when I was forty, but you didn't tell me what league it was going to be in."

So I came home smiling.

FROM THE

OCTOBER

HEROES

ERNIE SHORE

ERNEST GRADY SHORE
Born: March 24, 1891, East Bend, North Carolina; Died: September 24, 1980
Major-league career: 1912, 1914–1917, 1919–1920, New York Giants, Boston Red Sox, New York Yankees
Lifetime record: 63 wins, 42 losses

Ernie Shore has come down through baseball history as the author of the most unusual perfect game ever pitched. This rare feat has tended to obscure what was a most successful, albeit brief, big league career. From 1914 through 1917, Shore was considered the ace of a Red Sox pitching staff that was notable for its abundance of talent. In 1915 he won 18 games and posted an impressive 1.64 earned run average. In World Series competition, Shore won three of his four starts, with a Series earned run average of 1.82.

I can't tell you how many times it's happened in my life. I mention my name to somebody and they say, "Ernie Shore? You're the fellow who pitched that perfect game, aren't you?" That's the game that stands out in people's minds. But to tell you the truth, it was the easiest game I ever pitched.

It was on June 23, 1917, at Fenway Park, against Washington. Babe Ruth actually started the game for us, but he didn't stay in there very long. He walked the first batter, Ray Morgan. Babe didn't approve of some of Brick Owens' ball and strike decisions and let the umpire know about it. Babe got to jawing so much that Owens finally told him to start pitching again or be thrown out of the game. That seemed to set Babe off even more and he said something like, "If I go I'm going to take a sock at you on my way out." Well, Owens gave Babe the thumb right then and there. Ruth tried to go after Owens but a few of the boys stopped him, and a good thing too.

I was sitting on the bench and Jack Barry, our manager and second baseman, came running over to me and said, "Shore, go in there and stall around until I can get somebody warmed up."

You see, he never intended to have me go in there and finish the game. What he wanted me to do was go out to the mound and try to kill as much time as I could while he got somebody else ready in the bull pen. But there wasn't too much stalling I could do, because when a pitcher was thrown out of a ball game the next man was entitled to just five warm-up pitches. That's how it was back then; I don't know how they work it today.

I took my warm-ups and then started pitching to the next batter. Well, on my very first pitch, Morgan, the fellow Ruth had walked, tried to steal second and was thrown out. I threw two more pitches and retired the side.

When I came back to the bench Barry said to me, "Do you want to finish this game, Ernie?" My ball was breaking very sharply and he had seen that.

"Sure," I said.

"Okay," he said. "Go down to the bull pen and warm up."

So I did that and came back for the second inning. From then on I don't think I could have worked easier if I'd been sitting in a rocking chair. I don't believe I threw seventy-five pitches that whole game, if I threw that many. They just kept hitting it right at somebody. They didn't hit but one ball hard and that was in the ninth inning. John Henry, the catcher, lined one on the nose but right at Duffy Lewis in left field. That was the second out in the ninth. Then Clark Griffith, who was managing Washington, sent a fellow named Mike Menosky in to bat for the pitcher. Griffith was a hard loser, a very hard loser. He didn't want to see me complete that perfect game. So he had Menosky drag a bunt, just to try and break it up. Menosky could run, too. He was fast. He dragged a good bunt past me, but Jack Barry came in and made just a wonderful one-hand stab of the ball, scooped it up and got him at first. That was a good, sharp ending to the game, which I won by a score of 4–0.

It wasn't until after the season that they decided to credit me with an official perfect game. There had been a little controversy about it because I had faced just twenty-six men. But they decided to put it in the books as a perfect game and it's been there ever since.

I didn't even know I had a no-hitter going, much less a perfect game, until I sat down on the bench in the eighth inning. Then one of the fellows said to me, "Do you know they don't have a hit off of you?"

Well, I didn't know.

"Maybe they'll get one in the ninth," I said. Then I laughed and said, "And maybe they won't."

They didn't.

A lot of my career was tied in with the Babe. In 1914 we were both pitching for Baltimore of the International League when the Red Sox bought us. Later on we both went to the Yankees. We were always good friends, Babe and myself. He was always a larger-than-life sort of fellow, even way back when. I guess there are more stories told about him than about anybody else in baseball. There's the one they tell about Babe using my toothbrush when we were roommates. Well, that's a good one, but it's not true. It was my shaving brush. I keep telling people the true story but they go right ahead and keep telling it the other way. So you can see how certain stories go on and on, whether they're true or not. When it comes to wanting to believe something, people can be very stubborn.

It's generally believed that Babe made his name in New York, with the Yankees. But they loved him in Boston too. He was always popular. One time we checked into the hotel in St. Louis. As soon as we had signed the register the clerk handed Babe a big basket full of mail.

"For you, Mr. Ruth," the clerk said.

Babe looked at it for a few seconds and then said, "The hell with it."

He went upstairs, leaving the basket there. I said to the clerk, "Let's open that mail and see what's in it."

Well, we opened it and among that pile of mail we found over a hundred checks made out to Babe, from people wanting him to endorse this or that product. I brought those checks upstairs to him but he still wasn't interested. He told me to leave them on the table and he would look at them later. I don't know if he ever did look at them. Money didn't mean very much to him.

It broke Boston's heart when the Red Sox sold Babe to New York. But you know, I'd have to say that Babe belonged in New York. Given his abilities and his personality, that was just the place for him. He sure got the publicity there.

I liked New York myself, even though I was just a North Carolina farm boy. I was raised on my Daddy's farm. Originally he'd been in the liquor business. He'd been a distiller, until the state went dry sometime around 1906 or '07. Then he went into farming on a full-time basis. It was general farming—tobacco, wheat, peas, things like that. I grew up working on the farm. Did I like it? Well no. You take work like setting tobacco with a peg, it just kills your back. It wasn't for me.

I went to Guilford College, which was nearby in Greensboro. Later on I did a little teaching there between seasons. Mathematics. My ambition was to become an engineer, but baseball killed that. In the beginning I had no idea at all of going into baseball, even though I always loved the game. I can still remember all the excitement at the college during the 1910 World Series. The Cubs played the Philadelphia Athletics. The Cubs had some great pitchers that year: Three Finger Brown, Orval Overall, Ed Reulbach. In those days you had to wait until the next day to get the score. You just stayed on edge until you finally got hold of that newspaper. I can remember one of the fellows taking out his pocket watch one afternoon and looking at it and saying, "Well, they're started. The game's on." That was about as close as you got to it in those days—knowing when the game was on and trying to imagine what was happening.

Baseball just sort of came upon me, so to speak. Pitching for Guilford College for two years I won twenty-four games and lost one. One day I was pitching against the University of North Carolina. It was the day after Easter Sunday, I remember, in 1912. The New York Giants were in town, working their way back home from spring training. One of the Giant ball players umpired the game and after it was over they made me an offer. It was my intention to finish college, but that offer to go up with the Giants sounded pretty good, so I took it.

I couldn't believe my eyes when I arrived in New York. Just an unbelievable place. Bowled me right over. All of those people, and those buildings, and those lights! You didn't know where to look first. Oh, I liked it. I liked it just fine.

Christy Mathewson was still with the Giants then. I got to know him fairly well. He was a congenial fellow, and so was their other ace pitcher, Rube Marquard. No, I didn't talk pitching with them. I was just a rookie and they were way above me. In those days nobody taught me anything. You had to learn by observing. A rookie had to have a sharp eye and the capacity to learn on his own.

John McGraw? No, I'd better not tell you what I thought of him. We'll just leave that aside. Not my type of fellow. He was aloof, kept himself apart from the players. He could be very abusive too. Oh, no, he never bothered Mathewson. Mathewson was something special and McGraw never got after him.

I left the Giants because I wanted to finish college, which I did in 1914, before I joined the Baltimore club. No, I didn't want to play for the Giants. Not after what happened. You see, I was with the ball club all of 1912, pitching batting practice. Then when they won the pennant they sent me home before the World Series. They didn't want me to share in the Series money. That didn't sit too well with me, so I asked for my release and they gave it to me.

I had never followed any particular team. But I knew the names of most of the players, especially Walter Johnson. Everybody knew who Walter was. Later, when I was with the Red Sox I pitched against him. How fast was he? That's a hard question to answer, since most of the time you could hardly see the ball. But there was one game when I got two hits off of him. That was pure luck because I never got many hits. After the first one, when I came to bat again the catcher started to kid me. Then he yelled out to Walter, "Bear down now, this is a good hitter."

I laughed and stepped in. Darn if I didn't hit one like a bullet right past Walter. When I got to first he looked over at me and smiled.

"Say," he said, "you *are* a pretty good hitter, aren't you?"

But that was lucky. Walter was the fastest pitcher that's ever been up there. I never saw Smoky Joe Wood in his prime, but they told me he was just as good as Johnson. In 1912 Joe won thirty-four games and lost only five. But then shortly after that he hurt his arm. When I joined the Red Sox, Joe was still a good pitcher, though not as fast as he had been. But they said that in 1912 Joe Wood was as good a pitcher as ever lived.

Hitters? Cobb was a tough one. Lord, was he tough. But, you know, he wasn't the greatest hitter I ever faced. That was Joe Jackson. Why? He just hit everything you threw up there, that's why. And I mean he *hit* it. There's a difference between getting your bat on the ball and hitting it, if you know what I mean. He once lined a ball between my legs that didn't touch the ground until it got out behind second base. Good Lord, if that ball would have struck me it would have killed me.

Cobb, you see, was a scientific hitter. As great as he was, he still had to work at it. He would drag bunt, go to left field, punch it here and there. Jackson just walked up there and swung. And when he moved that bat it was the purest and most natural swing you ever saw. There was no way you could fool him with a pitch. Every time he put his bat on the ball it was a line drive. And they just whistled! If he had elevated the ball the way Ruth did, he would have hit just as many home runs as Babe, no question about it.

Best game I ever pitched? No, it wasn't any of the World Series wins. It wasn't the perfect game, either. It was a game I pitched against the Tigers in Boston in 1915. On September 18, 1915, as a matter of fact. We were one or two games ahead of them in first place and knew we were going to have to stand them off if we wanted to win the pennant.

We went along to the top of the twelfth inning without a run being scored. I was pitching against Harry Coveleski. He was one of the best. Lord, I'll never forget that game. It was on a Saturday afternoon. We had the biggest crowd that had ever attended a ball game in Boston, up to that time. There were so many people we had to let them stand in the outfield, behind ropes. That was done a lot in those days. Mounted policemen patrolled back and forth to make sure the people stayed behind the ropes.

Ty Cobb led off the twelfth inning and hit a fly ball into the crowd for a ground rule double. So now I've got this holy terror standing out on second base with nobody out, with Bobby

Veach and Sam Crawford coming up. That's a peck of trouble. And it was going to get even worse.

Veach put down a bunt and I fumbled it. That got Cobb over to third. Then I was looking at Sam Crawford. Well, I walked him on purpose to fill the bases.

They sent up Marty Kavanaugh to pinch-hit for George Burns. He hit one on the ground to Larry Gardner at third and we forced Cobb at the plate. Ty went in there like a lion out of a cage—that's the way he was on the bases—but we had him out with plenty to spare.

The next fellow was Ralph Young. Well, I gave it everything I had and he grounded into a double play. When I walked off that mound I got a mighty nice cheer from the Boston fans.

Then in the bottom of the inning we scored a run and won the game. That was the best I ever pitched, and not only because I shut them out for twelve innings, but because we were fighting them for first place and needed that game. It helped take some of the steam out of Detroit and get us into the World Series.

I was certainly looking forward to pitching in the World Series. We had a great team on the Red Sox in 1915. One of the best pitching staffs ever: Rube Foster, Babe Ruth, Joe Wood, Dutch Leonard, myself. Carl Mays was on that staff too, but we had so many starters he had to stay in the bullpen all year. You look at the records of that staff sometime. The highest earned run average any of us had was around 2.4. And we had one of the best outfields anybody ever saw—Tris Speaker, Harry Hooper, Duffy Lewis. And fellows like Dick Hoblitzell, Heinie Wagner, Everett Scott, Larry Gardner, Jack Barry. Just a fine team. Bill Carrigan was the manager and he was tops. Best manager in the world. He was close to his players, and he had their respect. I never heard a man ever speak ill of him.

Carrigan told me I was going to open the Series, which was just swell with me, and quite an honor considering the talent we had on our pitching staff. No, I wasn't a bit nervous. Why should I have been? There were only three things that could happen—I could win, I could lose, or I could tie. That's what I always told myself when I went into the pitcher's box. So there was nothing to worry about. And when I had my good stuff I nearly always won. I was a fastball pitcher. I threw a ball that dropped, a natural sinker. And it dropped fast, too; real fast. When I had it going for me they hit nearly everything to the infield, very seldom to the outfield.

I drew a pretty good opponent for myself in that game—Grover Cleveland Alexander. One of the best. He was one of the first pitchers to throw what they call a slider today. He threw a live fastball too, and had good control. The Philadelphia papers were filled with praise for him. He was their ace and they were very proud of him and were counting on him. They called him Alexander the Great, and he surely was a great one.

Alex beat me out in that first game. I can tell you just how it happened, too. It's sixty-three years ago as we sit here today, but I can remember it as clear as anything. I told you they didn't often hit me to the outfield. Well, in the eighth inning I gave up a couple of runs and not one ball left the infield the whole inning.

The score was 1–1 when we went into that last half of the eighth. With one out I walked Milt Stock. Then Dave Bancroft came up. He hit one right on the nose to Jack Barry, who made a terrific stop of it. But Everett Scott didn't cover second base, to this day I don't know why. Maybe he didn't think Barry would get it. When Barry wheeled to throw to the base, nobody was there, and he held the ball just long enough for Bancroft to beat it out.

The next man walked and the bases were loaded. Then Gavvy Cravath stepped in. He was the great home run hitter of the day, you know. He had hit something like twenty-four home runs that year, which was the new record for a single season. If I tell you that Cravath hit more home runs that year than most *teams* did, you'll get some idea of what a slugger he was. So you can bet I was careful with him. I got him to hit one on the ground, but the best we could do was get him at first, and a run scored.

Then a fellow named Fred Luderus came to bat. He hit a little nubber toward the mound. Well, it had rained the night before and the grass was still wet and slippery. In fact they had burned hundreds and hundreds of gallons of gasoline on the field before the game to try and dry it. It helped some, but not enough. I went after the ball and my feet just flew out from under me and down I fell. I still had a chance to throw him out but the darndest thing happened. You see, in those days they had a path from home plate to the pitcher's box, a skin track without any grass on it. You don't see that anymore. With the ground so wet from the rain, there were spike marks in that path about an inch deep. Well, the ball hit one of those marks and curved right on away from me. All I could do was sit there and watch that little white ball roll away—so slowly I could see each stitch—while the run crossed the plate. Talk about bad luck. I should have been out of that inning without a run scored. You put their hits end to end and they still wouldn't reach the outfield grass.

Alexander said after the game that I pitched in hard luck, that the breaks went against me. Well, he was right about that. The other run they scored came in the fourth inning, on a slow roller hit by Possum Whitted that he just did beat out. And wouldn't you know it was the only hit Whitted got in the Series? But you shouldn't complain about those things. You get your share of the breaks too, and then it's the other fellow's turn to moan. Anyway, Alexander pitched a beautiful game against us. Just because you were *un*lucky doesn't necessarily mean the other fellow was lucky. Alex worked a fine game and he deserved to win.

In the top of the ninth we had a man on first and one out and guess who came up to pinch-hit for me? First time he was ever in a World Series. Babe Ruth. Babe told me later that he was trying to hit one out to tie it up for me, but the best he could do that time was ground out.

President Wilson was there the next day. He was the first President ever to come to a World Series game. As a matter of fact, we had to delay the game for about twenty minutes until he showed up. There was some grumbling on the bench about that, because the boys were all warmed up and set to go and then had to sit down and wait. But it worked out all right because we won that game, and we won the next one.

I came back to pitch the fourth game, against George Chalmers. I beat him, 2–1. That was the third straight game we won by that score. I'll tell you how we scored one of our runs, just to show you how those breaks even out. In the third inning we had a man on first and Chalmers fell while fielding a bunt. Later on in the inning Harry Hooper beat out a slow roller to score a run. Just stay in there long enough and keep believing, and you'll get your share of the breaks.

In the sixth inning, Duffy Lewis doubled home the second run and I held on to beat them. Lewis was the best hitter in the pinch I ever saw. In the game that we beat Alexander, we got the winning run in the last of the ninth. With a man on first they walked Speaker on purpose to get at Lewis. That was a sad mistake. I never will forget it. As he walked up to the plate Duffy turned around and said to us, "Watch me hit that first curve ball." Well, that's just what he did. He waited for the curve and hit it right by Alexander's ear, over second base and into center field.

A very unusual thing happened in that World Series. When we moved back to Boston we didn't play our games in Fenway Park; instead we played in Braves Field because the seating capacity was so much greater. We drew over forty thousand for those games in Braves Field, which was a new World Series attendance record up to that time. Nobody complained about the shift because it meant more money all around. The winner's share amounted to $3780 apiece. That was a year's pay for a lot of people in those days.

We won the fifth game in Philadelphia and that gave us the championship. Just to show you what a strange game baseball can be, we won that game on home run power—Duffy Lewis hit a home run and Harry Hooper hit two. What's so strange about that? Why, over the course of the whole season we hit only fourteen home runs. That's right, fourteen home runs for the whole season. Then we go into that last game and hit three. Hooper hit as many that day as he did all year.

I was looking forward to getting back home. It's a long season you know. I went back to Yadkin County in North Carolina and spent the winter hunting quail. Was I the big hero in town? Well, there was no town. I lived five miles from East Bend, out in the country.

I took the train out of Boston the day after the Series ended. Went to Greensboro, and from there caught another train to Winston-Salem. From Winston-Salem I went to Donaha. That was the railroad station. Nothing there but the depot. I was the only one who got off the train. My Daddy was waiting for me with the horse and buggy. He took me home.

I was glad to be home. You look forward to the season

opening, you look forward to winning the pennant and getting into the World Series, and then you look forward to getting home again. I think that's pretty good—to always be looking forward to something nice.

We won the pennant again the next year, in 1916. There was a Red Sox dynasty in those years. Boston won the pennant and the World Series in 1912, 1915, 1916, 1918.

In 1916 we played Brooklyn. They were called the Robins at that time, after their manager Wilbert Robinson. It was the first pennant ever for Brooklyn and, yes, I'll say there was some excitement about it. They had brass bands parading and the flags were flying and I guess just about everybody in Brooklyn was worked up over that World Series.

Brooklyn had some of the old Giants I'd known during that year I spent with New York, fellows like Chief Meyers, Fred Merkle, Rube Marquard. Rube opened up the Series for them. He was an awfully good pitcher, Rube was, but we peppered him in that game. I was pitching for the Red Sox and had them beat 6-1 going to the top of the ninth. I had very good stuff that day. Too good. The reason I say that is because my ball was breaking so much I had difficulty in controlling it. In the ninth I walked a few men and hit one and they scored four runs. Fell just one shy. We won it 6–5.

The second game is probably still the best ever pitched in a World Series. You know who the pitcher was? Babe Ruth. That's right. By that time Babe had developed into a great pitcher, just great. He won twenty-three games for us that year. And what a game he pitched in that Series! In the first inning he gave up an inside-the-park home run to Hy Myers. And that was all he gave them. We got the run back in the bottom of the third—Babe knocked it in himself with a ground ball—and that's the way it stayed.

Sherry Smith pitched quite a game himself, for Brooklyn. It went to extra innings. Babe shut them out for thirteen innings, until we got a run in the bottom of the fourteenth to win it. He was quite a boy, the Babe, wasn't he?

Brooklyn had a few rough hitters in their lineup. I'm thinking of Zack Wheat and Jake Daubert, although I don't recall that they hurt us too much in that Series. The fellow who gave us the most trouble was Stengel. That's right, Casey was playing right field for Brooklyn. Casey always had something to say, even in those days. I remember, just before the first game, during batting practice, Duffy Lewis and I were walking across the outfield and as we passed him Stengel said, "Hello, boys. What do you think your losing share is going to come to?"

We just laughed at him. We didn't think it was possible for anybody to beat us. Out pitching was too good. Why, we had five strong starters. Along with Babe and myself, there was Rube Foster, Dutch Leonard and Carl Mays. The five of us started just about every game that season.

Brooklyn won just one game in the Series. Jack Coombs beat Mays in the third game. Then Leonard won and I came back to beat them again in the last one, against Jeff Pfeffer. He was a twenty-five-game winner for them that year. The score was 4–1. I had my good stuff that day and pitched a three-hitter. The only run they got came in on a passed ball. I still remember that pitch. It broke so much it missed the catcher's mitt entirely. That's what my fastball would do. It sank awfullly sharp and sometimes the catcher couldn't handle it.

My ball was breaking so sharply all through the Series that Wilbert Robinson couldn't believe it. He said later that I was putting licorice on the ball and then sticking dirt to it. Not true. I never did that in my life. And I told them so. But Robinson didn't believe it. He said those low pitches were taking too many funny shoots. They kept asking to see the ball the whole time. I was glad for them to do it; it gave them something extra to think about. But I wasn't monkeying with the ball. I didn't have to. What they were seeing was the natural break I had on it.

The nice thing about that last game was we won it right at home. Our fans let go a really good shout for us when it was over. We got a standing ovation. It was the third world championship the team had given them in five years and they showed that they appreciated it.

The Red Sox should have won a lot more pennants in those years, but they didn't. That's when the Yankee dynasty started, in 1921. I can tell you about that.

You see what happened, Harry Frazee, who owned the Red Sox, kept getting into debt because of theatrical investments that weren't panning out. He was always in the need of cash and he found the right man in Colonel Ruppert, who owned the Yankees. Ruppert had plenty of money and he desperately wanted a winner. Up to that time the Yankees had never won the pennant. New York belonged to McGraw and the Giants, and Ruppert wanted to change that.

So with those show business losses keeping Frazee in the soup, he started selling players to the Yankees. I was one of the first to go, along with Duffy Lewis, in 1919. My arm was shot by that time and I didn't play but one more year and not a very good year at that. But then Frazee started selling them one after another. Over the next few years do you know who he sold to New York? Well, Ruth of course. And then there was Everett Scott, Wally Schang, Joe Dugan, and all of those pitchers who won pennants for the Yankees—Carl Mays, Herb Pennock, Sam Jones, Bullet Joe Bush, Waite Hoyt. Every one of them were twenty-game winners for the Yankees at one time or another.

So when they talk about that Yankee dynasty, I always say it was really a Red Sox dynasty, in a Yankee uniform.

LES BELL

LESTER ROWLAND BELL
Born: December 14, 1901, Harrisburg, Pennsylvania; Died:
  December 26, 1986
Major-league career: 1923–1931, St. Louis Cardinals, Boston
  Braves, Chicago Cubs
Lifetime average: .290

*Playing with steady, quiet efficiency, Les Bell was one of the
National League's better third basemen in the 1920's. His finest
year was 1926, when the Cardinals won their first pennant and
went on to defeat the Yankees in the World Series. Bell batted
.325 that year, drove home 100 runs, hit 17 home runs, and
played an excellent third base.*

I can see him yet, to this day, walking in from the left-field
bull pen through the gray mist. The Yankee fans recognized
him right off, of course, but you didn't hear a sound from
anywhere in that stadium. They just sat there and watched
him walk in. And he took his time. Grover Cleveland Alexander was never in a hurry, and especially not this day. It was
the seventh game of the World Series, he had pitched nine
innings the day before, and he was coming in now to face a
tough young hitter with two out and the bases loaded. It was
the bottom of the seventh inning and the score was 3–2 in our
favor.

Yeah, I can still see him walking that long distance. He just
came straggling along, a lean old Nebraskan, wearing a Cardinal sweater, his face wrinkled, that cap sitting on top of his
head and tilted to one side—that's the way he liked to wear it.

We were all standing on the mound waiting for him—me

and Rogers Hornsby (who was our manager and second baseman) and Tommy Thevenow and Jim Bottomley and Bob
O'Farrell. When Alec reached the mound, Rog handed him the
ball and said, "There's two out and they're drunk"—meaning
the bases were loaded—"and Lazzeri's the hitter."

"Okay," Alec said. "I'll tell you what I'm gonna do. I'm
gonna throw the first one inside to him. Fast."

"No, no," Rog said. "You can't do that."

Alec nodded his head very patiently and said, "Yes I can.
Because if I do and he swings at it he'll most likely hit it on
the handle, or if he does hit it good it'll go foul. Then I'm going
to come outside with my breaking pitch."

Rog looked him over for a moment, then gave Alec a slow
smile and said, "Who am I to tell *you* how to pitch?"

Then, to show you what kind of pitcher Alec was and what
kind of thinking he did out there, he said, "I've got to get
Lazzeri out. Then in the eighth inning I've got to get Dugan,
I've got to get Collins, and I've got to get Pennock or whoever
hits for him, one, two, three. Then in the ninth I've got to get
Combs and I've got to get Koenig, one, two, so when that big
son of a bitch comes up there"—meaning Ruth, of course—
"the best he can do is tie the ball game." He had it figured out
that Ruth was going to be the last hitter in the ninth inning.

So we all went back to our positions—I was playing third
base—and Alec got set to work. He had gone nine the day
before, and if he got out of this jam he still had two more
innings to go today, he was nearly forty years old—but doggone, there wasn't another man in the world I would have
rather seen out there at that moment than Grover Cleveland
Alexander.

The first time I ever saw Grover Cleveland Alexander was
in 1915. I was thirteen years old at the time. My Dad, who
worked for the railroad, got a pass and took me from Harrisburg to Philadelphia to see a big league game for the first
time. We saw the Phillies play at Baker Bowl. Boy, that was
a big day in my life. Alec didn't pitch that day, but I saw him
throwing on the sidelines. Couldn't keep my eyes off him.
Another player I remember seeing was Gavvy Cravath—he
was the champion home run hitter at that time. When I got
back home I was the center of attention—none of my friends

had ever seen a big league game and they wanted to hear all about it. The next big league game I saw was eight years later, in 1923, when I was in the lineup for the Cardinals.

I was born and raised in Harrisburg. It was great growing up there in those years. Harrisburg was really a nice place. It was the capital city and it was a railroad town, the division point for the Pennsylvania Railroad between New York and Chicago and St. Louis. My Dad was a railroader all his life, a freight conductor, working in the yards in Harrisburg. When I came out of high school he said to me, "If you get a job on the railroad, I'll have you fired." Railroading was a tough job in those days, real tough. So it was the old story of a father wanting to see his son do better than he did. But I told him he didn't have to worry—I had my sights set on playing ball.

I was crazy about baseball. Always played it, as far back as I can remember. It was all I ever wanted to do. We always had a little pick-up team going. We'd get hold of gloves somehow—usually hand-me-downs—and we would make our own baseballs. We would take a little rubber ball and wrap twine around it and put friction tape on the outside. That's how it was done. And the darn thing would last a little while, too.

I went into semipro ball in 1919, after graduating high school. In those days semipro was a very good brand of ball around Harrisburg, and well organized. I played a few games a week in Harrisburg and then a few games in a little town called Columbia, not too far from Lancaster. All told I was making around seventy dollars a week playing semipro, which was decent money in those days.

Our manager in Columbia was Jimmy Sheckard, the old Cub outfielder. One day he said to me, "You interested in playing pro ball?" I told him I sure was. So he had a scout come in and look me over, a fellow named Billy Doyle from the Detroit Tigers. Doyle had his look and signed me and sent me down to Bristol, Tennessee. The funny thing was, I signed for two hundred dollars a month—less money that I was making in semipro. But that didn't bother me; I wanted a crack at pro ball. Sometimes you just feel that you've got to stretch yourself, see how good you are, and money is of secondary importance. I told myself I'd give it four years at most to see if I could make it to the major leagues, and if I couldn't, then I'd come back home and go to work.

Well, I went down to Bristol, stayed two weeks and got fired. Never did know why. The manager's name was Bell too, so maybe he figured one Bell on the club was enough.

When I got back home, Billy Doyle wrote me a letter and said not to worry, he would find me a job the next year. Which he did. Sent me out to Lansing, Michigan, in the Central League. I had no problems out there, played the whole season and hit .329. In the middle of the season the Cardinals bought me. They moved me around, to Syracuse, Houston, then to Milwaukee. In '23 they brought me up for a few games at the tail end of the season.

I'll never forget my first big league game. The club wasn't going anywhere, so they loaded the lineup with kids, me at third, another fellow at first, and so on. The first ball that was hit down to me I picked up cleanly and threw with everything I had. Listen, I had a strong arm. I sure did. I think I must have broken a seat ten or fifteen rows behind first base with that throw. A couple of innings later I had my second chance. This time that ball really flew, and I must have broken a seat *twenty* rows behind first base. When I came into the dugout after that inning I was feeling pretty blue. Who sits down next to me but the regular first baseman, Jim Bottomley. All he did that year was hit .371.

Jim put his arm around me and said, "Now, kid, Old Jim will be out there tomorrow playing first base. So when you throw the ball, just throw it in the *direction* of the base and Old Jim will get it."

That made me feel better, but I got to laugh now when I think of it. I was twenty-one and "Old Jim" was all of twenty-three. They called him "Sunny Jim" and he sure was all of that. What a fine gentleman he was, and a great ball player. He could do it all.

In 1924 I had a whale of a year with Milwaukee in the American Association, hitting .365. By that time I knew I could make the big leagues. I was itching for it. You can't hardly believe what a feeling it is when you know you're ready to bust out. In '25 I joined the Cardinals and became their regular third baseman.

I loved playing in the big leagues. Boy, I just loved it. It was everything I dreamed it would be and then some. What a way to make a living! I even enjoyed those long train rides, swinging back and forth across the country. I'd sit by the window and watch the farmland and small towns pass by, and now and then see a Model-T tooling along the country roads. You didn't see too many cars back then, especially in the boondocks.

The biggest day I ever had on a ball field was June 2, 1928, when I was with the Braves. We were playing Cincinnati at home and I hit three home runs in one game and came darned near a fourth. There was a screen that ran along the left field bleachers and stopped at an iron pole in center field. I hit a ball out there and it just hit that pole at the edge of the screen and ricocheted out into right-center. I got a triple out of it but had just missed another home run. I would have been the first man since Ed Delahanty in 1896 to hit four in one game. The funny thing about it was, I wasn't a home-run hitter; in fact that year I hit only ten. But I did get three of them in one game. It was a Saturday afternoon and the next morning I went out and bought every Sunday paper in Boston.

I had been traded to the Braves in 1928. We had an awful team. Just awful. In 1929 the owner of the ball club, Judge Fuchs, decided he would manage. I guess he figured it was an easy job and that he could save a few bucks by not having to pay a manager. In a sense it was an easy job; all you had to know was how to lose. John McGraw, Joe McCarthy and Connie Mack working together couldn't have done anything with that team. The Judge didn't know a thing about baseball, and he would sit on the bench and talk to the boys about one thing or another, not paying too much mind to what was going on out on the field. But he was a swell guy and the boys liked him. I remember one time Johnny Evers, who was one of our coaches, said to the Judge that the count was three and one on our batter and what did the Judge want the man to do.

"Tell him to hit a home run," the Judge said.

The year before, in '28, Hornsby was there, playing and managing. He led the league that year with .387. Paul Waner was chasing him most of the summer—I think Paul ended up around .370 or so. Anyway, toward the end of the year Pittsburgh came in for a series and the batting race was pretty close at the time. The papers made a big fuss over "The Battle for the Batting Championship." There wasn't much else to fuss over. Rog really went to town and got a carload of hits in the series while Waner didn't do too well. When it was over, Paul and Hornsby happened to be going back together through the runway underneath the stands to the clubhouses.

"Well, Rog," Paul said, "it looks like you're gonna beat me."

Rog scowled at him and said, "You didn't doubt for a minute that I would, did you?"

Hornsby was the greatest right-handed hitter that ever lived, I can guarantee you that. Maybe even the greatest hitter, period. He had the finest coordination I ever saw. And confidence. He had that by the ton. He just didn't think anybody could get him out. And damned few could. He was a picture up there. So rhythmic. He used a heavy bat—38 ounces and even heavier in the spring—and he held it back and up and he stepped into that ball so easily, from way back in the box. Everything so smooth. I copied him. They used to call me a pup out of Hornsby. I did all right, but nobody could hit like Rog.

Funny thing, I played for three different teams—the Cardinals, Braves and Cubs—and on each one, at one time or another, Hornsby was the manager. It got so that when I saw Rog starting to pack his bags I'd reach for mine.

I've heard a lot of ball players say he was a tough man to play for. I never found him that way. All he ever asked of anybody was that they give him all they had out on the field. "You're only out there for a couple of hours," he would say. Well, I don't think he was asking too much. Yes, I got along with him fine, wherever I played for him.

He was a lone wolf, you know. Even as a player, he never roomed with anybody. And you would never see him anywhere, outside of the hotel lobby. He wouldn't go to the movies because he said it was bad for the eyes. And about the only thing he would read was the racing form because he said reading was bad for the eyes too. Was he neurotic about his eyesight? Well, maybe he was. But there was that stretch over five years where he averaged around .400. So maybe Rog knew what he was doing.

There was another thing that Hornsby could do that a lot of people don't realize—he could run. When he was stretching out on a triple, he was a sight to see. If he had hit left-handed he probably would have hit .450. He was a streak going down that line. And you know, that infield in St. Louis cost him a lot of hits. Around the Fourth of July it had been baked out to concrete, and Rog always hit bullets—he seldom put his bat on the ball that it didn't whistle off. On that infield, those ground balls were in the infielder's glove in no time.

In 1926 we went to spring training in San Antonio. Hornsby was never much of a guy for holding meetings, but he held one on the first day of spring training. I'll never forget it.

"If there's anybody in this room who doesn't think we're going to win the pennant," he said, "go upstairs now and get your money and go on home, because we don't want you around here."

That's the attitude we all started with, right from the first day of spring training. And it carried us all the way, to the pennant, to the World Championship. And for me, personally, it was a great year. I hit .325, knocked in one hundred runs, was up among the league leaders in a lot of departments. I even outhit Rog that year, believe it or not—that was the only time over a ten-year stretch that he was under .360. Yeah, when I think of baseball, I think of 1926.

We won a very close pennant race that year. Beat out Cincinnati by two games. We finished up in the east, in the Polo Grounds. We opened up there on a Thursday and Cincinnati was playing in Philadelphia. All we needed was one win or one Cincinnati loss to clinch it. We kept watching the scoreboard all afternoon. I think we must have paid more attention to the Red-Phillie game than to our own. Anyway, we lost and the Reds won. So we still needed that one game. The next day we played the Giants again, but there was no score showing up for Cincinnati and Philadelphia. We figured they had been rained out. Well, we won, and then found out later that Hornsby had felt we had been too distracted by the scoreboard and he asked that no Cincinnati score be shown until our game was over. Sure ball players watch the scoreboard in a close pennant race. Don't think they don't.

I'll never forget what a thrill it was walking into Yankee Stadium for the first time, on the opening day of the '26 Series. That ball park was up for only a few years at that time but already there was a magic about it. It was big and beautiful and *important*-looking. And of course Babe Ruth played there. Maybe that was it: Babe Ruth.

I'd never seen so many people in my life—there were over

60,000 packed in there. In those days you had to come out through the Yankee dugout to get over to your own, and I guess when I walked onto the field and saw all those people I must have started shaking. Bill Sherdel, our little left-hander, put his arms around my shoulder and he calmed me down by saying, "Hey, Les, I'll tell you what to do."

"What's that, Bill?" I asked.

"You count 'em upstairs and I'll count 'em downstairs and we'll see how much money we're gonna make today.'"

I think a lot of people underestimated our ball club in that Series. The Yankees were top-heavy favorites. They had a great team with Ruth, Lou Gehrig, Earle Combs, Bob Meusel, Tony Lazzeri, Joe Dugan, Mark Koenig. And some first-rate pitchers in Herb Pennock, Waite Hoyt, Urban Shocker, Bob Shawkey. But we were fired up and we nearly won that dog-gone first game. Sherdel pitched beautifully but Pennock was a little bit better and beat us, 2–1.

Alexander got us even the next day, 6–2. Billy Southworth hit a home run with two on in the seventh and that was the clincher. Alec had them beating it in the dirt all day. I don't think there was more than one putout in our outfield. Alec was really on his game that day. When he was pitching like that the outfielders might just as well have set up a card table out there and played pinochle, for all they had to do.

You know, I was shut out those first two games. Went nothing for seven. Didn't get my first hit until we went back to St. Louis for the third game.

Man, what a parade they had waiting for us when we got back! You see, we had played most of our September schedule on the road and this was the first time we were back home in almost four weeks. So right in the middle of the World Series, St. Louis turned out for us, to celebrate the winning of the pennant. It was no ordinary pennant, you understand—it was the first ever for St. Louis. The Browns had never won one and neither had the Cardinals.

The train pulled in around three o'clock in the afternoon and they had a line of open touring cars waiting for us. We piled into the cars and they had this parade along Olive Street through downtown St. Louis. The streets were so packed there was just room enough for the cars to get through. Everybody was cheering and yelling and the ticker tape was pouring down like a blizzard. Why, we had trouble getting out of those automobiles into the hotel, what with everybody crowding around wanting to pat us on the back and shake our hands.

The next day Jess Haines started for us against Dutch Ruether. It was no score going into the bottom of the fourth. Then I started the inning off with my first hit of the Series, a single over second. Bob O'Farrell walked. Then there was an error in the infield on a double play ball that Tommy Thevenow hit to Lazzeri. Lazzeri flipped it to Koenig but Koenig's throw to first was wild and I scored the first run. Then Jess Haines, of all people, hit a home run into the right-field bleachers. He went on from there to shut them out, 4–0.

I'll tell you a funny story about that game. We scored those three runs in the fourth inning. Okay. Well, the inning before, Haines had led off with a hit and he got around to third base with one out and Hornsby and Bottomley coming up. Pretty good spot, wouldn't you think? But neither one of them could get him in. Now, there was a jewelry store in St. Louis that had put up as a prize a pocket watch for whoever scored the first Cardinal run in St. Louis. It was a beauty of a watch, too, with a baseball on it surrounded by diamonds. So there was old Jess standing on third with one out and Hornsby and Bottomley the hitters. Jess said later he could just feel that watch in the palm of his hand. But they never got him in. Then an inning later I score the first run. So I got the watch, and every time I showed it to Haines he would scowl and say, "Yeah, that ought to be mine."

The fourth game belonged to the Babe. No question about it. He was something to watch that day. What a show!

Flint Rhem started for us. Do you know about Flint? Well, he came from a well-to-do family down in South Carolina. As a matter of fact, I think the town was even named for his family: Rhems, South Carolina. Flint was Alexander's drinking buddy, which meant he had to be pretty good. One time we had a couple of off-days between Pittsburgh and Boston and Rog sent Flint and Alec to New York to rest up there and wait for the club to come in. Well, those two guys went on a binge that was unbelievable. When we pulled into New York, Flint, in particular, was so gassed up he could hardly see. When he sobered up, his explanation was a beauty: he said he didn't want Alec to get drunk, so he had kept drinking all the whiskey around them just to keep it away from Alec.

Flint won twenty games for us that year, but all the same it was a mistake to start him in the Series. In fact, Bill Killefer, one of our coaches, begged Hornsby not to do it.

"The Yankees will murder him," Bill said.

"Maybe," Rog said. "But he won for me all year. I'm a game up and I can afford to take the chance. He's earned it."

Flint's control wasn't that good, you see. You had to have control to pitch against the Yankees, otherwise they'd kill you, I don't care who you were. To give you an example, Flint started off the game by striking out Combs and Koenig. Then he got Ruth two quick strikes and decided he would throw the next one right on by Babe. Well, you couldn't pitch Ruth like that. He hit that ball over the doggone pavilion. Next time up he hit one out even farther. Then in the sixth inning—Flint was gone by this time—he hit the granddaddy of them all. He hit one out to center field that Taylor Douthit started in on. But that ball just kept rising and rising and ended by ricocheting in the top row of the center-field bleachers, 485 feet away. If the bleachers hadn't been there, I think that ball would have torn down the YMCA building across the street.

They thumped us good, 10–5.

Then we lost the fifth game in ten innings, 3–2. We should have won that son of a buck in nine. We were leading 2–1 going into the top of the ninth. Gehrig led off with a little Texas League double into left-center that just fell away from Thevenow, Wattie Holm, and Hafey. Lou eventually came around to tie it and they went on to win it in the tenth.

So we went back to New York, down three games to two, and there were a lot of people who wouldn't have given a plugged nickel for our chances. We were going to have to win two games in that big Yankee Stadium.

When we got to New York we saw in the papers that Miller Huggins was going to start Bob Shawkey. Bob was a good pitcher, but we figured we could hit him, and we did. Started right off in the first inning. We scored one run and had men on second and third and I lined a hit over Joe Dugan's head to score them. Alec was pitching and we were never headed. It was still fairly close going into the seventh, 4–1. We scored a few more and then I came up against Urban Shocker. I caught one and hit it into the left-field bleachers. That was the icing. Alec kept tooling right along and we won it by 10–2.

I'll tell you something else about that Ruth. He could throw. In the ninth inning I lined a hit into right-center. I figured I could get two out of it because Ruth had to go to his right and then turn around to throw. I thought it was a cinch double, but he came around and fired a strike right in there on one hop and got me. It came in with a zing, too. I had heard that you didn't take liberties with his arm, but there's always that little space between hearing something and believing it, and sometimes you just have to have it filled in for you, don't you?

So now it was all tied, three games apiece.

The next morning, it was gray and misty. We were staying at the Alamac Hotel, at 71st and Broadway, and when we woke up and looked out the window we didn't think there would be a game. It was a miserable day. Ordinarily we would have been out at the ball park by eleven thirty, but the day was so gloomy we just sat around the lobby waiting for word. Then Judge Landis called up and said, "Get your asses out there, boys, we're going to play." So we piled into taxicabs and headed up to the Stadium.

That number seven was a good ball game. In fact it was a great Series, any way you look at it, what with some good pitching and some very heavy hitting. But it was also a dramatic Series, for the simple reason of Alexander in that last game. I think it's one of the most dramatic things in all of baseball history, because it was Grover Cleveland Alexander who was involved. Anytime you have a really great athlete who's at the twilight of a long career come in and rise to the challenge, it's truly something to see and to remember.

After the sixth game, which Alec had pitched and won for us, we went into the clubhouse and Hornsby said to Alexander and Sherdel, "Alec, you're in the bull pen tomorrow and Sherry, you're in the bull pen."

Sherdel just nodded; it was fine with him. But Alec said, "All right, Rog. But I'll tell you, I'm not going to warm up down there. I've got just so many throws left in this arm. If you need me, I'll take my warm-up pitches on the mound."

And that's the way it was left. So when you hear those stories about how Alec didn't think he might be called on the next day and was out all night celebrating and how he was hung over when he came in, it's a lot of bunk. I saw him around the hotel the night before, for goodness sakes. I don't say he didn't have a drink, but he was around most of the night.

Haines started the seventh game for us and he pitched just fine. We got three runs in the fourth inning and I'll tell you, I should have got credit for a base hit on the ball that Koenig got his hands on. Why sure I remember it. You certainly do remember those hits that they took away from you. I can tell you just what happened. We were losing 1–0 to Ruth's home run. Then in the top of the fourth Jim Bottomley got a hit. I came up and hit one way over in the hole on the left side. Koenig went far to his right and fumbled the ball. They gave him an error on it but there was no way he could have thrown me out even if he had handled it cleanly. No way.

Then Chick Hafey lifted a little fly ball that fell into short left for a hit and the bases were filled. And then came a big break. Bob O'Farrell hit a fly ball to Meusel in left-center and Meusel dropped it. Just like that. Easiest fly ball you ever saw. What must have happened was he had set his mind on getting that ball and throwing home to try and catch Bottomley—Meusel had an outstanding arm. So he might have been thinking more about throwing it than catching it and maybe that's what brought about the error. But, gee, when that ball popped out of his hands the silence in that big ball park was really stunning. It was a hometown crowd, of course, and they couldn't believe what they had seen. Nobody could.

Then came the last of the seventh. The score was 3–2 now. With two out they loaded the bases against Haines and Tony Lazzeri was up. Haines was a knuckleball pitcher. He held that thing with his knuckles and he threw it hard and he threw it just about all the time. Well, his fingers had started to bleed from all the wear and tear, so he called a halt. Rog and the rest of us walked over to the mound.

"Can you throw it anymore?" Rog asked him.

"No," Jess said. "I can throw the fastball but not the knuckler."

"Well," Hornsby said, "we don't want any fastballs to this guy."

You see, we had been throwing Lazzeri nothing but breaking balls away and had been having pretty good luck with him.

So Rog said, "Okay, I'm going to bring in Pete," which is what we sometimes called Alexander.

So in came Alec, shuffling through the gloom from out in left field. You ever see him? Lean, long, lanky guy. An old Nebraskan. Took his time at everything, except pitching. Then he worked like a machine. That arm going up and down, up and down. If you didn't swing at the first pitch it was strike one, you didn't swing at the second pitch it was strike two. If he walked two men in a game he was wild. His control was amazing, just amazing. He could thread a needle with that ball. When he told you he was going to pitch a hitter a certain way and wanted you to play accordingly, you did it and that's all there was to it.

He came in there cold, took eight warm-up pitches on the mound and he was ready.

He wanted to get ahead of Lazzeri. That was his idea. But it had to be on a bad ball. He was going to throw that first one fast to Lazzeri, high and tight, far enough on the inside so that even if Lazzeri hit it solid it would have to go foul, because in order to get good wood on it, Tony would have to be way out in front with the bat. If he didn't get good wood on it, then he would be hitting it on the handle and maybe breaking his bat.

What made him think Lazzeri would be swinging at a bad ball? Well, Alec was a little bit of the country boy psychologist out on that mound. I guess a lot of your great pitchers are. He knew it was Lazzeri's rookie year, and that here it was, seventh game of the World Series, two out and the bases loaded and the score 3–2. Lazzeri *had* to be anxious up there. This is not to take anything away from Lazzeri—he later became a great hitter—but at that moment he was a youngster up against a master. And don't think when Alec walked in it wasn't slower than ever—he wanted Lazzeri to stand up there as long as possible, thinking about the situation. And he just *knew* Tony's eyes would pop when he saw that fastball.

There are so many legends associated with that strikeout. For instance, they say Alec was drunk, or hung over, when he came in. And they say that Hornsby walked out to left field to meet him, to look in his eyes and make sure they were clear. And so on. All a lot of bunk. It's too bad they say these things. Now in the first place, if you stop to think about it, no man could have done what Alec did if he was drunk or even a little soggy. Not the way his mind was working and not the way he pitched. It's true that he was a drinker and that he had a problem with it. Everybody knows that. But he was not drunk when he walked into the ball game that day. No way. No way at all, for heaven's sake. And as far as Hornsby walking out to meet him, that's for the birds too. Rog met him at the mound, same as all the rest of us.

So after the conference on the mound we all went back to our positions and Alec got set to work. Sure enough, the first pitch to Lazzeri is the fastball in tight, not a strike. Well, Tony jumped at it and hit the hell out of it, a hard drive down the left field line. Now, for fifty years that ball has been traveling. It has been foul anywhere from an inch to twenty feet, depending on who you're listening to or what you're reading. But I was standing on third base and I'll tell you—it was foul all the way. All the way.

And then you should have seen Tony Lazzeri go after two breaking balls on the lower outside corner of the plate. He couldn't have hit them with a ten-foot pole.

Then Alec shuffled off the mound toward the dugout. I ran by him and said something like, "Nice going, Alec." He turned his head toward me and had just the shadow of a smile on his lips. Then he took off his glove and flipped in onto the bench, put on his Cardinal sweater and sat down.

You know, a lot of people think that Lazzeri strikeout ended the game. You'd be surprised how many people I've spoken to through the years think it was the ninth inning. But hell, we still had two more innings to go.

Alec handled them like babies in the eighth, one, two, three, just like he knew he had to. In the bottom of the ninth they had their good hitters coming up—Combs, Koenig, Ruth, then Meusel and Gehrig.

Combs led off. He could run like a deer and I had to play in on the grass. He hit a doggone ball down to me and I got it in between hops and threw him out. Then Koenig came up and *he* hit one down to me off the end of the bat, spinning like crazy. I went to my right, picked it up and threw *him* out. You know, now and then during the winter I'd suddenly stop whatever I was doing and say to myself, "Boy, I wonder what the hell would have happened if I'd messed up one of those plays?" Those are the things you think about later.

So Ruth came up with two out and nobody on, just as Alec had wanted it. It would be nice to say that Alec struck him out to end it, and he nearly did. He nearly did. He took Babe to a full count and then lost him on a low outside pitch that wasn't off by more than an eyelash.

Ruth got to first and then, for some reason I've never been able to figure out, tried to steal second. Bob O'Farrell gunned the ball down to Hornsby, Rog slapped on the tag and that was it.

We all froze for a second, then rushed at Alec. We surrounded him, the whole team did, and pounded him around pretty good. He kept nodding his head and smiling and saying very softly, "Thanks, boys, thanks."

So many other things have come and gone now through the years. It's a long time ago, isn't it? More than fifty years. But whenever I think of Alec walking in from left field through the mist, it seems like yesterday. I can see him yet. . . .

LLOYD WANER

LLOYD JAMES WANER
Born: March 16, 1906, Harrah, Oklahoma; Died: July 22, 1982
Major-league career: 1927–45, Pittsburgh Pirates, Boston
    Braves, Cincinnati Reds, Philadelphia Phillies, Brooklyn
    Dodgers
Lifetime average: .316

*Though always overshadowed by his older brother Paul,
Lloyd Waner was a star in his own right. Ten times a .300
hitter, he had over 200 hits his first three major-league seasons,
including 234 in 1929, the year he led in triples with 20. His
198 singles in 1927 remain the single-season record. Remarkably swift of foot, he was considered one of the outstanding
center fielders of his time.*

Waner was elected to the Hall of Fame in 1967.

Some people find it unusual for two brothers to have gone up
to the big leagues and had long careers and in fact ended up
in the Hall of Fame together. Well, the way I look at it, Paul
and me had an advantage over most kids. There was only two
years and eleven months difference in our ages, so we never
lacked for somebody to play with. We loved baseball and we
played together all the time. Seems we were always swinging
something, be it a broomstick or a plain old stick or whatever
was handy. Our Dad made sure we had something to swing,
and he'd make us a baseball out of old rags and twine.

We were always pitching to each other, be it one of those old
rag-and-twine balls, or else corncobs. That's right, corncobs.
We would break them in two and then soak them in water so
they'd go farther when we hit them. You couldn't help but to

develop quick wrists swinging at those things because they broke in every direction. It was almost impossible to throw one straight. Broomsticks and corncobs. That's the beauty of baseball—anybody can play it and it doesn't have to be done too fancy.

I was born on a farm in Harrah, Oklahoma. Same place as my big brother. We had a really nice farm. At first we had cotton, but then the boll weevil started taking the cotton, so my Dad switched to alfalfa hay and wheat and corn and all sorts of vegetables.

My Dad had been a professional ball player himself you know, in Oklahoma City, when they first had the Western League. This was back in 1898. To get to the games he would ride his horse to Oklahoma City, leave it in the livery stable and then join the team. His salary was fifty dollars a month. But that looked like big money in those days. They played only three games a week, plus holidays.

He was a pretty good player, Dad was. As a matter of fact, at one time Cap Anson made him an offer to join the White Sox, but he didn't want to leave the farm. I guess not too many people remember Cap Anson's name today, but he was one of the greatest ball players of the last century.

Dad liked to kid Paul and me. When we were in the major leagues the roster was set at twenty-one players, not twenty-five like they have today. Well, he'd tell us that was pretty soft, because in his day, in the Western League, a club would carry only ten players. He was a pitcher and when he wasn't pitching, he said, they generally would put him in the out-field. Of course they played just three games a week, so we'd kid him back and tell him *that* was pretty soft.

He encouraged us to play ball. He sure did. Every chance he had he took us out to play catch. Now Dad was a good pitcher and he took some pride in that, especially in the curve ball he could throw, and it was a darned good one, too, very fast breaking. So when we went out to play catch he tried to take it easy, because we were so small. Also, we didn't have a catcher's mitt. I mean we had one, but Paul was left-handed and the mitt was right-handed. It was all right for me because I threw righty. So when Paul was catching Dad he had to do it with the mitt on the wrong hand. When Dad wanted to throw one of his great curve balls he'd tell us it was coming. Finally one day Paul said to him, "Throw anything you want. Don't make any difference, curve or not." So Dad figured he'd teach us a lesson and started mixing those pitches up, curves and fastballs. But we surprised him by catching everything he threw, and Paul especially surprised him because Paul had that mitt on the wrong hand.

Finally Dad stopped and put his hands on his hips.

"You fellows are all right," he said. "I'll swear, I'm throwing my best curves and I can't even fool you. You fellows sure have quick little hands."

I was around eight years old at the time and Paul was eleven.

Then Dad liked to see a good footrace. Every month or so he would measure off a hundred yards by strides and mark it off. Then he'd turn us loose. For a long while Paul used to beat me by a step or so. That was when we were younger. But then, after a while I started beating him until it got to where I was a step or two faster at a hundred yards than he was. And Paul could fly. But it was more than just a footrace, because my Dad used to coach us. He taught us to run on our toes, which he said was the main thing. You can't run fast if you're running flat-footed.

Dad managed a local team for a while, and one day he put me into the game as a pinch-hitter. I never will forget it. I was just twelve years old at the time and here I was getting into a game with grown men. I was so small that the other team thought Dad had put me in to try and work out a base on balls. But I hit at the first pitch I saw and poked it over the third baseman's head down the left-field line. We were playing in a cow pasture and the ball rolled into some weeds and got lost. I started running, so excited I was shaking. When I got to third base they were still out in the weeds looking for the ball. I stood there and didn't know what to do. Gee, I thought, the ball is lost. So I ran out there to help them look for it, too excited to hear my Dad yelling at me to come on across the plate. Well, they finally found the ball and whoever picked it up took one look at me and tagged me out. Dad never let me forget that one.

So you had that combination of things. The constant playing, the desire, the love for the game, the encouragement and good coaching from our Dad; it all helped to develop what God-given abilities we had.

We just had a lot of fun growing up, Paul and me. There was a river nearby and we'd go down there and fish some, set trout lines. Sometimes we'd go hunt possum. It was a nice time and a nice place for growing up.

Yes, Paul and me were always good buddies. Not only brothers but best pals. But you know, sometimes he'd get me in trouble. He was always egging me on to fight somebody. This one occasion has always stayed in memory. We were walking home from school—it was two-and-a-half miles from our farm to the schoolhouse—with some of the neighborhood boys. A gang of us were walking down the road. Paul started some trouble between me and a bigger boy. Finally the boy put his schoolbooks down in the road, hitched up his trousers and began rubbing his hands together.

I looked him over and then whispered to my brother, "Paul, he's a whole lot bigger."

He whispered back to me, "Just grab him by the legs and you got him."

So the fight started and I did what Paul said. I grabbed that boy by the legs and tumbled him off the road into a ditch where he landed right in a sandbur patch. Do you know what sandburs are? That's a weed that has burs growing on it and those burs are like needles. They can really hurt. Well, that boy came out of there covered with those things and just a-hollering and mad as blazes. He seemed twice the size now. I took one look at him and lit out for home fast as I could, with that boy coming after me, and Paul yelling from down the road, "Grab him by the legs! Grab him by the legs!"

Paul went into professional baseball two years before I did. He went out to San Francisco to play in the Pacific Coast League. He told the scout who had signed him about me and the fellow came by a year or so later and signed me to a contract. He said they would give me the same as they gave Paul his first year, which was four hundred dollars a month. I thought I was getting rich—that was big money back then, in 1925.

I was playing for a semipro team in Ada when I signed up. San Francisco promised to pay the team one thousand two hundred and fifty dollars and my Dad the same amount. Dad

wanted to use the money to get me through college. I'd promised him I would go to college after the season. Well, San
Francisco reneged on the agreement and wouldn't pay the
money. Paul talked to Joe Devine who was a scout for Pittsburgh, and Devine said I should get my release and Pittsburgh would sign me. Paul advised me to do it and I did what
he said. I got my release and the Pirates signed me. That
suited me just fine because Paul was already with the Pirates
and naturally I wanted to play with him. I was farmed out to
Columbia, South Carolina, in the South Atlantic League, had
a big year there and joined Paul in Pittsburgh the next season, 1927.

That was half the fun, I think, playing with old Paul. I sure
would have missed him if I had gone with somebody else. He
helped me out a whole lot, too. There were some pitchers in
the league I was having a little trouble with and he told me
what I was doing wrong against them. He got me to open my
stance against left-handers so I wouldn't pull away from them.
And he would tell me not to pay attention to the pitcher until
the ball was delivered so as not to be thrown off by the motion.
Paul was always helping me, telling me a lot of little old
things that made me a better hitter. The main thing he used
to tell me was to hit down at the ball instead of up. He said
that would give me a level stroke and I'd hit a lot of line
drives. That's the way he did it and he'd hit them through that
infield so fast they couldn't see them.

Paul used to lay the bat right on his shoulder and keep it
there until the last second, and then with those strong wrists
he'd whip it around and make that ball zing. I did it the same
way. I never will forget some of the managers around the
league saying we couldn't hit the inside pitch because we
wouldn't be able to get the bat around on it. But the inside
pitch never bothered us; in fact we hit it better. In our first
three years together at Pittsburgh, Paul hit .380, .370, .336,
and I hit .355, .335, .353, and we averaged better than 220 hits
a season apiece. So we were making pretty good contact.

They used to call us "Big Poison" and "Little Poison." A lot
of people have thought we had those nicknames because we
were "poison" to the opposing pitchers. But that isn't the way
it came about. It started in 1927, in New York. We were
playing the Giants in the Polo Grounds. There used to be this

Italian fellow who always sat in the center-field bleachers. He had a voice on him you could hear all over the ball park. When he hollered out you heard him no matter where you were.

Well, Paul and I were hitting well against the Giants. This one day we came out of the clubhouse between games of a doubleheader and this fellow started hollering at us. What it sounded like was "Big and Little Poison," but what he was really saying was "Big and Little Person." He was a real nice fellow and we would wave at him and he finally became our biggest rooter in the Polo Grounds. We got him an auto-graphed baseball one time. But whenever we came in there he would yell that and the newspapermen finally picked it up, except they thought he was saying "Poison" instead of "Person." It became a newspaper nickname, because no ball players ever called us that. And the name has stuck, right down to this day.

I thought that Bill Terry and Paul were the two best left-handed hitters in the league. And the best right-handed hitter was Hornsby. Boy, was he a hitter! You just didn't know how to play him out there because he would slam that ball where it was pitched. Line drives. Gee whiz, what line drives. He just powdered it. The only way to play him in the outfield was to try and get a jump on the ball, judging by his swing and where the ball was pitched. Joe Medwick was another great right-handed hitter, and so was Chick Hafey.

Lefty O'Doul was another top-notch hitter back then. He was strictly a pull hitter, sending practically everything to right field. You would have thought we would have been able to defend against him, but yet he led the league in batting a couple of times. He just powdered that ball down the line so hard nobody had a chance to move for it. Chuck Klein was another fellow who hit the ball to right field most of the time. He was more of a fly-ball hitter. He whacked a lot of home runs. Klein had an advantage when he broke in because his home park was that old Baker Bowl with the short, high fence out in right field. You didn't have to hit the ball good to make contact with that fence, you only had to get it up in the air, which Klein was able to do. But he wasn't a left-field hitter. I've always considered the good hitter the man you can't play on the straightaway, who can snap that ball into any field, like Bill Terry and Paul and Hornsby used to do.

We had a fellow with us on the Pirates throughout the 1930's who sure was an outstanding hitter and a fine shortstop. Arky Vaughan. I don't know why he's not in the Hall of Fame today. He's got a record that's better than a lot of them who are. He could hit and he could field and he could run. I'll say he could run. We had a contest on in Pittsburgh one time, things like running to first base, bunting and running, and so on. Arky and I tied in going to first base in bunting and running. Three and two-tenths seconds. Don't think that Arky Vaughan couldn't scamper. For going from home plate to second base I don't think there was anybody who could match him.

My first year up to the majors was 1927 and darn if we didn't win the pennant. Boy, I thought to myself, this looks like a cinch. But I hung around for eighteen more years and never saw another one.

We played the Yankees in the World Series that year. Of course everybody knows that the 1927 Yankees are supposed to be the greatest team ever put together, what with Babe Ruth, Lou Gehrig, Earle Combs, Bob Meusel, Tony Lazzeri, and the rest of them. The famous story that has come out of the 1927 World Series concerns the first day, when we were supposed to have watched the Yankees taking batting practice. According to the story, which I have read and heard so many times, Paul and me and the rest of us were sitting there watching those big New Yorkers knock ball after ball out of sight and became so discouraged that we just about threw in the sponge right then and there. One story that I've read I don't know how many times has me turning to Paul and in a whispery voice saying, "Gee, they're big, aren't they?"

That was the story. Well, I don't know how that got started. If you want to know the truth, I never even saw the Yankees work out that day. We had our workout first and I dressed and was leaving the ball park just as they were coming out on the field. I don't think Paul stayed out there either. We never spoke of it. I know some of our players stayed, but I never heard anybody talk about what they saw.

I don't know where the story came from. Somebody made it up out of thin air, that's all I can say. Every time I hear that story I tell people it's not so, but it just keeps on going. I don't think Paul ever saw anything on a ball field that could scare him anyway. He was such a great hitter in his own right that he never had to take a back seat to anybody.

This is not to say we weren't impressed by those Yankees during that Series. We sure were. They were just a fine ball club. And Ruth, well, that fellow always impressed you. I can remember when the Yankees let him go and he came over to the National League with Boston. This was in 1935. He was old, he was fat, he couldn't run, and he had lost a lot of his ability up at the plate. But he was still Babe Ruth. He came into Pittsburgh to play and after one of the games, I was leaving the ball park to go home and there's Babe signing autographs, surrounded by this big crowd. I'll swear that half the people who were to the game were waiting for him to sign. I stood there for a while watching and marveling at it. When I went home that crowd was still around him. The next day when I came to the park, somebody told me that Babe finally asked one of the policemen to get him a folding chair and Babe just sat there signing autographs.

"Till how long?" I asked.

"Till nearly ten o'clock at night," the fellow said. "He just sat and sat and sat till he'd made everybody happy."

But that's the way he was. He would never disappoint anybody if he could help it. You don't find them like that very often, I daresay.

It was in Pittsburgh that Babe had his last great day on the field. You could see he was near finished. He still had that beautiful swing, but he just wasn't hitting them anymore. But this one day he upped and amazed everybody. He hit three of them out in one game. The last one was hit farther than any ball I've ever seen. It went over the roof. I was standing in center field watching it go. You would have thought it had a little engine in it. It became a dot against the sky and then disappeared. My, did he hit it. But he could hardly get around the bases. His legs were shot, you see. We hit several balls out to Babe in right field in that game and he could hardly move after them. It was sad watching him out there. Matter of fact, he retired shortly after that game.

But in 1927 Babe was still in top form and he showed very well in that Series. It's true the Yankees beat us four straight, but they didn't run us off the field. There was only one lopsided game, where they beat us 8–1. Otherwise two of those games were settled by one run, and it seems to me that every game was close going into the late innings.

No, I wasn't nervous playing in the World Series. I'll tell you the only time I ever felt that way on a ball field—when I played my first major league game. After that I was never nervous again on a ball field. That's the truth.

I started off the Series in good fashion. First time up, Waite Hoyt hit me with a pitch. Paul doubled me around to third—he had a nice habit of doing that—and I scored on a fly ball. Later on in the game I doubled and came in on a base hit.

Ray Kremer pitched for us and he worked a good game. What beat him was errors. The Yankees got three runs in the third inning and I don't think a one of them was earned. They beat us by a run, 5–4. That was too bad; we should have won it.

In the second game I led off with a triple against George Pipgras. I remember that clearly. George threw me a good fastball and I just laid my bat on it and poked it down the left-field line. Then I scored on a fly ball. That was another close one until the eighth when the Yankees got three runs. I think that score was 6–2.

The third game was the only one where they beat us real bad. It was 8–1. But even so, it was close until the bottom of the seventh when they got six runs. That was one of the things about the Yankee team—they could explode right in your face at any time. Lee Meadows had been going along just beautifully for us for six innings, and then *wham!* Six runs. Babe Ruth hit a home run in that inning with a couple of men on. But do you know, for all their power, they only hit two home runs in the Series—both by Ruth. Do you know who hurt us in that Series? Mark Koenig, the shortstop. He hit .500. We just couldn't keep that fellow off the bases. And he was batting in front of Ruth and Gehrig. That's what did us in more than anything else, that fellow always being on base when those big guys came up. I'll tell you another interesting statistic about that Series somebody recently pointed out to me. In the four games the Yankees struck out twenty-five times to our seven. But all the same, no matter how many things you look at, it's still who scored the most runs, isn't it?

Something people tend to overlook with that Yankee team is their pitching. Everybody talks about Ruth and Gehrig, and well they might, but that was one fine gang of pitchers they

488 A DONALD HONIG READER

had. We saw four of them in the Series—Waite Hoyt, George Pipgras, Herb Pennock, Wilcy Moore. Pennock was rough. In the third game he retired the first twenty-two batters. He had a perfect game going until one out in the eighth. I remember it was Pie Traynor who broke it up. Pennock had fine stuff and A-1 control. Remember, our club had a .305 team batting average that season, but Pennock smoothed us out with very little trouble. He wasn't the type who threw the ball past you—he just made you hit it right at somebody.

The fourth game was a close one all the way and had a very unusual finish. In fact, I wonder if any World Series game ever ended the way this one did. It was played in Yankee Stadium. I led off with an infield hit and came around to score the first run. Later on Ruth hit a home run to put them ahead by two runs, but then we scored two in the top of the seventh to tie it up. It went on into the bottom of the ninth that way, 3–3.

That bottom of the ninth was a real oddball inning. Johnny Miljus was pitching for us. He was a relief pitcher and a real hard thrower. He could burn it in. He started off the inning by walking Earle Combs. Then Koenig beat out a bunt. First and second now, with nobody out. Then Miljus made it even worse by letting go a wild pitch, moving the runners up to second and third, with no outs. And all the Yankees have waiting in line for us are Ruth, Gehrig, Meusel and Lazzeri.

Naturally in a spot like that we put Ruth on. So now it's bases loaded and Gehrig up. But I told you, Miljus could really fire the ball, and that's just what he did. He leaned back and let it go. Struck out Gehrig. Then he struck out Bob Meusel. All of a sudden it's two out and the bases are still loaded. Then he got one strike across on Lazzeri. I was standing out in center field and I was beginning to think, "Maybe we'll get out of it yet."

Miljus wound up and fired the next one, but it went into the dirt and got away from the catcher, Johnny Gooch, and rolled all the way back to the screen. Combs ran home and the game was over. The World Series was over. For a couple of seconds I didn't budge, just stood out there in center field. Couldn't believe it, I guess. It's no way to end a ball game, much less a World Series, on a doggone wild pitch. That's how they scored it, a wild pitch. But Johnny Gooch said later that he should have caught it. Well, no matter. It was all gone and done with.

We were a little unhappy with the way things had gone. We

thought we were going to give a better showing than we did because we were a good hitting team, with Pie Traynor, Glenn Wright, Joe Harris, George Grantham, Clyde Barnhart, Paul and myself. In the Series I hit .400 and Paul .333, which wasn't bad. We outhit Ruth and Gehrig.

Paul and I went into vaudeville that winter. That's right. We were a vaudeville act. We traveled on the Loew's Orpheum circuit. We played ten weeks, going from St. Louis to Baltimore to New York where we played Loew's State for two weeks, then on to Pittsburgh and San Francisco and Los Angeles. Ten weeks altogether. We'd come out on the stage in our uniforms and play catch and tell some jokes about Babe Ruth and the World Series. Paul would go on the stage first and start calling into the wings asking where I was. Finally I'd run out with a ball in my hand and say, "I was running after the ball that Babe Ruth hit." The audience thought that was a good one.

Then we'd play burn-out. That was throwing the ball back and forth at top speed, making it pop in our gloves. Paul would say something like, "Say, you're pretty good." And I would say back to him, "You ought to see my brother." The people got a big kick out of it.

Then we played some music. You see, when we were going to school Paul took some lessons on the saxophone and I tried the violin. I never could get the hang of that thing, but I could carry a tune. So after the jokes and the running around on stage, the orchestra would strike up and we'd get our instruments and play along with them. Once in a while we'd hit the same note as the orchestra, but it didn't make much difference one way or the other because they made sure to play good and loud to cover us.

It was pretty good fun. We got a lot of standing ovations and sometimes had to come out and take a second bow. And we made more money those ten weeks in vaudeville than we did playing baseball for six months.

We did all right. They wanted us to go on for ten more weeks. But that would have thrown us over into spring training and the Pittsburgh ball club wouldn't let us do it. Paul was disappointed; he loved getting out there on the stage. But as far as I was concerned it was just as well. It had been a long season and I figured it was time to get on back home.

JOE WOOD

JOSEPH WOOD
Born: October 25, 1889, Kansas City, Missouri; Died: July 27, 1986
Major-league career: 1908–1922, Boston Red Sox, Cleveland Indians
Lifetime record: 114 wins, 58 losses
Lifetime average: .283

An arm injury suffered when Smoky Joe Wood was twenty-three years old curtailed what would unquestionably have been one of the greatest pitching careers in big league history. The year before the injury, 1912, Wood had what many consider the greatest single season ever enjoyed by a pitcher. He won 34 and lost 5, had 10 shutouts, 258 strikeouts, a 1.91 earned run average, and completed 35 of 38 starts. Wood capped off his remarkable season by winning three games against the Giants in the World Series.

A versatile and talented all-around ball player, Wood eventually switched to the outfield and in 1921 batted .366 for the Cleveland Indians.

That's right, when I was a boy growing up there was no such thing as a World Series. The first World Series wasn't played until 1903, when I was fourteen years old. As a matter of fact, for a long time I didn't even know what the big leagues were. Didn't know about John McGraw or Honus Wagner or Christy Mathewson or any of those fellows. All I knew about baseball was what I was doing myself, which was playing on a town team in Ouray, Colorado. This was in 1903, '04, parts of '05.

Those people out in western Colorado were crazy about

490

baseball. They used to have town teams and they'd cross the mountains to play each other. Everybody made a great hullabaloo out of those ball games. That was the center of it as far as we were concerned; we just didn't pay much attention to baseball anywhere else.

The first I heard about the World Series was when I got into professional ball with Hutchinson, Kansas. This was in 1907. I've got a very hazy recollection of hearing something about the Cubs and the Tigers. I seem to remember somebody talking about those great Chicago pitchers—Three Finger Brown, Orval Overall, Ed Reulbach, and that sharp little catcher they had, Johnny Kling, who was supposed to be one of the best ever. The Tigers had a young outfielder by the name of Ty Cobb. I heard his name mentioned. But I really didn't take much interest in the World Series.

I was born in Kansas City, Missouri, but soon after that we moved to Chicago and were there for ten years. Then my father got the gold fever and joined the Alaska gold rush. He spent some time there trying to make his fortune, same as a lot of other people. No, he didn't strike it rich. As a matter of fact he was lucky to get out alive. The Yukon River was frozen over, you see, and he had to walk out. He wrapped his feet up to his knees in gunnysacks and walked out, thirty miles a day. When he got out the doctors told him the only way he'd get the circulation and the feeling back in his legs was to go barefoot in the sand. So he went down to the gold strike in California and Nevada. The climate might have been better down there, but his luck stayed the same.

When he finally came home we got into a covered wagon and located way out in Ouray, Colorado. We were there for a few years, then came back to Kansas, then went on to the old family homestead in Pennsylvania. They talk about this being an on-the-go society today, what with the automobile and super highways and all that, but it seems to me that Americans were always a restless people. Back then those wagon wheels were always grinding, and wherever you went you met people going in the opposite direction.

But wherever I was I played baseball. That's all I lived for. When I sat up on the front seat of that covered wagon next to my father I was wearing a baseball glove. That showed anybody who was interested where *I* wanted to go.

I was a pretty good ball player, too. I could hit, I could run, and I could throw the ball hard. In 1908 I pitched for Kansas City in the American Association, struck out a few fellows, and in August was sold to the Red Sox. I was eighteen years old then.

Cy Young was on that Red Sox team. He was around forty years old at the time, but I don't think you could say he was over the hill since he pitched 300 innings that year and won twenty-one games. No, he didn't pay much attention to me. I don't think we talked to one another at all. I was just an unknown kid coming onto the club. Sure, I knew who he was. By that time I had heard of them all, and Cy Young was the greatest pitcher of his day. I don't suppose there are many people alive today who saw him in his heyday, but for a long time it was said he was the greatest pitcher who ever lived. I don't know how you can measure those things; I guess each generation has its candidates for the greatest this or the greatest that. As far as I'm concerned, Walter Johnson was the greatest pitcher that ever lived. I just never saw anyone else who had as much natural ability. He could throw the ball by you so fast you never knew whether you'd swung under it or over it.

Tris Speaker was a kid outfielder on that Red Sox team in 1908. Somehow or other we got together and were room-mates for fifteen years in the American League, with Boston and then later on with Cleveland. Among the men he played with and against, Speaker was always pretty much regarded as the best outfielder of all time. He simply did everything well. I don't think you could ask for a better all-around ball player.

As the years go by, some men naturally stand out sharper in memory than others. Cobb, of course. Nobody who watched him play could ever forget it. No, there was no way to pitch him except to throw him the best you had. But Cobb didn't give me near as much trouble as that other fellow they had, Sam Crawford. Sam was a big, strong hitter, and it was just tough trying to get the ball past him.

Lajoie was another top-notch player from those days. Some people called him Larry and some called him Napoleon. But whatever you called him, he could sock that ball! He drove a liner back to me one time that caught me in the leg and almost broke it in two. Great hitter. And graceful in the field. As graceful a ball player as I ever saw.

Ed Walsh got credit for being the greatest spitball pitcher there ever was. I guess he was the one who practically started it. But the fellow who threw the best-breaking spitter that I ever saw was Stanley Coveleski. Stanley and I were team-mates on the Cleveland ball club that won the world champi-onship in 1920, so I saw plenty of him. But you asked about Ed Walsh. Great, big, husky fellow, and a swell-looking guy. The year I came into the league he won forty games. That's four-oh. He used to come to Boston with the White Sox and pitch the first game and then like as not finish the next three. He was a workhorse. And never got paid for it. But of course nobody got very much money in those days, outside of Cobb and Speaker. The year I won thirty-four games I was getting something like four or five thousand, then had to battle like the devil to get seventy-five hundred the next year. How much would a thirty-four-game winner get paid today? I don't know. You tell me.

Rube Waddell was just leaving the league when I came in. He had had a great career, mostly with Connie Mack's A's, but he was with St. Louis when I knew him. He was still a fairly young man when he left baseball, maybe around thirty-two or thirty-three years old. He told me that Eddie Cicotte hit him on the wrist with a ball and that that was what finished him. Eddie Cicotte was with the Red Sox when I joined them, you know. He was one of our regular starters for a few years, then he was traded to the White Sox and later became involved in that 1919 scandal. The Black Sox scandal. That included Shoeless Joe Jackson, if you recall. And what a pity it was. I always maintained you couldn't blame Joe for anything. He was not a very well-educated fellow; they said he couldn't read or write. I guess somebody talked him into that mess. But one of the greatest ball players of all time. What a hitter! He'd carry that big black bat up there and whale away. You just had to admire him, even though he might be beating your brains out. How did you pitch to him? Same as with Cobb—try your best and hope it isn't his day. Hitters like that—Jackson, Cobb, Speaker, Lajoie—there's no set way to pitch them. They don't have a weakness. Their averages bear that out, and I mean the consistency of those averages—year after year they're anywhere between .350 and .400. Just because you got them out on a certain pitch one time didn't mean they weren't going to whack that same pitch next time up.

Seems nowadays everybody is down at the end of the bat. That's one of the reasons you have so many strikeouts today. You saw very little of that when I was pitching. They choked up and just swung to meet the ball. It takes a natural hitter to go down to the end of the bat. Jackson could do it, and Crawford and Lajoie and Speaker. Not too many of them. Cobb, for instance. He was up on that bat.

Eddie Plank? Well, he was a different sort of pitcher than, say, Johnson or Waddell. They were power pitchers. Plank was very studious out there. He used to pitch to spots, more so than most fellows of the day I would say. They do that more today, but Eddie Plank was doing it back then, in the first decade of the century, and doing it very well. I'll say. He was a 300-game winner. Connie Mack's three mainstays in those years were Plank, Chief Bender and Jack Coombs. Coombs was a thirty-game winner for Mr. Mack one year. He wasn't too fast but he had a big, beautiful curve ball. But it seemed to be that whenever Connie Mack had a very important game on, a game that meant a lot, Chief Bender was the pitcher. They had Bullet Joe Bush too in those days. I was Smoky Joe and he was Bullet Joe. I guess we both could throw the ball pretty fast.

The Philadelphia Athletics had great teams in those years. In fact, between 1910 and 1914 the only team to beat them out of a pennant was the Red Sox in '12.

In 1911 we finished fifth. All the same, when we got together for spring training in Hot Springs, Arkansas, the next year we had pennant on our minds. Jake Stahl had taken over as player-manager and he kept us on our toes. We won it by fourteen games, never letting up for a second. We went with a three-man rotation most of the time—Hugh Bedient, Buck O'Brien, and myself. The games we didn't start, Charley Hall and Ray Collins did. And everybody was ready to relieve, too, if need be. We'd get in a tough game going into the late innings and two or three of the fellows would come over to me and say, "How about it, Woodie?" And I'd go down in the corner and start throwing and be ready to go in. You see, today relief pitching is an art. The brigade heads down to the bull pen before the game starts. It wasn't like that back then. Nobody went down there until the middle of the game. There was no such thing as a relief specialist. You started and you relieved, you relieved and you started.

We won one hundred and five games that year, which was an American League record at the time. The five of us— Bedient, O'Brien, Hall, Collins, and myself—won one hundred and two of the one hundred and five games. That was the year I had my best record—thirty-four wins and five losses. Put together a sixteen-game win streak along the way. I was just twenty-two years old at the time, and as far as I was concerned still hadn't reached my peak.

I'd say that was quite a good team we had in Boston in 1912. In the infield we had Jake Stahl, Heinie Wagner, Steve Yerkes, and at third base one of the best, Larry Gardner. And we had three fellows in the outfield they're still talking about today: Harry Hooper, Tris Speaker and Duffy Lewis. Best defensive outfield ever. Bill Carrigan and Hick Cady were the catchers.

By the time September rolled around there was no question but that we were going to win the pennant. We just kept charging along, all keyed up. I was winning ball games wholesale and I suppose I was getting a lot of attention in the newspapers. Well, that seemed to upset somebody because I got a couple of threatening letters in the middle of September. I found one waiting for me in Cleveland and another in Detroit. Both from the same person and both with pretty much the same message: I would soon be no more. Sure, we had crackpots in those days, same as you have today. No, I didn't take it seriously. Maybe I should have, but I didn't. I think the only one I showed the letters to was Speaker. We just laughed them off and forgot about the whole thing. Nothing ever came of it.

That was the year Fenway Park opened, so you might say we got it off to a good start. There was plenty of excitement over that World Series. The Red Sox had a contingent of fans called the Royal Rooters. And they were just that. The most fanatical fans you could imagine. They had their own band and would parade on the field before a game. I'll tell you something about that Series. We played the Giants and the games alternated between New York and Boston. It was a seven-game Series and it was one day in New York, one day in Boston, and so on. Well, the Royal Rooters went back and forth on the train with us. So we didn't get much rest on the train rides because they were a noisy bunch; loyal and good-natured as all get-out, but noisy.

There was a good deal of excitement in New York too for that Series. We were staying at a hotel called Bretton Hall, which was uptown on Broadway, and when we went from the hotel out to the ball park we had to keep the blinds down in the taxicabs, otherwise we'd get pelted with rocks.

John McGraw had a good, tough ball club that year. I guess all of McGraw's teams of that era were good ones. They'd won the pennant the year before and they were going to win it again the next year. I would say they were probably the most famous team in baseball. I mean, people who didn't know anything about baseball might have heard of John McGraw and the Giants, just like years later they heard of Babe Ruth and the Yankees. And of course McGraw's most famous player was Christy Mathewson. Another candidate for greatest pitcher ever.

Mathewson wasn't a kid any longer by the time we got into the '12 Series. He was nearing the end of the trail, but still a great pitcher. I don't think he was as fast as he had once been. When I saw him his greatest asset was control and a beautiful curve ball that he'd start over your head and bring right down. I'd never seen a curve ball like it. He also threw what they called the fadeaway, which is the same as a screwball. As far as I know, he was the only one who threw it at that time.

Let's see who else I can remember from that Giant team. They had Larry Doyle, Fred Merkle, Chief Meyers catching, Buck Herzog, Art Fletcher, Fred Snodgrass, Red Murray, Josh Devore. That was a good, sharp ball club.

I knew I was going to get the first game in the Series. There was no question about my starting it off. I may not have heard about the World Series before, but I sure knew what it was now. When I went out to warm up that day at the Polo Grounds there were about 35,000 people sitting in the stands. I guess I felt a little extra pressure, but as quick as the game started it was gone. I think most ball players will tell you the same thing—they feel the special excitement of the World Series, but only until the first pitch is thrown, that first good fastball. That's right, I was primarily a fastball pitcher. I had a good curve too. Fastball and curve. That's all there was to it. Didn't throw anything else.

I started against Jeff Tesreau. In fact, I started three times in that Series and each time against Jeff Tesreau. I don't know why McGraw picked him over Mathewson to open. They also had Rube Marquard. But Tesreau was a good pitcher. He threw the spitball.

I was throwing hard that day, very hard. I struck out eleven. But even so, going into the top of the seventh I was down 2–1. In the last of the third the Giants had men on second and third with two out and Red Murray hit one into center to score them.

But then we got three runs in the seventh. Harry Hooper got a big hit in that inning and Steve Yerkes knocked in two runs with a hit. I didn't have any trouble in the seventh and eighth, but in the bottom of the ninth the Giants really threw a scare.

The last half of the ninth inning was quite a thrill for me. The Giants scored one run and had men on second and third with one out. The tying and winning runs. Art Fletcher was up. Same fellow who later coached on the Yankees under McCarthy. Well, I threw so hard I thought my arm would fly right off my body. I struck Fletcher out. That was two out and the fellows in the infield were yelling, "One more, Woodie." The batter was Doc Crandall. He had come in to relieve Tesreau. Crandall was a hard hitter and McGraw let him bat. One thing I was tickled to death about was that McGraw didn't use Beals Becker as a pinch hitter in that spot. Becker was sitting right there on the bench, and I was kind of looking out of the corner of my eye to see if he would get up. You see, I had played against him in the Western Association and he had always hit me pretty well. But I guess McGraw didn't know that.

I ran the count on Crandall to three and two. Fastballs, that's what I was throwing. Just burning them in and hoping for the best. Well, on the full-count pitch I threw one right on by him for strike three. That was the biggest thrill I ever had in baseball, those two strikeouts.

After pitching the opener I came back with only two days rest. I don't know why Stahl did that, he had those other starters. But it never bothered me any. I won both of those games. The score of the second one was 3–1 and I knocked in the third one myself with a base hit in the ninth inning. Say, I could swing the bat. After I hurt my arm I turned to the outfield and one year hit .366 for Cleveland. I took a lot of pride in that. As I said to somebody once, I was a *ball player*, not just a pitcher.

Then Hugh Bedient beat Mathewson 2–1 in Boston and we had them down three games to one. So it looked pretty good for us. But as I said, McGraw had a lot of first-rate players and they didn't quit; they came right back at us. Marquard beat O'Brien in the fifth game. O'Brien gave up five runs in the first inning and that was the ball game. Marquard beat us 5–2. You don't spot a pitcher like Rube Marquard five runs in the first inning and then expect to enjoy your dinner that night.

After the game, which was played in New York, we hopped the train back to Boston. Later on a story came out that said there had been an argument on the train between Jake Stahl and Jim McAleer, who owned the team, over who the starting pitcher should have been for that game. According to the story, Jake wanted to start me with two days' rest again but McAleer had insisted on O'Brien. Then another story had my brother having a fight with O'Brien on the train. Well, there wasn't a word of truth in any of it. It was absolutely false. How those stories get started I'll never know.

So I had three days' rest before my next start—and gave up six runs in the first inning! I was out of there before I knew what was happening. You know, there was a big ruckus just before the game. It seems that more tickets had been sold than there were seats, and it so happened that the people who were shut out were the Royal Rooters. Well, it took the mounted police to get them to go and when they finally did go they took part of the center-field fence with them. I was all warmed up and ready to start pitching and then that crowd broke down the fence. I had to go and sit down on the bench until it was fixed. Some people said that was why I got hit so hard in the first inning, that I had cooled off. But I don't think that had anything to do with it. I wasn't looking for any excuses. It was just one of those times when I couldn't get the ball by anybody. That would happen once in a while. Now and then there just wasn't anything on the fastball. Maybe two or three times a year it would happen. Not a darn thing you could do about it.

After the first inning we had little hope of catching up and the Giants ran away with it, 11–4. That tied the Series at three apiece. So there was going to be a seventh game. Actually it was the eighth game because one of the earlier games had ended in a tie because of darkness. But whatever number you want to call it, it was still the one that was going to decide everything.

That game has gone down in history as one of the most memorable ever played in a World Series. Things happened that day that are just as clear in my memory as this morning's breakfast. Mathewson, for instance. I can still see him and I can still hear him out there, making the most curious mistake in judgment for an experienced player. Sure he was the pitcher. That added to it. When you've got a Mathewson involved, or a Babe Ruth, or a Walter Johnson, that just adds to it.

Bedient started for us and Mathewson for them. They both pitched wonderfully well. Going into the bottom of the seventh—the game was played in Boston—we were losing 1–0. Then in the bottom of the seventh we put men on first and second with two out. Olaf Henriksen went up to hit for Bedient. It was Henriksen's one and only at bat in the Series. But he sure made it a good one—he banged out a double and tied the score.

They brought me on in the eighth. Against Mathewson. I don't know if I had any butterflies—it's a long time ago—but let's say I was definitely *impressed* by the situation. Not only is it the last game of the World Series and it's all tied up, but there's Christy Mathewson out there for the other side, and pitching just beautifully.

I held them in the eighth and ninth, but Mathewson stayed right with me. Then in the top of the tenth they scored a run. Red Murray doubled. Then Fred Merkle singled to score him, and when Speaker juggled the ball in center field Merkle went to second. I struck out Buck Herzog. Then Chief Meyers hit one back at me a mile a minute. I threw my bare hand out and the ball hit me on the wrist. I picked up the ball and got Meyers at first. That was three out. If I hadn't knocked down that shot and gotten Chief Meyers they would have scored another run and how many more we'll never know. But I knew I wasn't going to pitch anymore that day no matter what, because my hand started to swell up even before I reached the bench.

So we're into the bottom of the tenth down by a run, 2–1, with Christy Mathewson standing out there looking down our throats.

I was first up and ordinarily I would have batted for myself, but because of that injured hand I couldn't swing a bat. So they sent Clyde Engle up to bat for me. Clyde hit a soft fly ball out to Fred Snodgrass in center. Snodgrass dropped it. Maybe once a year a man would drop a ball like that. I'd seen it happen to Speaker, to Hooper, to all of them. No reason. It just happens. The ball hits your glove and falls out and that's all there is to it. If it happens in the middle of the season it's forgotten the next day. But in a World Series, and in particular *that* kind of situation, well, here we are, sixty-six years later, still talking about it.

Poor Fred Snodgrass. He'll always be remembered as the goat of that Series. But he didn't deserve it. What everybody forgets is that the next batter, Hooper, hit a real shot out to center and Snodgrass made a great catch of it. Nobody remembers that, but it was an outstanding play. Engle tagged up after the catch and went to third. Then Steve Yerkes got a walk and we've got men on first and third with Speaker up.

Then we got another break. This was the one that all of our fellows claimed was the turning point, more so than the dropped fly ball. What happened was, Speaker lifted a little pop foul between first and home. The first baseman, Fred Merkle, had the best shot at it. But instead of calling for Merkle to take it, Mathewson came down off the mound calling for Chief Meyers, the catcher. Merkle could have caught it easily, but Mathewson kept calling for Meyers, I'll never know why. You see, Merkle was coming in on the ball and the Chief was going with it. It's a much easier play for Merkle. But there was Matty, yelling for the Chief. I can hear him to this day. But Meyers never could get to it. The ball dropped. It just clunked down into the grass in foul ground and lay there. We couldn't believe it. Neither could Mathewson. You never saw a man as mad as he was when that ball hit the ground. But the way we saw it, it was his own fault. He called for the wrong man.

That's what we always felt won the Series for us. The write-ups in the papers never stressed that as much as they did Snodgrass dropping the ball in center field.

So Speaker had another shot, and you just can't do that with a hitter like Tris. Sure enough, he hit the next one into right field to tie the game. On the throw home the runners went to second and third. Duffy Lewis was next, but McGraw walked him to load the bases. That brought up Larry Gardner. Still just one out, remember. Larry was always a dependable fellow and he didn't disappoint us. He hit a long fly ball to right field to bring home Yerkes with the winning run—the world championship run.

I didn't realize it until later, what with all the excitement, but I was the winning pitcher in that game. It gave me three wins in the Series. It topped off a swell season for me. The winner's share in that Series came to $4024.70. Sure I remember the amount. Hell, it was just about equal to my whole year's salary.

So there I was, a thirty-four-game winner, three more in the Series, and a world championship. And not yet twenty-three years old. It sure looked like riding the rainbow for a long time. But I was quite unfortunate when it came to mishaps. For instance, one time we were monkeying around in the room, Speaker and I, and he slammed the door on my toe and broke it. Another time I got hit with a ball in batting practice that caused a blood clot in my foot and I had to have an operation to get it out. Things like that.

I hurt my arm the following spring and it was never the same again. I lost something on my fastball. It never came back. I could still pitch now and then—in 1915 I won fifteen games and led the league in earned run average—but I couldn't pitch more than every two weeks or so because of the pain in my arm after each game. The pity of it was that over the next half-dozen years the Red Sox were the best team in the league—they won pennants in '15, '16, and '18. No telling how many games I could have won with those teams.

But it's all a long time ago now, isn't it? It's funny how some things stand out and others fade away. I think it was around 1908 when I was warming up on the sideline and a sports reporter for the Boston *Post* named Paul Shannon was watching me. He turned to somebody and said, "That kid sure throws smoke." That was the origin of the nickname. It doesn't take much to get a nickname in baseball and once you've got it you might as well forget about ever getting rid of it. I'm eighty-eight years old now and people still call me Smoky Joe. But that's all right. I don't mind.

JOHNNY PODRES

JOHN JOSEPH PODRES
Born: September 30, 1932, Witherbee, New York
Major-league career: 1953–1967, 1969, Brooklyn and Los
 Angeles Dodgers, Detroit Tigers, San Diego Padres
Lifetime record: 148 wins, 116 losses

Johnny Podres' most memorable moment on a ball field occurred in the seventh game of the 1955 World Series when, in shutting out the Yankees he pitched the Brooklyn Dodgers to their first, and only, World Series victory. That single game overshadows a long and productive big league career, during which Podres also won three other World Series games. In 1957 he led the National League in earned run average and shutouts, and in 1961 his 18–5 record gave him the league lead in winning percentage.

There must have been twenty-five or thirty cops around me. I was right in the middle of them, like the President of the United States. They were escorting me to the team bus for the ride back to Brooklyn. There was no way I could have walked out of Yankee Stadium by myself that day.

In baseball—well, I guess it's true of any sport—if your name becomes identified with one game or one event it'll stick forever. Hell, it's more than twenty years ago now, but I still meet a lot of people who when they hear my name start talking about that game. Of course it wasn't just winning a World Series, although you can't ever underestimate that; it was the fact that it was the Dodgers' first Series win ever. I knew a little bit about Dodger history—they had been in seven World Series since 1916 and had never won one. Sure,

I knew that. You couldn't help but know it, the way the papers were playing it up in New York. But I don't think it was a factor one way or the other as far as I was concerned.

There was a hell of a party that night at the Hotel Bossert in Brooklyn. The champagne was really pouring. All you had to do was hold out your glass and somebody would fill it right up. The streets were filled with people and every so often I had to go out and wave to them, then go back inside again to the handshakes, the pats on the back, the champagne. Boy, the champagne! There was one guy there who kept telling me he'd been waiting for this since 1916. Can you imagine waiting thirty-nine years for something? I don't know how late that party went, or if it ever ended at all. The next morning a big limousine came by and picked me up and took me to the "Today" show. I must have still been feeling pretty good because I said, right out on the air, that I could beat the Yankees any day of the week. I was up so high I don't think I knew what I was saying. I didn't really come down until a few weeks later. I was at a deer camp in the Adirondacks, tramping through the woods by myself. It was a clear, crisp October day. All of a sudden I stopped and said to myself, "Hey, Podres, you beat the Yankees in the World Series!"

The next year, 1956, by rights should have been a great one for me. I was really riding a crest then. I had a tremendous amount of confidence and a certain amount of stature. I was only twenty-three years old at the time. I would ask myself: Where do you go from here, kiddo? Well, I'll tell you where I went: Into the United States Navy.

I still don't know how that happened. In 1952 I had been classified 4-F because of a back problem. Then all of a sudden I'm reclassified 1-A, and off I go. I'm not saying I shouldn't have gone in the Service; what I am saying is, why was I 4-F in 1952 and then all of a sudden 1-A in 1956? Was the World Series victory and all the publicity surrounding it a factor? It might have been. A lot of people probably said, "Here's this young, healthy guy, strong enough to win a World Series—why isn't he in the Service?" It might have created a public relations problem for somebody. I don't know.

Anyway, once I got into boot training my back didn't stand up under the gaff. They ended up putting me in a master-at-arms shack and got me a hospital bed to sleep on. I was living by myself. Then I went to Norfolk, pitched a few innings, and in six months they let me out. I missed the whole season in 1956.

A year after I got out of the Service the team moved to Los Angeles. We won the pennant there in '59 and played the White Sox in the Series. I won the second game, with some help from Larry Sherry. I started the sixth game and should have won that one, too. Hell, I had an 8–0 lead going into the bottom of the fourth and was really breezing. Never felt better. But I'll tell you what was happening. Early Wynn started for the White Sox and he knocked down a few of our guys. Early was pretty good for coming in close to a guy. They started grumbling on the bench. "Knock somebody on their ass."

So in the bottom of the fourth I figured it was a good time. I had a man out, nobody on base and an 8–0 lead. Jim Landis was the batter. I wanted to brush him back a little bit. So I threw one. It was a good brush-back pitch, high and inside. The problem was, Landis had decided to bunt, and damn if he didn't go right into the ball. The thing sailed up and got him square in the head. If he had been standing up straight nothing would have happened. But he got hit and fell to the ground. When he went down I started shaking. You never want to hit anybody like that. It turned out he wasn't badly hurt, but I didn't know it at the time.

Hitting him like that shook me up so bad I lost my composure. I walked the next guy, fell behind to Ted Kluszewski and grooved one which he hit into the right-field stands. Then I walked the next guy. The next guy who walked was Walter Alston and the one after him was me. Larry Sherry came in and finished the game.

I won another game in the '63 Series, against the Yankees. Yeah, I had pretty good luck in the World Series, winning four and losing only one. But the one everybody always remembers is that seventh game against the Yankees in 1955, the one that gave the Dodgers their first championship, and the only one they ever won in Brooklyn.

You know, it doesn't always pan out that you sign with your favorite team, but that's what happened with me. I was always a Brooklyn fan. When I was a kid I used to stay up at night listening to Red Barber and Connie Desmond announcing the games. Their voices became so familiar to me it was like they were members of the family. Did I ever dream about winning the World Series for the Dodgers? Well, maybe. If you're a kid who wants to be a big league ball player those thoughts are going to slip in now and then. What do you call it—the impossible dream?

The guys who were going to be my teammates a few years later were already there. Pee Wee Reese, Jackie Robinson, Gil Hodges, Duke Snider, Carl Furillo, Roy Campanella, Billy Cox, Preacher Roe. Many a quiet night I'd sit in my room listening to Barber and Desmond telling me what those guys were doing in Brooklyn, or in St. Louis or Cincinnati or Pittsburgh, or wherever they were. The nights were always quiet where I lived. That was Witherbee, New York. In the Adirondacks. Beautiful country. Just beautiful. That's where I started playing ball, throwing them back and forth to my father when I was six or seven years old. He was a semipro pitcher and I used to go and watch him pitch every Sunday. When I was old enough, I'd go out there in batting practice and shag balls, always making sure to put one or two in my pocket so I'd have a new ball to start the week off with.

There was one disadvantage growing up in the Adirondacks—the climate forced a short baseball season on you. Compared to the guys who grew up in, say, California or Florida, we barely had a chance to play. Our high school schedule was limited to ten or eleven games and sometimes a couple of those would be snowed out in the spring.

How did I get started in pro ball? Well, not many scouts come through Witherbee, New York. But I was lucky. My high school principal was a baseball fan and he took an interest in me. He knew a Dodger scout and got him to come up and have a look. The night the scout came up I pitched a no-hitter. He came back a second time to see me and I pitched another no-hitter. Then he invited me to come down to Brooklyn and work out at Ebbets Field with the Dodgers. This was in 1950. They signed me to a contract and I went away in 1951. I got a $6000 bonus. Actually $5200 was the bonus and $800 was my salary for 1951. Yeah, in 1951 I got paid $160 a month for five months.

They started me off at Newport News in the Piedmont League. I pitched there for a month and wasn't doing so hot and was sent down to Hazard, Kentucky in the Mountain States League. Class D ball. Screw up there and you're never heard from again. First game with Hazard I gave up seven runs in the first inning. I said to myself, "Boy, where do I go from here?" But then I got myself together and pitched shut-out ball the rest of the way and won the game. I ended up that season with a 21–3 record.

When I came home after the season I needed a job. I went over to Republic Steel—they had an office in town—and asked them if they'd hire me, in the mines or on the surface. With-erbee was a mining town in those days. My father worked his whole life in the mines, taking out iron ore. I wasn't crazy about the idea of going into the mines, but hell, I needed a job. I kept pestering them and finally they gave me a job on the surface, in one of the mills. But if I hadn't been a ball player I eventually would have had to go into the mines, like most of my friends.

The next year I went to spring training with the Dodgers. I almost made the club, too. That would have been a hell of a jump, from Class D to the big leagues. But they sent me to Montreal instead. A year later, though, I made the club, even though I didn't have such a good spring. I had come in at the right time, you see, when the Dodgers really needed left-hand pitching. The only other lefty on the team that year was Preacher Roe.

I joined the Dodgers a year or so ahead of Koufax. He was just a wild, hard-throwing left-hander then. It took him about five years, but he finally turned it around. I think the Dodgers were getting ready to give up on him, but then overnight he put it all together and for the next five or six years was the best pitcher I saw. He became a perfectionist out there. Hell, he got to the point where he'd get mad at himself for walking a guy. It was hard to believe this was the same pitcher who a few years before couldn't find the plate.

I would say that for the years I was watching him, Koufax was tops. But for the long haul, for year-after-year perfor-mance, Warren Spahn was the best I ever saw. He was just a master of his trade. When he was out there I couldn't take my eyes off him. I'd watch him work on the good hitters—he was always pitching them from behind so they would be swinging at the pitch *he* wanted them to hit. Great control. Watching him was an education. You know, the guy pitched over twenty years and hardly ever missed a turn. I don't think he knew what a sore arm was. And another thing about Spahn: He didn't win his first game in the big leagues until he was twenty-five years old, and he still ended up with 363 lifetime wins.

Robin Roberts was another great one. He pitched ball games just as good as he had to. I used to watch him time after time get into a jam, bases loaded and nobody out or something like that. You'd get the feeling on the bench: Okay, we got him now. One more hit will do it. But, damn, that hit wouldn't come. All of a sudden the guy is reaching back and firing harder and harder. Next thing you knew there were two strikeouts and a ground ball and you were wondering where the hell your rally went. Roberts always had it when he needed it.

But talk about talent, those Dodger teams in the 1950's had it. Pee Wee Reese, Jackie Robinson, Roy Camnpanella, Jim Gilliam, Carl Furillo, Gil Hodges, Duke Snider. For pitchers we had Don Newcombe, Carl Erskine, Clem Labine.

One of the problems with a club like that, with so many outstanding players, the sportswriters couldn't give each guy the coverage he deserved. When a team has two or three good players, then those guys get all the attention and the publicity. But with the team we had, with a couple of guys doing something spectacular every day with the bat or the glove, who were you going to focus on?

I'll tell you, it made me a much better pitcher, playing with those guys. And I don't mean just because they got me the runs and made the plays. It was just that being surrounded by so much talent made you work harder and play harder. There was no other way, if you wanted to stay on the same field with them.

Even when we lost the first two games to the Yankees in the '55 Series those guys were still confident they were going to win. We figured once we got them in Ebbets Field we'd knock them around a little.

I had no idea I'd be starting in the Series. We had Newcombe, Erskine, Roger Craig, Billy Loes, Karl Spooner. I honestly didn't think I'd get a start. You see, I really didn't have an outstanding year in '55. I started off okay, winning seven of my first ten, but then I hurt my shoulder. I was on the disabled list for a while and when I came back it took me some time to get squared away.

Then when I was okay again and getting back into the groove, I had a freak accident in September, at Ebbets Field. Batting practice was over and we were getting set to take infield. I had a fungo bat and was going to hit fly balls to the outfielders. Well, in Ebbets Field they used to wheel the batting cage across the diamond and out through a gate in center field. They started wheeling that thing and, jeez, they hit me right in the side with it. Banged up my ribs pretty good. For two or three weeks I could hardly breathe. It was so bad they were thinking of bringing somebody up from Montreal and putting me back on the disabled list, which would have kept me out of the Series.

But then after we'd cinched the pennant I pitched a game against the Pirates. This was about a week or so before the Series. I pitched four innings and had real good stuff, so they decided I was okay. If I hadn't looked all right in that game I don't think I would have pitched in the Series; I would have gone on the disabled list. Sometimes when I think of how close I came to not playing in the '55 Series I break out in a cold sweat.

Newcombe and Loes started the first two games at Yankee Stadium and we got beat. After the second game Alston told me to be ready tomorrow, that I was opening in Ebbets Field. I felt just great about it. The fact that he was picking me when we had our backs to the wall was a real compliment. It showed the confidence he had in me.

I beat the Yankees that third game, 8–3. Campanella got us going in the first inning with a home run off of Bob Turley, and we kept going. That game got us turned around. We won the next two and the Series went back to Yankee Stadium. We needed just one more to wrap it up. But Whitey Ford stopped us, 5–1.

We were all pretty blue after that game. I remember Reese was sitting in front of his locker with his head down and I said to him, "Don't worry, Pee Wee. I'll shut 'em out tomorrow." You've got to say something, what the hell.

Alston had told me before the sixth game, "You're the pitcher tomorrow if we don't win it today." So I knew. After we lost the sixth game, then I knew for sure. Well, I told myself, one more day's work to do. I went home that night and didn't think too much about it. I don't believe I ever in my life thought about a game I was going to pitch the next day. Why worry today about what you've got to do tomorrow?

I woke up that morning and had the same breakfast I'd had the day I pitched the third game. At the same time, too. Superstitious? No. Careful.

When I got out to the ball park, that's when I started getting keyed up. It wasn't just the seventh game either, it was walking into the ball park. That always keyed me up. Still does. That's when my clock starts to tick.

I remember I warmed up with Dixie Howell, who was our third-string catcher. When they announced the Yankee lineup I said to him, "Dixie, there's no way that lineup can beat me today." I guess I was trying to give myself a little boost.

One break I got was Mickey Mantle didn't play that day. He was injured. But so was Jackie Robinson. Neither one started.

You know, in the game I beat them 8–3 I threw a lot of change-ups. I had that pitch working just right and it really helped me. I think they were looking for it in the seventh game. I did throw some in the first three or four innings and again it was effective, but over the last five I stayed pretty much with the fastball. If you've got it, that's a good pitch to throw in Yankee Stadium that time of year, with the ball flashing from sunlight into shadow. No, we didn't deliberately change the pattern. Campy saw how well my hard stuff was working and he told me to stay with it, especially when those shadows started growing longer.

In the last of the eighth the Yankees had men on first and third and two out and I fanned Hank Bauer on as good a fastball as I ever threw in my life. I started it around his letters and when he swung and missed the ball was up at his shoulders.

But of course the play that everybody remembers in that Series is Sandy Amoros' catch. You can't talk about the '55 Series with anybody for more than a minute before they start talking about that play.

We were leading 2–0 in the bottom of the sixth and the Yankees got their first two batters on first and second. Gil McDougald on second, Billy Martin on first. Berra's the batter. He was a left-handed hitter and we played him to pull. He was a dead pull hitter. But the son of a gun lifted a ball out to left field. At first I wasn't worrying about it. In fact, when he hit it I bent over and picked up the rosin bag and said to myself, "Well, there's one out." But then I looked around and saw the ball keep slicing toward the line and I saw Amoros running his tail off. "Jeez," I said to myself, "he's got a hell of a run." The ball seemed to hang up in the air forever, and Amoros is *still* running. I started to think: *Is he going to get it?* I'll tell you, that's a helpless goddamned feeling, standing on the mound at a moment like that. The game was close, the tying runs are on base, all the marbles have gone up in the air on that ball, and there's your outfielder running for it and all of a sudden I started getting this sickly feeling that maybe he *wasn't* going to be there when the ball came down.

But he was, and, jeez, just barely. At the last moment, still going at top speed, he reached out and that baby dropped right into his glove. I let out a sigh—I guess I'd been holding my breath.

Martin, who was on second, hadn't gone off too far; but McDougald, who was on first, must have thought the ball was going to drop in. He had to be thinking that, because he was just about going around second base when Amoros made the catch, and he had to put the brakes on. We had McDougald hung out to dry and all we needed was a couple of good throws to get him. I remember Reese going out to take the cut-off. Just before he got the ball from Amoros, Pee Wee took a quick look around to see where the runners were, and then Amoros hit him with a perfect peg. As soon as Pee Wee got the ball he didn't hesitate a second—he knew where he had to send it.

I'm still standing there on the mound—all this is happening in a matter of seconds—watching it the same as everybody else. Pee Wee whips around and fires that ball to Hodges at first base. There's McDougald trying to get back. Pee Wee made a perfect throw and we had McDougald nailed from here to Christmas.

Boy, did that juice me up. I got the next guy out, got them out in the seventh and eighth, then nailed the first two men in the ninth. One more to go. I was so hepped up I could hardly stand still out there. I just *knew* I was going to get that last batter and couldn't wait. It was Elston Howard. I wanted to finish up with a strikeout and I threw him fastball after fastball—good, hard, riding fastballs—but he kept fouling them off. Campanella called for another fastball but I shook him off. I think it was the only time in the whole game I did that. I threw a change-up and Howard hit it down to Reese at short. When Pee Wee saw the ball coming at him a big grin broke across his face; I guess he couldn't help it. He made a low throw to first but Hodges picked it up without any trouble.

A lot of what happened after that is a blur. I wish I could remember it all, because I'm sure I had a hell of a good time.

JOE SEWELL

JOSEPH WHEELER SEWELL
Born: October 9, 1898, Titus, Alabama.
Major-league career: 1920–33, Cleveland Indians, New York
    Yankees
Lifetime average: .312

Joe Sewell is among the most remarkable hitters ever to play major-league ball. Statistically, he was baseball's most difficult strikeout—just 114 times in 7,132 official at bats. Though most assuredly a contact hitter, he met the ball with enough power to hit 436 doubles in his career, five times collecting over 40 in a season. Sewell batted over .300 nine times, with a high of .353 in 1923. In 1925 he struck out four times in 608 at bats, in 1929 four times in 578 at bats, and in 1932 three times in 503 at bats.

Sewell was elected to the Hall of Fame in 1977.

I grew up in Titus, Alabama. That was a little town, way out in the country. Fifteen miles from the railroad. There wasn't too much going on around there, so baseball, which was an early interest for me and my brother Luke, kept getting more and more important in our lives as we grew up.

Oh yes, I followed the big leagues. Ty Cobb was my idol. Not only was he a great player, but he was from Georgia, you see, and since I was from Alabama, I felt sort of a kinship with him. When I got to the big leagues in 1920 Cobb was still playing. We played in the American League together for eight years and I'll tell you, every time I got out on the same field with him it was a tremendous thrill for me.

I got to be very friendly with Cobb. He was one of the finest men I ever met. I know that a lot of people didn't like him, but that was because of the way he played ball. When he put on that uniform he was a different person. It became a blood war and he was determined to beat the fire out of you. But away from the field I found him to be as nice a person as I ever sat down with. Highly intelligent. Loved to talk.

He was the greatest ball player that I ever saw. The records bear it out; but there were a lot of things he could do to beat you that don't show up in the records. He was always outsmarting you, adapting to a situation, on the go before you knew what was happening. If you gave him the slightest opening he would spy it and take advantage. Now, Ruth was a great ball player, but Cobb could do more things out there than Babe. I'll say this though: For accuracy, Ruth was the greatest throwing outfielder that I ever played with. When there was a man on first and the ball was hit to right field I just went over and put the bag between my feet. That ball would come out of right field on one hop, smack into my glove. He seldom made a bad throw, maybe twice in the years I played on his side. For accuracy nobody could top him, not Speaker, not anybody.

To me it was very gratifying to think that I had enough ability to play with those fellows like Cobb and Ruth and Tris Speaker and Eddie Collins and Walter Johnson. Sometimes it's hard to believe what's happening to you. For years I read about Tris Speaker, about what a great all-around player he was, nearly the equal of Cobb. And then here I am one day joining the ball club where he's managing and playing center field, and he's calling me by my first name and treating me as an equal. I wish every boy who had the burning interest in baseball and the deep desire to play as I had, could have the chance to play in the major leagues.

Sure there was a lot of interest in Titus around World Series time. But what made it kind of frustrating for us boys was the fact that the scores didn't reach us until a day later. That's when we got the big city papers, from Birmingham or Montgomery. We would get yesterday's papers today. That was how we kept up with it.

One World Series I can still remember getting excited about was in 1914. That was the year the Boston Braves came from way behind to win the pennant and then upset Connie Mack's

Athletics in four straight games. Our papers were full of that. George Stallings was the manager of the Braves and he had those three mighty fine pitchers who seemed to do all of the winning for his team—Dick Rudolph, Lefty Tyler, and Bill James. That team stands out in my memory because what they did was quite a feat. Mr. Mack had just a fine, fine team, with his own good pitchers like Chief Bender, Eddie Plank, Bullet Joe Bush. Nobody—nobody in Titus, Alabama, anyway—believed that anybody could beat the Athletics that year, much less in four straight. We pondered that one for a long time.

I might have lived my whole life in Titus without anybody ever hearing about me, if not for baseball. But I was lucky. I'm sure there were any number of boys who would have had fine careers if they had just been given the opportunity. You see, back in those days it was very easy for even an outstanding young player to be overlooked. Today the big league clubs have scouts all over the country, plus a lot of other ways of conveying information about talented young players. It's unlikely that a boy would be overlooked today. But you couldn't say that when I was growing up, during those years after the turn of the century.

My father was a country doctor and he'd been to college. So he had seen the value of an education. There were six of us in the family and he was determined that each of us should have an education so as to be able to get the most out of whatever abilities we had. The school we attended was the University of Alabama. That's where we went, Luke and myself and our two brothers, while our sisters went to college in Montgomery.

I was supposed to be a doctor, like my father. In fact, I took premed; I was all set to study medicine. But at the same time I played baseball at the university. That was the ironic thing. The university had a highly developed and well-organized athletic program and it was through the exposure I got there that I landed with an industrial team in Birmingham. I played in the TCI League—that's the Tennessee Coal and Iron Company in Birmingham, a subsidiary of U.S. Steel. Each team represented a different town, like Tarrant City, Fairfield, Bessemer, and so on. It was a good brand of ball. Fellows went from that league up to the big leagues. I started there, so did my brother Luke, and so did Riggs Stephenson, one of the best hitters that ever lived.

It was playing in the TCI League that got me a contract with the New Orleans ball club, and they had an affiliation with the Cleveland Indians. Sure I was delighted when New Orleans offered me the contract. I never had any thought but to sign it. Was my father disappointed? No, he went along with it. You see, it was still my intention to study medicine, to go back to school after the season. But how could I have foreseen all the things that were going to happen to me over the next few months? I never did go back to school.

I came to the big leagues under the most tragic circumstances possible—to fill the job of a man who had died after being hit in the head by a pitched ball. To make it even more difficult for me, I had only about two months of professional experience under my belt, and to make it still more difficult, I was joining the ball club right in the middle of a red-hot pennant race.

I was in New Orleans when it happened. It was around the sixteenth or seventeenth of August, in 1920. I went downstairs to the hotel lobby in the morning and heard that the Cleveland shortstop, Ray Chapman, had died from the effects of being hit by a pitched ball thrown by Carl Mays of the Yankees. It never dawned on me that I was the next man in line for that job. What the heck, I was still pretty green. But then I was called into the office by the New Orleans manager, Johnny Dodds.

"How would you like to go to the big leagues?" he asked me.

I was a bit taken aback.

"I don't know," I said. I had never even seen a major league game, so I wasn't too sure.

"Well," he said, "the Cleveland Indians need a shortstop and you're the man they want."

"You reckon I can do the job?" I asked.

"You can play up there," he said. He seemed very positive about it. "In any event, you're leaving tonight. There's an eight o'clock train."

I played the ball game that afternoon, hit a double and a triple, and then hurried back to the hotel and got ready. I stepped aboard the train at eight o'clock still a little uncertain and bewildered—it was all happening so quickly. It took me that night and all the next day. I spent the night in Cincinnati, then caught the train the next morning and got into Cleveland in the middle of the afternoon. Excited? I'll say. Too excited even to talk. I don't think I said two words to anybody all the way to Cleveland.

But I'll tell you what happened. Remember now, I was coming out of New Orleans where it was real hot. When I got to Cincinnati, all I was wearing was a seersucker suit and a little sailor straw hat. Well, it was chilly up there—by my standards, anyway. I missed my train connection in Cincinnati and had to spend the night there. I checked into a little old hotel. I happened to mention to the desk clerk where I was going and that I needed heavier clothing.

"The stores are all closed," he said. It was after dark now. "But a friend of mine is a haberdasher. Let's see what we can drum up."

He called his friend and that fellow came down and opened his store and sold me a suit of clothes and a felt hat. While he was measuring me up, the haberdasher asked me why I was going to Cleveland. You know, just to make conversation.

"On business," I said.

I didn't tell him I was going up to the big leagues. I didn't think he would believe me. Heck, I still couldn't believe it myself.

Well, I finally got there, smack into a three-way pennant race between Cleveland, the Yankees, and the White Sox.

I never will forget the first game I saw. I wasn't in the lineup that day. I spent the whole afternoon on the bench. First of all, I almost fell off my feet when I saw that ball park—League Park. Biggest thing I ever saw in my life. Looked to me like they could get the whole city of Cleveland in there, if they wanted.

They were playing the Philadephia Athletics. Everything that happened that day is as clear in my mind as if it happened yesterday. Doc Johnston was playing first base for the Indians and he got five base hits for five times up, and in one inning he stole home. Elmer Smith of the Indians went after a ball in right-center and at the last second jumped up against the fence and caught that ball backhanded. Just took a high line drive right off of the fence. My goodness, I thought, what a great catch. I figured I had got to the big leagues just in time to see one of the most wonderful plays ever made. But then Tris Speaker made two catches in center field that were just as good, if not better. Tilly Walker, who was playing center field for the Athletics, threw a man out at home plate with a peg that looked to me like it was a half mile long. All through that game I just kept slumping down further and further in the corner of the dugout, telling myself, "I don't think you belong here, Joe." They'd take one look at me and send me right back. And what was I going to do with that heavy suit of clothes in New Orleans?

The next day Speaker put me out at short in infield practice. He got one of the coaches, Jack McAllister, to hit balls to me. Well, he couldn't get one by me. I was all over the place, going into the hole and crossing second base, just picking up everything. Then I took some batting practice and I hit the ball very well. When I went back into the clubhouse, Speaker collared me and said, "Joe, you're playing shortstop today."

"Are you sure?" I asked. I didn't know what to say.

"Yes," he said. "Aren't you?"

"I guess I am," I said.

He smiled at me and patted me on the shoulder. I think he understood that I was a little nervous.

First time at bat I hit a line drive that Tilly Walker caught in center field. Then I came up again. Fellow named Scott Perry was out on the mound. He wound up and threw it. I never will forget that pitch. A high curve ball on the outside. I reached out and hit it right over the third baseman's head for a triple. I dropped my bat and just flew around those bases. When I got to third I stood there and said to myself, "Shucks, this ain't so tough after all." And I haven't been nervous from that day to this.

That was the year, if you recall, that the White Sox scandal came to light. They had thrown the World Series the year before but it wasn't until September of 1920 that the story broke. It happened right after we played them a series in Cleveland. The whole bunch of them, Joe Jackson, Eddie Cicotte and all the others, were suspended. With two weeks of the season still remaining they were declared ineligible and that put the White Sox out of the running. But the Yankees were still there. When it came down to it though, we beat them out.

We played Brooklyn in the World Series. They were called the Robins then, because of their manager, Wilbert Robinson. The Brooklyn Robins.

Brooklyn had a good team. But so did we. We had some outstanding players. I'm thinking of Tris Speaker and Elmer Smith and Charlie Jamieson and Larry Gardner. We had some very fine pitchers, too. Jim Bagby won thirty-one games that year, Stanley Coveleski won twenty-four, Ray Caldwell won twenty. That's seventy-five wins right there, from three pitchers. You get that, you don't need much more.

Coveleski pitched the first game in Brooklyn and beat Rube Marquard by a score of 3–1. I didn't get many hits in that Series but I got one in the second inning that helped along a two-run rally, which was all Stanley really needed. But he had to pitch a close ball game because Marquard was a very tough pitcher, tough to hit. He had everything.

Burleigh Grimes shut us out the next day, 3–0. Burleigh was another good one. He had a live fastball and that spitball, the famous Burleigh Grimes spitball that was so hard to hit. We lost the third game too, 2–1, to Sherry Smith. Then the Series moved to Cleveland.

In the fourth game Stanley came back to beat them again, 5–1. Stanley was tough through the whole Series. But he was always tough. He was just a great pitcher, that's all.

Then came the fifth game. That's the famous one. One of the most historic games of baseball ever played. You just can't talk about World Series history without bringing up that game. As a matter of fact, I was on the scene for *two* of the most historic games ever played, and I'll tell you about the other one later. But this fifth one in 1920, just looking at the score doesn't tell you much. It was 8–1, a very easy win for us. So you've got to look twice to get the story.

To start off, Elmer Smith made history in the first inning when he hit the first grand slam home run ever in a World Series. And in the fourth inning Jim Bagby hit a home run with two men on—the first pitcher ever to strike a home run in a World Series. Now, many other players have achieved both of those feats since, but they were the first and they did it within a few innings of each other in the same game.

I can tell you how that first inning went, don't think I can't. Charlie Jamieson hit a single, Bill Wambsganss singled, Tris

Speaker beat out a bunt. First three men up. The fourth man was Elmer Smith. Burleigh Grimes was the pitcher. He got two quick strikes on Elmer. You know, years later, Burleigh and I landed together on the same club, the Yankees. We were sitting in the clubhouse one day and I decided to ask him about something that had been bothering me, bothering me for thirteen or fourteen years.

"Burleigh," I said, "I want to ask you one question. Why in the world did you throw Elmer Smith that high fastball in the 1920 World Series after you had got two strikes on him with spitballs?" He had thrown two beautiful spitters in there for strikes.

"Hell," he said, "I was trying to waste one. It was a bad ball."

"It sure was," I said. And it was. I think it was just about up to Elmer's cap bill. But you couldn't throw a fastball by Elmer Smith. When he saw one of those babies it was feastin' time— he'd go right after it. I've got a mental picture of that ball going over the fence, right now.

I'll tell you another story about that game. We hit Burleigh very hard that day. Which was unusual, believe me, because he was a tough man to hit, with that spitter of his. But we had picked something up. Every time Burleigh was going to throw a spitball, Pete Kilduff, the Brooklyn second baseman, would pick up a handful of sand and throw it down between his feet. Why he did that I don't know. Maybe to make sure his hand was dry in case he had to field the ball. Somebody on our club, I don't know who, noticed Kilduff doing it and so we watched him. I knew it; I watched Kilduff whenever I came to bat against Burleigh. Every time he picked up that dirt and threw it down I knew what was coming. Kilduff could read the catcher's signs, you see. So when he didn't pick up the dirt I knew to expect either the curve or the fastball. We knew when to lay off the spitter and wait for some other pitch to hit. If you wanted to guess, you'd go with the fastball, because that was Burleigh's other good pitch, along with the spitter. So we were in a pretty good position up there against him.

If Kilduff was doing that to make his hand dry I could understand it. Coveleski was a spitball pitcher too. He threw a beauty. He used to spit all over the ball and there were times when you could see the saliva flying off of it when he fired to the plate. There were also times when the ball was hit to me and it still wasn't dry and I'd throw a spitball to first base. You should have seen the first baseman dancing around trying to catch it! One time the darn thing was so wet that when I picked it up and threw it, it slipped right out of my hand and ended up in right field. When Coveleski was pitching and the ball was hit to me, if there was time I'd give it a little twist to dry it off before I threw it.

The story came out later about how we'd been watching Kilduff, and I'll bet Burleigh's neck turned a little red when he heard about it.

Okay, now we get to the fifth inning. That's one of the top moments ever in baseball. It's got to be, any way you look at it. And I'm standing right there, not more than a few yards away. Boy, it happened so fast—bang-bang-bang—hardly anybody knew what had taken place.

I can remember it just like it happened yesterday. The Dodgers got two men on base, Pete Kilduff on second and Otto Miller on first, with nobody out. The batter was Clarence Mitchell, a pitcher—he'd come in after we knocked out Burleigh. Clarence Mitchell was a good hitter, which is why they let him bat in that situation. Well, he hit it square all right. He drove a line shot that I thought was a base hit sure. No question in my mind but that it was going into the outfield. But our second baseman, Bill Wambsganss, was off and running the moment the ball left the bat. He ran toward second base and jumped just as high as he could and he took that ball right out of the air, backhanded. I can see him yet. In my memory he's still there, stretched out a little sideways in midair, his gloved hand thrown way up, and that ball is stopping dead in the center of his glove.

Everybody in the ball park thought it was going into the outfield, including Pete Kilduff and Otto Miller. They were moving as soon as the ball was hit. Well, Bill Wamby was running toward the bag anyway and he stepped on second and that was two out. But then he started to throw the ball to first base. I had been watching Otto Miller coming down the line— he was running full steam. I yelled to Bill, "Tag him! Tag him!" You see, Bill had run to the bag, made sure he touched it, but hadn't yet looked toward first base. He had his arm cocked to throw, but when he looked around there was Otto

Miller, running right toward him. Bill just went up to him and touched him on the chest with the ball, just as easy as saying hello. I think that was the first that Otto Miller realized the ball had been caught. When Bill touched him, Miller stopped in his tracks with the most dumbfounded look on his face. I've always said it was Otto Miller who completed that triple play because he just kept coming, right into Bill's arms. When the triple play had been completed I think Pete Kilduff was still running, around third base. That's how fast it all happened. The whole thing took maybe three seconds.

The jump that Bill made to grab that ball was just unbelievable. What made it possible was he had started running in the direction of second base the moment the ball was hit and his motion gave him just the little extra spring he needed. I'd never seen him jump that high before. Shucks, I don't think I've ever seen *anybody* jump that high for a line drive. Now, if I hadn't yelled out to him he may have thrown to first or he may have not. If he had thrown it would still be the triple play but not unassisted. That was the thing—an unassisted triple play. If it had been a plain triple play with other men handling the ball I daresay there would be some dust on it today; but since Bill did it all by himself it'll be up in lights forever.

For a few moments the fans couldn't quite grasp what had happened. There was a little lull. Then it sank in. You should have seen the scene then! It was the tag-end of the straw hat season and they started throwing those hats all over the field. We had to call time while some men came out with wheelbarrows to pick up the straw hats.

You know, just a little added note. Next time he came to the plate, Clarence Mitchell hit into a double play, first to short and back to first. I handled that one in the middle. So Clarence Mitchell made five outs in two consecutive times at bat.

Anyway, that's the story of your unassisted triple play. Only one ever made in a World Series, and not many others ever made, anytime, anyplace.

We went out the next day and beat them 1–0 with Walter Mails. That put us up four games to two. We still had to win one more. You see, the World Series that year was a best five-out-of-nine deal. They experimented with it that way for a few years, then went back to what it is today, four-of-seven. So the first three games were played in Brooklyn and the next four were scheduled for Cleveland. If there was to be an eighth or a ninth game we would have had to go back to Brooklyn to play.

Walter Mails did a fine job for us that day. I'll tell you something about that game. After he had finished warming up, Walter Mails came back and sat down on the bench. He picked up a towel and was drying himself off. Then he looked around and said to us, "You boys get me one run today and we'll win." I can still remember him saying that. Well, that's just what we got him, one run, and he made it stick. George Burns got a single and Tris Speaker scored him with a double. That was in the sixth inning, and Walter was as good as his word.

The next day Coveleski shut them out 3–0 to give us the championship. As soon as the celebrations were over—it was Cleveland's first pennant and first world championship—I got on the train and headed back to Alabama. My head was still spinning from all that had happened to me. In June, I had been at the University of Alabama, then I went to New Orleans to play, then in August to Cleveland, and in October I'm the shortstop on a championship team. My whole life had changed. I knew then I would never be a doctor. I was a major leaguer now.

I didn't get into a World Series again until 1932, when I was with the Yankees. It was against the Chicago Cubs and it was a rough-going Series, I can tell you. There was a lot of bad feeling on both sides and it just kept on getting worse. You see what happened, late in the season the Cubs lost their regular shortstop, Billy Jurges, to an injury. So they bought Mark Koenig to fill in. Mark did more than fill in; he played great ball for them. He hit over three hundred and fifty and pulled their infield together. A lot of people said the Cubs wouldn't have won the pennant that year without Mark Koenig. But when it came to dividing up the World Series money, the Cubs voted Koenig just a half-share.

Now, Koenig used to play for the Yankees and he still had a lot of friends on the club. So when it came out in the newspapers what the Cubs had done, you should have heard the talk in the Yankees clubhouse. The Cubs were called every kind of cheap, no good so-and-so's you could imagine. "If it hadn't been for Koenig they would be dividing up second-place money." That was the feeling in our clubhouse.

The Series opened in New York. After we'd taken batting practice on the first day, Ruth went and sat in the dugout near the runway where the visiting clubs came out. In those days the visiting club had to come through the Yankees dugout to get to the field. Well, Babe sat there and greeted every one of those Cub players. You never heard such goings-on, such yelling and cussing and ripping. Babe started it and then some of the other fellows picked up on it and they really laid it on the Cubs, because of what had happened with Koenig. Not one of the Cubs answered back; they just went out on the field. But they had to be steaming.

We beat them two straight in New York, pounding them around pretty good. Naturally that didn't improve their disposition any. They had started yelling back and we knew that when we moved on to Chicago it was going to be a rough time, because the newspapers were in on it now. A feud had started between the Yankees and the Cubs and it wasn't going to get any better.

Ruth was doing the loudest yelling. And he could pour it on, too. That was another department he led the league in. And of course the fact that Ruth was involved just made it bigger. Anytime that fellow was involved in anything, good, bad, or indifferent, everybody paid attention. You could love him, hate him, or be neutral, but you couldn't ignore him. There never was such a personality on a ball field. Talking about him can never do him justice. You had to be there, you had to see for yourself.

By the middle of the third game, in Chicago, it had got just plain brutal. I'd never known there were so many cuss words in the language or so many ways of stringing them together. But I'll tell you where it was all heading—right for the history books.

In the top of the fifth inning the score was tied, 4–4. I was batting in front of Ruth and I led off that inning. I grounded out. I went back to the dugout and sat down. Babe stepped up and just the sight of him was enough to set that place to jumping—the Cub players, the fans, everybody. Charlie Root was the pitcher. The Babe took one strike. Then two strikes. With each pitch the yelling was getting louder and louder.

Babe? He was just as calm as could be. He was enjoying it all, that son of a gun. You couldn't rattle Babe Ruth on a baseball diamond. No sir!

After the second strike Babe backed out and picked up some dirt. He rubbed his hands, looking square into the Cub dugout. What was coming out of there was just turning the air blue. He looked at Burleigh Grimes who was cussin' at him, and Babe cussed him right back. Burleigh had a towel around his neck, which he took and started to wave. Then Babe raised two fingers and pointed to the center-field fence. After doing that, he got back into the box and set himself. Charlie Root delivered the next pitch. The ball was just above Ruth's knees. A good pitch, a strike. Babe uncoiled one of those beautiful swings. *Crack!* I can still see that ball going out of Wrigley Field. Have you ever seen a golf ball take off? That's the way that ball shot into the air, just like a golf ball. It got so small in such a hurry it looked like it was shrinking as it went. It traveled out of the ball park and through a high tree standing out beyond. That tree was full of little boys and maybe some men, too, watching the game. When the ball went through the tree every one of them just rained out of there, dropping down to run after it.

By the time Ruth rounded third base it was something to see. The fans were throwing whatever was handy at him—cabbages, oranges, apples, just everything. What a show! What a circus! Babe Ruth. My heavens, that was some Babe Ruth.

After the game, which we won, 7–5, we naturally were congratulating Ruth on having done a good job. He hit two home runs in that game and so did Gehrig, but as usual Ruth was the center of things. Here's what he said:

"I was out at the hospital this morning and I told a little kid I was gonna hit him a home run today."

Mrs. Sewell told me later that when Babe came up in the fifth inning she heard Mrs. Ruth call out to him, "Remember the little boy." And that's when he pointed out and hit the home run. He'd already hit one, but I guess he figured that wasn't enough.

Do I believe he really called it? Yes sir. I was there. I saw it. I don't care what anybody says. He did it. He probably couldn't have done it again in a thousand years, but he did it that time.

That night Judge Landis wrote Joe McCarthy a very severe note, telling Joe to get his players to refrain from all the profanity. He told Joe that if we didn't calm down our vocabulary we would all be fined. You see, the yelling was so loud it was carrying to the stands. My wife could hear it. Joe McCarthy read that note to us in a meeting before we went out on the field the next day. Well, you could have heard a pin drop in our dugout during the game. We sat there like mummies. One thing you didn't do in those days was monkey around with Judge Landis. He was the *law* in baseball.

We let our bats do the talking for us in that game. It was a 5–5 tie into the seventh inning and we unloaded for four. I remember I got a single to right field to score two. I did all right that day, got three hits. We scored four more in the top of the ninth and beat them 13–6. That made it four straight and finished the World Series.

We mauled the Cubs in that Series. We really did. That was a pretty fair hitting team we had. Everybody talks about Ruth and Gehrig, but then just for good luck we had Bill Dickey, Tony Lazzeri, Ben Chapman, Earle Combs, Frank Crosetti, myself. By reputation the 1927 Yankees were supposed to be the greatest ball club ever, but I contend we had a good club in 1932. I may be a little prejudiced, but that was one heck of a team. You look at the lineup we put on the field for the first game of that World Series and you'll see we had six fellows in there who are in the Hall of Fame today—Ruth, Gehrig, Combs, Dickey, Red Ruffing, and myself.

I ought to point out that the Cubs were no patsies. Listen, they were a strong club. They had Billy Herman, Gabby Hartnett, Kiki Cuyler—they're all in the Hall of Fame—Charlie Grimm, Riggs Stephenson. Outstanding players, all of them.

Riggs Stephenson was a good friend of mine. Still is to this day. I can tell you a funny story about him. You know how it is in Yankee Stadium, how when it gets late in the season that sun can bother the dickens out of the left fielder. Well, your shortstop and third baseman can have a terrible time with the sun too, on balls hit up into the air. There are times when you see it and then lose it and just have to take a chance and grab where you think it's coming down. Well, Riggs Stephenson came to bat one time and he hit down on a ball that bounced off the plate and bounded way up in the air toward me at third base. I looked up and the sun was right there. All I had was a glimpse of the ball before I was blinded. I shut my eyes and put up my glove and wouldn't you know but that ball landed right in it. I was the most surprised person in Yankee Stadium. I took the ball and pegged it over and threw Steve out at first. I told him later, "Steve, I can catch those little old hoppers you hit down there with my eyes shut." Which is just what I did.

But he could hit a ball. There weren't many fellows who could swing the bat the way he could. I don't know why he isn't in the Hall of Fame. You just look at his averages sometime. And I'll say this, too, while we're on the subject—my brother Luke ought to be in there. He was a great catcher, year in and year out, and he could hit. A tremendous asset to a ball club. I'm not saying it because he's my brother, but because it's true.

That's right, I didn't strike out very often. I guess more than anything else, that's my reputation today—the man who didn't strike out. Once over the full season I struck out just three times, and then there were three years where I struck out only four times over the full season. Over the last eight years I played, I averaged around six strike-outs a season.

I suppose you've got to be blessed with good eyesight and judgment and coordination. But going way back, I can't remember when I couldn't throw a bottle cap or a rock up into the air and hit it with a broomstick handle. I used to carry a pocketful of rocks around with me and every now and then take that broomstick handle and swat at them. I wasn't even training myself to be a hitter; at that time I was no more thinking of being a ball player than I was of sitting on the moon. I just loved to hit at those things and see them go, and it made sense to me that if I wanted to hit them I had to keep my eye on them. That's the secret—and it sure isn't much of a secret, is it? You can't hit that bottle cap and you can't hit that rock—and you can't hit that baseball—unless you're looking at it.

Once I started playing ball around town I realized I could hit. I hit the ball just about every time I swung at it. I could see a ball leave my bat. A lot of people don't believe that's possible. But it sure is. All you have to do is watch it. It doesn't disappear when you put the bat on it. I watched a big league game not long ago and I saw some boys striking at balls that I swear they missed by a foot. They couldn't have been looking at those balls. You just know they couldn't.

The first thing you've got to learn if you want to be a good hitter is where the strike zone is. Another thing you've got to know is what kind of umpire you've got behind the plate. Some are keener than others. If you take a pitch a quarter of an inch outside of the strike zone it's a ball. And a good umpire will call it a ball. You've got to find out who they are and go accordingly. Bill McGowan, Tommy Connolly, they were good umpires. Billy Evans was a good umpire, but he missed some every once in a while. So I knew that when Billy Evans was umpiring behind the plate I couldn't take a pitch real close; not when I had two strikes on me anyway.

One of those years, when I struck out four times, I was in St. Louis and with two strikes on me the ball passed around the bill of my cap. Bill McGowan—who was one of the good umpires—said, "Strike three, you're out, oh my God I missed that." All in the same sentence. He sure had missed it. But I didn't say anything. I just turned and walked away. The next day before the game he came up to me and apologized.

"I did my best, Joe," he said.

"Good enough, Bill," I told him.

There was a fellow named Pat Caraway, a left-hander with the White Sox. He struck me out twice in one ball game. This was in Cleveland. It was a full house out there that day and the center-field bleachers were filled with white shirts. Pat Caraway didn't have very good stuff. You could have reached out and caught the ball he was throwing with your naked hand and tossed it back to him. But he had a herky-jerk motion and that day he was throwing that white ball in out of those white shirts and I never could find it.

Lefty Grove? I'll bet I was up around .400 against him. Sure he was tough to hit. But I could pick up the ball the moment he turned it loose and I followed it right on it. And it came right on in. With Grove you didn't have much time. Whoosh! But I let him furnish the power. All I did was flick my bat out at it and it would go. But he was fast. There were a lot of good fastball pitchers, but they weren't as consistently fast. Grove always was. Inning after inning, he never slowed up. I don't know where he got it all from. He could stand out there for a week and barrel it in at you. Never tapered off. Sometimes when the sun was out really bright he would throw that baseball in there and it looked like a flash of white sewing thread coming up at you.

One of the biggest thrills I ever had in my baseball career was the day I went five for five against Grove in Yankee Stadium. The last one was a home run into the right-field stands. When I hit that one Grove threw his glove way up in the air in disgust. Oh, he was sore. When I came around to the plate Ruth was standing there, waiting to hit next.

"Kid," he said shaking my hand, "thanks for doing my job for me."

Babe Ruth and Lefty Grove. Two of the greatest names in baseball. I'm proud to have been on the same field with fellows like that. And Cobb, too, and Speaker and Walter Johnson and Lou Gehrig and Jimmie Foxx and Al Simmons and Harry Heilmann and all the rest of them. Great players and wonderful people. Looking back on the years I see how fortunate I was. And sometimes I can't help thinking how strange the design was. We think we run our own lives according to our own plans. But we don't. Not always anyway. I've often wondered what my life would have been like if a ball hadn't gotten away from Carl Mays in Yankee Stadium in August 1920 and hit Ray Chapman in the head. Because the moment that ball left Carl Mays' hand, my life began to change.

FRED LINDSTROM

FRED CHARLES LINDSTROM
Born: November 21, 1905, Chicago, Illinois; Died: October 4, 1981
Major-league career: 1924–36, New York Giants, Pittsburgh Pirates, Chicago Cubs, Brooklyn Dodgers
Lifetime average: .311

A big-leaguer at the age of eighteen, Lindstrom batted over .300 seven times, with a peak of .379 in 1930. In 1928, and again in 1930, he collected 231 hits, leading the league in 1928. Ironically, he is most remembered for a ground ball that took a bad hop over his head in the final play of the 1924 World Series, a Series in which the eighteen-year-old prodigy rapped out ten hits.

Lindstrom was elected to the Hall of Fame in 1976.

It's possible that if it hadn't been for that ball bouncing over my head in the 1924 World Series a lot of people would have forgotten I ever existed. The association is made so often: Lindstrom, the bad bounce, the World Series. I still hear about it. Some people think I hit the ball, some think I scored the winning run. I have to refresh them on it. "I didn't do anything but just stand there," I tell them. "It was very easy. Anybody could have done it."

I don't think there's any doubt that baseball is the greatest sport for memories and reminiscing. One story always leads to another. I remember one time my wife and I had driven up to the Canadian Rockies for a vacation. This was years after I'd retired. We were coming home on the west side of the Rockies, into Montana. We were cruising along on the highway and I was listening to a ball game on the car radio. Dizzy Dean was doing the broadcasting. There was a lull in the game because the pitcher had been hit by a line drive and was being administered to on the mound. Having some time that he had to fill, Dizzy launched into a story.

"You know," he said, "this reminds me of the opening day of the 1935 season, in Wrigley Field. I had gotten the first two men out and Freddie Lindstrom came to bat." Well, my ears perked up at that. Here I am, driving along a highway in Montana and my name is coming over the radio.

"Boy," Dizzy said, "what an experience I had that day. I pitched Lindstrom what I thought was a good fastball outside and he wound up and hit that thing like a bullet right off of my knee. It knocked me down and I thought my kneecap was broken. They had to carry me off the field. That goldarn Lindstrom. I'll never forget it."

Well, there's the key right there—baseball people seem never to forget anything, whether it be something truly memorable like getting hit by a line drive, or some obscure thing that might have happened fifty years ago and for some reason has become locked in memory. One story or episode associates with another and you can go on forever. It's almost as much fun to talk about baseball as it is to watch or play. That's just one of the many things I love about the game.

My love for baseball was probably unavoidable. I was born and raised on the South Side of Chicago, just a short distance from the White Sox ball field, Comiskey Park. I suppose that automatically made me and everybody else in the neighborhood a White Sox fan. The Cubs were like people in a foreign country, as far as we were concerned.

Being a White Sox fan in those days was very enjoyable. I'm talking about the years during and just after the First World War, when the White Sox had some championship teams, with players like Joe Jackson, Buck Weaver, Claude Williams, Eddie Collins, Happy Felsch, Ray Schalk, Eddie Cicotte. Those were truly great ball clubs and naturally the neighborhood youngsters felt that the world began with them and ended with them. Of course when the scandal broke in 1920 and the White Sox were accused of having thrown the World Series to Cincinnati the year before, I was terribly disappointed. That anyone could, first of all, point an accusing finger at those fellows and then, second of all, substantiate the charges, was quite a disillusioning experience. There is that marvelous story of the young boy who accosts Joe Jackson outside of the courthouse and tugs on Joe's sleeve and says, "Say it ain't so, Joe." Well, that story might be apocryphal, but it nevertheless symbolizes what we felt, because we were so close to those fellows. By close I mean of course from the fan's perspective, and even though that is not at all intimacy it can lead to greater disillusionment because those players were part of our fantasies.

I went out to the ball park to watch them every opportunity I had. I didn't always pay to get in though, because in those days we kids used to shinny over the fence and get into the bleacher seats. The only time we would ever pay to get in was after we had been in the alleys junking for rags and bottles and things of that sort, which we would sell. Once we had raised the requisite amount of cash—two boys under the age of twelve could get in for a quarter—we would head for the ball park and enter like gentlemen. But most of the time we were scaling the wall. You put a big league game on one side of a wall and a couple of baseball-crazy kids on the other and you have set up quite a challenge to those kids' resourcefulness.

Once I got inside I used to stand behind the screen in left field and watch Joe Jackson in the outfield. I always marveled at the way he could take the ball and throw it to the plate. He had an overhand throw and later I found out that this was the correct way to throw the ball from the outfield, getting the overspin on it that would carry it three hundred and fifty feet. And his hitting, of course, never ceased to astound me. Simply one of the greatest natural hitters that ever lived.

I wanted to be a ball player, right from the beginning. When I was attending Loyola Academy in Chicago, Jake Weimer, our coach, who was a former big league pitcher, groomed me as a shortstop and as a ball player. It was Jake Weimer who first imbued me with the spirit of big league baseball.

In 1922, when I was sixteen years old, I had a chance to work out with the Cubs. This was arranged through a friend of Bill Killefer, who at that time was managing the Cubs. I worked out with them in the morning and took batting practice against Virgil Cheeves, who was one of their starting pitchers. I hit a couple of balls real well and felt I was doing all right. When I got into the clubhouse after the workout, Killefer asked me to write my name down on a piece of paper. When I did that he said, "We'll call you when we need you." I thought that would be next week. I didn't know this was their polite way of getting rid of you.

About three weeks later Dick Kinsella, a scout for the Giants, came through town. He was really on his way to the west coast to do some scouting, but at the behest of Jake Weimer he had agreed to stay over for a day and see me play. I played a game for Loyola that day and in the game I hit four consecutive doubles. I signed a contract with the New York Giants that night, in the Auditorium Hotel. My Dad had to come along with me and sign also because I was only sixteen years old. No, I wasn't disappointed in not signing with a Chicago team. After having been politely shoved off by the Cubs, I felt I was lucky to sign with anybody.

I must admit that my family was not overjoyed by my signing. They didn't want it at all. They wanted me to continue my schooling; but without the desire to learn I don't think I would have been a very good student. I had made up my mind: it was baseball or nothing. My head and my heart were too filled with baseball to make any other decision possible.

At the time I signed with them, the Giants were world champs and were going to be world champs again that year. In fact, they won four pennants in a row from 1921 through 1924. They were the great team of baseball, the glamour team, much as the Yankees became later on.

I played a few games at Toledo in 1922, stayed there the full season in 1923, and in 1924 came up to the big leagues. I was only eighteen years old when I joined the Giants.

John McGraw's Giants. That's what they were called and that's what they surely were. I don't know if any other manager before or since has ever had such a close identification with a ball club. The team reflected in its style of play his tactics and strategy, his ideas and attitudes, his businesslike approach to the game.

It was not an easy ball club for a rookie to break in with; no club was in those days, but I think the Giants were particularly difficult. The young fellows, like Bill Terry and myself, were more or less in another sphere—on the ball club but not part of it. The older players stood apart as a gang of their own and you remained isolated from them. They were a unit— George Kelly, Frankie Frisch, Ross Youngs, Irish Meusel, Frank Snyder, Art Nehf. The closeness was built upon success, you see—those four straight pennants. It took a while before anyone was allowed into that inner circle.

Frisch was a fiery ball player. He gave everything he had out there, but all the same, he and McGraw just couldn't get along. There was constant squabbling between them and they became terrible enemies at the end, before McGraw finally traded him. The problem lay, I think, in a similarity of personalities. They were both fighting types, aggressive and outspoken. McGraw had simply formed a dislike for Frisch and you could *feel* it whenever they came together. They had a brutal argument in St. Louis in '26. The name-calling became vicious. I can remember McGraw finally roaring at him, "You're through!" Ostensibly they were arguing about something that had occurred in the game, but what it really was was that personality clash again. Frisch was traded to St. Louis after the season, for Rogers Hornsby.

Now Ross Youngs, on the other hand, was one of McGraw's favorites. The old man always said that Youngs represented everything that he, McGraw, represented—meaning the bulldog attitude, the fierce determination to win. And Youngs certainly did possess those attributes. If you had nine guys like Ross Youngs on the ball club that club wouldn't need anyone to prod them on to greater efforts. He never stopped hustling, never stopped trying to win. Youngs didn't hustle any more than Frisch did, but he was by nature a very quiet person where Frisch was outspoken, and it was this difference in them that made McGraw like the one while disliking the other.

Youngs was still a young man when he developed a kidney disease in 1926. It began to slow him down, more and more. With a nonstop hustler like Youngs, it became more apparent than it would have with an ordinary ball player. McGraw became so concerned that he assigned a male nurse to travel with Youngs when we went on the road. But Youngs' condition kept worsening. I can remember one day in Philadelphia, at the hotel there, the elevator door opened and he came walking out, accompanied by the nurse. We hadn't seen Ross for a week or so and I was startled by what I saw. His legs were so bloated up that they eliminated the creases in his trousers. That's what the illness was doing to him. It was a short time later, maybe even the next day, that he was taken to the hospital. This was the beginning of the end. We never saw him again. He sat out the entire 1927 season and then died that fall. He was thirty years old. McGraw was badly shaken when Youngs died. They say only two photographs ever hung in McGraw's office—one of Christy Mathewson and one of Ross Youngs.

We had Irish Meusel in left field. His brother Bob seems to have gotten more publicity through the years; maybe because Bob played on the 1927 Yankees and people are always writing about that team. But Irish was quite a good ball player in his own right. I would say he was as reliable a man as I ever saw for driving in the winning run. Put that winning run on second base with two outs and, boy, was he tough. How would I account for that? I think it's probably psychological. Certain fellows simply respond to the pressure better than others. There was something about those clutch situations that brought out the confidence in Irish Meusel and made him a tough hitter. Maybe his concentration became more intense, or maybe he was one of those fellows who didn't worry about being up in crucial situations. And of course we shouldn't overlook a very practical aspect of it: Irish was a good low-ball hitter and often in those situations, with the winning run parked out there, the pitcher will throw breaking balls and try to keep them down. And that was right in Irish's alley.

We also had Hack Wilson on the Giants in those early years, in center field. A lot of people forget that Hack started his career with the Giants and by rights that's where he should have stayed. He of course later became a great star with the Cubs and losing him was the biggest mistake the Giants ever made. You see what happened, McGraw decided Hack needed some more seasoning in the minors and sent him out. But somebody in the front office, through a clerical oversight, failed to protect our recall rights to him and left him unprotected in the draft, and the Cubs picked him up for a few thousand dollars. I can just imagine what McGraw said when he heard about it; he knew what an outstanding talent Hack was.

Losing Hack Wilson was one of the most costly things that ever happened to the New York Giants. If we had had him with us through the late twenties and early thirties we would have won pennant after pennant, because he was having tremendous years—for the Cubs. In '27 and '28 we lost the pennant by two games each time. And we were close again in 1930. With Hack in center field there's no question in my mind but that we would have won in each of those years. You see, we didn't have a good, steady center fielder at that time. McGraw was rotating different men in and out of there. As a matter of fact, he finally pulled me from third base and put me out there. This was in 1931.

Look at it this way. In 1930 Hack set those National League records that are still up there: fifty-six home runs and one hundred ninety runs batted in. Well, if he had been with the Giants in 1930 and done only *half* of that, I think we would have won it. His home run mark may well be broken some day, but the RBI record is just awesome. It's seldom that anybody comes within even fifty of that record.

We had a good, tough team with a good, tough manager. McGraw was tremendously successful with that era of ball player. Later on, however, when he began to be associated with the more modern-day players he didn't have the ability to cope with them. I'm thinking of men like Bill Terry. The players that were coming in had a different approach to baseball—times were changing—and McGraw was just not able to adapt. You see, his style of dealing with someone who had made a mistake on the field was to chew them out unmercifully. He could be brutal. He thought nothing of humiliating a man in front of the whole team. For years he was able to get away with it. But Frisch wouldn't take it, and then Terry wouldn't take it, and I wouldn't take it.

McGraw and I had some very rambunctious arguments. He could be very unfair at times. I would talk back to him at these times, trying to be very logical in presenting my side of the story. But he didn't like that. Of course it wasn't until I felt very secure as a ball player that I started talking back to him. This was in 1928. I had a very good year in 1928, hitting .358, getting two-hundred thirty-one hits, driving in over one hundred runs, and had a good year in the field. I resented being second-guessed, which he did on a couple of occasions. I remember one time, with the bases loaded and one out, I picked up a ground ball hit to my left and went to second base to try and start a double play. Well, we got only the top man, missing the runner at first by an eyelash. A run scored and eventually we lost the game in extra innings. Later, McGraw contended I should have come home with the ball. I felt that was second guessing. I didn't appreciate it and let him know about it. We had a loud shouting match over it.

It ate his craw to have anyone talk back to him, to challenge not only his authority but his expertise. But I wasn't trying to do either; I was simply trying to defend myself. Nevertheless he held me in high esteem. I know that, because in 1931 when asked by the *New York Journal* to pick the twenty greatest ball players he ever saw he ranked me ninth on his list.

Finally a hassle began to develop between McGraw and the Giant organization. By the Giant organization I mean Mr. Stoneham, who owned the ball club. This was Charles Stoneham, Horace's father. He decided the time had come to get rid of McGraw, which was not going to be an easy task because the man had been there for so many years and had become an institution. And then it also became a question of who was going to succeed him. It finally boiled down to Terry or me. Well, Stoneham promised me the job. So did Jim Tierney, who was his right-hand man and the club secretary.

As a matter of fact, when Tierney first approached me on the subject of managing the Giants, Terry was in the room. This was in the Alamac Hotel in New York. Terry and I were sitting around talking when Tierney came in and broke the news to us that Stoneham was going to replace McGraw. Both Terry and I said, more or less in unison, "How can that be? McGraw has a contract that goes for three more years."

"True," Tierney said. "But McGraw owes Stoneham $250,000." That was from McGraw's horce racing affairs in Havana. "The old man is going to forget it if McGraw agrees to step aside."

Naturally we were curious as to who Mr. Stoneham had in mind as a successor.

"He does have somebody in mind," Tierney said to me. "You."

"Did he give me any consideration?" Terry asked.

"Yes he did," Tierney said. "But he figured you two fellows were such close friends that you would go along with it."

We didn't have to ask why the move was being made. Mc-Graw had become old and crotchety and had lost much of his effectiveness. He no longer had control of the ball club. But still, he was John McGraw and it wasn't going to be easy to get him to step aside. And if he had not owed that money I'm sure Stoneham couldn't have got him to agree to it.

As I look back upon the situation now and realize how deeply in debt McGraw was, I can see that it was bound to create an unstable position for him to work from. It had to make him less positive in his thinking and less logical in his rationale than he would have been if he had been free of such financial woes. It had to be a major distraction for him as well as a constant source of tension and irritation. You blend that with the normal tensions and irritations of managing a big league ball club and you don't have a very serene situation.

There was no question in our minds that he had lost a lot of effectiveness as a manager. As I mentioned before, times were changing, players were changing. It was a different caliber of man now and tactics that had been successful before were no longer applicable. You now had to manipulate your players more diplomatically. I don't mean to imply that you had to coddle them; it's just that the days of brutally dressing down a ball player for a mistake were gone. John McGraw's career had begun in 1891 and been in many ways quite remarkable. It was just unfortunate that he had remained inflexible when everything else was changing around him.

All this was taking place in 1931. That was the season I made the switch from third base to the outfield. Well, midway through the season I broke my leg, in Philadelphia. While I was laid up in St. Francis hospital there, Jim Tierney came to visit.

"We're making that change we spoke about next year," he said. "McGraw is going out and we want to make you manager. We're not doing it this year because of your broken leg. Mr. Stoneham and I have decided to postpone it until next year."

It was supposed to be a secret, but it leaked out and McGraw heard about it. Well, he was quite bitter. He seemed to feel that I had undermined him, which of course was not true. But this was what he believed.

Nothing happened until June of the next year, 1932. Then one day Bill Terry called me into the office at the Polo

Grounds, shut the door and said, "They've made me manager."

I was dumbfounded. "You don't mean it," I said.

"It's true," he said.

It was like the grandstand falling on my head. Terry, who was a very good friend of mine and still is to this day, knew that I had been considered for the job and what a terrible disappointment this was to me.

What happened, I suppose, was McGraw continued to believe I had been undermining him and even though he and Terry weren't very good friends had probably been instrumental in selecting Bill to succeed him.

My career with the Giants terminated shortly after McGraw's. When Terry took over the ball club I'm sure he thought it would be better for both of us if I went to another team. So I was traded to Pittsburgh. Two years later the darndest thing happened, or I should say almost happened.

It was November, 1934, and I was attending the baseball meetings. I was having breakfast with Warren Brown, a Chicago sportswriter. Terry came over and sat down.

"How's it going?" Warren asked him.

"Fine," he said. "And I've got a bit of news for you. I'm going to get Freddie back with me on the Giants."

"How are you going to do that?" Warren asked.

Terry mentioned someone on the Giants he was going to trade to Pittsburgh for me.

I didn't say anything. It was Warren who told Terry.

"You're out of luck," Warren said. "A deal has just been consummated. Lindstrom and Larry French to the Cubs for Jim Weaver, Guy Bush and Babe Herman."

Terry looked at me. "Is this true?" he asked.

"A half-hour ago," I said.

Do you know what that was all about? It had been Terry's intention to trade for me to bring me back to New York to manage the ball club, while he would move up to another position with the Giants—I presume general manager.

So that was twice I missed out on becoming manager of the Giants.

It seemed there was always something happening around the Giants during the McGraw years. Sometimes it was due to the force of McGraw's personality, and sometimes there were other factors involved, like what happened at the end of my rookie year in 1924.

After winning a close pennant race against Brooklyn and Pittsburgh—on the last weekend of the season, as a matter of fact—there was some doubt that we would play in the World Series. Do you remember the Jimmy O'Connell scandal? That was really something. It came down to Judge Landis sitting in a hotel in New York trying to decide whether or not the Giants would be eligible to play. For a while there was the clear possibility that he might disqualify us because of what had happened. This was just four years after the Black Sox scandal had broken, remember, and people were very touchy about the slightest taint of suspicion upon baseball.

We had a young outfielder named Jimmy O'Connell. McGraw had bought him from the Pacific Coast League a year or so earlier for a lot of money. O'Connell was a pretty good ball player and a likable fellow, but at the same time he was sort of naive and gullible. Anyway, we were in Philadelphia to play our last series of the season, against the Phillies. If we could beat them one or two games it would assure us of the pennant. The Phillies were a weak club and we were very confident we could run over them without any trouble.

Well, according to the story, O'Connell is alleged to have approached one of the Phillies' infielders, Heinie Sand, on the field before the game. They had known each other in the Coast League.

"Look," O'Connell is supposed to have said, "we're old buddies from the coast. How about looking the other way when the ball is hit at you?"

Sand later reported the conversation to his manager, Art Fletcher, who in turn relayed it to the league president, who in turn informed Judge Landis. Landis came immediately to New York, took a room at the Waldorf Astoria and called O'Connell to his suite. He told O'Connell what he had heard and then asked, "Did you say this to Heinie Sand?"

O'Connell admitted that he had. And then he implicated one of our coaches, Cozy Dolan, and three of our players—Frankie Frisch, Ross Youngs and George Kelly. O'Connell claimed that Dolan had passed the word to him, with the connivance of those three players, to attempt to bribe Sand.

He insisted that in the clubhouse they were the ones who had put the idea into his head.

When he heard that, the Judge didn't waste any time. I think it was about two or three o'clock in the morning that he called those three players to his suite. They denied any knowledge of the whole business, were very clear and emphatic about it, and Landis took their word. But when Landis asked Dolan if he knew anything about the alleged bribe, all Cozy would say was, "I don't remember. I don't remember."

That really shook Landis. "You don't remember?" he demanded. "It happened only a couple of days ago and you don't remember?"

Dolan's vagueness didn't sit too well with Landis and he declared both O'Connell and Dolan ineligible. In other words, they were banned forever from organized ball.

You know, the whole story has never ceased to mystify me. Why would O'Connell try to bribe Sand? That was the thing I could never understand. The only explanation I can think of is that O'Connell was, as I said, a naive sort of fellow. And a youngster on that ball club was kidded and booted around quite a bit. There was always a lot of foolery and horseplay in the clubhouse. It's quite possible that somebody might have made a facetious remark and O'Connell picked up on it. I think that's what it finally amounted to, O'Connell taking seriously something said in jest and actually going ahead with it, trying to pull a fast one.

But once Landis had spoken to Frisch, Youngs and Kelly the cloud was lifted and we went ahead. Nevertheless there was a day or two in there when we couldn't be sure what would happen. It was well within his power for the Judge to disqualify us and put the second place team—the Dodgers—into the Series. That would have been a heck of a thing.

So that situation was cleared up and we got set to meet the Washington Senators in the World Series.

I guess I'm still the youngest player ever to participate in a World Series. I was a month or so short of my nineteenth birthday. And all of a sudden I found myself penciled in as the starting third baseman. You see what happened, Heinie Groh, who was the regular at third base, hurt his knee toward the end of the season and was sidelined. This meant that I was going to be the third baseman in the Series, a position I really hadn't played all that much during the season. In fact, I had been a utility man, filling in for Groh at third and Frank Frisch at second. Actually, some people felt shortstop was my best spot. But in any event, I was going into the Series playing a position I hadn't had too much experience at.

Was I nervous? No, honestly I wasn't. I was so young I think I was unconscious of the seriousness of the whole thing. Sometimes a person's innocence can work to his advantage. I was simply unawed by the glamour and unaware of the excitement and unaffected by the tensions that were building up. I was much more excited and emotionally wrought up in the '35 Series when I was with the Cubs, because by that time I was much more familiar with all the trappings and all the seriousness.

McGraw didn't go out of his way to calm me down. In the first place, as I said, I wasn't excited. And in the second place, that sort of thing wasn't done in those days. They just put you on the field and let you play. If you did the job you stayed, if you didn't you left. I can't ever remember McGraw teaching me very much. I think his feeling was that if you wore a big league uniform you were expected to be able to play big league ball.

You know, not only was I playing in a World Series at such a tender age, and at a relatively unfamiliar position, but when I walked up to the plate as the first batter in the Series, who was standing out there on the mound getting ready to pitch to me but Walter Johnson. It was certainly a very special experience, but at the same time I have always contended that because I was so young I was just dumb enough not to be aware of his greatness. To me he was just another pitcher. The fact that he was one of the greatest pitchers who ever lived and that he was supposed to have a fastball that created smoke as it was thrown to the plate did not faze me. As I say, at eighteen I was too young and too dumb to be as impressed as I should have been. But at the same time I had a youngster's self-confidence. I simply thought I could hit anybody.

Johnson was up in years by that time but he could still throw. He had what I would describe as a slingshot delivery. It was a nice, easy movement, which didn't seem to be putting any strain at all on his arm. But he could propel that ball like a bullet. I remember talking once about Walter with Eddie

Ainsmith, who had caught him in Walter's younger days. "If you tried to hit against him on a dark day," Eddie said, "you were out of luck. I had all I could do to *see* the ball when he let fly." He said there was many an occasion when he just got his glove up in time, because he actually had not been able to follow the flight of the ball, it was coming in there with such a rush.

You know, it was ironic. Johnson had come to the big leagues in 1907—when I was around a year and a half old—and this was his first World Series. And there I was, just a green kid, playing in a World Series in my rookie year. So naturally there was a lot of sentimental rooting for Walter. All of that was very nice, but neither I nor my teammates shared any of those feelings. We beat Walter in the first game, 4–3 in twelve innings.

I didn't have any luck with Walter that day. He turned me back five times. But George Kelly and Bill Terry hit home runs, and as a matter of fact we peppered Johnson fairly well, even though he chalked up a lot of strikeouts. We pitched a good lefty, Art Nehf, and he went all the way for us.

We had them beat 2–1 going into the bottom of the ninth when they scored a run to tie. Then we scored two in the top of the twelfth and they came back with one and darn near tied it up again. It was a heck of an exciting game and you might say that it set the tone for the whole Series, because nearly every game was nip-and-tuck.

The second game was won by the same score, 4–3, but this time we were on the short end. Again there were some ninth-inning heroics. We were losing 3–1 when we scored two in the top of the ninth. I can remember Hack Wilson rapping out the base hit that scored George Kelly with the tying run. But then in the bottom of the ninth they got a man to second base with one out and Roger Peckinpaugh drove a two-base hit past me down the left field line to win it.

We moved the Series up to New York the next day and beat them 6–4. I drove in what proved to be the winning run with a double in the sixth inning. I really had not done too much hitting up to that point, going something like 2 for 12 in the first three games. But then I got hot.

They beat us in the fourth game to tie the Series at two apiece, in spite of my three hits. Johnson came back at us in the fifth game and that's one I'll always remember. Against Walter I singled in the first inning, singled in the third inning, singled in the seventh, and then once again in the eighth. It was a nice afternoon's work under any circumstances, but particularly so in a World Series. Four hits in a game is still the record for a Series, one which is held by a number of men. What made it so memorable for me, of course, was getting them against Walter Johnson. And what made it important, naturally, was that we won, 6–2. So that was twice we had beaten Walter, who was such a sentimental favorite.

Then we went back to Washington needing only one more win to wrap it up. The sixth game was a very smooth pitchers' battle. Art Nehf for us against Tom Zachary, two good left-handers. That was a game we should have won. You've heard that one before, I guess. Well, it's true. But I suppose the loser of every 2–1 game ever played has made that statement. Okay, let's give Zachary some credit too. He was a tantalizing pitcher. He had a little nickel curve and a little nickel knuckleball and he seemed to be able to put those pitches right where you couldn't do very much with them.

We scored a run in the first inning on hits by Frisch and Kelly. But then in the bottom of the fifth, with men on second and third, Bucky Harris hit a single to drive them in and there was the ball game. Harris was the manager and second baseman for Washington and he played just a great Series, an inspired Series you might say. He hit a couple of home runs, got a lot of hits, drove in a lot of runs, was outstanding in the field.

Now it was all tied up at three apiece and it was anybody's Series. You know, I have heard people say that that seventh game in 1924 is perhaps the greatest ball game ever played, in terms of importance and excitement and drama. That might be so. It sure had everything. I've always felt that the seventh game of the World Series, which by definition is the most important contest of the season, should be a good one. Well, that game certainly filled every expectation.

Right off the bat there was a tactical battle of wits. A jockeying for advantage. You see, McGraw had been playing Terry against right-handers and sitting him down against lefties. Well, that strategy had paid off because Bill was just beating their brains out. So Bucky Harris did some juggling.

He started a right-hander, Curly Ogden, in order to get Terry in there. Ogden pitched to two batters and then they immediately took him out and brought in George Mogridge, a left-hander, one of their top pitchers. That forced Terry out of the lineup in the middle of the game for a right-handed pinch hitter, and when that happened they brought in a right-hander, Fred Marberry, who was another top pitcher.

Did McGraw read it? I can't say for sure what he thought when he saw Ogden warming up. I do know that Washington claimed a lot of credit later on for outfoxing him. And outfoxed he was, because they succeeded in squeezing Terry out of there in the middle of the game. What did I think of it all? Listen, I was that dumb young kid, remember. All I was concerned with was playing my position to the best of my ability and trying to get a few hits to win the ball game. I was content to leave the heavy thinking to McGraw. That's what he was paid his forty thousand for, to do the thinking. And he did it, all of it. Do you know what the cardinal sin was on that ball club?—to begin a sentence to McGraw with the words "I thought. . . ." "*You* thought?" he would yell. "With *what?*"

Virgil Barnes started that game for us. In the bottom of the fourth, Bucky Harris hit a home run to put us a run down. But then in the sixth inning we broke through for three runs and maybe started to smell a world championship.

Then we went into the bottom of the eighth, ahead 3–1. Boy, I'll never forget that inning. You know, what people remember most about the 1924 Series is the ball that took a bad bounce over my head in the bottom of the twelfth and cost us the Series. But not many people remember another bad bounce that occurred, one which was just as important. It was the beginning of a series of events that finally made some of our boys throw up their hands and say, "It wasn't meant to be."

Washington loaded the bases with two out. Bucky Harris came to bat. He hit a ground ball down to me. It looked like an easy chance and I was set to play it when all of a sudden the ball hit a pebble and bounced high over my head into left field. Two runs came in and the game was tied.

So we went into the top of the ninth and here came Walter again, walking in from the bull pen. The Senators had pinch-hit for their pitcher in the eighth, and with everything up for grabs now, Harris brought in his best, even though Johnson had had only one day of rest. It was very dramatic, because here was this great veteran, this fine gentleman, being given another chance to win a Series game.

It was an October afternoon and the shadows were getting longer, which certainly didn't hurt Walter any, the way he could throw that ball.

We had a crack at him in the ninth. Frisch tripled with one out. They put Youngs on first. Then Walter bore down and struck out Kelly and also retired the next batter. That strike-out of Kelly, that was the big one.

It went along to the bottom of the twelfth. That's another one I'll never forget. Not only will I never forget it, but there are times when I still can't believe it. We got the first man out. Then Muddy Ruel stepped up. He lifted a high foul ball over toward the grandstand. Hank Gowdy, our catcher, threw his mask aside and went after the ball. But then the wind began carrying the ball back toward the plate and Hank moved with it. It still looked like an easy out. But then one of those fluke things happened. As he moved under the ball, with his glove up waiting to make the catch, Hank stepped right into that mask, lost his balance, slipped and fell, and the ball came down on the grass alongside of him.

By that time, I suppose, even a callow, eighteen-year-old boy like myself, who knew nothing about fate, should have begun to see the light. Washington was supposed to win this game and that's all there was to it. Because sure enough, given that second chance, Muddy Ruel smacked a double into left field.

Johnson was the next batter. I guess it would have been most poetic if he would have won his own game. But that's not what happened. There was very little poetry in this inning, let me tell you. What did happen was Walter hit a ground ball to Travis Jackson at shortstop. Jackson booted it. He said later than Ruel, coming down the line from second, had obscured the play for a moment and made him lose the cadence of the ball for just that split second. Whatever happened, he booted it. Ruel, thinking that Jackson would make the play, had reversed himself and gone back to second. So instead of three out, there was one out and men on first and second.

I was standing there with my hands on my hips wondering what could possibly happen next. I soon found out.

Earl McNeely was the batter. Jack Bentley, who was pitching for us, and pitching well, got McNeely to hit a ground ball down to me. Well, it happened again. The ball hit a pebble—maybe the same darned pebble that Harris' ball had hit—and took a big kangaroo hop over my head and went out into left field. And here's Muddy Ruel charging down from second base with the winning run. You know, I don't think he could have scored if Irish Meusel in left field had anticipated my not taking the ball. If Meusel had been running in the moment the ball was hit I don't think Ruel, not a fast runner, a slow runner in fact, would have even tried to score. But Meusel had no way of knowing that thing was going to bounce the way it did. By the time he got to the ball it was too late. He just picked it up and put it in his pocket. The game was over.

So they won it. Jack Bentley, who was something of a philosopher, I think summed it up best after the game. "Walter Johnson," Bentley said, "is such a lovable character that the good Lord didn't want to see him get beat again." You couldn't argue with that. But after all that had happened, I think if Washington hadn't won it in the last of the twelfth, even the Lord might have withdrawn his support of Walter.

No, McGraw didn't have much to say about it. He had seen enough baseball in his life to know when something had been taken out of his hands. You know the old saying, "That's the way the ball bounces." Well, it was never more appropriate than in the seventh game of the 1924 World Series.

As a matter of fact, I didn't talk to McGraw until later that evening, on the train going back to New York. He was in his drawing room with some of his brother Lambs from the Lambs Club who had come down to see the game. He called me in and gave me a couple of shots of bourbon, to get me to quiet my nerves and forget about what had happened. I drank that whiskey on an empty stomach, had no resistance whatsoever to it, and it knocked me out. And I stayed knocked out, all the way home. When we got to New York, big George Kelly picked me up and threw me over his shoulder and carried me through Pennsylvania Station. I guess a lot of people who saw us must have wondered what happened. But it was just a kid coming home from his first World Series.

FROM
THE MAN
IN THE
DUGOUT

BOBBY BRAGAN

ROBERT RANDALL BRAGAN
Born: October 30, 1917, Birmingham, Alabama
Managerial career: Pittsburgh Pirates, 1956–57; Cleveland
    Indians, 1958; Milwaukee-Atlanta Braves, 1963–66

Versatile as a ballplayer, Bobby Bragan was colorful and innovative as a manager. After a playing career that saw service with the Philadelphia Phillies and the Brooklyn Dodgers, Bragan went on to manage three major league clubs. He later became president of the Texas League and is now president of the National Association.

I was with the Dodgers in 1947 when Jackie Robinson was promoted from Montreal. This was a big moment—the first black player in the big leagues. Branch Rickey had laid an awful lot of groundwork in getting ready for it. He'd spent countless hours with Jackie, readying him to accept all the abuse and name-calling that he knew was going to come Jackie's way.

In spring training there were newspaper stories about some of the southern boys on the Dodgers not wanting to play on the same team with a black man. So Mr. Rickey asked several of them to come to his quarters to talk, one at a time. I was one of them. I was born and raised in Birmingham, Alabama, which I suppose is just about as southern as you can get. When I walked into the room, the only other person present besides Mr. Rickey was Arthur Mann, a writer and a very good friend of his. Mr. Rickey came right to the point.

"I understand that there's a conspiracy going on around here to get Robinson off the club and that you're part of it."

"I'm not part of any conspiracy," I said. "And if there is one going on, I don't know anything about it. But I do know there's some resentment."

He lifted those big bushy eyebrows and said, "Oh, is there?" pretending to be surprised.

"Yes, sir," I said. I'd made up my mind that I was going to be as honest with him as I could.

"Well, I'm going to tell you this," he said. "I don't care if a man's got pink skin or green skin or black skin. If he can go farther to his left or farther to his right than the man who's out there now, he's going to play. Do you understand that?"

"Yes, sir. I understand it."

"So if you'd rather be on another club, if you want to be traded, we'll accommodate you."

"That's fine with me," I said. "I'd just as soon be traded. I don't want a big fuss made of it, but I'd just as soon be on another team."

He stared at me for a while, very thoughtfully, and said, "I appreciate your honesty, Bobby."

And that was the start of a great friendship between Mr. Rickey and me. That's right. He didn't take offense at what I'd said because he knew I was born and raised in Alabama. He knew that I'd grown up surrounded by a way of thinking that had been there long before I came on the scene and that I couldn't help but have it imparted to me. He understood that for me it was going to be a tremendous adjustment to play alongside a black man. He took it all into account; he took *everything* into account. He was a great student of human nature, that man, a great psychologist.

A few days later Arthur Mann came to me and said, "Bobby, Mr. Rickey really appreciated what you told him in there. You were honest with him."

Of course, a month or so later any resentment that anybody had left them because it soon became apparent that there wasn't any way we were going to win without Jackie. The guys who had been reluctant to sit down with him in a dining car were sitting down now. I wasn't traded; I stayed with the club all year, and we won the pennant and got into the World Series.

And I'll tell you, Jackie won the respect of everybody by sheer guts and ability. Nobody ever came into the big leagues under less favorable circumstances, and he handled himself beautifully and he played like a demon. He was one of the greatest ballplayers ever to come down the pike.

Being Jackie Robinson's teammate was one of the best breaks I ever got. Watching what he had to go through helped me. It helped make me a better, more enlightened man, and it helped me to have a future in baseball as a manager because later on I was going to have to manage fellows like Felipe Alou, Maury Wills, Henry Aaron, and plenty of other black players. If I hadn't had that experience with Jackie, I don't think I could have done it. It was a breakthrough for me, a great experience that I learned from and built upon later in life.

Jackie and I became good friends. Side by side we mourned our great loss in the same pew at Mr. Rickey's funeral. The respect and admiration that we shared for our mutual "father" served to cement our friendship.

Branch Rickey was the greatest man I ever met. I don't know who's in second place, but there's quite a gap between them. You can't praise that man enough for his achievements. You can't give him enough credit. And I know that, above everything else, he was proudest of having had a hand in breaking down the color barrier in baseball.

You want to know why the National League is the stronger league? why it's dominated for so many years? why it draws more fans? Branch Rickey. He's the answer. Pure and simple. He signed Robinson. Then he signed Campanella and Newcombe. Then the other teams in the league started to get the message, and here come Willie Mays and Monte Irvin and Frank Robinson and Ernie Banks and Henry Aaron, and so on. All in the National League. All due to Mr. Rickey's leadership. The American League was left holding the sack for a long, long time, and it's going to be a long, long time before they catch up.

When you're managing, you always want to improve your ballplayers. I suppose every manager thinks he can do that. But you can't always do it, and you shouldn't always want to try it. That's something I learned from Mr. Rickey. He'd have us all together at meetings in Vero Beach, all the minor league managers and coaches and scouts. He'd have these big meetings, with charts and blackboards. One day he was talking about a kid hitter in camp. "This fellow's got an unusual batting stance. Boys, I don't want you to fool with a man who's got an unusual batting stance." Then he turned and wrote on the blackboard *In extremis*. "How many of you fellows know what that means?" he asked. "That's Latin for 'extreme circumstances.' " Then he went on to tell a story. He was always illustrating his points with stories.

"I had an uncle," he said. "An avowed atheist. Never believed in a supreme being. In his eighty-third year he took ill and his doctor said to him, 'It grieves me to tell you this, but for you it's just a matter of a few hours.' My uncle looked up at the ceiling and said, 'God help me.' First time in his life he'd ever uttered those words." Then Mr. Rickey gave us all a very stern look and said, "Mr. Manager, when that hitter comes to you and says 'Would you help me?' that's when I want you to experiment with his stance and his approach to hitting. And not until then. Otherwise *the finger of guilt will point at you the rest of your career.*"

So after you've heard that and you go back and take over your club and a guy goes 0 for 14, you don't get too excited about it.

Time and time again he'd drive his point home with a story. One night, not long before we broke camp and scattered around the country, he told us, "You managers are all going to different cities, some of you for the first time. First time you've been in Pueblo, first time you've been in Valdosta," and so on down the list. "Now, I want you to go in there and be part of that community. All it takes is a little bit of the right kind of effort." And then came the story.

"There used to be an old boy who'd sit in the railroad station and wait for the trains to come in. Once in a while a man would get off, put his bag down, and say to the old boy 'What kind of town is this?' Invariably the old boy would say, 'What kind of town did you come from?' 'Oh,' the man might say, 'everybody cutthroat—hooray for me, the hell with you.' "That's the kind of town this is,' the old boy would say. A few days later another train would stop and another man get off. He'd see the old boy sitting there and ask him the same question, 'What kind of town is this?' The old boy would give him the same answer: 'What kind of town did you come from?' 'Oh,' the man might say, 'very cooperative. Everybody helping one another.' 'That's the kind of town this is,' the old boy would say."

That was Mr. Rickey's way of telling us that if we went into these towns with positive, cooperative attitudes, we'd find positive, cooperative people. Managing to him was more than strategy and developing ballplayers; it was becoming part of a community and getting a community to become part of a team.

I came up to the big leagues as a shortstop with the Phillies in 1940. That was fortunate for me because we had the worst team in the National League. If I had gone to St. Louis, where they had Marty Marion, or to Brooklyn, where they had Pee Wee Reese, or with most any other team, I would have been sent right back to the minors. But the Phillies needed a lot of help, and Doc Prothro, who was managing, opened the door for me to play short. Sometimes there's an advantage to being on a bad ball club. Later on, when our catchers were injured, I volunteered to go behind the plate. Being able to catch helped keep me in the big leagues a few more years.

It was different for a manager in those days. All he had to do was walk into the dugout and say "Sic 'em," and we'd take off for our positions hell-bent for leather. If the manager asked you to run through the wall, why you'd run through the wall. Blind loyalty. The kind that doesn't exist anymore. No question in my mind about it. How do I account for it? Change of times. Everything has changed, not just baseball. The whole social fabric—all the attitudes, perspectives, what have you. I suspect that today there's less concern for the team as a whole; individual accomplishment supersedes everything else. But it's no different from any other business.

It's a different breed of player today, and consequently a different breed of manager. There was a time when the manager didn't give a damn if anybody in the clubhouse liked him or not. He'd dress you down in front of everybody else or call you into the office and take a thousand dollars from you for loafing on the field and not really be concerned about repercussions or feelings. Today, you take a guy's money for loafing or for not showing, you get a call from the Players Association the next morning or from the general manager wanting to see you in his office to thrash it out. It makes running the club more difficult.

After Prothro left, Hans Lobert took over. He was an old-timer from the McGraw era. Lobert was unique in one respect—he had a different sign for every ballplayer in the lineup. My bunt sign might be somebody else's hit-and-run sign. He had four or five different signs for each player and remembered what each one of them was. He was the only manager I ever played for who had that particular system. He had to have a hell of a memory.

Lobert was a wonderful fellow, with a fine sense of humor. But I saw him do something one day I'll never forget. He was coaching third, and one of those raucous fans in Philadelphia got on him and stayed on him the whole game. Wouldn't let up. With the small crowd we had, everybody in the ball park could hear this loudmouth giving it to Hans. Inning after inning Hans came back to the bench and never said a word. Here's the mark of a real veteran, I thought, somebody who's been around long enough to ignore the vituperation. Calm, cool, above it all. But as soon as that last out was made, Hans took off. He must have been over sixty years old at the time, but he went over the railing like a kid and went tearing up the steps to the upper deck where that guy was. He grabbed him by the collar and was really going to work on him, but a couple of ballplayers who had gone up after him interceded. So I guess you might say that those fires never went out in Hans Lobert.

That couldn't happen today—at least it's very unlikely—because the manager is seldom out there on the coaching lines anymore. Managing has become a specialized field. A lot of things have become specialized. The manager used to be out there coaching third base himself because that's the most important coach you've got, that fellow at third. He can't afford to make mistakes. He knows the contours of the fence in every park; he knows which outfielders have got the good arms and which ones you can run on; he knows his own runners, which ones he can send home and which ones he'd better stop, given the circumstances. It's a science all in itself, and to put the extra responsibility on yourself, if you're managing, takes away from your efficiency.

That's one way the game has become more sophisticated today. You've got all these specialists—on the lines, in the dugout, in the bull pen. In the old days all you had was one or two coaches. It made managing a bit more difficult, but a guy who's equipped to manage a big league ball club has got to be knowledgeable in every facet of the game, whether it's base-running or throwing a curveball or breaking up a double play. He really doesn't need a coach to impart all that.

I was traded to Brooklyn in 1943. Durocher was managing there then. Best manager I ever played for. Never heard a ballplayer second-guess him. He never missed a move. On most teams there will be a game now and then when you hear a player say "I sure wish we'd have bunted that man over," or a similar comment. I never heard those remarks when Durocher was managing. Not once. His players had implicit faith in his moves and maneuvers on the field.

Leo had an aggressive personality. He wanted to win. That came first with him, ahead of everything else. Not everybody cottoned to him. He could irritate some people. You either loved him or you didn't; there wasn't any in-between. But by and large they all respected him.

We had some great ballplayers on the '43 Dodgers—fellows like Dolph Camilli, Billy Herman, Arky Vaughan, Dixie Walker, Paul Waner, Joe Medwick, Whit Wyatt, Kirby Higbe, Bobo Newsom, Johnny Allen. That's quite a cluster of veteran ballplayers, some of them real individuals. But there was only one master on that ball club, and they all knew who he was. In the clubhouse the manager is king, and nobody was ever more so than Leo Durocher. He was so knowledgeable and so adept at making the right moves that he just forced you to respect him, which was all he wanted. Didn't mean a damn to him whether you liked him or not.

We had a kid join the team that year—in '43—who could throw the hell out of the ball. Rex Barney. There's an awful lot of guys who will tell you Rex Barney was the fastest pitcher they ever saw. Speed to burn. Now and then somebody will ask me what happened to him, what went wrong, why a boy with an arm like that never became a star. Well, I don't know. I've seen him down at Vero Beach in what they called the string area. Mr. Rickey had devised this area where he had strings constructed to form the strike zone. If the pitcher threw the ball between those strings, you knew he was throwing strikes. Well, one day Leo tells me to go over there and warm up Barney because he might use him in the eighth or ninth inning of this game we're playing.

I went over with Rex and began warming him up. Every pitch he threw went right through those strings. Fastballs and curves. Then Leo calls him in. Rex promptly walks two men on eight pitches. Seeing a batter up there with a bat in his hand made a difference.

Then another time, we're playing the Giants in the Polo Grounds. This is in 1947, when Burt Shotton was managing. Barney is pitching for us, and the score is either tied or we're a run ahead. There's a runner at second and Sid Gordon is the hitter. Shotton sends Clyde Sukeforth, one of our coaches, out to the mound with a message: "Throw the fastball. Stay with the fastball." Sukeforth does that and then comes back and sits down next to Shotton. The next pitch Barney throws is a curve that bounces on home plate and goes over the catcher's head, and the guy scores from second.

After the game, when we got in the clubhouse, Shotton called Barney over and said, "What did Sukeforth tell you when he came to the mound?" Barney looked at him and said, "Sukey? He didn't come to the mound." He hadn't even been aware that Sukeforth had been out there to talk to him. That's hard to believe, isn't it? But that's probably one of the things that kept him from being a great pitcher—his mind wandered while he was working, and the ball wandered with it. It was heartbreaking because he probably threw as hard as any man who ever lived. And a nice fellow, too. Very likable.

After I'd played for about four or five years, I started to think about managing. When I was with the Dodgers, I used to spend as much off-time as I could talking baseball with Clyde Sukeforth and with Gene Mauch, who was just a rookie then but always a keen student of the game. One time Mickey Owen, Eddie Stanky, and I were having a baseball confab in the club car of a train going to Indianapolis, where we were going to stop off to play an exhibition game before going on to Chicago. Well, we got so engrossed that when the train stopped at Indianapolis and the team got off, we went right on with our baseball strategy session, not taking any notice at all, and rode on to the next stop. That's how deep some of that talk got.

There's an awful lot of thinking that goes along with the job, and a lot of discussing and theorizing. I remember one time down at Vero Beach, when I was managing in the Dodger organization, there was a difference of opinion among some of the managers as to how to make the double steal with men on first and third. Some had the opinion that if you're on third you can wait until the catcher's peg got by the pitcher on its way to second before you headed home. We went out and disproved that. In other words, that runner on third has got to have a good lead and he's got to run as soon as the catcher releases the ball; otherwise two throws back and forth will nail him every time. What happens if the pitcher cuts it off? You lose.

Some of the old, acquired wisdom has to be tested, too, occasionally. When I was making the transition from short-stop to catcher, one of the things they used to teach in that situation was to look the runner back to third before you threw to second. Well, if I've looked down there a thousand times, I still haven't seen anything. I look, all right, but as far as seeing if he's got a twenty-foot lead or a ten-foot lead or if he's standing on the bag, I would never see it because if you look long enough to actually see what's there, there's no way you're going to throw the man out at second.

Now, these things are very fine slices out of a ball game, but they can make the difference between winning and losing. You can keep refining this game until it becomes very, very subtle. Sometimes you wait all season to pull a certain play. For instance, with a man on first and the count two and two on the hitter, the next pitch eludes the catcher and the runner goes to second. You might want to walk the batter to set up the double play, or you might *pretend* you want to. You have two different signs to give the catcher. You get his attention and hold up four fingers—that means you want the batter put on. Or you point to first base—that means you want him to pretend the fourth ball is coming up and you want the pitcher to throw a good hard strike to surprise the batter.

I got away with that a few times. You might strike out a guy once or twice a season that way, but when you do it, it can mean a ball game. I pulled it on Minnie Minoso once, when I was managing in Cuba. The situation came up and I made a big production out of yelling "Put him on. Put him on." The catcher moved out and in this case the pitcher, Billy O'Dell, threw a change of pace up there, a little lollipop that floated right over the plate. Minoso didn't even see it. He had his head turned and was in conversation with the umpire. In the middle of the conversation the umpire said, "Minnie, I'm afraid you're out."

How did I become a manager? In June of '48, Mr. Rickey came up to me one day and said, "Burt Shotton has spoken highly of you, Bobby. We both think you've got managerial possibilities. If a job comes up in the organization, would you like to try it?"

"Yes, sir," I said.

Later in the month they let the manager at Fort Worth go. Mr. Rickey offered me the job and I took it. I stayed at Fort Worth for five years and then went on to manage Hollywood in the Pacific Coast League. Again it was through Mr. Rickey. Hollywood was a Pirate affiliate, and by that time Mr. Rickey had left Brooklyn and taken over at Pittsburgh. Then in '56 I got the Pittsburgh job. When I arrived there, Mr. Rickey was moving out of his office to make room for Joe Brown; his last official act had been to bring me in to manage the club. Looking back now, I suppose I should have appreciated Joe Brown, since he was taking over as the new general manager, but my allegiance and my loyalty and my respect were for Mr. Rickey. I even invited him down to spring training to get the benefit of his advice. Politically, that probably wasn't the smartest thing to do.

The Pirates were a last-place club when I took over, but there was some potential there. We had Dale Long, Dick Groat, Bob Skinner, Bill Mazeroski, Roberto Clemente, and a few good pitchers, like Bob Friend, Vern Law, and Roy Face.

Clemente was just a kid then, his second year up. He was a real introvert. Very quiet, morose almost. But he performed; man, did he perform! And he had tremendous pride. But I learned one thing about him early on—if he didn't feel like playing, you'd better let him sit. Wherever I managed, two hours before the game started, that lineup was posted on the board. I always wanted a man to know if he was starting. Now and then Clemente would come to me and say, "I don't feel like playing." If it had been somebody else, I would have asked him what the hell he was talking about. But not Clemente. When he didn't want to play, he wouldn't play, and that's all there was to it. It didn't happen very often, but it happened. It was usually a backache that he complained about. How serious it was, I don't know, but I do know that he believed it was serious and that he was sincere about it. Remember, this was before he was a great star, so you had to believe he was sincere about his aches and pains and not trying to take advantage of his status.

I tried to innovate when I was managing. For instance, I had a theory that your best hitter should lead off, your second best should bat second, and so on. I discussed this with Mr. Rickey and he said, "A manager cannot be faulted for batting his best hitter first. There's no way you can fault him for that." You see, the first inning is the only time a manager controls who will hit. So if one batter on your ball club is going to go to bat five times and the rest of them are going to go four, I'd rather have DiMaggio go for me, or Ted Williams, than, say, Dick Groat or Eddie Stanky or Maury Wills because I may be one run behind when he's up there for that fifth time. And on the other hand, if DiMaggio or Williams is leading off the game for me, I may suddenly be one run ahead.

Then the argument comes up. What about the pitcher? Your best hitter is always batting behind the pitcher. But you can take care of that by moving the pitcher up to the seventh spot and dropping your normal two leadoff men down to the eighth and ninth spots, so your big hitter is still batting behind them. You see, you bat your big hitter third, not fourth, to insure he's going to come up in the first inning; otherwise he's liable to be leading off the second inning for you. So why not hit him first? For one thing, it's a deterrent against intentional walks—that's 162 times you know he's going to be pitched to.

Based on the 154-game schedule, which I operated under, the leadoff man would go to bat 17 times more than the number two man. And the number two man would go 17 times more than the number three man. Same thing for numbers three and four. So that's 51 more at bats than if he's hitting fourth. That can be four or five more home runs, which can mean four or five ball games for you.

I tried it out at Pittsburgh for about 65 games. What happened? We continued to lose. It was a last-place club any way you wrote out the lineup. But we had some fun with it. Frank Thomas was my leadoff man. Dick Groat was normally the second hitter, but under the new lineup it meant he was hitting ninth. He was a sensitive man and very proud. I must have had fifteen guys standing around waiting for Groat to come in and read his name in the ninth hole. He came in and took a look—wanted to know what the hell was going on. It went on, all right. I still think it's a good idea if you've got the right horses.

I had another theory—hitting and running with a man on third. You've got to have the right man up at the plate, of course. Take a Groat or an Alvin Dark or a Billy Herman—guys that you know can hit the ball and get a piece of it. If the man on third is running, he'll score on a ground ball. If it's a fly ball, there's still time to go back and tag up. So you've got two shots at getting the run home. Sure, it's a gambling play. You need a man who can lay the bat on the ball and who's not going to hit a line drive down third and decapitate your runner. We tried it a few times—that particular situation doesn't come up that often, of course—and more times than not it worked.

We had another play all primed when I was with Pittsburgh—men on first and third, less than two out, and a pop foul hit down the line to either the first baseman or the third baseman. I want that runner from first to break for second after the catch. If he draws a throw, the runner on third will score. But I'll be damned, the play never came up.

I was let out in Pittsburgh in the middle of '57, after a year and a half. I don't know if it was because I was Rickey's man or not. Anyway, Joe Brown gave me the word in Chicago. I'll tell you what happened the night before, in Milwaukee. I had been thrown out of five games and all five times by the same umpiring crew. In this particular game in Milwaukee, Groat thought that a runner had missed touching second base going from first to third, and he made an appeal play to the umpire, Stan Landis. Well, as soon as Landis disallowed it, he took about four steps toward me in the dugout and said, "He's safe, Bobby. What do you think of that?"

I held my nose and then said, "That's what I think of it, right there."

He took a few more steps and gave me the old "Get out of

here." He's throwing me out of the game for that! So I came running out and said, "This is five times you guys have thrown me out. I don't know why this crew always gives me trouble, but I'm going to find out. And I'm going to be comfortable while I'm finding out. I'll be right back."

I went back to the dugout and told Danny Murtaugh—he was one of my coaches—to get me a hot dog and a cold drink. All they could rustle up was an orange drink with a straw in it, and I took that and went back out there.

"Now let's talk about it," I said to Landis. "What have you guys got against me? Would you like a sip of orange drink while we discuss it?"

He got provoked and told me to get out. Eventually I did, of course, but I thought I'd made my point. Warren Giles, the league president, fined me a hundred or two, but that was all right.

The next day is an off-day in Chicago and Joe Brown flies in. He came up to my room and gave me the word. He was upset about it, but I told him not to shed any tears for me. There's the old saying about managers—you've heard it a thousand times—"Hired to be fired." Sure, it hurts your pride, but you know it's inevitable.

Did the orange juice have anything to do with it? Well, it was something to hang it on. The pot had been boiling, and that made it boil over. A cup of cold orange juice.

I guess I've pulled a few antics on the ball field as manager. One time when I was managing in the Pacific Coast League, I had a little run-in with an umpire. I thought a pitched ball had struck the hitter's bat. The umpire said no, that it had hit the man's hand, and awarded him first base. I went out to him and said, "Would you ask the other umpire if he heard a wood sound?"

"I don't need to ask anybody," he said. "I know what it hit."

"Oh," I said, "you've got all the answers, is that right? You know everything, is that it?"

"That's right," he said. "I'm in charge out here."

"You are, are you?" I said. "Well, I'm going to show you how much respect I've got for your authority. I'm going to lay down here and go to sleep. What do you think of that?"

And I did that. Stretched right out on the grass. He was

flabbergasted. Then the other umpire came over, looked down at me, and said, "Bobby, he's thrown you out of the game."

"That's right," I said. "But I'm not ready to go just yet."

So I got the reputation for doing the unorthodox thing. I wouldn't say that that reputation was unjustified. Another time I sent my batboy out to coach third base. This was out in Hollywood. Ed Runge was umpiring behind the plate—this is before he went up to the American League. We had a disagreement about something and I was ejected. I went into the dugout and said to the batboy, "Hey, go coach third base." So the kid takes off for third base. He's about thirteen years old. Runge stops him. "Listen," he says to the kid, "don't let Bragan make a fool out of you." "Oh, he's not," the kid says. "This is great." And he runs up to the third-base coaching box and starts clapping his hands to get a rally going, whereupon Runge runs him right back to the dugout.

Then one night we're playing extra innings in Hollywood against Oakland. And I mean extra innings—we're in the bottom of the 21st. Allen Gettel pitched all the way for Oakland. Now, you can't start an inning after five minutes to one, and there are two clocks on the wall indicating two minutes to one. So I use a pinch hitter for my pitcher, Bob Hall, who's been pitching a hell of a ball game, figuring this is the last inning. We don't score, and when the inning is over, it's one o'clock by the clocks on the wall. But the umpire behind the plate shows me his watch and says, "This is the official time, and I've got six minutes to one. Start another inning."

I didn't even have a pitcher warmed up, so I had to do that in a hurry, after letting the umpire know what I thought of his watch. Well, we lose the game in the 22nd inning. Oakland gets four runs.

So the next night I sent my coach, Gordie Maltzberger, up to home plate with the lineup cards, and he's got wristwatches running up and down both arms and an alarm clock around his neck. The umpire pretended not to notice.

That was my way of getting to them. I never believed in going out there and calling them all kinds of names. Had my own approach. Another time in the Coast League we lost the first game of a doubleheader on what I felt were a couple of questionable calls. Late in the second game we're losing big, around 12–1, and another dispute comes up. I went out to talk to the plate umpire.

"Listen," I said, "you guys are making a farce of the game, do you know that? Now if you really want to make it a farce, I'll show you how to operate."

Lee Walls was the batter. I took him back to the dugout with me and sent up a pinch hitter, Mel Queen, a pitcher. I gave him instructions. "Don't stay up there long enough for the pitcher to throw you a ball." He's announced, gets into the box, and then steps back out. Time. I send up a pinch hitter for him. Same instructions. Kept doing that. Sent up eight pinch hitters in the same slot and didn't let any of them look at a pitch. Just having a little fun, trying to get under the umpire's skin.

I don't want to sound like a wise guy. I really do have great respect for authority. When I was managing Fort Worth, Mr. Rickey decided to economize a little. Instead of the managers wiring in their reports, he told us to airmail them. A little while later he sends me a telegram: "Do you need a shortstop or can you go with your present infield?" So in order to save money, I wired him back a one-word telegram—"Yes." He wires me back, "Yes what?" And I wire him back, "Yes, sir."

In the winter of '57 I was managing in Cuba, and Hank Greenberg came down and hired me to manage the Indians. A few weeks later Hank left the job and there I was, again working for a man who hadn't hired me. This time it was Frank Lane. He was an unusual fellow. Nice guy, but impetuous. He was inclined to second-guessing. Out loud. One day we're getting beat 2–1 by the Orioles in the bottom of the ninth with two out. Billy O'Dell is pitching for them and Russ Nixon is scheduled to hit. That's lefty against lefty, so I bring in J. W. Porter to hit for Nixon.

Lane is sitting in the press box and he says, "Who's that coming up to hit?"

"J. W. Porter," somebody says.

"Automatic strikeout," Lane says.

Porter steps in and the first pitch is around his cap bill and he swings at it. Strike one. Next pitch is neck high and he swings at it for strike two. The next pitch is right down the middle and he takes it, but the umpire calls it a ball. That started a big furor which saw Paul Richards, the Orioles' manager, get ejected. After things quieted down, J. W. hit the next one out of sight, over the left center-field fence.

Lane starts yelling in the press box, "That's my boy, J. W. Porter. I signed him. Signed him to his first contract."

Somebody says to him, "But, Frank, you said he was going to strike out."

Lane looks at him and says, "Dammit, he did. The umpire didn't call it, that's all."

Isn't that beautiful? What do you do with a guy like that?

Another time I'm sitting beside Lane in spring training and Minnie Minoso walks up to hit. The count goes to three balls. Lane yells, "Atta boy, Minnie, that's the way to watch that ball." Strike one called. "That's all right, Minnie, you're still way out in front." Strike two called. "Don't take too many now, Minnie." Strike three called. Lane stands up and yells, "You look like a big bag of shit with a cherry on top!" Prerogatives of the general manager.

So I knew how unpredictable he was. I was out of there by the middle of July. But we're good buddies today. Frank Lane is Frank Lane, that's all.

In '63 I took over the Braves. They were still in Milwaukee then. I managed them right through their first year in Atlanta. Had Henry Aaron on my club. What kind of player was he to manage? A dream. Just a dream—on and off the field. I made only one contribution to Henry Aaron as a manager. In my second year there I said to him one day, "Henry, you're making about seventy thousand dollars and Willie Mays is making a hundred and twenty. There isn't a thing he does that you can't. The only difference is he runs. From now on you've got the green light whenever you want to run." He went out and stole something like 31 bases out of 37 attempts. Later on, in evaluating the managers that he'd played for, he said, "Bobby was the one that made me a complete player." That was very nice to hear. But that was the only contribution I ever made. He made plenty of contributions to me—kept me in business for almost four years.

After the All-Star Game in 1966, I started to hear the rumors again. In fact, I went to John McHale, the general manager, and told him I knew that the owners were putting some pressure on him and that if it would make it more comfortable for him, I would be glad to step aside. He told me to sit tight. But the string was running out, and I was fired before the end of the season.

I'll tell you frankly, I wasn't that brokenhearted. It was around that time that things were starting to change. The demands were starting to come in. There were complaints that the temperature inside the bus wasn't 72 degrees and that the ride to the airport was too long. Transistor radios blared music on the bus. Hair dryers started showing up in the clubhouse. More and more demands for this and that. It seemed that the fun was going out of it—at least it was for me. Times had changed and baseball was changing along with them. I found I didn't have the patience to go along with it.

"Hired to be fired." You've always got to remember that. That's one part of this game you've got to be realistic about. If you're a player, no matter how great, you're going to slow down one day and be released. If you're a manager, you're going to lose your job. It's basic—part of the whole pattern.

One night, when I was managing the Braves in Atlanta, I was attending a banquet honoring Gale Sayers and Henry Aaron. I was sitting at the front table next to the president of a southern university. Midway through the evening he leaned over to me and said, "Mr. Bragan. That job you have as manager of the Braves, it's a very precarious job, isn't it?"

"Yes, it is," I said. "But like they've said before, 'Managers are hired to be fired.'"

He said, 'You know, there's a lot of philosophy in that statement. I'll tell you, a lady made a statement to me not too long ago that had a lot of the same philosophy in it."

"What was that?" I asked.

"She said, 'If you come into this world, you will leave it.'"

BURLEIGH GRIMES

BURLEIGH ARLAND GRIMES
Born: August 18, 1893, Clear Lake, Wisconsin; Died: December 6, 1985
Managerial career: Brooklyn Dodgers, 1937–38.

After a long and distinguished career working the mounds of the National League for six different teams, Burleigh Grimes took over a floundering, near-bankrupt Brooklyn Dodger team as manager in 1937, doing the best he could with a team of preordained losers.

Grimes was elected to the Hall of Fame as a player in 1964.

They used to call me Ol' Stubblebeard. That's because I'd let my beard grow the day before I was going to pitch. Did that deliberately. Some people thought I wanted to give myself a mean look out there, but that wasn't the reason. You see, I never used resin because it would smart my skin. All the other fellows used it though, and it was on all the towels. I perspired a lot when I pitched, and I hated picking up a towel that had resin on it because it would burn my face. So I let my whiskers grow to give my skin a little protection.

I was the last of the spitball pitchers—the legal ones. I always threw that pitch. I brought it into pro ball with me. I had an uncle who was a cattle buyer, you see, and one time he let me ride down with him to St. Paul, to the stockyards. This was in 1903. I was ten years old then. First time in the big city. Hell, I'd never even seen a streetcar before. After transacting his business, my uncle took me to a ball game with him, at old Lexington Park. Toledo and St. Paul were playing. The pitcher for St. Paul kept going to his face all the time. I'd never seen that before, and I asked my uncle what he was doing.

"He's loading it up," he said.

"Loading what up?" I asked.

"The ball. He's throwing spitballs."

That was the first I'd heard of that. When I got back to the farm, up in Wisconsin, I talked to an old catcher about it. Then I tried throwing it. About the second or third one I threw did something. He got all excited and told me to try some more, and I did, and that's how I got started throwing that thing.

I used to chew slippery elm—the bark, right off the tree. Come spring the bark would get nice and loose and you could slice it free without any trouble. What I chewed was the fiber from inside, and that's what I put on the ball. That's what they called the foreign substance. That ball would break like hell, away from right-handed hitters and in on lefties.

It wasn't necessarily my number one pitch—the fastball generally was. The spitter was always a threat. When I got into trouble, then they started looking for it, and when I knew they were looking for it, I'd give them something else. But you get a reputation and what can you do about it? People meet me today and they say, "Oh, Burleigh Grimes? You were the spitball pitcher." Well, hell, I threw a fastball, curve, slider, change, screwball. One time I pitched 18 innings against the Cubs, beating Hippo Vaughan 3–2, and I threw only three slow spitters in the ball game. The rest were all fastballs.

I was always interested in baseball. So was my father. He played a little amateur ball around here in Wisconsin back in the 1890s. One day they were playing over near New Richmond and this pitcher threw a curveball to him. Right then and there he quit. He said, "When they get so they can start a-curvin' that thing, I'm through." He retired, and I'll tell you, bud, that curveball has retired a hell of a lot of guys. It's like the fellow said, whoever invented that thing took all the fun out of the game.

We had a kid team called the Redjackets. We played baseball because we loved it, that was all. I was ten or twelve years old at the time, so this was around 1905. No, I didn't have any idols as a kid. Hell, I hadn't heard of anybody yet. I knew there was such a thing as big league baseball, but I'd never heard of Honus Wagner or John McGraw or Christy Mathewson or any of those fellows. The news hadn't got through the timber yet.

I played some semipro ball around home and then decided to take a crack at the pros. This was in 1912. There was a team down in Eau Claire. My dad gave me fifteen bucks, and I went to Eau Claire and asked the manager if I could work out with the team if I paid my own expenses. He said I could. I had fifteen bucks for three weeks—five bucks a week to live on. You could do that in those days, even if you didn't enjoy it a hell of a lot.

After three weeks they came to where they were going to cut down. They were going to send me away. So I went to the manager.

"Mr. Bailey," I said, "I paid my own expenses. You ought to give me at least one shot anyway."

He said all right and took me along with them. I pitched batting practice and did one thing and another for a while. Still hadn't signed a contract though. Then we were playing in Rochester, Minnesota, and I was on the gate. Taking the tickets, you see. I was the visiting player assigned to the gate. That's how good they thought I was. In the first inning one of the guys comes running around and says Bailey wants me. So I went inside and he told me to warm up.

I came in with the bases full and nobody out. First pitch I made is belted and two runs come in. And that was the last hit they got for the rest of the game. After it's over, the catcher comes out to shake my hand and he says, "Kid, he's going to offer you sixty dollars. Get eighty out of him." I reach the dugout and Bailey is all smiles. He tells me to come into the clubhouse with him.

"I'm signing you up," he says. "Sixty a month."

"I think I ought to get eighty," I said.

His smile went away. "Somebody told you that," he says.

"That's right."

"All right," he says. "I'll give you eighty."

That was my first contract.

I stayed in the minors for four years and in 1916 the Pirates bought me from Birmingham. I came up in the latter part of the season. Honus Wagner was still playing ball, though near the end now. Yeah, by that time I'd heard of him. He was forty-two years old then and was still something to watch out there at shortstop. To look at him, you'd have thought he was anything but a ballplayer. Bowlegged as all get-out. But then you saw him move on a ball field and you just sat there and watched him with plain old awe.

He was a cutey too. One day he was batting against a young pitcher who had just come into the league. The catcher was a kid, too. A rookie battery. The pitcher threw Honus a curveball, and he swung at it and missed and fell down on one knee. Looked helpless as a robin. I was kind of surprised, but the guy sitting next to me on the bench poked me in the ribs and said, "Watch this next one." Those kids figured they had the old boy's weakness, you see, and served him up the same dish—as he knew they would. Well, Honus hit a line drive so hard the fence in left field went back and forth for five minutes.

Then I was pitching against the Dodgers in Ebbets Field. This is 1916 and they're fighting for the pennant. It's late in the game, the score is 1–1, I've got a man on first, and there's one out. Wagner walks in from shortstop.

"Hey, kid," he says. "Make this guy hit it to me and I'll get you a double play."

"Okay," I said. Now, of all things, in those days I certainly couldn't make a guy hit a ball in any particular direction. So I threw it in there and darn if it doesn't go down to shortstop. Boy, I was pleased as hell with myself! Figured I'd impressed old Honus. He comes in and the ball hits his shoe and goes off into right center field, the runner scores, and the batter goes to third.

After the ball came back into the field, here's Honus walking it back to the mound. I can see him to this day—pounding it into his glove, staring at it as he came over, never looking at me. I was wondering what he was going to say.

"Those goddamn big feet were always in my way," he said.

Babe Adams was on that club. Real fine pitcher. Quiet fellow. Never talked much. But he was one of the best pitchers the Pittsburgh ball club ever had. Wilber Cooper was another one. A left-hander with a good fastball. And they had Max Carey in center field. Hell of a ballplayer.

The year I came into the league, Grover Cleveland Alexander won 33. The year before he'd won 31; the year after, 30. That's who he was. If anybody was ever a better pitcher than that guy, I wouldn't know what his name was. It was just a pleasure to watch him work, even though he was beating your brains out most of the time. Smooth and easy—always smooth and easy. I used more effort winding up than he did in pitching nine innings. He threw a sinker and a curve. Always kept them down. He was fast, too. I'll say he was! That thing would come zooming in and then kick in about three inches on a right-handed hitter. He'd throw you that fastball and that curve, and you couldn't tell which was which because they didn't do anything until they were right on top of you. And once they showed you what they were going to do and where they were going to do it, your bat was someplace else. Yeah, he's my pitcher, Alex.

In 1918 I was traded over to Brooklyn in a deal that sent Stengel to the Pirates. I liked playing in Brooklyn, and I liked managing there. Those fans were all right—a little peculiar at times, but all right. They'd tear the hide right off of you, but just let a stranger come in and say one wrong word to you and they'd throw him out. Boily. That's who I was. "Hey, Boily," they'd yell. "Throw harder. We don't hear you gruntin'." When I was managing there, I had Waite Hoyt, and one day it's in the papers he's got an injury. The next day I go out on the field and some guy yells at me, "Hey, Boily, I hear Hert's hoit."

Had a few good ballplayers there in 1918. Zack Wheat. He won more ball games for me than any other individual. He was just terrific. A great hitter in the pinch, particularly after the seventh inning.

We had Jake Daubert at first base. Gentleman Jake, they called him. Why? Well, he was a gentleman. Conducted himself very nicely. And quite a good hitter—he led the league in batting twice. But they traded him soon after I got there. You see, when the Federal League started up in 1914, Gentleman Jake told Mr. Ebbets that he was going to jump unless the Dodgers gave him a five-year contract at $9,000 a year. Ebbets had no choice but to pay and hated Daubert for it. Traded him first chance he got. Was nine thousand a lot of money in those days? I wouldn't say it was a lot; I'd say it was *all* of it.

Christ, I was paid around eighteen hundred my first year in Brooklyn.

I played there for Wilbert Robinson. Uncle Robbie. Great old fellow. I sure liked him. He's the guy that made a pitcher out of me. I'd been just a throw-in in the Stengel deal; hell, I was 3 and 16 for the Pirates the year before. Nobody was interested in Grimes. But I turned right around and won 19 for Uncle Robbie. Somebody asked him, "What'd you do to that guy?" "Hell," he said, "all I did was just give him the ball." Some managers would have filled a billboard telling all that they had done for me, but not Robbie. What he said was what he did—he simply gave me the chance to pitch, and that's all I needed. There was no baloney with him.

How did he handle his players? Well, I think they handled him more than he handled them. It was his clubs, you know, that got called Daffy Dodgers. We had Ivy Olson. Shortstop. He wanted to make a hit in every ball game. Very laudable. But the problem was he never wanted to bunt. Uncle Robbie always sat in back of that concrete post we had in the dugout. When Olson was up and he knew a bunt was in order, he'd keep moving around in the batter's box to keep that post between him and Robbie so Robbie couldn't flash him the sign. We'd watch Robbie move in one direction, Olson in the other. The bunt sign was a clenched fist, and here's Robbie sliding around on the bench with that fist clenched, looking like he wanted to punch somebody, and there's Olson up at the plate ducking around to keep that post between them. Finally Robbie would say, "Ah, the hell with it."

Then we had Chick Fewster. Second baseman. One day he made the double play backwards. Instead of crossing the bag and going to his right while he threw to first, he took the throw from the shortstop and spun all the way around, making a complete circle, and did it that way. When he came into the dugout, Uncle Robbie said, "I've been in baseball for forty years, and I want to ask you a question. What the hell kind of a way is that to make a double play?"

"How'd you like it?" Fewster asked.

"I didn't," Robbie said.

Then there's that famous story about Uncle Robbie trying to catch a ball dropped from an airplane. This happened in Daytona Beach, during spring training in 1916. I was with the

Birmingham club then and by chance we were in Daytona that day. We heard some talk in the morning about Ruth Law, who somebody said was the only woman aviator of the day. It seems that some damn fool idle talk had built up as to whether a man could catch a baseball that had been dropped from an airplane. Uncle Robbie said he could do it. He had been a good catcher in his day, you know, and took a lot of pride in that.

So they set it up. Ruth Law would take the plane up and a fellow named Kelly, the Dodgers' trainer, would go with her. He was going to drop the ball. Naturally everybody went out to see it. There was Uncle Robbie, with his catcher's mitt, very serious about the whole thing. Well, the way I heard it, this fellow Kelly thought it would be funny if he traded the baseball for a grapefruit. The plane took off and sailed overhead and this thing dropped out. Robbie went running for it, holding out his mitt, and he caught it all right and was knocked right over with the impact. Of course, the moment the grapefruit hit his glove, it broke and the juice covered his face, and he yelled, "Jesus Christ, I'm all blood!" Then he had a look at what the hell he had caught and everybody was laughing. When he found out who'd done it, he fired him. Fired Kelly's ass right off the Dodger club.

Nineteen twenty was a hell of a year. We won the pennant and had some real fun along the way doing it. That was the year we played that 26-inning 1–1 game with the Braves. That's one of the most famous games in baseball history. And one of the things people like to talk about is the fact that the two starting pitchers went all the way—Joe Oeschger for them and Leon Cadore for us. And most everybody else played all the way, too—that's what people forget. So here's my theory on that. While everybody marvels at the stamina of those two pitchers, they forget that those guys were pitching to two very, very tired ball clubs. You never saw so many lazy bats; they couldn't get a ball out of the infield. Oeschger and Cadore were just throwing that thing right in there. Toward the end of that game Jeff Pfeffer, Sherry Smith, and myself—all pitchers—were agitating Uncle Robbie to put us in the outfield. We were all pretty good hitters, and we were fresh. And by the end of the game Oeschger was throwing just our speed. But Robbie wouldn't do it. So we played until it got dark and nobody won.

You want to hear the payoff on it all? The next day I pitch 13 innings against the Phillies and lose. The day after that we're playing the Braves again and we go 19 innings and lose that one. Christ, there's 58 innings of baseball in three days, and we don't win a game.

We had some other lovely experiences in the World Series that year, against the Indians. I pitched a shutout in the second game, beat them 3–0. I should have stayed in bed after that. You know, after I pitched that shutout, Tris Speaker, who was playing and managing for the Indians, told a newspaperman, "Grimes won't win another game in the Series." What's cooking now? I wondered. That was a hell of a statement for Speaker to make, particularly since he wasn't a pop-off sort of guy. But he was right because he knew something I didn't, and I'll tell you what happened and then I'll tell you how it happened.

I start the fifth game and goddamn it in the first inning they get four runs. Elmer Smith hit a grand slammer off of me, first one ever hit in a World Series. I've got that distinction. They were taking my spitters, you see—taking real good tight pitches. So I came in there with a fast one and he whaled it. Four runs. You know what else happened in that game? I was out by then, but that's the game where Bill Wambsganss pulled the unassisted triple play on us. Only time *that* ever happened in a World Series.

Now get this. We had a fellow named Pete Kilduff playing second base. He's out there and he can see the catcher's signs. Before each pitch he's picking up some sand and putting it in his glove. If it's not a spitter, he drops the sand. If it's going to be a spitter, he keeps it in his glove. He's doing that, you see, so if the ball is hit to him, he'll get some of the wet off of it so it won't slip when he throws it. Christ, I don't know why the hell he had to do that—fellows were throwing it from short, from third. Anyway, it didn't take long for somebody to pick that up and all the hitters had to do was watch Kilduff. We found out about it after the Series. I had some words with Kilduff. He denied doing it, but he never cared a hell of a lot for me after that.

Dazzy Vance joined us in 1922. I've never seen anybody who could throw harder. Bob Feller, Van Mungo, Vance—all out of the same barrel. If you could have measured their speed, you wouldn't have found too much of a separation to make a difference.

A funny thing about that Vance. He'd been knocking around for years with all that great stuff. Hell, he was thirty-one years old when he joined us and finally put it all together. He'd never been able to find that missing link. But I've always believed he found it all at once one day in Pittsburgh. You see, he had that tremendous stuff, but when he pitched to a hitter, he'd hold back just a little. I don't know why—maybe afraid of killing somebody. It's not unusual to see that. The sight of a guy standing up there with a bat in his hand has taken the bloom off many a pitcher.

On this day in Pittsburgh, it was his turn to pitch, and because of a rain delay or something, he went down to warm up in front of the Pittsburgh clubhouse. Some of the Pirates came out to watch him, and he made their eyes pop. You never saw a ball do such tricks. Not only did he have that blazer, but he had a curveball that came in there like a scared snake. One of the Pirates said, "For Christ's sakes, if you threw that way in a game, nobody could touch you." Vance believed him, I guess, because from then on he went and became a great pitcher. Finally made it to shore.

I was traded over to the Giants in '27. I wasn't at all unhappy about it. I always wanted to play for McGraw. I think most everybody in the league wanted to play for McGraw. Sure, he was a strict disciplinarian, but he played the best baseball. He was the smartest man I ever played for. He showed me one simple thing that made me a better pitcher. You see, the way my spitter broke to right-handed batters, they'd hit it to right field in a majority of cases. That's the way I'd been pitching for ten years, and with pretty good success. When I joined McGraw, he said to me, "Burleigh, how's your curveball?"

"Mediocre," I said.

"Pitch it over the middle of the plate and down," he said. "Make them pull the ball to left field. Don't let them hit behind the runner all the time."

You see, if somebody gets a base hit to right field with a man on first, you've got runners on first and third. But if the same guy hits it to left field, you've got runners on first and second. So instead of throwing that spitter all the time and having them snub it into right field on me, I threw the curve over the plate when I had a man on base and made them hit it in front of the runner. My chances of getting the double play were better, and the base hit didn't hurt me as much.

So I pitched that way and had a fine year, 19–8. Then I went over to Pittsburgh the next year and kept pitching that way and won 25 games, something I'd never done before. I ended up winning 270, but I could've won 300 if I'd learned how to pitch sooner keeping those right-handed hitters out of right field. McGraw proved he knew what he was talking about, which didn't surprise me at all.

He used to have a saying. If you'd made a bad play he'd say, "Son, come over here and sit down by me." You'd do that and he would say, "Now, why did you make that play that way?" Usually the fellow would say, "I thought—" and McGraw would interrupt and say, "What with? You just do the playing. I'll do the thinking for this club." Bill Terry tipped me off about that when I joined the club. "Don't ever say 'I thought' to him," he warned me. I never did. I did my share of thinking, but I never told McGraw about it.

You had to sign in in the mornings, you know. He had an alarm clock in the clubhouse at the Polo Grounds. You had to be there by ten o'clock—and in those days a game started around three or three-thirty. At ten o'clock that alarm went off, and if your name wasn't on that list, it cost you. That's the way he ran things. But he was a great guy.

He had this reputation for being rough on his players—for chewing them out unmercifully. I asked him about that once, how he accounted for it.

"Burleigh," he said, "I pay the highest price for players in baseball. When I get them here to New York and they have two or three good games, the newspapers blow it all up. So then everybody in this town gets interested, all the sharpies and chorus girls. If I can save that guy from himself for two years, I've got me a ballplayer." That come pretty close to answering it? He puts the knuckle on them and lets them know it's going to cost them. His philosophy was to put a little scare into a guy and get a better ballplayer. He knew there was no place like New York, and he tried to put himself between the city and his ballplayers.

McGraw was a great manager because he had his kind of team, and he had his kind of team because he'd been given time on the job to put it together and prove himself. That's what I tried to do when I took over the Dodgers, put together my kind of team. If you can do that, get the boys to play the way you want to manage, then you're a good manager. But you don't do that overnight. It takes time. The average ball-player who comes along can only play his type of baseball. So on the short term you've got to play what he can play, which limits your game as a manager.

McGraw's was an aggressive game. He was a slasher. He'd run on you, play hit-and-run, suck you in for the bunt, and then hit by you. He liked those guys who'd hustle and break their necks to win a game, like Frisch and Ross Youngs—guys who could do the unexpected and get away with it, who were daring, daring but never reckless. He was that kind of man-ager, and when that kind of manager gets his kind of players, you can't beat him.

He was secure in his job, you see, so he wasn't afraid of the newspapers' second-guessing him, and he wasn't afraid of making himself look bad. You can avoid ever making yourself look bad by playing a book game. Bunt when the book says to, take when the book says to, and so on. But if you hit in a bunt situation and you're successful, you've just broken it wide open. On the other hand, if you ram into a double play, you've just blown your ball game. Either way it's the manager who makes the first guess and takes the responsibility. And McGraw, more than any other manager who I ever saw or heard about, wasn't afraid of taking on responsibility.

This is not to say you can't win as a book manager. Bill McKechnie was that way. I never saw anyone like him. He always played it the same way, whether he had a good ball club or a horseshit ball club. Always by the book. And he was pretty successful; he won four pennants. Bill was a long-run manager. You knew he was going to be around a long time because he played pure, conservative baseball. Steady. Those kind of guys always have a job, and they'll win for you now and then. Nothing wrong with them.

I stayed with McGraw only a year. I didn't want to leave, but they wouldn't pay me what I wanted. They offered me

$15,000, and I wanted more. I would liked to have stayed, but you've got to go where the money is, don't you?

So I was traded to Pittsburgh. That's where I had the pitcher's best friend playing behind me at third base—Pie Traynor. He was a miraculous fielder. Now more than ever it made sense to get them to hit it to the left side. He was always in front of it. One day he dusted me off. Somebody hit a shot down there, and I knew it was a base hit—hell, I'd been around long enough. I was so disgusted I didn't even look around. Next thing I know somebody is yelling at me. Traynor had come up with it and was firing across to first. I ducked just in time; otherwise that ball would have flattened me. That had never happened behind me before. Yes sir, he was that good. There was a line I heard once: "Hornsby doubled twice down the line and Traynor threw him out each time." You can believe it, too.

I was traded over to the Cardinals in the middle of 1930, and that was the best thing that could have happened to me, since they were going to take pennants that year and the next. Had some good ballplayers—Frisch, Jim Bottomley, Chick Hafey, Taylor Douthit, Jimmie Wilson. Hell of a ball club. In 1930 all eight regulars hit over .300. Today a guy hits .300, they cover him with roses.

We got into the Series both times against the Athletics. Oh, Connie Mack had sweet teams in those years. We'd heard about Lefty Grove, how hard he could throw. But I'll tell you, the guy we thought threw the hardest was Earnshaw. Big George Earnshaw. But Grove could throw hard, no doubt about that. He beat me in the opening game and then again later on, in relief. That game was a heartbreaker. It was 0–0 to the top of the ninth. I walked Cochrane on a 3–2 spitter with two out. Geez, that pitch didn't miss by much. It was just a little tight. Then I threw Jimmie Foxx a curveball, and he knocked the concrete loose in the center-field bleachers. He hit it so hard I couldn't feel sorry for myself.

We got hunk with them the next year, beat them in seven games. That's the one they call the Pepper Martin World Series. Pepper went hog-wild, got 12 hits and stole a passel of bases. They blamed Cochrane for it, but the truth was he was running on Grove and Earnshaw because neither of them knew how to hold a man on. Cochrane never had a chance. Every time poor Mickey looked up, there was Pepper sliding around to one base or another. I beat Earnshaw in the seventh game, and we had ourselves a World Championship. It'd been a long time coming.

Then the next year I'm traded again—to the Cubs—and get into another World Series. This was getting to be a nice habit. Rogers Hornsby was the manager up until August, when he had some sort of dispute with ownership and they let him go. Charlie Grimm took over.

I got along all right with Hornsby. He spoke his mind and I'd do the same. One day I'm pitching and there are men on second and third. I hear from behind me, "Grimes." I turn around and here's Hornsby walking over from second base with some advice.

"Don't give him anything good, but don't walk him."

I looked him in the eye and said, "How the hell do you want him pitched to? Do you want him pitched to, or do you want him walked?"

He turned around and went back to second base.

But Hornsby was all right. Blunt as hell, but he never gave you any bullshit. You might not have liked what he had on his mind, but you always knew what it was.

That Cub team was a good one. We had Billy Herman—just a kid then—Billy Jurges, Grimm, Kiki Cuyler, Gabby Hartnett, Riggs Stephenson. Stephenson was the best hitter on the club. We had some good pitchers, too, and mean ones—Lon Warneke, Guy Bush, Pat Malone, Charlie Root. They'd saw you off. Yours truly wasn't too shy about those things either. Look, this was for the bread and butter. Either he got it or you got it, and if you wanted it, you had to be tough. I think that anybody who doesn't help his own cause is foolish. You have to be careful though. Got to know what you're doing. Bill Terry, for instance. He had trouble getting out of the way. He used to fall out of the box instead of going down. I was always afraid of hitting him. So I'd throw at his feet, make him skip a little rope. I liked Bill a lot, but what the hell, he'd hit .400. Wasn't that enough?

You know who we had that year, who pitched one inning for

us? Bobo Newsom. Normally you don't remember a guy who comes in and pitches just one inning, but you have to remember Bobo. Just a kid. Could run like a deer. Outran every man on the club except Cuyler, who could fly, and Cuyler wouldn't run him. Then a few years later a mule gave Bobo a kick and broke his leg, and he couldn't run so good after that.

We played the Yankees in the Series that year. A mean Series. Lots of bench jockeying, and some of it got pretty damned nasty. That was the one where they say Ruth called his shot. You want to know about that, huh? All right. I'll give it to you the way I saw it. I'm sitting on the bench next to Guy Bush. Charlie Root's doing the pitching, and he's got two strikes on Ruth. Our bench is on Ruth pretty heavy, with Bush leading the tirading. After the second strike Bush yells, "Now, you big ape, what are you going to do now?" So Babe holds up his fingers as if to say, "I've got the big one left." He's looking right at Guy Bush. Then he hits the next one out.

The next thing you know some newspapermen are saying he'd pointed to the center-field bleachers, and people are believing it. Ruth went along with it, and why not? Just to show you how people can be led along, I had a good friend who was at the game, and he swore to me later that Ruth pointed to the bleachers. "Forget it," I'd tell him, "I don't want to hear about it."

A couple of years later I was a Yankee myself. This was in 1934, my last year as an active player. I joined Joe McCarthy's Yankees. I liked Joe. Different type of manager from McGraw. With McGraw the ball club was like a machine and you played machine-type baseball. With McCarthy you played power. Joe had it there—Ruth, Gehrig, Lazzeri, Dickey—and that's the way he played it.

Joe was a sound baseball man, and he could be strict. He had his hot spots. Didn't like pipe smokers you know. We had a few on the club, including myself, and when we wanted to do some fanning and puff on our pipes, we'd go up to Gehrig's room and smoke there. Lou was a pipe smoker and so were Ruffing and Crosetti.

McCarthy and Ruth barely spoke to one another. Babe wanted that job of managing the Yankees. He didn't particularly care for Joe. There wasn't a hell of a lot Joe could do about Ruth. Christ, the man was an institution. But Babe was at the end of the line then, and Joe just bided his time and waited for the problem to go away on its own, which it did at the end of that season when Babe went over to the National League.

I'll tell you, when I quit as an active player in '34, I wanted to go to umpiring. In fact, I had a job waiting for me in the New York–Penn League. It was Larry MacPhail and Branch Rickey who talked me out of it. They got me to go into the Cardinal farm system as a manager. I managed a couple of years in the minors and then took on the Dodger job in 1937. A few more years managing in the minors wouldn't have hurt, to tell you the truth. I don't think a fellow can be too smart.

After the season in '36, I went on up to New York for the World Series. The Yankees were playing the Giants that year. I was walking across the field after a game when somebody took hold of my arm and said, "Hey, we want to talk to you." It was somebody from the Dodger management. We talked and they offered me the job as manager. It wasn't a big money job, but I decided I would take it because it was an opportunity and because of a loyalty I felt to the Brooklyn organization.

You know who I replaced as manager, don't you? Casey Stengel. The newspapermen didn't like the idea of seeing him go. He was always a favorite with those guys, and with good reason. In fact, they didn't even invite me to their dinner that winter. They were sore at me because I'd taken Casey's job. Hell, I didn't take his job. He lost it, and somebody was going to get it. I was a different kind of a guy. After they'd had Casey in there, they figured I was too serious. Well, I can tell you, I didn't have a hell of a lot to laugh about.

First year with the Dodgers I went out to the minor league meetings in Milwaukee with Andy High and Ted McGrew—a coach and a scout for me—and all of us paid our own expenses out there. When we sat down on the train, I said, "Boys, we sure have got a hell of a lot to look forward to." The ball club didn't have a dime; they were in debt up to their ears. A lot of Brooklyn bankers were sitting on the board of directors and they weren't turning loose very many dollars. So I had a pretty good idea of what it was going to be like, except I underestimated it—I didn't think it was going to be that bad.

But you see, every man thinks that he can do something that somebody else can't do when he starts managing. I'll give you a nickel's worth of philosophy: Don't have hope and optimism and you'll never be disappointed.

When I took over the Dodgers in 1937, Van Lingle Mungo was the only valuable asset that I had. I don't know of anybody who was any faster. His problem was he couldn't carry it for nine. He was like a three-quarter horse. He would come out from the first pitch firing as hard as he could, but by the sixth or seventh inning he would start to lose it. I tried to get him to spread it out a little, to throw a few changes here and there, but he couldn't do it. That's a problem with strikeout pitchers. They like to throw that fastball past everybody. But let's say it takes five pitches to whiff a guy. Isn't it better to throw one pitch and get him to ground out? The fewer pitches you make in a ball game, the better chance you have of winning. That's the way I tried to pitch and the way I tried to get my boys to—let the batter hit it. Give him a piece of the ball. If you've got good stuff and good control, you've got nothing to worry about.

You know, I could have made a whopping good deal with the Cubs for Mungo and Buddy Hassett. We could have got five players for them—Clay Bryant, Ripper Collins, Augie Galan, Clyde Shoun, and I think Joe Marty. Now, what I was going to do was take those fellows and trade them to the Phillies for Bucky Walters and Dolph Camilli. So I could have had, in effect, Walters and Camilli for Mungo and Hassett. But the officers of the Dodgers, those bankers, turned it down. Wouldn't let me make the deal. I'd say that was quite a mistake, wouldn't you? Hassett was traded eventually anyway, while Mungo won very few games for the Dodgers after 1938. They did buy Camilli from the Phillies, but it cost them $65,000, and they never got Bucky Walters. Do you know what a fellow like Walters would have meant to the Dodgers? Just about the best damned pitcher in the league for the next few years.

We had a lot of older ballplayers on the team. They seemed to hang around longer in those days. Heinie Manush had a great year for me, hit around .330. Hustling son of a gun. And we had Waite Hoyt, and Fred Fitzsimmons, who I got from the Giants. That was a good deal. I got Lavagetto from the Pirates

and traded four players to the Cardinals for Durocher, who I'd
always liked.

When Larry MacPhail came in as general manager in 1938,
he would occasionally sic a detective on the club, just to find
out what was going on. He wouldn't tell me about it, but I'd
get a tip now and then. The detective would go around check-
ing rooms and then file a report to MacPhail. When I knew
something was up, I'd call some of the boys—certain ones, you
know—and tell them to be in on time because they were
getting a caller tonight. One night I knew one of my pitchers
had a woman in his room after midnight, which was against
the rules. I'd been tipped off about the detective that morning,
so I got a passkey and went up to this guy's room. I knew that
if MacPhail found out what was going on, it would cost this
guy plenty.

I knocked on the door and told him I knew he had a girl in
there and to get her the hell out because it was after midnight.

"Who's that?" he said. I could tell he was stewed.

"Burleigh Grimes," I said.

"No it isn't," he said.

"Well, yes, it is," I said. I was getting sore. Here I am
standing in a hotel corridor being told through a closed door
who I'm not by some son of a bitch who's breaking half the
club's rules and regulations all at once. I rattled the key in the
door and told him I was coming in.

"Hold it," he yelled. "I'm coming out."

He came out into the corridor and started to give me some
baloney. I fined him five hundred bucks right on the spot and
suspended him for three days. And it would have been a hell
of a lot worse if MacPhail had caught him.

Well, I never figured to keep his money. I was going to hold
it over him for the rest of the season to get performance out of
him. I had something on him now, right?

On the fourth day, when his suspension was up, I put him in
a game to relieve. He pitched good ball and in the ninth
inning hit a home run to win the game. On the way back to
the clubhouse, a newspaperman detained me for a few minutes to talk about one thing or another, and then I went in. I
walked up to this guy and said, "Hey, come here." We put our
heads together and I said, "I'm going to give you a hundred of
that back." His face got all bright, and I figure I've got a good

thing going with this guy for the rest of the season. He's really going to be busting his tail for me. But then later I find out that MacPhail has been there ahead of me and given him *two* hundred back. So he had three hundred back already, and I didn't have much more to use on him.

I guess I got thrown out of my share of games when I was managing—maybe more than my share. There were some umpires who would run me out for saying hello to them. One time I was suspended by the league for three days for having a to-do with a man in blue, and Ford Frick called me up to his office. He was president of the National League at that time.

"How come," I asked him, "that some managers in this league can say the same thing that I do and get away with it?"

"Well," he said, "I guess it's the way you say it."

I said, "Boy, I must have awfully good diction."

Of course, managing a second-division club doesn't help your disposition any. There are a lot of things you don't realize or think about when you take over a bad club until you start going through the season with them. You're playing a good team and they've got nine positions all filled with good ballplayers. The best you can put on the field is maybe five pretty fair ones. So, as a fellow says, you've got to get a well-pitched ball game, and the ball can't be hit to your poor fielders, though it usually is. So there you go. And those losses start piling up, and under that pile are all the high hopes of spring. You've got just so much to work with and that's all there is; there isn't any more.

You may be the nicest and softest guy in the world, but when you're out there managing, you've got to be absolutely ruthless about putting in your best men and winning. Otherwise you're going to second-guess yourself, and you don't need that. Was I second-guessed much? No, I don't think so. They couldn't second-guess me too much because with what I had to work with, I was lucky to be able to get in my one guess.

It's a hell of a job. Even if you're playing .500 ball, winning 77 and losing 77, that's still 77 nights you're eating your heart out. And what about a club that loses 90 or 100 games a season? Of course when you have a ball club like that, your worries don't last too long, since nobody is too shy about canning a manager. Very often the fault lies with the team's general manager. What the hell, he's the one who's supplying you with the players. But how often do you hear of a general manager getting fired? The manager is the one who gets it in the neck because he's visible, he's out there, and the fans know him.

Listen, there are so many things that enter into this game of baseball. Physical condition. Mental condition. Mental condition—that's very important. If you're the manager, you've got to take that into consideration. If a man isn't eating and sleeping well, it's going to affect him physically. But if he isn't eating and sleeping well, then something's bothering him mentally. He's got problems. Maybe he's got family trouble or money trouble. This is a high-tension profession—this baseball—and when you mix it in with a man's personal problems, anything can pop. A manager's got to know a hell of a lot about his players. Some of them can handle themselves better than others, and you've got to make that leash tighter or looser, depending on the man and your knowledge of him.

A lot of it comes down to this: Can you handle individuals or can't you? A good manager can. That's all there is to it. Don't ask me how or why some men can do it and others can't. It's just something a man has inside of him or he doesn't.

A sense of humor doesn't hurt either. Sometimes that'll do more for you than a three hundred and fifty hitter. We were down in spring training one year and I'm coaching first base. The steal sign—when we were fortunate enough to get a man on base—was a wink of the eye. Not very elaborate, but friendly. In the middle of the game, I had to leave the field for a few minutes and I said, "Put somebody in to coach first." I didn't know Max Butcher was going to run out there. Max had an affliction, I think they called it St. Vitus dance—his eyes were always blinking, always blinking away.

When I came back on the field, there's a baserunner, Gibby Brack, running like a bastard for second, with nobody out, and we're behind in the game. Jesus, he's thrown out from here to Canarsie. When they came in off the field later, I asked Brack, "What the hell kind of a play was that? Who sent you?"

He jerked his thumb at Butcher. "He did," he said.

"Max," I said, "what the hell did you give him the go sign for?"

"I didn't give him the go sign," Max said, blinking away.

"You're giving it to me right now," Brack yelled.

Another time Brack is on third base, Manush is on first, and my good hitter, Babe Phelps, is up there. This is during the season now. I'm one run behind, and the next hitter behind Phelps can't hit anything. So I decide I'm going to run Manush and open up a hole for Phelps to shoot at. Now, I figure if Phelps misses, the catcher—it was Ernie Lombardi—won't throw through but will let the pitcher cut it off and try to catch Brack napping at third.

I'm coaching at third and I move over to Brack. "Now this is going to be a hit-and-run," I tell him, "and you stay here. I don't want you to budge."

"Okay," he says.

The pitcher delivers, Manush goes, Phelps swings and dammit misses, and sure enough Lombardi doesn't go all the way with it but throws it to the pitcher. So I'm still in good shape because now I've got men on second and third and a hit puts me ahead. Except that the moment Lombardi fired the ball, off goes Brack. I couldn't believe it. I ran down the line after him; so help me, I was trying to tackle him. He slides in and of course Lombardi slaps it on him. Brack is kneeling there on all fours, shaking his head, and I'm so damned mad I run up and boot him right in the ass.

"What'd you do that for?" he asks.

"What'd I tell you?" I yelled.

"You told me to stay there."

"So how the hell did you get up here?"

"I don't know," he says.

He didn't know.

A few weeks or so before the close of the season in 1938, MacPhail called me in and told me there was going to be a change.

"I expected that," I said.

"Not surprised, eh?" he said.

"Can't say that I am," I said.

"Not really your fault," he said.

"You'd better be careful what you say," I told him, "or else I'll ask you why you're letting me out." We both laughed. Then he asked me if I had any suggestions as to who my successor ought to be.

"Yes," I said, "I think I do. You've got a guy right on the

club now who's pretty smart, has got a lot of guts, and ought to be a damned good manager."

"Who's that?" he asked.

"Durocher," I said.

"Do you think so?"

"Yes, sir," I said. "I certainly do."

Shortly after that they signed Leo.

I'll tell you a funny tag to the whole thing. In the early twenties, when I was pitching for the Dodgers, Uncle Robbie sent me out to watch a game between Harvard and Princeton. He wanted me to look at a pitcher and if I liked him sign him up. Well, I went to the game, sized up the pitcher, and decided I didn't like him. But there was another fellow in the game, playing shortstop for Princeton. I liked him and brought him in and he stayed in the big leagues for fifteen years. It was Moe Berg. You didn't know that I brought Moe Berg to the Dodgers as a shortstop around 1923, did you? That's right.

Now, later on, in 1938, this other guy—this pitcher—is sitting on the board of directors of the bank that's controlling the Dodgers. God, you never know when they're going to turn up, do you? And he knew damned well I'd scouted him fifteen years before and put the kibosh on him. I can't believe that had anything to do with my getting canned in Brooklyn, but I couldn't help wondering if I didn't make a mistake back then in not signing the son of a bitch up.

PAUL RICHARDS

PAUL RAPIER RICHARDS
Born: November 21, 1908, Waxahachie, Texas; Died: May 4, 1987
Managerial career: Chicago White Sox, 1951–54; Baltimore Orioles, 1955–61; Chicago White Sox, 1976.

After a playing career that included service with the Brooklyn Dodgers, New York Giants, Philadelphia Athletics, and the Detroit Tigers, Paul Richards turned to managing and soon developed a reputation as one of baseball's keenest and most respected minds. After being out of uniform for fifteen years, Richards returned to the field as manager of the Chicago White Sox for the 1976 season.

As far back as I can remember, the only thing I ever wanted to do was play baseball. My father was a schoolteacher, so I was taught pretty early on to read, and my favorite reading was the box scores and accounts of ball games that came down with the Dallas newspapers.

I started out as a third baseman and pitcher in high school. Strangely enough, I was an ambidextrous pitcher and actually did some ambidextrous pitching in professional ball at Macon, Georgia, and Muskogee, Oklahoma. At Macon, in 1930, our club had a few of its catchers get hurt, and there was a call for volunteers to go behind the plate. I volunteered and all of a sudden I'm a catcher, and I stayed a catcher for the rest of my career.

I played on a high school team that won 65 consecutive games. Naturally that attracted some attention. So a bird-dog scout from Dallas came down to Waxahachie to see us play.

He went back and called the Brooklyn Dodgers and spoke to Wilbert Robinson, who was managing them at that time. Uncle Robbie sent his old ace pitcher Nap Rucker to Texas to look the team over, and Nap signed me to a Brooklyn contract.

He was a great fellow, Nap was. One of those homespun country gentlemen, a good storyteller and a very interesting character. He'd had the experience of breaking into the old South Atlantic League with a fellow named Tyrus Raymond Cobb. They were roommates, and he told many stories about Cobb's early days—how Ty fought and scratched and scrambled to be first, whether it was going to bed first or taking a bath first or getting to breakfast first. Whatever it was, Cobb had an obsession about being first, even way back then at the very beginning.

Incidentally, the Detroit Tigers trained right here in Waxahachie around 1917, in a park that was then called Jungle Park and is now called, excuse me for saying so, Richards Park. John McGraw's Giants were training not too far away in Marlin Springs, and they came up here for an exhibition game. Naturally I went out to see the game. Well, in the very first inning Cobb dropped an easy fly ball that was right in his hands. I've never forgotten that. The greatest player in the world drops a ball. It's odd the things you remember, isn't it? If he had gone four for four, I would probably have forgotten it a long time ago because he was supposed to do that. But I can still see that easy fly ball dropping out of his hands to the grass.

Years later, when I was managing in the big leagues, Cobb would call me whenever we were in the same town together and he would come over to talk. The interesting thing that I noticed about him was that he was always hesitant about answering questions, but he would ask you questions by the hour—about various players, about techniques, about how they were doing this or that today. He wanted to know everything that was going on in baseball, but he didn't want to tell you anything.

He was a fascinating character. They say that playing against him was always an experience. The drive he had to excel was incredible, and sometimes frightening. You know, you just don't become a Ty Cobb when you put your spikes on.

There's got to be something more to it, something born in you along with the natural ability. There was a force in Cobb that demanded he excel no matter the cost, and there was a cost— he was very unpopular with his teammates as well as with the opposition. And it didn't seem to bother him in the least. Certainly he didn't court popularity.

Did I ever see another ballplayer with that kind of inner drive? Well, yes. I'd say that Ted Williams had it as a hitter. The intensity of his concentration and determination at the plate was awesome. And I'd say that in some respects, without the ultimate ability of a Cobb, certain players that I knew had it, like George Kell, Nelson Fox, Minnie Minoso, and Brooks Robinson.

Did I always want to manage eventually? Well, even as a youngster of ten or twelve years old I had my own teams. We used to hitchhike to various little towns around the county to play. Later on, in pro ball, I always observed the moves the managers made and occasionally talked to them later about their strategy and tried to analyze their thinking.

Donie Bush, whom I played for at Minneapolis, was very influential in my career. He was a strict manager, even with the former big leaguers who came down, fellows like Jess Petty and Rube Benton and Carmen Hill. I liked that. I liked the way he handled men. And he was a student of the game, always bringing things to your attention, no matter how minute. One thing I learned from him, and always remembered and drilled into my players when I was a manager, was that no player should ever be doubled on a line drive with nobody out. And we actually went seven years in Baltimore when I was managing without ever having a player doubled with the bases full and nobody out. Sometimes you see a man doubled off on a line drive and later on somebody will say, "He couldn't help it." Well, that's wrong. He could help it. He could have stayed on the bag, for one thing, although I'm not advocating that. But you can teach a fellow not to break until he *knows* that ball is in the outfield or on the ground.

Another thing Bush insisted on was, with runners on first and third and one out, the man on first should never be tagged when a ground ball is hit to the second baseman, which can prevent that run from scoring. Yet it happens quite often, and they say, "Well, he went a little too far." That's exactly right.

He went a little too far. The second baseman charged the ball, tagged him, and threw on to first for the double play. The run doesn't count. But if he can make the second baseman throw the ball to first and *then* run him down, that man on third is going to score. How do you do it? It's very simple—just don't run when the ball is hit to the second baseman. Now, that is a fundamental. The fundamentals start and end with the simplest things you can think of, and I actually get embarrassed talking about them because they are so simple. But these fundamentals are not observed in the major leagues the way they should be. How many times have you seen a man on first go to third on a base hit and the batter wind up on second because the outfielder threw the ball to third? The next batter hits a ground ball which should be a double play, but it isn't.

You would think they'd learn these things in the minor leagues. Well, let me tell you something about the minor leagues. You can bring a boy up and tell him something, and he'll say he never heard of it. The chances are he was told about it but probably didn't pay any attention. There's the old story about hitting a mule over the head with a two-by-four to get its attention. Well, you can't hit your ballplayer over the head, but you've got to get his attention and stamp the lessons into him. How many times have you heard a third-base coach say he told that guy to tag up on line drives to the outfield? "I told him twenty times." Okay. But maybe he should have told that guy *fifty* times because twenty wasn't enough—because the guy still broke when the ball was hit and then wasn't able to get back and tag up and score when it was caught.

But those things aren't the player's fault. They're the manager's fault. He's responsible for everything that happens on that field, good or bad. If he's got good players and trains them well, it's to his credit. And let's say the player does something out of the ordinary that's good, something that the manager hasn't taught him. Well, in my contention, the manager gets credit for it because he has trained his player to expect these situations, to be instinctively alert for them, and to take advantage of them. On the other hand, if the player misses third base while he's scoring the winning run, that's the manager's fault. He should teach his players to touch those bases. Everything that happens on the field during the course of the game is either something good for the manager or something bad. What the fan is seeing is the end product of what the manager has done before the game.

And I've often wondered how much of this game of baseball the fan actually sees and perceives. The competition between the pitcher and the hitter, for instance, can be quite interesting for the perceptive fan. He can see the outfielders and the infielders move a step or so, which tells them the pitcher is going to try and pitch a certain way to the hitter, and sometimes he'll see the hitter adjust himself a little to try and meet the challenge. It's all quite subtle and interesting, if you know what to look for and how to watch it. I've always contended that baseball is made up of very few big and dramatic moments, but rather it's a beautifully put together pattern of countless little subtleties that finally add up to the big moment, and you have to be well versed in the game to fully appreciate them.

I'll say this. It is much, much easier to teach winning baseball on a winning team than it is on a losing team because a little failure in the third inning on a losing team doesn't make a whole lot of difference if you're getting beat 10–2. But if you get beat 2–1 in eleven innings, that failure in the third inning beat you. So the winning team gets into the clubhouse and they say, "Wait a minute. We'd have won that game if it hadn't been for that one little thing." So those things go together. You can teach the game better if you're winning than if you're losing because those little mistakes are all the more glaring and obvious. It means the losing manager has got a tougher job, and he's got to stay with it longer.

One thing you can't do—that's fool your players. A ballplayer knows when he's wrong, and he doesn't mind being told about it. And this business of being tough, don't try it unless you know you're right, and not a hundred percent but a hundred and ten percent because once you start down that road, there's no turning around.

All players are not alike. That's another very simple thing to know and to understand, and you had better know it and understand it. You've got twenty-five different players and each one calls for different handling, and you'd better give them that handling. You see, when you take over a ball club, you have to prove to the ballplayer that you know what you're doing and that what you're doing is best for the ball club.

Now, the player may not like it, but deep down he will respect it. You may be sitting him down against left-handed pitching, for instance, and he's going to gripe about it, but he knows that this is right. You've got to prove to them that your moves are the right ones for the ball club. You've got to get their respect. You don't necessarily have to have them like you. Managers who try to get too close to their ballplayers are making a mistake because invariably you'll get too close to two or three and leave the others out in the cold, and they're not going to like that.

Is it easy for a club to lose confidence in a manager? It sure is. Very easy. If it's obvious that he's playing up to the sportswriters or he's playing up to the general manager and not giving full attention to what's going on on the field, sure he's going to lose his players' respect. And you'd be surprised how many managers will do that in order to keep the newspapers from criticizing them. Sometimes they'll use strategy that goes against their better judgment, just to appease the newspapermen, rather than do what they know they should do and stick with it.

The newspapermen have their job to do, of course, and it's up to you to get along with them. You have to be a pretty good diplomat and sell yourself to them in a manner that does not in any way reflect adversely on your ballplayers. The writers come right on into the clubhouse after a game, and there are a few who try to get somebody to say something controversial. They work at it. The manager has to be very careful. If you've got a player who messed up your ball game for you, your first reaction many times is to say, "Well, if so-and-so hadn't booted that ball, we'd have won it." Or the writer may say to you, "What do you think of so-and-so making that error?" My answer to that sort of question was always this: "Well, I remember last week when he made a great play and saved the game. That's what I prefer to remember."

It gets back to what I've always felt is absolutely essential for being a good manager. It's wrapped up in one word, one thing you must by all means be sure that you're capable of understanding, and that is restraint. He must restrain himself when things are tough, when things are not going well. Restraint under duress is absolutely necessary. And, boy, I can tell you, sometimes that's not easy—sometimes the more restraint you're trying to exercise, the more duress you put yourself under.

You know, the problem of disciplining a player has changed considerably since the time I came up to the big leagues. Back then, you could do almost anything you wanted to a ballplayer. Not anymore. Today they've got player representatives and they've got Marvin Miller. Today it is absolutely necessary for the manager to be one hundred percent right in a dispute with a ballplayer. He can no longer be arbitrary or unduly severe in dealing with a player. He knows that his decisions might well be contested by a labor relations law and all other facets of that particular union. You get back to the manager not having so much to exert discipline as to exact respect from the players so that they will keep themselves in condition and be ready to play. If you can't get them to respect you, you're in trouble.

I came up to the Dodgers in 1926, stayed on the bench for a couple of months, and then was shipped out. Wilbert Robinson was the manager, and they had Dazzy Vance, Zach Wheat, Rabbit Maranville, and Burleigh Grimes, among others—and, by the way, they're all in the Hall of Fame today. Wilbert Robinson was more or less a manager who took the older players and put them on the field and just let them play. He didn't do a whole lot of managing or instructing. In fact, I don't think any team in baseball did less instructing than the Dodgers in those days.

I came back to Brooklyn again, briefly, in 1932. Hack Wilson was on the club at the time, a little past his peak but a great personality. We had Van Lingle Mungo, who had a world of stuff but was saddled with a mediocre team; and Lefty O'Doul, who was one of the brightest, most observing ballplayers that I was ever around and a very fine hitter.

The Giants bought me in 1933, and I joined them under Bill Terry. Terry was probably the finest defensive manager that I knew in baseball. He concentrated almost entirely on defense. His theory was not to let the other club score and they'd beat themselves. Naturally most ball games are lost rather than won. Terry took it far beyond anybody I ever knew—his entire approach to every game was defense. He didn't hit-and-run. He didn't go for the stolen base or any fancy offensive plays at all. He just figured to score three or four runs. And he had the good pitching staff to win—Carl Hubbell, Hal Schumacher, Roy Parmelee, Fred Fitzsimmons—and a good bull pen.

Could a fellow like Terry have managed differently with a different type of team? I don't think so, and I think perhaps he proved it later on, that without the great pitching staff and without the good defense his managing fell apart. I don't think he was able to adjust to another type of managing. His whole concept was defense, and when he didn't have it, he couldn't manage. But when he did have his kind of club on the field, he was very skillful in leading it.

Terry was not a personality manager. He had no feelings for the ballplayers, no particular friends except those who courted him. He had a couple of players who made a point of doing that, and he wasn't aware of the fact that that was what they were doing. That sort of thing was to the detriment of the other players, and they criticized it severely.

Terry was a marvelous ballplayer. A lot of people don't know this, but he was the fastest man going down to first base in the National League. He was a superb fielder. And he hit .400. Terry had only one weakness. When he was at bat and the pitcher was winding up, Terry had a tendency to drop his bat slightly while he timed the pitcher's motion and then brought it back up again. When the pitcher was holding a man on and working out of a stretch, Terry did the same thing, only this time he had a tendency to drop the bat too fast and then couldn't get it back. You know, he got the reputation for not driving in runs. Well, if the bases were full, he could drive in runs because the pitcher was winding up. That was Terry's only weakness.

Did I ever mention it to him? No. He was hard to talk to. I stayed as far away from him as I could, frankly. I can give you an example. Roy Parmelee was one of our good pitchers on the Giants. I had him down in the bull pen one day. He had a sailing slider-fastball kind of pitch which was effective. I asked him if he could sort of let it out a different way, with his big finger instead of his forefinger. He tried it and it sank like a spitball. I told Terry about it and asked him to watch it and see what he thought of it.

"Leave him alone," he said. "He's doing fine."

So I forgot about it. But I'll always feel that Roy Parmelee could have been one of the real great pitchers if he could have used that pitch—if somebody had demanded he use it. I always felt that under no circumstances do you rule out a certain pitch for a pitcher until you know it's not effective. The Tigers, when Cobb was managing, got rid of Hubbell because he had a screwball. They just didn't think much of that particular pitch in those days.

I don't think that experience with Terry was lost on me. When I was managing, I wanted a player to feel free to come to me with what he felt were constructive suggestions. It's true that I wanted to keep them at arm's length, but no further. The door was always open, as far as baseball was concerned, but "Please don't ask me to have dinner with you or a drink with you or go visit your family."

I don't mean you should be cold and unrelated to a ballplayer. If he's got a serious problem and he comes to you for advice, sure, help him, do whatever you can. But it depends entirely on circumstances. I'll tell you something that I've stated many times, and I'll repeat it: I learned more as a player what not to do than what to do. You learn more through the mistakes of the managers you play for than you learn through their good points.

Another thing I tried to hold firm was that the players not bring their kids when they come to the ball park. Some managers say it's going to be one big family—that the kids are welcome, the wives are welcome, and so on. Well, I'll tell you, the worst thing you can have is one of the players' kids in the clubhouse. He gets in somebody's way, maybe a guy who's mad about something, and pretty soon you've got trouble on your hands, trouble that's absolutely unnecessary.

I caught Hubbell in quite a few games. Who called the game when he was pitching? Well, I did, but I will have to say that he did not have to accept any sign that I gave. But after I'd caught him a couple of games—and I think he'd verify this—he seldom, if ever, shook me off.

Catchers and pitchers are another category entirely. When I was managing, I tried to teach our catchers, and especially young fellows catching older pitchers, that you don't try to be too smart. You try to figure your pitcher out and determine what he would like to throw, early in the game especially. If you're giving him the pitch that he likes to throw early, then along about the eighth and ninth innings, when he's tired and undecided about what he wants to throw, he'll go along with you. You've convinced him you've been right all day, why aren't you right now? That gives him confidence. But you almost never insist on asking a pitcher to throw a certain pitch because in most cases if you do that, he will not give it the good effort. So I learned that if a pitcher was strongly in favor of a certain pitch at a certain time, I'd rather he give me his pitch good than my pitch bad. Essentially it's a combination of things wherein the catcher has to gain the complete confidence of the pitcher for the time when the tough situations arise late in the game.

Of course, it doesn't always pan out. You know, there are certain personalities about baseball people. There are some players who remember only the games they win. There are other players who only remember the games they lose. Dizzy Dean never remembered a game he lost. Hubbell seldom remembers a game he won. Well, as a catcher, I go back through the years, and I remember the bad calls I made rather than the good ones. I remember Joe Cronin pinch-hitting against us one time when I was catching for Detroit. We threw him five consecutive fastballs and ran the count to three and two. I figured now's the time for the curve. So I called for it and the pitcher busted off as good a curve as you could throw, and Cronin hit it in the seats. I've never been able to understand that. Was he guessing? How could he be guessing after five fastballs? To this day it worries me.

I saw Pie Traynor when I was in the National League. He had a bad arm then, but he could get the ball away quickly and that compensated for his errant throws. He had a marvelous ability to dive for balls. That was what impressed me about him. I really think, though, that Brooks Robinson is his superior as a fielder. Brooks is the greatest defensive third baseman that ever lived. There's no doubt about it as far as I'm concerned. Of course, I can't go back to the guy the old-timers say was the greatest, Jimmy Collins. But I saw Ken Keltner, George Kell, Traynor, and Billy Cox, and I'd have to say that Brooks just made plays that nobody else makes, or ever made, as far as I saw.

Would I call Brooks a natural? No, I wouldn't. In fact, we had two scouts bring in bad reports on him. We only signed him after our third scout went down and saw something in him. He had a little trouble with his hitting when he first came up, but his defensive ability was so good that the pitchers didn't care whether he ever got a hit or not. They wanted him in there.

The best throwing arm I ever saw on a catcher probably belonged to Gabby Hartnett. And he was accurate. He was just a great throwing catcher. Better than Johnny Bench? Yes. The fans used to come out early to watch infield practice just to watch Hartnett throw the ball around. That's quite a tribute to a fellow's throwing arm, wouldn't you say? He didn't go through infield practice as a matter of routine. He made a theatrical performance out of it because he knew the fans liked to see him pop that ball to second base and to third base, and you could hear it all over the park.

Another one of my favorites behind the plate was Ernie Lombardi. One of the nicest people I ever met in my life. He came to the Brooklyn club one spring when I was there—a big, powerful kid from California. He reported with a little cap on and a satchel about the size of one a doctor would carry. The ballplayers put together some money to buy him a hat. Everybody liked him. The first game he caught he was catching Dazzy Vance. Somebody swung at a ball and Lombardi ducked and the ball hit him on top of the head and bounced all the way back to the bench. A blow like that would have knocked out an ordinary man, but Lombardi just crouched down and gave another sign, just as if nothing had happened. I've seen him catch hard-throwing pitchers with his bare hand and just toss the ball back to them. Carl Hubbell once said that Lombardi was the one hitter he didn't want to pitch to. The only way you could get him out was pitch him low outside, and if you didn't throw it perfectly, he was liable to hit it back through the box and kill you. Ernie was a great hitter, and if he would have had just normal speed afoot, there's no telling what he would have hit.

In 1935 I was traded to the Philadelphia Athletics. Had a chance to play for Connie Mack. To tell you the truth, I wasn't terribly impressed with the way he managed. I'm sure he was a very learned baseball man, but he didn't seem to be stretching himself that year. We had a team that included Jimmie Foxx, Eric McNair, Wally Moses, Bob Johnson, Pinky Higgins, and Doc Cramer, which is a pretty good team. But nothing was done with them. Nobody seemed to pay much attention, and we finished last.

I wasn't in the American League all that long at that time, but I did have an opportunity to see some of the great players they had there then. Charlie Gehringer was one of the best. Nobody in the league knew how to pitch to him. Most of the time he'd spot you a strike, for some reason or other. But then at the most inopportune or unexpected time he would not do that, and he'd hurt you. When it came down to driving in the tying or winning run in the ninth inning, Gehringer is the man that you wanted at the plate, above all others in my opinion.

In the field he was just as great. He made the double play beautifully and covered tremendous ground. He was, along with Bobby Doerr, one of those second basemen who could run toward the base and pick up a ball backhanded and flip it out of his glove to the shortstop. He started many a double play doing that that he might not otherwise have made. It's not an easy play to make; there are some second basemen who won't even try it.

Lefty Grove was throwing a fork ball when I batted against him. He was no longer real fast. I never hit at him in his heyday, but I did see him pitch. He was terrifically fast. You know, a left-hander's ball has a tendency to tail a little bit, but Grove threw it so hard it didn't tail—it didn't have time. It was on top of you before you knew it. Lefty had the type of fastball they tell me Satchel Paige had. You thought it was waist-high when you swung at it, but it was actually letter-high. The ball was four or five inches higher than you thought it was, which made the hitters think it was jumping, but it wasn't jumping. It came so fast it created an illusion.

Bill Dickey and Mickey Cochrane? I'd have to pick Dickey. He didn't have the fire that Cochrane did. Cochrane had a lot of flair, and he was a great catcher and a good hitter. But he didn't have the arm Dickey had, and he didn't have the power Dickey had. So I would take Dickey over all the catchers I've known. He's number one. And I'll tell you something else—

that Berra's not too far behind. I remember one time a New York sportswriter came into our clubhouse moaning about Berra not hitting—Yogi was around .270 or so at the time.

"I'll tell you what," I said to him. "You go back to the hotel tonight and check back through your scorebook and see what Berra's hitting when the seventh inning starts."

He showed up the next day with a sheepish look on his face and said, "Well, I give up. From the seventh inning on he's hitting .430."

That's right, from the seventh inning on. And in close games that's when they change the marbles, right there. Berra was a game winner, and he was a better thrower than people gave him credit for being. And you know, in spite of what some of the Yankee pitchers said, he was a little smarter than they gave him credit for. He knew what was going on.

When you get to talking about hitters, there's no doubt that Ted Williams has to be the best left-handed hitter I ever observed. No doubt about it at all. Up at the plate he had the concentration and determination of a Cobb and it blanked out everything except what he was up there trying to do. I remember one day we were playing them a doubleheader in Detroit. This was the year they won the pennant, 1946. In the first game Williams hit a couple of home runs and a double, and the times we got him out, he nailed the right fielder to the fence with line drives.

Freddie Hutchinson is going to pitch the second game of this doubleheader. I don't think there was ever a tougher competitor on the mound than Hutchinson, or one who got angrier while he was at it. I'd caught the first game that day and gone out for a pinch hitter late in the game. I went into the clubhouse and Freddie's on the table getting rubbed down. He's telling the trainer that he doesn't care what Williams was doing out there or how great a hitter he was, he just wasn't going to hit Freddie that way. Freddie was going to knock Ted down the first time up. The game hasn't started yet, but Hutch is already steamed up.

The second game starts and he goes out to pitch. Williams comes up the first time and Fred throws one close, which didn't faze Ted. Second pitch he really knocked him down. Ted gets up and steps back in, snapping that bat back and forth. Never blinked an eye. Then Hutch threw the next one in. I can

see it to this day. You know, along around Thanksgiving I
read in the paper where some writer asked Ted what was the
longest home run he'd ever hit in his life. Ted said that there
had been one Sunday in Detroit when he caught the wind
going out in the second game of a doubleheader and Freddie
Hutchinson gave him a fastball which went for a pretty good
ride.

Hutch didn't last very long in that game. Just an inning or
two. I had to go into the clubhouse and there he is, good and
mad. He's throwing chairs and equipment and whatnot. I got
over near the door and said, "Hutch, boy you really scared
that Williams." I closed that door just as a chair came crash-
ing against it.

So that was Ted Williams. No use throwing at him. First of
all, you're not going to hit him. And second of all, you're not
going to bother him. Best thing to do with him was to let him
do what he was going to do anyway and then concentrate on
getting the next man out.

In 1936 I went back to the minors, with Atlanta. I managed
at Atlanta for five years, then later on, after the war, managed Buffalo for three years and Seattle for one, before taking
over the White Sox in 1951.

I was always willing to try out a new idea. One year,
when I was at Buffalo, Sam Jethroe was tearing the league
apart with his base running. In 1949 he stole 89 bases. You
just couldn't stop him. We were playing Montreal one day
and a situation came up that we had talked about. It was
the eighth inning, we were leading by a run, there were two
out, and the Montreal pitcher was at bat. Jethroe was on
deck. If we get the pitcher out, we have Jethroe leading off
the ninth. Well, if he leads off in the ninth and gets on base,
he's going to steal second and very possibly third. We had it
figured out that anytime he led off an inning and got on
first, his chances of scoring were ninety percent. We had
statistics on it.

So, if we walk the pitcher intentionally and let Jethroe hit
with the pitcher on first base and two out, the only way that
Jethroe's going to hurt us in that particular situation is with
a triple. If he gets a hit, the chances are the pitcher is only
going to second, and even though Jethroe is on base, he can't

hurt us with his speed because he's got the pitcher in front of him. So we tried it, and it worked.

Branch Rickey, running the Dodgers at that time, who owned Jethroe, happened to be in the ball park and he carried that story back with him to the All-Star Game, and it upped the price on Jethroe from $25,000 to $75,000. Mr. Rickey actually told me that himself.

That maneuver drew some attention to me, and so did another one. This one involved putting a pitcher at third base, bringing in a relief pitcher to work to one man, and then taking him out and putting the first pitcher back on the mound. That got a lot of publicity because it happened in a big league game. And you'd be surprised at the baseball people who didn't know you could do that.

What happened was, I had Harry Dorish pitching against the Red Sox in the top of the ninth. Ted Williams was leading off, and I wanted a left-hander to pitch to him. So I moved Dorish over to third base and brought Billy Pierce in. Pierce got Williams out and I took him out of the game and put Dorish back in to pitch to the right-handed hitters. Was I worried about Dorish having to handle a difficult play at third? Well, no. I'd never seen Williams hit a ball to the third baseman.

Billy Pierce was quite a pitcher. You know, I first ran into him when I was playing with Detroit in 1945 and he was working out with them. In fact, he got into a few games that year. He was just a kid. His father owned a drugstore about a block from where I was living. I'd go in now and then to buy something, and there was this kid clerking behind the counter. I never paid any attention to him. Then out at the ball park we had this little left-hander who I'd warm up occasionally. One day he walked up to me on the field and said, "You know, you won't even speak to me when you come into our drugstore."

"What are you talking about?" I asked.

"That's my father's drugstore," he said. "You were in there last night."

I took a good hard look at him and, sure enough, he was the clerk.

You know, the Tigers made a mistake with him. They traded him before anybody knew what a fine pitcher he was going to be. Sent him over to the White Sox, which was fine for me because when I took over that club in 1951, there he was. I worked a little with him on his windup to help his delivery and convinced him that he had to throw a slider and an occasional change of pace, and that was all he needed.

Billy had a nice sense of humor. He's pitching against the Yankees one day and they're hitting him pretty well, but Jim Busby out in center field is catching everything they hit. I went out to ask Billy how he felt and he said, "Don't ask me how I feel, ask Busby how he feels."

I went back out in the eighth inning and asked him again. I know he's got to be tired by this time.

"I'm all right," he said. "I'll stay out here and lose it."

"No you won't either," I said. "We'll let somebody else lose this one." He was a real cute kid. I was fond of him.

Another one of my favorites with the White Sox was Nelson Fox. I think a fellow like Nelson Fox is a tremendous compliment to baseball, as well as a great asset. Here's a fellow who didn't posses overwhelming physical ability but still went out and made himself into a fine ballplayer.

I've never seen anybody who wanted to play more than Fox did. In spring training you had to run him off the field to get him to rest, and I mean just literally run him off. During the season Frank Lane, who was the general manager, would get on me from time to time to give Fox a rest. I didn't want to, but finally I said all right. So I took him out of the lineup one day in Detroit. The game starts, I'm sitting up there at the end of the bench, and here comes Fox. He sits down next to me and starts yelling at the pitcher, yelling and yelling, giving him hell, calling him everything. He goes on for nine innings like that, loud as he could. Doing it on purpose, you see, just to give me a headache.

Finally I turned to him. "Foxie," I said, "let me tell you something right now. This is the last time you're ever going to sit on this bench with me. I don't care if Lane or anybody else says you need a rest, you're not going to get it. Just remember that."

Well, that satisfied him. He didn't want a rest. He never wanted a rest. And I sure didn't want him sitting next to me for nine innings screaming his head off.

Minnie Minoso was another favorite of mine. To my way of

thinking he was undoubtedly the most colorful player of his era. I once heard another ballplayer say that with Minoso on the club, if you don't hustle, you really look bad. He had an effect on the whole team. I asked Billy Pierce one day who he thought would lead the team in stolen bases, Busby or Minoso.

"Busby," he said.

"Why?" I asked.

"Because Minoso doesn't stop at first," he said.

That was the way he played ball, all the time. He was one of the great people in baseball—one of the finest, most lovable men.

In 1955 I was offered the job at Baltimore and I accepted it. What we were faced with there was a complete rebuilding job, practically from scratch. I got myself a lot of scouts, and we signed a lot of ballplayers, a lot of them. What we were doing was using the old Branch Rickey formula, which was "There's got to be some quality in quantity." And that proved to be right. We went out on a limb several times with players. We took a little chance on a guy like Brooks Robinson. Milt Pappas had a bad knee, but we took him. We had a scout out in California who picked up Chuck Estrada and Jerry Walker and Wes Stock. Then we added Steve Barber and Jack Fisher. All good young pitchers. They called it the Kiddie Korps. In addition we had Jim Gentile, Ronnie Hansen, Marv Breeding, and Brooks.

It was a fine young team, and it came right along. In 1960 we made a run at the Yankees. We played them a four-game series in New York in September, when it was all up for grabs, and they wiped us out. That was always the problem, during all my years of managing—the Yankees. They always seemed to have a little more—more power, more pitching. They out-manned you; they outgunned you. Well, I guess I'm not the first manager who's sung that song.

Handling pitchers? Well, I guess I had my own approach, my own system. You know that a certain pitcher must have four days' rest or five days' rest. Once in a while you run into a guy that can pitch with three days' rest, but with night baseball that runs into problems. You don't recover from night pitching as you do from day pitching. Night pitching stiffens you up more. You have to know how to use your staff to maximum efficiency. So many times you have a star pitcher who wants to pitch with three days' rest regardless of anything. Well, that upsets your whole pitching staff. It means one guy might have to take six days' rest, another five, and so on. If somebody needs the extra throwing, let him get it on the sidelines. I don't care what pitcher it is, he's got to have more stuff with four days' rest than he has with three. I'm a firm believer in that. He'll have more stuff, harder stuff. He may not have as sharp control, but let me tell you—hitters worry about stuff more than they do about control.

Some managers will work their top pitchers with three days' rest. All right. They'll win 20 games for you, but they'll also lose 14 or 15. You're not getting maximum efficiency from them. Also, you're wearing them out and at the same time not developing a pitching staff.

You've got to come back to the fundamentals. I can't say that often enough. My drilling of my players did not stop when spring training ended. It continued on throughout the season. You cannot assume a player has been taught a particular fundamental and then when he messes up in a ball game, blame him for it. You have to *know* that he's been instructed along those particular lines. Game conditions, the score, the inning, everything is a factor. John McGraw used to have an automatic fine, and I had one also, if his coaches didn't know how the wind was blowing. If my coaches couldn't tell me when I walked into the clubhouse if the wind was blowing to right field or left field, they were fined. The coaches have to know so they can tell the players.

I don't care how experienced a player is, you've got to keep after him. There are an awful lot of small details that add up to the winning of a ball game, and it's up to the man in charge to see that his players are always drilled in and constantly alert to those things. So if anybody tells you a manager has no effect on a ball club, he's telling you that he doesn't know baseball.

OSSIE BLUEGE

Oswald Louis Bluege
Born: October 24, 1900, Chicago, Illinois; Died: October 15, 1986
Managerial career: Washington Senators, 1943–47

Ossie Bluege spent his entire big league career with the Washington Senators as player, coach, and, in 1943 through 1947, as manager. In 1945 Bluege took a team that had finished last the year before and brought it to near victory, missing the pennant by a narrow margin.

I used to watch McGraw when I was a kid. He'd bring his Giants to Chicago to play the Cubs—that was a great rivalry in those days. I was lucky growing up in a town that had two big league clubs. I saw my first big league game when I was ten years old. That would be 1910. So I saw all those fellows—Tinker, Evers, Chance, Three-Finger Brown, Honus Wagner, Ed Walsh, Smoky Joe Wood, Nap Lajoie, Shoeless Joe Jackson. Then there were some that I saw that I had the opportunity to play on the same field with later on, like Ty Cobb, Tris Speaker, Babe Ruth, Eddie Collins, and Walter Johnson.

I loved to play baseball, always enjoyed it, but who the devil ever thought about becoming a big leaguer? I was never very big, but I had a lot of nervous energy and was always keyed up out there.

I was going to school at night, taking accounting courses, and holding down a job during the day with International Harvester. Through a fellow named Jack Doyle, an ex-major-leaguer, I started playing some pretty fast semipro ball around Chicago. I was getting fifteen dollars a game—not bad money in those days. As I was leaving the ball park one day, I was stopped by a fellow named Bill Jackson.

"Listen," he said, "I'm the manager of the Peoria Tractors in the Three-I League. I watched you play today, and I've got a contract for two hundred a month for you."

This was in 1920. I was still a minor, so he told me to take the contract home, have my father sign it, and then join the Peoria ball club in Rock Island. I was flattered—I didn't know I was that good. So I took the contract home and showed it to my father. He didn't know too much about baseball. He was a strict old German gentleman who believed in hard work and in going to church on Sundays and holding the Bible up in your hands where everybody could see it. He wasn't too impressed with that contract.

"You want to give up all your accounting training, all your schooling?" he asked.

"Dad," I said, "they make five and six thousand dollars a year playing major league ball."

He couldn't believe that. "They pay men that much money to chase that ball around?"

"That's right," I said. I told him I didn't have to give up my accounting, that I could always go back to it.

So we talked and talked, and finally I told him that if I didn't make the big leagues in three years' time, I'd come back and push the pencil. That satisfied him, and he signed the contract.

The next day I caught the night train to Rock Island and got there at four in the morning. I checked into the hotel, slept a few hours, and at 7:30 was up and ready to go. That was my normal routine—get up early and go to work. I hung around the lobby until nine o'clock, and nobody had showed up. What is this? I asked myself. So I rang Jackson's room and told him I was there.

"What the hell are you calling me up at this hour of the morning for?" he asked.

"It's time to go to work, isn't it?" I asked.

"For who?" he asked.

That's when I began to get the idea that this was going to be a different life.

I was there for just a little while when Bill Jackson said to me, "Kid, next year you're going to be sold to a major league ball club." Boy, when he told me that, the wheels started turning in my head. You know how it is when you're a kid. You've got all that ambition, and it doesn't take too much to get your imagination warmed up. But he knew what he was talking about because next year, sure enough, Joe Engel of the Washington club came by and bought my contract for $3,500.

I split the '22 season between Washington and Minneapolis and in '23 became the Senators' regular third baseman. Donie Bush was the manager in '23. Then Bucky Harris took over in 1924 as playing manager. He was the one who put me in the lineup to stay. You see, I'd hit only .245 my first year, and they felt the team needed some more punch in the lineup. So they brought a few guys in and tried them out at third while I sat on the bench. I didn't say anything—didn't make any fuss. But I could see that things were happening around third base that shouldn't be happening, and we were losing ball games. Then early in May we lost a couple of games because of some shenanigans around third base. I'll never forget this. I was in the shower after the second game, cleaning up. Bucky walked by, and I could tell by his face he was annoyed. Suddenly he looked at me and said, "You're playing third base tomorrow and from here on in, come hell or high water."

From that day on we went. We started clicking. We won the pennant and the World Series.

I can remember John McGraw and Bucky Harris having a managerial battle of wits before the seventh game of the 1924 World Series. Looking back on it now, it was really something. Here is the young Harris, in his first year as a manager, trying to outsmart the Giants' great John McGraw.

You see, McGraw was platooning at first base. He was starting George Kelly against the left-handers and Bill Terry against the righties. Terry was murdering us, and we wanted him out of there. So Griffith and Bucky did a little scheming. There was a lot of rivalry there, between Griffith and McGraw. You have to go way back on this. Griff was the first manager to represent the American League in New York. He managed the Yankees in 1903, when they were known as the Highlanders. McGraw didn't like that; old John J. thought New York was his private kingdom. There was an enmity there for years and years.

So Bucky started Curly Ogden, a right-hander, and Mc-
Graw put Terry in the lineup. Ogden pitched to two batters
and then we brought in George Mogridge, a lefty and a good
one. We were leading them 1–0 in the sixth inning and, sure
enough, McGraw hit for Terry. Then Bucky turned around
and brought in Fred Marberry, a right-hander. Bill Terry told
me later that they were telling McGraw right from the start
not to pay attention to what we were doing, not to platoon,
otherwise they'd get caught short. But McGraw didn't listen.

We were tied at the end of nine innings, 3–3, and we brought
Walter Johnson in at that point. The shades of night were
falling now, and Walter was throwing bullets. The Giants had
roughed Walter up twice in the Series, but they weren't hitting him now.

Then we got lucky in the bottom of the twelfth. Muddy Ruel
hit a double and then Earl McNeely hit one down to Freddie
Lindstrom at third that hit a pebble and bounced over Freddie's head just as he was getting set to make the play. That
was it, brother. Muddy came in with the winning run, Walter
was a winner, and we all were winners. That was the greatest
thrill of my life, winning that Series—the only one the Washington Senators ever won.

It was a good ball club. Do you remember Joe Judge? He
was our first baseman, and I'll tell you, he was a better first
baseman than Sisler ever was. This is not to take anything
away from Sisler, but Joe was a genius around that bag. And
we had Roger Peckinpaugh, Muddy Ruel, and Sam Rice. Sam
was a heck of a ballplayer. He's in the Hall of Fame today.
You want to hear something? Sam ended up with 2,987 hits.
That's right, just 13 short of 3,000. Why didn't he go on and
get those last 13? I don't know; I guess he wasn't interested.
Ballplayers didn't pay as much attention to their records in
those days as they do today. Today they wouldn't let a man
retire under those circumstances. They'd make a big promotion out of his getting those last few hits.

We weren't a power team. We hit only 22 home runs that
year. That's right—22 home runs for the entire season. And
Goose Goslin got 12 of them by himself. Goose was a great
hitter. You couldn't throw the fastball by him. They would
try. They would set him up for it with other stuff and then try
to slip it by, and he would always zing it. He was a character,

too. I remember one time he was going stinko. There was a guy up in the grandstands, one of those louts with the foghorn voices, and he was on Goose something terrible. "Goose," he's yelling, "where were *you* last night?" Things like that. Boy, that Goslin, he was coming in every inning getting redder and redder in the face.

Finally the old man, Griffith, who was sitting right behind our dugout, sent a note down to Bucky. The note said, "Take Goslin out of there. Let him take care of that guy." So Bucky took him out, and Goose went back to the clubhouse, changed into his streetclothes, and went up into the stands and took that guy by the collar and gave him a good shaking.

To me the two greatest thrills in joining the Washington ball club were playing in the nation's capital and playing on the same team with Walter Johnson. Walter was like a little god as far as I was concerned. Playing behind him was a pleasure. If you booted a ball, he'd come over and say, "That's all right. You'll get the next one."

When I saw him, he'd already been pitching for about fifteen years, and he was still as fast as anyone in the league. He used to like to pitch batting practice, so I had the chance to bat against him quite a bit. He used to sort of flip that thing up there sidearm, almost underhand, and you'd think that ball was going to come right at you, and you'd back off and swipe at it, but it was right over the plate. That ball would rise; it would swoosh and rise. Try and hit it. And when Walter got in a tough spot in a game, he could reach back for that little extra. Very few pitchers can do that. Walter always seemed to have a little in reserve. But he was something to watch when he was in trouble out there. First he would put his glove down on the mound. Then he would open his belt and pull it in a notch. Then he would pick up a little dirt and let it ooze through his fingers. When he did that, brother, look out—the current was on. He had turned the switch.

After Bucky left as manager for the first time, in 1928, Griff hired Walter. Walter was not a good manager. You know what his chief weakness was? He didn't know how to handle his pitchers. That may sound strange, but the truth was, Walter didn't know very much about pitching. All he knew was that you reached back and fired—that was the way he had done it for twenty years, and nobody ever did it better.

And that's what he expected his pitchers to do. Bucky, who was a second baseman, knew more about pitching than Walter did.

I think Griff knew about Walter's weaknesses, but he hired him anyway. The old man was something of a sentimentalist. He liked to hire his own boys to manage. He put Clyde Milan in there, then Bucky, then Walter, then Joe Cronin, then Bucky again, then me, then Joe Kuhel.

Ty Cobb? Sure, I saw plenty of him. Old Tyrus Raymond. I don't think the fires ever went out in him, not till the day he died. I remember one game late in the season in 1928. We were playing the Athletics in Philadelphia. They were fighting the Yankees for the pennant that year. As a matter of fact, they lost out by only a game or two. That was the year Connie Mack had Cobb, Speaker, and Eddie Collins on the team, all of them right at the end of the line. Collins was a player-coach, but Cobb and Speaker got into quite a few games. In this one game it was the bottom of the ninth, one out, Collins is on third, we're leading them by a run, and Mack sends Cobb up to pinch-hit. Tyrus Raymond himself.

Naturally the infield was pulled in, especially with that Cobb up there. Well, he hit one down to Harris at second on two big bounces. Collins breaks for the plate and Harris throws the ball home, to Muddy Ruel. I come in from third, and we've got Collins in a rundown. Now, here was a play we'd worked on in spring training. Instead of throwing that ball back and forth, which gives the batter time to get to second, Harris wanted us to run the base runner back and then at the last split second throw the ball. That way, there's a minimum amount of ball handling, and you can keep the batter from taking that extra base. Well, we worked it to perfection. Muddy got the ball, Collins put on the brakes, Muddy ran him back, I came in, Muddy gave me the ball, and I put it on Collins. Then I turned around and there's Cobb racing to second. I fired the ball to Harris, and he put the tag on Cobb. Boom—double play and the game is over. Tyrus Raymond couldn't believe it. He figured Collins would have jockeyed around long enough for him to get to second. He just stood there with his hands on his hips and yelled, *"How* long has that guy been playing ball?"

Cobb was a smart ballplayer. Shrewd. Don't you think he wasn't. But so was Griffith. Do you know what the old man used to do when he was managing and they were playing the Tigers? He would have one of his ballplayers get on Cobb. Ty had a low boiling point, you know. Finally it would get to the point where Cobb couldn't take it any longer, and he would go after the guy. There would be a fight, and they'd both be thrown out of the game. That's how Griff dealt with Tyrus Raymond.

Cobb was always thinking out there, always doing something to irritate you. If he stepped out of the batter's box to get some dirt on his hands, he always bent over with his backside to the pitcher. He always had contempt for the opposition, nothing but contempt, and he wanted you to know it.

I can give you another illustration of the way Cobb played ball. I was just a rookie. Ty's on first base and Harry Heilmann hits a line drive single to right field. Well, Cobb seldom stopped at second. He just kept on going and you had to throw him out, that's all there was to it. On this particular play Sam Rice picked up the ball in right field and fired it in to me, and now I've got the ball at third base just as Cobb is rounding second. And he doesn't care; he's coming. I'm thinking to myself, this is going to be interesting! Instead of waiting at the base, I took a few steps out to meet him, in a little bit of a crouch, waiting to tag him. Well, this is no exaggeration now. He didn't slide. He just took off and came at me in midair, spikes first, about four or five feet off the ground, so help me just like a rocket. He hit me in the upper part of my arm, just grazing the flesh but tearing open the sleeve. I made the play. I tagged him out, but I was so mad I was going to konk him with the ball while he was lying on the ground. But Billy Evans, the umpire, pulled me away. Then he threw Cobb out of the game for making such a vicious slide.

The next day I was standing around the batting cage waiting my turn to hit when up walks Mr. Tyrus Raymond. Just as sweet as apple pie. He's apologizing.

"Son," he said, "I hope I didn't hurt you."

"I'm all right," I said.

"Good," he said. Then the look in his eyes changed just a little, his face got mean, and he said, "But remember—never come up the line for me."

But that wasn't what had got him mad. I'll tell you what got him mad—he knew he was going to be out. That was like waving a red flag in a bull's face. When he knew you had him, it seemed to make him a little crazy, like a cornered animal. That's when he was most dangerous.

As an infielder, I always tried to take everything into consideration, anticipating every possibility—if the ball was hit to me and at what speed; who is the runner on first and if he runs like a deer or a donkey; who was covering the bag in case I had to throw there, the second baseman or the shortstop? And it's all got to be automatic because you don't have time to think out there. If you've got to stop and think out there, you'd better quit.

I used to try and drill these lessons into my players when I was managing. You see, I was known as a pretty good fielder in my day and I prided myself in that. To my mind, fielding is the artistry of the game. You watch a third baseman coming in to scoop up a ball bare-handed and throw a man out on a bunt, or you watch the double play being made or the outfielder making the fine running catch. This is all very beautiful when it's being executed well. And the fans appreciate it too; don't think they don't. A great play in the field always gets a standing ovation, whether it's for the home team or against.

I couldn't emphasize some of these things enough to my players. I used to tell them that we were not all gifted alike, that some of us had quicker reflexes and better hands than others, but at the same time I would let them know how they could become better ballplayers simply through observation and anticipation. Sit on the bench when the other team is taking batting practice, study those hitters, and never mind going into the clubhouse and sitting around because in batting practice the opposing hitter will show you where his strength is. And watch him when he bunts one because he's going to tell you something then too—whether he squares off to bunt or just drops the bat on the ball. If you can pick up those little tip-offs, then you're going to be able to get a split-second jump on him, and that often can make all the difference.

Another thing I would tell my infielders was not to watch

the pitcher during the game. Too many of them used to watch the pitcher wind up and throw. Forget that, I'd tell them. You study that hitter, you keep your eye on *him* because if you're keen enough, you can almost instinctively know what he's going to do. When I was playing third base, I never took my eyes off the hitter, and in time I got to where I could almost sense when he was going to knock one down my way. You don't believe that, do you? Well, it's true. And that's why I was able to go to my right as well as my left. I know this sounds egotistical, but anybody who saw me play ball will tell you I could do those things. And it was the product of hard work and observation, that's all. You can get a lot more out of your God-given abilities if you keep your eyes open.

I mentioned that seventh game of the 1924 World Series against the Giants. Okay, we're in extra innings now. Here again I'm talking about observation. The Giants came in from the field, and I was looking over at their dugout. There's McGraw talking to Freddie Lindstrom, who was going to lead off. Lindstrom had pretty good foot, he could run. I said to myself, Oh-oh, something's up. Extra inning ball game, the man is leading off, you know they want to try something. So I got even with the bag and watched his bat. I was *anticipating,* you see. Sure enough, he dropped it down. And it was a perfect bunt, rolling up the third-base line. But I was moving in the moment he moved that bat. I got that ball and fired it to Joe Judge at first base, never straightening up, and nailed Lindstrom.

After we'd won that game, and the Series with it, McGraw came into our clubhouse to congratulate Harris. And before he left, he came over to me and shook my hand and said, "Son, you're the best ever." Well, coming from John McGraw, who was an old third baseman himself and sparing with his praise, it just made my chest swell out and I never forgot it. I don't want to sound like I'm popping off; I made plenty of errors too. But when John McGraw makes a statement like that to you, you can't help but be proud of it.

Right after the season closed in 1942, I went to Chicago to visit my family. One day I got a phone call from Griff.

"When are you coming home?" he asked. Home was Washington.

"I'm not sure," I said.

"Well, why don't you get in your wagon now and get back here?" he said. "I want to talk to you."

I knew right then and there what it was all about. Bucky had been released as manager shortly before, you see. It was the second time for Bucky. So I drove back and when I got to Washington, I went out to Griff's house. He took me into his study, and we sat down.

"Well," he said, "I had to release Bucky." And when he said it, tears came into his eyes. That's how he felt about Harris. You don't always want to let a manager go; sometimes you just have to. Then he said, "Do you want the job?"

To tell the truth, I never had any ambitions to be a manager. I never thought I was cut out for it. I had been working as a coach under Bucky, and after having been in the big leagues for more than twenty years as a player and a coach, I knew all the problems one had to deal with. You had to be a teacher and an instructor and a psychologist, and some players take it kindly and some don't. I always felt, Why go through it? But of course it's easy to settle all that in your mind when nobody has made you an offer. I guess that's human nature—you say you're not interested in something, until somebody offers it to you.

I knew it would be a real challenge. I felt confident that I knew the game well enough. Of course, I knew I'd be managing players who had been my teammates, which is sometimes rough. But you don't like to say no, do you? Not many men are asked to manage a big league club, and when you're asked, it's very hard to refuse.

So I said yes, and we shook hands on it. He said he couldn't pay me a lot of money, but that was of no concern to me. I was never a materialistic man. I knew he would be as fair as he could be, and that was good enough.

Then we assessed the ball club, the strengths and weaknesses. We had some good ballplayers, like Mickey Vernon, Jerry Priddy, George Case, Stan Spence, and Jake Early, and a few good pitchers like Early Wynn, Dutch Leonard, and Mickey Haefner. We went over the rosters of the other ball clubs to see who might be available. The war years were upon us then. A lot of fellows had been drafted or were about to be, and good ballplayers were hard to come by. Bob Johnson of the

Athletics had retired, but we induced him to come back and play for us. He gave us some power and was a pretty good outfielder. We needed a third baseman, and we got Harlond Clift from the Browns, still a solid ballplayer even though he'd seen his best days. In those war years you had to do a lot of cutting and pasting to make a ball club.

We finished second in 1943, which was the highest a Washington club had been since 1933. In 1944 it turned completely around and we finished last. You see, in those years, with ballplayers going into service, your whole team could change overnight. But then the next year, in 1945, we turned it right around again and almost won the pennant. We finished second to the Tigers by a game and a half. I think that was the most peculiar end of a pennant race there ever was. We finished the schedule a week ahead of everybody else because Griff had agreed to give the Washington Redskins the use of the field. At the time the agreement was made, nobody expected us to be in the race. What the heck, we'd been dead last the year before. So it was very peculiar that last week. We were fighting for the pennant, only we weren't fighting—we were sitting around to see what the Tigers were going to do.

We wound up our season with a doubleheader against the Philadelphia Athletics, and I'll never forget that. Of course we knew that every game was going to be precious to us. I had Dutch Leonard going for me in that first game, and we were ahead by a run or two in the late innings. Buddy Lewis had come back from military service in the middle of the year and was in right field. Late in the game somebody hit a ball into short right field. Buddy came in for it and caught the ball and in almost the same motion started to flip it to George Myatt, the second baseman, who had come running out. Well, when he started to flip the ball, Buddy dropped it. Eddie Rommel was the umpire, and he ruled that Buddy hadn't had possession of the ball long enough for the batter to be out, which was plain nonsense.

Now, I had seen that Rommel hadn't been watching it all that closely. So I went charging out there.

"Eddie," I said, "I was watching you, and you weren't anywhere near the play."

He knew he was wrong. I could tell by his reactions. I kept chewing him up until finally he said, "That's enough out of you. You want to stay in this game, you'd better clear out of here."

That made me even madder.

"You want to throw me out for arguing something that you know you're dead wrong about?" I said. Oh, I really started to give it to him then. "You want to throw me out?" I said. "Then go ahead." I don't think I was ever hotter on a ball field.

Well, he did throw me out. His bum call cost us the ball game. Anyway, I went back to the clubhouse and the clubhouse man said to me, "Os, Tommy Connolly is in the ball park. He's sitting right behind the dugout." Tommy Connolly was the American League's chief of umpires. When I heard he was there, I got dressed and went out to look for him. I was still burning. When I got upstairs to the box seats, he wasn't there. He had scooted.

I sat there and watched us lose that game, and after it was over, I headed for the umpire's room. That's sanctum sanctorum you know; nobody's allowed in there. I knocked on the door and Tommy Connolly opened it.

"May I come in, Tommy?" I asked. "I'd like to talk to you."

"Come on in," he said.

Rommel and the other umpires were there, and Rommel's face was flushed. Tommy must have just got finished eating him out.

"Tommy," I said, "I'm not going to discuss that play. You know how I feel about that. All I'm asking is that you grant me permission to sit on the bench and direct the ball club in the second game."

You see, in those days the rule was if you're thrown out of the first game of a doubleheader, you're out for the whole day. Well, we were fighting for a pennant, and I wanted to be in there, especially after having been thrown out for disputing a call like that.

He looked at me and grunted and in his Irish brogue said, "No, I can't do that. Those are the rules."

"Tommy," I said, "this is something special. You can waive that rule at this stage of the game. This is the last day we've got to play. I'm sure the league would back you up on it."

"Can't do it," he said. He was an old-timer from the old school. Strict.

That was it. I went back and sat behind our dugout for the

second game. And I had to be careful. I was dying to give some signs and instructions during the game, but if my coaches had been caught looking at me or if I had started doing some wigwagging, it would have been a violation. So I had to sit there like a wooden Indian the whole game, which we won anyway. But if we had won that first game, it might have been a different story at the end because we lost by just a game and a half. The Tigers won on the last day of the season when Hank Greenberg hit a grand-slam home run in the ninth inning against the Browns.

And that was the only game I was ever thrown out of as a manager.

I never argued with the umpires very much. They seldom change their decisions, as you know. But you do have to go out there from time to time to put in your two cents worth. There are reasons for it. Sometimes you try to lay the groundwork for the next close call that comes up. If you handle it nicely, you might get that call. If you run out there like you're going to fight a pack of wolves, you're only going to get them mad at you, and that's not going to help your cause any. What you try to do is convey to them that they *may* have missed it. After all, they're not infallible, and they know that. If he was out of position to call that particular play, you go out there and let him know that you know it.

Another thing is, if one of your players is arguing, you've got to go out there and back him up, even if you think he's wrong. In those cases you might run out there and get in a little wink at the umpire while you're hollering at him, just to let him know that you know what the story is. He knows you've got to come out there and wave your arms. The fans enjoy it, your ballplayer is satisfied, and there's no harm done. Another reason you're out there is to prevent your player from getting thrown out of the game. You'll see the first thing a manager does when he goes out is to get between his ballplayer and the umpire.

I can tell about one experience I had with Bobo Newsom. I don't have to tell you what a character he was. He was like a big kid, playful and easy going. But at the same time he could drive you nuts out there. I knew him well enough after so many years. I could tell when he was getting tired on the mound—he'd start yapping at the umpires. In fact, that's a good rule of thumb to use with certain pitchers. Different pitchers show it differently when they're getting tired, and with a lot of them it's barking at the umpire. Particularly if it's a close ball game. That's when you know they're losing it, because every pitch is becoming labor to them and they want every close call. This was Bobo.

One day we're in a one-run ball game, and everything is going along fine. All of a sudden around the seventh inning Bobo starts giving the plate umpire a going-over on every other pitch. It was big Cal Hubbard, one of the best. Bobo is walking down off the mound, yelling, and walking back. He got out of the inning all right, and between innings Hubbard called me out.

"Os," he says, "you'd better get somebody ready because that guy isn't going to be around much longer. The next time he comes walking down to give me his opinions, I'm going to run him out. I'm telling you as a friend."

Sure enough, the next inning Bobo starts up with him again. Now, I knew he was getting tired, but he was still getting them out, and I wanted to keep him in there as long as I could because a tired Bobo was still better than what I had fresh in the bull pen at the moment. So I went charging out there. He's storming around on the mound.

"For Pete's sake," I said, "calm down and pitch." He gave me some lip and I lost my patience and said, "Listen, you big fathead, do you know where that last pitch was? It was high. So what are you yelling about?"

"You think that pitch was high?" he said. Now he's mad at me.

"That's right," I said.

"Nuts," he said.

"Nuts to you," I said.

So there's the manager standing out on the mound in a close ball game arguing with his pitcher. All I was trying to do was keep the big lout in there. I managed to do that, and he struggled through to win it. But that's the kind of guy he was. He could drive you crazy. But he was harmless and lovable and a good pitcher. He was always being traded back and forth. I think he was with the Washington ball club four or five different times. Griff kept getting rid of him and kept bringing him back.

But when he was out there, he had the heart of a lion. I can tell you that right out of experience. This happened on opening day in 1936. We were playing the Yankees. Ben Chapman laid down a bunt, and I came in for it. I had to hurry because Ben could run. It was one of those do-or-die plays, when you line first base up in your mind and come up throwing, which I did—and there's that big hulk of a Bobo standing there. The ball hit him right in the jaw. He came staggering over to me and said, "What'd you do that for?"

"Why didn't you duck?" I said.

"I don't know," he said.

You know something, he had a broken jaw—they wired it up later—but that son of a gun wouldn't come out of there. He stayed in and finished the game and won it. That was Bobo.

You know, I went out and pitched batting practice practically every day of my managerial life. That's right. And I would hit fungoes too. Joe McCarthy used to say to me, "Ossie, that's against all rules of the union." I pitched batting practice because I loved it, but the reason I had to hit the fungoes was because I didn't have anybody else to pick up the bat. I wanted Clyde Milan, my coach, to keep his eye on things during the workout. We didn't have all the specialists around that you have today. The manager had to get out there and work.

One of the great things about baseball is it's an unpredictable business. You never know when something interesting or exciting is going to happen, and that's why you can't wait to get out to the ballpark every day, no matter how many years you've been at it. I can give you an example. We had a tryout camp at Sanford, Florida, one spring. I think it was '37. Joe Engel was running it. Naturally a lot of kids showed up for it. One day in walks this big, robust kid wearing dungarees and a work shirt. He was only seventeen, but he looked like he could take care of himself. He walked up to Joe Engel and said, "I want to play ball."

Joe looked him over and said, "What are you?"

"I'm a pitcher," the kid said. "And I can hit, too."

"You can, eh?" Joe said.

"That's right," the kid said. He didn't lack for confidence. So they gave him a uniform and let him work out, and on the strength of what they saw, they signed him to a contract. That's how the Washington ball club got Early Wynn. Just walked in and announced himself. A few years later he was in the big leagues, on his way to the Hall of Fame. But I'll tell you something, he didn't become a real good pitcher until we traded him to Cleveland. When he pitched for me in the early forties, he had a good fastball, but that was it. When he went to Cleveland, Mel Harder got hold of him and taught him how to throw the good curveball and change-up, and that's when Early became a great pitcher.

Signs can be a troublesome thing, although they shouldn't be, particularly with big leaguers. But you know, on opening day, after spring training, you call a meeting and go over the signs with your ball club. This is the bunt. This is the take, the steal, the hit-and-run, and so on. Everybody got them? They nod their heads. Okay. But the minute you turn around, they start putting their heads together and whispering to each other, "What's the bunt sign? What's the take?" I saw it as a player and I saw it later on as a manager.

Of course, you're going to have problems with individual players. Sometimes the fans see a man thrown out stealing second and they want to know why a guy was stealing in that particular situation. Well, the truth is he wasn't stealing— the batter missed a hit-and-run sign and the runner was shot down. That's when a manager gets gray. No, I never fined a player, for that or anything else. I never believed in taking a man's money. I always tried to reason with them. Sit down and have a talk. And sometimes that can make you even grayer. I'll tell you what I mean.

I had a fellow named George Binks playing for me during the war. Bingo Binks. He was a good ballplayer. One day he's on first base and Rick Ferrell is up. Rick was slow afoot and was an easy double-play man, so very often he would hit-and-run. I let him call it anytime he wanted to because I trusted his judgment. Well, he put it on, but Binks didn't go. Now, this wasn't the first time that had happened. Rick was pretty frustrated. He pulled me aside after the game and said, "Os, that Binks just can't get a sign."

"Okay," I said. "I'll talk to him."

The next day I called Binks into my office.

"George," I said, "do you know all the signs?"

"Sure," he said.

"What are they?"

He went through them and he had them right.

"Good," I said. "Now, do you know the hit-and-run signs of the players that are hitting in back of you?"

"Sure," he said.

"What's Rick Ferrell's sign?"

He told me.

"Okay," I said. "Now we're getting to the question. You were on first base yesterday and Rick gave you the hit-and-run sign."

"That's right," he said.

"Well, you didn't go. Why didn't you run when the ball was pitched?"

He looked at me very seriously and said, "I was afraid he was going to miss it."

That was the answer. And so the manager gets gray. And grayer.

AL LOPEZ

Alfonso Raymond Lopez
Born: August 20, 1908, Tampa, Florida
Managerial career: Cleveland Indians, 1951–56; Chicago
  White Sox, 1957–65, 1968–69

In fifteen full years as a manager, Al Lopez's ball clubs were never out of the first division, and only three times were they lower than second place. Lopez's 1954 Cleveland Indians set an American League record with 111 wins. Lopez holds the major league record for lifetime games for a catcher—1,918. He was elected to the Baseball Hall of Fame in 1977.

In 1925 a team of big leaguers came barnstorming through Tampa right after the World Series, planning on playing each other or playing against a local pick-up team. When they got to Tampa, they thought it might be a good idea to get one of the local kids to play with them, to attract some customers. I was only seventeen years old at the time and had caught just one season in the Florida State League, so you can imagine how scared and excited and delighted I was to play with big leaguers.

"Great," I said. "Who's pitching?"

"Walter Johnson," they said.

"Walter Johnson!" I asked. This was a little more than I expected.

"Do you think you can catch him?"

"I don't know," I said. "But I'll try."

So they advertised it: Walter Johnson pitching. Al Lopez catching. I thought that was pretty funny, me being an equal drawing card with Walter Johnson. But they figured it would attract a lot of people from over in Ybor City, where I lived.

Johnson was very nice. Just before we went out to warm up, he came over to me and said, "Look, I'm not going to really let out. I'm going to bear down on just two fellows—Ike Boone and Jack Fournier. They hit me pretty good, so I'm going to bear down on them. You be ready when they come up."

He bore down on them all right. He pitched just five innings that day, so he faced those guys twice each and he struck them out twice each. Johnson must have been around thirty-eight years old then, but still a great pitcher. He could still fire it when he wanted to. And you know, he was easy to catch. You could follow his ball, and he was always around the plate. After it was over, he told somebody, "That boy did real well back there. Handled himself fine." You can bet that made me feel good.

The Dodgers bought my contract and brought me up from Macon, Georgia, at the end of the year in '28. I sat around on the bench the last few weeks, not doing anything until the last weekend of the season. We were playing the Pirates and all of a sudden Wilbert Robinson put me in to catch. I found out later the reason I caught was because Burleigh Grimes was pitching against us that day and none of the other catchers liked to hit against him. Burleigh was kind of mean.

I caught that day and went 0 for 4. The next day we had a doubleheader and Robbie let me catch both ends. This is when the Pirates had Pie Traynor and Glenn Wright on the left side of their infield. Well, I was strictly a pull hitter and I hit some good hard shots to the left side. I'd take off for first figuring I had myself a hit, but each time to my astonishment I saw that peg zinging into the first baseman's glove. I knew, I just *knew,* that at Macon those would have been hits. It was practically impossible to hit a ball past Traynor or Wright. I was 0 for 8 in that doubleheader and went home that fall wondering what a fellow had to do to get a base hit in the big leagues.

Wilbert Robinson—we all called him Uncle Robbie—was a fine man, very easygoing. It really hurt his feelings if one of his players disliked him. He tried to have everybody's good-will. I think that's the reason he traded away Grimes; he and Burleigh didn't see eye to eye all the time. Dazzy Vance was one of his pets. Robbie liked big strong pitchers who could throw hard, and Vance was just that. Dazzy also had one of the finest curveballs I ever saw.

Dolf Luque was there too. He was a real old-timer when I joined the club. To me he was a real pitcher; by that I mean he was a craftsman out there. He could spot that ball anywhere he wanted. He was strictly overhand, with a curve that broke straight down—they called it a drop. He could pitch to left-handed hitters better than he could to righties by throwing them that curve. Catching him was a real education. I learned an awful lot about pitching to hitters from catching Luque.

Babe Herman was another one of Robbie's favorites. Babe was a great hitter, one of the best I ever saw. I roomed with him a couple of years, and the funny thing is I had good years with the bat then. Maybe it rubbed off. You know, he had the reputation for being clumsy in the field, but the truth is he became a good outfielder. He was a fine ballplayer for the Dodgers. One year he hit .393—and didn't lead the league. That was 1930, which was probably the biggest hitting year the league ever had. I believe the National League as a whole averaged over .300 in 1930. It was a good ball to hit that year, very lively.

They changed the ball after 1930. I think McGraw complained about it, and McGraw had a lot to say about things then. When he said something, they listened. The Giants were the powerhouse of the National League, and probably of base-ball, when it came to influencing things.

I can remember one game very distinctly. The Giants had a pitcher by the name of Roy Parmelee, a wild, hard-throwing right-hander. He was pitching against us this day in the Polo Grounds, the bases were loaded, and Glenn Wright was up—he was with the Dodgers now. Parmelee threw him a fastball; his fastball had a natural sliderlike break to it. Glenn started to swing, saw the pitch breaking away, and kind of half threw his bat at the ball, almost one-handed. He got out in front of it and hit it down the left-field line. Remember the Polo Grounds, how short it was down the lines? Well, Glenn hit it just hard enough for the ball to drop in for a grand-slam home run. We could see McGraw throw up his hands in the dugout, and, we heard later, he said, "What kind of baseball is this?" I think he made up his mind right then and there that the ball was too lively and that something had to be done. The way I understand it, that was the beginning of softening the ball up a bit.

McGraw was tough as nails on the field. He wouldn't tolerate mistakes, whereas Robbie would. You could get away with mistakes with Robbie. But McGraw made a fine impression on me as a manager. I didn't know the man personally, but when you played against his team, you knew you were playing against one of the best. They weren't going to make too many mistakes. There was something about them that made you know they were in good shape to play baseball, especially in the spring. I heard that he really drove them in the spring because he wanted to get off to a good start. Another thing, when they threw the ball around during infield practice, they really fired it; that's the way he wanted them to do it. When you watched that Giant team on the field, you could always feel McGraw's hand everywhere. He was all business on a ball field, and so were they. There was never any clowning on that club, not even around the batting cage. With every other team the guys would get around the batting cage and there would be a lot of kidding, but not with the Giants.

What you saw with the Giants was discipline. That was the way McGraw worked. In those days a ball game started at three o'clock in the afternoon. Well, McGraw insisted his players be in the clubhouse by ten o'clock in the morning, and if they weren't there on time, they'd be in trouble. No, there's no way a manager could run his team like that today—there'd be a revolution.

But with all his strictness, McGraw had the respect of his players. You can get away with all the strict discipline if your players respect you. And I think that's the main thing in managing. That's all I ever wanted when I was managing. It's not too difficult to earn their respect. All you have to do is treat them the way you wanted to be treated when you were a player. I understood that a man was going to make a mistake, and as long as he didn't do it over and over again, I'd go along with him. You don't want to be rough on players who are trying their best.

Bill Veeck once said that if I had a weakness as a manager, it was that I was too decent. Well, I never took that as a negative comment. In fact, it was nice to hear that said. I'd like to think I'm a decent guy. Nothing wrong with that, is there?

A ball club can reflect the manager's personality. McGraw was businesslike and efficient, and so were his ball clubs. Uncle Robbie was easygoing, and so were his clubs. Of course, they weren't the "Daffy Dodgers" any longer when I got there, but some of those guys could still be pretty tricky. One day I had an argument with Bill Klem over a close play. We had a good go at it, and that was that. The next day there was a picture in the paper of that play, and it showed Klem was wrong. One of the guys—I think it was Mungo—cut the picture out, taped it over home plate, and then covered it with dirt. I didn't know anything about it.

Just before the first pitch was thrown, Klem went around to clean off the plate. I was crouched there watching him. He bent down and started whisking his little brush back and forth. He uncovered a corner of the picture, turned his head, and gave me a dirty look. Then he went on brushing, his hand moving slower and slower, his face getting redder and redder. Little by little he cleared off the whole picture. I tried not to laugh because I could see how sore he was. He thought I had done it and, boy, was he burned up! "You dumb busher," he said. "I didn't do it, Bill," I said. But I don't think he even heard me because he just kept chewing me out.

Klem, by the way, was a great umpire. The best I ever saw.

You know, when you're managing a ball club, you're constantly being interviewed. The writers are always around looking for a story. Well, you've got to be darned careful not to say anything that's going to offend anybody. Remember that crack Bill Terry made when he was managing the Giants: "Is Brooklyn still in the league?" Well, that was just a flip remark made on the spur of the moment in spring training. But I think he probably was sorry later on that he ever said it.

You see, we came down to the last two games of the season playing the Giants at the Polo Grounds. This was 1934. The Giants were tied for first place with the Cardinals. We were going nowhere. We were down in sixth place, I think. Now, that remark of Terry's had never bothered the Dodger players any, but it seemed to have rankled the fans. They took it up and made a big thing of it. I think there must have been more

Dodger fans than Giant fans in the Polo Grounds at those two games. They were running up and down the aisles waving banners and yelling and really cheering us on.

We were up for those games. Van Lingle Mungo beat them the first game, and the next day we came from behind to beat them again. That knocked the Giants right out of the pennant. You can imagine what went on there. You should have heard those fans. It couldn't have been any wilder out there if we had won the pennant ourselves, but I guess knocking the Giants out of it was just as sweet to the Dodger fans. You can't believe how bitter that Dodger-Giant rivalry used to be. You don't have anything these days to compare to it.

Stengel was managing the Dodgers at that time. He told me something afterwards about that last day. After we'd beaten the Giants, he was going to go to their clubhouse and tell Terry how sorry he was that they'd lost out. But then he thought better of it, figuring that Terry was probably feeling pretty lousy about things. The Giants had led most of the season, you see. So Stengel went on home. Then at the winter meetings he met Terry. "You know, Bill," he said, "I was going to come in after that last game and pay my respects." Stengel said Terry was still burning from what had happened, and Bill scowled at him and said, "Well, it's a goddamn good thing you didn't. You would have been thrown out on your ass."

I don't know if Terry's wisecrack had anything to do with the way we played those last two games, but when everything was over, it made him look bad. I'll tell you, I learned my own lesson soon after I joined the Dodgers. A writer came to me one day and asked me which pitchers I liked to hit against. "Listen," I said, "they're all tough." That's what you're supposed to say, right? But I wanted to be a nice guy and give him some kind of answer, so I went on and added, "But I've had pretty good luck with Bill Walker." Bill Walker was a left-hander with the Giants, and a good one. Anyway, that's what I said. But it came out in the paper that I said Walker was easy for me to hit. You can imagine what he thought when he read that. I had a devil of a time with him after that. He really bore down against me, pushed me back, knocked me down. I didn't blame him. All he knew was what he'd read in the paper. But I'd never said what was attributed to me.

*   *   *

I used to warn my players not to antagonize anybody unnecessarily, especially the cellar clubs. Don't wake them up. Be nice to them, joke with them, get them relaxed—and then go out and beat their brains out. In a nice way.

Durocher seemed to want to do the opposite. He'd stir you up. I remember one time when I was with the Pirates and Durocher was managing the Dodgers, he got into an argument with Vince DiMaggio. Leo yelled something over from the Dodgers' dugout, and it got Vince angry. Vince had a short fuse anyway. Next time up, he popped out, and that made him angrier. They spent the rest of the game yelling back and forth at each other.

In the ninth inning we're one run behind. This was in 1941, and the Dodgers were fighting for the pennant. Every game means something to them. Anyway, DiMaggio comes up in the ninth with one out and doubles off of Hugh Casey. Somebody hits a ground ball to second and Vince moves over to third. That made two out and I'm the hitter. Now, Casey had a way of going down to the ground in his windup and then coming up. Just as he goes down for his windup, DiMaggio makes a tear for the plate, as if he's going to steal home. He came so far down the line I actually thought for a moment he was coming all the way, but then he stopped. He must have distracted Casey because Hugh hesitated for just a fraction in his motion—I thought he did anyway so I jumped out of the batter's box and yelled "Balk!" Then the umpire, big George Magerkurth, ripped off his mask and yelled "Balk!" He saw it the same way I did. So DiMaggio is waved in and scores the tying run.

Well, you should have seen the commotion. Leo led a charge of Dodgers out to Magerkurth, and they went at it. Finally Leo got kicked out and play resumed. I'm still up at the plate and Casey is out there boiling. The first pitch is right at my head. Second pitch, same thing. I'm ducking, and so is Magerkurth. Finally Mage says to me, "Hey, Lopez. Is he throwing at you or is he throwing at me?"

"I don't know," I said, "and let's not try and find out—he's mad enough as it is."

"The hell with this," Mage says. "I want to know." And out he goes to talk to Casey. Well, when that happens, here comes

Leo again—he must've been hiding in the runway behind the dugout—along with Charlie Dressen, Fred Fitzsimmons, and some others. They go at it again. Magerkurth finally clears them off, throwing Leo out again.

So I step in again and look at Casey. He's got murder in his eyes. He throws two more at me. The fourth ball almost took my head off. I go down to first base. The next hitter is a fellow named Alf Anderson. Alf isn't too much with the stick, but don't you think he hits the first pitch just fair down the right-field line? I start running as hard as I can, while Dixie Walker is chasing the ball down in right field. The ball hugs the line all the way, and I score from first base—and that's the ball game.

The moment I crossed the plate, Leo comes running back onto the field and follows Magerkurth all the way to the umpires' dressing room, jawing away at him. I understand he tried to break down the door there, which is not such a good idea since those doors are heavy and the fines for trying to break them down are even heavier.

But what hurt the Dodgers most was Leo getting on Vince DiMaggio. He should have left Vince alone. Instead he got him so worked up that Vince provoked Casey into balking, which got Casey so provoked he couldn't pitch to me. It ended up costing them the ball game. So when you hear somebody say "Let sleeping dogs lie," you'd better believe there's a lot of good sense to it.

Stengel was a great guy and a fine manager. He loved to teach. He would get a young fellow and sit with him by the hour and talk to him about baseball. I think he tried to pattern himself after McGraw in many ways. Of course, he was a different personality from McGraw, though he could eat you out on the bench if he had to. The difference between them was that a little while later he'd be kidding with you, which I don't think McGraw would ever have done.

My path and Casey's kept crossing in baseball. I was traded three times during my career and two of those times by Casey. In the winter of 1935 I came up to New York on some business. I was having drinks in my room at the St. George Hotel with some friends when Casey came by. This was about three o'clock in the afternoon. Casey was such an interesting talker that the next thing we knew it was about nine o'clock, and we hadn't had our dinner yet. I suggested we go out and get something to eat. I invited Casey to come along, and he said he'd join us on one condition—that we let him pick up the check. We argued back and forth, but he was insistent. So we went across the street to a restaurant, ate dinner, listened to him talk some more, and then went back upstairs to my room. At two o'clock in the morning we were still talking. Finally my friends left, and Casey sat around to have one more drink. He became quiet for a few minutes, and I could see he had something on his mind.

"Dammit, Al," he said all of a sudden, "I'm going to have to make a trade. It's either you or Mungo, and I'd like to keep Mungo because he's younger and because he brings people into the park."

I could see it was bothering him. I guess it had been on his mind the whole time, and he had been sitting all afternoon and all night figuring out how to tell me.

"Casey," I said, "don't feel bad. If you think you can make a good deal, go ahead and make it."

"Okay," he said. "But if I trade you, it's going to be to a good club, a contender."

Soon after I got back to Tampa, I heard about the trade. Casey's intentions about sending me to a contender were well meant, I'm sure, but he ended up trading me to Boston, who the year before had set the league record by losing 115 games. Then a few years later he comes over to manage Boston and trades me to Pittsburgh.

I was a teammate of Al Simmons' at Boston in 1939. Here was one of the greatest right-handed hitters who ever lived, but on the decline now. Something happened that year that I'll never forget. The Braves had acquired Eddie Miller from the Yankees to play shortstop. For the Braves, who didn't have much money, it was a pretty big deal. They laid out some cash and gave up about four or five ballplayers for Eddie. And he was worth it, too. He was a good ballplayer.

One day there was a fly ball hit into short left, and Miller and Simmons went for it. It was one of those situations where you just want to close your eyes because you can see the collision coming, and there's not a thing you can do about it.

They ran into each other with a smack and went tumbling to the grass.

Everybody went running out there to see how Miller was. He was the bright young ballplayer, the one they had the investment in. Hardly anybody paid any attention to Simmons. Well, Miller was all right, but Simmons had a hairline fracture above his ankle, and was out for quite a while. One day he came into the clubhouse and sat down next to me. He had a wistful little smile.

"You know something, Al?" he said. "Ten years ago, when I was playing for Mr. Mack, if that collision had happened, they would have sent a goddamned kid shortstop nine hundred miles from Philadelphia for running into me."

I'll never forget him saying that.

In 1946, after the Pirates let Frankie Frisch go, a Pittsburgh newspaper took a poll to see who the fans wanted to manage the club. It turned out that I was their choice. But the new owners, Frank McKinney and his associates, wanted Billy Herman. That was fine with me. I thought Billy was a great guy and would be a good manager. But at the same time it left me in kind of an uncomfortable position. I knew that sooner or later we'd have a few bad games and the fans would start yelling "We want Lopez." I didn't want that to happen, so I went to the front office, explained how I felt, and asked to be traded. They sent me to Cleveland. I played there in '47, which was my last active year in the big leagues. I was thirty-nine years old then.

After the season in '47 Bill Veeck, who owned the Indians, and Lou Boudreau got into some kind of a hassle. I forget what it was about, but there was a story in the paper saying that Boudreau might not be back to manage in '48. At the same time I was in New York for the World Series and was also shopping around for a job as a coach or a minor league manager. I got a call from Veeck. We were both at the New Yorker hotel, and he wanted to see me. So I went up to his room.

"You get a job yet?" he asked me.

I told him that I had a few feelers out and that things looked promising.

"Look," he said, "don't do anything until I get back. I'm

going to Chicago to talk to Boudreau. If things don't pan out, you might have the job."

"Bill," I said, "I don't want the job. I was there one year as a player, and I don't want people thinking I was after the job, that I might have been undermining Boudreau."

I told him I'd prefer going out somewhere to manage, to get that experience, and then if later on he still wanted me, I'd be glad to work for him. So he went to Chicago and straightened things out with Boudreau, and I wound up in Indianapolis, where I managed for three years. Eventually I did get up to manage the Indians, but it wasn't until 1951.

That's when I began chasing the New York Yankees. I spent year after year chasing them. I finished second to the Yankees nine times. I did manage to beat them out a couple of times, in 1954 with Cleveland and again in 1959 with the White Sox. Those were the only years between 1949 and 1964 that the Yankees didn't win the pennant. In '52 we finished two games out of first place. The frustrating thing about that was we won something like 18 of our last 21 games, and the Yankees did the same thing. We just couldn't gain an inch on them.

A manager has to adapt his style to what material he's got. There's no other way to do it. In 1954 with Cleveland I didn't have too much speed on the club—we only stole around 30 bases—but we did have guys who could hit the ball out of the park, like Vic Wertz, Al Rosen, and Larry Doby. So our game was to hold the other side with our good pitching and wait for somebody to sock one out.

Now, my other pennant winner, the White Sox, was set up differently. Outside of Sherman Lollar we didn't have any really serious long-ball threats. It was a Punch and Judy team, with fellows like Luis Aparicio, Nellie Fox, Jim Landis, and Billy Goodman. But you see a guy like Aparicio, how well he can run the bases, and you turn him loose. Just give him the go sign. His percentage of steals was over 90 percent that year, so it's hardly a profound tactical move to put a fellow like that on his own.

Letting Aparicio try to steal meant we didn't have to hit-and-run with Nellie Fox, who was behind him in the lineup. The hit-and-run is more of a defensive play than an offensive one, you see. You use it to keep out of the double play. And you have to hit at whatever the pitcher throws, his pitch rather than yours. So why should you have to handicap Nellie Fox, who's a .300 hitter, by hitting-and-running with him when you can get Aparicio to steal second base? You don't have to be much of a genius to dope that out.

I never believed in having one particular pattern for my pitchers to follow. The old wisdom used to be pitch high inside and low outside. Today I think they concentrate mostly on pitching low. They claim it's harder to hit the low ball for distance, but I don't think so. If you're a low-ball hitter, you're going to hit it. And suppose your best stuff is high? If you're a high-ball pitcher with a riding fastball, I think you should pitch high, no matter who's up there. It's your strength against his.

When I managed Cleveland, I thought I had the best-balanced pitching staff ever in baseball, with Bob Lemon, Early Wynn, Mike Garcia, Bob Feller, and Art Houtteman for starters, plus Don Mossi and Ray Narleski in the bull pen. Well, when we held a meeting to go over the hitters, you found out there was no one way to pitch a man because everybody was a different type of pitcher. Wynn was a high-ball pitcher. Lemon threw a sinker and kept it low. Garcia was just overpowering, and he tried to pitch the right-handed hitters tight all the time because his ball bore into them. Houtteman pitched a little bit like Lemon. Feller no longer had the great speed, so he'd throw them curves and sliders in tight. They were entirely different pitchers, so I left them on their own.

I played for many managers and of course you learn a little from each one. I think I learned more about pitching from Bill McKechnie than from anybody else. He liked to keep his pitchers in rotation, no matter what. I tried to do that when I managed. Of course you plan ahead and set them up. I always wanted to have Lemon, Wynn, and Garcia ready for the Yankees because that was the club you had to beat if you were going to go anywhere. And Stengel was sure to shoot Raschi, Reynolds, Lopat, and Ford at us.

In 1954, when I was managing Cleveland, we finally caught the Yankees. It wasn't easy because they won 103 games. But we won 111, which is still the American League record. Then we went into the Series against the Giants and didn't win a game. We just got cold, that's all, and the Giants played great ball. They made the plays. Remember that ball Vic Wertz hit with the bases loaded at the Polo Grounds that Mays made the great catch on? Heck, that would have been a home run just about anyplace else. And nobody gives their third baseman, Henry Thompson, much credit, but he made some of the greatest plays I ever saw. And Dusty Rhodes got those big pinch hits.

They say anything can happen in a short series. Well, I knew that. I just never thought it was going to be *that* short.

ROGER PECKINPAUGH

ROGER THORPE PECKINPAUGH
Born: February 5, 1891, Wooster, Ohio; Died: November 17, 1977
Managerial career: New York Yankees, 1914; Cleveland Indians, 1928–33, 1941.

Managing the New York Yankees for 17 games in 1914 at the age of twenty-three made Roger Peckinpaugh the youngest manager in major league history. After a long and distinguished playing career with the Yankees, Cleveland Indians, Washington Senators, and Chicago White Sox, Peckinpaugh returned to managing.

When I was a kid growing up on Hough Avenue in Cleveland, I lived right across the street from Napoleon Lajoie. I used to sit out in front of my house just to watch him come home. He was my idol. I might even have become an infielder because he was, though he was a second baseman and I was a shortstop.

Sure I played ball when I was a kid. There were a lot of vacant lots around in those days, and that's all you need to produce ballplayers. We had a gang of kids, and we'd play every day after school and keep playing until either it got dark or we'd lost the ball. It wasn't a real ball either, just a lot of stuffings that we bound together and wrapped tape over.

When I got further along, I played on the semipro teams. One day a scout from the Cleveland ball club came over during a game and asked me if I'd like to sign up to play professional ball. I wanted to play, all right, but wasn't too sure what I should do. You see, in those days professional ballplayers didn't have very good reputations; people thought they just hung around barrooms all the time and played baseball as an excuse for not working.

So I talked it over with my old high school principal, and he said he didn't see anything wrong with the idea if I could make good in three years. He said I shouldn't spend more than three years in the minor leagues. Well, I made it to the top in two years.

That was in 1909. In 1910 I was playing with the Indians. Can you believe that? I played the last fifteen games or so after having been farmed out to New Haven. New Haven's season closed Labor Day, and that's when the Indians brought me up to finish the season. I'll say it was a thrill. But the biggest thrill was playing alongside Nap Lajoie, my boyhood idol.

Lajoie was one of the greatest. Fine fellow, too. Big, good-hearted Frenchman. During the game sometimes I couldn't help but glance over at him from shortstop, just like I was still a kid sitting up in the stands—that same kind of feeling. He was a graceful fielder, could pick up anything, and of course the glove that he wore—the gloves that we all wore back then—was little more than the glove you wear today when you're driving a car. He was a line-drive hitter; he'd send that ball all over the lot like rifle shots.

Addie Joss was on that team too. It was his last year. He died the next spring; I think he was around thirty years old. He was a great pitcher, that fellow. He would turn his back toward the batter as he wound up, hiding the ball all the while, and then whip around and fire it in. He threw the good fastball and the good curve. Very tough to hit.

I never batted against Joss, but I did against Smoky Joe Wood, Walter Johnson, and Lefty Grove, and I managed Bob Feller in his heyday. Who was the fastest? That's the million-dollar question, isn't it? I would say Walter Johnson. Now Bobby was fast all right, but he had that great big curveball to go along with it. Walter only threw a fastball. No curve to speak of. When he threw his curve, he'd come up over his head with it and everybody in the ball park knew what was coming—otherwise he always fired that thing in sidearm. But he was fast—just pure speed—and that ball was alive. I'll tell you another thing about his ball—you could hear it go by you with a *swish!* I never heard that from anybody else. And you know, my first game in the major leagues was against Washington, and Walter was pitching. He was the guy I broke in against. Can you imagine that! A year before I was in high school, and now here's Walter Johnson staring down at me. I fouled out twice and was tickled to death for it.

Joe Jackson was on that Cleveland team too. He was a great hitter, one of the best I ever saw in my life. He used a big black bat and swung it right from the end, and he could hit a ball further than anybody, until the Babe came along.

Jackson couldn't read or write, you know. He was a big, likable country boy from South Carolina. We'd go in for breakfast and the waitress would hand him a menu. Well, he knew they always had ham and eggs and that's what he would order. But we'd go in for dinner and if the waitress went to him first for his order, he'd say, "I haven't made up my mind yet. See what they want." Then he'd listen to what the rest of us were ordering and he'd pick out something we said. That's how he got by in the dining room.

It was a pity what happened to him, getting mixed up in that World Series scandal. That was in 1919. You know, in 1920, when I was with the Yankees, we finished three games out of first place, and I'll never know whether we should have won it or not. The White Sox—they call that team the Black Sox today, don't they?—were monkeying around so much during the year you could never be sure. The scandal didn't come full bloom until near the end of the season. We'd play them one series and they would look terrible; we'd play them the next time and they'd look like the best club in the world. That's the way they set themselves up that year.

I remember one time we went into Chicago and little Nemo Leibold came up to me. He was on the White Sox but wasn't part of the shenanigans, but he smelled a mouse.

"Listen," he said, "something screwy is going on here. I don't know what it is, but it's something screwy all right. You guys bear down and you ought to take all four games."

You just never knew when they were going to go out there and beat your brains out or roll over and play dead. Somebody was betting on those games, that's a cinch. When they wanted to play, you had a hard time beating them, that's how good they were.

Eight of them were kicked out of baseball. Let's see, there

was Happy Felsch, Buck Weaver, Chick Gandil, Joe Jackson, Eddie Cicotte, Swede Risberg, Fred McMullin, and Lefty Williams. I knew them all. Gee, I haven't thought of them for a long time. They're all dead now, I believe. That Happy Felsch was a hell of a ballplayer. And Eddie Cicotte was some pitcher. He had one of those phony pitches, a shine ball.

You know, when they barred the spitball, it wasn't the spitball exactly they wanted to bar. They wanted to get rid of all those phony pitches. All of those pitches were in the disguise of the spitter. You see, the pitchers went to their mouths, but then they might throw you a shine ball or a mud ball or an emery ball. Russell Ford, the old Yankee pitcher, was the originator of the emery ball. His own teammates didn't know what he was throwing. They thought it was a spitter. But it was an emery ball. He'd rough up the cover and get it to sail. He had a hole in his glove and under it was a piece of emery paper. Then he wore a ring on his finger with a piece of emery paper wrapped around it. The ring was on a rubber band, and when he pulled it off, it went up his sleeve. Nobody knew what he'd been doing until he went out of the league, and then his catcher, big Ed Sweeney, told us. Sweeney was the only one who'd known.

So, as I understand it, the only way they could stop them fooling with that baseball was to bar the spitter, not let the pitcher go to his mouth. If a pitcher didn't go to his mouth and still threw one of those freak pitches, the umpire would know damn well that guy was doctoring the ball. That's how they stopped it.

You know, when I first came to the big leagues they never threw a ball out of the game. It could be black as ink and the cover could be soft, but they still kept it in. The only time a ball went out of play was when it was fouled into the stands. Many a time if I was leading off an inning and there was a ball that had been in the game two or three innings, it was my job to try and foul it into the stands to get rid of it. Today, if there's a spot on the ball, they holler and throw it right out.

Cobb was the greatest of all, in my book. In addition to everything else, he was a smart ballplayer. He never had one spot where he stood in the batter's box. He stood in different places for different pitchers, according to what they had and how they pitched him. I never saw another hitter do that. They have one spot and that's it. I'll tell you, they never threw at Cobb very much. If they did, he'd step out and warn them. "Don't do that again," he'd say. And if they did, he would drag a bunt down to first, and if the pitcher covered, Ty would knock him for a loop. So they seldom threw at him. He was a tough monkey, that guy. A real tough monkey. He played a slashing game out there. You could be behind ten runs, and he'd still come into second base and bat you around.

Nobody liked Cobb, including his own teammates. He was sort of a loner. Didn't get along with anybody. And I can tell you how deep those feelings went. We were in New York for an old-timers game once. A group of us were sitting around a table. Cobb wanted to buy the boys a drink, but they wouldn't take one from him.

I can tell you another story about how people felt about Cobb. This happened in 1910, my first year up. We were finishing out the season with a doubleheader in St. Louis. The Chalmers automobile people were giving away a car to the leading hitter in the league. Cobb and Nap Lajoie had been battling for the title all year. On the last day Cobb was hitting .385 and Lajoie was seven or eight points behind him. Cobb took himself out of the lineup that last day, so it meant Nap had to get something like eight hits in the doubleheader to catch him and win that car.

Here's how much they disliked Cobb: The manager of the Browns, Jack O'Connor, told his third baseman to play way back on the grass for Lajoie. The first time up Nap socked a triple, but after that he noticed where the third baseman was playing him. So he began dropping down bunts and beating them out. He went four for four in the first game. We all knew what was going on, but it was none of our business. Lajoie didn't say anything. If they wanted to give him base hits, he would take them.

The second game was the same thing—Nap got four for four again and I think three of them were bunts. He went eight for eight in the doubleheader and everybody figured he'd won the title. But when it was all over and the statistics came out, he was still a fraction of a point behind Cobb. When word got around what had happened, Ban Johnson, who was president of the American League, saw to it that Jack O'Connor lost his job.

In 1913 they traded me to the Yankees. You see, they had Ray Chapman coming along, and he had a tremendous amount of promise. And of course he turned out to be a wonderful ballplayer. You know, I was at shortstop for the Yankees when Ray got hit in the head with a pitched ball and was killed. That was in 1920. Carl Mays was the pitcher, and I'd say that pitch was almost a strike. Chapman crowded the plate more than anybody in the league; in fact he hit with his head practically in the strike zone. What happened was at the last second he turned his head and got hit right in back of the ear. The ball hit so solidly that it went out toward third base in fair ground, and Mays fielded it and threw it to first base—he couldn't tell from the sound whether it had hit the bat or not. That's how hard Chapman got smacked.

I managed the Yankees the last few weeks of the season in 1914. I was only twenty-three years old then, so I guess I'm the youngest man ever to manage a big league club. Sometimes I look at some of these twenty-three-year-old kids today, and I have to laugh and think to myself, "Gee, when I was that age, I was managing the New York Yankees."

Frank Chance was the manager; he'd had a hassle with the owners and quit. He came to me and said, "I've recommended they put you in charge of the club the rest of the season." They went along with Frank's recommendation and I ran the club for those few weeks, got my first experience managing, and picked up a few extra bucks in the bargain.

Frank was a good manager and got along okay with the players. He'd managed the Cubs earlier and had some great years there, winning a few pennants. They had some wonderful ball clubs in Chicago. Tinker to Evers to Chance. Three-Finger Brown. Johnny Kling. I don't recall if Frank talked about those teams very much. It's getting to be a long while back. That's sixty years ago!

Of course, the Yankees at that time were what we used to call a joy club. Lots of joy and lots of losing. Nobody thought we could win and most of the time we didn't. But it didn't seem to bother the boys too much. They would start singing songs in the infield right in the middle of a game. There wasn't much managing to do outside of selecting the starting pitcher and hoping we didn't get beat too badly.

I don't think there was a great deal of difference in the game then as compared to today. The home run is the biggest difference, I'd say. Today pretty near anybody in the lineup can hit the ball out of the park. In my day, before they started feeding that baseball Wheaties, you had two or three fellows who could do that, and that was all.

I think today the manager has a little tougher job than when I was there because, I would guess, at least, a third of the players that are in the major leagues today should not be there. They should still be playing minor league ball. But the scarcity of players makes it necessary to bring these kids up when they show signs of anything at all. Watching them out there now and then, I see them making a lot of mistakes that they should be making in the minor leagues. You see, back when I was playing and managing, there were only sixteen big league clubs and barely enough players to fill a roster. Today you've got twenty-four clubs. Where are you going to get that many players from? So I would say a manager today has a lot more on his hands because he has so many inexperienced players.

When I broke in, a rookie had a hard time of it. You didn't get much cooperation from anybody because they didn't want you coming along and taking their jobs. That's the way it was most of the time. Anyway, they only had one coach on a club, and he generally had enough to do without bothering with a rookie. They had only one umpire, too. He worked in back of the plate until a man got on first, then he went in back of the pitcher and called balls and strikes from there. Even so, he couldn't watch everything. There was a lot of cheating in a ball game then; the smart runners were chopping off three or four feet when they went around second base on their way to third.

Hal Chase was first baseman when I joined the Yankees. Prince Hal. He later was suspected of betting on games. I was just a kid breaking in, and Hal Chase had the reputation of being the greatest fielding first baseman of all time. I remember a few times I threw a ball over to first base, and it went by him to the stands and a couple of runs scored. It really surprised me. I'd stand there looking, sighting the flight of that ball in my mind, and I'd think, "Geez, that throw wasn't that bad." Then I'd tell myself that he was the greatest there was, so maybe the throw was bad. Then later on when he got the smelly reputation, it came back to me, and I said, "Oh-oh." What he was doing, you see, was tangling up his feet and then making a fancy dive after the ball, making it look like it was a wild throw.

I don't know if anybody suspected anything at the time, but I do know they got rid of him later in the season.

Ballplayers weren't the celebrities then that they came to be later on, with a few exceptions of course, like Cobb and Walter Johnson. But the Babe changed that. He changed everything, that guy. So many, many people became interested in baseball because of him. Why, they would be drawing 1,500 a game in St. Louis. We'd go in there with the Babe and they'd be all over the ball park; there would be mounted policemen riding the crowd back. Thousands and thousands of people coming out to see that one guy. Whatever the owners paid him, it wasn't enough—it couldn't be enough.

Miller Huggins took over the Yankees in 1918, and then they got Ruth from Boston and the Yankees began to move. Huggins was a fine manager, one of the best I ever played for. He understood men, and he got along all right with everybody but the Babe. Babe was going to throw him off the train one night coming back from Boston. Huggins hadn't handled the pitching the way Mr. Ruth thought it should have been handled. So Babe had a few drinks and then went looking for Hug with the intention of throwing him off the train. He meant it, too. He was storming around looking for Hug. Finally three of us wrestled him down to the floor and held him there until he simmered down.

I had two very good years with the Yankees in 1920 and '21, but after the '21 season I was traded to Washington. I can tell you just how that happened to come about. Babe and Huggins were feuding all the time, and then Babe started openly announcing that they should get rid of Huggins and appoint me manager. Well, it turned out just the opposite—they got rid of me and kept Huggins. Babe thought he was doing me a favor, I guess, but it didn't work out that way.

I'll tell you what upset me about that trade. I was home

trimming the Christmas tree when the phone rang. I picked it up and there was a reporter on the other end of the line.

"Hey," he said, "what do you think of the trade?"

"What trade do you mean?" I asked.

"Oh," he said, "didn't you hear? You've been traded to Boston."

It was a three-way deal, you see. I went from New York to Boston to Washington in one big swap. But that's the way I learned about it—from a reporter calling me up.

Bucky Harris took over the Washington club in 1924, and we won two pennants under Bucky, in '24 and '25. He was a tough, aggressive ballplayer, but I wouldn't call him a hard-driving manager. As far as I'm concerned, that kind of manager seldom made good. You take Rogers Hornsby. He was made manager of the Cardinals. So what does he do? He makes rules for the clubhouse that nobody likes. You had to check in by the clock. No smoking in the clubhouse, no eating, no card-playing. The players were unhappy, which is the last thing you want. I don't say you should cater to them, but for heaven's sake, you don't want to antagonize them.

I've often said that a bad manager can ruin a good ball club. But you put an ordinary manager in charge of a good club and they're going to win. Don't saddle them with too many rules; don't make them unhappy. That's the secret. Managing might make the difference of one or two games over the whole season. The third-base coach probably has more to say about winning or losing a ball game than the manager. He's the one who's got to send those runners in, or not send them. His judgment can be crucial.

People talk about a good manager. Well, what's a good manager? It's somebody who can get the most out of his players. Strategy? There's nothing mysterious about that, is there? Geez, don't I know what you're going to do, and don't you know what I'm going to do? I'm talking about most of the time. Give a manager those old Yankee teams like McCarthy and Stengel had, and it's hard for him to make a mistake. The ability is all there. The players can do practically anything the manager asks them to do. It's got to turn out right. All you have to remember is not to do anything to make them hate your guts.

We won the Series against the Giants in '24, then lost it the next year to Pittsburgh. That was the Series where Sam Rice made his great catch on a ball hit by Earl Smith. Boy, I'll never forget that one. Sam dove into the bleachers for the ball, just left his feet and disappeared with the ball in his glove, and when he came out, he still had it. There was a loud argument about it, the Pirates claiming he'd lost the ball in the bleachers and then picked it up again. That controversy went on for a long time. Then just before Sam died, he said he'd written a letter to be opened after his death which would tell the truth about that catch. Well, after he died, that letter was opened and in it Sam said that it had been a fair catch all the way. Under those circumstances, a man talking practically from his deathbed, you've got to believe him. I'll tell you, it was a whale of a catch.

Did I ever want to become a big league manager? Well, I hadn't thought about it too much, to tell you the truth. I was finishing out my playing career with the White Sox in 1927, which was around the time the Cleveland ball club was purchased by Alva Bradley and his associates. He hired Billy Evans as the general manager and me as field manager. I was from Cleveland and so was Billy, which made it nice.

I took over in 1928. Managing was all new to me, of course, but I'd had seventeen years' experience under some pretty good managers and had an idea of what it was all about.

That first year I was there Billy Evans made a trip out to the Coast League to look at an outfielder named Roy Johnson. When Billy got there, he learned that Johnson had already been sold to Detroit. But in talking with the players out there, he kept hearing that the best ballplayer in the league was a fellow named Earl Averill. So he wound up buying Averill, who became one of the all-time Cleveland greats. Then we got Dick Porter, and we had Eddie Morgan and Johnny Hodapp and Joe and Luke Sewell. We had plenty of hitting but were a little shy on the good pitching. We did have Mel Harder and Willis Hudlin and Wes Ferrell, but it wasn't enough. Wes was one of the best but very temperamental. He'd get mad at himself if anybody got a base hit off of him, and if they got two in a row, he was liable to fly right off the top.

But it was a tough time to be in that league. We were up

against two great ball clubs. On the one hand you had Connie Mack's Athletics, with Foxx, Simmons, Grove, Cochrane. And on the other hand there were the Yankees, with Ruth, Gehrig, Lazzeri, Dickey, Combs, and those fellows. It was discouraging. You knew you were doomed the day the season opened, with those two monsters in the league.

I was let out of the job in the middle of the season in 1933. I got in Dutch with the newspapers, which is very easy to do if you don't keep your mouth shut. Some of the Cleveland writers got on me and just rode me unmercifully. I remember a story Ed Bang had. We got beat 1–0 one day. The next day Bang had a big story about the game. The other team had got a man on and they bunted him down and that led to the winning run. Apparently somewhere along the line I'd had a man on, and Bang thought I should have bunted him down. So he wrote that the other manager was not afraid to have his men sacrifice, and then he went on to give me hell.

I went up to the team office and checked the records, just for the hell of it. Well, I found out that the Cleveland club was leading the league by far in sacrifice hits. I cut that out and went up to the paper the next morning to see Bang.

"Ed," I said, "that story you wrote about me—did you ever look up to see what you're writing about?"

"Why?" he said. "What's wrong?"

"Take a look at this," I said and showed him the records. He looked at the figures and said, "That's very interesting."

"You're goddamned right that's interesting," I said.

He was apologetic. Or chagrined—I think that's the better word for it. "What do you want me to do?" he asked.

"It's too late to do anything," I said. "The fans have got the other story fixed in their heads now. Anytime I don't bunt, they're going to give me hell." Which they did.

That's how some of these things get started—one guy not knowing the figures and everybody else believing what he writes.

How do you get a man out of a slump? There's no set way, really. Very often those slumps are mental. A fellow gets it into his head that he's not going to hit the ball, and consequently he doesn't hit it. What happens is you go up to the plate and look around and all you see are fielders. There's no room for you to hit it anyplace. I'll tell you what happened one time with Averill. He was having tough going, which was unusual for him. One day somebody gave me a bat that was a little burned. It had been given some kind of special heat treatment. I looked at that bat and had an idea. I brought it over to Averill.

"Look, Earl," I said, speaking in a very confidential way. "See what I have here. I want you to try this bat out. But just once. I don't want to take a chance on you breaking it; otherwise we'll both be in the soup. And for heaven's sake, don't tell any of the other boys about it."

So he goes up to the plate with that bat and *whack!* A line shot for a base hit. He came back to the bench later all smiles.

"Remember," I said. "Not a word to anyone about it."

You know, that snapped him out of it and he started hitting like hell. What kind of bat was it? Just an ordinary bat that somebody had put in an oven and burned a little. No different from any other bat, except that Earl thought it was different. You see, that slump had become a mental thing with him, and all he needed to break out of it was some oddball notion.

You can have slumps in the field, too, you know. In 1925 I had that lousy Series against Pittsburgh. I made eight errors, though some of them were stinko calls by the scorer. And if you don't think ballplayers have long and stubborn memories, listen to this. Some of those calls were on balls hit by Max Carey. Well, whenever I run into Max in Florida, he still raises the devil about them, claiming they should have been base hits.

"For goodness sakes, Max," I tell him, "that's fifty years ago."

"All the same," he says, "they should have been base hits."

I still hold that darned record of eight errors by a shortstop in a World Series. But up to that time, as I understand it, Honus Wagner had the record with six. So I tell people that I once broke one of Honus Wagner's records, but I don't tell them what it was!

INDEX

Holm, Wattie, 473
Holmes, Tommy, 411–16
Homestead Grays, 134, 137
Hooper, Harry, 91, 457, 459–60, 495, 497, 500
Hope, Bob, 325
Hopp, Johnny, 184, 272, 370
Hornsby, Rogers, 69, 95, 110–11, 143, 144, 465, 468–70, 472–77, 484, 534, 579, 580, 645
House of David, 140
Houston Astros, 356, 424, 433, 448
Houtteman, Art, 420, 635
Howard, Elston, 377, 511–12
Howell, Dixie, 510
Hoyt, Waite, 102, 280, 463, 471, 487, 488, 572, 583
Hubbard, Cal, 206, 210
Hubbell, Carl, 42, 84, 109, 113, 190–91, 339, 360, 596–99, 620
Hudlin, Willis, 25, 137, 646
Hudson, Johnny, 342
Hudson, Sid, 372
Huggins, Miller, 102, 103, 473, 644
Hughson, Tex, 372, 382, 426
Hunnefield, Bill, 28
Hutchinson, Freddy, 79, 385, 601– 2
Hyland, Dr., 233–34, 369, 374–75

International League, 63, 65, 82, 93, 183, 269, 323, 453
Irvin, Monte, 304, 388–97, 553

Jackson, Bill, 608–9
Jackson, Shoeless Joe, 89, 456, 493, 494, 518, 531, 532, 607, 639, 640
Jackson, Travis, 546
Jacobson, Baby Doll, 67, 91
James, Bill, 515
Jamieson, Charlie, 519
Jansen, Larry, 394
Jay, Joey, 404
Jenkins, Irvin, 64
Jethroe, Sam, 602–3
Johnson, Ban, 641–42
Johnson, Bob, 600, 616–17
Johnson, Judy, 141
Johnson, Roy, 351, 646
Johnson, Walter, 10, 11, 19, 26, 39–40, 42, 62, 66–67, 92, 106, 141, 158, 217, 445, 455, 492, 494, 499, 514, 529, 542–47, 607, 610–12, 624– 625, 644
Johnston, Doc, 517
Jones, Deacon, 179
Jones, Sam, 102, 463
Jones, Willie, 438
Joost, Eddie, 360
Joss, Addie, 638
Judge, Joe, 610, 615
Judnich, Walter, 416
Jurges, Billy, 112, 115, 116, 523, 580

Kamm, Willie, 91
Kansas City Athletics, 268, 356, 364, 378–79, 380
Kansas City Monarchs, 134, 140, 147
Kavanaugh, Marty, 457
Kell, George, 358, 359, 598

Kelleher, Frank, 177
Keller, Charlie, 77, 78, 177, 185, 214, 215, 247, 255, 258, 412
Kelly, George, 534, 540, 541, 543, 544, 546, 547, 609
Keltner, Ken, 127, 416, 598
Kennedy, Monte, 85–86
Kerr, Buddy, 273–74
Kilduff, Pete, 520–21, 575
Killefer, Bill, 227–28, 473, 533
Kinder, Ellis, 266, 381–82, 426–27
Kiner, Ralph, 81, 321–28
King, Clyde, 241
Kinsella, Dick, 533
Klein, Chuck, 109, 116–18, 484
Klein, Lou, 170, 171
Klem, Bill, 199, 628
Kling, Johnny, 491, 642
Klinger, Bob, 84, 375
Kluszewski, Ted, 431, 440, 505
Koenig, Mark, 465, 471–73, 475, 477, 487, 488, 523–24
Konstanty, Jim, 440, 442
Koslo, Dave, 394
Koufax, Sandy, 31, 157, 217, 361, 420, 507
Koy, Ernie, 343
Kramer, Jack, 426
Kremer, Ray, 487
Kress, Red, 137
Krichell, Paul, 277, 280, 347, 412
Krist, Howie, 370
Kubek, Tony, 362
Kucks, Johnny, 379
Kuhel, Joe, 612
Kurowski, Whitey, 167, 168, 184, 370, 371, 375

Laabs, Chet, 209–10
Labine, Clem, 379, 396, 508
Lajoie, Napoleon, 492–94, 607, 637, 639, 641
LaManno, Ray, 272
Landis, Jim, 430, 505, 634
Landis, Kenesaw Mountain, 46, 205, 207–8, 224, 232, 249–51, 340, 474, 526, 540–41
Landis, Stan, 562–63
Lane, Frank, 565–66, 604
Lanier, Max, 163–74, 370
Larsen, Don, 379
Lary, Frank, 177
Lary, Lyn, 346, 348
Lary, Otis, 64
Lavagetto, Cookie, 179, 231, 242, 264, 265, 313, 342, 583
Law, Ruth, 574
Law, Vern, 560
Lazzeri, Tony, 13, 102, 111, 157, 257, 346, 347, 465, 471, 472, 475–77, 485, 488, 526, 647
Lee, Bill, 46, 84, 114, 115, 119, 315, 581
Lee, Thornton, 180, 323
Leibold, Nemo, 639
Lemon, Bob, 182, 419, 420, 427, 635
Leonard, Buck, 141
Leonard, Dutch, 190, 295, 457, 462, 616, 617
Lewis, Buddy, 264, 290, 296, 331, 617
Lewis, Duffy, 452, 457, 460, 462, 463, 495, 501
Lincoln Giants, 147
Lindell, John, 266, 381